LOEB CLASSICAL LIBRARY

FOUNDED BY JAMES LOEB 1911

EDITED BY

JEFFREY HENDERSON

SELECT PAPYRI

III

LCL 360

SELECT
PAPYRI

POETRY

TEXTS, TRANSLATIONS, AND NOTES BY
D. L. PAGE

HARVARD UNIVERSITY PRESS
CAMBRIDGE, MASSACHUSETTS
LONDON, ENGLAND

First published 1941

LOEB CLASSICAL LIBRARY® is a registered trademark
of the President and Fellows of Harvard College

ISBN 978-0-674-99397-6

*Printed on acid-free paper and bound by
The Maple-Vail Book Manufacturing Group*

CONTENTS

CONTENTS

CONTENTS

MIDDLE COMEDY AND NEW COMEDY, 4TH AND 3RD CENTURIES B.C.

CONTENTS

CONTENTS

CONTENTS

CONTENTS

CONTENTS

PREFACE

This book professes to contain all the Greek poetry which has been recovered from papyri; except (1) texts already published in other volumes of the Loeb Classical Library, (2) texts destined for publication in other volumes (*e.g.* the fragments of Callimachus), (3) fragments which are too small and broken to be either coherently translatable or—in our opinion— worth reprinting here for any other cause.[a] A few texts from ostraca and parchment have been included for special reasons. The contents therefore exclude the fragments of Hesiod, Alcman, Alcaeus, Bac- chylides, Timotheus, Herodes and others; Sappho, Pindar and Corinna are sparsely represented; there remain (1) all the papyrus-fragments of Tragedy,[b] (2) all of Comedy, except the greatest part of

---

[a] Texts of importance to the scholar but not yielding a sufficiently connected sense to be worth reprinting here include among others the following: *Berliner Klassikertexte*, v. 1, p. 67; *P. Oxy.* nos. 419, 676, 1823; *Cat. Lit. Pap. B.M.* nos. 51, 53, 57; *P. Ryl.* no. 1; *P. Hibeh*, nos. 10, 11; *Archiv für Papyrusforschung*, iii. p. 1; *Raccolta Lombroso*, p. 29; *P. Vindob.* 29779. *P.S.I.* iii. no. 157 is omitted because I can make no sense of it; and I have ventured to think that no useful purpose would be served by republishing the fragments of Dioscorus of Aphroditopolis.

[b] Except the fragment commonly ascribed to Aeschylus, *Carians* (see H. Weir Smyth, Loeb *Aeschylus*, vol. ii.).

PREFACE

Menander, (3) all of Mime (despite its want of poetry), (4) a considerable number of fragments in lyric, iambic, elegiac and hexameter verse : altogether, about four thousand two hundred lines of Greek poetry.

The edition of these texts was originally undertaken by Mr. C. H. Roberts, Fellow of St. John's College, Oxford. Engaged in heavier labours he transferred the task to me ; but not before he had nearly completed a catalogue of all fragments to be taken from publications up to the summer of 1933 [a] ; this catalogue was seen and so far approved by Hunt himself. Mr. Roberts handed to me at the same time a book of notes, the result of long and ingenious labour on the Tragic and Comic fragments : although I started the work again from the beginning, I derived great profit from his researches, and here express my gratitude.

The reader will find that the text and translation of each piece are preceded by a short bibliography and an introductory note. I must briefly explain both these and the texts themselves.

At the head of each text stands a full reference to the *editio princeps*, followed by abbreviated references to books, articles, reviews and notes which deal with the whole or some part or aspect of the text. These little bibliographies do not always aim at completeness; which, for such pieces as *Hypsipyle* and *Ichneutae* among others, was beyond both my power and the scope of my book. And I have of course excluded

---

[a] The *editiones principes* referred to in this catalogue are scattered over four dozen different books and periodicals, a few of which are almost—one or two quite—unobtainable in England. I have at last had access to all except the *ed. pr.* of no. 129 (written in Russian, which I cannot read).

references to works (especially reviews) which seemed to add nothing to the subject. I hope that the bibliography often includes all that contributes to the elucidation of the text ; but I am unhappily certain that there must be some, and may be many, regrettable omissions.

The bibliographies are often followed by introductory notes, which try very briefly to illuminate the texts against their literary and historical background, to elucidate their general meaning, to comment on divers matters of interest and importance such as authorship, style and date, and to give wherever possible—often, I fear, where it was not possible—the context of the fragment itself. Such notes are unusual in this series of volumes ; but they may be justified by the fragmentary nature of the texts, which are often difficult to understand without some preliminary exposition and explanation : often enough both text and translation depended on matters which are discussed in the introductory note. In a few instances the notes do nothing more than justify readings in the text or points in the translation : that this was necessary, will be admitted freely by those who have studied the latest fragments of Euphorion, or followed the controversy which rages around the *Niobe* of Aeschylus. These introductions were written or revised after perusal of the works to which the bibliographies refer ; I am therefore heavily indebted to those works, however much I modify them or go beyond them.

As for the texts : again, I could not conform to the custom of this series, because I could rarely find a " received " text which I might adopt and reprint ; I must therefore construct my own. My practice

PREFACE

has been to start with the *editio princeps* as a basis, and to embellish it with such modifications as were dictated by later research and by my own study.[a] I am not a papyrologist; consequently it signifies little that I have read many of my texts in the original papyri, the great majority of them in photographic reproductions—most published, others bought and borrowed. In my study of some of these texts, especially nos. 1, 30 and 121, I had the incomparable benefit of Mr. Edgar Lobel's assistance; those familiar with his standards will not need the reminder that his assistance in my study by no means implies his approval of my result.

A word about supplements. I began eager to fill every gap with flawless fragments of my own composition; I ended with the desire—too late—to remove all that is not either legible in the papyrus or replaceable beyond reasonable doubt. At the eleventh hour, indeed, I expelled handfuls of private poetry: yet far too much remains, hard though I tried to print nothing which is inconsistent with spaces and traces in the papyrus, and to be guided, for the sense of my supplements, by certain or probable indications provided by the legible text.

Of my translations I cannot think with any satisfaction. The insuperable difficulties of rendering Greek poetry into English are in no way mitigated

---

[a] In publishing the result, I have usually printed what I considered to be the best text hitherto produced; footnotes then refer only to divergences from that standard. Such basic texts are denoted by asterisks in the bibliographies. Where no asterisk appears, it must be understood that for special reasons I have been unable to adopt any single text as basic; in such cases, the authors of *all* supplements, etc., are named in the footnotes.

PREFACE

when the Greek is a disjointed fragment, often obscure and controversial, sometimes highly unpoetical. The only purpose which my versions can serve is to make it clear how I have understood the Greek—if I have made it clear, and if I did understand it. Had my predecessors (most of them) had even this ideal, my task would have been much easier. Many of these fragments have not been translated before.

Since October 1939 I have been altogether unable to give either the time or the attention necessary to a proper reading of the proofs.[a] But Mr. Roberts —equally distracted by new duties—has exercised unceasing vigilance. And late, but not too late, Professor J. D. Beazley performed a miracle of deep and painless surgery on every page : to him above all my readers owe whatever state of convalescence they may find in this volume ; they will never know how ill it was before.

D. L. P.

October 1940

[a] In particular, I have been unable to take account of works which were published, or became accessible to me, while this book was being printed, *e.g.* Mette, *Supplementum Aeschyleum*, Berlin, 1939 (p. 31 = no. 20, p. 22 = no. 35, p. 47 = no. 1, p. 71 = no. 2) ; Edmonds, *Mnemos.* 1939, 1 and Schmid, *Philol.* 93, 413 (= no. 40) ; Szantyr, *Philol.* 93, 287 (= no. 17) ; Schmidt, *Phil. Woch.* 59, 1939, 833 ; Collart, *Rev. Et. Gr.* 52, 1939, 222. Murray, in the introduction to his *Aeschylus* (Oxford, 1940) gives a clue to part of the contents of the forthcoming volume of *Oxyrhynchus Papyri.*

The whole of the first edition was destroyed by enemy action, and the translator has revised this reprint.

November 1941

AIDS TO THE READER

Π throughout in notes = the original papyrus of the text.

Dates at the head of each piece refer to the age of the papyrus (3 B.C., 1 A.D. of course mean " the third century B.C., the first century A.D.," not the third and first years of those centuries).

Dates in the index of contents refer to the time, certain or probable, when the fragments were composed.

Square brackets [ ] enclose letters which are lost in lacunae in the original papyrus, conjecturally restored by modern scholars. Round brackets ( ) indicate the omission in the original of the letters enclosed, either by accident or through deliberate abbreviation (as in nos. 77, 113).

Dots under letters signify that the letters are not certainly read ; dots inside brackets represent the approximate number of missing letters. A dash (*paragraphus*) in the text or margin of the Greek denotes change of speaker ; where a speaker's name appears in brackets, in full or abbreviated, it is to be understood that the papyrus has a *paragraphus* in that place or else provides an indication that one must be restored.

Abbreviations of authors' names and of titles of works are chiefly those adopted by the latest edition of Liddell & Scott's Lexicon ; any others will no doubt explain themselves readily.

TRAGEDY

ΑΙΣΧΥΛΟΣ

1 **[2 A.D.]** ΝΙΟΒΗ

Ed. pr. Vitelli-Norsa, *Bulletin de la société royale d'archéologie d'Alexandrie*, no. 28, 1933, p. 108 with Plate. Republished *ibid.* no. 29, 1934, p. 229. See Körte, *Hermes*, 68, 1933, 249 and *Archiv*, xi. 1935, 248 ; Maas, *Gnomon*, 9, 1933, 249 ; Latte, *Gött. Nachr.* 1933, 22 ; Cazzaniga, *Rend. Ist. Lomb.* 66, 1933, 843 ; Pfeiffer, *Philol.* 89, 1934, 1 ; Schadewaldt, *Sitzb. Heidelb. 1933-1934*, Abh. 3, 1934 ; Reinhardt, *Hermes*, 69, 1934, 233 and *Sophokles*, 1933, p. 246 ; Pickard-Cambridge, *Greek Poetry and Life ; Essays presented to Gilbert Murray*, 106 ; Rostagni, *Riv. di Fil.* 62, 1934, 117 ; Lesky, *Wiener Studien*, 52, 1 ; Schmid-Stählin, *Gr. Lit.* ii. 1934, 117, 2 ; C.-E. Fritsch, *Neue Fragm. d. Aisch. u. Soph.*, diss. Hamb. 1936, 25 ; Zimmermann, *Phil. Woch.* 57, 743 ; Kloesel, *Hermes*, 72, 1937, 466.

I am bound to append the following notes in explanation of my text of this desperately difficult fragment.

V. 1. Niobe must be the speaker : at least, our Papyrus certainly ascribed the lines to her. Reading ἐποιμώζουσα as it does in v. 7, it must have had a finite tense (first person) in the beginning of v. 8, e.g. ἔκλαυσα. Otherwise the Papyrus could have made no sense at all ; and that there is no reason whatever to assume. Though ἐποιμώζουσα may well be an incorrect reading, there is no reason to assume a further corruption—to suppose that the intrusion of this word, if indeed it is intrusive, destroyed or at all altered the general grammar and construction of the sentence.

2

AESCHYLUS

NIOBE [2 A.D.]

The Papyrus, then, certainly ascribed the lines to Niobe : and to my mind, the arguments hitherto brought against the ascription are singularly weak :—

(1) Hesychius quotes v. 7 in the form τέκνοις ἔπωζε τοῖς τεθνηκόσιν : here I agree with Körte that the third person of the verb in this citation is too easily explicable in other ways (see Körte, Hermes, loc. cit. p. 238) to be a good reason for altering our fragment to suit it :—Hesychius is clearly paraphrasing, not quoting ; hence his imperfect tense (which no editor accepts for our fragment) and the incompleteness of his line (which he leaves two—or three— syllables short).ᵃ

(2) The tone of the speech. Niobe has long been silent, sitting on her children's tomb : when at last she speaks, will her utterance be so calm, so gnomic, so philosophical ? We must answer that we do not know the tone of the speech as a whole ; and cannot be certain of that of our own small fragment. There is nothing cogent in the assertion that the tone and spirit of these lines, so far as we apprehend them, are such that the Niobe of Aeschylus could not—or even probably

---

ᵃ It is quite possible that Hesychius's citation comes from some other part of the same play : repetitions of a striking metaphor within one play are a common feature of Greek tragedy.

3

would not—have spoken thus. As few scholars make use of this argument, I say no more about it.

(3) *Some of those who read* ἐπώζει, ἐπωάζουσα, *in v. 7, with the meaning " sit on eggs," allege that such a metaphor in a description of Niobe by herself is intolerable. This is anyway a matter of opinion. But the argument may be ignored by those who believe (as I do) that in the original text the offensive metaphor had no place at all. See note on v. 7.*

(4) *If* ἀναστενάζε[ται *is read in v. 1, the question is of course settled. But the reading in that place is extremely uncertain. So dubious are the traces that the possibilities range over* αναστεναζε[ται, αναστεναζο[μαι, αναστεν[ε]ιν ο[, αναστεν[ε]ιν θ[, αναστεν[ε]ιν ε[, αναστεναζο[μεν.

(5) *If* τῆσδε *in v. 11 refers to Niobe, the reference should normally (in Aeschylus) be made about Niobe by another person, not by herself : i.e. the pronoun* ὅδε, ἥδε *is not used in Aeschylus to denote the speaker, without further qualification. But since we do not know the meaning or reading of that line—since indeed we do not even know whether the word in question refers to Niobe at all (v. Lesky, ad loc.)—this argument must be dismissed. If, for example, we read* ψυχῆς] κόμιστρα τῆσδ' ἑκὰς πεφρ[ασμένος, *the objection disappears altogether.*

(6) *Some scholars have objected that Niobe should not lament the loss of her beauty in v. 8 : it is an " intolerable lapse into sentimentality " for Niobe to regret the passing of her " poor vanished beauty." But where is the loss of Niobe's beauty mentioned ? Not in the Papyrus. Niobe may possibly be weeping because of some consequence of her beauty ; but so far as our text goes, she is not lamenting for the loss or destruction of it. Indeed the beauty may even be that of her children, which had proved fatal to them, cf. Parthenius 33* εἰς ἔριν ἀφικομένην Λητοῖ περὶ καλλιτεκνίας, *and Pearson's note on Soph. fr. 448—in one version, evidently,*

*the beauty of the children was an essential element in the
story. However that may be, it is certain that Niobe's pride
in her own beauty was an important factor (Ovid, Metam.
vi. 181 and Lesky,* loc. cit. *p. 2) : so Niobe may be weep-
ing not the destruction of her beauty, but the consequences
of it.*

Vv. 1-4. *Niobe cannot say, without some qualification,
that she does nothing but mourn her father (or, mourns
nobody but her father).—She must have mourned her children
first. No doubt the preceding lines made vv. 1-4 easily
intelligible—Niobe, having mourned her children, turns for
a moment at the end of her speech to consideration of her
father, who will be heart-broken when he learns these events.—
I agree with Lesky in his supposition that Tantalus does not
know what has happened : he is coming in the hope of finding
a happy daughter and grandchildren—he will find the one in
mourning and the others buried. Well may Niobe, having
abundantly lamented her children's fate, exclaim on the eve
of Tantalus's arrival " Long have I mourned my children,
and now I only mourn Tantalus, who will be distraught
through this calamity." The conclusion of the first line cannot
be restored with certainty (see above). To ἀναστενάζομαι
(or ἀναστενάζεται) there is the considerable objection that
the middle form is being specially invented for this passage.
In Soph. Eurypylus, ed. pr., fr. 5 col. 1 line 15, ἐστενάζετο
is read, and the first editors called it a middle ; but there is
nothing to show that it is not a passive. We may quote such
rarities as στένομαι Eur.* Ba. *1372,* μεταστένομαι Med. *996,
μετακλαίομαι* Hec. *214 ; but it is not certain that these
are adequate parallels for a verb in -άζω. And we must
already accept sufficient oddities in this mysterious piece
without creating more. For instance* δόντα *in v. 2. It
seems to equal* ἐκδόντα. *Half a dozen apparent parallels can
be quoted ; but (as Schadewaldt observes) in all of them (e.g.*
Med. *288) the context assists the meaning of* δοῦναι *greatly,*

5

—*whereas here it does not so (though possibly the preceding lines assisted it).*

In vv. 2-4 I construe : εἰς οἷον βίον ὁ Φοῖβος τὸν Τάνταλον ἐξώκειλε.

V. 5. τοὐπι[τ]είμιον *would be preferable here to* τοὐπι- [τ]έρμιον *if only it were the likelier reading—partly to avoid yet another peculiarity (the use of* τὸ ἐπιτέρμιον *as a noun), partly because the sense is more powerful and explicit. But* τοὐπι[τ]έρμιον *is the likelier reading of the Papyrus.*

V. 6. τριταῖ]ον *is highly praised, and may be correct. To call it " an absolutely certain supplement " is uncritical. We do not after all know exactly how many days Niobe sat there. (Unless we require no more evidence than a variant reading in a Life of Aeschylus.)*

Vv. 7-8. The most reasonable solution of the difficulties here seems to be this :—the original reading was ἐπωάζουσα, *and it meant " crying* ὠά," *i.e. mourning. For this, the easier reading* ἐποιμώζουσα *was later substituted (for such alterations in the text of Aeschylus, v. Quintilian x. 1. 66). The sources of Hesychius, who paraphrases* ἔπωζε, *read* ἐπ- ωάζουσα *and mistakenly interpreted it as* ἐπικαθημένη τοῖς ὠοῖς.

Vv. 10-13. The great objection to giving these lines to e.g. the Chorus is that this device does not remove the difficulty which prompted it—the apparent awkwardness of connexion, especially of the μέν *and* δέ. *And the difficulty itself may not seem very great, especially if the supplement* μάτην *is removed from v. 10. Read e.g.* αὖθις *in its place, and the piece runs smoothly enough. V. 9 is the gnome which rounds off the description of Niobe's present sufferings and attitude (vv. 1-8). Then comes a move forward to another theme : " Tantalus will soon be here ; meantime I will tell you the origin of these sufferings which you have just observed."*

V. 11. The end of this line is mysterious. πεφα[, not πεφρ[,ᵃ is the reading at the end according to ed. pr. And even if this were not so, such a line as (e.g. ζητῶν)] κόμιστρα τῆσδε καὶ πεφρ[ασμένος is not very good. καὶ πεφα[σμένων (from *φένω) is no better ; τῶν πεφασμένων is required, and we have already tolerated or introduced sufficient oddnesses. Rather than endure either of these, I would read (e.g. ἐπ' ἀγ)]κόμιστρα τῆσδ' ἑκὰς πεφα[σμένος (from φαίνομαι).ᵇ It is by no means certain that τῆσδε could not be used by Niobe with reference to herself ; though it would be one more oddness introduced into the text.

V. 12. μῆνιν τίνα, not μῆνίν τινα, should be read, to avoid producing a line without a caesura.

V. 19. For the beginning of this, we read that ἀλλ' οἱ μὲν is " certainly too long," but (in the same breath) ἀλλ' οἱ γὰρ " fits the space." I imagine that this is a mere oversight ; it is of course impossible to estimate differences so nicely in this Papyrus.

V. 20. At the end, [εὐπραξίαν is warmly praised by some, not despite the adjacent εὖ πράσσοντες but because of it. I agree with those who find the repetition offensive ; e.g. [ὄλβου χάριν would be better ; but the mot juste remains to be found.

V. 21. Lobel advises me that καλλισ[τεύμασι is at least as probable as the singular, if the reference is to the beauty of the children. And it is equally possible that some case of κάλλισ[τος should be read.

ᵃ Aesch. fr. 438 N. πεφρασμένος· παρεσκευασμένος εἰς τὸ φρασθῆναι, προσεκτικὴν ἔχων διάνοιαν Αἰσχύλος : this is said to make πεφρ[ασμένος " certain " here, despite the evidence of Π ; I know of no evidence for the connexion of the two passages. ᵇ Or, if πεφρ[is—despite ed. pr.—possible : ψυχῆς] κόμιστρα τῆσδ' ἑκὰς πεφρ[ασμένος.

LITERARY PAPYRI

—— νῦν] οὐδὲν εἰ μὴ πατέρ' ἀναστεν[
τὸν] δόντα καὶ φύσαντα Ταντάλου β[ίαν
εἰς οἷ]ον ἐξώκειλεν ἀλίμενον βίον
Φοῖβ]ος· κακοῦ γὰρ πνεῦμα προσβ[άλλε]ι
    δό[μοις.
αὐταὶ] δ' ὁρᾶτε τοὐπι[τ]έρμιον γάμου·   5
τριταῖ]ον ἦμαρ τόνδ' ἐφημένη τάφον
τέκν]οις ἐπωάζουσα τοῖς τεθνηκόσιν
ἔκλα]υσα τὴν τάλαιναν εὔμορφον φυήν.
βροτὸ]ς κακωθεὶς δ' οὐδὲν ἄλλ' εἰ μὴ σκιά.
    αὖθις] μὲν ἥξει δεῦρο Ταντάλου βία   10
. . . . .] κόμιστρα τῆσδε καὶ πεφα[
Φοῖβος] δὲ μῆνιν τίνα φέρων 'Αμφίονι
πρόρρι]ζον αἰκῶς ἐξεφύλασεν γέν[ος,
ἐγὼ πρ]ὸς ὑμᾶς, οὐ γάρ ἐστε δύσφρονε[ς,
λέξω·] θεὸς μὲν αἰτίαν φύει β[ροτοῖς   15
ὅταν κα]κῶσαι δῶμα παμπήδη[ν θέληι·
τέως δ]ὲ θνητὸν ὄντα χρὴ τὸν ἐ[κ θεῶν
ὄλβον π]εριστέλλοντα μὴ θρασυστομ[εῖν.
οἱ δ' αἰὲν] εὖ πράσσοντες οὔποτ' ἤλπισαν
πίπτον]τες ἐκχεῖν ἣν ἔχουσ[20
καὐτὴ γ]ὰρ ἐξαρθεῖσα καλλισ[

1 e.g. ἀναστένειν ἔχω, ἀναστενάζομαι.   2 Ed. pr.   3
Schadewaldt.   4 Beginning D. L. P., end Latte.
5 Schadewaldt.   6 E. Wolff.   7 τέκνοις from Hesychius;
εποιμωζουσα Π, corr. Immisch, Kloesel, from Hesychius

2   [2 A.D.]   ΔΙΚΤΥΟΥΛΚΟΙ

Ed. pr. *Vitelli-Norsa, *Bulletin de la société royale d'archéologie d'Alexandrie*, no. 28, 1933, p. 115 with Plate; *ibid.* no. 29, 1934, p. 247 ; *Mélanges Bidez*, ii. 1934, p. 66.
8

AESCHYLUS

NIOBE. Now I only mourn my father, strong
Tantalus, who begot me and gave me forth in
marriage; to such a life without a haven has he
been driven aground by Phoebus; the high winds of
calamity assault our house. Your own eyes behold
my wedding's end : three days already sitting here
upon the tomb, moaning above my children dead, I
mourn the misfortune of their beauty. Man brought
to misery is a shadow, nothing else.

Strong Tantalus will presently come hither, . . .
So now, the anger of Phoebus against Amphion,
wherefore he has destroyed his house with outrage,
root and branch, I will expound to you—you are not
enemies. God first creates a fault in man, when He
is minded utterly to ruin his estate. Man must
attend meantime to the good fortune that God gives
him, and guard his lips from insolence. They whose
turn it is to prosper never think that they shall
stumble and spill forth the (welfare) of to-day. For
see, I too, exultant in the beauty . . .

(ἔπωζε).   8 Lobel.   9 Eduard Fraenkel.   10
D. L. P.   11 Perhaps ἐπὶ ἀγ]κόμιστρα τῆϲδ' ἑκὰς πεφα-
[σμένος, or ψυχῆς] κόμιστρα τῆϲδ' ἑκὰς πεφρ[αϲμένος.   13-15
Ed. pr.   15-16 From Plato, Resp. ii. 380 A.   17 τέως
D. L. P.   17-18 ἐκ θεῶν ed. pr., ὄλβον Latte.   19
Lesky.   20 Lobel.   21 καλλιστεύματι ed. pr., -μαϲι
Lobel : or some form of κάλλιϲτος.

DICTYULCI   [2 A.D.]

See Körte, Hermes, 68, 1933, 267 and Archiv, xi. 1935, 249 ;
Goossens, Chron. d'Egypte, 19, 1935, 120 ; Vitelli-Norsa,
Papiri Greci e Latini, xi. 1935, no. 1209, p. 97 ; Fritsch,

LITERARY PAPYRI

Neue Fragm. d. Aisch. u. Soph., diss. Hamb. 1936, 7 ;
Pfeiffer, *Sitzb. Bayer. Akad.* 1938, 2, p. 3 ; Schmid-Stählin,
Gr. Lit. vii. 1, 2, 1934, p. 262 ; Zimmermann, *Phil. Woch.*
57, 541.

Fragment of the prologue of a Satyric drama. Danae and Perseus arrive at the shore of Seriphus enclosed in a chest.

[? ΔΙΚΤΥΣ] ξυνῆκ[ας;
—— ξυνῆκα· [
[ΔΙ.] τί σοι φυλάσσω; [
   εἴ που θαλάσσης [
[ΔΙ.] ἄσημα· λεῖος πόν[τος   5
—— δέρκου νυν ἐς κευ[θμῶνα τόνδε πλησίον.
[ΔΙ.] καὶ δὴ δέδορκα τῷδετ[
   ἔα· τί φῶ τόδ᾽ εἶναι; πότερα [πόντιον τέρας,
   φάλαιναν ἢ ζύγαιναν ἢ κῆ[τος, βλέπω;
   ἄναξ Πόσειδον Ζεῦ τ᾽ ἐνά[λι᾽, οἷον τόδε   10
   [δ]ῶρον θαλάσσης πέμπετ᾽ [ἐλπίδος πέρα.
—— [τί] σοι θαλάσσης δίκτυον δ[ῶρον στέγει;
   [π]εφυκ[ίωτ]αι δ᾽ ὥστε δαγνο.[

   (*Here follow fragments of two lines*)

——   ]εστι τοὔργον οὐ χωρεῖ πρόσω.
   [καὶ δὴ β]οὴν ἵστημι τοῖσδ᾽ ἰύγμασιν·   15
   [ἰού· π]άντες γεωργοὶ δεῦτε κἀμπελοσκάφοι,
   [βοτήρ τ]ε ποιμήν τ᾽ εἴ τίς ἐστ᾽ [ἐ]γχώριος,
   [πάραλ]οί τε κἄλλο [πᾶν ἁλιτ]ρύτων ἔθνος,
   [ἄγρας βαρείας τῆσδ᾽] ἐναντιωτάτης
   [ἡμῖν ξυνάπτεσθ᾽]   20

6 τόνδε πλησίον D. L. P.   9 κῆ[τος Lobel.   10 οἷον
τόδε D. L. P.   11 End D. L. P.   12 Schadewaldt.

They are caught in the fishing-net of Dictys, who is one of the two speakers in our fragment (the word Δικτυν, probably a proper name, occurs in fr. b 2, ed. pr. Hyginus 63. 3: Dictys was the name of the fisherman who found the chest). In vv. 16 sqq. the Chorus of fishermen is summoned to help bring the heavy load to shore.

? Dictys. You understand . . . ?
—— I understand. . . .
Dictys. What are you asking me to watch . . . ?
—— In case . . . of the sea. . . .
Dictys. Not a sign ; the sea's a millpond. . . .
—— Look now at this hollow, this one near me.
Dictys. All right, I'm looking. . . .
Good Lord, what are we to call this ? A sea-monster ? A grampus, or a shark, or a whale ? Poseidon and Zeus of Ocean, a fine gift to send up from the sea to unsuspecting mortals !
—— (*Tragically*) What gift of Ocean does your net conceal ? Covered with seaweed like . . .

(Here follow fragments of two lines)

. . . the job's not getting on. Listen, I'll raise a hue and cry :—Hallo ! Farmers and ditchers, here, all of you ! Herdsmen and shepherds, anyone in the place ! Coastfolk and all you other seadogs ! Help us take hold of this catch, it's heavy and it pulls against us. . . .

---

13 Beginning D. L. P. and Goossens simultaneously: end ? δαίμο[νος κάρα | Γλαύκου, cf. Plato, Resp. 611 D.   16 ἰού Beazley (extra metrum, like ἔα v. 8).   17-20 Pfeiffer.

ΣΟΦΟΚΛΗΣ

3 [2 A.D.]   ΑΧΑΙΩΝ ΣΥΛΛΟΓΟΣ

Ed. pr. Schubart-Wilamowitz, *Berliner Klassikertexte*, v. 2,
p. 64, 1907, Plate III.   See *Pearson, *Fragments of Sophocles*,
i. p. 94 ; Hunt, *F.T.P.* ; Pickard-Cambridge, *New Chapters*,
iii. 78 ; Körte, *Archiv*, v. 1913, 565 ; Wecklein, *Sitzb.
Münchn. Akad.* 1909, 13 ; Diehl, *Suppl. Soph.* 29 ; Srebrny,
Journ. d. Minist. für Volksaufklärung, N.S. 48, 1913, 523 ;
Fromhold-Treu, *Hermes*, 69, 1934, 333 ; Webster, *Bull.
Rylands Library*, 1938, 22, 2, p. 543 ; Schubart, *Pap. Graec.
Berol.* Plate 30b, Text xxiv.   For the case in favour of ascrib-
ing this fragment to Euripides' *Telephus* see E. W. Handley
and J. Rea, *Bulletin of the London Inst. of Class. Studies*,
Suppl. No. 5 (1957).

*The following is the outline of the legend on which this play
was based :—Telephus (born by Auge to Heracles in Arcadia)
succeeded Teuthras as king of Mysia, where the Greeks
landed by accident (having lost their way) while sailing
against Troy.   During a conflict between Greeks and
Mysians, Achilles wounded Telephus.   The Greeks departing
from Mysia were scattered by a tempest : and reassembled
in Argos, where they prepared a second expedition against
Troy.   Now Telephus, who had been advised by Apollo that
his painful wound could be healed by none but its author,
came to the Greek army at Argos in search of Achilles.   There
were obstacles to be overcome ; but in the end Achilles healed
Telephus, who in return guided the Greek fleet to Troy.*
    Of the course of Sophocles' play we know—
    (1) *From fr. 144 N.:—a roll of the assembled Achaeans*
12

SOPHOCLES

GATHERING OF THE ACHAEANS

[2 A.D.]

*was called early in the play ; and it probably transpired
that Achilles was absent.*

*(2) From our fragment and from the story as a whole :—
Telephus arrives, eager to be treated by Achilles. It is likely
that he offers his services as guide in return for reconciliation
with Achilles. This offer the Greeks decline, perhaps because
they think that Telephus is a foreigner (possibly an oracle
had said " no foreigner shall be your guide "). It then
appears that Telephus is after all a Greek by parentage ; and
his offer is accepted. It remains therefore only to persuade
Achilles to heal Telephus and to accept him as guide : this is
to be done through the mediation of Odysseus, portrayed as a
diplomatic go-between. It is clearly expected that Achilles
will prove difficult. The sequel can only be inferred from
the legend : Achilles was persuaded to heal Telephus with rust
from the spear which wounded him, and to consent to his
appointment as guide.*

*In our fragment, Telephus (addressed in the vocative case,
v. 3) has just left the scene, having been accepted as guide for
the fleet, which prepares to sail presently. Achilles enters,
and is waylaid by Odysseus.*

*So much is clear enough : but I do not understand the part
which Achilles played. Why is he expected to prove an
obstacle ? And especially, how is it that he expects to sail at
once ? Either he does not know (or does not consider) that a
guide is necessary ; or he has already appointed some other*

*guide. The first alternative is possible but unlikely : he was
a member of the previous expedition, and therefore knows the
disadvantage of sailing without a guide. In the second
alternative, it is impossible (only for want of evidence) to
identify the guide upon whom his choice had fallen (it could
hardly be himself : if he was a sufficient pilot, how could he
explain his failure on the occasion of the first expedition ?).*

[χο.] ἢ νότ[ου ἢ] ζεφύρ[ο]ιο δίνα
    πέμ[ψει Τ]ρωιάδας ἀκτάς.
    σύ τε π[ηδ]αλίωι παρεδρεύ[ων]
    φράσε[ις τῶι] κατὰ πρῶ(ι)ρα[ν]
    εὐθὺς Ἰ[λίο]υ πόρον   5
    Ἀτρει[δᾶν ἰ]δέσθαι.
    σὲ γὰρ Τε[γ]εᾶτις ἡμῖν,
    Ἑλλάς, οὐ[χ]ὶ Μυσία, τίκτει
    ναύταν σύν τινι δὴ θεῶν
    καὶ πεμπτῆρ' ἁλίων ἐρετμῶν.   10

ΑΧΙΛΛΕ[ΥΣ] μῶν καὶ σὺ καινὸς ποντίας ἀπὸ χθονὸς
    ἥκεις, Ὀδυσσεῦ; ποῦ 'στι σύλλογος φίλων;
    τί μέλλετ'; οὐ χρῆν ἥσυχον κεῖσθαι π[ό]δα.

ΟΔ. δοκεῖ στρατεύειν καὶ μέλει τοῖς ἐν τέλει
    τάδ'· ἐν δέοντι δ' ἦλθες, ὦ παῖ Πηλέως.   15

ΑΧ. οὐ μὴν ἐπ' ἀκταῖς γ' ἐστὶ κωπήρης στρατός,
    οὔτ' οὖν ὁπλίτης ἐξετάζεται παρών.

ΟΔ. ἀλλ' αὐτίκα· σπεύδειν γὰρ ἐν καιρῶι χρεών.

ΑΧ. αἰεί ποτ' ἐστὲ νωχελεῖς καὶ μέλλετε,
    ῥήσεις θ' ἕκαστος μυρίας καθήμενος   20
    λέγει, τὸ δ' ἔργον [οὐ]δαμοῦ πορεύεται.
    κ[ἀγ]ὼ μὲν ὡς ὁρᾶ[τ]ε δρᾶν ἕτοιμος ὢν
    ἥ[κ]ω, στρατός τε Μ[υρ]μιδών, καὶ πλεύ-
       σ[ομαι]
    [τὰ τ]ῶν Ἀτρειδᾶ[ν οὐ μένων] μελλήματα.

14

SOPHOCLES

Sophocles' Gathering of the Achaeans (produced sometime before Euripides' Telephus in 438 B.C.) was the third of Sophocles' trilogy on the subject of Telephus (see esp. the inscription from Aexone—or Halae Aexonides—including the sentence Σοφοκλῆς ἐδίδασκε Τηλέφειαν ; Fromhold-Treu, loc. cit. p. 324). The first two plays were Aleadae (see Fromhold Treu, ibid. p. 326) and Mysians (ibid. p. 329). It is possible that the anonymous fragment on p. 140 comes from our play.

CHORUS. . . . a swift wind from south or west shall speed us to the shores of Troy ; you, seated at the rudder, shall show the sailor at the prow, for him to see, a passage for the sons of Atreus straight to Ilium. The land of Tegea—Hellas, not Mysia— brought you to the light to be our sailor, surely by the favour of a god, and escort of our oars over the sea.

ACHILL. Odysseus ! You too, but lately come from your island home ? Where are our comrades gathered ? Why are you all delaying ? This is no time to rest our feet at ease.

ODYSS. It is resolved, the army sails ; the commanders attend to it. Son of Peleus : you are come in the hour of need.

ACHILL. Yet I see no bands of oarsmen on the beach, nor of soldiers present to answer the call.

ODYSS. It shall be presently. Man's haste should be as the time requires.

ACHILL. Ever idle and delaying ! Each one of you sits and makes a thousand speeches, and the work progresses nowhere ! Myself, as you see, am here and ready for action, I and my army of Myrmidons ; I shall sail without waiting for the Atridae's tardiness.

---

24 Suppl. D. L. P., *cf. I.A.* 818, Aeschin. *Ctes.* § 72 : for the form Ἀτρειδᾶν in iamb. trim., *v. P. Petr.* i. 3. (2) μήνιμ' Ἀτρειδᾶν.

LITERARY PAPYRI

4 [2 A.D.] ΕΥΡΥΠΥΛΟΣ

Ed. pr. Grenfell-Hunt, *P. Oxy.* ix. 1912, no. 1175, p. 86,
Plates III, IV.   See *Pearson, *Fragm. of Soph.* i. 146 ;
Körte, *Archiv,* v. 1913, 563 ; Pickard-Cambridge, *New
Chapters,* iii. 82 ; Milne, *Cat. Lit. Pap. B.M.* no. 66 ; Diehl,
Suppl. Soph. p. 21 ; Brizi, *Aegyptus,* 8, 1927, 3 (and litera-
ture, *ibid.* p. 3, n.) ; Reinhardt, *Sophokles,* p. 235.

The authorship of Sophocles is suggested[a] *by the coincidence
of fr. 5. i. 9 (ed. pr.) with a fragment attributed to Sophocles
(on a theme evidently the same as that of our fragments) by
Plutarch,* De cohib. ira *10, p. 458 D.   The attribution is sup-
ported by the style of the fragments, and by the relation of* Π
to the Ichneutae *papyrus (see ed. pr., pp. 86-87).   It is clear
from the lines themselves that the play was concerned with
the death of Eurypylus (cf. vv. 26-28, Priam mourns the son
of Telephus, i.e. Eurypylus) who was slain in a duel with
Neoptolemus (Homer, Od. xi. 519).   That Sophocles wrote a
play entitled* Eurypylus *is not certain, but had already been
inferred by Tyrwhitt from Plutarch, loc. cit., cf. Weil, Rev.
Et. Gr. iii. 343 : a play with that title is mentioned by Aris-
totle, Poet. 23, 1459 b 6.*

The story on which this play was based was probably as

[ΧΟ.] . . . ἐπεὶ κτησίων φρενῶν ἐξέδυς.
[ΑΣΤ.] ὦ δαῖμον ὦ δύσδαιμον ὦ κείρας [ἐ]μέ.
[ΧΟ.] ἀγχοῦ προσεῖπας, οὐ γὰρ ἐκτὸς ἑστὼς
    σύρει δὴ φύρδαν.
[ΑΣΤ.] ἐπισπάσει δίκα με.   5
[ΧΟ.] δίκα, ναί.
[ΑΣΤ.] ἀλλ' ὡς τάχιστ' ἄριστα.

---

[a] It is not proved, for a line ending χ]αλκέων ὅπλων may
not be unique : but the coincidence is striking.

16

SOPHOCLES

EURYPYLUS [2 A.D.]

follows :—Priam sent to his sister Astyoche (wife of Telephus and mother of Eurypylus) a golden vine, given to Laomedon (or Tros) in compensation for the rape of Ganymede ; hoping thus to persuade her to send her son forth to fight against the Greeks at Troy. She sent him ; and he performed many heroic deeds before he was slain in a duel by Neoptolemus.

In our fragments, Astyoche laments the death of her son in dialogue with the Chorus. There follows immediately the concluding portion of a Messenger's speech, relating the sequel of the death of Eurypylus. Evidently this 'Αγγελία was strangely divided into two parts, separated by a short dialogue between Astyoche and the Chorus. The presence of the Mysian queen at Troy is less surprising since we know that she and her sisters were among the women taken captive after the fall of Troy (Tzetz. Lycophr. 921, 1075). The further course of the play is unknown, but probably included lamentation and preparation for the burial of Eurypylus. In the first part of his divided speech, the Messenger narrated the duel of Eurypylus and Neoptolemus. Beyond this all is uncertain. (See Brizi, loc. cit.: the scene of the action is Troy, probably in front of Priam's palace ; Priam himself was probably one of the actors ; Neoptolemus was certainly not.)

CHORUS. . . . now that you have wandered from your proper wits.

ASTYOCHE. O spirit, O spirit of sorrow, O my destroyer !

CHORUS. Face to face you speak to him, he stands not far away, he draws and drags you.

ASTYOCHE. Justice will catch me !

CHORUS. Justice, aye !

ASTYOCHE. Soonest is best !

[ΧΟ.] ἐέ·
　　τί φήσομεν, τί λέξομεν;
[ΑΣΤ.] τίς οὐχὶ τοὐμὸν ἐν δίκαι βαλεῖ κάρα;　　　10
[ΧΟ.] δαίμων ἔκειρεν ἐν δίκαι σε δαίμων.
[ΑΣΤ.] ἦ κἀμβεβᾶσι τὸν [ν]εκρὸν πρὸς τῶι κα[κ]ῶι
　　γέλωτ’ ἔχ[ο]ντες ἀ[δρ]ὸν ’Αργεῖοι βίαι;
[ΑΓΓ.] οὐκ ἐς τοσοῦτον ἦλθον ὥστ’ ἐπεγχαν[ε]ῖν,
　　ἐπεὶ πάλαισμα κοιν[ὸ]ν ἠγωνι[σ]μένοι　　　15
　　ἔκειν[τ]ο νεκροὶ τυ[τ]θὸν [ἀ]λλήλων ἄπο,
　　ὁ μὲν δ[ά]κῃ τόσ’, ὁ δὲ [τὸ] πᾶν [ἀ]σ[χη-
　　　　μόν]ως
　　[λ]ύμην ’Αχαι[ῶν δὶς τ]όσῃ[ν ἠικισμέ]νος.

(*Fragments of twelve lines*)

[το]ιαῦτα πολλῶ[ν λυγρὸ]ν ἐρρ[ό]θει στόμα·
[π]ολλὴ δὲ σινδὼν [πολ]λὰ δ’ ’Ιστρ[ι]ανίδων　　20
ὕφη γυναικῶν ἀνδ[ρὸ]ς ἐρριπτ[ά]ζετο
(γέρας θανόντος, οἷα προσέφερον Φρύγες)
νεκρῶι διδόντες ο[ὐδ]ὲν ὠφελ[ο]υμένωι.
ὁ δ’ ἀμφὶ πλευραῖς καὶ σφαγαῖσι [κ]είμενος
πατ[ὴρ] μὲν οὔ, πατρῶια δ’ ἐξαυδ[ῶ]ν ἔπη　　25
Πρί[αμος] ἔκλαιε τὸν τέκνων ὁμαίμονα,
τὸν [π]αῖδα καὶ γέροντα καὶ νεαν[ία]ν,
τὸν οὔτε Μυσὸν οὔτε Τηλέφου [κα]λῶν,
ἀλλ’ ὡς φυτεύσας αὐτὸς ἐκκαλούμ[εν]ος·
οἴμοι τέκνον προὔδωκά σ’ ἐσχάτη[ν ἔχων　　30
Φρυξὶν μεγίστην (τ’) ἐλπίδων σωτ[ηρία]ν.
χρόνον ξενωθεὶς οὐ μακρὸν π[ολ]λῶν κακῶν

11 ου δικαι Π, corr. Roberts, *cf.* vv. 5–6.　　12 και
βεβασι Π.　　17 δ[·]κητός· Π.　　22 Supplied *ex grat.*
by Pearson, to fill a presumed lacuna of one line in Π.
18

CHORUS. Alas ! What shall we say, what shall we say ?

ASTYOCHE. Whose hand were unrighteous, if he shall smite this head ?

CHORUS. A spirit has destroyed you—it is just—a spirit.

ASTYOCHE. Are they trampling him with violence, do the Argives loudly mock his corpse, to crown this evil ? [a]

MESSENGER. Not so far they went, as to mock him with insult. The dead had fought the common strife ; their bodies [b] lay just apart one from the other—one with but a few wounds, the other all shamefully disfigured twice as much by Achaean swords. . . .

(Fragments of twelve lines)

So rose the mournful clamour from many lips. And many a linen robe, and many that Istrian women weave were thrown upon him (in honour of his death, such garments as the Phrygians brought) and gave unto the corpse that had no benefit of them. And Priam, prostrate about his wounded body, not father he, yet with a father's words bewept the kinsman of his sons : calling him boy and man and elder [c]—no Mysian, no child of Telephus, but his own son, so did he invoke his name :—" O my son, whom I have betrayed ! though in you I found the last and greatest salvation of my hopes for Phrygia ! Not many days our guest, yet manifold the sorrow whose memory

[a] For this (doubtful) rendering of these difficult lines, see Pearson *ad loc.* [b] Those of Eurypylus and one of his earlier victims ; see Pearson. [c] *i.e.* E. combined the best qualities of different ages—son, warrior and counsellor.

32 The last word in this line is preserved in a small scrap of papyrus published in *P. Oxy.* xvii. (2081 b 2).

LITERARY PAPYRI

μνήμην παρέξεις τοῖς λ[ελειμμέν]οις Ἄ[ρεως,
ὅσ᾽ οὔτε Μέμν[ω]ν οὔτε Σα[ρπήδων ποτὲ
π[έν]θη π[οήσ]α[ς κ]αίπερ αἰχ[μητῶν ἄκροι   35

5 [c. 200 A.D.]   ΣΚΥΡΙΟΙ

Ed. pr. Hunt, *P. Oxy.* xvii. 1927, no. 2077, p. 30.   See
Körte, *Archiv*, x. 1932, 48 ; *Pfeiffer, *Philol.* 88, 1933, 1 (he
first identified the play, observing that fr. 511 N. coincides
with part of this fragment) ; Pearson, *Fragm. of Soph.* ii.
p. 191 ; Fritsch, *Neue Fragm. d. Aisch. u. Soph.*, diss. Ham-
burg, 1936, 44 ; Zimmermann, *Phil. Woch.* 57, 747.

The course of the action is highly uncertain.   In general,

(a) —— ἢ ποντόναυται τῶν ταλαιπώρων βροτῶν]
      οἷς οὔτε δαίμων οὔτε τις θνητῶν γέμων]
      πλούτου ποτ᾽ ἂν νείμειεν ἀξίαν χάριν.]
      λεπταῖς ἐπὶ ῥοπαῖσιν ἐμπολὰς μ]ακρὰς
      ἀεὶ παραρρίπτοντες] οἱ πολύφθ[οροι   5
      ἢ ᾽σωσαν ἀκέρδαν]αν ἢ διώλεσαν.
      ὅμως δὲ θαυμάζω] τε κἀπαινῶ βροτούς,
      οὓς χρὴ κατ᾽ ἦμαρ] χειρὶ τῆι δυστλήμονι
      . . . . πο]ρσύνειν βίον.

(b)   (*Fragments of nine lines*)

   —— εἰέν· τί δ[ράσω; κῦμα πληθῦον βλέπω   10
      νῦν πᾶν, κατάξ[ειν δ᾽ αὐτίκ᾽ ἐλπίζουσί νιν,
      πλοίοις Ἀχαιῶν καὶ [συνωμότηι στρατῶι·
      ὧν εὐλαβείας οὔνεκ᾽ ἂ[ν θᾶσσον πόδα
      καθεῖμεν ἐκ τῆσ(δ᾽) ἀμφ[ικύμονος χθονὸς
      πρὸς ἄνδρα Χαλκώδον[τα, πατρῶιον ξένον,   15
      ναίοντά που κευθμῶν[ας Εὐβοῖδος χθονός.

20

SOPHOCLES

you will bequeath to those whom War has left: causing such lamentations as never Memnon nor Sarpedon, though foremost of fighters, . . .

SCYRIANS [c. 200 A.D.]

the play dealt with the bringing of Neoptolemus to Troy from Scyros. Odysseus and Phoenix were perhaps the Greek envoys. Perhaps there was a plot contrived by Lycomedes and Deidameia to frustrate their designs upon Achilles' son. See further Pfeiffer, Pearson, loc. cit.

TRULY are mariners counted among unhappy mortals !—to whom neither god nor man however full of riches can ever give their due reward ! Too slender the chance whereon they ever risk their distant enterprise, amid disasters, whether they save or lose their profit. Yet I revere and praise him whose long-suffering hands must provide a livelihood from day to day. . . .

(Fragments of nine lines)

Well now : what must I do ? Behold, the seas on every side abound with Greek vessels and confederate army, hoping to carry him home without delay : for guard against them, let us begone with all speed from this sea-girt land to a man, his father's friend, Chalcodon, who dwells somewhere in the

1-6 = Nauck fr. 511. 2 θεῶν νέμων MSS., corrupt: μέδων Pfeiffer: text Meineke. 7 D. L. P. 8 Pfeiffer. 10-12 D. L. P. 13 D. L. P. after Körte (ἂν βάδην πόδα). 14 Pfeiffer: τῆς Π, τῆσδ' Fritsch. 15 D. L. P. after Körte (πατρικὸν ξένον). 16 Hunt.

21

LITERARY PAPYRI

κεἰ πλοῦς ἔθ' ἡμᾶς πει[
κατῆγ' ἀνῆγέ θ' αὐτὸς ὃς γ[

6 [2 B.C.]   ΙΝΑΧΟΣ ΣΑΤΥΡΙΚΟΣ

Ed. pr. Hunt-Smyly, *Tebtunis Papyri*, iii. 1, 1933, p. 3, no. 692, Plate I. See Körte, *Archiv*, xi. 1935, 252 ; Schmidt, *Phil. Woch.* 1934, 1302 ; Fritsch, *Neue Fragm. d. Aisch. u. Soph.*, diss. Hamb. 1936, 33 ; *Pfeiffer, *Sitzb. Bayer. Akad.* 1938, 2, 23 (to this I am especially indebted, though I have not followed Pfeiffer's text in all details).   See further Pearson, *Fragm. of Soph.* i. p. 197.   Fragments of Π too small for inclusion here reveal the new words πορπαφόρος (" wearing a brooch "), οἴζομαι (" lament ").

The ascription of this text to Sophocles is not absolutely certain (see Körte, p. 253) : but Pfeiffer has shown it to be probable, in the course of his commentary (e.g. pp. 46-47, 57-59).

The scene of the action of Sophocles' Inachus *was probably the Argolis.   Fr. (a) below is preceded by fragments which reveal* σύριγγο[ς] δὲ κλύω, σ]ταθμοῦ, τὴν [. .]σιν βοῶ[ν *: hence it is likely that the speakers are near or among the cattle-herds of Inachus.*

From this text I (following Pfeiffer, to a certain extent) make the following inferences about the course of the action of this Satyric play :—

(a) Zeus sent Hermes to procure for him Io, who has been transformed into a cow and is guarded by Argus.   Hermes demands her surrender from Inachus (father of Io), whose refusal leads to a quarrel.   Inachus is obdurate : Hermes departs with his mission unaccomplished, but threatening to return : the Chorus is summoned to form an additional protection for Io.   [The quarrel between Hermes and Inachus certainly occurred early in the play, Pfeiffer, p. 56.]

22

glens of Euboea. If the voyage still . . . the same
one brought him hither and took him home . . .

INACHUS [2 B.C.]

(b) *Hermes returns, wearing the Cap of Hades, which
renders him invisible : thus he may elude the Chorus and
the myriad eyes of Argus, whom he will lull to slumber with
the music of a shepherd's pipe : he enters playing the pipe.
The Chorus is alarmed, but confident that Hermes will fail
again.—They tell him, he will try in vain a second time :
the first failure was of course his earlier dismissal by Inachus
(cf. v. 22 αὖ).*

*The further course of the action is quite uncertain : except
that Hermes succeeded in disposing of Argus. The play may
have ended with the departure of Io on her travels ; or with
a reconciliation between Zeus and Hera, and the liberation of
Io (Iris certainly appeared and conversed with Hermes :
perhaps she was a messenger of peace, Pfeiffer, p. 56).*

*Frs. (b) and (c) come from consecutive columns. The
position of fr. (a) is quite uncertain ; I have placed it before
the others, because the sequence of events seems to demand it.
We have two scenes.—(1) A quarrel between Hermes and
Inachus : Hermes, who is not yet invisible, clearly comes
with a command from Zeus, and clearly comes in vain.
(2) Hermes enters invisible, and the Chorus says " you will
fail again " : both this observation of the Chorus, and the
change from visibility to invisibility—from direct to deceitful
methods—suggest to me that the former scene must precede,
and explain, the latter.*

*I agree with Pfeiffer (p. 55) in rejecting the common
inference from fr. 279 (Pearson) that the transformation of
Io into a cow actually occurred in the course of this play.*

23

(*a*) [ΕΡΜΗΣ   ] ταῦτα· μὴ λέξῃς πλέω.
[ΙΝΑΧΟΣ ἀλλ' αὖθις εἶ]πον Ζηνὸς αἰάξαι λάτρι[ν.
[ΕΡΜΗΣ δὶς οὗτος οὐ] πάρεστιν Ἰνάχωι λόγ[ος.
[ΙΝΑΧΟΣ Διὸς πεφυκὼς] ὀλίγον ἰσχύεις ὅμ[ως.

(*b*) [ΧΟΡΟΣ ΣΑΤΥΡΩΝ] πολὺ πολυιδρίδας   5
             ὅτις ὅδε προτερῶν
             ὄνομ' εὖ σε θροεῖ,
             τὸν Ἀιδοκυνέας
             σκότον ἄ(β)ροτον ὑπαί.
[ΧΟ. Α] —— τὸν Διὸς μὲν οὖν ἐρώτων ἄ[γγ]ε-
        λον, μέγαν τρόχιν,   10
[ΧΟ. Β] ⟨——⟩ εἰ[κ]άσαι πάρεστιν Ἑρμῆν
     α′   π[ρὸ]ς τὰ σὰ ψοφήματα,
[ΧΟ. Γ] —— αὐτὸν ὄντα σ' αὐτὸν ὅς μοι δεῦρ'
     β′   ἀνέστρεψεν πόδα·
[ΧΟ. Δ] —— δευτέρους πόνους ἔοικας πρὶν μύ-
         σαι κενοὺς ἐλᾶν.
Χ[ΟΡΟΣ] ὠή· ε(ἰ)σορᾷς;
        †εις τον ατο† πόδ' ἔχειν.   15
        μανία τάδε κλύειν.
        σὺ γὰρ οὖν, Ζεῦ, λόγων
        κακὸς εἶ πίστεως·
        δι' ἄχη θεοβλαβ[

(*c*) [ΧΟ.] ψιθυρᾶν μάλ' αἰολᾶ[ν.   20
—— πάντα μηχανᾶι τὸ Δῖον, ὡς [τὸ Σισύφου,
        γένος.
—— ἦ ῥα τάχα Διὸς αὖ,
—— Διὸς ἄρα λάτρις ὅδε;

2-4 Beginnings D. L. P.: dialogue between H. and I.
recognized by Pfeiffer.   6 προτερῶν Körte, προτέρων edd.
9 ἄβροτον Fritsch, Pfeiffer : ἄροτον Π.   15 εἰς may be

SOPHOCLES

(*a*) HERMES. . . . Say no more !

INACHUS. I say again, the devil take the lackey of Zeus !

HERMES. No Inachus shall say that twice !

INACHUS. You may be son of Zeus, but you're still a weakling. . . .

(*b*) CHORUS. Wise, very wise is he who utters here your name aright before you tell him ! [a] The unearthly darkness of the Cap of Hades [b] hides you.

—— The prince of footmen, the messenger of the amours of Zeus,

—— It's a fair guess that you are Hermes from the sound you make,

—— Hermes himself, yes, Hermes, who has turned back toward us.

—— It's not the last futile errand you'll be running before you're much older. [c]

—— Oho, you see ? . . . It drives you mad to hear it ! [d] So you, Zeus, are a poor hand at keeping promises ! Through sorrows, stricken of God . . .

(*c*) —— . . . of whispers, very rapid. Sons of Zeus, like sons of Sisyphus, are up to every trick.

—— From Zeus again, can it be ?

—— The footman of Zeus is here ?

[a] Or, (with προτέρων) "whoever of the Front Row," ref. to ζυγά or rows of Satyrs in the dance. [b] The "Cap of Hades" rendered its wearer invisible ; see Homer, *Il.* v. 844-845, and Pfeiffer, p. 33. [c] Or, "before the day is over" (before you close your eyes in sleep) : but *cf.* τάχιον ἢ ἀναμῦσαι, and Eur. *Ba.* 747. [d] "It" : *sc.* the pipe of Hermes, *cf.* Aesch. *P. V.* 574.

———

ἐκ: τον is certain : ατο may be απι (Pfeiffer) : *faute de mieux*, (κρ)εῖσσον ἀπὸ πόδ' ἔχειν, "better keep away ! "

—— ἐπί με πόδα νέμει,
—— ἐμὲ †χερακονιει†.   25
—— μέγα δέος ἀραβεῖ.

(*Fragments of tetrameter dialogue, beginning* τῶν ἐναν-
τίων τὸ τάρβ[ος, τῶν κάτω Διὸς φαλάγγ[ων,
δωμάτων γ' εἰ μὴ 'πελᾶι[ς, ποῦ δὲ χρὴ πόδα
στατίζε[ιν)

24 After this verse a line was later inserted in smaller

7   [Late 2 A.D.]   ΙΧΝΕΥΤΑΙ

Ed. pr. Grenfell-Hunt, *P. Oxy.* ix. 1912, no. 1174, p. 30,
Plate II.   See *Hunt, *F.T.P.* ; Pearson, *Fragm. of Soph.* i.
p. 244 (to which my debt is especially great) ; Diehl, *Suppl.
Soph.* p. 3 ; Pickard-Cambridge, iii. 87 ; Bethe, *Ber. Sächs.
Ges. d. Wiss.* 1919 ; Robert, *Hermes,* 47, 536 ; Walker, *The
Ichneutae of Sophocles* ; Körte, *Archiv,* v. 1913, 558 ; Milne,
Cat. Lit. Pap. B.M. no. 67 ; Walton, *Harvard Class. St.* 46,
1935, 167.

The Dramatis Personae *are Apollo, Silenus, a Chorus of
Satyrs, Cyllene, and Hermes. The scene of the action is
Mount Cyllene in Arcadia. Apollo has lost his cattle ; he
has sought them vainly in Northern Greece, and has now
come to the Peloponnese. He promises a reward to their
discoverer. Silenus enters and offers the aid of himself and
his sons the Satyrs, in return for a prize of gold and release
from slavery. After a short ode, the Chorus and its leader
advance on the track of the cattle. Confused prints are dis-
covered, leading to the entrance of a cave. The Chorus is
suddenly alarmed by a strange sound, which appears to issue
from the cave. Silenus reproaches the Satyrs for their*

SOPHOCLES

—— He's coming at me !
—— At me . . .
—— There's terror in the sound of him ! [a]

(Fragments of tetrameter dialogue)

[a] Or " My teeth chatter with a great fear," ed. pr., *cf.* Homer, *Il.* x. 375-376. The Satyrs hear the approach of Hermes, whom they cannot see because he wears the Cap of Hades. The sounds of his pipe put fear and madness into them.

letters, . . . με πόδα νέμει (ἔχς με· κτλ. Pfeiffer). 25 ἐμὲ
χερὶ κλονιεῖ or κλονέει Pfeiffer.

THE SEARCHERS [Late 2 A.D.]

cowardice, and contrasts therewith the courage which he himself frequently displayed when he was young. The chase is resumed ; but the strange sound is heard again, and panic ensues. At last they beat loudly on the roof of the underground cave ; Cyllene emerges and inquires the meaning of their uproar. She informs them that she is nursing a son of Zeus and of the daughter of Atlas. This child—Hermes—, grown marvellously in a few days, has fashioned an instrument of music from the shell of a tortoise.—From this comes the noise which alarmed the Satyrs. Now it appears that Hermes has used a cowhide to stretch over the tortoise-shell ; and the Satyrs at once presume that the possession of this cowhide proves that Hermes is the thief of Apollo's cattle. The fragment ends with a quarrel between Cyllene and the Chorus ; she denying, and they insisting, that he must be the thief.

The conclusion of the play is not preserved. In col. xvii. 18-19 ed. pr., Apollo seems to admit that Silenus and his Satyrs have earned the promised reward. Thereafter prob-

27

*ably Hermes, confronted with Apollo, appeased his anger by
giving him the lyre. The analogy of Euripides' Cyclops
makes it likely that " the dénouement may not have occupied
more than another two or three hundred lines " (ed. pr.).*

*It was not previously known that Sophocles had treated this
story. He diverges from the detail of the Homeric Hymn to
Hermes (with which he was familiar, Pearson, p 228) in
several points.—In Sophocles (1) the theft of the cattle pre-
cedes the invention of the lyre, (2) the scene is Mount Cyllene,
not Triphylian Pylos, (3) the Satyrs are the hunters of the
stolen cattle, (4) Cyllene, not Maia, is the nurse of Hermes.
Ichneutae, which is probably an early work of Sophocles
(Pearson, p. 230), immediately invites comparison with the
only other extant satyric drama, Euripides' Cyclops. The
comparison is largely a contrast. Sophocles' play reveals—
so far as we can tell—much less both of humour and of
indecency : further, its diction is predominantly tragic,
admitting only a very few vulgar phrases, and numerous
exclamations which are below the tragic level : in its iambic
metre, Ichneutae is again more regular than Cyclops,
admitting anapaests in the first foot only, and violating the*

[ΑΠΟΛΛΩΝ κήρυγμ' Ἀπόλλων πᾶσι]ν ἀγγέλλω βρο-
    το[ῖς
    θεοῖς τε πᾶσι· δῶρ' ὑπισ]χνοῦμαι τελεῖν,
    βοῦς εἴ τις ἐγγὺς εἶδεν εἴτ' ἀ]πόπροθεν·
    δειν]ὸν [γὰρ οὖν ἄλγημα δύσ]λοφον φρενὶ
    ἔπεσ]τ' ἀ[φαιρεθέντι βο]ῦς ἀμολγάδας   5
    μόσ]χους [τε πάσας καὶ νόμευμ]α πορτίδων.
    ἅπα]ντα φρ[οῦδα, καὶ μάτη]ν ἰχνοσκοπῶ
    λαθ]ραῖ' ἰόν[των τῆλε βου]στάθμου κάπης
    ἀφα]νῶς τεχνά[σματ'· ἀλλ' ἐ]γὼ οὐκ ἂν
        ᾠόμην
    οὔτ' ἄ]ν θεῶν τιν' [οὔτ' ἐφημ]έρων βροτῶν   10

SOPHOCLES

canon of the final cretic once only (v. 269, a gentle offence). The lyrics, as in Cyclops, are short and slight in size, structure, and metres.   Unique is the dialogue in iamb. tetram. acatal. (vv. 238 sqq.).

A difficult problem arises out of v. 45.   Apollo promises freedom to Silenus and his Satyrs.   Whose slaves then were they ?   Now Cyllene (vv. 171 sqq.) refers to their master as following in the train of Dionysus with fawnskin and thyrsus. From this it follows that Dionysus himself—otherwise the likeliest candidate—was not their master.   Further, how can Apollo liberate the slaves of Dionysus *?   Pearson (whose account I followed until the last moment) suggests that Apollo himself is the master.   But Professor Beazley has convinced me (too late, I fear, to make a necessary alteration in the text) that this Dionysiac Apollo is an impossible creation, and that Pearson's references to Aesch. fr. 341, Eur. fr. 477 do not assist his argument.   Beazley (following Robert) suggests that a line has dropped out after 171 (e.g. καὶ τῶι φιλοίνωι—or κρατίστωι—πατρί, Σιληνὸν λέγω) : then the δεσπότης of 171 is Dionysus, ὅς in 172 is Silenus, and all is natural and requires no further comment (ἐγγόνοις νύμφαισι 175 is now free from difficulty—unintelligible, if Apollo is the subject of these lines).*

APOLLO. To every man and every god proclaims Apollo : if anyone has seen my cattle, near or far, to him I promise a reward.   Grievous and heavy pain is in my heart ; someone has robbed me of my cows and all my calves and herds of heifers.   Not one is left. All are gone unseen, far from the stables : vainly I follow the traces of their stealthy plot.   I never should have thought that any god or mortal man

---

1-4 D. L. P., after Hunt, Rossbach.   5 Pearson.
8, 9 Pearson.

δρᾶσ]αι τόδ' ἔργ[ον ὧδε] πρὸς τόλμαν πεσεῖν.
ταῦτ'] οὖν ἐπείπερ [ἔμα]θον, ἐκπλαγεὶς ὄκνωι
ζητ]ῶ, ματεύω, παντελὲς κήρυγμ' ἔχων
θεοῖ]ς βροτοῖς τε μηδέν' ἀγνοεῖν τάδε·
. . . . .]υθίαι γὰρ ἐμμανὴς κυνηγετῶ.   15
. . . . .]ων δ' ἐπῆλθον φῦλα, τ[οῦ] παντὸς
    στρατ[οῦ
ζητῶν] τίς [

(A gap, then fragments of three lines)

τὰ Θεσσαλῶν [τ' ἔγκαρπα πεδί' ἐ]πεσσύθην
Βοιωτίας τε γ[ῆς πολυκτήτου]ς [πό]λ[εις]
ἔπει]τα δ' [20

(A gap of about four lines)

       ]ς Δωρικο[
     γει]τον' ἔνθ[εν
    ] ἥκω ξὺν [τ]ά[χει
    Κυλ]λήνης τε δυ[
    ] τε χῶρον ἐς δυ[25
ὡς εἴτε ποι]μὴν εἴτ' ἀγρωτή[ρων τις ἢ
μαριλοκαυ]τῶν ἐν λόγωι παρ[ίσταται
ἢ τῶν ὀρ]είων νυμφογεννή[του γένους
θηρῶ]ν τίς ἐστι, πᾶσιν ἀγγέλ[λω τάδε,
τὰ ἔλ]ωρα τοῦ Παιῶνος ὅστις ἂ[ν λάβηι,   30
τῶιδ' α]ὐτόχρημα μισθὸς ἔσθ' ὁ κε[ίμενος.
[ΣΙΛΗΝΟΣ Λύκειε,] σοῦ φωνήμαθ' ὡς ἐπέκλυον
βοῶ]ντος ὀρθίοισι σὺν κηρύγμασι,
σπουδῆι τάδ' ἢ πάρεστι πρεσβύτηι [μαθών,
σοί, Φοῖβ' Ἄπολλον, προσφιλὴς εὐε[ργέτης   35
θέλων γενέσθαι τῶιδ' ἐπεσσύθην δρ[ό]μ[ωι,

would dare to do this deed. Since I have heard the news, distracted with alarm I hunt and search and make full proclamation to gods and men, that none may be unaware . . . I follow frantic in pursuit. I visited the tribes . . . seeking, which man of all the host . . .

(A gap, then fragments of three lines)

I rushed to the fruitful plains of Thessaly [a] and the wealthy cities of Boeotia, and then . . .

(A gap of about four lines)

Doric [b] . . . neighbour, whence . . . I have come swiftly . . . and of Cyllene . . . and to a place. . . . So if any shepherd, farmer, or charcoaler is at hand to hear me, or any nymph-born wild-man of the mountains, to one and all I make this proclamation : whoever catches the prey taken from Apollo, earns forthwith the reward that lies ready here.

SILENUS. I heard your voice, Apollo, raised in loud proclamation. Fast as an old man may, when the news came, eager to be your friend and benefactor, Phoebus, I hurried—running as you see—to find if

---

[a] Traditionally the scene of Apollo's pastures. [b] Marks the progress of Apollo from North to South Greece in his search.

---

13 Murray, Wilamowitz. 15 ἀκολο]υθίαι Wilamowitz, δυσπε]υθίαι Murray, πολυμ]υθίαι Pearson. 16 Θραικ]ῶν Hunt, with Wilamowitz : but *v.* Pearson *ad loc.* 17 Murray, Hunt. 23 Mekler. 30 τὰ ἕλωρα Pearson ; τοῦ II ; τῶν Hunt, after Wilamowitz. 32 Diehl.

ἄν πως τὸ χρῆμα τοῦτό σοι κυνηγέσω.
τ[ὸ] γὰρ γέ[ρα]ς μοι κείμενον χρ[υ]σο[σ]τεφὲ[ς

(Fragment of one line)

παῖδας δ' ἐμ[οὺ]ς ὅσσοισι [
πέμποιμ' ἄ]ν εἴπερ ἐκτελεῖς ἅπερ λέγεις.   40
[ΑΠ. σπουδὴν ἐπαιν]ῶ· μοῦνον ἐμπ[έδου τ]άδ[ε.
[ΣΙ.] τὰ[ς βοῦς ἀπάξω σ]οι· σὺ δ' ἐμπέδου [δόσι]ν.
[ΑΠ. ἕξει σφ' ὅ γ' εὑ]ρὼν ὅστις ἔσθ'· ἐτ[οῖ]μ[α] δέ.

(Fragments of four lines)

[ΣΙ.] τί τοῦτο; πο[ίαν δωρεὰν ἄλλην λέγ]εις;
[ΑΠ.] ἐλεύθερος σὺ [πᾶν τε γένος ἔσται τέκν]ων.   45
ΧΟ[ΡΟΣ] ΣΑΤΥ[ΡΩΝ]

(Fragments of twelve lines)

ξὺν ἅμα θεὸς ὁ φίλος ἀνέτω
πόνους προφήνας
ἀρίζηλα χρυσοῦ παραδείγματα.
ΣΙΛΗΝΟ[Σ] θεοὶ τύχη καὶ δαῖμον ἰθυντήριε,   50
τυχεῖν με πράγους οὗ δράμημ' ἐπείγεται,
λείαν ἄγραν σύλησιν ἐκκυνηγέσαι
Φοίβου κλοπαίας βοῦς ἀπεστερημένου.
τῶν εἴ τις ὀπτήρ ἐστιν ἢ κατήκοος
ἐμοί τ' ἂν εἴη προσφιλὴς φράσας τάδε   55
Φοίβωι τ' ἄνακτι παντελὴς εὐεργέτης.

*(Fragments of five lines, two by Silenus, three by
the Chorus)*

38 Pearson.   40 Diehl.   41 σπουδὴν ἐπαινῶ Pear-
son.   47 σύναμα Hunt: corr. Pearson.   56 προστελὴς
Π: corr. Pearson.

I could hunt this treasure down for you. The prize
of a golden wreath awaiting me . . .

(Fragment of one line)

and my sons, sharpeyed . . . I will send forth if you
will keep your promise.

APOLLO. Your zeal comes not amiss ; only make
good your word.

SILENUS. I will restore to you your cattle ; only
make good your gift !

APOLLO. The finder gets it, whoever he is. It is
waiting for him.

(Fragments of four lines)

SILENUS. What's this ? What is this other gift you
mention ?

APOLLO. Freedom : for you and all your sons.[a]

CHORUS OF SATYRS.

(Fragments of twelve lines)

. . . now at our side let the god who is dear to us,
who shewed us those glittering samples of gold, bring
our task to fulfilment.

SILENUS. O Gods, O Fortune, O Guiding Spirit !
Grant me success in the quest whereat my course is
aimed, to track the loot, the spoil, the plunder, the
stolen cattle that Phoebus has lost ! If anyone has
seen them or heard of them, let him speak out ; he
shall be my friend, and King Phoebus's greatest
benefactor.

*(Fragments of five lines, two by Silenus, three by
the Chorus)*

---

[a] The Satyrs were nevertheless *not* represented as slaves
of Apollo ; see Introd. Note.

[ΣΙ.] φησίν τις, ἢ [οὐδείς φησιν εἰδέναι τάδε;
ἔοικεν ἤδη κ[ἀμὲ πρὸς τοὖργον δραμεῖν.
ἄγ᾽ εἶα δὴ πᾶς σ[
ῥινηλατῶν ὀσμ[αῖσι   60
αὔρας ἐάν πηι πρ[
διπλοῦς ὀκλάζω[ν
ὔποσμος ἐν χρῶι [
οὕτως ἔρευναν καὶ π[
ἅπαντα χρηστὰ κα[ὶ . . . . τε]λεῖν 65

[ΗΜΙΧ.] θεὸς θεὸς θεὸς θεός· ἔα [ἔα·
ἔχειν ἔοιγμεν· ἴσχε· μὴ . ρ[. . . .]τει.

[ΗΜΙΧ.] ταῦτ᾽ ἔστ᾽ ἐκεῖνα τῶν βοῶν τὰ βήματα.

[ΗΜΙΧ.] σῖγα· θεός τις τὴν ἀποι[κία]ν ἄγει.

[ΗΜΙΧ.] τί δρῶμεν, ὦ τᾶν; ἢ τὸ δέον [ἄρ᾽] ἤνομεν; 70
τί; τοῖσ[ι] ταύτηι πῶς δοκεῖ; [ΗΜΙΧ.] δοκεῖ
πάνυ.
σαφῆ γὰρ αὔθ᾽ ἔκαστα σημαίνει τάδε.

[ΗΜΙΧ.] ἰδοὺ ἰδού·
καὶ τοὐπίσημον αὐτὸ τῶν ὁπλῶν πάλιν.

[ΗΜΙΧ.] ἄθρει μάλα·   75
αὔτ᾽ ἐστὶ τοῦτο μέτρον ἐκμε[μαγ]μένον.

[ΗΜΙΧ.] χώρει δρόμωι καὶ τα[. . . . .]ν ἔχου
. . . .]οπ[. . .]μενος
ῥοίβδημ᾽ ἐάν τι τῶν [. . . πρὸ]ς οὖς [μόληι.

ΡΟΙΒΔΟΣ

[ΗΜΙΧ.] οὐκ εἰσακούω πω [τορῶ]ς τοῦ φθέγματος, 80
ἀλλ᾽ αὐτὰ μὴν ἴχ[νη τε] χὠ στίβος τάδε
κείνων ἐναργῆ τῶν βοῶν μαθεῖν πάρα.

[ΗΜΙΧ.] ἔα μάλα·

---

58 Roberts.   59 For the aspiration, v. ed. pr. *ad loc.*
66 This was v. 100 of the complete play (stichometrical α in

Who says he knows? Anyone or no one? It seems high time for *me* to set to work. Come, everyone . . . nosing the scent . . . somewhere perhaps a breath of wind . . . squatting double . . . follow the scent closely . . . so . . . the search, and . . . everything fine, and . . . bring to an end.

SEMICHORUS OF SATYRS. A god, a god, a god, a god! Hullo, hullo! I think we have them! Stop, don't . . .

SEMICH. Here it is! The cattle's trail!

SEMICH. Be quiet! A god is leading our colony.[a]

SEMICH. What must we do, sir? Were we doing our work aright? Well? What say our friends over there?

SEMICH. They approve: each mark here is certain evidence.

SEMICH. Look, look! The very imprint of their hooves again!

SEMICH. Look close: here is a moulding of the very size!

SEMICH. Run hard, and . . . if a noise from those . . . should reach your ear.

Noise[b] (*off stage*)

SEMICH. I can't yet hear their lowing clearly, but here are the very steps and trail of Apollo's cattle, clear to see.

SEMICH. Good gracious! the footprints are re-

[a] *i.e.* simply "is in charge of our expedition." [b] The noise is that of the lyre; the chorus hears it indistinctly and supposes that it proceeds from the cattle.

---

margin, col. iv., v. 14, ed. pr.). 76 Pearson. 79 τῶν [ἔσω etc. Pearson: but the reference to the cave or *inmates* of anything is premature. Perhaps τῶν [βοῶν.

παλινστραφῆ τοι ναὶ μὰ Δία τὰ βήματα.
εἰς τοὔμπαλιν δέδορκεν· αὐτὰ δ' εἴσιδε.　85
τί ἐστὶ τουτί; τίς ὁ τρόπος τοῦ τάγματος;
εἰς τοὐπίσω τὰ πρόσθεν ἤλλακται, τὰ δ' αὖ
ἐναντί' ἀλλήλοισι συμπ[επλεγ]μένα.
δεινὸς κυκησμὸς εἶχ[ε τὸν βοη]λάτην.

[ΣΙ.] τίν' αὖ τέχνην σὺ τήν[δ' ἄρ' ἐξ]εῦρες, τίν' αὖ, 90
πρόσπαιον ὧδε κεκλιμ[ένος] κυνηγετεῖν
πρὸς γῆι; τίς ὑμῶν ὁ τρόπος; οὐχὶ μαν-
θάνω.

ἐχῖνος ὥς τις ἐν λόχμηι κεῖσαι πεσών,
ἤ τις πίθηκος †κυβαποθυμαινεις† τινί·
τί ταῦτα; ποῦ γῆς ἐμάθετ', ἐν ποίωι τόπωι; 95
σημήνατ', οὐ γὰρ ἴδρις εἰμὶ τοῦ τρόπου.

[ΧΟ.] ὖ ὖ ὖ ὖ.
[ΣΙ.] τ[ί τοῦτ' ἰύζεις;] τίνα φοβῆι; τίν' εἰσορᾶις;
τ[ί δεῖμ' ὄπωπ]ας; τί ποτε βακχεύεις ἔχων;
α[. . . . .]ι κέρχνος ἱμείρεις μαθεῖν. 100
τ[ί δῆτα] σιγᾶθ', οἱ πρὸ τοῦ [λαλίστ]ατοι;
[ΧΟ.] σ[ίγα μὲν οὖν.]
[ΣΙ.] τ[ίν' ἔστ' ἐκεῖθε]ν ἀπονοσ[φίζ]εις ἔχων;
[ΧΟ.] ἄ[κουε δή.]
[ΣΙ.] καὶ πῶς ἀκούσ[ω μηδεν]ὸς φωνὴν κλύων; 105
[ΧΟ.] ἐμοὶ πιθοῦ.
[ΣΙ.] ἐμ[ὸν] δίω[γμά γ' οὐδα]μῶς ὀνήσετε.
[ΧΟ.] ἄκουσον αὖ τοῦ χρ[ήμα]τος χρόνον τινά,
οἵωι 'κπλαγέντες ἐνθάδ' ἐξενίσμεθα
ψόφωι τὸν οὐδεὶς π[ώπο]τ' ἤκουσεν βροτῶν. 110

85 αὖ· τάδ' Hunt: αὐτὰ δ' Pearson.　91 κεκλιμένος
Pearson.　94 κυβαποθυμαίνεις Π, δ written above by the
second hand.　κύβδ' ἀποθυμαίνεις Hunt: but that would be

36

SOPHOCLES

versed! Just look at them! They face backwards!
What's this? What sort of order is it? The front
marks have shifted to the rear ; some again are en-
tangled in two opposite directions! What a strange
confusion must have possessed their driver !

SILENUS. And *now* what trick have you invented ?
what's the game ? What *is* it, I say ? this new one—
hunting on your bellies like that! What sort of
method do you call this ? It's a mystery to me.
Lying on the ground like hedgehogs in a bush, or
(stooping) like an (amorous) ape ! What is this
foolery, and where on earth did you learn it ? Tell
me : I never heard of such behaviour.

CHORUS. Ow !

SILENUS (*addressing members of the Chorus severally*).
What are you howling for ? Who's frightening you ?
Whom are you looking at ? Have you seen a bogey ?
Why do you keep dancing like dervishes? . . . you
want to find out . . . that scraping sound . . .?
(*A pause.*) Why silent now ? You used to talk
enough !

CHORUS. No, no, be quiet !

SILENUS. What is it there, that you keep turning
from ?

CHORUS. Listen, do !

SILENUS. How can I listen when I hear no voice ?

CHORUS. Do what I say.

SILENUS. A lot of help you will give me in my
chase !

CHORUS. Listen to the thing again a moment; a
noise that terrifies us here and maddens us ; no
mortal ever heard it yet !

the only instance of an anapaestic foot outside the first foot
in this play.   100 ἀ[γχοῦ τίς ἤχε]ι Hunt.

[ΣΙ.] τί μοι ψόφον φοβ[εῖσθε] καὶ δειμαίνετε,
μάλθης ἄναγνα σώματ' ἐκμεμαγμένα,
κάκιστα θηρῶν ὄντ[ες, ἔ]ν πάσηι σκιᾶι
φόβον βλέποντες, πάντα δειματούμενοι,
ἄνευρα κἀκόμιστα κἀνελεύθερα   115
διακονοῦντες, [σ]ώ[μ]ατ' εἰ[σ]ιδ[ε]ῖν μόνον
καὶ γλῶσσα καὶ φαλῆτες; εἰ δέ που δέηι,
πιστοὶ λόγοισιν ὄντες ἔργα φεύγετε.
τοιοῦδε πατρός, ὦ κάκιστα θηρίων,
οὗ πόλλ' ἐφ' ἥβης μνήματ' ἀνδρείας ὕπο   120
κεῖται παρ' οἴκοις νυμφικοῖς ἠσκημένα,
οὐκ εἰς φυγὴν κλίνοντος, οὐ δειλουμένου,
οὐδὲ ψόφοισι τῶν ὀρειτρόφων βοτῶν
πτήσσοντος, ἀλλ' α[ἰχ]μαῖσιν ἐξειργασμένου
ἃ νῦν ὑφ' ὑμῶν λάμ[πρ' ἀ]πορρυπαίνεται   125
ψόφωι νεώρει κόλακι ποιμένων ποθέν;
[τί] δὴ φοβεῖσθε παῖδες ὣς πρὶν εἰσιδεῖν,
πλοῦτον δὲ χρυσόφαντον ἐξαφίετε
ὃν Φοῖβος ὑμῖν εἶπε κἀνεδέξατο,
καὶ τὴν ἐλευθέρωσιν ἣν κατήινεσεν   130
ὑμῖν τε κἀμοί; ταῦτ' ἀφέντες εὕδετε.
εἰ μὴ 'νανοστήσαντες ἐξιχνεύσετε
τὰς βοῦς ὅπηι βεβᾶσι καὶ τὸν βουκόλον,
κλαίοντες αὐτῆι δειλίαι ψοφήσετε.
[ΧΟ.] πάτερ, παρὼν αὐτός με συμποδηγέτει,   135
ἵν' εὖ κατειδῆις εἴ τίς ἐστι δειλία.
γνώσηι γὰρ αὐτός, ἂν παρῆις, οὐδὲν λέγων.
[ΣΙ.] ἐγὼ παρὼν αὐτός σε προσβιβῶ λόγωι
κυνορτικὸν σύριγμα διακαλούμενος.
ἀλλ' εἶ', [ἀ]φίστω τριζύγης οἴμου βάσιν,   140
ἐγὼ δ' ἐν ἔργοις παρμένων σ' ἀπευθυνῶ.
ΧΟ.   ὗ ὗ ὗ, ψ ψ, ἇ ἇ, λέγ' ὅ τι πονεῖς.

SOPHOCLES

SILENUS. Why should a mere noise alarm and scare
you ? Tell me, you damned waxwork dummies,
you worthless animals ! You see an ogre in every
shadow, a bogey everywhere ! Useless assistants—
spineless, slovenly, unenterprising ! Just flesh and
chatter and wantonness ! in every crisis you profess
loyalty, but fly from action. Yet your father, you
worthless brutes, was a youth whose valour set up
many a splendid trophy in the nymphs' abodes ; he
never yielded to flight, never lost courage, never
ducked at noises made by cattle grazing on the hill ;
he performed feats in battle whose lustre now you
tarnish at some shepherd's new wheedling call.
Scared as babies before you even see ! You throw
away the golden riches that Phoebus promised and
guaranteed, and the freedom he agreed to give us,
you as well as me. You give it all up and go fast
asleep ! Come back and search out where the cattle
and the cowman went, or you'll be sorry—you shall
pay for making such a noise out of mere cowardice !

CHORUS. Father, come here and guide me your-
self : you'll soon find out if there is any cowardice.
Come here, and you'll learn what nonsense you are
talking.

SILENUS. I'll come, and win you to my way of
thinking, with a cheer for all like the call of the hunter
to the hounds. Come on, no more standing at the
cross-road ! I will stay on the scene of action and
put you on your path.

CHORUS. (*Sundry noises of alarm and encourage-*

---

112 σώματ᾽ P. Oxy. 2081 (a) i.   117 φαλῆτες P. Oxy.
2081 (a) i.   122 Nicander (see Hunt, App. Crit.):
δουλουμένου Π, Hunt.   124, 125 Pearson.   127
Pearson.   140 [ἀ]φίστω Pearson.

τί μάτην ὑπέκλαγες ὑπέκριγες
ὑπό μ᾽ ἴδες; ἔχεται
ἐν πρώτωι τίς ὅδε τρόπ[ωι;   145
ἔχει· ἐλήλυθεν ἐλήλ[υθεν·
ἐμὸς εἶ, ἀνάγου.
δεῦτ᾽, ὤ, τίς ὅδε [. . . . . .]της
ὁ δράκις, ὁ γράπις [

(*Fragments of nineteen lines*)

πάτερ, τί σιγᾶις; μῶν ἀληθ[ὲς εἴπομεν;   150
οὐκ εἰσακούεις, ἢ κεκώφη[σαι, ψόφον;
[ΣΙ.] σί[γα.] [ΧΟ.] τί ἔστιν; [ΣΙ.] οὐ μενῶ. [ΧΟ.]
        μέν᾽, εἰ θέλεις.

[ΣΙ.] οὐκ ἔστιν, ἀλλ᾽ αὐτὸς σὺ ταῦθ᾽ [ὅπηι θέλεις
ζήτει τε κἀξίχνευε καὶ πλού[τει λαβὼν
τὰς βοῦς τε καὶ τὸν χρυσόν, [ὡς ἐμοὶ δοκ]ε[ῖ 155
μὴ πλεῖστ[ον] ἔτι μ[έ]ν[οντα διατρίβειν]
        χρόνον.

[ΧΟ.] ἀλλ᾽ οὔ τι μ[ή σοι] μ᾽ [ἐκλιπεῖν ἐφήσομαι
οὐδ᾽ ἐξυπελ[θεῖ]ν τ[οῦ πόνου πρίν γ᾽ ἂν
        σα]φῶς
εἰδῶμεν ὄν[τιν᾽] ἔ[νδον ἤδ᾽ ἔχει στέγη.
ἰὼ γ[160
φθέγμ᾽ ἀφύσ[ε]ις[
.]ηδ[. . . μισ-]
θό[ν δ]όμοισιν ὀλβίσηις.
ὁ δ᾽ οὐ φανεῖται τοῖσιν· ἀλλ᾽ ἐγὼ τάχα
φέρων κτύπον πέδορτον ἐξαναγκάσω   165
πηδήμασιν κραιπνοῖσι καὶ λακτίσμασιν
ὥστ᾽ εἰσακοῦσαι κεἰ λίαν κωφός τις ἦι.
[ΚΥΛΛΗΝΗ] θῆρες, τί τόνδε χλοερὸν ὑλώδη πάγον
ἔνθηρον ὡρμήθητε σὺν πολλῆι βοῆι;

ment.) Say, what is your trouble? What's the good
of groaning and gibbering and glowering at me?
Who is this who is caught at the very first bend?
You're caught—here he comes, here he comes! I
have you! Off to prison you go! Hither—hullo!—
who is this . . . ? The wizard, the wizened . . .

(Fragments of nineteen lines)

Father, why silent? Didn't we speak the truth?
Can't you hear the noise, or are you stone-deaf?

SILENUS. Be quiet!

CHORUS. What is it?

SILENUS (*hearing the noise*). I'll not stay!

CHORUS. Do stay—please!

SILENUS. Impossible. You look and search them
out as you please, and catch the cattle and the gold
and get rich quick. I'm determined not to spend
much more time waiting here.

CHORUS. I'll not allow you to desert me and sneak
away from the job before we know for certain who
lives beneath this roof.

Hallo . . . you shall pour forth a voice . . . pro-
vide a rich reward for our house.

He won't shew himself for *that*. I'll apply another
method—make the ground ring with repeated jumps
and kicks; I'll soon force him to hear me, however
deaf he is.

CYLLENE. Wild creatures, wherefore have you
attacked this green and wooded hill, haunt of wild
beasts, with loudest uproar? What tricks are these?

---

150 This was line 200 of the complete play (stichometrical
β in margin, col. viii., v. 13, ed. pr.). 152 *sqq.* For the
arrangement of those lines, *v.* Pearson, whom I follow. εἰ
θέλεις Π, εἰ δύναι Wilamowitz, from a *v.l.* on ὅπηι θέλεις v. 153
in margin of Π. 155, 156 Pearson.

τίς ἥδε τέχνη, τίς μετάστασις πόνων   17(
οὓς πρόσθεν εἶχες δεσπότηι χάριν φέρων,
ὑμῖν ὃς αἰεὶ νεβρίνηι καθημμένος
δορᾶι χεροῖν τε θύρσον εὐπαλῆ φέρων
ὄπισθεν εὐίαζετ’ ἀμφὶ τὸν θεὸν
σὺν ἐγγόνοις νύμφαισι καὶ παίδων ὄχλωι;   17ᵃ
νῦν δ’ ἀγνοῶ τὸ χρῆμα, ποῖ στροφαὶ νέ[ω]ν
μανιῶν στρέφουσι· θαῦμα γάρ· κατέκλυον
ὁμοῦ πρέπον κέλευμά πως κυνηγετῶν
ἐγγὺς μολόντων θηρὸς εὐναίου τροφῆς,
ὁμοῦ δ’ ἂν αὐτι[ς . . . .]αι φωρ[18(
γλώσσης ἐτείνε[τ’ ε]ἰς κλοπὴν [. . . . . .]έναι
αὖτις δ’ ἀ[. . . .]τ[   ] μένων [   ]α
κῆρυκ[. . . .]ι[. . . . . .] κηρυγμα[
καὶ ταῦτ’ ἀφεῖσα σὺν ποδῶν λακ[τίσμασι
κληδὼν ὁμοῦ πάμφυρτ’ ἐγειτν[ία στέγηι.   18ᵃ
[καὶ] ταῦτ’ ἂν ἄλλως ἢ κλ[. . . . .]μ[
[φων]ῶν ἀκούσασ’ ὧδε παραπεπαισμένων
. . . . . .]φ[. .]η[. . . .]νων ὑμᾶς νοσεῖν
νό[σ . . τί νύμφη]ν ἔτι ποεῖτ’ ἀναιτίαν;

ΧΟ.   νύμφα βαθύζωνε π[αῦσαι χόλου   19(
τοῦδ’, οὔτε γὰρ νεῖκος ἥ[κω φέρων
δάιου μάχας οὐδ’ ἄξενό[ς που σέθεν
γλ[ῶ]σσ’ ἂν μάταιός τ’ [ἀφ’ ἡμῶν θίγοι.
μή με μὴ προσψαλ[άξηις κακοῖς,
ἀλλ’ εὐπετῶς μοι πρ[όφανον τὸ πρᾶγ-   19ᵃ
μ’, ἐν τόποις τοῖσ[δε τίς νέρθε γᾶς ὧδ’ ἀγα-
στῶς ἐγάρυσε θέσπιν αὐδά[ν;

[ΚΥ.]   ταῦτ’ ἔστ’ ἐκείνων νῦν [τρόπων πεπαιτέρα,
καὶ τοῖσδε θηρῶν ἐκπύ[θοιο μᾶλλον ἂν
ἀλκασμάτων δ[ειλή]ς [τε πειρατηρίων   20(
νύμφης· ἐμοὶ γὰ[ρ οὐ]κ [ἀρεστόν ἐστ’ ἔριν

42

What is this change from that task wherewith of old
you pleased your master?[a] . . . who, clad in hide of
fawn, bearing the light thyrsus, was ever wont to sing
for you that holy song in the god's train, accompanied
by nymphs, his descendants, and a youthful company.
But this—I know it not, whither your latest madcap
whirlwind spins you. 'Tis strange indeed. I heard a
cry like the call of hunters when they come near the
brood of a beast in its lair, and in the same moment
again . . . thief . . . your words referred to a theft
. . . and to a proclamation . . . then, dropping that,
your shouting, together with stamping of feet, in one
roar of confusion came to live on the roof above me.

. . . hearing such crazy shouts . . . what would
you still do to a harmless nymph?

CHORUS. Stay your anger, stately nymph: I do
not come to bring you strife of wars and enemies:
nor do I think that any unfriendly foolish word from
us shall reach your heart. Ah no, assail me not with
taunting, but readily disclose the secret—who is it
here below the ground, who spoke with a voice divine
to amaze us?

CYLLENE. Come, that's a gentler manner than the
other: if you hunt like *this*, you will learn far more
than by violence and attempts upon a frightened
nymph. I do not like loud quarrels started in argu-

---

[a] δεσπότηι 171 is Dionysus; a lacuna should be marked
after 171; ὅς 172 is Silenus. See Introd. Note.

---

191 Diehl.

ὀρθοψάλακτον ἐν [λ]όγο[ισ]ιν [ἱστάναι.
ἀλλ' ἥσυχος πρόφαινε καὶ μ[ή]νυ[έ μοι
ὅτου μάλιστα πράγματος χρείαν ἔχεις.
[χο.] τόπων ἄνασσα τῶνδε, Κυλλήνης σθένος,   205
ὅτου μὲν οὕνεκ' ἦλθον ὕστερον φράσω·
τὸ φθέγμα δ' ἡμῖν τοῦθ' ὅπερ φωνεῖ φράσον,
καὶ τίς ποτ' αὐτῶι διαχαράσσεται βροτῶν.
[κτ.] ὑμᾶς μὲν αὐτοὺς χρὴ τάδ' εἰδέναι σαφῶς,
ὡς εἰ φανεῖτε τὸν λόγον τὸν ἐξ ἐμοῦ,   210
αὐτοῖσιν ὑμῖν ζημία πορίζεται.
καὶ γὰρ κέκρυπται τοὔργον ἐν [θ]ε[ῶ]ν ἕδραις,
Ἥραν ὅπως μ[ὴ πύ]στ[ι]ς ἵξεται λόγου.
Ζ[εὺ]ς γ[ὰρ] κρυφ[αίαν ἐς στέ]γην Ἀτλαντίδος
τήνδ' ἧκε νύκτωρ, διὰ δ' ἐπαρθέν]εύσατο   215
          ]ν[. .] φίλας
. . . .] λήθηι τῆς βαθυζώνου θεᾶς.
κατὰ σπέ]ος δὲ παῖδ' ἐφίτευσεν μόνον,
τοῦτον δὲ] χερσὶ ταῖς ἐμαῖς ἐγὼ τρέφω·
μητρὸς γ]ὰρ ἰσχὺς ἐν νόσωι χειμάζεται·   220
κάδεστ]ὰ καὶ ποτῆτα καὶ κοιμήματα
πρὸς σπ]αργάνοις μένουσα λικνῖτιν τροφὴν
ἐξευθ]ετίζω νύκτα καὶ καθ' ἡμέραν.
ὁ δ' α]ὔξεται κατ' ἦμαρ οὐκ ἐπεικότα
μέγι]στος, ὥστε θαῦμα καὶ φόβος μ' ἔχει.   225
οὔπω γ]ὰρ ἕκτον ἦμαρ ἐκπεφασμένος
. . . . .]ς ἐρείδει παιδὸς εἰς ἥβης ἀκμήν,
κἀξορμενίζει κοὐκέτι σχολάζεται
βλάστη· τοιόνδε παῖδα θησαυρὸς στέγει.
δυσεύρε]τός [τ' ἔτ'] ἐστὶ τοῦ πατρὸς θέσει.   230
ἀφανεῖ δ' ὃ πεύθηι φ]θέγμα μηχανῆι βρέμ[ον
καὶ π[όλ]λ' ἐθά[μβεις, αὐτὸ]ς ἡμέραι μιᾶι
ἐξ ὑπτίας κ[. . . . . γ' ἐμηχ]ανήσατο·

ment. Now be calm, and tell me clearly just what you want.

CHORUS. Queen of this region, mighty Cyllene, I will tell you later why I came. Explain to us this voice that is sounding, and tell us who in the world is setting our teeth on edge.

CYLLENE. You must understand clearly that if you do not keep my story to yourselves, there's a punishment in store, and you will be the sufferers. The facts are a secret, guarded in Heaven, to prevent the news coming to Hera. Zeus came by night to this hidden dwelling of Atlas's daughter, and ravished her . . . unknown to the stately goddess; in the cave he begot an only son, whom in my own arms I nurse, since his mother's strength is wasted in storms of sickness. So night and day I stay beside the cradle and look to his infant needs, food and drink and rest. Every day he grows bigger and bigger, it seems unnatural; I am surprised and frightened by it. Born less than six days ago, he is already thrusting forward . . . to the full bloom of boyhood, sprouting and shooting up with no more delay. Such is the baby whom in our strong-room we hide. We are still concealing him, to humour his father. As for the voice you ask about, which surprised you so much, ringing out as it did from some invisible instrument,—he invented it himself, in a single day, out of an upturned . . . ! That is the kind of thing it is—a vessel invented

---

215 D. L. P.   227 γυίοι]ς Hunt.   233 κίστης edd.

τοιόνδε θη[ρὸς ἐκ θανόντ]ος ἡδονῆς
ἔμμεστον ἄ[γγος εὗρε κ]αὶ κάτω δ[ονεῖ.   235

(*Fragments of seven lines*)

[χο.]   . . . . . ἐ[κ θανόν-
τος πορίζειν τοιάνδε γᾶρυν.

[κτ.] μὴ νῦν ἀπίστει, πιστὰ γάρ σε προσγελᾶι θεᾶς
ἔπη.

[χο.] καὶ πῶς πίθωμαι τοῦ θανόντος φθέγμα
τοιοῦτον βρέμειν;

[κτ.] πιθοῦ· θανὼν γὰρ ἔσχε φωνήν, ζῶν δ' ἄναυ-
δος ἦν ὁ θήρ.   240

[χο.] ποῖός τις ἦν εἶδος; προμήκης ἢ 'πίκυρτος
ἢ βραχύς;

[κτ.] βραχὺς χυτρώδης ποικίληι δορᾶι κατερρικνω-
μένος.

[χο.] ὡς αἰέλουρος εἰκάσαι πέφυκεν ἢ τως πόρ-
δαλις;

[κτ.] πλεῖστον μεταξύ, γογγύλον γάρ ἐστι καὶ
βραχυσκελές.

[χο.] οὐδ' ὡς ἰχνευτῆι προσφερὲς πέφυκεν οὐδ' ὡς
καρκίνωι;   245

[κτ.] οὐδ' αὖ τοιοῦτόν ἐστιν, ἀλλ' ἄλλον τιν'
ἐξευροῦ τρόπον.

[χο.] ἀλλ' ὡς κεράστης κάνθαρος δῆτ' ἐστὶν
Αἰτναῖος φυήν;

[κτ.] νῦν ἐγγὺς ἔγνως ὧι μάλιστα προσφερὲς τὸ
κνώδαλον.

[χο.] τ[ί δ' αὖ τὸ] φωνοῦν ἐστιν αὐτοῦ, τοὐντὸς ἢ
τοὔξω, φράσον.

[κτ.] φωνεῖ μὲν αἰό]λο[ν φ]ορίνη σύγγονος τῶν
ὀστράκων.   250

46

out of a dead animal, brimful of pleasures ; he keeps playing it down there.

(Fragments of seven lines)

CHORUS. . . . . to contrive such utterance from the dead.

CYLLENE. Don't be so sceptical, when a goddess greets you with the truth.

CHORUS. I can't believe that so loud a voice comes from a corpse.

CYLLENE. You must believe it. In death the creature got a voice, in life it had none.

CHORUS. What sort of shape was it ? Long ? Humped ? Or short ?

CYLLENE. Short, pot-shaped, shrivelled, with a spotted skin.

CHORUS. Like a cat or a panther, perhaps ?

CYLLENE. Enormously different ; it's round and has short legs.

CHORUS. Not like a weasel or a crab ?

CYLLENE. No, not like that either ; find some other sort.

CHORUS. Well, perhaps it is like a horned beetle, one from Etna ?

CYLLENE. Now you've nearly guessed what the creature resembles most !

CHORUS. What part of it makes the noise ? Tell me, the inside or the outside ?

CYLLENE. It is the crust that rings the changes, exactly like a shell.

---

239 This was v. 300 of the complete play (stichometrical γ in margin, col. xii., v. 3, ed. pr.).   245 ἰχνευτῆι and καρκίνωι II.   250 Marx (*Rh. Mus.* 78, 224).

[ΧΟ. ποῖον δὲ τοὔνομ᾽ ἐν]νέ[πει]ς; πόρσυνον, εἴ
τι πλέον ἔχεις.
[ΚΥ. τὸν θῆρα μὲν χέλυν, τὸ φωνο]ῦν δ᾽ αὖ λύραν
ὁ π[αῖς κ]αλεῖ.

(Fragments of nine lines, then a gap of one or two)

καὶ τοῦτο λύπης ἔστ᾽ ἄκεστρον καὶ παρα-
ψυκτήριον
κείνωι μόνον, χαίρει δ᾽ ἀλύων καί τι προσ-
φων[ῶν μέλος
ξύμφωνον· ἐξαίρει γὰρ αὐτὸν αἰόλισμα τῆς
λύρας.   255
οὕτως ὁ παῖς θανόντι θηρὶ φθέγμ᾽ ἐμη-
χανήσατο.

ΧΟ. ὁ(ρθο)ψάλακτός τις ὀμφὰ κατοιχνεῖ τόπου,
πρεπτὰ (δ᾽ αὖ) διὰ τόνου φάσματ᾽ ἔγ-
χωρ᾽ ἐπανθεμίζει.
τὸ πρᾶγμα δ᾽ οὗπερ πορεύω βάδην,   260
ἴσθι τὸν δαίμον᾽ ὅστις ποθ᾽ ὃς
ταῦτ᾽ ἐτεχνήσατ᾽, οὐκ ἄλλος ἐστὶν κλοπεὺς
ἀντ᾽ ἐκείνου, γύναι, σάφ᾽ ἴσθι.
σὺ δ᾽ ἀντὶ τῶνδε μὴ χαλε-
φθῆις ἐμοὶ (μη)δὲ δυσφορηθῆις.   265

[ΚΥ. τίς ἔχει πλά]νη σε; τίνα κλοπὴν ὠνείδισας;
[ΧΟ. οὐ μὰ Δία σ᾽, ὦ πρέσ]βειρα, χειμάζειν [θέλω.
[ΚΥ. μῶν τὸν Διὸς παῖδ᾽ ὄ]ντα φηλήτην κα[λεῖς;
[ΧΟ. ὅν γ᾽ ἄσμενος λάβοιμ᾽] ἂν αὐτῆι τῆι κλοπῆι.

(Fragments of seven lines and a gap of perhaps two)

[ΚΥ. . . . .] ἄρτι μανθάνω χρόνωι   270
πονηρέ, σ᾽ ἐγχ]άσκοντα τῆι 'μῆι μωρίαι.
δρᾶις δ᾽ ὑγιὲς ο]ὐδέν, ἀλλὰ παιδιᾶς χάριν.
σὺ δ᾽ οὖν τὸ λοιπὸ]ν εἰς ἔμ᾽ εὐδίαν ἔχων

CHORUS. What is the name you give it ? Out with it, if you have any more detail.

CYLLENE. Our baby calls the animal a tortoise and the noisy part a lyre.

(Fragments of nine lines, then a gap of one or two)

CYLLENE. And it's all he has to cure and comfort him when he is unhappy. He enjoys being crazy, singing in harmony with it ; it simply transports him to ring changes on the lyre. So that is how Baby invented a voice for a dead animal.

CHORUS. Loud is the voice that goes forth over the land ; clear are the fantasies that the strings make to flit around us everywhere. But here's the point I am slowly coming to—you may be sure, good lady, that whoever may be the god who invented this, the thief is none other than he.[a] Now don't be angry with me for saying this ; don't take it too hard.

CYLLENE. What delusion possesses you now ? What is this charge of theft ?

CHORUS. I swear I don't like to distress you, lady, but——

CYLLENE. Are you calling the son of Zeus a thief ?

CHORUS. Yes. How gladly I would take him red-handed !

(Fragments of seven lines and a gap of perhaps two)

CYLLENE. At last I understand, you scoundrels are simply grinning at me for an idiot. You're full of rotten tricks, all for the sake of foolery. For the

---

[a] In the previous lacuna, Cyllene must have explained that Hermes made his lyre by stretching *ox-hide* across the shell.

εἴ σοι φέρει χάρ]μ' ἢ τι κερδαίνειν δοκεῖς
ὅπως θέλεις κά]χαζε καὶ τέρπου φρένα·   275
τὸν παῖδα δ' ὄ]ντα τοῦ Διὸς σαφεῖ λόγωι
μὴ βλάπτε κιν]ῶν ἐν νέωι νέον λόγον.
οὗτος γὰρ οὔτε] πρὸς πατρὸς κλέπτης ἔφυ
οὔτ' ἐγγενὴς μ]ήτρωσιν ἡ κλοπὴ κρατεῖ.
σὺ δ' ἄλλοσ', εἴ τ]ίς ἐστι, τὸν κλέπτην σκόπει,   280
. . . . . . ἄ]καρπον· τοῦδε δ' οὐ πεινῆι δόμος.
ἄθρ]ει γένος, πρόσαπτε τὴν πονηρίαν
πρὸς ὄντιν' ἥκει· τῶιδε δ' οὐχ οὕτω πρέπει.
ἀλλ' αἰὲν εἶ σὺ παῖς· νέος γὰρ ὢν ἀνὴρ
πώγωνι θάλλων ὡς τράγος κνήκωι χλιδαῖς.   285
παῦου τὸ λεῖον φαλακρὸν ἡδονῆι πιτνάς.
οὐκ ἐκ θεῶν τὰ μῶρα καὶ γέλοια χρὴ
χανόντα κλαίειν ὕστερ'; ὡς ἐγὼ λέγω.
[ΧΟ.] στρέφου λυγίζου τε μύθοις, ὁποί-
αν θέλεις βάξιν εὕρισκ' ἀπό-   290
ψηκτον· οὐ γάρ με ταῦτα πείσεις
ὅπως τὸ χρῆμ' οὗτος εἰργασμένος
ῥινοκόλλητον ἄλλων ἔκλεψεν βοῶν
που δορὰς ἢ 'πὸ τῶν Λοξίου.
μή με τᾶ[σδ' ἐ]ξ ὁδοῦ βίβαζε.   295

(About six lines missing)

[ΧΟ. εἴ] τοι πονη[ρὰ δρᾶι, πονηρὸς ὢν κυρεῖ.
[ΚΥ.] κακῶς ἀκού[ειν οὐ πρέπει Διὸς γόνωι.
[ΧΟ.] εἰ δ' ἔστ' ἀλη[θῆ, χρή με καὶ λέγειν τάδε.
[ΚΥ.] ο]ὐ μὴ τάδ' [εἴπηις

(A gap, then fragments of eight lines)

[ΚΥ.] πο[ῦ] καὶ βόας νέμουσι τ[300
[ΧΟ.] πλείους δέ γ' ἤδη νῦν [
50

future, if it gives you any pleasure or hope of profit,
laugh at me to your heart's content, enjoy yourselves
at your ease so far as I'm concerned.   Only don't
slander a child who can prove that his father is Zeus.
Stop inventing new crimes against new-born babies.
He was not born a thief on the father's side and there
are no light-fingered gentry in his mother's family.
You try and find your thief elsewhere . . . a poor
harvest ; there is no hunger in *his* home.   Remember
his parentage ; fix the crime where it belongs, not
upon *him*—it's not proper.   You always did behave
like a baby.   You're a full-grown man with a beard,
but you are as saucy as a goat among the thistles.
It's time that bald skull stopped fluttering with
ecstasy.   The gods do make folk sorry for silly
jokes and chatter : such is my opinion.

CHORUS. Wriggle, twist, the tales you tell ! Invent
what smart remark you will ! One thing you will
not persuade me : that he who made this thing by
sticking hides together, stole them from any other
cattle than Apollo's. Don't try to shift me from
this path. . . .

(About six lines missing)

CHORUS. He is a villain, if he acts like one.
CYLLENE. A son of Zeus may not be slandered !
CHORUS. But if it's true, how can I help saying so ?
CYLLENE. You must not . . . !

(A gap, then fragments of eight lines)

CYLLENE. Where do they graze their cattle . . . ?
CHORUS. More now already . . .

278-280 Pearson.

[ΚΥ.] τίς, ὦ πόνηρ', ἔχει; τί πλ[

[ΧΟ.] ὁ παῖς ὃς ἔνδον ἐστὶν ἐγκεκλημένος.

[ΚΥ.] τὸν παῖδα παῦσαι τὸν Διὸς [κακῶς λέγων.

[ΧΟ.] παύοιμ' ἄν, εἰ τὰς βοῦς τις ἐ[ξάγοι, λόγον. 305

[ΚΥ.] ἤδη με πνίγεις καὶ σὺ χα[ὶ βόες σέθεν.

305 This was v. 400 of the complete play (stichometrical δ
in margin, col. xv., v. 20, ed. pr.).   Suppl. Pearson.

CYLLENE. Villain ! Who has them ? . . .

CHORUS. The infant who is shut up in there.

CYLLENE. Stop slandering the son of Zeus !

CHORUS. I'll stop, if someone will bring out those cattle !

CYLLENE. You and your cattle will be the death of me.

ΕΥΡΙΠΙΔΗΣ

8   [3 A.D.]   ΑΛΚΜΕΩΝ ΔΙΑ ΚΟΡΙΝΘΟΥ

Ed. pr. *Grenfell-Hunt, *P. Oxy.* xiii. 1919, no. 1611, fr. 1, col. iv. 90-93, p. 134. See Körte, *Archiv*, vii. 240 ; Deubner, *S.-B. Heidelb. Akad.* 1919, Abh. 17, p. 5.

Quotation in an essay in literary criticism : introduced by the phrase δύναται δὲ τὸ αὐτὸ (*D. L. P.*[a] : διὰ τούτου Π) καὶ τὸ

κἀγὼ μὲν ἄτεκνος ἐγενόμην κείνης ἄπο·
Ἀλκμέωνι δ' ἔτεκε δίδυμα τέκνα παρθένος.

[a] Deubner keeps διὰ τούτου, supplying (ἀπολυθῆναι).

9   [1 B.C.]   ΑΛΕΞΑΝΔΡΟΣ

Ed. pr. Crönert, *Nachrichten der Gesellschaft der Wissenschaften zu Göttingen*, 1922, p. 1. Revised text in *Snell, *Hermes, Einzelschriften*, v. 1937, pp. 1 *sqq.* See Lefke, *de Euripidis Alexandro*, Diss. Münst. 1936 ; Luria, *Aegyptus*, 1924, 326 and *Hermes*, 1929, 491 ; Körte, *Archiv*, vii. 255 ; Wilamowitz, *Hermes*, 1927, 288 ; Pickard-Cambridge, *New Chapters*, iii. 137.

This play was produced together with Palamedes *and* Troades *at Athens in* 415.

The nature and sequence of events are not certainly or fully known.

EURIPIDES

ALCMEON THROUGH CORINTH

[3 A.D.]

παρ' Εὐριπίδηι ἐν 'Ἀλκμέωνι τῶι διὰ Κ[ο]ρίνθου λεγόμενον ὑπὸ θεοῦ. *The story is given in Apollod. iii. 7. 7. The παρθένος is Manto, daughter of Teiresias ; the two children (παῖδας δύο Apollod., i.e. not—as here—twins) are Amphilochus and Tisiphone ; the speaker is Apollo. From the prologue.*

AND I was without child by her : but she bore to Alcmeon twin children, yet unwed.

ALEXANDER
[1 B.C.]

The following is a brief summary of Snell's painstaking reconstruction (loc. cit.). Even this bare outline is in many points hypothetical.

(1) Prologue spoken by Cassandra.—She tells of the dream of Hecuba, who imagined that she gave birth to a torch from which there issued serpents. Apollo's oracle declares that Hecuba's baby must die. Priam sent the baby forth to be slain ; but it was only exposed, and later found and reared by shepherds. Now games were instituted in honour of the baby whom Priam and Hecuba mourned. The baby was Alexander (Paris).

(2) *Parodus, followed by a short dialogue between Hecuba
and Cassandra. Cassandra withdraws ; Hecuba and the
Chorus mournfully recall the child whom they suppose to
have died many years ago. Cassandra returns and foretells
the doom of Troy. Hecuba and Cassandra quarrel. (Vv.
1-2 belong to this part.)*

(3) *Stasimon.*

(4) *Episode.*—*Priam is informed by a shepherd that a
youth named Alexander is intending to compete in the games
which are about to take place. A bull has been sought to be
the prize, and the choice has fallen upon one which was a
favourite of this young countryman Alexander ; who there-
fore, though a slave, is determined to compete and to win
the prize.*

(5) *Stasimon (during which the games take place).*

(6) *Episode.*—*A messenger reports the story of the games,
and the surprising victory of Alexander therein. This
report was probably made to Hecuba. There followed the
entrance of Deiphobus and Hector, her sons, both vanquished
by Alexander. Deiphobus is enraged at his defeat ; Hector
takes it easily and endeavours to pacify his brother. (Vv.
3-12, 13-25 belong to this part.)*

(7) *Stasimon.*

(8) *Episode.*—*A debate between Deiphobus and Alexander,
whom the former accuses of unfair competition : being a
slave, he was not entitled to compete, let alone to win prizes.*

(*a*) [χορος καὶ μὴν δέ]δορκα παῖδα Κ[ασάνδραν
       σέθεν
    ἤκουσα]ν ἀδύτων ὧ[δε Φοιβείων πάρος.

(*b*) [χορος] τύχηι δ[ίδω]μι πά[ντα
    [αγγελος] κρείσσω(ν) πεφυκὼς [ἔφερε τἀπινίκια

4 D. L. P.

Priam referees their argument, and decides in favour of Alexander.

(9) *Stasimon.*

(10) *Episode.—Hecuba and Deiphobus determine to murder Alexander.* (*Vv. 26-38 belong to this part.*)

(11) *Stasimon.*

(12) *Exodus.—Hecuba and Deiphobus attempt to kill Alexander: but at the last minute it is revealed that he is son and brother of his would-be murderers. How this recognition was effected is unknown. Perhaps (as Snell suggests) Alexander cried out at the point of death.*

> οἴμοι θανοῦμαι διὰ τὸ χρήσιμον φρενῶν,
> ὃ τοῖσιν ἄλλοις γίγνεται σωτηρία.[a]

Thereupon Hecuba inquires his meaning, and he reveals that he is not after all a slave; he knows that he is the son of noble parents, but has promised his shepherd-guardian to keep his knowledge secret: otherwise the latter may incur penalties for saving a child whom he had been commanded to slay. He possesses tokens to prove his story. These are brought forward, and Hecuba recognizes them as belonging to the baby whom many years before she had been forced to expose—her Alexander.

In the end, it is likely enough that a divinity (Aphrodite) appeared and forecast the future, thus making a transition to Palamedes, *the second play of the trilogy (if indeed it was a trilogy).*

(*a*) CHORUS. Lo ! I behold your child Cassandra coming hither before the shrine of Phoebus.

(*b*) CHORUS. All things I yield to fortune . . .

MESSENGER. He was the champion ; he carried off the prize.

[a] Fr. 58 Nauck.

[ΧΟ.] ἦ καὶ στέφουσιν αὐτὸ[ν ὄντα δυσγενῆ; 5
[ΑΓ.] καί φασιν εἶναί γ' ἄξιον [
[ΧΟ.] ὁ δ' ὧδε μορφῆι διαφέρ[ων ἴσον σθένει;
[ΑΓ.] ἅπανθ', ὅσ' ἄνδρα χρὴ [τὸν εὐγενῆ, τελεῖ.

(*Fragments of two lines*)

[ΧΟ.] ἀγῶνα ποῦ κ[ρίνουσι;
[ΑΓ.] Πρίαμος τίθησιν [10
[ΧΟ.] εἰς τόνδε νικητ[ήρι' ἦλθε δὴ τίνα;
[ΑΓ.] ἱερός τ' [ἐλ]αιδ[ος θαλλός

(*c*) [ΧΟΡΟΣ ἀλλ' εἰσορῶ γὰρ] Ἕκτορ' ἐξ ἀγωνίω[ν
        ἥκοντα μό]χθων σύγγονόν τε, παῖδε σώ·
        πάρεισι δ',] εἶς θ' ἄμιλλαν ἥκουσιν λόγων. 15
[ΔΗΙΦΟΒΟΣ ἐπήινεσ' οὐ]δέν' ὅστις ἐστὶ δυσχερὴς
        ἁλοὺς δὲ τοῖ]ς κακοῖσι μαλθάσσει φρένας.
[ΕΚΤΩΡ μάταιος ὅσ]τις μίκρ' ἔχων ἐγκλήματα
        δεινὸν νο]μίζει καὶ συνέστηκεν φόβω[ι].
[ΔΗ. πῶς γάρ, κα]σίγνηθ' Ἕκτορ, οὐκ ἀλγεῖς
        φρένα[ς]   20
        δούλου παρ'] ἀνδρὸς ἆθλ' ἀπεστερη-
        μέν[ος];
[ΕΚ. λίαν ἀθυ]μεῖς, Δηίφοβε· τί γάρ με δεῖ
        μισεῖν νιν; οὔ τοι] καιρὸς ὠδίνειν φρ[έ]-
        νας.
[ΔΗ. ἀργοῦντι θυμῶ]ι ῥαιδίως φέρεις τάδε,
        ἥσσων δὲ δούλου Φρ]υξὶν ἐμφανὴς ἔσηι. 25

5 Schadewaldt.   7 D. L. P. (διαφέρων Crönert).
8 D. L. P. (after Luria).   11 D. L. P.   12 Snell
(θαλλός Schadewaldt).   15 D. L. P.   16 Münscher.

CHORUS. And do they crown him, albeit ignobly born ?

MESSENGER. Yes ; and they call him worthy . . .

CHORUS. So handsome, yet so strong ?

MESSENGER. All that the nobleman must do, he does.

(Fragments of two lines)

CHORUS. Where do they decide the contest . . . ?

MESSENGER. Priam appoints . . .

CHORUS. What were the prizes that came to him ?

MESSENGER. A holy branch of olive, and . . .

(c) CHORUS. I can see Hector and his brother, your sons, arriving, fresh from the labour of the games. Here they come !—they start a quarrel !

DEIPHOBUS. Shame on all men who are first indignant, then—captives of misfortune—abate their temper !

HECTOR. Only a fool is led by petty grievances to think it disaster, and join battle through fear.[a]

DEIPHOBUS. Hector, my brother ! Robbed of the prize by a slave—are you not heart-broken ? How can it be ?

HECTOR. You are too despondent, Deiphobus. Why should I hate him ? there is no cause for broken hearts.

DEIPHOBUS. An idle spirit persuades you to bear it lightly. All Troy will see that a bondman has beaten you !

[a] Doubtful translation of an obscure phrase: this is perhaps the best that can be done without altering the text.

18 D. L. P.   23 Snell (οὔ τοι D. L. P.).   24 D. L. P.
25 Lefke.

LITERARY PAPYRI

(d) [ΕΚΑΒΗ] καὶ τοὺς λάθραι λέ[γοντας ὡς ἐλεύθερα
    δούλης γυναικὸς [παῖς ἐνίκησεν τέκνα.
    μή νυν ἔτ' εἰσὶν τ[
    ἀλλ[ὰ ο]ὐκ, ἰώ μοι, δ[υνατὰ ταῦθ' ἡμῖν
      φέρειν,
    κεῖνον μὲν ὄνθ' ὃς ἔστι θαυμάζειν Φρύγας, 30
    Πριάμου δὲ νίκ[ηι μὴ] γεραίρεσθαι
    δόμους.
[ΔΗΙΦΟΒΟΣ] πῶς οὖν (μ)ε[ταβα]λεῖ ταῦτά γ'
    ὥστ' ἔχειν καλῶς;
[ΕΚ.] ο[ὐ δῆλον ὡς σφε τῆ]ιδε χειρὶ δεῖ θανεῖν;
[ΔΗ.] οὐ μὴν ἄτρωτός γ' εἰσὶν εἰς Ἅιδου
    δόμους.
[ΕΚ.] ποῦ νῦ[ν ἄ]ν εἴη καλλίνικ' ἔχων στέφη; 35
[ΔΗ.] πᾶν ἄστυ πληροῖ Τρωικὸν γαυρούμενος.
[ΕΚ. . . . .] δεῦρ', εἰς βόλον γὰρ ἂν
    πέσοι.
[ΔΗ. . . . . ε]ἰδῆις γ' ὅτ[ι κρ]ατεῖ τῶν
    σῶν τέκνων

Supplements by D. L. P. except 26 λέγοντας, 29 ἀλλὰ οὐκ
(and δυνατὰ) Snell; 34 εἰσὶν Lefke (εστιν Π); 35 Wilamowitz.
    28 *e.g.* εἰσὶν Τ[ρῶες, οἳ τιμῶσί νιν;   31 Π has νικωμισις
according to Crönert; Wilamowitz conjectured νικῶνθ' ὡς.

10   [3 B.C.]   ΑΝΤΙΟΠΗ

Ed. pr. Mahaffy, *The Flinders Petrie Papyri*, i. 1891, no. 1,
p. [1], Plates I and II. See especially *Schaal, *de Euripidis
Antiopa*, diss. Berlin, 1914 (revised text); Taccone, *Riv di
Fil.* 1905, 32 and 225; Wecklein, *Philol.* 1923, 51; von
Arnim, *Suppl. Eur.* 1913, 18; Pickard-Cambridge, *New*

(d) HECUBA. . . . and secret gossip, how the son of
a slave girl overcame the children of free men . . .
Ah no, we cannot endure it,—that he, being what he
is, should be the wonder of all Troy, while the house
of Priam is robbed of the victor's honour !

DEIPHOBUS. Well, how shall we change things for
the better ?

HECUBA. Is it not clear ?—this hand must slay
him !

DEIPHOBUS. Deep-wounded shall he go to his
grave !

HECUBA. Where would he be now, the victor and
his noble crowns ?

DEIPHOBUS. All over the city of Troy, boasting
success.

HECUBA. (If only he would come) hither—so might
he fall into the snare.

DEIPHOBUS. . . . know that he is master of your
sons . . .

---

which is consistent with the traces according to Snell : if so,
Π was certainly corrupt.   32 πως ουν ε[·]·[·]ει Crönert,
πως ουν ο[κελ]λει Snell : I add (μ) as omitted by haplography
after ουν, and conjecture *faute de mieux* (μ)ε[ταβα]λει.
37 εἰ πως μόλοι] *et simil.* are too long.   38 μηπώποτ'
ἐπ]ίδηις Snell.

ANTIOPE   [3 B.C.]

Chapters, iii. 105 ; Roberts, *C. Qu.* 1935, 134 (revision of
parts of text) ; Milne, *Cat. Lit. Pap. B.M.* no. 70.

*The action of this play, which was produced in or about
408 B.C., was probably as follows : (1) Prologue : a shepherd
explains how he discovered and reared the exposed twins*

LITERARY PAPYRI

Zethus and Amphion, who are now grown to manhood. He knows that Antiope is their mother, but does not know that Zeus is their father. The sons know nothing of either parent. Antiope is to-day a slave and prisoner in the palace of King Lycus and Queen Dirce.

(2) *Parodus : a chorus of old men, Attic shepherds, comes to hear Amphion play the lyre. Conversation between these two about the invention of the lyre and about music.*

(3) *Episode : the celebrated controversy between Zethus and Amphion ; the latter defending the contemplative life of the artist and philosopher, the former representing the soldier and statesman. The centre of the discussion is, " which life is of greater service to the state ? " Euripides is indirectly explaining and defending his own manner and ideal of life.*

(4) *Episode : (probably) conversation between Antiope— who has been miraculously released from prison—and her sons. Neither party is aware of the relationship. Antiope*

[ΑΜΦΙΩΝ . . . . . . το]ύσδε μήδ' ὅπως φευξούμεθα.
ἀλλ' εἴπερ ἡμ]ᾶς [Ζεὺ]ς ἐγέννησεν πατήρ,
σώσ]ει μεθ' ἡμῶν τ' ἐχθρὸν ἄνδρα τείσεται.
ἱ]κται δὲ πάντως εἰς τοσόνδε συμφορᾶς
ὥ]στ' οὐδ' ἂν ἐκφύγοιμεν εἰ βουλοίμεθα   5
Δί]ρκης νεωρες αἷμα μὴ δοῦναι δίκην.
μένου]σι δ' ἡμῖν εἰς τόδ' ἔρχεται τύχη
ὡς ἢ] θανεῖν δεῖ τῶιδ' ἐν ἡμέρας φάει,
ἤ τοι] τροπαῖα πολεμίων στῆσαι χερί.
καὶ σοὶ μ]ὲν οὕτω, μῆτερ, ἐξαυδῶ τάδε,   10
σοὶ δ' ὃς τ]ὸ λαμπρὸν αἰθέρος ναίεις πέδον
λέγω τ]οσοῦτον, μὴ γαμεῖν μὲν ἡδέως
σπείραντ]α δ' εἶναι σοῖς τέκνοις [ἀνω]φελῆ·
οὐ γὰρ κ]αλὸν τόδ', ἀλλὰ συμμαχεῖν φίλοις.
πιθοῦ] πρὸς ἄγραν τ' εὐτυχῆ θείης [μολ]εῖν 15
ὅπως ἔ]λωμεν ἄνδρα δυσσεβέστατον.

tells all her story and laments her servitude and present danger.

(5) *Hereafter must have been described the recognition of her sons by Antiope and of their mother by Zethus and Amphion. It is not known how the recognition was effected. Later enters Dirce with a chorus of Bacchanals : she takes Antiope and the twins away for punishment.*

(6) *A messenger narrates the rescue of Antiope and death of Dirce at the hands of Zethus and Amphion.*

(7) *Exodus : represented by our fragments. Zethus and Amphion, having just killed Dirce, plot to destroy King Lycus also. Lycus enters, eager to capture Antiope and her confederates. Led by the shepherd, he enters their retreat. His death is prevented at the eleventh hour by Hermes, who appears* ex machina *and commands Lycus to yield the dominion of Thebes to the sons of Antiope.*

AMPHION. . . . these men, nor how we shall escape. If Zeus was indeed our own father, he will rescue us and at our side chastise the man we hate. We have come anyway to such a pass that we could not, even if we would, escape the penalty for the blood of Dirce newly shed. If we wait here, our fortunes come to this : either the light of this very day shall see us die, or our own hands shall set a trophy up above our enemies. So much I say, my mother, to you. And this I say to you, who dwell on the bright plain of heaven : do not go marrying for your pleasure and then prove useless to the children you create. Not that, but fighting beside your friends, is the way of honour. Hear us, and grant us to come with good fortune upon our prey, that we may catch this impious man.

---

1 το]ύσδε Roberts. 2 ἀλλ' von Arnim, εἴπερ Wilamo-witz. 5 ὥστ' von Arnim. 9 Von Arnim.

[ΧΟΡΟΣ ὅδ' αὐτό]ς, εἰ χρὴ δοξάσαι τυραννικῶι
   [σ]κ[ή]πτρωι, Λύκος πάρεστι· σιγῶμεν φίλοι.
[ΛΥΚΟΣ] ποῦστ' Ἀντιόπη [   ]αι πέτραν
   δρασμοῖς ἐπ[20
   τίνες δὲ χοὶ συνδρῶντες ἐκ ποίας χθο[νός;
   σημήνατ', εἴπαθ', ὡ[ς ἔ]ν[εστ' αὐ]τοὺς ἐλε[ῖν].
   δεινὸν νομίζων, αὐτὸς οὐκ ἀτιμάσας
   ἦλθ[ον

(Here follow small traces of three lines, then a gap
of thirty lines)

[ΒΟΥΚΟΛΟΣ . . . . σε κομί]σας ἥδομαι κα[κ]ῶν
   ἕκας.   25
  [ΛΥ.] οὐκ ἀσφαλὲς τόδ' εἶπας, ἄνθρωπε, στέγος.
  [ΒΟ.] δρᾶν δεῖ τι· κείνους δ' οἶδ' ἐγὼ τεθνηκό[τας.
  [ΛΥ.] καλῶς ἄρ', εἴπερ οἶσθα, ταξώμεσθα νῦν.
  [ΒΟ. τάξιν τίν'] ἄλλην ἢ δόμων στείχειν [ἔ]σω
     ἐς τήνδ'] ἵν' ἡμεῖς καὶ πρὶν οἰκοῦμ[εν πέτραν; 30
  [ΛΥ. ἄφρων γ' ἂν εἴην,] τοὺς ξένους ἐῶν μ'
     [ἐλεῖν.
  [ΒΟ. ἀτὰρ λιπεῖν χρὴ] δορυφόρου[ς] ἔξω θύρας.
  [ΛΥ. καλῶς ἔλεξας· πά]νθ' ἵν' αἴ[ρω]σιν φό[βον.
  [ΒΟ. τὰ δ' ἔνδον ἡμ]εῖς καὶ σὺ θήσομεν καλῶς.
  [ΛΥ. πόσοι δὲ καὶ τὸ πλ]ῆθος εἰσὶν οἱ ξένοι; 35
  [ΒΟ. . . . .] δ' οὐκ ἔχουσιν ἐν χεροῖν.
  [ΛΥ. ἀλλ' ἄγετε δή,] φρουρεῖτε περίβολον πέτρας
     πάντηι βλέπο]ντες· κἄν τις ἐκπίπτηι δόμων

21 καὶ Π, corr. D. L. P.   22 Roberts.   25
Roberts, D. L. P.   30 ἐς τήνδ' and πέτραν D. L. P.
31-33 D. L. P. (θύρας 32 read by Roberts).   34-35 Von
64

Chorus. The king himself, if we may guess from his royal sceptre !—Lycus is here ! Silence, friends.

Lycus. Where is Antiope ? She has escaped me, . . . (to this ?) rock ; . . . And who are her accomplices ? Where do they come from ? Tell me, point them out—I have a chance to catch them ! In indignation, I thought it not beneath me to come in person . . .

(Here follow small traces of three lines, then a gap of thirty lines)

Cowman. I'm glad I have brought you well away from danger.

Lycus. There is peril in the shelter, fellow, if you speak truly !

Cowman. It is high time to act. They, I know, are dead.

Lycus. Since you are certain, let us make good arrangement . . .

Cowman. Arrangement ? What other than advance into the house, this rock which long has been my home ?

Lycus. I should be mad to let the strangers catch me !

Cowman. Still, you must leave your bodyguard outside the door.

Lycus. Well said !—to remove all cause of fear . . .

Cowman. Indoors, you and I will arrange everything.

Lycus. How many of these strangers are there ?

Cowman. (Only a few ;) and they carry no (spears).

Lycus. Away then, guard the circle of the cavern, watch every side. Seize all who are driven from the

---

Arnim.　　36 παῦροί γε· λόγχας] Roberts (much too long for the space).　　38 Von Arnim.

λάζυσθ'· ἐγὼ] δὲ παῖδα Νυκτέως ἐμῆι
θέλω φονεῦ]σαι χειρί· καὶ τάχ' εἴσεται   40
θεοὺς τὸ πρὶν φιλοῦ]ντας, ὡς μάτην λόγωι
ἐκόμπασ', ὄντας συ]μμάχους ἀνωφελεῖς.

[ΧΟ. ὅδ' ἀρκύων ἄιδρ]ις, ἂν θεὸς θέληι,
πληγεὶς πεσεῖται] τήνδ' ἀνὰ στέγην τάχα.

. . . μακα]ρίων σθένος βρόχοισι καταδεῖ   45
     τὸν ἄδικον]· βροτῶν δ' αὖ τέχναις
     [τ]ί[ς ἔφυγεν θε]όν;

[ΛΥ.] ἰώ μοί μοι.

[ΧΟ.] ἔα ἔα·
    [κ]αὶ δ[ὴ πρὸς ἔργω]ι τῶν νεανίων χέρες.

[ΛΥ. ὦ] πρόσπ[ολοι δραμό]ντες οὐκ ἀρήξετε;   50

[ΧΟ.] ἀλαλάζετ[αι στέ]γα·
     βοᾶι [. . . . .] μέλος.

[ΛΥ. ὦ] γαῖα Κάδ[μου κ]αὶ πόλ[ισ]μ' Ἀσωπικόν.

[ΧΟ.] κλύεις, ὁρᾶ[ς];
    π[αρα]καλεῖ πόλιν φοβερός· αἵματος
    δίκ[α τοι δί]κα χρόνιος ἀλλ' ὅμως
    ἔλαβεν ὅταν ἴ[δ]ηι [τ]ιν' ἀσεβῆ βροτῶν. 55

[ΛΥ.] οἴμοι θανοῦμαι πρὸς δυοῖν ἀσύμμαχος.

[ΑΜ.] τὴν δ' ἐν νεκροῖσιν οὐ στένεις δάμαρτα σήν;

[ΛΥ.] ἦ γὰρ τέθνηκεν; καινὸν αὖ λέγεις κακόν.

[ΑΜ.] ὁλκοῖς γε ταυρείοισι διαφορουμένη.

[ΛΥ.] πρὸς τοῦ; πρὸς ὑμῶν; τοῦτο γὰρ θέλω
     μαθεῖν.   60

[ΑΜ.] ἐκμανθάνοις ἂν ὡς ὅλωλ' ἡμῶν ὕπο.

[ΛΥ.] ἀλλ' ἦ τι[νων π]εφύκαθ' ὧν οὐκ οἶδ' ἐγώ;

39 λάζυσθε D. L. P. : Νυκτέως Roberts.   41 D. L. P.
42 Murray.   45 φονίοις μακα]ρίων Wilamowitz, Schaal.
52 [θανάσιμον] Wilamowitz : all but the μ seems to fit the

house. As for the child of Nycteus, my own hand shall slay her. She shall soon find that the gods who used to love her,—as she idly boasted—are but feeble comrades in arms ! (*Exeunt Lycus and the Cowman.*)

CHORUS. Ignorant of the toils, if it be God's will, this king shall soon fall wounded in the house. . . . The might of the blest gods binds down the unrighteous man in the meshes of a snare : what mortal ever escaped from God by cunning ?

LYCUS. (*Groans within.*)

CHORUS. (*A cry of joyful surprise.*) Those youthful hands are turned to their task !

LYCUS. Come quick, my servants, rescue me !

CHORUS. The roof resounds, it cries . . . a sound of sorrow !

LYCUS. Oh land of Cadmus, city of Asopus !

CHORUS. Listen to him ! look at him ! He calls to the city in his hour of terror ! Justice for murder done, aye, justice long delayed, yet sees unrighteous men and catches them !

LYCUS. Unhappy ! Death is at hand ! I have no comrade, my foes are twain !

AMPHION. (*Also within.*) Have you no tears for your wife, who lies among dead corpses ?

LYCUS. What ! She is dead ? Another grief for me to hear !

AMPHION. Yes. Dragged by a bull and torn to pieces.

LYCUS. Who did it ?—I want to know—was it you ?

AMPHION. Be assured, she perished at our hand.

LYCUS. Are you the sons of parents whom I know not to be such ?

---

traces.   53 ὁρᾶι[ς D. L. P.   53-55 Suppl. *ex fragm.* 223 Nauck.   επεσεν ελαβεν Π, corr. Wilamowitz.

[ΑΜ.] τί τοῦτ' ἐρευν[ᾶ]ις; ἐν νεκροῖς πεύσει θανών.
[ΕΡΜΗΣ παῦσαι κελ]εύω [φόν]ιον ἐξορμ[ωμ]ένους
ὁρμήν, ἄνα]ξ 'Αμφῖον· [ἐ]ντολὰς δὲ σοὶ   65
'Ερμῆς ὁ Μ]αίας τ[ῶι τε . . . .
        μ]ένωι
τῶιδ' ἐκ Δι]ὸς κήρυγ[μ' ἀφικόμη]ν φέρων.
καὶ πρ[ῶ]τα μέν σφ[ιν μητρὸ]ς ἐξερῶ πέρι,
ὡς Ζεὺς ἐμείχθη [. . . ἀ]παρνῆται τάδε

(Here follow small fragments of three lines)

αὐτή τε δεινῆς [συμφορᾶς ἀπη]λλάγη   70
παῖδάς τε τούσδ' [ἐφηῦρε]ν ὄντας ἐκ Διός.
ὧν χρή σ' ἀκούειν [καὶ] χθονὸς μοναρχίαν
ἑκόντα δοῦνα[ι τοῖσδε Κ]αδμείας, ἄναξ.
ὅταν δὲ θάπτηις ἄλοχον εἰς πυρὰν τιθεὶς
σαρκῶν ἀθροίσας τῆς ταλαιπώρου φύσιν   75
ὀστᾶ πυρώσας "Αρεος εἰς κρήνην βαλεῖν,
ὡς ἂν τὸ Δίρκης ὄνομ' ἐπώνυμον λάβηι
κρήνης [ἀπό]ρρους, ὃς δίεισιν ἄστεως
πεδία τ[ὰ Θή]βης ὕδασιν ἐξαρδῶν ἀεί.
ὑμεῖς δ' [ἐπε]ιδὰν ὅσιος ἦι Κάδμου πόλις   80
χωρεῖτε, [παῖδε]ς, ἄστυ δ' 'Ισμηνὸν πάρα
ἑπτάσ[τομ]ον πύλαισιν ἐξαρτύετε.
σὺ μὲν †[. . . . .]ντο πνεῦμα πολεμίων
        λαβών†,
Ζήθωι [τάδ' εἶ]πον· δεύτερον δ' 'Αμφίονα
λύραν ἄ[νωγ]α διὰ χερῶν ὡπλισμένον   85
μέλπειν θεοὺ[ς ὡι]δαῖσιν· ἔψονται δέ σοι
πέτραι τ' [ἐ]ρυμναὶ μουσικῆι κηλούμεναι
δένδρη τε μητρὸς ἐκλιπόνθ' ἑδώλια,

AMPHION. Why ask the question ? Die, and find out among the dead !

HERMES. Stop, I command you ! Stop, King Amphion, your murderous attack ! Hermes, the son of Maea, speaks : I come with orders for you and a summons from Zeus for (your victim) here.

Now first, I will tell them their mother's history, how Zeus embraced her . . .

(Here follow small fragments of three lines)

and herself was freed from distress, and discovered these her sons, whom she bore to Zeus. You shall obey them, king, and freely give to them the throne of Cadmus's country. And when you do your wife's obsequies and set her on the pyre,—when you have gathered in one place the limbs of your unhappy queen—burn her bones and throw them into the spring of Ares ; so shall its outflow, that goes through the city and ever waters the plain of Thebe, receive from her the name of Dirce. And you, when the city of Cadmus is purified, go, sons, and establish a city with seven gates beside the Ismenus. Your task . . .—I speak to Zethus ; next I command Amphion arm his hand with the lyre, and celebrate the gods in song : and mighty rocks shall follow you, spellbound by your music, and trees shall leave their abodes in Mother Earth, making

---

66 τ[ῶιδέ τ' ἐκπεπληγμ]ένωι Schaal.   67 τῶιδ' ἐκ
D. L. P.   68 Roberts.   69 [κοὐκ ἀ]παρνήσηι Schaal :
ἀ]παρνῆται Roberts.   72 [καὶ] χθονὸς Π acc. to Roberts.
73 Wilamowitz.   83 Obscure and perhaps corrupt : see
Roberts, *loc. cit.*   84 Roberts.   85 Wilamowitz.

ὥστ' εὐμ[ά]ρειαν τεκτόνων θήσει χερί.
Ζεὺς τήνδε τίμην, σὺν δ' ἐγὼ δίδωμί σοι,   90
οὗπερ τόδ' εὕρημ' ἔσχες, Ἀμφίων ἄναξ.
λεύκω δὲ πώλω τὼ Διὸς κεκλημένοι
τίμας μεγίστας ἕξετ' ἐν Κάδμου πόλει.
καὶ λέκτρ' ὁ μὲν Θηβαῖα λ[ήψ]εται γαμῶν,
ὁ δ' ἐκ Φρυγῶν κάλλιστον ε[ὐ]νατήριον   95
τὴν Ταντάλου παῖδ'· ἀλλ' ὅσον τάχιστα χρὴ
σπεύδειν θεοῦ πέμψαντος οἷα βούλεται.
[ΑΥ.] ὦ πολλ' ἄελπτα Ζεῦ τιθεὶς καθ' ἡμέραν,
ἔδειξας [εἰς φῶς] τάσδ' ἀβουλίας ἐμὰς
ἐσσφρα[. . . .] δοκοῦντας οὐκ εἶναι Διός.   10
πάρεστε καὶ ζῆθ'· ηὗρε μηνυτὴς χρόνος
ψευδεῖς μὲν ἡμᾶς, σφῷν δὲ μητέρ' εὐτυχῆ.
ἴτε νυν, κρατύνετ' ἀντ' ἐμοῦ τῆσδε χθονὸς
λαβόντε Κάδμου σκῆπτρα· τὴν γὰρ ἀξίαν
σφῷν προστίθησιν Ζεὺς ἐγώ τε σὺν Διί.   10
Ἑρμ[ῆι δ]ὲ [πίσυν]ος Ἄρεος εἰς κρήνην
       [β]αλῶ
γυναῖκα θάψας, τῆς[δ' ὅπως] θανοῦσα γῆς
νασμοῖσι τέγγηι πεδία Θηβαίας χθονός,
Δίρκη παρ' ἀνδρῶν ὑστέρων κεκλημένη.   11
λύω δὲ νείκη καὶ τὰ πρὶν πεπραγμένα

94 γάμων edd.   99 εἰς φῶς Blass.   100 ἐσσφρα

11   [Parchment 2-3 A.D.]   ΚΡΗΤΕΣ

Ed. pr. *Schubart-Wilamowitz, *Berliner Klassikertexte*,
v. 2, p. 73, Plate IV. See Schubart, *Pap. Graec. Berol.* Text
xxiii, Plate 30a ; Roberts, *C. Qu.* 1935, 164 ; Pickard-
Cambridge, *New Chapters*, iii. 129 ; Hunt, *F.T.P.* ; von

light labour for the builder's hand. This honour,
King Amphion, you owe to Zeus, and to me also, the
inventor of your gift. You shall both be called the
White Steeds of Zeus, and enjoy great honours in
the city of Cadmus. For marriage, one shall win
and wed a Theban, the other the noblest bride of
Phrygia, daughter of Tantalus. Now make all speed,
for Zeus has sent you all his will.

Lycus. O God, through whom are brought to pass
so many things unlooked-for, day by day, you have
discovered to the light my foolish plot. . . . I never
thought them sons of Zeus ! Live here among us.
Time the revealer has shown that we are false, your
mother fortunate. Go now, and rule this land in my
stead, take the sceptre of Cadmus. Zeus grants you
the dignity and I grant it with him. Obedient to
Hermes, I will cast the ashes of my wife into Ares'
fountain, when I have done her obsequies, that from
her grave she may flood this Theban plain with
flowing waters and be called " Dirce " by men that
come after us. My quarrels I dissolve, and my
former deeds . . .

[. . . .] Π, *ut vid.* εἰς φῶς, γένος δοκοῦντας : ἐς φράτορας,
δοκοῦντας edd. Perhaps ἐσσφραγίσα[ς] (Roberts).   106
Ερμη[. . .]σ . [. .]τος Ἀρεος Roberts : Ἑρμῆι [δὲ πεισθεὶς ῎Αρ]εος
Schaal.

CRETANS   [Parchment 2-3 A.D.]

Arnim, *Suppl. Eur.* 22 ; Croiset, *Rev. Et. Gr.* 28, 1915,
217.

*Ignored by anthologists, lexicographers, and probably
mythographers too, this play had survived hitherto only in a
single quotation and a handful of references. From Ar.*

LITERARY PAPYRI

Ran. *849 Schol.* we learn that its plot was concerned with the passion of Pasiphae for a bull, and the birth of the Minotaur (cf. Joh. Malal. p. 86, 10 ; p. 31, 6 ; Libanius, Decl. vol. iii. p. 375, p. 64, τὸν Μίνω δεινὰ πασχόντα ἐπὶ τῆς σκηνῆς καὶ τὴν οἰκίαν αὐτοῦ διὰ τοῦ τῆς Πασιφάης ἔρωτος ἐν αἰσχύνηι γεγενημένην). From Ar. Ran. *1356 Schol.* we hear that the play included a monody by Icarus, the son of Daedalus : this fact, combined with the evidence of Etruscan urns and a sarcophagus (references ed. pr. p. 78 n. 1), suggests that the plot covered the punishment of Daedalus, who made the wooden cow-frame in which Pasiphae enclosed herself. The solitary quotation (from Porphyrius, Nauck, T.G.F. fr. 472) consists of introductory anapaests recited by a chorus of Initiates devoted to the service of Idaean Zeus.

The outline of the story as it was known to later mythographers (Apollod. iii. 8—not necessarily following Euripides' play) was this :

Minos defended his claim to the dominion of Crete by the argument that the gods had given it to him. To prove this, he asserted that the gods would fulfil whatever he might demand of them. For an instance, he prayed Poseidon to send up a bull out of the sea, promising that he would then sacrifice it. Poseidon heard his prayer : but Minos sent the bull to join his herd, and sacrificed another in its place (or else made no blood-offering at all, see ed. pr. p. 78). Poseidon therefore inflamed Pasiphae, wife of Minos, with passion for the bull : with which she was united, after enclosing herself in a wooden frame shaped like a cow. She gave birth to the Minotaur. Minos discovered the monster and imprisoned it in the labyrinth.

In our fragment, Minos has just discovered the new-born Minotaur, and confronts Pasiphae with her abominable sin. Pasiphae defends herself, with the assistance of the Chorus, who allege that the fault lay chiefly with a confidante (v. 1, cf. v. 47). But Minos condemns his wife and her accomplice

EURIPIDES

*to the dungeon. Nothing is certainly known of the sequel :
but Croiset's inferences from our fragment are both interest-
ing and probable.*

*There is nothing to suggest that (as ed. pr. thought)
Euripides employed a chorus of Mystics in this play in order
to attack the doctrines which they represent. On the contrary
our fragment makes it clear that the characters of Minos and
the Chorus were contrasted in a manner uncomplimentary to
the former. The men of peace and self-control are clearly
opposed to the violent and brutal king. Minos, who has but
lately ascended his throne, is portrayed as a savage and
barbaric despot, according to the Tragic convention (Plato,
Minos 312 ʋ ʻΡαδάμανθύν γέ φασιν δίκαιον ἄνδρα, τὸν δὲ Μίνων
ἄγριόν τινα καὶ χαλεπὸν καὶ ἄδικον.—ʼΑττικόν, ὦ βέλτιστε, λέγεις
μῦθον καὶ τραγικόν). Vv. 35-39 are not ironical : they refer
to barbaric conduct about which the earlier part of the play
will have given more information. With this character, then,
the Chorus stands in sharpest contrast. Minos cannot
ignore the Mystics, for they are the high priests of his father's
temple. They counsel moderation, mercy and self-control.
At the end of the play, perhaps, a divinity appeared ex
machina, rescued Pasiphae (Hyginus 40 : Pasiphae remains
at liberty), and bade Minos conform to the discipline of
the Chorus—foretold that he must soon become a man of
peace and piety, a wise legislator and a great ruler of his
nation.*

*If it be thought improbable that the Chorus played so
important and integral a part in the play, we can point to
the title Κρῆτες in support of Croiset's theory. The play
was named after the Chorus, not after Minos or Pasiphae :
this fact alone proves that the part of the chorus was of great,
if not supreme, importance in the action of the drama. On
the relation of the Chorus's religion to Orphism, see Mr.
Guthrie's admirable* Orpheus and Greek Religion, *pp. 111,
199.*

[χο.] οὐ γάρ τιν' ἄλλην φημὶ τολμῆσαι τάδε·
    σὺ †δ' ἐκ κακῶν†, ἄναξ,
    φρόντισον εὖ καλύψαι.

ΠΑΣΙΦΑ[Η] ἀρνουμένη μὲν οὐκέτ' ἂν πίθοιμί σε,
    πάντως γὰρ ἤδη δῆλον ὡς ἔχει τάδε.   5
ἐγ[ὼ] γὰρ εἰ μὲν ἀνδρὶ προὔβαλον δέμας
τοὐμὸν λαθραίαν ἐμπολωμένη Κύπριν,
ὀρθῶς ἂν ἤδη μάχ[λο]ς οὖσ' ἐφαινόμην·
νῦν δ', ἐκ θεοῦ γὰρ προσβολῆς ἐμηνάμην,
ἀλγῶ μέν, ἐστὶ δ' οὐχ ἑκο[ύσ]ιον κακόν.   10
ἔχει γὰρ οὐδὲν εἰκός· ἐς τί γὰρ βοὸς
βλέψασ' ἐδήχθην θυμὸν αἰσχίστηι νόσωι;
ὡς εὐπρεπὴς μὲν ἐν πέπλοισιν ἦν ἰδεῖν,
πυρσῆς δὲ χαίτης καὶ παρ' ὀμμάτων σέλας
οἰνωπὸν ἐξέλαμπε περ[καί]νων γένυν;   15
οὐ μὴν δέμας γ' εὔρ[υθμον ὧδε ν]υμφίου·
τοιῶνδε λέκτρω[ν εἴνεκ' εἰς] πεδοστιβῆ
ῥινὸν καθεῖσ[ηι σῶμ' ὅδ' ἐξοργίζε]ται;
ἀλλ' οὐδὲ παίδων φ[ύτορ' εἰκὸς ἦν] πόσιν
θέσθαι· τί δῆτ' ἂν τῆι[δε μαι]νοίμην νόσωι;   20
δαίμων ὁ τοῦδε κἄμ' ἐ[νέπλησεν κα]κῶν,
μάλιστα δ' οὗτος οἴσε[ται ψόγον βροτ]ῶν·
ταύρου γὰρ οὐκ ἔσφαξ[εν ὃν κατηύ]ξατο
ἐλθόντα θύσειν φάσμα [πο]ντίω[ι θε]ῶι.
ἐκ τῶνδέ τοί σ' ὑπῆλθ[ε κἀ]πετείσ[ατο   25
δίκην Ποσειδῶν, ἐς δ' ἔμ' ἔσκηψ[εν τάδε.
κἄπειτ' αὐτεῖς καὶ σὺ μαρτύρηι θεοὺς
αὐτὸς τάδ' ἔρξας καὶ καταισχύνας ἐμέ.
κἀγὼ μὲν ἡ τεκοῦσα κοὐδὲν αἰτία

2 Perhaps σὺ δὲ κατὰ κακόν, ἄναξ.   8 μάχ[λο]ς Hunt,
Wilamowitz.   16 ὧδε D. L. P.   18 D. L. P. (καθ-
εῖσα σῶμα μή τις ἤδεται; Büchener, *Neue Phil. Rundsch.* 12,

EURIPIDES

CHORUS. I say that she,[a] none other, dared this deed. Consider, my king, and hide well . . .

PASIPHAE. Denial will no longer convince you, for the fact is already manifest. If I had given my body to a man, selling my love for secret hire, how justly were I then exposed for a wanton! As it is, God visited me with madness; so though I suffer, my sin was not freely willed. There is no reason in it. What could I see in a bull, to wound my heart with such distress, so shameful? Was it the sight of his pretty clothes? The gleam of wine-red light that shone from his eyes and auburn hair? The beard that was dark upon his chin? I swear my bridegroom was less handsome! Is this the passion that tempted me into an animal's hide?—Is this the cause of your distemper? I could not even expect to make such a husband father of my children: why, why was I likely to go mad of *that* malady? The evil spirit of this king has loaded me too with misfortune: and he shall be the one to bear the burden of man's blame: because he did not slay that bull, that apparition, which when it came he swore to sacrifice to the Sea-god. Therefore Poseidon has pursued you and taken vengeance; and on *my* head this woe is fallen. And then *you* cry aloud and call the gods to witness—you that wrought these deeds and my disgrace! I, the mother,

[a] The nurse, or whoever else was *confidante*, of Pasiphae.

226). 20 τιδηταντηι[. . . .]νομην Π: corr. D. L. P.; τί δῆτα τῆι[δ' ἐμαι]νόμην Wilamowitz. 22 G. Zuntz: οἷς ἔ[δρασ' ἔνορκος] ὢν Croiset. 23 ταῦρον ΜS., corr. Beazley, cf. Soph. *Tr.* 507 φάσμα ταύρου. ὃν D. L. P. 26 τάδε D. L. P. 27 κἀπιμαρτύρηι Wilamowitz, Hunt.

ἔκρυψα πληγὴν δαίμονος θεήλατον,　　30
σὺ δ', εὐπρεπῆ γὰρ κἀπιδείξασθαι καλά,
τῆς σῆς γυναικός, ὦ κάκιστ' ἀνδρῶν φρονῶν,
ὡς οὐ μεθέξων πᾶσι κηρύσσεις τάδε.
σύ τοί μ' ἀπόλλυς, σὴ γὰρ ἡ 'ξ[αμ]αρτία,
ἐκ σοῦ νοσοῦμεν.　πρὸς τάδ' εἴτε ποντίαν　35
κτείνειν δοκεῖ σοι, κτεῖν'· ἐπίστασαι δέ τοι
μιαιφόν' ἔργα καὶ σφαγὰς ἀνδροκτόνους·
εἴτ' ὠμοσίτου τῆς ἐμῆς ἐρᾷς φαγεῖν
σαρκός, πάρεστι· μὴ λίπῃς θοινώμενος.
ἐλεύθεροι γὰρ κοὐδὲν ἠδικηκότες　　40
τῆς σῆς ἕκατι ζημ[ία]ς θανούμεθα.

[ΧΟ.] πολλοῖσι δῆλον [ὡς θεήλατον] κακὸν
τόδ' ἐστίν· ὀργῆι [μὴ λίαν εἴξῃι]ς, ἄναξ.

ΜΙΝ[ΩΣ] ἆρ' ἐστόμωται; μ[ᾶσσον ἢ ταῦρος] βοᾶι.
χωρεῖτε, λόγχη[ι δ' ἥδ' ἴτω φρουρο]υμένη·　45
λάζυσθε τὴν πανο[ῦργον, ὡ]ς καλῶς θάνηι,
καὶ τὴν ξυνεργὸν [τήνδε, δ]ωμάτων δ' ἔσω
[ἄγο]ντες αὐτὰς ἔρ[ξατ' ἐς κρυπτ]ήριον,
[ὡς μ]ηκέτ' εἰσίδ[ωσιν ἡλίου κ]ύκλον.

[ΧΟ. ἄ]ναξ, ἐπίσχ[ες· φρο]ντί[δος] γὰρ ἄξιον　50
τὸ πρ[ᾶγ]μα· [νηλ]ὴς δ' ο[ὔτις] εὔβουλος
βροτῶν.

[ΜΙ.] κ[αὶ δὴ] δ[έδοκται] μὴ ἀναβάλλεσθαι δίκην.

12　[2-3 A.D.]　　ΥΨΙΠΥΛΗ

Ed. pr. (a) Grenfell-Hunt, P. Oxy. vi. 1908, no. 852, p. 19,
Plates II and III. See Herwerden, Euripidis Hypsipylae
Fragmenta, 1909; *Hunt, F.T.P. 1912; von Arnim, Suppl.

innocent of all, hid the affliction that a spirit sent
from heaven : you, maddest of madmen, proclaim
your wife's disgrace—a proud and proper theme for
exhibition !—to all the world, as if you will have no
part in it ! It is *you* who have ruined me, *yours* is the
sin, *you* are the cause of my malady. Come then, if
it is your will to slay me in the seas, slay on—you are
no novice in bloody deeds and murder of men. Or if
you lust to feed on my raw flesh, you may ! Feast
on, and never pause ! Free and innocent of all, we
shall die to answer for your crime.

CHORUS. Many the signs, my king, that shew this
curse to be the will of God. Yield not too far to
passion.

MINOS. Well, is she muzzled ? a bull does not
bellow thus ! Away, let her go hence under armed
guard ! Abandoned woman ! Seize her, let her die
her noble death,—and *her* too, the accomplice : take
them indoors and pen them in the dungeon : so shall
they look no longer on the circle of the sun !

CHORUS. My king, stay your hand ! The matter
deserves your thought. It is never good counsel to
be ruthless.

MINOS. I am determined ; justice shall wait no
longer.

---

36 ῥίπτειν . . . ῥῖπτ' ed. pr.   44 Herwerden.   45
D. L. P.   48 Herwerden.   52 C. H. Roberts.

HYPSIPYLE   [2-3 A.D.]

Eur. 1913, 46; Morel, *de Eur. Hypsipyla,* diss. Leips. 1921;
Italie, *Eur. Hypsipyla,* diss. Berlin-Ebering, 1923, and litera-
ture cited there, pp. xi-xii; Pickard-Cambridge, *New Chapters,*

iii. p. 120 ; Körte, *Archiv*, v. 1913, 567 ; Lobel, *Class. Rev.*
38, 1924, 43 ; Milne, *Cat. Lit. Pap. B.M.* no. 74 ; Tobias,
L'Hypsipyle d'Euripide, Brussels, 1928. (*b*) Mahaffy, *The
Petrie Papyri*, ii. 1893, no. xlix (c) p. [160]. See Petersen,
Hermes, 49, 1914, 156 ; Italie, *ad loc.*

It is possible that *P. Petrie* no. xlix (d) p. [161] *ibid.* is a
fragment of our play (iambic trimeters ending ἐμφανῆ παιδὸς
μόρον, καί φησιν κτανεῖν, ποινὰς ὅπως : all of which would
occur very suitably in a speech by *e.g.* Eurydice, relating to
the death of Opheltes. καί φησιν κτανεῖν " she admits she
killed him " would harmonize very well with Murray's
theory that Hypsipyle confessed her deed to Eurydice, *cf.*
ἐμφανῆ παιδὸς μόρον). See Milne, *Class. Rev.* 40, p. 64.

*The following reconstruction of the course of events is
based on that of ed. pr., with such modification as later re-
search has made necessary. The story of the play was hitherto
known from* (a) *the scanty fragments of the play* (*Nauck,
752-770*) ; (b) *Clem. Alex. Schol. p. 105* ; (c) *Apollod. iii. 6.
4* ; (d) *P. Nem. Schol.* ; (e) *Hyginus, fab. 74* ; (f) *Statius,
Theb. v. 500 sqq.* ; (g) *Anth. Pal. iii. 10: see Welcker*, Gr.
Trag. ii. *557, Hartung*, Eur. Restitut. ii. *430. The play
was written between 412 and 406 B.C.* (v. *Italie, ix-xi*).

*The framework is dictated partly by the natural order of
events discernible in the fragments, but especially by the
stichometric letters which are read in the margins in six
places :*

δ = *line 400 of the play, fr. 1 col. v. 3 ed. pr.* (*small fragm.
of iambic dialogue between Amphiaraus and Hypsi-
pyle*).

ζ = *line 600 of the play, fr. 25 col. ii. 1* (*metre and subject
unknown*).

η = *line 700 of the play, fr. 26, 2* (*metre and subject un-
known*).

θ = *line 800 of the play, fr. 27, 1* (*metre iambic, subject
probably dialogue between Hyps. and Eurydice*).

λ = *line 1100 of the play, fr. 57, 17* (*part of a choral lyric
which included references to Dionysus*).

EURIPIDES

$\pi = line$ *1600 of the play, fr. 64 col. ii. 79 (from the dialogue between Hyps. and her sons).*

Dramatis Personae : Hypsipyle, formerly wife of Jason, now nurse of the child Opheltes in the palace of Lycurgus and Eurydice at Nemea.

Thoas ⎱
Eunêus ⎰ *sons of Hypsipyle.*

Amphiaraus, a seer, one of the Seven against Thebes.

Eurydice, queen of Nemea, and wife of Lycurgus.

Opheltes (later Archemorus), son of Eurydice and Lycurgus.

Chorus of Nemean Women, well-disposed toward Hypsipyle.

Scene : Before the palace of Lycurgus at Nemea.

Prologus. 1-200 ᵃ : Hypsipyle narrates her past history and present circumstances : she was formerly queen of Lemnos, but is to-day a servant in the palace at Nemea, and nurse of the royal child Opheltes. She returns to the palace. Enter Eunêus and Thoas. They knock on the door. Hypsipyle appears with Opheltes in her arms. They are admitted to the palace : Hypsipyle is left alone with Opheltes, to whom she sings (vv. 1-29 of my text).

Parodus. 200-310. A chorus of Nemean women enters. They sing a strophe and antistrophe, each with a lyric response from Hypsipyle. The chorus wonders that she is still thinking of her distant home while such great events are occurring in Nemea—the march of the Seven through Nemea against Thebes. Hypsipyle replies that her heart is far away with the Argonauts and Lemnos. The chorus quotes other heroines whose plight was similar to hers, but worse. Hypsipyle refuses to be comforted (vv. 30-98 of my text).

First Episode. 310-480 (proved by stichometric δ). Amphiaraus arrives. He makes himself known to Hypsipyle; explains the expedition of the Seven against Thebes ; and tells

ᵃ These figures in each case represent *approximately* the lines of the complete play.

*the story of Eriphyle's necklace.   He appeals to Hypsipyle to
shew him a stream of pure water for holy libation on behalf
of his army.   Hypsipyle consents (Fr. 753 Nauck, δείξω μὲν
᾽Αργείοισιν ᾽Αχελώιου ῥόον).   They depart together (vv. 99-
152 of my text).*

*First Stasimon.   480-550.   The chorus sings of the quarrel
of Tydeus and Polynices at Argos ; and of their marriage
with the daughters of Adrastus (vv. 153-162 of my text).*

*Second Episode.   550-770.   Hypsipyle returns distraught.
She describes the death of her charge Opheltes, how she left
him lying on the ground while she conducted Amphiaraus to
a stream, and how, when she returned, she found that a
serpent had stung him to death.*

*[Herein I follow ed. pr. pp. 24-25.   There are, of course,
other possibilities, but the objections to them are grave.   Vv.
163 sqq. (of my text) must be part of a description of
Opheltes' death—it is highly improbable that they are part of
a passage in which Hyps. described the stream to Amphiaraus;
she would thus emphasize her forgetfulness and carelessness
later in leaving Opheltes exposed ; and above all it is indis-
pensable that the audience should be acquainted with the
manner of Opheltes' death, in some detail, long before
Amphiaraus's brief description of it (vv. 248 sqq. of my text,
between vv. 1150-1350 of the complete play).   It is possible
that not Hypsipyle but a messenger reported his death : but
I agree with ed. pr. in thinking it more likely that Hypsipyle
herself was the speaker.   V. 206 (of my text) then becomes, as
Murray first explained, intelligible : " in vain was my com-
punction ! " cries Hypsipyle, meaning that her self-surrender
to Eurydice had not saved her from the extreme penalty.   See
further p. 78 above].   Thereafter Hypsipyle considers a plan
of escape.   In the end, perhaps, she resolves to confess her
story to Eurydice (vv. 163-183 of my text).*

Second Stasimon.   700-770.   [Subject unknown.]

Third Episode.   770-1080.   [Here there is a gap in our

knowledge of the action. There is not much doubt about the course of events so far ; their nature is dictated by the fragments themselves, and their position in the play fairly secured by the stichometrical sign for line 400. We tread safe ground again at v. 1100, from which point the fragments and two stichometric letters define the course and position of events very clearly. But between v. 770 and v. 1100 we have very little to guide us. It is however possible to say this much :— corresponding to this gap of 300 lines, there is obviously a gap in the action of the play. For Hypsipyle later recognizes Eunêus and Thoas to be her own sons : these two must therefore have played a part of some importance in the play—yet so far they have done nothing except enter the palace in the Prologus. Further, since it is Amphiaraus who makes her sons known to Hypsipyle, there must have been a scene in which his knowledge of her sons (whom he has not yet met) was explained. How this was done is obscure. Possibly Eunêus and Thoas were appointed executioners of Hypsipyle —Eurydice might well turn to them in the absence of Lycurgus ; then Eurydice, having yielded later to the plea of Amphiaraus, might mention them to him. Or perhaps Hypsipyle sent Eunêus and Thoas to fetch Amphiaraus to help her in return for her earlier courtesy to him. [So ed. pr. : their objection, that Amph.'s return seems spontaneous, *is not a very strong one]. Conceivably the sons were helping Hypsipyle to escape : but, if so, it is hard to see how this could have brought them into contact with Amphiaraus ; except in connexion with the theory that they enlisted the help of Amphiaraus in her rescue. Whether one or two episodes are missing is of course unknown.]*

? Third Stasimon. 1080-1150 (proved by stichometric λ). *The Chorus sings praise of Dionysus and implores his aid for Hypsipyle.*

?Fourth Episode. 1150-1350. Hypsipyle is led out to her death. She pleads with Eurydice, in vain. She is in despair

81

LITERARY PAPYRI

*when at the eleventh hour Amphiaraus arrives and recounts
the true story of Opheltes' death. Eurydice had charged
Hypsipyle with deliberate murder : Amphiaraus explains
that the death was accidental, caused by a serpent while
Hypsipyle was performing a pious service for the Argive
army. He foretells the failure of the Theban expedition, and
the institution of the Nemean Games in memory of Opheltes.
Eurydice listens to him, and spares Hypsipyle (vv. 184-292
of my text).*

(From the Prologus)

[ΤΨΙΠΤΛΗ] ἥξε[ι πατὴρ οὐ] σπά[νι' ἔχων ἀ]θύρματα
      ἃ σὰς ὀδυρμῶν ἐκγαλη[νιεῖ φ]ρένας.
      ὑμεῖς ἐκρούσατ', ὦ νεανία[ι, πύλα]ς;
      ὦ μακαρία σφῶιν ἡ τεκοῦσ', ἥτις ποτ' ἦν.
      τί τῶνδε μελάθρων δε[όμε]νοι προσηλθέτην; 5
ΘΟΑΣ στέγ[η]ς κεχρήμεθ' [ἐ]ν[τὸς ἀ]χθῆναι, γύναι,
      εἰ δύ[να]τον ἡ[μῖν νύκτ' ἐ[ναυλίσ]αι μίαν.
      ἔχομεν δ' ὅσων δεῖ· τ[ί] πο[τε] λυ[π]ηροὶ
            δό[μοις
      ἐσόμεθα τοῖσδε; τὸ δὲ σὸν ὡς ἔχει μ[εν]εῖ.
[ΤΨ. ἀδέσ]ποτος μ[ὲν ο]ἶκ[ο]ς ἀρσένων κυρεῖ 10

(*A few lines missing : fragments of two survive*)

[ΤΨ.] Λυκοῦρ[γος αὐτὸς τυγχάνει θεωρὸς ὤν,
      γυνὴ δ[ὲ Νεμέας Εὐρυδίκη τὰ νῦν κρατεῖ.
  ΘΟ. οὐκ ἐν ξε[νῶσι τοῖσδ' ἄρ' ἀναπαυσαίμεθ' ἄν,
      πρὸς δ' ἄ[λλο δή τι δῶμ' ἀφορμᾶσθαι χρεών.
[ΤΨ.] ἥκιστ[α· καὶ γὰρ δώματ' οὐκ ἐπίσταται 15
      ξένο[υς ἀπωθεῖν οὐδ' ἀτιμάζειν τάδε,
      ἀεὶ δὲ [φιλίαι τὸν μολόντ' ἐδέξατο.

15-17 Suppl. *ex gr.* D. L. P., after Eur. *Alc.* 566-567.
82

EURIPIDES

?Fourth Stasimon. 1350-1375. [Subject uncertain.]

Exodus. 1375-1720 (proved by stichometric π). Amphi-araus makes mother and sons known to each other. He departs, and they converse. Dionysus appears ex machina *(his name is written in the margin of fr. 64 col. iii. 2 ed. pr.). He probably directed Eunêus to go to Athens and found the famous guild of musicians there called* Εὐνεῖδαι *(ed. pr. p. 28).—Dionysus Melpomenus was the object of their family cult (vv. 293-341 of my text).*

(From the Prologus)

HYPS. Father comes soon![a] Many a pretty toy he brings you to soothe your heart from sorrow.—
(*She observes Thoas and Eunêus.*) Was it you, gentlemen, who knocked on the gate? How enviable your mother, whoever she was! What need you of our palace, that you come here?

THOAS. Lady, we wish to be brought inside the house, if we can lodge here a single night. All that we need, we have. We shall make no trouble here; you shall remain undisturbed.

HYPS. It happens, the house has no master here . . .

(*A few lines missing : fragments of two survive*)

HYPS. Lycurgus himself chances to be on pilgrim-age; his wife—Eurydice—at present rules in Nemea.

THOAS. Then we will not rest in these lodgings; we must be off to some other house.

HYPS. Ah, no! It is not the practice of this palace to turn the newcomer away disregarded : rather, it welcomes every stranger. . . .

[a] This was about v. 180 of the play (see ed. pr. pp. 21, 23).

83

(Fragments of two more lines : then a gap)

[ΓΨ. . . . . . .] ὡς ἐνόπτρου
[κελαιν]οφαῆ τιν' αὐγάν·
[ἀοιδῆι δ'] αὔξημα τὸ σὸν   20
[προ]μνήσωμαι, τέκνον, εὐ-
ωποῖς ἢ θεραπείαις.
ἰδοὺ κρότος ὅδε κροτάλων·
⟨. . . . . . ⟩
οὐ τάδε πήνας, οὐ τάδε κερκίδος
ἱστοτόνου παραμύθια Λήμνια,   25
Μοῦσα, μέλει με κρέκειν, ὅ τι δ' εἰς ὕπνον
ἢ χάριν ἢ θεραπεύματα πρόσφορα
παιδὶ πρέπει νεαρῶι,
τάδε μελωιδὸς αὐδῶ.

(Parodus)

[ΧΟΡΟΣ] τί σὺ παρὰ προθύροις, φίλα;   30
πότερα δώματος εἰσόδους
σαίρεις, ἢ δρόσον ἐπὶ πέδωι
βάλλεις οἷά τε δούλα;
ἢ τὰν 'Αργὼ τὰν διὰ σοῦ
στόματος ἀεὶ κληιζομέναν   35
πεντηκόντερον ἄιδεις,
ἢ τὸ χρυσεόμαλλον
ἱερὸν δέρος ὃ περὶ δρυὸς
ὄζοις ὄμμα δράκοντος
φρουρεῖ, μναμοσύνα δέ σοι   40
τᾶς ἀγχιάλοιο Λήμνου
τὰν Αἰγαῖος ἑλίσσων
κυμοκτύπος ἀχεῖ,
δεῦρ' ὅτ' ἂν λειμῶνα Νέμει-
[ον] ἐπάγει χαλκέοισιν ὅπλοις   45

EURIPIDES

(Fragments of two more lines : then a gap)

Hyps. . . . like the dark gleam in a mirror : that with song, while you grow from babe to boy, I may [a] woo you, or with smile and service. Look at the rattle ! There, it sounds !

.   .   .   .   .   .

No chant of Lemnos, no song to comfort me beside my weaving, beside the shuttle pressed upon the web, O Muse, is mine to sing : only what is apt to charm a little child to sleep or joy or comfort—this is the burden of my song.

(Parodus)

Chorus. What make you at the doorway, friend ? Sweeping the entrance to the palace, or sprinkling water on the ground, like a slave ? Are you singing of Argo's fifty rowers—her tale is ever on your lips— or the holy fleece of golden wool which on the oak- tree's bough the unsleeping dragon guards ? Are your thoughts with island Lemnos, that rings with the thunder of the Aegean's rolling waters ? Hither meantime, over the meadows of Nemea, Adrastus, armed with bronze, fleet of foot, brings war apace,

---

[a] The construction of προμνήσωμαι in the Greek text is (because of the preceding gap) altogether uncertain.

19-21 D. L. P.   21 It seems clear that there is space
for 3 letters in the gap.   24 Π indicates an omission here.
34 ἤ edd., corr. D. L. P.   45 ἐπάγει D. L. P.: ἀπάγει Π.

'Αργεῖον πεδίον πα[ρεὶς
ἐπὶ τὸ τᾶς κιθάρας ἔρυμα
τᾶς 'Αμφιονίας ἔργον [χερὸς
ὠ[κυ]πόδας Ἄ[δρ]ασ[το]ς [Ἄρη θοόν;
ὁ δ' ἐκάλεσε μένο[ς   50
ποικίλα σάματα [
τόξα τε χρύσεα [
καὶ μονοβάμονε[ς
ἀειρόμενοι χθ[ον

. . . .

[ΥΨ. . . . . . Θ]ραικίαν   55
. . . . .]σ[.]μένης ὀρού-
σας ἐπ' οἶδμα γαλανεί-
ας πρυμνήσι' ἀνάψαι,
τὸν ἀ τοῦ ποταμοῖο παρθ-
ένος Αἴγιν' ἐτέκνωσε Πη-   60
λέα, μέσωι δὲ παρ' ἱστῶι
'Ασιάδ' ἔλεγον ἰήιον
Θρῆισσ' ἐβόα κίθαρις 'Ορφέως
μακροπόλων πιτύλων ἐρέτηισι κε-
λεύσματα μελπομένα, τότε μὲν ταχύ-   65
πλουν τότε δ' εἰλατίνας ἀνάπαυμα πλά-
τας. τάδε μοι τάδε θυμὸς ὑδεῖν ἴε-
ται, Δαναῶν δὲ πόνους
ἕτερος ἀναβοάτω.

ΧΟ. παρὰ σοφῶν ἔκλυον λόγους   70
πρότερον ὡς ἐπὶ κυμάτων
πόλιν καὶ πατρίους δόμους
Φοίνικας Τυρία παῖς
Εὐρώπα λιποῦσ' ἐπέβα
Διοτρόφον Κρήταν ἱερὰν   75
Κουρήτων τροφὸν ἀνδρῶν,

(he is past the plain of Argos) against the lyre-built fortress,[a] work of Amphion's hand. He has summoned the might . . . blazons manifold . . . and gilded bows . . . and marching singly . . . rise over earth . . .

.   .   .   .   .   .

HYPS. Thracian . . . over the swell of the calm sea, speeding to make the cables [b] fast : he, Peleus, son of Aegina,[c] maiden of the river.[d] Beside the mast amidships the Thracian lyre of Orpheus rang with an Asiatic dirge of sadness, playing the rowers a measure for their long sweep of oars—now a swift stroke, now a pause for the blade of pine. This, this is the song that my spirit is eager to chant : let another sing loud the labours of the Greeks.

CHORUS. I have heard wise men relate the tale of the Tyrian maid Europa, how she left of old her father's home and city, left Phoenicia and went over the waves to holy Crete, where Zeus was cradled and the Curetes nursed. Three children [e] she bore, and

---

[a] Thebes, cf. Eur. Ph. 823-824.   [b] Of the ship Argo.
[c] Usually P. is her *grandson*.   [d] Asopus.   [e] Minos, Rhadamanthys, Sarpedon.

---

62 Ἀσιὰς Π: corr. Beazley.   67 ἰδεῖν Π: corr. Wilamowitz (though ὑδεῖν not elsewhere known before Alexandrian poetry).

ἃ τέκνων ἀρότοισιν
τρισσοῖς ἔλιπεν κρά[τος]
χώρας τ' ὄλβιον ἀρχάν.
'Αργείαν θ' ἑτέραν κλύω   80
[οἶσ]τρωι βασίλειαν 'Ιὼ
[πάτ]ρας ἀμφὶς ἀμεῖψαι
[κερ]ασφόρον ἄταν.
[ταῦ]τ' ἂν θεὸς εἰς φροντίδα θῆι σοι,
[στέρξ]ε[ι]ς δή, φίλα, τὸ μέσον,   85
[ἐλπὶς δ' οὐκ] ἀπολείψει
[ἔτι σε τὸν π]ατέρος πατέρα
[ῥύσεσθαί πο]τ'· ἔχει σέθεν [ὥραν,
αὐτίκα δ'] ὠκύπορο[ς] μετανίσσεται

(*Fragments of six more lines : then a gap*)

[ΥΨ.]   -νεμον ἄγαγέ ποτε   90
κυναγόν τε Πρόκριν,
τάν πόσις ἔκτα,
κατεθρήνησεν ἀοιδαῖς.
θάνατον ἔλαχε· τὰ δ' ἐμὰ πάθεα
τίς ἂν ἢ γόος ἢ μέλος ἢ κιθάρας   95
ἐπὶ δάκρυσι μοῦσ' ἀνοδυρομένα
μετὰ Καλλιόπας
ἐπὶ πόνους ἂν ἔλθοι;
[ΧΟ.] ὦ Ζεῦ Νεμέας τῆσδ' ἄλσος ἔχων,
τίνος ἐμπορίαι τούσδ' ἐγγὺς ὁρῶ   100
πελάτας ξείνους Δωρίδι πέπλων
ἐσθῆτι σαφεῖς πρὸς τούσδε δόμους
στείχοντας ἐρῆμον ἀν' ἄλσος;

(*First Episode*)

ΑΜΦΙΑΡ[ΑΟΣ] ὡς ἐχθρὸν ἀνθρώποισιν αἵ τ' ἐκδημίαι
88

left them empire and happy lordship of lands. Another too, I hear, royal Io from Argos, gadfly-stung far from her native land, changed her state to carry horns—her doom. If God set this in your heart, beloved, the path of moderation shall content you : and Hope shall not fail you that your father's father [a] shall save you still. He cares for you, and swiftly journeying, soon comes in quest . . .

(*Fragments of six more lines : then a gap*)

HYPS. . . . brought of old, sang a lament for Procris,[b] the huntress whom her lover slew. Death was her portion ; but, for my woes—what wailing or lamenting, what music of mourning lyres and weeping, though Calliope assist, could approach my sufferings ?

CHORUS. Zeus, lord of our Nemean grove, for what business are they come, these strangers?—I see them close, in Dorian raiment, plainly, approaching : toward the palace they stride through the lonely grove.

(*First Episode : Amphiaraus enters with armed attendants*)

AMPHIARAUS. How hateful to a man is travel : and

---

[a] Dionysus (who appeared *ex machina* at the end of the play).   [b] Procris, daughter of Erechtheus, accidentally killed by her husband Cephalus while hunting, Apollod. iii. 15. 1.

---

85 Suppl. Radermacher.

ὅταν τε χρείαν εἰσπεσὼν ὁδοιπόρος   10
ἀγροὺς ἐρήμους καὶ μονοικήτους ἴδηι
ἄπολις ἀνερμήνευτος ἀπορίαν ἔχων
ὅπηι τράπηται· κἀμὲ γὰρ τὸ δυσχερὲς
τοῦτ᾽ εἰσβέβηκεν· ἄσμενος δ᾽ εἶδον δόμους
τούσδ᾽ ἐν Διὸς λειμῶνι Νεμεάδος χθονός.   110
καί σ᾽, εἴτε δούλη τοῖσδ᾽ ἐφέστηκας
          δόμοις
εἴτ᾽ οὐχὶ δοῦλον σῶμ᾽ ἔχουσ᾽, ἐρήσομαι,
τίνος τάδ᾽ ἀνδρῶν μηλοβοσκὰ δώματα
Φλειουντίας γῆς, ὦ ξένη, νομίζεται;
ΥΨΙΠΤΛ[Η] ὄλβια Λυκούργου μέλαθρα κλήιζεται
          τάδε,   11
ὃς ἐξ ἁπάσης αἱρεθεὶς ᾽Ασωπίας
κληιδοῦχός ἐστι τοὐπιχωρίου Διός.
ΑΜ. ῥυτὸν λαβεῖν [χ]ρ[ήιζοι]μ᾽ ἂν ἐν κρωσσοῖς
          ὕδωρ
χέρνιβα θεοῖσιν ὅ[διον] ὡς χεαίμεθα.
στατῶν γὰρ ὑδάτων νάματ᾽ οὐ διειπετῆ,   120
στρατοῦ δὲ πλήθει πάντα συνταράσσεται.
ΥΨ. τίνες μολόντες καὶ χθονὸς ποίας ἄπο;
[ΑΜ.] ἐκ τῶν Μυκηνῶν ἐσμὲν ᾽Αργεῖοι γένος,
ὅρια δ᾽ ὑπερβαίνοντες εἰς ἄλλην χθόνα
στρατοῦ προθῦσαι βουλόμεσθα Δαναϊδῶν.   12
[ἡ]μεῖς [γὰρ ὠ]ρμ[ήμεσ]θα πρὸς Κάδμου
          πύλας,
[εἴ πως θεοὶ πέμποιεν ε]ὐτυχῶς, γύναι.
[ΥΨ. τί δὲ στρατεύεσθ᾽, εἴ γε] σοῦ θέμις μαθεῖν;
[ΑΜ. κατάγειν θέλοντες φυγ]άδα Π[ολυνεί]κη   13
          πάτρας.
[ΥΨ. σὺ δ᾽] ὦ[ν τίς . . . .]ας θηρᾶις
          [. . . . .

90

in the wanderer's hour of need, to see fields empty
and solitary homes! No city, no informant, no way
of knowing where to turn! Such vexation is now my
own. How gladly I saw this house in the meadows
of Zeus at Nemea! Now you—whether as slave you
watch over the house, or not a slave, I ask you : what
man is called master of these halls, madam, where
sheep are pastured in the land of Phlius ?

HYPS. Men call it the happy dwelling of Lycurgus,
elect of all Asopia to be the priest of Zeus, god of
our country.

AMPH. It is my wish to fill our pitchers from running
waters, to pour the traveller's libation to the gods.
Streams of standing water are not clear, all muddied
by our unnumbered host.

HYPS. Who are you ? From what country do you
come ?

AMPH. Mycenae ; we are Argives ; crossing our
frontiers to another land, we wish to make sacrifice
for the Danaid army. We have set forth towards the
gates of Cadmus, lady,—if only the gods may speed
us with good fortune.

HYPS. Why do you march—if I may learn this
of you ?

AMPH. To restore Polynices, now in exile from his
land.

HYPS. And who are you, so eager . . . ?

---

130 ἄλλων πημον]ὰς θηρᾶι[ς λαβεῖν Hunt.

[ΑΜ.] παῖς Οἰκ[λέους τοι μάντις] Ἀμφιάρ[εως
ἐγώ.

.   .   .   .

ὄνομα [τὸ σὸν νῦν καὶ γένος λέξον, γύναι.
[ΤΨ.] ἡ Λημ[νία χθὼν Ὑψιπύλην ἔθρεψέ με.

.   .   .   .

[ΑΜ.] γυ[νὴ στρατεῦσαί μ' οὐχ ἑκόντ' ἠνάγκασεν.
[ΤΨ.] ὅσια φ[ρονοῦσ', ἢ καί τινος κέρδους χάριν;   135
[ΑΜ.] ἐδέξ[αθ' ὅρμον χερσὶ Πολυνείκους πάρα.
[ΤΨ.] πόθεν μ[
[ΑΜ.] ἔγημ' ὁ κλε[ινὸς Ἁρμονίαν Κάδμος ποτέ.
[ΤΨ.] εἰς ἦν τις, ὡ[ς ἤκουσα, τῶν θεοῖς φίλων.
[ΑΜ.] ταύτηι δίδωσ[ιν ὅρμον Ἀφροδίτη καλόν.   140
[ΤΨ.] θεοὶ θεῶν γὰ[ρ παισὶν εὐμενεῖς ἀεί.
[ΑΜ.] Πολύδωρος οὖ[ν ἐκλήιζεθ' οὐξ αὐτῶν γόνος.
[ΤΨ.] εἴ που θεᾶς φὺ[ς θεῖ' ἐδέξατ', εἰκότως.
[ΑΜ.] τούτου δὲ παῖ[ς τὸν ὅρμον ἔσχε Λάβδακος.

(Fragments of two lines)

[ΤΨ. ἐ]δέξατ' οὖν ἔξουσα δύ[σφημον κλέος;   145
[ΑΜ. ἐδέ]ξαθ', ἥκω δ' [οὔ]ποτ' ἐκ [μάχης πάλιν.   146
[ΤΨ. εἰς χρησμὸν οὖν σοι θα[νάσιμον πορευτέον;   147
[ΑΜ. χρὴ γὰρ στρατεύειν μ', εἴ[περ ἀξιοῖ γυνή.   148
[ΤΨ. πάλα]ι σαφῶς [σοι] θάνατ[ος ἦν πεπρωμένος;
[ΑΜ. οὐκ ἔ]στι νό[στος] ἀν[δρὶ τῶιδε πρὸς δόμους.   150
[ΤΨ. τί δῆ]τα θύειν [δεῖ σε κατθανούμενον;

134 D. L. P. after Arnim (οὐ θέλοντ' ἠνάγκασεν).   139
Arnim.   145-150 The text here is that of Italie, who
discovered that fr. 49 (Hunt) belongs to these lines. The
supplements come from Mr. C. H. Roberts and Dr. G. Zuntz
(except 148, by Italie).   145-146 post 147-148 Roberts.
On ἔξουσα v. 145, see Lobel, C.R. 1924, 43.

AMPH. The prophet Amphiaraus, son of Oecles.

.   .   .   .   .   .

AMPH. Now tell me, lady, your name and family.
HYPS. I am Hypsipyle ; Lemnos was my home.

.   .   .   .   .   .

AMPH. My wife compelled me—against my will—
to march.
HYPS. With honest purpose, or had she some hope
of profit ?
AMPH. She was given a necklace by Polynices—
HYPS. Whence came it . . . ?
AMPH. Famed Cadmus took Harmonia once to
wife—
HYPS. He was one, I have heard, whom the gods
loved !
AMPH. To her Aphrodite gave a lovely necklace—
HYPS. Aye, God is generous—to a child of God.
AMPH. Polydorus was the name they gave their
son.
HYPS. Divine of birth, divinely endowed ! It was
just.
AMPH. His son was Labdacus ; who got the neck-
lace.

(Fragments of two lines)

HYPS. She took the chain then, though she should
earn dishonour ?
AMPH. She took it : I shall not return from war.
HYPS. So you must go to fulfil an oracle of doom ?
AMPH. I needs must march ; my wife demands it.
HYPS. Death has long since been your certain fate?
AMPH. For me, there is no homecoming.
HYPS. Why sacrifice then, if you must surely
die ?

93

[ΑΜ. ἄμεινον·] οὐ[δεὶς κάματος εὐσεβεῖν θεούς.

(*After a gap of five lines, come the initial letters
of nine more*)

(*From the first Stasimon*)

[ΧΟΡΟΣ] νυκ[τὸς . . . .] ἐν κοίταισι παρ'
    αὐλᾶι
ἔριδ[ας θάμ' ἀ]μειβόμενοι
σιδ[άρου τ' εἰρ]εσίαι   15
σφαγᾶι [τε δῆ]λον
κλισίας π[ερ]ὶ νυκτέρου
γενναίων πατέρων
φυγάδες δορὶ θυμόν.
Φοίβου δ' ἐν[ο]πὰ[ς] β[ασ]ιλεὺς ἐνύχευ-   16
εν Ἄδραστος ἔχων
τέκνα θηρσὶν [ζ]εῦ[ξ]αι

    .   .   .   .   .

(*From the second Episode*)

[——] κρήνη [σ]κιάζ[εταί τις, ἥνπερ ἀμφέπει
δράκων πάροικ[ος, φοινίοισιν ὄμμασι
γοργωπὰ λεύσσω[ν, κρατί τε ξανθὴν ἔπι   16
πήληκα σείων, οὗ φόβ[ωι φεύγουσ' ἀεὶ
ποιμένες, ἐπεὶ σῖγ' ἐν [βοτοῖς ἑλίσσεται

    .   .   .   .   .

[ΤΨΙΠΤΛΗ] ὦ φ[ίλα]ται γ[υναῖκες, ὡς ἐπὶ ξυροῦ
    ἔστηκα [
ἀνά[ξι'] ἕξειν· οἱ φόβοι δ' [ἔχουσί με.   17

151-152=Fr. Adesp. Nauck 350, first placed here by
Italie.   153 δ' ἐποίουν] ἐν Hunt.   154 *sqq.* These
supplements, which leave δορί 159 almost inexplicable, are
even more than usually doubtful.   163-167 Supplements

EURIPIDES

AMPH. It is better so ; no labour, to worship God.

(After a gap of five lines, come the initial letters of nine more)

(From the first Stasimon)

CHORUS. . . . by night . . . where they lay in the courtyard ; strife answered strife ; with slaughter and stroke upon stroke of iron, heroes in exile, they revealed the temper of their noble fathers in battle, fighting about their couch by night. And King Adrastus lay in his bed ; he had the word of Phoebus, that he should wed his daughters to wild animals [a] . . .

.   .   .   .   .   .

(From the second Episode)

HYPSIPYLE (?). There is a shady fountain; and there dwells a serpent and watches over it ; fiercely he glares with blood-shot eyes, and on his head quivers a yellow crest.[b] In dread of him the shepherds ever turn to flight, when silent he glides among their herd . . .

.   .   .   .   .   .

HYPS. Dear friends, I tremble on the brink ! . . . to suffer undeserving. My terrors master me.

[a] Polynices of Thebes and Tydeus of Calydon, fugitives from their homes, met at Argos, and quarrelled in front of Adrastus's palace concerning their lodging for the night. Adrastus made peace between them : and believing them to be the Lion and Boar who, an oracle foretold, would become husbands of his daughters, married those to them and undertook to return them to their homes.   [b] Cf. Verg. *Aen.* ii. 206-207, Statius, *Theb.* v. 572.

---

by D. L. P. (except 164 and σκιάζεταί τις 163, φοιν. ὄμμ. 164, ἐν βοτοῖς 167 Arnim).

[ΧΟΡΟΣ] εὔελπ[ι δ' ο]ὔτι [ῥῆμ'] ἔχεις ε[ἰπεῖν φίλαις;
[ΤΨ.] δέδοικα θανάτωι παιδὸς οἷα πείσομαι.　　(3)
[ΧΟ.] οὔκουν ἄπειρός γ' ὦ τάλαινα σ[υμφορῶν.　　(4)
[ΤΨ.] ἔγνωκα κἀγὼ τοῦτο καὶ φυλάξ[ομαι.　　(5)
[ΧΟ.] τί δῆτά γ' ἐξηύρηκας εἰς ἀλκ[ὴν κακῶν;　　(2) 175
[ΤΨ.] φεύγειν.　στί[β]ων τῶν[δ' ἵ]δρ[ις εἰ γὰρ ἦ
　　　μόνον.　　　　　　　　　　　　　　　　(1)
[ΧΟ.] ποῖ δῆτα τρέψηι;　τίς σε δέξεται πόλις;
[ΤΨ.] πόδες κρινοῦσι τοῦτο καὶ προθυμία.
[ΧΟ.] φυλάσσεται γῆ φρουρίοισιν ἐν κύκλωι.
[ΤΨ. ν]ικᾶι[ς]· ἐῶ δὴ τοῦτό γ'· ἀλλ' ἀπέρχομαι.　180
[ΧΟ.] σκόπει, φίλας [γὰ]ρ τά[σδε] συμβούλους
　　　ἔχεις.
[ΤΨ.] τί δ' εἰ τιν' εὕροιμ' [ὅστ]ις ἐξάξει με γῆς;
[ΧΟ. οὐκ ἔστιν ὅστις βούλεται] δούλους ἄγειν.

．　　．　　．　　．　　．　　．

(From the fourth (?) Episode)

[ΧΟΡΟΣ] γενν[αῖ' ἔ]λε[ξας σωφρονοῦσί τ' εὐπιθῆ·
　　　ἐν σώφροσιν [γ]ὰρ κἄμ' ἀριθμεῖσθα[ι θέλω.　183
[ΕΤΡΥΔΙ]Κ[Η] τί ταῦτα κομψῶς ἀντιλάζυσαι λ[όγοις
　　　καὶ γούνατ' ἀμπ]έχουσα μηκύνεις μ[ακράν,
　　　κτανοῦσ' Ὀφέλ]την, τῶν ἐμῶν ὄσσων [χαράν;

(Fragments of one line)

．　．　．　．　．　．　．　．] παιδί θ' ὃν διώ[λεσας.

172-176 rearranged by Zuntz. The small numbers on
the right indicate the sequence in Π, which is kept by Hunt.
175 κακῶν Wilamowitz, σ' ἄγον Hunt.　　185-204 are
partly preserved in *P. Petrie*, ii. 49c: Petersen, *Hermes*, 49,
156, first identified this fragment.　　Supplements : 184
Bury, Arnim.　　185 Wilamowitz.　　186, 187 D. L. P.
(μ[ακράν C. H. Roberts ; for the μ[see Milne, *P. Lit. Lond.*
96

CHOR. Have you no word of hope to tell your friends ?

HYPS. I dread what I shall suffer for the baby's death.

CHOR. Poor lady ! Already no stranger to sorrow !

HYPS. I know it well ; and will be on my guard.

CHOR. What defence from ruin have you discovered then ?

HYPS. Flight ! If only I had knowledge of these paths !

CHOR. Where will you turn, then ? What city will welcome you ?

HYPS. My feet and ready spirit shall decide.

CHOR. The land is guarded by sentinels round about.

HYPS. You win : that plan I abandon. But go I will.

CHOR. Reflect : in us you have friends to counsel you.

HYPS. Suppose I found a guide to take me from the land ?

CHOR. No man will want to guide a slave.

. . . . .

(From the fourth (?) Episode)

CHOR. Your words are noble, and to the wise ring true—I would count myself among the wise.

EURYDICE. Why do you cling thus to subtle argument ? Why embrace my knees, and plead so long ? You killed Opheltes, who was my eyes' delight ! . . .

(Fragments of one line)

and to my son, whom you destroyed.

---

p. 53)—ανλαζεσαι *P. Petr.*, corr. Roberts. 188 Morel.
189 Petersen.

[ΥΨΙΠΥΛΗ] οὕτω δοκεῖ μ[ε, π]ότνι', ἀποκτείν[ειν
        κακῆι   19

ὀργῆι πρὶν ὀρθῶς πρᾶγμα διαμαθ[εῖν τόδε;
σιγαῖς, ἀμείβηι δ' οὐδέν· ὦ τάλαιν' ἐγ[ώ,
ὡς τοῦ θανεῖν μὲν οὕνεκ' οὐ μέγα [στέν]ω,
εἰ δὲ κτανεῖν τὸ τέκνον οὐκ ὀρθ[ῶ]ς δοκῶ,
τοὐμὸν τιθήνημ', ὃν ἐπ' ἐμαῖσιν ἀγκάλαις   19
πλὴν οὐ τεκοῦσα τἄλλα γ' ὡς ἐμὸν τέκνον
στέργουσ' ἔφερβον, ὠφέλημ' ἐμοὶ μέγα.
ὦ πρῶιρα καὶ λευκαῖνον ἐξ ἅλμης ὕδωρ
Ἀργοῦς, ἰὼ παῖδ', ὡς ἀπόλλυμαι κακῶς.
ὦ μάντι πατρὸς Οἰκλέους, θανούμεθα.   20
ἄρηξον, ἐλθέ, μή μ' ἴδηις ὑπ' αἰτίας
αἰσχρᾶς θανοῦσαν, διὰ σὲ γὰρ διόλλυμαι.
ἔλθ', οἶσθα γὰρ δὴ τἀμά, καὶ σὲ μάρτυρα
σαφέστατον δέξαιτ' ἂν ἥδ' ἐμῶν κακῶν.
ἄγετε, φίλων γὰρ οὐδέν' εἰσορῶ πέλας   20
ὅστις με σώσει· κενὰ δ' ἐπηιδέσθην ἄρα.
[ΑΜΦΙΑΡΑΟΣ] ἐπίσχες, ὦ πέμπουσα τήνδ' ἐπὶ σφαγὰς
δόμων ἄνασσα· τῶι γὰρ εὐπρεπεῖ σ' ἰδὼν
τοὐλεύθερόν σοι προστίθημι τῆι φύσει.
  [ΥΨ.] ὦ πρός σε γονάτων ἱκέτις Ἀμφιάρεω πίτνω 21
καὶ πρὸς γενείου τῆς τ' Ἀπόλλωνος τέχνης·
καιρὸν γὰρ ἥκεις τοῖς ἐμοῖσιν ἐν κακοῖς·
[ῥ]ῦσαί με· διὰ γὰρ σὴν ἀπόλλυμαι χάριν,
μέλλω τε θνήισκειν, δεσμίαν τέ μ' εἰσορᾶις
πρὸς σοῖσι γόνασιν, ἢ τόθ' εἱπόμην ξένοις· 2
ὅσια δὲ πράξεις ὅσιος ὤν· προδοὺς δέ με
ὄνειδος Ἀργείοισιν Ἕλλησίν τ' ἔσηι.
ἀλλ' ὦ δι' ἁ[γνῶ]ν ἐμπύρων λεύσσων τύχας

190, 191 Wilamowitz.   193 μετα P. Petr., corr.
Wilamowitz.   194 εἰ δὲ Hunt, acc. to Italie: τοῦ δὲ

Hyps. Is it your pleasure, queen, to slay me in evil temper, before you learn all the truth of this ? What, silent ? No answer ? Woe is me—I have not many tears for death, only for the false thought that I killed your son, the babe I nursed, whom in my arms I fed, whom in all—save that I bore him not—I loved as my own child, my own great comfort. O prow of Argo, and water whitening from the spray, O my two sons, how miserably I perish ! O prophet, son of Oecles, death is upon me. Come, save me, see me not suffer death from a shameful charge ! For your fault I die. Come—for you know my story—and the queen may accept your word as true witness of my woe. Take me—I see no friend at hand to save me. It seems, my compassion was in vain.[a]

(Amphiaraus enters)

Amph. Stop ! You that send this woman to her doom !—Queen of this palace you must be : for at a glance I see in you nobility as well as grace.

Hyps. Now at your knees I implore you, Amphiaraus, falling here, and by your beard and by Apollo's art ; timely in your hour of danger you are come. Save my life ! It is for your sake I am ruined and about to die, at your knees, as you behold, in chains—lately companion of your foreign host. You are a holy man ; holy shall be your deed ; betray me, and your name shall spell disgrace to Argos and to Hellas. You that see the fortunes of the Danai in

---

[a] Her " compassion " was the sympathy which led her to assist Amphiaraus: or else her free confession to Eurydice.

Hunt (edd. 1 and 2).   197 εφερβον ωλεναις μο[*P. Petr.*, εφερον επωφελημα Π.

Δαναοῖσιν, [εἰπ]ὲ τῆιδε συμφορὰν τέκνου,
παρὼν γὰ[ρ οἶσ]θα. φησὶ δ' ἥδ' ἑκουσίως   220
κτανεῖν με παῖδα κἀπιβουλεῦσαι δόμοις.
[ΑΜ.] εἰδὼς ἀφῖγμαι τὴν τύχην θ' ὑπειδόμην
τὴν σὴν ἃ πείσηι τ' ἐκπεπνευκότος τέκνου,
ἥκω δ' ἀρήξων συμφοραῖσι ταῖσι σαῖς,
τὸ μὲν βίαιον οὐκ ἔχων, τὸ δ' εὐσεβές.   225
αἰσχρὸν γὰρ εὖ μὲν ἐξεπίστασθαι παθεῖν,
δρᾶσαι δὲ μηδὲν εὖ παθόντα πρὸς σέθεν.
πρῶτον μὲν οὖν σὸν δεῖξον, ὦ ξένη, κάρα·
σῶφρον γὰρ ὄμμα τοὐμὸν Ἑλλήνων λόγος
πολὺς διήκει. καὶ πέφυχ' οὕτως, γύναι,   230
κοσμεῖν τ' ἐμαυτὸν καὶ τὰ διαφέρονθ' ὁρᾶν.
ἔπειτ' ἄκουσον, τοῦ τάχους δὲ τοῦδ' ἄνες·
εἰς μὲν γὰρ ἄλλο πᾶν ἁμαρτάνειν χρεών,
ψυχὴν δ' ἐς ἀνδρὸς ἢ γυναικὸς οὐ καλόν.
[ΕΤ.] ὦ ξένε πρὸς Ἄργει πλησίαν ναίων χθόνα,   235
πάντων ἀκούσασ' οἶδά σ' ὄντα σώφρονα·
οὐ γάρ ποτ' εἰς τόδ' ὄμμ' ἂν ἔβλεψας παρών.
νῦν δ', εἴ τι βούληι, καὶ κλύειν σέθεν θέλω
καί σ' ἐκδιδάσκειν· οὐκ ἀνάξιος γὰρ εἶ.
[ΑΜ.] γύναι, τὸ τῆσδε τῆς ταλαιπώρου κακὸν   240
ἀγρίως φέρουσάν σ' ἤπιον θ[έσθαι θέλ]ω,
οὐ τήνδε μᾶλλον ἢ τὸ τῆς δίκης ὁρῶν.
αἰσχύνομαι δὲ Φοῖβον, οὗ δι' ἐμπύρων
τέχνην ἐπασκῶ, ψεῦδος εἴ τι λέξομεν.
ταύτην ἐγὼ 'ξέπεισα κρηναῖον [γά]νος   245
δεῖξαι δι' ἁγνῶν ῥευμάτων [ὅπως . . . .
στρατιᾶς πρόθυμ', Ἀργεῖον ὡς δ[ιεκπερῶν

(*Three lines missing : then fragments of four more*)

the flame of holy sacrifices, tell her what befell her
son! You know it, you were there. Of set purpose,
she says, I killed him—I made a plot against the
palace!

AMPH. I knew before I came; I divined your fate,
and all you must suffer because her son has breathed
his last. And I am here to aid you in your distress,
armed not with power but piety. For I should be
ashamed if I had skill to win a kindness from you;
then having won it, to do no kindness in return. (*To
Eurydice*) Now first, unveil your head, stranger queen.
Far goes the tale through Hellas, that my gaze is
modest. And this, lady, is my nature—self-dis-
cipline, and a discerning eye.[a] Next listen, and stay
your haste. Err about all things else; but not against
the life of man or woman—that is sin!

EURY. Stranger, whose land is Argos's neighbour,
from all men's words I know your modest temper;
else you had never stood and looked upon these eyes.
Now, if you will, I am ready to hear you and to inform
you. For you deserve it.

AMPH. Lady, it is my will to appease your temper,
seeing you bear so harshly this poor woman's wrong:
respecting not her so much as justice. I should feel
shame before Phoebus, whose art I practise through
the flame of sacrifice, if I speak any falsehood. By
me persuaded, this woman made known to us a
sparkling fountain, that with holy waters I might
(make) an offering for the army, crossing the bounds
of Argos . . .

(*Three lines missing: then fragments of four more*)

[a] Literally, " and to see essential qualities."

246 [ὅπως λάβω edd.

θῦσ]αι θέλ[οντες· ἀλλὰ κείμενον χαμαὶ
δράκων ἀσ[ήμωι παῖδ᾽ ὑφειμένος βέλει
ἠκόντισ᾽, α[250
καί νιν δρομ[
εἵλιξεν ἀμ[φὶ παῖδα
ἡμεῖς δ᾽ ἰδό[ντες παντόθεν προσβάλλομεν,
ἐγὼ δ᾽ ἐτόξευσ᾽ [αὐτόν· ἦν δ᾽ ἀνήνυτον·
ἀρχὴ γὰρ ἡμῖν [πημάτων πολλῶν θανὼν   255
Ἀρχέμορος ε[ἰς τὸ λοιπὸν ὀνομασθήσεται.
σὺ δ᾽ οὐχὶ σαυτῆ[ς μόνον ἀφῃρέθης τέκνον,
ὄρνιθα δ᾽ Ἀργείο[ισι γενόμενον κλύεις.

(*Fragments of two more lines*)

πολλοὶ δ[ὲ νικηθέντες εἴξουσιν μάχηι
Κάδμου [πολίταις· παῦρος ἐκ πολλῶν λεὼς   260
νόστου κυρήσ[ει· φεύξεται δ᾽ ἐχθρῶν χέρας
Ἄδραστος, ἥξει τ᾽ Ἄρ[γος ἐκ Θηβῶν πάλιν
ἑπτὰ στρατηγῶ[ν ἐκσεσωσμένος μόνος.
τὰ μὲν γενόμεν[α δὴ σαφῶς ἐπίστασαι,
ἃ δ᾽ αὖ παραινῶ, ταῦτά μοι δέξαι, γύναι.   265
ἔφυ μὲν οὐδεὶς ὅστις οὐ πονεῖ βροτῶν·
θάπτει τε τέκνα χἄτερα κτᾶται νέα
αὐτός τε θνήισκει· καὶ τάδ᾽ ἄχθονται βρότοι,
εἰς γῆν φέροντες γῆν· ἀναγκαίως δ᾽ ἔχει
βίον θερίζειν ὥστε κάρπιμον στάχυν,   270
καὶ τὸν μὲν εἶναι τὸν δὲ μή· τί ταῦτα δεῖ
στένειν, ἅπερ δεῖ κατὰ φύσιν διεκπερᾶν;
ἃ δ᾽ εἰκὸς Ἀργο[ῦς ἐξάγουσι πρόσφορα
θάψαι δὸς ἡμ[ῖν παῖδ᾽ ἀειμνήστοις τάφοις·
οὐ γὰρ καθ᾽ ἡμ[έραν γε ταῦτ᾽ ἔσται μίαν,   275

248-254 D. L. P. (248 θῦσαι θέλοντες Wecklein, Hunt).
256-258 Arnim (γόνον 257).   259-260 Roberts.   261
102

. . . eager to sacrifice. But, as he lay upon the ground, a serpent lurking struck your son with hidden sting. We rushed upon him ; . . . wrapped his coils about the child . . . We, when we saw it, attacked from every side ; and I shot it down, but all to no purpose. He died, and his death begins our many woes—Archemorus [a] shall be his name hereafter. You have not merely lost a son, your own : I tell you of a portent that has come to pass for Argos. . . .

(Fragments of two more lines)

Many shall yield to the men of Cadmus's town, vanquished in battle : many go, but few shall come home again. Alone of seven commanders Adrastus shall be saved, shall escape the foeman's grasp and come back from Thebes to Argos. Thus what has come to pass, clearly you understand. What now I counsel, lady, take in good part from me. No man was ever born, but he must suffer ; he buries his children and gets others in their place ; then dies himself. And yet men bear it hard, that only give dust to dust ! Life is a harvest that man must reap like ears of corn ; one grows, another falls. Why should we moan at this, the path of Nature that we must tread ? Give us your son, that we—bringing from Argos all that our duty owes—may bury him in a grave of remembrance everlasting. These things shall not be

[a] The name is derived from *archein* (begin) and *moros* (doom).

D. L. P.   262 D. L. P.: ιξεταρ[Π, ιξετάρα Hunt. See Aes. *Hic.* 176 ἱκετε mss., ἤκετε Porson ; Aes. fr. 6 ἤκουσ' mss., ἱκουσ' edd. pler.   274-281 D. L. P. (275 omitted by a mistake in ed. pr. and in Hunt, *F.T.P.* ; 277 C. H. Roberts, 278 Hunt).

ἀλλ' εἰς τὸν ἀε[ὶ δῆτα πήμασιν χρόνον
τοῖ[ς σο]ῖς βρότε[ιον πᾶν συναλγήσει γένος.
κλεινὸς γὰρ ἔσ[ται τάφος ἐν ἀνθρώποις ὅδε,
ἀγῶνά τ' αὐτῶι [στησόμεσθα, φυλλάδος
στεφάνους διδ[όντες· ὁ δὲ κρατῶν καθ'
    Ἑλλάδα   280
ζηλωτὸς ἔστ[αι καὶ περίβλεπτος βροτοῖς.
ἐν τῶιδε μὲν [λειμῶνι συλλεχθεὶς στρατὸς
μνησθήσετα[ι σοῦ παιδός, Ἀρχέμορος ὅτι
ἐπωνομάσθη, [πρῶτος ὡς ἄρξας μόρου,
Νεμέας κατ' ἄλσ[ος. τήνδε δ' οὖν λῦσαί σε
    χρή,   285
ἀναιτία γάρ, τοῖς [δὲ σοῖς κλέος φέρει·
σὺν γὰρ καλῶι σό[ν, ὦ γύναι, πένθος τέλει
θήσει σε καὶ παῖδ' [εἰς τὸ λοιπὸν εὐκλεεῖς.

    (Fragments of two more lines)

[ΕΥ.] πρὸς τὰς φύσεις χρὴ καὶ τὰ πράγματα
    σκοπεῖν
καὶ τὰς διαίτας τῶν κακῶν τε κἀγαθῶν·   290
πειθὼ δὲ τοῖς μὲν σώφροσιν πολλὴν ἔχειν,
τοῖς μὴ δικαίοις δ' οὐδὲ συμβάλλειν χρεών.

   .   .   .   .   .

    (From the Exodus)

  . . . τέκνα τ' ἀνὰ μίαν ὁδὸν
ἀνάπαλιν ἐτρόχασεν
ἐπὶ φόβον ἐπὶ   295
χάριν ἑλίξας,
χρόνωι δ' ἐξέλαμψεν εὐάμερος.
ΑΜΦΙΑΡ[ΑΟΣ] τὴν μὲν παρ' ἡμῶν, ὦ γύναι, φέρηι
    χάριν,

for a single day, but for all time all men shall suffer in your sorrow. A memorable tomb in the eyes of men this one shall be ; and we shall found Games [a] in honour of it, and award crowns of leaf ; the winner shall be envied throughout Hellas and all men shall look up to him. So in this meadow the host assembled shall call your son to mind, how he was called Archemorus, because he first began our doom, in the grove of Nemea. But this woman must go free, for she is innocent ; indeed she brings glory to your house : since your misfortune has a happy ending, lady, and will make your son and you renowned for all time to come.

(Fragments of two more lines)

EURY. One must look to man's character and deeds, and the lives of the evil and the good : and have much confidence in the righteous, but with the unrighteous not consort at all. . . .

.   .   .   .   .   .

(From the Exodus)

HYPS. . . . the wheel of Fortune has sped my sons and me back again along a single road. Now to terror, now to joy it turned us ; at long last she has shone forth serene.

AMPH. Thus, lady, you gain my service.   You

[a] The celebrated Nemean Games.

---

282 Roberts.   283-284 Arnim.   286 D. L. P.
287 πένθος D. L. P. : πάθος Hunt.   289-292 = fr. 759 N.

ἐπεὶ δ' ἐμοὶ πρόθυμος ἦσθ' ὅτ' ἠιτόμην
ἀπέδωκα κἀγώ σοι πρόθυμ' ἐς παῖδε σώ.   300
σῷζ' οὖν σὺ τέκνα, σφὼ δὲ τήνδε μητέρα,
καὶ χαίρεθ'· ἡμεῖς δ' ὥσπερ ὡρμήμεσθα δὴ
στράτευμ' ἄγοντες ἥξομεν Θήβας ἔπι.
ΟΙ ΤΨΙΠ[ΤΛΗΣ] ΤΟΙ εὐδαιμονοίης, ἄξιος γάρ, ὦ ξένε.
—— εὐδαιμονοίης δῆτα· τῶν δὲ σῶν κακῶν,   305
τάλαινα μῆτερ, θεῶν τις ὡς ἄπληστος ἦν.
ΤΨΙΠ[ΤΛΗ] αἰαῖ φυγὰς ἐμέθεν ἃς ἔφυγον,
ὦ τέκνον, εἰ μάθοις, Λήμνου ποντίας,
πολιὸν ὅτι πατέρος οὐκ ἔτεμον κάρα.
[ΕΤΝΗΟΣ] ἦ γάρ σ' ἔταξαν πατέρα σὸν κατακτα-
νεῖν;   310
[ΤΨ.] φόβος ἔχει με τῶν τότε κακῶν· ἰὼ
τέκνον, οἷά τε Γοργάδες ἐν λέκτροις
ἔκανον εὐνέτας.
[ΕΤ.] σὺ δ' ἐξέκλεψας πῶς πόδ' ὥστε μὴ θανεῖν;
[ΤΨ.] ἀκτὰς βαρυβρόμους ἱκόμαν   315
ἐπί τ' οἶδμα θαλάσσιον, ὀρνίθων
ἐρῆμον κοίταν.
[ΕΤ.] κἀκεῖθεν ἦλθες δεῦρο πῶς τίνι στόλωι;
[ΤΨ.] ναῦται κώπαις
Ναύπλιον εἰς λιμένα ξενικὸν πόρον   320
ἄγαγόν με δουλοσύνας τ' ἐπέβασαν, ὦ τέκνον,
ἐνθάδε Δαναϊδῶν μέλεον ἐμπολάν.
[ΕΤ.] οἴμοι κακῶν σῶν.
[ΤΨ.] μὴ στέν' ἐπ' εὐτυχίαισιν.
ἀλλὰ σὺ πῶς ἐτράφης ὅδε τ' ἐν τίνι   322
χειρί, τέκνον ὦ τέκνον;
ἔνεπ' ἔνεπε ματρὶ σᾷ.
[ΕΤ.] 'Αργώ με καὶ τόνδ' ἤγαγ' εἰς Κόλχων πόλιν.
[ΤΨ.] ἀπομαστίδιόν γ' ἐμῶν στέρνων.

met my entreaty with goodwill, and I in turn shewed goodwill toward your sons. Now keep your children safe—and, children, keep your mother. Farewell; we must begone, leading our host to Thebes, as we set forth to do.

SONS OF HYPS. (*a*) Blessings upon you, stranger, as you deserve!

(*b*) Aye, blessings. Poor mother, surely some god was insatiate of your sufferings!

HYPS. O! If you should know my banishment, my son, banishment from Lemnos in the sea, because I cut not my father's grey head off.

EUNÊUS. What, did they bid you slay your father?

HYPS. I tremble for those woes of old! Oh my son, like monsters they slew their husbands in their beds!

EUN. And you—how did you steal away from death?

HYPS. I went to the roaring beach and swell of the sea, where the birds lie in loneliness—

EUN. How came you hither? What convoy brought you thence?

HYPS. Carried by sailors, rowed to a foreign harbour, Nauplia: and they brought me to servitude, my son, a weeping woman bought for gold by daughters of Danaus!

EUN. I share your sorrows, and lament!

HYPS. Weep not in our good fortune. But how were you and your brother reared, my son? Whose hand was it? Tell me, oh tell your mother.

EUN. Argo took me and him to the city of Colchians—

HYPS. Torn from my breast!

107

[ΕΥ.] ἐπεὶ δ' Ἰάσων ἔθαν' ἐμός, μῆτερ, πατήρ   330

[ΤΨ.] οἴμοι, κακὰ λέγεις, δάκρυά τ' ὄμμασιν,
    τέκνον, ἐμοῖς δίδως.

[ΕΥ.] Ὀρφεύς με καὶ τόνδ' ἤγαγ' εἰς Θράικης
    τόπον.

[ΤΨ.] τίνα πατέρι ποτὲ χάριν ἀθλίωι
    τιθέμενος; ἔνεπέ μοι τέκνον.   335

[ΕΥ.] μοῦσάν με κιθάρας Ἀσιάδος διδάσκεται,
    τοῦτον δ' ἐς Ἄρεως ὅπλ' ἐκόσμησεν μάχης.

[ΤΨ.] δι' Αἰγαίου δὲ τίνα πόρον
    ἐμόλετ' ἀκτὰν Λημνίαν;

[ΕΥ.] Θόας κομίζει σὸς πατὴρ τέκνω δύο.   340

[ΤΨ.] ἦ γὰρ σέσωσται; [ΕΥ.] Βα[κ]χ[ίου] γε μη-
    χαναῖς.

. . . .

13   ΜΕΛΑΝΙΠΠΗ ΔΕΣΜΩΤΙΣ

[(a) 2 B.C. (Schub.-Wil.)
and 1 A.D. (Grenf.-H.)]
[(b) Parchment 5 A.D.]

Ed. pr. (a) Schubart-Wilamowitz, *Berliner Klassikertexte*, v. 2, 1907, p. 125. Vv. 1-12 also Grenfell-Hunt, *P. Oxy.* xi. 1912, no. 1176, fr. 39, col. xi. pp. 153-154.
(b) Blass, *Aegyptische Zeitschrift*, 1880, p. 37 ; *Rh. Mus.* 25, p. 390. *Cf.* Nauck, *T.G.F.*[2] fr. 495. Revised text in *Schubart-Wilamowitz, *ibid.* p. 85.

N. Lewis suggested that the fragment which he published in *Etudes de Papyrologie*, vol. iii. (republished by Snell, *Hermes, Einzelschr.* v. p. 78), belongs to this play : but there is no good evidence for this ascription, nor sufficient for Snell's tentative attribution to *Melanippe the Wise*.

See further Wilamowitz, *Sitzb. d. k. preuss. Akad. d.*

Eun. And when my father Jason died, mother—

Hyps. Alas! Your story is my sorrow, son; tears to my eyes you bring—!

Eun. Orpheus brought me and him to a part of Thrace.

Hyps. How shewed he gratitude to your unhappy father? Tell me, son!

Eun. He taught me the music of the lyre of Asia, and schooled my brother for Ares' weapons of war.

Hyps. And what way did you go over the Aegean to the shores of Lemnos?

Eun. Thoas, your father, conveyed both your sons—

Hyps. Is he safe then?

Eun. Yes, by the skill of Bacchus. . . .

* * * * * *

MELANIPPE CAPTIVE

[(a) 2 B.C. (Schub.-Wil.)
and 1 A.D. (Grenf.-H.)]
[(b) Parchment 5 A.D.]

Wiss. 1921, 63 (including notes of H. Petersen); Pickard-Cambridge, *New Chapters*, iii. 117; Beloch, *Hermes*, 19, 604; Wünsch, *Rh. Mus.* 49, 91; von Arnim, *Suppl. Eur.* p. 32; *Hunt, *F.T.P.*

Aeolus, discovering that his daughter Melanippe had borne twins, disbelieved her story that Poseidon was the father. He sent her to Italy in the charge of the king of Metapontum, who happened to be travelling in Thessaly (Diod. Sic. iv. 67 Αἴολος . . . παρέδωκε τὴν Ἄρνην Μεταποντίωι ξένωι κατὰ τύχην παρεπιδημοῦντι, προστάξας ἀπάγειν εἰς Μεταπόντιον: *Arne is the lady who replaces Melanippe in Diodorus's version).*

Melanippe bore twins, Boeotus and Aeolus, in the house of the Italian king. These were exposed, but reared by shepherds. Years later, Metapontius (as we will call the king) adopted them as successors to his throne [a] : no one was then aware of their identity, except perhaps an old shepherd, who so far held his peace.

Now the king's wife (Theano, Hyginus 186 ; Autolyte, Diod. iv. 67) bore sons thereafter, and plotted to destroy Boeotus and Aeolus, against whom she conceived a natural jealousy for their favour with the king. Melanippe discovered the plot—which was, that the queen's uncles should kill Boeotus and Aeolus while hunting—and learnt too that the doomed boys were her own sons. [Perhaps the old shepherd, who had reared them and knew their identity, heard the plot and discovered all to Melanippe, imploring her to assist them.] But the queen learnt the truth, and imprisoned Melanippe—who may have held some position of menial trust in the palace, like that of Hypsipyle at the court of Nemea. It is possible that the absence of the king may explain his queen's opportunity to act thus.

The plot failed. Our second fragment describes the assault upon the sons of Melanippe, who defended themselves successfully and slew their would-be murderers, the brothers of the queen : but not before these had explained to the youths their "ignoble" birth—evidently the queen's brothers knew (perhaps the queen told them) that the youths were exposed children, reared by a shepherd on the hills.

Boeotus and Aeolus returned, and heard (perhaps from the

[a] If it seems unlikely that the king should not recognize children whom he himself had exposed in his own territory some years ago, remember the certain parallel of Eur.'s *Alexander* and the probable one of Sophocles' *Tyro.*

chorus) that Melanippe was imprisoned for intervention on their behalf. They liberated her, and she proved to them that they were her sons. We do not know how the scene was composed. It is possible that it was very brief (see below): Melanippe greeted the youths as her sons ; they were sceptical ; Melanippe had no sure means of proof; but Poseidon appeared and told all the truth—the god from the machine prophesied the wanderings of Aeolus and Boeotus, and perhaps ordained a wedding between Melanippe and the king (who may have returned to find his wife and her brothers dead, and therefore was about to punish Melanippe and her sons). We do not know exactly how and at what point the suicide of the queen occurred.

This is a typically Euripidean plot : my summary is based upon the fragments themselves, Hyginus 186, and Diodorus iv. 67. It is of course only hypothetical : for none of the fragments except the Messenger's Speech is very helpful ; Hyginus is clearly, as that very speech proves, not paraphrasing Euripides' play ; and Diodorus gives a version in which Melanippe plays no part at all, the role usually assigned to her being given to one Arne. All we can say is that the above summary (including a few traits from the fragments) is true of what Eur. found before him when he composed his play. How far he diverged from it, we do not know.

The above reconstruction solves the three problems hitherto held insoluble (but v. Pickard-Cambridge, loc. cit.)—first, the part played by Melanippe herself. The person after whom a play is named is usually, if not always, an important character in it. On my view, Melanippe may have played a part almost as important as that of Hypsipyle in the play which bears her name : her imprisonment may have occurred more than half way through the play, her release towards the end (after the Messenger's speech).—Second, the manner in which Melanippe came to Metapontum. Thessaly is too far away : there can be no direct contact between it and Meta-

LITERARY PAPYRI

*pontum (which is certainly the scene of this play, see Strabo
vi. 265 ἐνταῦθα (sc. in Metapontum) καὶ τὸν Μετάποντον
μυθεύουσι καὶ τὴν Μελανίππην δεσμώτην καὶ τὸν ἐξ αὐτῆς
Βοιωτόν, and Wilam. Sitzb. preuss. Akad. p. 69) in this
play : and Aeolus cannot have had any part in it. Melanippe
herself must have been in Metapontum from the start.—
Thirdly, though Melanippe must, for this play, bear her sons
in Metapontum, she must not know that these are her sons*

(a) (Probably spoken by Melanippe)

μάτην ἄρ᾿ εἰς γυναῖκας ἐξ ἀνδρῶν ψόγος
ψάλλει κενὸν τόξευμα καὶ λέγει κακῶς·
αἱ δ᾿ εἰσ᾿ ἀμείνους ἀρσένων. δείξω δ᾿ ἐγώ.
ταῖς μὲν γάρ ἐστ]ι ξυμβόλαι᾿ ἀμάρτυρα

(*Fragments follow of four lines, ending* καὶ οὐκ
ἀρνούμεναι, ἀλ]λήλας πόνους,] αἰσχύνην ἔχει
(φέρει B),]ωτος ἐκβαλεῖ γυνή)

νέμουσι δ᾿ οἴκους καὶ τὰ ναυστολούμενα   5
ἔσω δόμων σῴζουσιν, οὐδ᾿ ἐρημίαι
γυναικὸς οἶκος εὐπινὴς οὐδ᾿ ὄλβιος.
τὰ δ᾿ ἐν θεοῖς αὖ πρῶτα γὰρ κρίνω τάδε·
μέρος μέγιστον ἔχομεν· ἐν Φοίβου τε γὰρ
χρησμοῖς προφητεύουσι Λοξίου φρένα   10
γυναῖκες, ἀμφὶ δ᾿ ἁγνὰ Δωδώνης βάθρα
φηγῶι παρ᾿ ἱερᾶι θῆλυ τὰς Διὸς φρένας
γένος πορεύει τοῖς θέλουσιν Ἑλλάδος.
ἃ δ᾿ εἴς τε Μοίρας τάς τ᾿ ἀνωνύμους θεὰς
ἱερὰ τελεῖται, ταῦτ᾿ ἐν ἀνδράσιν μὲν οὐχ   15
ὅσια καθέστηκ᾿, ἐν γυναιξὶ δ᾿ αὔξεται
ἅπαντα. ταύτηι τἀν θεοῖς ἔχει δίκης
θήλεια. πῶς οὖν χρὴ γυναικεῖον γένος

EURIPIDES

when this play begins, nor must they know that she is their mother. Later, they must recognize each other.

Beyond this we cannot venture : except to say that (1) *the prologue must have been spoken by a divinity (Poseidon), since none of the human characters could have given the necessary explanation about Melanippe's sons ;* (2) *the play must have ended fairly soon (about 350 lines ?) after the Messenger's speech (see Wilam. loc. cit., and ed. pr. p. 87). In this interval, we must imagine that Melanippe was liberated, Theano died, and Poseidon spoke from the machine.*

(a) *(Probably spoken by Melanippe)*

VAIN is man's evil speaking and blame of women —the twanging of an idle bowstring. For they are better than men, and I will prove it.—Their covenants have no witness . . .

(Fragments follow of four lines)

They manage the home, and guard within the house the sea-borne wares. No house is clean or prosperous if the wife is absent. And in religion —highest I judge this claim—we play the greatest part. In the oracles of Phoebus, women expound Apollo's will ; and at the holy seat of Dodona, beside the sacred oak, woman conveys the will of Zeus to all Greeks who may desire it. As for the holy rites performed for the Fates and the Nameless Goddesses—they are not holy in the hands of men ; among women they flourish all. So righteous is woman's part in holy service. How then

---

4 Suppl. D. L. P.   10 χρησμο[ι]ς Π. Oxy.: δομοις Π. Berl.   15 μενευ Π: μὲν οὐ edd.: μὲν οὐχ D. L. P.

113

κακῶς ἀκούειν; οὐχὶ παύσεται ψόγος
μάταιος ἀνδρῶν, οἵ τ' ἄγαν ἡγούμενοι   20
ψέγειν γυναῖκας, εἰ μί' εὑρέθηι κακή,
πάσας ὁμοίως; διορίσω δὲ τῶι λόγωι·
τῆς μὲν κακῆς κάκιον οὐδὲν γίγνεται
γυναικός, ἐσθλῆς δ' οὐδὲν εἰς ὑπερβολὴν
πέφυκ' ἄμεινον· διαφέρουσι δ' αἱ φύσεις. . .   25

(β)   (*Spoken by the Messenger to the Queen*)

[ΑΓΓΕΛΟΣ] τίς ἦν ὁ τἄ[ργον τόδε βέλος μ]εθεὶς
    ἐμοί;
ὡς δ' οὐκ ἐφαινόμεσθα, σῖγα δ' εἴχομεν,
πρόσω πρὸς αὐτὸν πάλιν ὑποστρέψας πόδα
χωρεῖ δρομαίαν, θῆρ' ἑλεῖν πρόθυμος ὤν,
βοᾶι δέ· κἂν τῶιδ' ἐξεφαινόμεσθα δὴ   30
ὀρθοσταδὸν λόγχαις ἐπείγοντες φόν[ον.
τὼ δ' εἰσιδόντε δίπτυχον θείοιν κάρ[α
ἤσθησαν εἰπόν τ'· εἶα συλλάβεσθ' ἄγρα[ς,
καιρὸν γὰρ ἥκετ'. οὐδ' ὑπώπτευον [δόλον
φίλων προσώπων εἰσορῶντες ὄ[μματα.   35
οἱ δ' εἰς τὸν αὐτὸν πίτυλον ἤπειγ[ον δορός·
πέτροι τ' ἐχώρουν χερμάδες θ' ἡ[μῶν πάρα
ἐκεῖθεν, οἱ δ' ἐκεῖθεν, ὡς δ' ἤιε[ι μάχη
σιγή τ' ἀφ' ἡμῶν, γνωρίσαντ[ε δὴ τὸ πᾶν
λέγουσι· μητρὸς ὦ κασίγν[ητοι φίλης   40
τί δρᾶτ'; ἀποκτείνοντες ο[ὓς ἥκιστα χρῆν
φωρᾶσθε. πρὸς θεῶν δρᾶτ[ε μηδαμῶς τάδε.
σὼ δ' αὐταδέλφω χερμ[άδ' αἴρουσιν χεροῖν
λέγουσί θ' ὡς ἔφυσα[ν ἐκ δούλης ποθέν,
κοὐ δεῖ τύρανν[α σκῆπτρα καὶ θρόνους
    λαβεῖν   45

20-21 For the construction (apparent omission of *e.g.*

114

should her kind be fairly abused ? Shall they not
cease, the vain reproaches of men ; and those who
deem too soon that all women must be blamed alike,
if one be found a sinner ? Let me speak on, and
distinguish them : nothing is worse than the base
woman, and nothing far surpasses the good one.
Only their natures differ. . . .

(b) (*Spoken by the Messenger to the Queen*)

" Who was it cast this vain shaft at me ? "
Now since we revealed not ourselves, but stayed in
silence, far off he turned again towards him, and
came running, eager to catch the prey. Then he
cried out. At once we revealed ourselves, standing
upright, and our lances brought death on apace.
They, when they saw their uncles twain, were glad
and spoke : " Come, help us with the chase !—You
are come at the hour of need ! "—suspecting never a
plot, for friends were they whose gaze they met.
Forward your brothers pressed to share the spear-
men's onslaught ; from us came stones and boulders,
some on this side, some on that : but as the battle
advanced, and there was silence on our side, they
understood all at last and spoke : " Brothers of our
dear mother, what are you about, that we catch you
slaying those whom you should treat so least of all ?
For God's sake, do not so ! "

Your brothers lifted a great stone, and cried,
" You are the sons of some slave-girl ; you have no

δεῖν) *cf.* Eur. *Or.* 555-556, Thuc. ii. 42, Plato, *Prot.* 346 в.
31 I have not followed Headlam and others in removing
this example of violated caesura : *cf.* Eur. *Hec.* 1159, *Hic.* 695,
Ba. 1125 (all in " Messengers' " speeches) ; *El.* 546, *Hel.* 86,
Pseudo-Eur. *I.A.* 630.   34 Blass.   45 Weil,
Wecklein.

πρεσβεῖ' ἔχοντ[ας δυσγενεῖς τῶν εὐγενῶν·
κἀπεὶ τάδ' εἰσή[κουσαν . . . . .

(*Fragments of three lines : then a gap*)

ἔσ]φηλέ τ' εἰς γῆν [τὸν βίον τ' ἀφεί]λετο.
ἡμῶν δ' ἐχώρει κωφὰ πρὸς γαῖαν βέλη,
δ]υοῖν δ' ἀδελφοῖν σοῖν τὸν αὖ νεώτερον   50
λόγ]χηι πλατείαι συοφόνωι δι' ἥπατος
παίσ]ας ἔδωκε νερτέροις καλὸν νεκρὸν
Βοιω]τός, ὅσπερ τὸν πρὶν ἔκτεινεν βαλών.
κἀντεῦ]θεν ἡμεῖς οἱ λελειμμένοι φίλων
κοῦφον] πόδ' ἄλλος ἀλλόσ' εἴχομεν φυγῆι.   55
εἶδον δὲ τ]ὸν μὲν ὄρεος ὑλίμωι φόβηι
κρυφθέν]τα, τὸν δὲ πευκίνων ὄζων ἔπι,
οἱ δ' εἰς φάρ]αγγ' ἔδυνον, οἱ δ' ὑπ' εὐσκίους
θάμνους κα]θῖζον. τὼ δ' ὁρῶντ' οὐκ ἠξίουν
δούλους φονε]ύειν φασγάνοις ἐλευθέροις.   60
τάδ' οὐκέτ' ὄντων σ]ῶν κασιγνήτων κλύεις.
ἐγὼ μὲν οὖν οὐκ] οἶδ' ὅτωι σκοπεῖν χρ[ε]ὼν
τὴν εὐγένειαν· τού]ς γὰρ ἀνδρείους φύσιν
καὶ τοὺς δικαίους τῶ]ν κενῶν δοξασμάτων,
κἂν ὦσι δούλων, εὐγεν]εστέρους λέγω.   65

(*Fragments of seven more lines*)

14   ΜΕΛΑΝΙΠΠΗ Η ΣΟΦΗ

Ed. pr. *Rabe, Rheinisches Museum*, 63, 1908, p. 147.
See Wilamowitz, *Class. Phil.* iii. 226, note ; *Sitzb. preuss.
Akad.* 1921, 63 ; Pickard-Cambridge, *New Chapters*, iii.
113 ; von Arnim, *Suppl. Eur.* 26.

*Hippo, daughter of Chiron, bore Melanippe to Aeolus.
During Aeolus's absence in exile for a year, Melanippe, a girl*

right to seize the royal sceptre and throne, ignoble masters of noblemen!" Now when they heard this . . .

(Fragments of three lines : then a gap)

tripped him to the ground, and took his life away. Our shafts fell idly to the ground ; the younger of your two brothers was struck through the heart by the broad spear destined for the boar ; and his fine corpse was given over to the dead by him, Boeotus, who struck the former one and slew him. Thereupon we, the remnant of his friends, turned our nimble feet to flight, each a different path. One man I saw hidden in the leafy forest on the mountain, another on the boughs of a pine ; others climbed down to a ravine, some crouched beneath dark shadowy bushes. They saw us, but thought it not well that swords of noblemen should butcher slaves. This is my story : your brothers are no more. For my part, I know not whereby one must judge nobility. Men brave in character and just, albeit sons of slaves, are nobler, I say, than the vain pretentious.

(Fragments of seven more lines)

---

46 Weil.   47 Nauck.   61 Von Arnim.

MELANIPPE THE WISE

of singular beauty, bore twin sons to Poseidon ; who bade her conceal the fact from Aeolus by hiding the twins in a cattle-shed. When Aeolus returned, he was told that two infants had been found being suckled by cows : regarding them as monsters, βουγενῆ τέρατα, he determined to burn them, and

*bade Melanippe attire them in funeral clothes. Melanippe
tried desperately to save the babies' lives: and as a last
resort confessed that they were her own. (Or perhaps her
secret was betrayed by a nurse to whose care she had com-
mitted her babies in the cattle-shed.) Aeolus in anger was*

(From the Prologue)

[ΜΕΛΑΝΙΠΠΗ] Ζεύς, ὡς λέλεκται τῆς ἀληθείας ὕπο,
  "Ελλην' ἔτιχθ', ὃς ἐξέφυσεν Αἴολον·
  οὗ χθών, ὅσον Πηνειὸς 'Ασωποῦ θ' ὕδωρ
  ὑγροῖς ὁρίζον ἐντὸς ἀγκῶσι στέγει,
  σκήπτρων ἀκούει πᾶσα καὶ κικλήσκεται   5
  ἐπώνυμος χθὼν Αἰολὶς τοὐμοῦ πατρός.
  ἐν μὲν τόδ' ἐξέβλαστεν "Ελληνος γένος.
  πτόρθον δ' ἀφῆκεν ἄλλον εἰς ἄλλην πόλιν

(Lacuna of at least one line, referring to the
adventures of Δῶρος)

  κλεινὰς 'Αθήνας Ξοῦθον, ὧι νύμφη ποτὲ
  θυγάτηρ 'Ερεχθέως Κεκροπίας ἐπ' αὐχένι   10
  "Ιων' ἔτικτεν. ἀλλ' ἀνοιστέος λόγος
  ἐπ' ὄνομα τοὐμὸν κεῖσ' ὅθενπερ ἠρξάμην.
  καλοῦσι Μελανίππην (με), Χίρωνος δέ με
  ἔτικτε θυγάτηρ Αἰόλωι· κείνην μὲν οὖν
  ξανθῆι κατεπτέρωσεν ἱππείαι τριχὶ   15
  Ζεύς, οὕνεχ' ὕμνους ἦιδε χρησμωιδὸς βροτοῖς
  ἄκη πόνων φράζουσα καὶ λυτήρια.
  πυκνῆι θυέλληι δ' αἰθέρος διώκεται
  μουσεῖον ἐκλιποῦσα Κωρύκιον ὄρος.
  νύμφη δὲ θεσπιωιδὸς ἀνθρώπων ὕπο   20
  'Ιππὼ κέκληται σώματος δι' ἀλλαγάς.
  μητρὸς μὲν ὧδε τῆς ἐμῆς ἔχει πέρι.

*about to slay the children and punish Melanippe, when the
intervention of Hippo (or Poseidon) stayed his hand. The
divine parentage of the babies was revealed, and their future
fame as eponymous heroes of Boeotia and Aeolis was pro-
phesied.*

(From the Prologue)

MELANIPPE. Hellen—so runs the tale of truth—
was son of Zeus ; and son of Hellen was Aeolus ;
whom all the land obeys, that Peneus's and Asopus's
floods protect and limit with their winding streams.
The land is called Aeolis, after my father's name.—
This was one race that sprung from Hellen.

But he sent forth other branches to other cities . . .

(Lacuna of at least one line, referring to the
adventures of Δῶρος)

and Xuthus to famous Athens ; to him of old, on
the neck of Cecrops' land, his bride the daughter
of Erechtheus bore Ion.

Now I must recall my tale to the point where I
began—to my own name. They call me Melanippe ;
the daughter of Chiron bore me to Aeolus. Her—
because she chanted songs of prophecy to men, ex-
pounding remedies and release from pain[a]—Zeus
covered with the plumage of bay horse's hair ; thick
fell a tempest from Heaven, and she was driven forth,
and left the Corycian mountain of the Muses. That
nymph of prophecy is called Hippo by the world, by
reason of her body's change.

Such is the truth about my mother. . . .

---

[a] *i.e.*, because she gave these benefits to mankind, Zeus
punished her ; *cf.* his punishment of Prometheus.

1-2=fr. 481 N.

15 ΠΕΙΡΙΘΟΟΣ

Ed. pr. (b) *Rabe, *Rheinisches Museum*, 63, 1908, p. 145;
(a and c) *Hunt, *P. Oxy.* xvii. 1927, no. 2078, p. 36 (2 A.D.).
See von Arnim, *Suppl. Eur.* 40 ; Pickard-Cambridge,
New Chapters, iii. 148 ; Wilamowitz, *Analecta Euripidea*,
p. 161 ; *Sitzb. preuss. Akad.* 1907, 1 ; Kuiper, *Mnemosyne*,
35 ; Körte, *Archiv*, x. 1931, 51

*The story of the tragedy was this :—Pirithous went to
Hades accompanied by Theseus to seek the hand of Persephone
in marriage. He was dreadfully punished for his presump-
tion, being chained to a rock guarded by serpents. Theseus
would not desert his companion, and elected to live in Hades.*

*Then Heracles, sent by Eurystheus to fetch Cerberus,
accomplished his labour and delivered both Pirithous and
Theseus. (Herein was a great innovation : the common
story ended with the deliverance of Theseus only.)*

*In our first fragment Pirithous (perhaps in the Prologos)
describes the sin and suffering of his father Ixion. In the
second fragment, Aeacus observes the approach of Heracles ;
challenges him, and receives his answer. In the third frag-
ment, Theseus implores Heracles for deliverance.*

*The great authority of Wilamowitz (who however did not
treat the problem fully or in detail) has led many scholars
to follow him in denying that Euripides wrote this play.
Their only direct evidence is the sentence in Athenaeus
(496 b) ὁ τὸν Πειρίθουν γράψας, εἴτε Κριτίας ἐστὶν ὁ τύραννος ἢ
Εὐριπίδης, and the statement in a Life of Euripides that
Tennes, Rhadamanthys and Pirithous were "spurious"
dramas.*

*Kuiper, loc. cit. adequately refutes the charges, (1) that the
cosmogony implied in fr. 593 Nauck is impossible for Eur.,
(2) that Pir. fr. 598 is inconsistent with Eur.'s views about
human character, (3) that there is anything un-Euripidean in
the language, (4) one or two minor and even more weakly*
120

EURIPIDES

PIRITHOUS

founded charges. He also shews that there is no reason to believe that the doubtful ascription to Critias in Athen. 496 b (cf. Vit. Eur.) is based on good or early authority : on the other side, Pirithous is included among the plays of Eur. on the Piraeus stone (Wilam. Anal. Eur. p. 138)—a most weighty consideration—and is attributed to Eur. by Plutarch, Clement, scholiasts, anthologists, lexicographers and others. The comparative freedom from resolution of the iambic trimeters may only indicate that Pirithous was not among Eur.'s later plays (a conclusion provisionally accepted by Zielinski, Trag. Lib. Tres, p. 228). Hunt's inference from v. 8 of our first fragment is wholly arbitrary (he suggested, from comparison of Or. 36-37, El. 1253, that τροχῶι μανίας should be taken together as a metaphor, i.e. that Ixion's wheel was in this play made a mere figure of speech, his myth rationalized : this would not be surprising if the poet were the Critias who wrote Sisyphus fr. 1 Nauck, where the same rationalizing tendency can be observed in the allegation that the gods are only an utilitarian invention. But (1) since the ends of the lines are missing, we do not know whether μανίας should be taken with τροχῶι or not—it is very easy to avoid taking it so ; (2) even if the myth was thus rationalized— which we do not know—it would not be the first instance of such rationalism in Euripides : no need to look beyond him to a Critias).

It is further alleged that the scene of the action must have been set partly in Hades, partly on earth : the principal events certainly occurred in Hades ; but the Chorus, which sings to Zeus, and calls upon the Aether, must have been outside Hades in the daylight. This is very far from certain. It is most reasonable to suppose that the Chorus was a band of Initiate Souls in Hades, like the Chorus of Initiates in Aristo-

phanes' Frogs.[a] *There need be no change of scene. And
even if there was a change of scene, and if Hades as the scene
is itself considered strange and unprecedented, I do not see
that the ascription to Critias at the end of Euripides' life is
a better solution than the ascription to Euripides himself a
few years earlier.*

In conclusion : the direct testimonies, quoted above, create

(*a*) [ΠΕΙΡΙΘΟΟΣ] θεὸς δὲ μανία[ς ἀρτίως ἐλευθέρωι
ἔπεμψεν ἄτη[ν· ἁρπάσας δ' ἠικασμένην
νεφέλην γυναικ[ὶ δυσσεβέστατον λόγον
ἔσπειρεν ἐς τοὺς Θε[σσαλούς, ὡς δὴ Κρόνου
θυγατρὶ μίσγοιτ' ἐ[ν φυταλμίωι λέχει.   5
τοιῶνδε κόμπω[ν δ' ὕστερον καταξίους
ποινὰς θεοῖς ἔτεισεν [
μανίας τροχῶι περι[
οἰστρηλάτοισιν ὤχ[μασεν, κἄπειθ' ἑλὼν
ἄπυστον ἀνθρώποι[σιν αἰθέρος βάθει   10
ἔκρυψεν. ἀλλὰ βορε[άσιν πνοαῖς ἐκεῖ
διεσπαράχθη συμμ[έτρωι κομπάσμασιν
πατὴρ ἁμαρτὼν εἰς θε[οὺς τιμωρίαι.
ἐγὼ δ' ἐκείνου πήματ' ἀ[ινιχθέντ' ἔχων
[Περίθους ὀνόματι καὶ τύχας εἴληχ' ἴσας.]   15

(*b*) [ΑΙΑΚΟΣ] ἔα, τί χρῆμα; δέρκομαι σπουδῆι τινα
δεῦρ' ἐγκονοῦντα καὶ μάλ' εὐτόλμωι φρενί.
εἰπεῖν δίκαιον, ὦ ξέν', ὅστις ὢν τόπους
εἰς τούσδε χρίμπτηι καὶ καθ' ἥντιν' αἰτίαν.

1-15 restored *ex grat.* by Housman.   7 [ὧν πάντων
πατὴρ Housman.   8 περι[φερὲς ἐν δίναις δέμας Housman.

---

[a] Ar. *Ran.* was certainly influenced by *Pirithous* : *cf.*
further the part of Aeacus. If the chorus of *Pirithous* was

EURIPIDES

a sense of uncertainty which nothing can dispel ; but modern scholarship has failed to add much, if any, strength to them. On the whole the balance of evidence is in favour of Euripidean authorship : though we still know far too little about the play to permit a definite conclusion. I defer to the consensus of ancient opinion in publishing the play under the name of Euripides.

(*a*) Pirithous. Now when he was just freed from madness, God sent infatuation upon him ; he seized a cloud, made in the likeness of a woman, and spread among the Thessalians an impious rumour,—that he embraced the daughter of Cronus in fruitful union. For that vain boast thereafter he paid to heaven a just penalty ; . . . Zeus took and hid him in the sky's abyss, far from the knowledge of man. There he was torn asunder by northern gales—he, my father, his retribution suited to his boasting, whereby he had sinned against the gods. And I, bearing his agonies riddled in my name,[b] am called Pirithous, and my fortunes are like his. . . .

(*b*) Aeacus. What is this ? I see a figure hastening hither apace—bold is his spirit indeed ! Stranger, you must tell me who you are that come near these regions, and what matter brings you.

indeed a band of Initiates, a reason must have been given why they should appear in the same scene as Pirithous ; their normal haunts would of course be separate from his place of punishment. But a reason could easily have been found : Pirithous is being punished for a crime against Persephone —the chorus, if (like that of Ar. *Ran.*) it consists of " dead " Eleusinian Initiates, is a devotee of Persephone. It would not require much ingenuity to bring together Persephone's worshippers with her captive enemy. [b] He derives his name from *peri* and *thoos, circling* and *swift*—Ixion his father was bound to a *wheel.*

[ΗΡΑΚΛΗΣ] οὐδεὶς ὄκνος πάντ᾽ ἐκκαλύψασθαι
    λόγον.   20
  ἐμοὶ πατρὶς μὲν Ἄργος, ὄνομα δ᾽ Ἡρακλῆς,
  θεῶν δὲ πάντων πατρὸς ἐξέφυν Διός.
  ἐμῆι γὰρ ἦλθε μητρὶ κεδνῆι πρὸς λέχος
  Ζεύς, ὡς λέλεκται τῆς ἀληθείας ὕπο.
  ἥκω δὲ δεῦρο πρὸς βίαν, Εὐρυσθέως   25
  ἀρχαῖς ὑπείκων, ὅς μ᾽ ἔπεμψ᾽ Ἅιδου κύνα
  ἄγειν κελεύων ζῶντα πρὸς Μυκηνίδας
  πύλας, ἰδεῖν μὲν οὐ θέλων, ἆθλον δέ μοι
  ἀνήνυτον τόνδ᾽ ὤιετ᾽ ἐξηυρηκέναι.
  τοιόνδ᾽ ἰχνεύων πρᾶγος Εὐρώπης κύκλωι   30
  Ἀσίας τε πάσης ἐς μυχοὺς ἐλήλυθα.

(c) [ΘΗΣΕΥΣ . . . . . .] πιστὸν γὰρ ἄνδρα καὶ
    φίλον
  αἰσχρὸν πρ]οδοῦναι δυσ[με]νῶς εἰλημμένον.
  [ΗΡΑΚΛΗΣ σαυτῶι τε], Θησεῦ, τῆι τ᾽ Ἀθηναίων
    πό[λει
  πρέπουτ᾽ ἔλεξας· τοῖσι δυστυχοῦσι γὰρ   35
  ἀεί ποτ᾽ εἶ σὺ σύμμαχος. σκῆψιν [δέ τ]οι
  ἀεικές ἐστ᾽ ἔχοντα πρὸς πάτραν μολεῖν.
  Εὐρυσθέα γὰρ πῶς δοκεῖς ἂν ἄσμενον,
  ἔμ᾽ εἰ πύθοιτο ταῦτα συμπράξαντά σοι,
  λέγειν ἂν ὡς ἄκραντος ἤθληται πόνος;   40
  [ΘΗΣΕΥΣ] ἀλλ᾽ οὔ σὺ χρήιζεις π[αντελῶς] ἐμὴν
    ἔχεις
  εὔνοιαν, οὐκ ἔμπλ[ηκτον ἀλλ᾽ ἐλ]ευθέρως
  ἐχθροῖσί τ᾽ ἐχθρὰ[ν καὶ φίλοισι]ν εὐμενῆ.
  πρόσθεν σ᾽ ἐμοὶ τ[οιοῦτον ὄνθ᾽ αἱρ]εῖ λόγος,
  λέγοις δ᾽ ἂν [ἤδη καὶ σὺ τοὺς αὐ]τοὺς
    λόγους.   45

EURIPIDES

HERACLES. I fear not to unfold all my story. My fatherland is Argos, my name is Heracles. And I am son of Zeus, the father of all the gods : for Zeus—so runs the tale of truth—came to my good mother's bed. And I come hither perforce, obedient to the commands of Eurystheus who sent me and bade me fetch the hound of Hades living to the gates of Mycenae,—not that he wished to see it, but he deemed that he had found therein a labour that I could not accomplish. In quest of this business I have travelled round about to the farthest ends of Europe and of all Asia. . . .

(c) THESEUS. . . . for it is shameful to betray a loyal friend, when captive of the foe.

HERACLES. Theseus, your speech does honour due to Athens and yourself. You were ever champion of the oppressed. Yet it were shame for me to return home with excuses on my lips. How gladly, think you, would Eurystheus say—if he heard I did this with your help—that my task and toil were unfulfilled ?

THESEUS. For your desire, all my goodwill is with you : not given in heat, but freely, hating them that hate, but to friends favourable. Such were you once to me, as all men tell ; and now you shall say the same. . . .

---

23 End probably corrupt: κεδνὸν ἐς λέχος Dobree.   41
παντελῶς D. L. P.

16   ΣΘΕΝΕΒΟΙΑ

Ed. pr. Rabe, *Rheinisches Museum*, 63, 1908, p. 147. See
Wilamowitz, *Class. Phil.* 3, 1908, 225 ; Croiset, *Rev. de
Phil.* 34, 1910, 216 ; Sellner, *de Eur. Stheneb. quaest. select.*
1910 ; Sechan, *Et. sur la trag. grecque*, 494 ; *Pickard-
Cambridge, *New Chapters*, iii. 131 ; von Arnim, *Suppl. Eur.*
43 ; Stahl, *Rheinisches Museum*, 63, 626.

*Bellerophon had fled from Corinth to the palace of Proetus
at Tiryns, where he was purified of homicide. Stheneboea,
wife of Proetus, made advances to him, which he rejected (she
employed a Nurse as go-between). In the prologue, Bellerophon
resolves to leave Tiryns, in order to avoid dishonour for him-
self if he yields to Stheneboea, and for Proctus if he should
denounce the queen. Proetus however listened to the slanders
which his humiliated wife uttered against his guest, and sent
Bellerophon to King Iobates of Caria with a secret message
bidding Iobates to slay him. Iobates sent Bellerophon forth
to fight the Chimaera, thinking that he would not return ; but
Bellerophon accomplished this labour, and returned enraged
to Tiryns, borne by Pegasus. Finding there another plot to*

[ΒΕΛΛΕΡΟΦΩΝ] οὐκ ἔστιν ὅστις πάντ᾽ ἀνὴρ εὐδαι-
       μονεῖ·
   ἢ γὰρ πεφυκὼς ἐσθλὸς οὐκ ἔχει βίον,
   ἢ δυσγενὴς ὢν πλουσίαν ἀροῖ πλάκα.
   πολλοὺς δὲ πλούτωι καὶ γένει γαυρουμένους
   γυνὴ κατήισχυν᾽ ἐν δόμοισι νηπία.   5
   τοιᾶιδε Προῖτος γῆς ἄναξ νόσωι νοσεῖ·
   ξένον γὰρ ἱκέτην τῆσδ᾽ ἔμ᾽ ἐλθόντα στέγης
   λόγοισι πείθει καὶ δόλωι θηρεύεται

7 ἐπελθόντα ms. : ταῖσδ᾽ . . . στέγαις Wilam., Pick.-Camb.,
text von Arnim.

EURIPIDES

STHENEBOEA

destroy him, he feigned compliance with Stheneboea's reiterated advances; he proposed to her that she should fly with him on Pegasus to Asia Minor. She assented: but while they were flying near Melos, Bellerophon threw her down into the sea. Her body was recovered by fishermen, who brought it to Corinth; whither Bellerophon also returned, and justified himself before Proetus.

This was a remarkable tragedy. The introduction of Pegasus—a real horse, probably, adorned with artificial wings—on to the stage, had perhaps no precedent, and was certainly a bolder innovation of its kind than anything since the chariot of Oceanus in Aeschylus's Prometheus. *Even more surprising is the disrespect for the common unity of time.—Two long intervals must have elapsed during the action of the play, (1) while Bellerophon went to Asia Minor and performed labours at the command of Iobates; (2) while Bellerophon and Stheneboea flew away from Corinth on their winged horse.*

Further, the duplication of the plots against the life of Bellerophon, and of his temptation by Stheneboea, is indeed astonishing. (It is probable that Stheneboea's death at the hands of Bellerophon was an Euripidean innovation in the story.)

BELLEROPHON. No man in the world is happy in all ways : either his birth is noble, but he has no livelihood ; or he ploughs wealthy fields, but his birth is humble. Many are proud of riches and noble birth together, yet a foolish wife at home brings shame upon them. Such is the affliction of Proetus, who rules this country. I came here as a guest and suppliant of this palace ; her tongue beguiles me

127

κρυφαῖον εὐνῆς εἰς ὁμιλίαν πεσεῖν.
αἰεὶ γὰρ ἥπερ τῶιδ' ἐφέστηκεν λόγωι   10
τροφὸς γεραιὰ καὶ ξυνίστησιν λέχος
ὑμνεῖ τὸν αὐτὸν μῦθον· ὦ κακῶς φρονῶν
πιθοῦ· τί μαίνηι; τλῆθι δεσποίνης ἐμῆς

(At least one line missing)

κτήσει δ' ἄνακτος δώμαθ' ἐν πεισθεὶς
   βραχύ.
ἐγὼ δὲ θεσμοὺς Ζῆνά θ' ἱκέσιον σέβων   15
Προῖτόν τε τιμῶν, ὅς μ' ἐδέξατ' εἰς δόμους
λιπόντα γαῖαν Σισύφου φόνον τ' ἐμῆς
ἔνιψε χειρὸς αἷμ' ἐπισφάξας νέον,
οὐπώποτ' ἠθέλησα δέξασθαι λόγους,
οὐδ' εἰς νοσοῦντας ὑβρίσαι δόμους ξένος,   20
μισῶν ἔρωτα δεινόν, ὃς φθείρει βροτούς.
διπλοῖ γὰρ εἴσ' ἔρωτες ἔντροφοι χθονί·
ὁ μὲν γεγὼς ἔχθιστος εἰς Ἅιδην φέρει,
ὁ δ' εἰς τὸ σῶφρον ἐπ' ἀρετήν τ' ἄγων ἔρως
ζηλωτὸς ἀνθρώποισιν, ὧν εἴην ἐγώ.   25
†οὐκοῦν νομίζω καὶ θανεῖν γε σωφρονῶν·
ἀλλ' εἰς ἀγρὸν γὰρ ἐξιέναι βουλήσομαι†
οὐ γάρ με λύει τοῖσδ' ἐφημένον δόμοις
κακορροθεῖσθαι μὴ θέλοντ' εἶναι κακόν,
οὐδ' αὖ κατειπεῖν καὶ γυναικὶ προσβαλεῖν   30
κηλῖδα Προίτου καὶ διασπάσαι δόμον

and her wiles pursue me, to share her bed in secret.
Ever and again that aged nurse who is charged
with this message, and conspires to make the union,
chants the same story: " Yield, foolish man !
Whence comes this madness ? Be bold, (obey) my
queen's (command) ; . . .

(At least one line missing)

one little act of yielding, and your prize shall be this
palace ! "

But I have good respect for law and Zeus, the sup-
pliant's god ; and esteem for Proetus, who received
me into his house when I left the land of Sisyphus,
and washed my hands clean of murder, with blood of
new slaughter shed above them ; so never yet have
I consented to listen to her plea, nor to offend against
this stricken house, where I am a guest : and I ab-
hor that dangerous passion which destroys the soul
of man. Two kinds of love there are, that live on
earth :—one, our worst enemy, leads to death ; the
other leads to virtue and a good life—coveted by
men such as I would be ! Better, I think, that a
man be virtuous, though he should die for it. (?)

Now I would go forth into the fields. I do myself
no service sitting in the palace, and listening to abuse
because I will not sin : nor yet denouncing her and
bringing shame on the wife of Proetus, and rending
the house in twain . . .

17-18 φόνων τ' ἐμὰς ἔνυψε χεῖρας cod., Pick.-Camb. Text
von Arnim.   26-27 senseless and (27) unmetrical:
Roberts suggests plausibly ἐξάγειν for ἐξιέναι.

LITERARY PAPYRI

17   [2 B.C.]   ΤΗΛΕΦΟΣ

Ed. pr. *Calderini, *Aegyptus*, xv. 1935, p. 239. See Goossens, *Chroniques d'Égypte*, 11, 1936, 508 (and 139); Körte, *Archiv*, xiii. 1938, 98; Buchwald, *Stud. zur Chronol. d. Att. Trag.*, diss. Königsb. 1939, 26.

For the plot of this famous play, see J. Schmidt in Roscher's Lexicon, *v. col. 274*; Schwenn in P.-W.-K. *ix. col. 362*; and esp. Wilamowitz, Berliner Klassikertexte, *v. 2. 69*. For the legend see our preface to Sophocles' Ἀχαιῶν Σύλλογος : from which it will be evident that Sophocles' treatment of the theme gave little scope for tense or profound drama. But the Telephus of Euripides was a most original and interesting character. The action of the play was partly concerned with a dissension in the Greek army ; Agamemnon being eager, and Menelaus reluctant, to abandon the expedition against Troy. And Telephus himself took for his model the crafty Athenian politician, a cunning fellow thriving on stratagem and deception. First, he disguised himself as a beggar in rags ; then he sought to win Agamemnon over with sly argu-

(*From the Prologue*)

[ΤΗΛΕΦΟΣ] ὦ γα[ῖα πατρίς], ἣν Πέλοψ ὁρίζεται,
    χαῖρ’, ὅς τε πέτραν Ἀρκάδων δυσχείμερον
    Πὰν ἐμβατεύεις, ἔνθεν εὔχομαι γένος·
    Αὔγη γὰρ Ἀλέου παῖς με τῶι Τιρυνθίωι
    τίκτει λαθραίως Ἡρακλεῖ· σύνοιδ’ ὅρος   5
    Παρθένιον, ἔνθα μητέρ’ ὠδίνων ἐμὴν
    ἔλυσεν Εἰλείθυια, γίγνομαι δ’ ἐγώ.
    καὶ πόλλ’ (ἐ)μόχθησ’· ἀλλὰ συντεμῶ λόγον·
    ἦλθον δὲ Μυσῶν πεδίον, ἔνθ’ ε(ὑ)ρὼν ἐμὴν
    μητέρα κατοικῶ, καὶ δίδωσί μοι κράτη   10
    Τεύθρας ὁ Μυσός, Τήλεφον δ’ ἐπώνυμον
    καλοῦσί μ’ ἀστοὶ Μυσίαν κατὰ χθόνα·

EURIPIDES

TELEPHUS [2 B.C.]

*ments; being unsuccessful, he boldly seized the infant Orestes
and held him as hostage until Agamemnon yielded. [This
feature was not invented by Euripides : vases prove it to be
earlier, and tradition assigned it to Aeschylus, see Wilamo-
witz, loc. cit. pp. 69-70.] Finally he prevailed upon Achilles
with another display of specious and sophistical argument.
The fragments do not allow us to follow Telephus pleading his
own cause as if he were another person, and later betraying
his own identity; but there was evident occasion for surprise
and subtlety. We see clearly how Euripides could transform
a slow and stately legend into a breathless drama of intrigue
and suspense; and how obviously he merited the accusation
that he was abasing the dignity of his profession. But the
Athenians never forgot the rags and tatters of his Telephus.*

The play was produced in 438 B.C. together with Alcmeon
through Psophis, Cretan Women, *and* Alcestis. *Vv. 1-7
(to* Εἰλείθυια) =fr. 696 N. : v. 13 =fab. incert fr. 884 N.*

(From the Prologue)

TELEPHUS. I greet my fatherland, where Pelops
set his boundaries ; and Pan, who haunts the stormy
Arcadian crags, whence I avow my birth. Auge, the
daughter of Aleus, bore me in secret to Heracles of
Tiryns. Witness Parthenion, the mountain where
Ilithyia released my mother from her pangs, and I
was born. And long I laboured—but I will make my
story brief ; I came to the plain of Mysia, where I
found my mother and made a home. Teuthras, the
Mysian, granted me his empire. Men call me
Telephus in the towns of Mysia, since *far from*

1-7 (Εἰλείθυια) Nauck, fr. 696.   9 ερων Π: corr.
Goossens.

131

τηλοῦ γὰρ οἴκων βίοτον ἐξιδρυσάμην.
"Ελλην δὲ βαρβάροισιν ἦρχον ἐκπονῶν
πολλοῖς σὺν ὅπλοις, πρίν (γ᾽) Ἀχαϊκὸς μολὼν 15
στρατὸς τὰ Μυσῶ[ν πε]δί᾽ ἐπ[ε]στράφη
παγ[

(Obscure fragments of four more lines)

13=Nauck, fab. incert. fr. 884.　　14 ηρχετεκτονων Π:
ἦρχον D. L. P., ἐκπονῶν Goossens.　　15 So ed. pr. : πολ-

18　[(a) 2 A.D.]　　FRAGMENTS
　　[(b) 5 A.D.]

(a) Ed. pr. *Grenfell-Hunt, P. Oxy. ix. 1912, no. 1176
(from Satyrus's Life of Euripides) (1) and (2)=fr. 38, col. iii.
p. 143 ; (3)=fr. 39, col. ii. p. 144 ; (4)=fr. 39, col. iv. 33-38,
p. 147 ; (5)=fr. 39, col. vi. 4-12, p. 148 ; (6)=fr. 39, col. vi.
12-15, p. 148.　See von Arnim, Suppl. Eur. 3.

(a) (1)　　　　　　　　Βοσπό]ρου πέρα
　　Ν[είλου] τε ναυστολοῦσι χρημάτων χάριν
　　ἀστρο[σκο]ποῦντες [ἐνα]λίαν τρικυ[μί]αν.

(2) θύραθεν [οὐ] θέλοιμ᾽ ἂν [ἐλθ]οῦσαν μα[κρὰν
　　χρυσοῦν [τὸν] "Ιστρον [οὐ]δὲ Βόσπο[ρον
　　λα]βών.　　　　　　　　　　　　　　　5

(3) [——— λ]άθραι δὲ τού[τ]ων δρωμένων τίνας
　　　　φοβῆι;
　　[———] τοὺς μείζονα βλ[έ]ποντας ἀ[ν]θρώπων
　　　　θεούς.

(4) κτήσασθ᾽ ἐν ὑστέροισιν εὔ[κ]λειαν χρόνοι[ς,
　　ἅ]πασαν ἀντλή[σαν]τες ἡμέρα[ν πόν]ον
　　ψυχαῖς.　　　　　　　　　　　　　　　10

EURIPIDES

home ^a my life was settled. Over barbarians I ruled,
a Hellene, at my task beside me were a thousand
spears; until the Achaean army came, and turned
to the plains of Mysia . . .

(*Obscure fragments of four more lines*)

^a A play on the Greek name Τήλεφος.

λοισινενβλοιειν Π. 16 στρατοσθεμνσω . . διονεπ[ι]στροφην-
παγ[Π: corr. Goossens (ἐπεστρώφα Körte). παγ[is corrupt:
πο[δί Goossens.

FRAGMENTS [(*a*) 2 A.D.]
[(*b*) 5 A.D.]

These fragments are not explicitly ascribed to Euripides in
the Papyrus; we can only say that the contexts render the
ascription probable.

(*b*) Ed. pr. *Vitelli, *Papiri Greci e Latini*, ii. 1913, no. 126,
p. 27. (See p. 254, line 70-71.) Quoted in a fragment of a
comedy, and explicitly ascribed to Euripides.

(*a*) (1) Beyond the Bosporus and the Nile they
sail in quest of gold, watching the stormy ocean high
as heaven. . . .

(2) I would not have her . . . going far from home,
not though I gained the Bosporus and Ister turned
to gold. . . .

(3) —— These things are done in secret : whom do
you fear ?
—— The gods ; farther than men they see. . . .

(4) Go, get you fame for all time to come, and
every day drain labour to the dregs within your souls !

5 [τὸν] von Arnim.

133

(5)　　　] τεκόν[τι] π[α]τρὶ δυσμενέστατοι·
　　　δόμ]ων γὰρ ἄρχε[ι]ν εἰς ἔρωτ' ἀφιγμένοι
　　　τοῖς φιλτάτοις κυρ[ο]ῦσι πολεμιώτατοι.
(6)　σμικρ[οὶ] γέροντι πα[ῖ]δες ἡδίους πατρί.

(b)　　　　　　　　　　τὰς γὰρ συμφορὰς　　　　15
　ἀπροσδοκήτους δαίμον[ες δι]ώρισαν.

(5) . . . hate their own father most : they come to yearning for rule over the house, and prove the bitterest foes to their nearest friends.

(6) An aged father has more joy of little children. . . .

(*b*) The gods appointed man's misfortunes to be unexpected.

---

15 γὰρ may not be part of the original Euripidean text.

ΙΩΝ

19   [3 A.D.]   ΟΜΦΑΛΗ

Ed. pr. *Grenfell-Hunt, *P. Oxy.* xiii. 1919, no. 1611, fr. 2, col. i. 124-127, p. 134. See Körte, *Archiv*, vii. 240; Schmidt, *G.G.A.* 1922, 97; Blumenthal, *Ion von Chios* (Berlin 1939), p. 35.

Quotation in an essay in literary criticism, introduced by the phrase ὁ ἐν τῆι Ἰωνο[ς Ὀμφ]άλη(ι) κατ' ἀρχὴν λεγόμε[ν]ος Ἡρακλέους βόρειος [ἵπ]πος. *Omphale was a Satyric play: its scene was Lydia. For the* βόρειος ἵππος *cf. Homer,* Iliad *xx. 221* τοῦ τρισχίλιαι ἵπποι . . . τάων καὶ Βορέης ἠράσσατο

ὅρων μὲν [ἤ]δη Πέλοπος ἐξελαύ[νο]μεν,
Ἑρμῆ, βόρειον [ἵπ]πον· ἄνεται δ' ὁδός

ANONYMOUS

20   [1-2 A.D.]   ? ΑΙΣΧΥΛΟΣ: ΜΥΡΜΙΔΟΝΕΣ

Ed. pr. Vitelli-Norsa, *Mélanges Bidez, Annuaire de l'Institut de philologie et d'histoire orientales*, ii. 1934, p. 968 with Plate. See Körte, *Archiv*, xi. 1935, 250; Sulzberger, *L'Antiquité Classique*, 3, 1934, 447; Vitelli-Norsa, *Papiri Greci e Latini*, xi. 1935, no. 1211, p. 102, with Plate; Kalén, *Eranos*, 33, 1935, 39; Schadewaldt, *Hermes*, 71, 1936, 25; Fritzsch, *Neue Fragmente der Aisch. und Soph.*, diss. Hamburg, 1936, 16; Zimmermann, *Phil. Woch.* 57, 745; Stella, *Rend. Ist. Lomb.* 69, 1936, 553.

ION

OMPHALE

βοσκομενάων. *The subject of* ἐξελαύνομεν *may be the Satyrs.*
" Possibly Heracles had been sent by Omphale to fetch one of
the horses sprung from Boreas which belonged to Pelops ; cf.
the legend of the capture of the horses of Diomedes, which
Heracles gave to Eurystheus (Apollod. ii. 5. 8) " (ed. pr.).
See Blumenthal, pp. 36-37 for details.

At length from the boundaries of Pelops we drive
forth, O Hermes, the North Wind's horse ; and our
journey is at its end . . .

ANONYMOUS

?AESCHYLUS, *MYRMIDONS* [1-2 A.D.]

The ascription of these lines to Aeschylus is based upon the
form διαί *at the end of v. 8 : for the only other iambic tri-*
meter which ends with this form of the preposition (i.e. in
which the form, when it occurs in an iambic trimeter, is not
required by the metre) is Aeschylean, viz. Cho. 656 ; cf.
Aesch. fr. 296 Nauck, διαί *at the end of a trochaic tetrameter.*
This evidence is surely insufficient ; there is no reason why

Sophocles, Euripides and others should not have used the form in this way ; the fact that it is not so used in their extant works is a reply that may be confuted by the next discovery of a tragic fragment in a papyrus. It is not as if forms of this kind were in themselves peculiarly Aeschylean. διαί *occurs only in Aeschylus (also Agam. 448, 1133, 1453, 1485, Cho. 610 lyrics) ; but* ὑπαί, *found in Aeschylus, Agam. 892, 944, Eum. 417, occurs also in Sophocles, El. 711, Ant. 1035 (all in iambic trimeters) ; Aesch. Agam. 1164, Cho. 615 (both lyric, and both probably false readings) ; Euripides, El. 1187 (lyric) ; and in the fragment (p. 22) which is probably part of Sophocles' Inachus, a satyric play, v. 9 (lyric) ; cf. Aristophanes, Ach. 970, Av. 1426 (iambic trimeters, parodies of tragic style).*

If we turn to the style of the fragment, we find that although it is perhaps more like that of Aeschylus than that of Sophocles or Euripides, it is not really like the style of Aeschylus. It lacks the power and colour and metaphor of Aeschylean language ; it is indeed very simple and direct, clear and unadorned [a] *; its boldest metaphors are " shepherd " for Agamemnon and " healer of evils "—perhaps introduced with an apology—for death ; the only word in the vocabulary which might suggest Aeschylus is* πολυσκεδεῖς *v. 16, a new (but comparatively tame) compound.*

The details of the linguistic evidence, apart from διαί, *afford no helpful criterion. There are several points of construction, vocabulary, etc., which do not occur in Aeschylus : but there is perhaps nothing that could not have occurred in*

[ΑΧΙΛΛΕΥΣ] λεύσουσι τοὐμὸν σῶμα· μὴ δόκει ποτὲ
πέτρ[ο]ις καταξανθέντα Πηλέως γόνον

---

[a] Stella observes that the *Myrmidons* of Aesch. was specially chosen by Aristophanes in the *Frogs* as an example of particularly pompous and grandiose writing.

ANONYMOUS

his work. The rare word προδοσία *v. 20 is not found else-where in Tragic iambic trimeters (or in indeed in Tragedy at all, except Eur. Hel. 1633, troch. tetr.), but no secure infer-ence can be made on this basis. The details can be found in Stella,* loc. cit.*: with whom I agree further that the character of Achilles here is not typically Aeschylean ; he is psycho-logically more advanced, more sophisticated and argumenta-tive, more interested in himself and his own motives and actions, than we expect in Aeschylus. True, the nature of the action may have demanded such a character : the point is that although such a character is not impossible for an Aeschylean play, it certainly is not typical of one.*

The most that can be said in favour of the ascription to Aeschylus is this : that the fragment comes from just such a scene as we imagine Aeschylus's Myrmidons *to have included ; that the form of a preposition in -αί, used without metrical necessity, does not in fact occur in Tragic iambics outside Aeschylus ; and that the style and character of the speaker, though not Aeschylean, are not impossible to reconcile with Aeschylus.*

This evidence, though not lightly to be dismissed, is in-sufficient for the important conclusion which it purports to prove. It remains undeniable that the fragment may pro-ceed from the hand of another writer. If Sophocles and Euripides are thought unlikely candidates for authorship, we must still remember that Achilles was the hero of plays written by Astydamas, Carcinus and others ; and we have long ago been forced to abandon the assumption that a tragic fragment found in a papyrus of the 1st or 2nd century A.D. must auto-matically be ascribed to one of the three great Tragedians. It is clear that the only scientific verdict must be :—" Anony-mous ; perhaps from the Myrmidons *of Aeschylus."*

ACHILLES. . . . they will stone me ! Stoning and **torture** of the son of Peleus shall prove no blessing—

Δαναοὺς ὀ]νήσειν Τρωικὴν ἀνὰ χθόνα·
ἀλλ'] ἡμένοισι Τρωσὶ τὴν ἄ[ν]ευ δορὸς
νικᾶ]ν γένοιτ' ἄν, εὐπετέστερ[ον] δ' ἔχοις   5
. . . .] τοῦτο δὴ βροτοῖσιν ἰατρὸν πόνων.
τάρβε]ι δ' Ἀχαιῶν χεῖρ' ἐφορμήσω δορὶ
μαιμ]ῶσαν ὀργῆι ποιμένος κακοῦ διαί;
ἀλλ' εἴ]περ εἷς ὤν, ὡς λέγουσι σύμμαχοι,
τροπὴ]ν τοσαύτην ἔκτισ' οὐ παρὼν μάχηι,   10
οὐκ εἴ]μ' ἐγὼ τὰ πάντ' Ἀχαιικῶι στρατῶι;
τοιόν]δ' ἀφεῖναι τοὖπος οὐκ αἰδώς μ' ἔχει·
τίς γὰρ] τοιούτ[ο]υς εὐγενεστέρους ἐμοῦ
. . . . . ἄ]ν [εἴ]ποι καὶ στρατοῦ ταγ[εύ]-
μᾶτα;
] ὑμᾶς εἷς ἀνὴρ ἠ[ι]κ[ί]ζετο   15
τ]αράσσων καὶ πολυσκεδεῖς [τι]θ[ε]ὶς
] τεύχ[η π]ερὶ νέοις βρα[χίο]σιν

(Fragments of nineteen more lines, including πάνθ'
ὑμῶν στρατόν 18, εὐμαρῶς ἐτ[ρέ]ψατο 19,
ἀ]νδ[ρ]ὸς προδοσίαν 20, ἄ]νδρα τόνδ' α[ἰ-
σχρῶς] θανεῖν 21, τόνδ' ἀποφθερεῖ στρατόν
27, ϝμ]ῆνις ὡς ὁρᾶν πάρα 28, ἐμ]φανῶς
κατηγόρος 30, ἐλε[ύ]θερον λέγεις 31, ο]ὐ-
δαμῶς πρέπει τάδε 34, διαλ[λα]γαί 34, μει-
λί[γ]ματι 36)

ANONYMOUS

21   [2 A.D.] ?ΣΟΦΟΚΛΗΣ: ΑΧΑΙΩΝ ΣΥΛΛΟΓΟΣ

Ed. pr. *Roberts, Catalogue of the Greek Papyri in the
John Rylands Library, Manchester, iii. 1938, no. 482, p. 91,
140

never think it—to the Greeks on Trojan soil. No : rather the Trojans shall sit in ease and win the victory that comes without a battle. And you shall more easily meet your friend the " Healer of man's sorrow."

Shall fear of Greeks drive my hand to seize the spear, this hand that trembles now with anger through the fault of their vile master ? Comrades in arms are saying that I alone—my absence from the fighting—have made this mighty rout : so am I not all in all to the Greek army ? No modesty forbids me to speak so, for who would call such generals nobler than me ? Such leaders of your army ? . . . one man has done you violence . . . shaken and shattered you . . . armour on youthful shoulders . . .

(Fragments of nineteen more lines)

3-5 D. L. P.   In v. 3, *either* ed. pr. are mistaken in giving room for only 6 letters at the beginning of the line *or* their facsimile is altogether misleading (the N of O]ΝΗΣΕΙΝ comes under the IT of ΛΕΥΣΣΟΥΣΙΤΟΥΜΟΝ v. 1).   For ὀ]νήσειν *cf.* Eur. *Held.* 705, *Hic.* 373.   6 τὸν] is certainly too short for the space ; πρὸς] hardly makes sense. 11 Schadewaldt.   12 Körte : τοῖον] δ' ed. pr.   13 Fritsch.   14 ἀρχοὺς ἂ]ν Fritsch, too long for the space ; ἀγοὺς Schadewaldt, unpleasant with ταγεύματα following.

ANONYMOUS

? SOPHOCLES, *GATHERING OF THE ACHAEANS* [2 A.D.]

Plate IV. See Webster, *Bulletin of the John Rylands Library,* *Manchester*, vol. xxii. no. 2, Oct. 1938, p. 543.

*The following reconstruction of this fragment is based on
the assumption, likely but far from certain, that it proceeds
from a play on the subject of Telephus's adventures in Hellas.
In one account of the legend (Nauck, T.G.F. p. 579; Pearson,
The Fragments of Sophocles, i. 94) Telephus prevailed upon
Achilles to heal the wound which he himself had inflicted, by
seizing the infant Orestes and threatening to kill him unless
Achilles complied. Our fragment may belong to a play on
this theme. It will then deal with the following portion of
the plot :—Telephus is to win over the fleet; then someone is
to assist him to penetrate the royal palace; there has been a
proclamation—designed specially to impede Telephus—that
no foreigner may be admitted to the palace; so Telephus will
go dressed as an ἀστός, an ordinary citizen. Vv. 5-8 mean
that Telephus will enter the palace on the pretext that he has
come to seek justice, which has been denied him by the chief-
tains of the state. Once inside, he will take his opportunity
to seize Orestes. (His enterprise was traditionally made
easier by the complicity of Clytemnestra.) Webster (loc.
cit.) argues differently. In his view, our fragment ends
shortly before the fragment of Ach. Syll. (p. 12) begins :
it is the end of the scene before the arrival of Achilles.
Odysseus here is sending Telephus to the fleet, himself await-*

—— ἔπειτα καταβά]ς, Τήλε[φ'], ἐς τὰ πε[
σήμαινε] να[ύτα]ις καὶ κ[υ]βερνή[ταις τάδε,
. . . . π]αρὼ[ν] ἐκ νυκ[τός]· εἶτα σ[ὸν
ἔργον· σὺ] μὲν [σύ]μβουλο[ς] ἐλθὲ τῶι
[στόλωι.
ἐπεὶ] γὰρ ἡμῶν, ὡς ὁ [μῦ]θός ἐστ', ἀ[γοὶ   5
δίκηι τὰ π]ρῶτα καὶ νόμ[ο]ις Ἑλληνι[κοῖς
εὔργο]υσι χρῆσθαι, τ[ῆ]ς τύχης ἀμ[αρ]τάνων
τολμᾶι δόμ]οισιν ἐμπε[σ]εῖν· ἀστὸς γὰ[ρ] ὡς

ing Achilles, whom he must persuade to heal Telephus. κηρύ-
κειον *refers to a proclamation made in deference to an oracle
that " no foreigner may lead the Greek army to Troy." This
idea has in its favour the close connexion between our frag-
ment,* ἀστὸς γὰρ ὡς *etc., and the passage in the Ach. Syll.
fragment in which Telephus, who has clearly been accepted as
guide already, is emphatically denoted as " a Tegeate, no
child of Mysia," i.e. a Greek, not a foreigner. But it leaves
vv. 8-9 very difficult : Webster (reading ξένον or ξένους at
the beginning of v. 7) translates " Foreigners, as the decree
runs, the chiefs forbid to use Greek right and law " (my
romans). Apart from the sense given to ὡς ὁ μῦθός ἐστι, this
is a most unnatural way of saying that the chiefs forbid
foreigners to guide the Greek fleet to Troy (which, in Webster's
view, was the content of the decree).*

*But the whole problem is difficult : I do not say that
Webster's view is more open to objection than that of Roberts
and myself. The divergence and doubt shew clearly how
dangerously hypothetical these reconstructions may be. The
evidence for Sophocles' authorship itself is not very strong.
There is nothing to contradict it : the words* ἀμνηστεῖν,
κηρύκειον *(elsewhere in Tragedy adjectival) and* ὑπεξελεῖν *(in
the sense " remove objections ") are found in Sophocles, but
not in Aesch. or Eur. It is clear that evidence for Sophocles'
authorship could well be a good deal stronger. The ascription
to a play concerned with Telephus is based on the vocative*
Τήλεφ' *in v. 1.*

—— Then, Telephus, go down to the . . . appear
by night and give this signal to the sailors and the
pilots. Then . . . the task is yours : go and assist
the fleet in counsel. For since our chieftains (thus
our story runs) forbade him from the first the use of
justice and the laws of Hellas, failing of that good
fortune he makes bold to assail the palace. He shall

εἶσ', ὃν τὸ] κηρύκειον ο[ὑ] δάκνει πλέον·
σὺ δ' ἐξά]γοις ἂν τῆσδ' ἀφ' ἑσπέρας γνάθο[υ· 10
οὐ γάρ, τάδ'] ἦν ε(ὐ) θώμεθ', ἀμνηστεῖν σε
χρὴ
τῶν εἰσέπει]τα· σοὶ δ' ὑπεξελεῖν πάρα
τῶνδ' εἴ τι] μὴ πρόσχο[ρδ]ον, ὡς ἀνὴρ μόλῃ.
—— ἄγε σ]ὺν τούτοις τ[ῶι] μὲν ξείνωι
συμπλε]ῖν πομπού[ς] παρατασσέσθω   15
. . . να]ύαρχός τις [ἀν]ὴρ ἔσται·
τὸ δ' ἄρ'] ἐκ τούτω[ν αὐ]τὸς ἐγὼ πᾶν

ANONYMOUS

22   [3 B.C.]   ?ΣΟΦΟΚΛΗΣ: ΝΙΟΒΗ

Ed. pr. Grenfell-Hunt, *New Classical Fragments and other
Greek and Latin Papyri*, Series ii. 1897, no. 6, p. 14. See
*Pearson, *Fragm. of Soph.* ii. 94 ; Blass, *Lit. Centralbl.*
1897, 334, and *Rh. Mus.* lv. 96 ; Pickard-Cambridge, *New
Chapters*, iii. 84 ; Robert, *Hermes*, 36, 368.

*Blass conjectured that this fragment is part of a scene in
which Artemis (v. 1) drives or has driven from the house
(v. 2) someone (probably a girl, v. 10) who is in danger of
death at her hands (v. 9) ; probably Artemis is shooting at
her with bow and arrows (v. 3).*

*He suggested further that the fragment comes from
Sophocles' Niobe. Apollodorus (iii. 47) relates that Niobe
returned to Lydia after her children's death : now Hom. Il.
xxiv. 602 Schol. Townl. states that this was a feature of
Sophocles' Niobe. It is therefore inferred that Apollodorus
is following Sophocles when he says that Artemis shot down*

144

go as a citizen, whom the edict stings no more than
another. But you must begone from this promontory
when evening falls. And if success attends us here,
what follows you must not forget. You may remove
whatever makes no harmony with our plot, that the
man may arrive.

CHORUS. Let him post an escort for the stranger,
to sail with him, together with these men . . . he
shall be captain of a ship. All that follows, I will . . .

ANONYMOUS

? SOPHOCLES, *NIOBE*   [3 B.C.]

*the daughters of Niobe in the house, and Apollo slew the sons
while hunting on Mount Cithaeron.*

   *So it is inferred that our fragment represents the shooting
of one of the daughters by Artemis. Since however the
inferences both about the action of our fragment and about
the nature of Sophocles' plot are by no means certain, I have
not included this piece among the fragments of Sophocles.
The evidence, which I have given (see further Pearson, p. 96),
for believing that Apollodorus gives the story of Sophocles'
play, is not very strong.[a] As for the fragment itself, it is not
certain that Artemis plays any direct part in its action;
there is no mention of Niobe or a Niobid. All that is fairly
certain is that a girl (v. 10) is on the stage in danger of death
(v. 9). So far as we can judge, the fragment suggests the
slaying of a Niobid by Artemis; but this is no more than a*

---

   [a] In other respects (*e.g.* the sparing of one son and one
daughter) it is generally agreed that Apollodorus is *not* giving
the Sophoclean version.

145

LITERARY PAPYRI

*likely guess. However tempting the inference may seem,
there is nothing in the fragment itself which proves that the
girl was in fact killed. That she was killed on the stage is
a still more doubtful inference, which has no support in*

[ΧΟΡΟΣ . . . ἀλ]λὰ Φοίβου τῆς θ' ὁμοσπόρο[υ φόβωι
    πόδ' ἐ]ξελαύνεις δωμάτων τ' [ἀφειμένη
    κατ]αστοχίζηι πλευρὸν εἰσε[

[ΚΟΡΗ   ]α τὴν πολύστονον σ[
           ] ἐκεῖσε τῆιδ' ἐπουρίσω πόδα   5
           ]ες δὲ μύχαλα τάρταρά τε [γᾶς
           ]οι πόδα καταπτήξω
           ]α λίσσομαι δέσποινα [
           ]ντο . . . μηδ' ἐμὲ κτά[νηις

[ΧΟ.   ἀθ]λία κόρη   10

ANONYMOUS

(Subject uncertain ; commonly ascribed to

23   [2 A.D.]   SOPHOCLES, *TANTALUS*)

Ed. pr. Grenfell-Hunt, *P. Oxy.* ii. 1899, no. 213, p. 23,
Plate IV. See Pearson, *Fragm. of Soph.* ii. p. 209 ; Pickard-
Cambridge, *New Chapters*, iii. 86 ; Crönert, *Archiv*, i. 511 ;
Wecklein, *Phil. Woch.* 1900, 508 ; Wilamowitz, *G.G.A.*
1900, 34 ; Robert, *Hermes*, 49, 1914, 634 (with readings of
F. Petersen) ; Fritsch, *Neue Fragm. d. Aisch. und Soph.*,
diss. Hamb. 1936, 27 ; Reinhardt, *Hermes*, 69, 1934, 251 ;
Zimmermann, *Phil. Woch.* 57, 745 ; Milne, *Cat. Lit. Pap.
B.M.* no. 68 ; Pfeiffer, *Sitzb. Bayer. Akad.* 1938, 2, 21 n. ;
Morel, *Burs. Jahresb.* 259, 1938, i. 33.

*A fragment of wholly uncertain reference, context and
authorship, commonly ascribed to the* Tantalus *of either
Aeschylus or Sophocles. It is assigned to Sophocles on the*

146

ANONYMOUS

Apollodorus or indeed in any ancient testimony, including this papyrus.

[*I must add that Pearson, who includes this among the fragments of Sophocles' Niobe, admits that " the identification is of course not certain."*]

(CHORUS ?) . . . For dread of Phoebus and his sister you are driven forth ; free of the house, your body is target of their bows.

(NIOBID ?) . . . the mournful . . . thither, hither you have sped your way . . . depths and nether world of Earth . . . I will crouch . . . mistress I implore . . . nor slay me . . .

(CHORUS ?) . . . unhappy maid . . .

---

7 ὀτοτοτοτοτοτ]οῖ ed. pr.   8]ᾁλῳσομαι Pearson :]α λίσσομαι Blass.

ANONYMOUS

(Subject uncertain ; commonly ascribed to
SOPHOCLES, *TANTALUS*)   [2 A.D.]

grounds (1) that the postponement of ἐπεί v. 2, if we read τῶνδ' ἐπεὶ κτλ., is found twice in S., but not in A. But the reading ἐπεὶ is not certain. (2) σθένειν with the in- finitive is found in S. but not in A. But this depends on reading λιθ]ῶσαι in the next line, and wilfully governing it by σθένει v. 8. (3) τοιγαροῦν is found in S. but not in A. But both τοίγαρ and γὰρ οὖν are common in A. (4) S. is fond of λιθο- compounds, A. has none. The fragment is alleged to belong to a play about Niobe on the grounds (1) that the description λιθουργὲς εἰκόνισμα is especially appropriate

147

to her, (2) *it is easy enough to restore the lines to make* e.g. *a speech of Tantalus on first observing Niobe turned to stone on Mount Sipylus. But the reading of* Π *in v.* 5 καὶ μάγους πάγας *is difficult to reconcile with a reference to Niobe : it would certainly suit* e.g. *Medea or Circe better. And* λιθ. εἰκ. *might easily be part of an allusion to Niobe in a passage which concerns some other character ; or it might refer to Medusa.*

> πο]νήρων παυ[
>]πε τῶνδεπιμωνος φόβων
> λι]θουργὲς εἰκόνισμα †ειδητερα
>]αι κωφαῖσιν εἴκελον πέτραις
>]εινης οἶδα καὶ μάγους πάγας   5
>]υγρωι κάλυβι κοιμηθήσεται
> έ]σχον θάμβος· ἢ γὰρ †πνεύμεθα
>]δίοις πέτραισι νῦν πάλιν σθένει
>   ]ωσαι· τοιγαροῦν †θ[. .]ρειταιμοι
>]εν οἰκτρὰ συμφορὰ δάπτει φρένας   10
>]ναι μολόνθ' ἑκουσίους μ[ά]χας
>] μοιρῶν †ἀντιααζον[. . . . . .]τοι

2 ἐπεὶ μόνος φόβων edd.   3 ἰδεῖν πάρα edd.: *e.g.* ἤδη τέρας would do less violence to the text.   4 ἴκελον πετροις Π.   5 μορφὴν δ' ἐκ]είνης οἶδα κώμματοσταγεῖς (or χαίματοσταγεῖς) edd.: but Π is perfectly clear. δόλους δ' ἐκείνης οἶδα καὶ μ. π. Maas.   6 ὑγρῶι, διύγρωι, καθύγρωι. καλαβι

ANONYMOUS

24   [Early 3 A.D.]   ? ΣΟΦΟΚΛΗΣ : ΤΗΡΕΥΣ

Ed. pr. Vitelli-Norsa, *Studi e Testi,* vol. 53 ; *Il Papiro Vaticano,* XI. ; Città del Vaticano, Biblioteca Apostolica
148

ANONYMOUS

The weakness of the evidence, both for ascription to Sophocles and for assignment to a play about Niobe, is obvious: following a hint from Pfeiffer, loc. cit., I have returned to the text of the papyrus itself, and printed it as an anonymous and unidentified fragment. (Arguments from a second fragment, ed. pr. ibid. = Pearson, 595, are worthless, because its connexion with our fragment is uncertain.)

  . . . of bad . . .
  . . . of these terrors . . .
  . . . stone-image . . .
  . . . like dull crags . . .
  . . . I know . . . wiles of sorcery . . .
  . . . shall be laid to rest in a watery bower . . .
  . . . astonished . . .
  . . . rocks, now again is strong . . .
  . . . therefore . . .
  . . . pitiable misfortune rends the heart . . .
  . . . entering battles wilfully . . .
  . . . fates . . .

Π.   7 πνεῦμ' ἔνι, ἔτι edd.   μέγιστον ἔ]σχον edd.   8 ἀκαρδίοις ed. pr. much too short for the space (about eight letters before διοις): πετροισινυμπαλιν Π : πέτραισιν, ἢ ᾿μπαλιν edd.   9 θεὸς λιθ]ῶσαι ed. pr. θεωροῦντι, θαρσοῦντι, θαρρεῖτε, θροεῖτε μοι edd.   10 παιδὸς μ]ὲν edd.   11 ἢ θεοῖσι]ν ἔμολεν εἰς ἑκουσίους edd., violently.   12 The second α of αντιααζον is uncertain : perhaps αντιλαζον[.

ANONYMOUS

? SOPHOCLES, *TEREUS* [Early 3 A.D.]

Vaticana, 1931, with Plate. See Maas, *Deut. Litt.-Zeit.* 1931, 1210 ; *Cazzaniga, *Rend. Ist. Lomb.* ii. 67, fasc. vi-ix,

LITERARY PAPYRI

1934 ; Buchwald, *Stud. zur Chronol. d. att. Trag.*, diss. Königsb. 1939, pp. 37, 56. Quotations contained in Favorinus's περὶ φυγῆς (early 1st cent. A.D.). (a) = col. vii. 44-46 ; (b) = col. ix. 25-27 ; (c) = col. xi. 3-8.

Fr. (b) *is quoted in conjunction with* Soph. Tereus *fr. 532,*

(a)   φοιτᾶι γὰρ ἐπ᾽ οἶδμά τε πόντου
        γᾶν τε καὶ λειμῶνας εὐφύλλους
        διαπε . . α[. . . .]οιον ὕδωρ
        Ζεὺς ὁ πάντ᾽ ἐποπτεύων.

(b)   εἷς μοῦν[ος] ἀνθρώποις θεὸς [. . . .]το
            κοινὰν   5
        ἁλίου μοῖραν

(c)   . . . μῶρος δ᾽
        ὅστις ἀνθρώπων πόλιν
        (τὰν) θεὸν κείναν σεβίζειν
        μοῦνον ἐλπίζει καλῶς.   10
        εἰσὶν γάρ εἰσιν
        ἀξιοπάμονες ἄλλαι
        ταὶ μέλονται
        πρός τινος ἢ Διὸς ἢ γλαυκᾶς Ἀθάνας.

ANONYMOUS

25   [3 B.C.]   ? ΣΟΦΟΚΛΗΣ : ΤΥΡΩ

Ed. pr. *Grenfell-Hunt, *Hibeh Papyri*, i. 1906, no. 3, p. 17, Plate II. See Pearson, *Fragm. of Soph.* ii. p. 270 ; Pickard-Cambridge, *New Chapters*, iii. 104 ; Körte, *Archiv*, v. 1913, 565 ; Wilamowitz, *Sitzb. preuss. Akad. d. Wiss.* 1921, p. 76 n. 1 ; Rasch, *Sophocles quid debeat Herodoto*, p. 61 ; Weil, *Journal des Savants*, 1906, 513 ; Robert, *Hermes*, 51, 1916, 273.

150

ANONYMOUS

1-2 Nauck (=fr. 591, 1-2 Pearson), and is probably part of the same context. The case for ascribing the other two fragments to the same source (Cazzaniga) is much weaker; ed. pr. had suggested Pindar as the author, without much probability.

(*a*) He roams on the swell of the sea, and the land and the leaves in the meadow . . . water, Zeus, who keeps watch over the world.

(*b*) One god alone . . . for mankind . . . a common share in the sunlight . . .

(*c*) The man is a fool, who hopes our goddess honours none but *that* city well! Others there are, yes others, worth possessing, who enjoy the care of God, be it of Zeus or of grey-eyed Athene.

---

9 (τὰν) add. D.L.P.   10 καλοῖς Π, corr. D. L. P.

ANONYMOUS
? SOPHOCLES, *TYRO*   [3 B.C.]

The story of Tyro was in outline as follows (there are many divergences in detail) :—

Tyro, daughter of Salmoneus and Alcidice, bore Pelias and Neleus to Poseidon. She exposed them in a little boat. When they grew up, they discovered their mother and slew her stepmother Sidero, by whom she had been persecuted.

151

LITERARY PAPYRI

Little is known about the detail of the action of this story in Sophocles' Tyro. The recognition of mother and sons occurred towards the end of the play (Eur. Or. 1691 Schol.), and was effected by means of tokens (πηρίδιον γνωρισμάτων Menander, Epitr. 114, referring to this play) and the boat in which they were exposed (Aristotle Poet. 16, 1454 b 25, Aristoph. Lys. 158 Schol., bronze situla in Pickard-Cambridge, p. 104). We know further that the result of Sidero's maltreatment of Tyro was portrayed by means of an actor's mask (Pollux 4. 141). From Men. Epitr. loc. cit. we infer that the exposed children were discovered and reared by a shepherd, who later told them his story, and sent them forth with the "little box of tokens" to find their parents.

It is likely that the recognition took place when Tyro was drawing water from a well (archaeological evidence, see Engelmann, Arch. Stud. p. 40); and that in the end Poseidon appeared ex machina and announced that he was indeed the father of the children (Ar. Lys. 138). It is highly probable that Salmoneus was still alive and played a part; and that Poseidon ordered his brother Cretheus to marry Tyro (Pearson, p. 273).

δ]εῖμα νύκτερος

. . . .

εὔνους δὲ καὶ τάσδ' εἰσορᾷς πεν[θητρί]ας

. . . .

[φό]βος τις αὐτὴν δεῖμά τ' ἔννυχον πλανᾷι

. . . . .

καλ]λίρουν ἐπ' Ἀλφειοῦ πόρον

. . . .

[. . .] . ας ἀρωγὸν πατέρα λίσσομα[ι μολεῖν] 5
[ἄν]ακτα πόντου μητρί

152

ANONYMOUS

The investigation is complicated by the fact that Sophocles wrote two plays on this subject: perhaps, as Welcker believed, the second Tyro was only a revision of the first. At any rate, there is not evidence enough to determine fully the action of one Tyro, let alone two.

Now what is the evidence that our fragment belongs to this obscure play? [a] (1) *The reference to the river Alpheus (v. 4) is consistent with the fact that Elis was the adopted home of Salmoneus: it is uncertain but likely that Elis was the scene of the action in Sophocles (Pearson, p. 273). (2) The terrible dream in vv. 1, 3 " fits certain extant fragments of the Tyro (especially fr. 660, 661); but this is a very lame argument, as may be seen by a reference to the passages in question"* (Pearson). (3) *" The prayer in vv. 5-6, addressed to Posei-don, is entirely appropriate to the sons of Tyro "* (id.). (4) *If the reading* Πελι]ας *were secure in v. 5, the case would be greatly strengthened. (It would not be " decisive ": Carcinus and Astydamas also wrote plays on this theme.) But the reading is extremely uncertain in that place: the* σ *is doubtful; the* α *is very doubtful; the* ι *is a mere trace which could belong to any one of several letters. This evidence is very weak.*

. . . terror, at night . . .

Good friends are these mourning women too, whom you behold.

A dread and terror by night distracts her.

. . . to the fair waters of Alpheus's ford.

. . . I implore my father to come and aid me.

Lord of the sea . . . to mother . . .

[a] The ascription, suggested by Blass, was warmly sup-ported by Wilamowitz, approved by Weil, and accepted by Pearson.

---

5 [Πελι]ας (ed. pr.) is by no means a certain restoration. See Introd. Note.

ANONYMOUS

26   [2 A.D.]   ? ΕΥΡΙΠΙΔΗΣ : ΑΛΕΞΑΝΔΡΟΣ

Ed. pr. Grenfell-Hunt, *P. Oxy.* ix. 1912, no. 1176, fr. 38, col. ii. p. 143. Partly coincides with fr. 960 N., ascribed to

[ΧΟΡΟΣ]   ἔνι γὰ[ρ] π[ό]νος· ἀλλ'
            ὅτ[ωι] πάρεστιν τὸ πονεῖν
            τῶν τ' ἀγαθῶν κεκλῆσθαι,
            φίλος ὢν ἐμ[ὸ]ς λεγέσθω.
            τί μάταν βροτοὶ δ[ὲ] πολλ[ὰ   5
            π]έπασθε, πλο[ύτ]ωι δὲ δοκε[ῖτ']
            ἀρετὰν [κατε]ργάσεσθα[ι;
            τί] δ' εἴ τιν' Αἴτν[α]ς πάγον
            Π[ιερ]ίαν τε πέτραν χρυσήλατον
            ἐν θαλάμοις ἔχοιτε   10
            πασ[ά]μενοι πατρώ[ι]οις,
            οὔτοι τ[ό] γε μὴ πεφυ[κὸς

            . . . .

            ἐν ἐσθλοῖς δὲ †καθήσεσθ'† ἄνολβοι.

27

ANONYMOUS

    [3 B.C.]   ? ΕΥΡΙΠΙΔΗΣ : ΜΕΛΕΑΓΡΟΣ

Ed. pr. *Page, *The Classical Quarterly,* xxxi. 1937, p. 178. See Körte, *Archiv,* xiii. 1938, 99.

The attribution of this fragment to the Meleager *of* Euripides *(or of any other poet) is wholly uncertain : see ed. pr. for the evidence.*

154

ANONYMOUS

? EURIPIDES, *ALEXANDER* [2 A.D.]

Alexander by Hartung without sufficient evidence. See
*Snell, *Hermes, Einzelschr.* 5, 1937, p. 20; Wilamowitz, *Gr.
Versk.* p. 328.

. . . for labour lies therein. He who can undergo
labour, and attain a good man's name, shall be
called my friend. Mortals ! Why have you heaped
your empty gains ?—thinking that you shall achieve
excellence through riches ? What though you had
acquired a crag of Etna or Pierian rock of solid gold,
and had it in your father's house ? What was not
so from birth . . . you will abide unblest among the
good.

5-7 = fr. 960 N. (Possibly fr. 959 N. is part of the same
lyric.) 13 κάθησθ' Nauck (fr. 960).

ANONYMOUS

? EURIPIDES, *MELEAGER* [3 B.C.]

The plot of Euripides' Meleager was briefly as follows [a] :
*In the prologue, Artemis explained that Oeneus, king of
Calydon, had forgotten her when sacrificing the first fruits of
the harvest to the gods : she had therefore sent a boar to
ravage the land. Among the heroes assembled to chase the
boar was Meleager, who insisted (in spite of his companions*

[a] See *P.-W.-K. s.v.* Meleager; Séchan, *Ét. sur la
tragédie grecque,* 423 sqq. ; ed. pr., *loc. cit.*

*and of his mother Althaea) that Atalanta should be permitted
to take part in the adventure. This quarrel between Althaea
and Meleager and Atalanta was portrayed in the play. The
story of the chase and its fateful end were narrated by a
Messenger :—Oeneus had promised the boar's hide to its
slayer. In the event, Atalanta first wounded the boar, Am-
phiaraus second ; then Meleager killed it. He gave the hide to
Atalanta. But the Thestiadae, brothers of Althaea, and
uncles of Meleager, took it from her, alleging that it belonged
to them as next of kin, if Meleager renounced his claim.
Meleager in anger killed the Thestiadae and restored the hide
to Atalanta, whom he loved. When Althaea heard the
Messenger's story, she extinguished the torch which, being*

—— θαύμαστ' ἔλεξας, εἰ] τόδ' αἰτιώμενος
τολμᾶι σφ' ἀναιρεῖ]ν· κεῖνο δ' εἰδέναι θέλω,
θηρὸς τίς ἐνθένδ' ἔλαβε]ν ἀγρίου δέρος;
—— σοί τ' οὐκ ἀρεστὰ ταῦτ]α, δέσποτ', εἰδέναι,
κἀγὼ λέγειν τὰ μὴ φίλ' οὔ] χρήιζω δόμοις. 5
—— μή νύν με κρύψηις, εἴ τι τῶνδ'] εἰπεῖν ἔχεις.

*(Two lines missing, and the fragmentary end of a
third : then it continues :—)*

αὖθι]ς αὖ
τιμῆς ἔκατι παρθένωι Σχοινηίδι]
ἔδωκε τἀριστεῖον ἐς χέρας] λαβεῖν·
μάλ' ἀξία γὰρ ἡ τὸ πρὶν δ]εδεγμένη.   10
—— καὶ νῦν φράσον μοι ποῦ 'στιν] 'Αταλάντη,
γέρον;
—— τέρψει σε, δέσποτ,' οὐδ' ἐκεῖ]ν· οὔπω πάλαι

*(Here follow fragments of nineteen lines, including a
reference to a pursuit (δ]ιώκειν), and to ματαίους
ἀφρο[σύνας, the recent behaviour of Meleager or
of the Thestiadae.)*

*quenched, was destined to end the life of Meleager. Towards
the end of the play it is likely that Meleager was brought dying
on to the scene, and that Althaea killed herself. The play
closed with a divine epiphany.*

*Our fragment, if indeed it belongs to this play, comes from
the end of the Messenger's narration ; he concluded with the
death of the Thestiadae ; his interlocutor, probably Oeneus, is
appalled at the tidings, but goes on to ask what happened to
the prize afterwards. The Messenger says that it was re-
stored to Atalanta. Asked what now Atalanta is about, he
perhaps replied that she had fled with Meleager ; Oeneus, if
Oeneus it is, may then have left the scene to comfort Althaea
for her brothers' death and to dissuade her from violent
revenge.*

OENEUS. Strange, if he made bold to slay them on
such a charge ! Now this I want to hear : who was
the next to seize the wild beast's hide ?

MESSENGER. Master, the hearing will not please
you : and I have no wish to bring unwelcome tidings
to your house.

OENEUS. Hide it not from me, if you know anything
about it.

*(Two lines missing, and the fragmentary end of a
third : then it continues :—)*

MESSENGER. . . . he gave the prize back into the
hands of her, the maiden daughter of Schoeneus, to
do her honour. It was indeed her right, for she had
won it long ago.

OENEUS. Now tell me, old servant, where is Atalanta
now ?

MESSENGER. Master, that also will displease you.
Not long ago . . .

(Here follow fragments of nineteen lines)

—— ἀλλ' ἔργ[ον ἤδη τοῖς ὁμαίμοσιν μέλει·
ἐγὼ δ' ἄπ[ειμ' ἐς οἶκον, Ἀλθαίαν ὅπως
μολ[ὼν ἐπίσχω μὴ παρὰ γνώμην τι δρᾶν. 15

ANONYMOUS

28   [Early 3 B.C.]   ? ΕΥΡΙΠΙΔΗΣ : ΟΙΝΕΥΣ

Ed. pr. Grenfell-Hunt, *Hibeh Papyri*, i. 1906, no. 4, p. 21,
Plate I + Grenfell-Hunt, *New Classical Fragments and other
Greek and Latin Papyri*, Series ii. 1897, no. 1, p. 3, Plate I.
See *von Arnim, *Suppl. Eur.* 39 (revised text of vv. 5-8: but
I have not accepted his combination of fr. a, col. ii. with fr. g ;
the " fortlaufender Zusammenhang " of v. 4 is not impressive,
and of v. 2 may easily be a mere coincidence ; and vv. 1, 5
become extremely difficult) ;   Milne, *Cat. Lit. Pap. B.M.*

λαμπρὸν σί]δηρον μ[έλανι βάψαν]τες φόνωι
(*Fragments of one line*)

νῦν οὖν, τέλο]ς γὰρ τῶν ἐ[μ]ῶν λόγων ἔχεις,
ἐφ' ἣν ὑφηγ]εῖ πρᾶξιν [ὁ]ρμήσω ποδί,
τῶι πατραδ]έλφ[ωι] Μελεάγρωι δ[ω]ρήματα
ὅπως γένηται κἀποπληρωθῆι τάφος,   5
τύχηι δ' ἀγώνων τῶν κεκαλλιστευμ[ένω]ν,
ὥσπερ τυράννοις ἀνδράσιν [νομίζεται.

χοροῦ μ[έλος

ὅσον ταραγμ[ὸ]ν [ἡ δυ]σπραξία
ψυχαῖσιν ἐμ[βέβληκε] τλημόνων βροτῶ[ν·
ἐγὼ γὰρ [εἶδ]ο[ν ἄρτι τὸ]ν τεθνηκότα   10

ANONYMOUS

Oeneus. . . . Action lies now with her own kins-men. I will go home and stop Althaea, when I arrive, from any unexpected deed. . . .

ANONYMOUS

? EURIPIDES, *OENEUS* [Early 3 b.c.]

no. 59 (*revised text of 9-11); Pickard-Cambridge, *New Chapters*, iii. 154.

All that is clear is that somebody is about to pay honours to the tomb of Meleager. If πατραδέλφωι were a correct restoration in v. 4, the speaker would be Diomedes : but the supplement is only a guess. In Euripides' Oeneus, Oeneus was expelled from his kingdom by Agrios or the sons of Agrios; Diomedes came to Aetolia, slew Agrios and his sons, and restored Oeneus to the throne.

In dark blood steeping the bright steel . . .

(*Fragments of one line*)

Now, therefore, since you hear the end of all I have to say, I will go forth to the deed whereto you guide me ; so shall his gifts be made to Meleager, brother of my father ; his burial rites shall be complete and he shall have Games of splendour unsurpassed, such as are due to royal princes.

(*Choral song*)

What confusion . . . misfortune casts upon the soul of long-suffering man ! For lately I saw the dead . . .

ANONYMOUS

29   [(*a*) 2 B.C.]   ? ΕΚΤΩΡ
    [(*b*) c. 100 B.C.]

Ed. pr. (*a*) Grenfell-Hunt, *Amherst Papyri*, ii. 1901, no. 10, p. 1, Plate II. See Weil, *Journal des Savants*, 1901, 737 ; Radermacher, *Rh. Mus.* 1902, 138 ; *Pickard-Cambridge, New Chapters*, iii. 152 ; Crönert, *Archiv*, ii. 355.
   (*b*) *Snell, *Hermes, Einzelschriften* v. 1937. See Körte, *Archiv*, xiii. 1938, 100.

The scene is before Troy. Unwelcome tidings—presumably an assault by Greeks—are announced to Hector, who calls for his armour and the captured shield of Achilles.

(*a*) —— ἄνδρες πρ[ὸ]ς ἄ[στυ
       ταῦτ' ἀγγελῶν σοῖς οὐ καθ' [ἡδονὴν δόμοις
       ἥκω. σὺ δ', ὦναξ, τῆς ἐκεῖ φρ[ουρᾶς
         μολὼν
       φρόντιζ', ὅπως σοι καιρίως ἕ[ξει τάδε.
[ΕΚΤΩΡ] χώρει πρὸς οἴκους, ὅπλα τ' ἐ[κκόμιζέ μοι, 5
       καὶ τὴν Ἀχιλλέως δοριάλωτ[ον ἀσπίδα.
       ἔξω γὰρ αὐτὴν τήνδε κα[ὶ
       ἀλλ' ἐκποδών μοι στῆθι, μὴ [διεργάσηι
       ἡμῖν ἅπαντα. καὶ γὰρ εἰς λα[γῶ φρένας
       ἄγοις ἂν ἄνδρα καὶ τὸν εὐθα[ρσέστατον. 10

(*b*) [ΑΓΓΕΛΟΣ] ἀ[μ]βὰς κολων[ὸν
          (*One line missing*)
       ὁ μὲν [γ]ὰ[ρ] Ἕκ[τωρ
       ελαμ[
       σείων ἐπ' αὐτὸ[ν
       Ἕκτωρ δὲ πρῶτ[ος   **15**

ANONYMOUS

? HECTOR

[(*a*) 2 B.C.]
[(*b*) c. 100 B.C.]

*The time of the action then is later than the death of
Patroclus: therefore it is improbable that this fragment is a
part of the* Hector *of Astydamas, whose play certainly con-
tained an incident which occurred much earlier in the story
(Iliad vi. 472 Schol., v. Pickard-Cambridge, loc. cit.).*

In fr. (b), *Snell observed the difference between Homer, Il.
xxii. and this play.—Here it is Hector who shoots first, and
Achilles who stoops to avoid the missile. Achilles then strikes
Hector with his sword (ἔπαισεν, not used of attack with
spears), which falls in vain upon the shield—his own shield,
now carried by Hector.*

*There is no evidence, except coincidence of subject-matter,
that these two fragments proceed from the same play.*

(*a*) MESSENGER (?). To the city, men. . . . Such is
the cheerless message that I came to bring to your
palace. Go, king, and take heed for our defence
there ; so shall all be as the time demands.

HECTOR. Indoors ! bring me my armour out, and
the shield of Achilles, prize of my spear ! I will
carry it—none other—and . . . Stand out of my path,
or you will ruin all ! Why, you would bring even the
bravest man to have no more heart than a rabbit . . . !

(*b*) MESSENGER. . . . climbing a hill . . .

(*One line missing*)

as for Hector, he . . . seized (?) . . . brandished
against him. . . . But Hector first . . .

LITERARY PAPYRI

(One line missing)

ἔπτηξεν . . [
ἄκραν δ' ὑπὲρ ἴτυν ξυμ[
ὥ(ς) δ' εἶδ' Ἀχιλλεὺς Ἕκτορο[ς μάτην
  πέσον
εἰς γῆν κελαινὸν ἔγχος, ἡδο[νῆς ὕπο
ἀνηλάλαξε· καὶ δι' ὧν διε[πλάγη   20
οὐδ' αὐτός, αὐτὰ πρόσθε τ[ιμηθένθ' ὅπλα
ἔπαισεν· ἀσπὶς δ' οὐ διῆκ' εἴσ[ω ξίφος
ἀλλ' ἴσχεν αὐτοῦ, δεσπ[ότην δ' ὁπλι-
  σμάτων
τὸν καινὸν οὐ προ(ΰ)δωκ[ε

ANONYMOUS

30 [1 A.D.]   ? ΕΚΑΒΗ

Ed. pr. *Lobel, *Greek Poetry and Life : Essays presented to Gilbert Murray*, 1936, p. 295 with Plate. See Morel, *Phil. Woch.* 1937, 558 ; Körte, *Archiv*, xiii. 1938, 100.

This fragment is preceded in Π by remnants of a column of iambic trimeters in which] τάφον, χ]ώρας ἄπο,] γύναι,] λιτάς,] χοάς *can be read at the ends of lines. It appears to be a part of a tragedy composed about events which occurred immediately after the fall of Troy. Ed. pr. observes that for lexical reasons (ἐστέρεσεν, βλαβερά, μακαριστότατον) the fragment is likely to be of post-Euripidean date ; and suggests that in the iambic trimeters an unsympathetic character, e.g. Talthybius, warns a Trojan captive, e.g. Hecuba or Andromache, that she must prepare to depart with her new master ; thereupon follows the captive's lament.*

162

ANONYMOUS

(One line missing)

cowered . . . over the rim's edge . . . Now when Achilles saw the dark spear of Hector fall idly to the ground, he cried aloud for joy : and smote those arms that once he honoured, through which himself was never struck. The shield let the sword not through, but stayed it there, and betrayed not the new master of that armour . . .

Supplements by ed. pr., except 18 (πέσον μάτην ed. pr.), 20, 21 D. L. P.

ANONYMOUS

? HECUBA [1 A.D.]

The lines present insoluble difficulties ; of which the chief concerns the identity of the speaker. It is certain that a woman speaks : the lines in general, and the references to Hector and to a child in particular, suggest Hecuba or Andromache ; the child in v. 23 will then presumably be Astyanax. If the choice is to be made between Hecuba and Andromache, the former seems slightly preferable. The plural in τέκ]νων ὄνομα ἥδιστον speaks for Hecuba ; the phrase τί γὰρ ἡ τλήμων πάθος οὐκ ἀντλῶ is reminiscent of Eur. Tro. 106 τί γὰρ οὐ πάρα μοι μελέαι στενάχειν—spoken by Hecuba ; further, a certain generality of sentiment and breadth of outlook—reference to the fall of Priam's palace, and of Troy, to the instant fate of Trojan virgins (κοῦραι κοῦραι δύσνυμφοι cries Hecuba, Eur. Tro. 144)—are better suited to the conventional Hecuba than to the conventional Andromache (who would

163

perhaps not have postponed her reference to Astyanax so long).   Finally, in vv. 24-25 μετὰ μητρὸς ὅμ[ως οὐ] γειναμένης (= *Hecuba*) *is a better and more convincing supplement than* μετὰ μητρὸς ὁμ[οῦ τῆς] γειναμένης (= *Andromache*)—μετὰ . . . ὁμοῦ *is a singular combination.   These are indeed inconclusive grounds ; but at the same time far from negligible.*

The next difficulty :—these anapaests are written in Π *in a column (short, only 21 vv.) without any regard for metrical lines.   The right-hand side of the column is missing.   It is therefore quite uncertain how much is missing.   Where a line ends* μακαριστότατον π[, *followed by* μέλαθρον *in the beginning of the next line, it is obviously tempting to reconstruct the first line on the assumption that* π[*is* π[ριάμου, *and that no more is wanting.   But the assumption may be false, and the lacunae at the ends of lines much longer.   I have however made the assumption, for (1) most of the lines thus admit an easy restoration of good sense ; (2) if half a dozen letters only are added to the anapaestic column, that column will be much the same in breadth as the preceding column of iambic trimeters (which did observe the metrical line as a unit).   Once more, these reasons are insufficient, but neither are they negligible.*

τέκ]νων

ὄνομ' ἥδιστον καὶ δῶμα φίλον

το[. . . . .]το δ' ἴσον καὶ ἐμοί

ποτε νυμφίδ[ιον . . . . .] ἐστέρεσεν

φθόνος ἢ βλαβερὰ [. . . . .]   5

τί γὰρ ἡ τλήμων πάθος οὐκ ἀν[τλῶ

. . . .] φρεσίν; ἢ γὰ[ρ] ἐμαῖς

ἐπὶ δυστυχ[ίαις νῦν δὴ] πέλανος

προλέλοιπε γοῶν· [οἴμοι μελέα,]

1-26 Supplements, other than those of ed. pr., by D. L. P.

ANONYMOUS

*In 20 of these 23 " lines " (as written in Π) the scribe begins
a new line with a new word, does not divide a word between
two lines. In two lines ª he does make such a division. In
one line there is some doubt. The 19th line of col. ii. begins in
the Papyrus .ΕΤΥΧΛΣ : the doubtful letter before* E *looks like*
N, *but the ink has both run and faded, and* M—*though I admit
it seems a fraction too broad for the space—is not impossible.
At least, then, it is clear that the scribe did sometimes divide
a line between two words ; and his reason for doing so was
probably, as ed. pr. suggests, to enable him to keep his columns
fairly even. The Papyrus ends for its last 11 lines (vv. 13-
end, in my text) two or three letters later than it ends for the
first 8 lines (vv. 1-12). If no more than* π[ριάμου *is to be
supplied after* μακαριστότατον *in* Π's *12th line, we proceed
with the assumption that some five or six letters are missing
at the ends of the last 11 lines in* Π ; *and therefore some
seven or eight, perhaps eight or nine, at the ends of the first
8 lines in* Π.

[*Morel, loc. cit., conjectures that our fragment comes from
a play which was the original of Ennius's* Andromache
Aechmalotis : *I find no evidence for this view in his article.
Körte, quoting Aristotle,* Eth. Eud. vii. 4, 1239 a 37, *sug-
gests Antiphon as the author of the piece.*]

. . . dear home, and sweetest name of children !
Malice or . . . injurious . . . stole the bridal . . .
from me of old.   Unhappy, surely there is no suffer-
ing sore-lamented that in my heart I drain not to the
depth ?   Now at last in my misfortunes fails my

ª The first of the anapaestic lines (v. 20 of col. i.) ends
μονον αλλ ε, and must therefore have divided a word between
this line and the next.   The next line ends ΟΝΟ followed by
ΜΙΔΙΣΤΟΝ at the beginning of col. ii. v. 1.

---

5 [τις Ἐρινύς Maas : but the letter following βλαβερὰ in
Π was certainly not a τ.   8 πέλαγος Schadewaldt.

φθιμένου μελέα σέθεν, Ἕκτορ, [. . . .   10
. . . . . .] πάτραι καὶ ἐμοὶ μέγα φῶς,
ἅμα σ[οὶ δ᾽ οἴκων] ὄλετ᾽ ὄλβος.

(*Traces of two lines*)

θάλαμόν τ᾽ ὀ[λο]ῶι πυρὶ δα[ιόμ]εν[ον,
καὶ] πρίν ποτε δ[ὴ] μακαριστότατον
Π[ριάμου] μέλαθρον [στε]φάνας θ᾽ ἱερὰς   15
χθο[νὸς Ἰδαίας], διὰ δ᾽ οὐχ ὅ[σιον]
λέχος αἰνογάμου [. . . . . .] Ἑλένης
ἀδ[όκ]ητα κόραις καὶ ἀ . .[. .] κλύειν
ἄμ[α Τρ]ωιάσιν δέμνι᾽ Ἀχαιῶ[ν
ἤδη] παρὰ ναυσὶ[ν ἐ]χούσαις.   20
ἀλλ᾽ ἐπὶ τ[οῖς σοῖς] τύμβοισι μό[ν]ην
τὰς σὰς θρηνεῖν [συνέβη] με τύχας.
δύστη]νε τέκνον, στεῖχε .[. . . . . .
βάσιν εὐθύν[ω]ν μετὰ μητρὸς ὁμ[. .
. .] γειναμένη[ς· π]οῖ μ᾽ ὦ φιλ[ία   25
Τρώω[ν . . .

10-11 [ἐπεί σ᾽ ἔτεκον] if Hecuba is the speaker.   17 *e.g.*
[περίεσθ᾽].   18 Not ἄτερπνα, ἄπιστα, ἀπευκτά, ἄτλητα; A is
certain; next comes Π or Τ; next letter very doubtful.
ἄτιμα seems to me possible, but I defer to Mr. Lobel's adverse
judgement. Beazley suggests ἀτηρὰ (with crasis of καί).

ANONYMOUS

31   [2 A.D.] ?ΟΙΝΕΥΣ, Η ΣΧΟΙΝΕΥΣ, Η ΦΟΙΝΙΞ

Ed. pr. Grenfell-Hunt, *P. Oxy.* viii. 1911, no. 1083, p. 60.
See *Hunt, *F.T.P.* ; Körte, *Archiv,* v. 1913, 570 ; Pickard-
Cambridge, *New Chapters,* iii. 101 ; Blumenthal, *Ion von
Chios,* p. 56.

offering of lamentation.[a]   Woe, woe is me, Hector, in your death : . . . the sunlight of my life and of our land ; with you the happiness of our home is perished.

(Traces of two lines)

. . . and the chamber consumed in the fatal fire, and the hall of Priam, so happy long ago, and the sacred coronal of Ida's land ; through Helen's unholy love—a curse lay on her wedding !—our maids of Troy are destined to hear . . . unexpected ; already they have their beds beside the Achaean ships.   My fortune it is to mourn your fate alone above your tomb.   Come, guide your steps, unhappy child, with me—your mother. . . . Whither, dear land of Troy . . . ?

[a] *i.e.* I have lamented so much already, that I have no groans left to give as an offering to the dead (πελανος, *e.g.* Aes. *Cho.* 92).   πέλανος γόων " an offering of groans " is an odd phrase : but we know nothing of this writer's style.

---

20 κοίλαις] Körte.   21 μά[τ]ην (Maas, Körte) was not the reading of Π.   23 στεῖχ' Ἀ[στυάναξ is possible ; στεῖχε [πρὸς οἴκους Morel, is not.   στεῖχε ν[εογνὸν Körte. 24-25 ὅμ[ως οὐ] if Hecuba is the speaker.

ANONYMOUS

? OENEUS, or SCHOENEUS, or PHOENIX
[2 A.D.]

Evidently a Satyric drama.   The daughter of Oeneus (or possibly—but less probably—Schoeneus) is the prize of a contest in which Satyrs are competing.

167

LITERARY PAPYRI

Oeneus is known to have arranged such a contest for the hand of his daughter Deianeira; in which Heracles overcame Achelous. Phoenix (who is party to a dialogue in fr. 4 ed. pr., is mentioned in fr. 14 and in a note on fr. 19) was probably another competitor : for he married Perimede, another daughter of Oeneus (Asius ap. Paus. vii. 4. 1)—perhaps, as Hunt suggests, a consolation prize. (Schoeneus also promoted such a contest for the hand of his daughter Atalanta ; here too Phoenix is at home, for he took part in the chase of the Calydonian boar.)

The style seems unlike that of Aeschylus or Euripides

(*a*) [ΟΙΝΕΥΣ] ἀλλ᾽ ἐξεροῦμεν· ἀλλὰ πρῶτα βούλομαι
γνῶναι τίνες πάρεστε καὶ γένους ὅτου
βλαστόντες· οὐ γὰρ νῦν γέ πω μαθ[ὼν ἔχω.
ΧΟ[ΡΟΣ] ΣΑΤΥ[ΡΩΝ] ἅπαντα πεύσηι.   νυμφίοι μὲν
ἤ[κομε]ν,
παῖδες δὲ νυμφῶν, Βακχίου δ᾽ ὑπηρέται,   5
θεῶν δ᾽ ὄμαυλοι· πᾶσα δ᾽ ἥρμοσται τέχνη
πρέπουσ᾽ ἐν ἡμῖν· ἔστι μὲν τὰ πρὸς μάχην
δορός, πάλης ἀγῶνες, ἱππικῆς, δρόμου,
πυγμῆς, ὀδόντων, ὄρχεων ἀποστροφαί,
ἔνεισιν ὠιδαὶ μουσικῆς, ἔνεστι δὲ   10
μαντεῖα πάντα γνωτὰ κοὐκ ἐψευσμένα,
ἰαμάτων τ᾽ ἔλεγχος, ἔστιν οὐρανοῦ
μέτρησις, ἔστ᾽ ὄρχησις, ἔστι τῶν κάτω
λάλησις· ἆρ᾽ ἄκαρπος ἡ θεωρία;
ὦν σοι λαβεῖν ἔξεστι τοῦθ᾽ ὁποῖον ἂν   15
χρήιζηις, ἐὰν τὴν παῖδα προστίθηις ἐμοί.
ΟΙ. ἀλλ᾽ οὐχὶ μεμπτὸν τὸ γένος· ἀλλὰ βούλομαι
καὶ τόνδ᾽ ἀθρῆσαι πρῶτον ὅστις ἔρχεται.

(*b*) [Α φρο]ῦδον, οὐδ᾽ ἀποδέρκ[ομαι
]άσω χθονὸς σελήνα[20

ANONYMOUS

*(though there is no definite criterion). Sophocles (who wrote
a Φοῖνιξ, and perhaps an Οἰνεύς) is a likelier candidate for
authorship; Hunt points to Soph. fr. 855, 3-5 Nauck, for a
good parallel to the anaphora of ἔστι in vv. 9 sqq. of our frag-
ment. Wilamowitz was inclined to attribute the lines to Ion
of Chios, who wrote a Φοῖνιξ ἢ Καινεύς and a Φοῖνιξ δεύτερος.
But all this is merest guesswork; there is not sufficient
evidence for a decision. [P. Iand. v. p. 179, no. 76, a tiny
fragment, may belong to the same play.]*

(a) OENEUS. We will speak out: but first I wish to
know who you are that come, and of what family—I
have not learnt this yet.

CHORUS OF SATYRS. You shall hear everything.
We come as suitors, we are sons of nymphs and
ministers of Bacchus, and neighbours of the gods.
Every proper trade is part of our equipment:—
fighting with spears, contests of wrestling, horse-
racing, running, boxing, biting, hitting below the
belt; here you have songs of music, here you have
oracles fully known—not forged,—and tests for
medicines; we know the measuring of the skies,
we know the way to dance, we know the lore of
the world below,—say, is our study fruitless? You
may choose whatever of these you will, if you assign
your daughter to me.

OENEUS. With your family I find no fault. But
first I wish to see who this man is who comes
here. . . .

(b) —— . . . gone, nor do I see . . . of the land . . .
the moon. . . .

LITERARY PAPYRI

[Β ἰδ]ού, τὸ φῶς βέβηκεν, οἴχετα[ι σέλας·
ἀλλ' ἦι τι νυκτὸς ἄστρον ἢ [μήνης κέρας
θνήισκει πρὸς αὐγὴν ἡλίο[υ μαυρούμενον,
ἐκπνεῖ δὲ τόνδ' αὖ μέλανα βό[στρυχον
καπνοῦ.

ANONYMOUS

32   [2–3 A.D.]   ? ΦΡΙΞΟΣ

Ed. pr. Vitelli, *Revue Egyptologique*, N.S. 1, 1919, p. 47.
See Vogliano, *Riv. di Fil.* 1926, 206 ; *Schadewaldt, *Hermes*,
63, 1928, 1 ; Körte, *Archiv*, x. 1931, 49 ; Pickard-Cam-
bridge, *New Chapters*, iii. 97.

*Ino, wife of Athamas, jealous of her rival Nephele, roasted
the corn-seed to make it unfruitful. She then gave it to an
old man to sow. Athamas, ignorant of these things, con-
sulted the oracle : but Ino persuaded the envoys to report
that the ground would not become fertile unless Athamas
would sacrifice his son Phrixus, child of Nephele. Phrixus*

[ΙΝΩ σὺ δ' οὖν] ἔλεγχ', εἰ τοῦτ' ἐν ἡδονῆι τί σοι.
[ΑΘΑΜΑΣ ἐξενν]έπειν χρὴ π[ά]ντα τἀληθῆ, γέρον.   5
[ΠΡΕΣΒΥΣ λέξω] παρούσης ταὐτὰ κἀπούσης, ἄναξ,
    ἐκ τῆσ]δε χειρὸς σπέρμα δέξασθαι τόδε
    σπείρε]ιν τ' ἀρούρας· ὤφελον δὲ μὴ λαβεῖν.

2 ἐξεννέπειν Beazley.   5 σπείρειν Vitelli.

---

[a] This line is spoken by Ino, not by the Old Man who
would not say to the king " Ask away, if it's any pleasure to
you." It is clear from v. 3 that there has been some discus-

170

—— Look, how the light is gone,[a] the flame is vanished ! Like a star at night or the moon's horn fading to death before a ray of sunlight !

And see, it breathes out a black curl of smoke ! . . .

[a] The light of a torch or altar has been extinguished (Hunt).

ANONYMOUS
? PHRIXUS [2–3 A.D.]

was brought to the altar : but thereupon the old man who had sown the seed betrayed Ino's secret.

The authorship of this fragment is altogether uncertain, for want of sufficient evidence. It could be the work of Sophocles ; but nothing proves it. Schadewaldt argues for Euripides : but fails to produce a single strong (let alone conclusive) argument. The fragment may be the work of either of these two poets, or of an unknown poet of the 5th (or even 4th) century. We cannot nowadays assume that a tragic papyrus of the 2nd or 3rd century A.D., however finely written and produced, is a work of one of the three great Tragedians.

Ino. Go, question, if it gives you any pleasure.[a]

Athamas. Old servant : you must tell the whole truth.

Old Man. My tale will be the same whether she be present or away, my king,—that from her hand I took this seed and sowed the fields. I would I had not taken it.

sion whether Ino should be present while the king questions his servant. She finally consents to remain.

171

[ΙΝΩ ἀπώμο]σ', ὅρκου τ' ἐκτὸς οὐ ψευδῆ λέγω,
μὴ ταῦτ'] ἐμῆς τὸν δοῦλον ἐκ χερὸς λαβεῖν.
[ΑΘ. ἀρνῆι, γύν]αι, σπεύδου[σα] δύστηνος φόνον
ἢ τοῖς] πολίταις ἢ [τέ]κνοισι τοῖς ἐμοῖς;
σιγᾶις; σὺ λέξο]ν, σπέρμα τίς δίδωσί σοι; 10
[ΠΡ. κινεῖς] τὸν αὐτὸν μῦθον; ἐκ τίνος δ' ἐγὼ
λόγου δι]ώλλ[υν τούσ]δε, δοῦλος ὢν σέθεν;
γύναι,] τάχ' ἂν τοῦδ' ἀνδρὸς ἄρσενος τύχ[ο]ις
τὸν παῖδ'] ἀποκτείνουσ'· ἐγὼ δ' ἔτ' ἐν
σκότωι
κεύθω] τὰ πλείω, πόλλ' ἔχων εἰπεῖν ἔπη. 15
[ΙΝΩ σὺ δ' εἰσακ]ούεις ἄλοχος οἵ' ὑβρίζεται;
[ΠΡ. καὶ μὴν ἐγὼ] βλέπ[ω] γε τοῦδ' ἐς ὄμματα,
κοὔ πήματ'] εἰκῇ προσμένων ψευδῆ λέγω.

7 So I conjecture for the reading ΤΟΝΔΩΛΕΝΗΣ, which
must surely be a corruption. (ΤΟΝΔΟΥΛΟΝΕΚ is palaeographically very close to Π's ΤΟΝΔΩΛΕΝΗΣ.)   10
σιγᾶις; D. L. P.   σὺ λέξον Maas.

ANONYMOUS

33   [2 A.D.]   ? ΕΠΤΑ ΕΠΙ ΘΗΒΑΣ

Ed. pr. *Vitelli-Norsa, *Annali della reale Scuola normale
superiore di Pisa*, Serie ii. 4, 1935, p. 14. See Körte,
Archiv, xiii. 1938, 102.

(a) *This fragment is described by ed. pr. as a "rifacimento" of Euripides'* Phoenissae, *apparently a schoolroom
exercise. But I believe that it is part of an original Greek
Tragedy written in (or not much later than) the 4th century
B.C.*

For (1) *no line, indeed no single phrase, of this fragment*

172

INO. I swear—and even apart from oath, I speak no falsehood,—this slave did not get it from my hand.

ATHAMAS. Woman, do you deny that you were bent on murder, unhappy, to destroy either our people or my children? What, silent? (*To the Old Man*) Speak, you! Who gave the seed to you?

OLD MAN. The same tale again? For what reason should I, your slave, try to destroy these children? Woman, you would murder his son: but you may yet find your man a man indeed! I still hide the greater part in darkness, though I have much that I might say.

INO. (*To Athamas*) You hear how he insults your wife?

OLD MAN. But I can look him in the eyes: I do not speak untruth and rashly await the penalty.

ANONYMOUS

? SEVEN AGAINST THEBES   [2 A.D.]

was borrowed from Euripides' Phoenissae. There is not even a linguistic coincidence worthy of the name. Further, the style and vocabulary, though generally based upon tragedy of the 5th century, are by no means particularly Euripidean (see below).

(2) There is an obvious similarity of outline to Eur. Ph. *443 sqq. Jocasta has contrived an interview between her sons, hoping that they may still be reconciled by debate and mediation. But there the similarity ends, and the remarkable differences begin. I draw attention to some of them.—*

LITERARY PAPYRI

Vv. 1-2. A good instance of this poet's complete independence of phraseology : the thought is much the same as that of Eur. Ph. *364-366 (cf. 272-273).*

V. 3. Polynices hands his sword over to his mother : this feature is new, not in Eur.'s play : a spectacular innovation.

V. 4. A new and striking element: Jocasta bids Polynices swear that after the ensuing debate he will abide by her verdict. This feature too is absent from Eur. Ph. *Here apparently, the brothers have agreed to meet and try to settle their differences by arbitration. In* Ph., *Jocasta hopes thus to reconcile them ; Polynices is willing and faintly hopeful (435-437) ; Eteocles humours his mother (446 sqq.), but plainly does not intend to be conciliated. Nowhere in Eur. does either brother formally promise to accept and abide by his mother's verdict at the end of the debate. In our fragment there was evidently a dramatic moment when Jocasta insisted that both sons should give to her their swords before the debate began.*

V. 6. In Eur.'s play, neither brother addresses the other by name in this scene. Indeed neither speaks directly to the other until the violent quarrel at the end (cf. 455 sqq., they will not even look at each other). Here they begin at once speaking to each other, and Polynices actually addresses his brother by name. This follows from the poet's innovation observed on v. 4 :—the brothers here have agreed to start at least by aiming at a definite reconciliation; therefore their animosity is at first suppressed, their spirit outwardly milder.

And here is a great difference in structure:—In Eur. Ph., *the brothers begin at once by stating their cases in alternate ῥήσεις ; Jocasta then speaks, and the debate is over ; thereupon the brothers quarrel violently in stichomythia in trochiac tetrameters.*

In our fragment, the brothers begin their debate in iambic stichomythia. ῥήσεις may or may not have followed this or interrupted it ; but certainly the debate and quarrel go

ANONYMOUS

together at the beginning, in iambic stichomythia.   Our poet is going out of his way to be different from Euripides.

V. 10. Cf. vv. 13, 23 : in Eur., Polynices never, in the presence of Eteocles, speaks of his bringing the Argive army to Thebes, though he does once speak of taking it away ; a delicate point, which eluded our poet.

Vv. 11-17. These lines, like so many others in this fragment, do not appear to be based on anything in Eur.'s play, either in sentiment or in phraseology.

V. 19. This sentiment is not expressed in Eur. Ph.

Vv. 22-23. V. note on v. 10.

Vv. 28-29. Nothing corresponding to this sentence (εἰ γὰρ Κύκλωπος εἶχον . . . ψυχὴν ἄθελκτον) occurs in the Euripidean scene.

There are other differences ; but these are sufficient to make it clear that this is a fragment of an original Tragedy. The relation to Euripides' Phoenissae is confined to a broad and—with this subject—inevitable similarity of outline.   In phraseology, in incident, in structure, and often in spirit and sentiment, the new fragment exhibits not similarity to Euripides, but remarkable divergences from his example. And these divergences are unintelligible except in relation to the whole of which this fragment is part : i.e. the fragment really is a fragment, not a complete and self-contained " exercise."

(b) There follows a brief commentary which is intended to shew that there is nothing here to compel us to assign these lines to a date later than the 4th or 3rd century B.C.

V. 2. φιλτάτη τεκοῦσα : I have not observed another example in Tragedy of τεκοῦσα vocative without ὦ, nor of the combination φιλτάτη with τεκοῦσα vocative.   But there is no good reason to deny the phrase to a Tragedian of the 4th century (or indeed of the 5th).

παρεθέμην : παραθέσθαι τί τινι " deposit something with someone " is good prose (Hdt., Xen.).   παραθέσθαι not in

175

Aesch. or Soph., in Eur. only Cycl. 390 (in a different sense).

V. 3. αὐτῆι=σεαυτῆι : *a peculiar usage, based on such passages as Soph. O.C. 1356* τὸν αὐτὸς αὐτοῦ (= σεαυτοῦ) πατέρα τόνδ᾽ ἀπήλασας, *ibid. 929-930* αἰσχύνεις πόλιν τὴν αὐτὸς αὐτοῦ (=σεαυτοῦ). *Kühner-Gerth, i. 564-565 quotes only examples of the idiom where the nom.* αὐτὸς *occurs too, as in the above citations from Sophocles. Perhaps* αὐτὴ παρ᾽ αὐτῆι *was the original reading here :* ΑΥΤΗ *could easily be corrupted to* ΑΙΤΩ.

V. 6. Ἐτέοκλες : *perhaps read* Ἐτεοκλῆς, *nom. for voc. as often (form* -κλῆς *Eur. Ph. 443, 1407) ; less probably,* Ἐτεόκλεες.

V. 7. πάντοτ᾽ : *perhaps* πᾶν τότ᾽ ; *but* πάντοτ᾽, *familiar from Menander, Philemon, could hardly be denied to a Tragedian of the 4th century.*

V. 9. παρὰ | βροτοῖς : *the rhythm is rare, but cf. Ion 931, Ba. 940, I.A. 1164, Eur. Inc. Fab. 953, Theodectes fr. 8, 5. Ph. 538 is similar.*

V. 10. σὺ γὰρ οὐκ : *anapaest in first foot as in vv. 13, xviii. dactyl vv. 6 (proper name), 14, 28 ; tribrach vv. 8 (proper name), 24. Resolutions elsewhere not specially frequent : 2 tribrachs in 2nd, 2 in 4th foot ; 2 dactyls in 3rd. This is rather a heavy allowance for the first foot ; cf. however Ph. 529 sqq., eleven resolved first feet in 56 lines (one proper name) ; I.A. 431-437, 507-509, 1199-1201.*

στρατούς : *plural not elsewhere in Tragedy ; Iliad xviii. 509, of two armies.*

V. 11. I suggest a lacuna here, as ed. pr. did at v. 15. The writer is evidently not copying the passage consecutively, but only certain portions of it. I do not see how v. 11 can be interpreted to follow v. 10 : and vv. 12-13 sqq. make it clear enough that Eteocles has argued meantime, " You have brought an army to attack your own country."

V. 13. φέρειν : *here and v. 15 ="fetch," "bring."*

ANONYMOUS

V. 14. The rhythm εἰ γὰρ ἐμέριζες *at the beginning of the line is unusual, but has parallels in Eur.* Or. *2* οὐδὲ πάθος οὐδέ, Ba. *285* ὥστε διὰ τοῦτον. *The phrase* μερίζειν τὸ διάδημα *is remarkable; but* μερίζειν *is common in historians and philosophers of the 4th century (it means of course " divide," not " share "). And* διάδημα, *the emblem of royalty for the Great King and for Alexander, is not an improbable flight of fancy for a Tragedian of the 4th century. The word could be used by any poet after Xenophon at latest; and the combination* μερίζειν τὸ διάδημα *is very passable poetry for " divide the supreme authority." There are stranger things in our scanty fragments of 4th-century Tragedy.*

V. 15. ἀνάγκη τοῦ φέρειν : *I have not found a parallel to the construction ; but the analogy of other words (e.g.* αἰτία τοῦ *c. infin.) explains it easily.*

V. 16. κέλευέ μοι: *see Kühner-Gerth,* i. *pp. 410-411. Normal in Homer ; but dative not elsewhere in Tragedy. Cf. however Cycl. 83* προσπόλοις κελεύσατε *(usually emended), and, for a clear example in the 4th century, Menander,* Perik. *224* τί δ᾿ ἐστὶν ὁ κελεύεις ἐμοί ; *(The dative may be merely " ethic," as Prof. Warmington suggests.)* Π *gives this line to Eteocles—(change of speaker is denoted by* ἔκθεσις *of the first line of each new speech)—but the next line suggests that it should be said by the speaker of this one.*

V. 19. πραῖον : *word not in Aesch. or Soph. (who has* πραΰνειν). *In Eur.* Ba. *436 only.*

ἐνετράπη : *for the scansion (lengthening of syllabic augment before mute and liquid) see A.* Pers. *395, Agam. 536, Eur.* Hcld. *646,* H. *150, Hel. 1188, Or. 12 ; Porson on* Or. *64, Tucker in* C.R. *xi. 1897, 341 (Ph. 586* ἀπότροποι).

V. 28. ἄθελκτον : *word not in Eur. or Soph. ; Aesch. only Hic. 1055.*

The conclusion is :—though there are several points which forbid us to call this a fragment of 5th-century Tragedy,

there is nothing to prevent us assigning it to an author of the
4th century or soon after. It is not a " rifacimento " of Eur.
Ph. ; *it is not a schoolmaster's or schoolboy's exercise ; it*

[ΠΟΛΥΝΕΙΚΗΣ] . . καντε . . ν σοι τ[ήνδε τὴ]ν ψυχὴν
    ἅπαξ
    σοί, φιλτάτη τεκοῦσα, παρεθέμην μολ[ών.
    αἰτῶ, παρ' αὐτῆι τὸ ξίφος φύλασσέ μοι.
[ΙΟΚΑΣΤΗ] μάλιστα. λέξον· ἐμμενῶ μητρὸς κρίσει.
  [ΠΟ.] καὶ μὴν φανεὶς πονηρὸς οὐδὲ ζῆν θέλω.   5
    ἀλλ', Ἐτέοκλες, πίστευσον, οὐ φανήσομαι.
    σὲ δ' ἐξελέγξω πάντοτ' ἠδικηκότα.
[ΕΤΕΟΚΛΗΣ] Ἐτεοκλέης δοὺς σκῆπτρα συγγόνωι
    φέρειν
    δειλὸς παρὰ βροτοῖς, εἰπέ μοι, νομίζεται;
  [ΠΟ.] σὺ γὰρ οὐκ ἂν ἐδίδους μὴ στρατοὺς ἄγοντί
    μοι.   10

          (? *Lacuna*)

  [ΕΤ.] τὸ μὴ θέλειν σόν ἐστι, τὸ δὲ δοῦναι τύχης.
  [ΠΟ.] ἐμοὶ προσάπτεις ὧν σὺ δρᾶις τὰς αἰτίας·
    σὺ φέρειν γὰρ ἡμᾶς πολεμίους ἠνάγκασας.
    εἰ γὰρ ἐμέριζες τὸ διάδημ' ἄτερ μάχης,
    τίς ἦν ἀνάγκη τοῦ φέρειν στράτευμ' ἐμέ;   15

          (? *Lacuna*)

  [ΠΟ.] κοινῆι πέφυκεν· ὥ[σ]τε μὴ κέλευέ μοι·
    ἄλλοις τύραννος τυγχάνεις, οὐ συγγόνωι.
[?ΕΤ.] . . . εμ . . . [.] . . . ες . . . ουν γενή-
    σομαι.
  [ΠΟ.] τὸ πρᾶιον ἡμῶν, μῆτερ, οὐκ ἐνετράπη·
    ὅθεν ἐξ ἀνάγκης . . . . λοιπὸν φράσω. 20
    γαίας γὰρ αὐτὸς ἀκ[λ]εῶς μ' ἀπήλασεν·

178

is a piece of an ancient Tragedy, based upon one of Eur.'s most popular plays, but going beyond its model in content, and avoiding imitation of it in style.

POLYNICES. . . . dearest mother, by coming here I have entrusted my life to you once for all. I beg you, guard my sword beside you.

JOCASTA. Gladly.—Repeat : " I will abide by my mother's judgement."

POLYNICES. I swear, if I prove a villain, I would not even live. But I shall not prove so—believe me, Eteocles : though I shall convict you of wrong at every time.

ETEOCLES. Shall Eteocles give up his sceptre for his brother to bear,—tell me—and be thought a coward by the world ?

POLYNICES. Aye, coward, for you would not have offered it, had I not brought armies hither !

(? *Lacuna*)

ETEOCLES. Not to wish is in your power : granting your will, in Fortune's.

POLYNICES. The blame you fasten on me, but the deeds are yours ! It was you that compelled me to come with enemies. If you were for dividing the crown without a battle, what need had I to bring an army ?

(? *Lacuna*)

POLYNICES. . . . it is for all alike. Cease then to give me orders : to others you may be king, but not to your brother.

ETEOCLES. . . . I shall be. . . .

POLYNICES. Mother, he took no heed of my gentle spirit, so I must speak henceforth (in anger). He, none other, drove me without honour from the land :

179

LITERARY PAPYRI

Ἄργους δὲ γῆ μοι συμμάχους παρέσχετο,
καὶ πλείον᾽ αὐτὸς στρατὸν ἔχων ἐλήλυθ[α
. . . αν[
τοιγὰρ [
προσφ[25
ὃ παρεθέμην σοι [
—— οὐδ᾽ εἰ Κύκλωπος εἶχον [
ψυχὴν ἄθελκτον [
τί γὰρ τυραννεῖς τιλ[
ἡλίκον ἐφ᾽ ὑμῖν π[30
—— κληθεὶς σύναιμος οὐκ ἐ[
τὸ ῥῆμα τοῦτο διαφερ[
—— ἀδελφὸν ὄντα δεῖ με [

*(Here follows a free space : the copying of the
original did not proceed beyond this point)*

ANONYMOUS

34   [160 B.C.]   SPEECH OF A HEROINE

Ed. pr. Weil, *Un papyrus inédit : nouveaux fragments
d'Euripide et d'autres poètes grecs : Monuments Grecs
publiés par l'association pour l'encouragement des études
grecques en France*, no. 8, 1879, p. 2 with Plate.

Ascribed to Euripides by the Papyrus, followed by ed. pr. ;
Cobet, Mnemos. 8, 1880, 56 ; Blass, Rh. Mus. 35, 1880,
76 ; cf. Bergk, ibid. 245 ; Kock, ibid. 269. Euripidean
authorship disproved by Tyrrell, Hermath. 4, 1883, 99 ;
cf. Wilamowitz, Hermes, 15, 1880, 491 and Herakles, i.
p. 41, n. 82. Assigned to New Comedy by Robertson, Class.
Rev. 36, 1922, 106, suggesting the lines were the ἀντίρρησις

180

ANONYMOUS

Argos provided me with comrades in arms, and I have come with a greater army . . .

therefore . . . which I entrusted to you . . . not even if I had the implacable soul of Cyclops. . . . For why are you monarch . . . despite the name of brother . . . this utterance . . . though I am his brother, I must . . .

(Here follows a free space : the copying of the original did not proceed beyond this point)

ANONYMOUS

SPEECH OF A HEROINE [160 B.C.]

of Pamphile to the ῥῆσις of Smicrines in Menander, Epitr. ; cf. *Jensen*, Rh. Mus. *76, 1927, 10 ; this suggestion contested by Körte, Hermes, 61, 1926, 134, who however supported the attribution to New Comedy ; cf. Robertson, Hermes, ibid. 348 ; Körte, ibid. 350 ; Platnauer, New Chapters, iii. 155 and 168 ; the fragment appears in *Nauck, T.G.F.², p. 666 as Eur. Incert. Fab. fr. 953 ; in Jensen, Menandri reliqu. p. 132 (praef. xxvi) ; Körte, Menander, 3rd ed. 1938, praef. lxi, text p. 143.*

*   The papyrus belonged to the Macedonian Ptolemaeus, the famous recluse of the Serapeum at Memphis. Wilcken (Urk. d. Ptolemäerzeit, 111, 115) observed that the text on the verso (v. 1, note) was written by Ptolemaeus himself,*

181

and the subscriptio *to the text on the recto by his brother
Apollonius, who was then only 13 or 14 years old.*

*There can be no doubt that the attribution to Euripides,
or to any Tragedian of the 5th century, is mistaken. The
elision of -αι in v. 44, the phrases μέχρι πόσου v. 32, τυχὸν ἴσως
v. 9, the perfects ἠδίκηκε, ἡμάρτηκε, ἠπόρηκε, and the rhythms
(possible but very rare)* τῶι μὲν διὰ τέλους *v. 15,* τῶν μὲν ἀγαθῶν
v. 25, are sufficient proof, even if ἀντείπαιμι *is " corrected,"
and a few other things tolerated.*

*But the assignment to New Comedy is by no means free
from objection. The plain fact is that there is no extant
speech in New Comedy, comparable in length, which combines
comparatively Tragic metre with comparatively Tragic diction
and spirit to the extent which we discover in our fragment.
Damoxenus fr. 2 Kock (C.A.F. iii. p. 349), which has been
quoted as a parallel, is fairly regular in metre ; but openly
comic in spirit, style and language. Menander, Perik.
338 sqq. is a good imitation—half parody, half serious
imitation—of Tragic metre and style ; but since it is a passage
of stichomythia, the parallel is wholly inadequate ; and the
style seems to me not nearly so consistently on the Tragic level
as it is in our fragment. In fact, our fragment reads (to
my ear) even less like Menander than like Euripides. I
am therefore bound to seek some other context for it, until
someone can shew me a comparable passage from New
Comedy.*

*Now it is by no means impossible that this fragment pro-
ceeds from a Tragedy written in the 4th century* B.C., *or even
later. As for the metre :*—(1) *The elision of -αι has 4th-
century parallels in Pseudo-Eur. I.A. 407 ; cf. Agathon
fr. 29 (=Sthenelus fr. 1) ; Eur. Incert. Fab. fr. 1080.
(2) The unusual rhythm of v. 15* τῶι μὲν διὰ | τέλους *has
parallels in Eur. Ion 931, Ba. 940, I.A. 1164, Theodectes
fr. 8, 5, Anonymous, no. 29, v. 17, v. 9, Anonymous, no. 33,
v. 9. (3) The unusual rhythm in v. 25 has a parallel in Pseudo-*

ANONYMOUS

Eur. I.A. *1409* ἐξελογίσω. (4) *Porson's canon is violated
in v. 10 : but there are several such violations even in 5th-
century Tragedy,* Aes. Pers. *321,* Soph. Ai. *1101,* Phil. *22,
Eur.* Hcld. *529,* Ion *1,* Tro. *1182,* Pseudo-Eur. *I.A. 635, cf.
Descroix,* Le trimètre iambique, *pp. 300 sqq. As for the
language and grammar :—*καίτοι γε *has a parallel in Eur.*
I.T. *720, cf. Denniston,* Gk. Particles, *p. 564. And the
other forms and phrases which have given offence are all
admitted in prose or poetry of the 4th century (see Körte,* loc.
cit., *for details). In the present state of our ignorance we
cannot dogmatize about what was and what was not possible
for a Tragedian writing in the age of Menander or soon after-
wards.* μέχρι πόσου *is not the diction of 5th-century Tragedy,
but I know no reason to deny it to Tragedy in the late 4th
century. (As for the " non-Tragic" word* μέχρι, μέχρις *in
Soph.* Ai. *571 has never been properly explained.)* ἁρμόττει,
ἀντείπαιμι *are not the forms of 5th-century Tragedy : but
neither is out of place in good prose and poetry of the late
4th century. No objection can be brought against the con-
struction of* ἁρμόττει *v. 2-3 (cf.* Soph. Tr. *731) or against that
of* λοιπόν ἐστι *v. 4 (Plato,* Resp. *466 D, Xen.* Symp. *iv. 1).* οὐσία
means " property," as here (v. 30), in Eur. H. *337,* Hel.
1253. For the rest, we have only to consider (1) the phrase
τυχὸν ἴσως *v. 9, (2) the meaning of* ἠπόρηκε *v. 19—*ἀπορῶ *does
not mean " am poor " in poetry before the 4th century.
Körte has shewn how well these things were established in the
New Comedy. Could they have been used in a Tragedy written
during or soon after the lifetime of Menander ? We do not
know ; but have not sufficient reason to suppose the contrary.
N.B. too that small changes in this ill-written papyrus would
remove several of the divergences from the style of earlier
Tragedy—v. 2* ἁρμόζει *for* ἁρμόττει *(Weil) ; v. 10* ἀντείποιμι
for ἀντείπαιμι *(Weil) ; v. 9* τυγχάνουσ' *for* τυχὸν ἴσως
(Nikitin), with ταῦτ' οὐκ *(Πα) for* οὐσ' οὐκ *in v. 10 ; v. 19*
εὐπόρηκε δ' οὔ *for* ἠπόρηκε δέ *(D. L. P.). Such changes*

183

(though I do not recommend them) would leave little in the language, as there is nothing in the metre, which could not find a parallel in Tragedy of the 5th and 4th centuries. We should only have to suppose further that such a phrase as μέχρι πόσου was—as well it may have been—as characteristic of Tragedy in the late 4th or early 3rd century as are the perfect tenses εὐπόρηκεν, ἡμάρτηκεν, ἠδίκηκεν.

In conclusion : there will, I hope, be some who agree with me that the comparative regularity of these lines in their tragic metre and language, combined with the serious and earnest tone, the impassioned and elevated spirit which inform them, precludes the possibility of their ascription to a New Comedy : whereas there is nothing which precludes the likelihood of their ascription to a Tragedy written in the 4th century B.C., or soon afterwards.

Another possibility is this : that the passage is not part of a complete Tragedy, but is an isolated speech written—as an exercise, or for pleasure—in deliberate imitation of Euripides

Ὦ πάτερ, ἐχρῆν μὲν οὓς ἐγὼ λόγους λέγω,
τούτους λέγειν σέ· καὶ γὰρ ἁρμόττει φρονεῖν
σὲ μᾶλλον ἢ 'μὲ καὶ λέγειν ὅπου τι δεῖ.
ἐπεὶ δ' ἀφῆκας, λοιπόν ἐστ' ἴσως ἐμὲ
ἐκ τῆς ἀνάγκης τά γε δίκαι' αὐτὴν λέγειν.   5
ἐκεῖνος εἰ με μεῖζον ἠδίκηκέ τι,
οὐκ ἐμὲ προσήκει λαμβάνειν τούτων δίκην;
εἰ δ' εἰς ἔμ' ἡμάρτηκεν, αἰσθέσθαι με δεῖ.
ἀλλ' ἀγνοῶ δὴ τυχὸν ἴσως ἄφρων ἐγὼ
οὖσ'· οὐκ ἂν ἀντείπαιμι. καίτοι γ', ὦ πάτερ,   10
εἰ τἆλλα κρίνειν ἐστὶν ἀνόητον γύνη,
περὶ τῶν γ' ἑαυτῆς πραγμάτων ἴσως φρονεῖ.
ἔστω δ' ὃ βούληι· τοῦτο, τί μ' ἀδικεῖ, λέγε.

ANONYMOUS

by a would-be poet of the late 4th or early 3rd century. In favour of this theory are the facts (1) that—if the few stylistic lapses are overlooked—the spirit and style of the piece are really remarkably Euripidean, (2) that "Euripides" is written at the head (and foot) of the piece,—the natural title to a passage written in imitation of Euripides. But it is hard to think of a good reason why such a tour-de-force should have been included in the same "anthology" as fragments from Aeschylus, Poseidippus, Euripides himself. Mr. Roberts justly observes that the plot of the play (as deduced especially from vv. 20-21), is consistent rather with New Comedy than with Tragedy: but it remains clear that the treatment of the plot was Tragic. This fine speech hovers alone in a by no means lucid interspace of world and world. We do not even know whether 4th century Tragedians dealt occasionally with more or less Menandrean themes.

THE words I speak, father, you should be speaking: it is fitting that you should be wiser than I, and speak what the time demands. Now, in your default, it remains for me, I think, perforce to plead myself the cause of justice. If my husband has done me a great injury, is it not for me to exact a penalty therefor? And if he has wronged me, must I not perceive it? Perhaps I am a fool and know it not.—I will not answer no: and yet a woman, father, though a fool in judgement of all else, may perhaps have good sense about her own affairs. But be it as you will. Only tell me this, wherein he

---

1 Text written in Π twice, once on recto (= Πa), once on verso (= Πb).   2 ἁρμόζει Weil.   6 εἰ μὲν Π, corr. D. L. P.   10 ταυταουκαν Πa, ου . αουκαν Πb, corr. Blass, ἀντείποιμι Weil.   12 ισωσκοπει Πb.

ἔστ᾽ ἀνδρὶ καὶ γυναικὶ κείμενος νόμος,
τῶι μὲν διὰ τέλους ἣν ἔχει στέργειν ἀεί,   15
τῆι δ᾽ ὅσ᾽ ἂν ἀρέσκηι τἀνδρί, ταῦτ᾽ αὐτὴν ποεῖν.
γέγονεν ἐκεῖνος εἰς ἔμ᾽ οἷον ἠξίουν,
ἐμοί τ᾽ ἀρέσκει πάνθ᾽ ἃ κἀκείνωι, πάτερ.
ἀλλ᾽ ἔστ᾽ ἐμοὶ μὲν χρηστός, ἠπόρηκε δέ·
σὺ δ᾽ ἀνδρί μ᾽, ὡς φής, ἐκδίδως νῦν πλουσίωι   20
ἵνα μὴ καταζῶ τὸν βίον λυπουμένη.
καὶ ποῦ τοσαῦτα χρήματ᾽ ἐστίν, ὦ πάτερ,
ἃ μᾶλλον ἀνδρὸς εὐφρανεῖ παρόντα με;
ἢ πῶς δίκαιόν ἐστιν ἢ καλῶς ἔχον
τῶν μὲν ἀγαθῶν με τὸ μέρος ὧν εἶχεν λαβεῖν,   25
τοῦ συναπορηθῆναι δὲ μὴ λαβεῖν μέρος;
φέρ᾽, ἐὰν ὁ νῦν με λαμβάνειν μέλλων ἀνὴρ
(ὃ μὴ γένοιτο, Ζεῦ φίλ᾽, οὐδ᾽ ἔσται ποτέ,
οὐκ οὖν θελούσης οὐδὲ δυναμένης ἐμοῦ)
ἢν οὗτος αὖθις ἀποβάληι τὴν οὐσίαν,   30
ἑτέρωι με δώσεις ἀνδρί; κᾆτ᾽, ἐὰν πάλιν
ἐκεῖνος, ἑτέρωι; μέχρι πόσου τὴν τῆς τύχης,
πάτερ, σὺ λήψει πεῖραν ἐν τῶι ᾽μῶι βίωι;
ὅτ᾽ ἦν ἐγὼ παῖς, τότε σ᾽ ἐχρῆν ζητεῖν ἐμοὶ
ἄνδρ᾽ ὧι με δώσεις, σὴ γὰρ ἦν τόθ᾽ αἵρεσις·   35
ἐπεὶ δ᾽ ἅπαξ ἔδωκας, ἤδη ᾽στιν, πάτερ,
ἐμὸν σκοπεῖν τοῦτ᾽, εἰκότως· μὴ γὰρ καλῶς
κρίνασ᾽ ἐμαυτῆς τὸν ἴδιον βλάψω βίον.
ταῦτ᾽ ἔστιν. ὥστε μή με, πρὸς τῆς Ἑστίας,
ἀποστερήσηις ἀνδρὸς ὧι συνώικισας.   40
χάριν δικαίαν καὶ φιλάνθρωπον, πάτερ,
αἰτῶ σε ταύτην. εἰ δὲ μή, σὺ μὲν βίαι

wrongs me ? For wife and husband there is a law
laid down :—for him, to love his woman for ever till
the end ; for her, to do whatever gives her husband
pleasure. All I demanded, my husband has been to
me ; and all that pleases him, father, pleases me. You
say he is good to me but he is poor !—so now (you tell
me) you give me in marriage to a man of wealth, that
I may not live all my life in distress. Where in the
world is all that money, father, which—if I have it—
will cheer me more than the man I love ? How is it
just or honourable, that I should take my share of
the good things he had, but in his poverty take no
share at all ? Say, if the man who is now about to
take me (which dear God forbid, nor shall it ever be !
—at least not of my will, nor while I can prevent it)—
if he should lose his substance hereafter, will you give
me to another man ? And then to another, if he too
loses all ? How long will you use my life, father, for
your experiments with fortune ? When I was a
child, that was the time for you to find a husband to
give me to, for then the choice was yours. But when
you had once given me, father, at once it was for me
to look to my own fate. And justly so, for if I judge
not well, it is my own life that I shall injure. There
is the truth. So by the Goddess of our Home, do not
rob me of the man to whom you wedded me.
This favour I ask you—a just one, father, and full of
lovingkindness. If you refuse, you shall do your

27 φερεανυν . . λαμβ. Πα, . ερεοαν . . υνλανβ. Πb, corr.
D. L. P. 33 δελημψει Πα, τελημψει Πb, corr. Weil.
37 κακωσ Παb, corr. Blass.

πράξεις ἃ βούληι· τὴν δ' ἐμὴν ἐγὼ τύχην
πειράσομ' ὡς δεῖ μὴ μετ' αἰσχύνης φέρειν.
στίχοι μδ'
Εὐριπίδης ΣΜΟΔΡΕΓΑΤΗΣ.

44 πειράσομαι δὴ Th. Gomperz.   46 σπο(υ)δεργάτης
Radermacher (*Hermes*, 61, 350).   Perhaps σπευδεργάτης, *i.e.*
ψευδεργάτης "forger."   Perhaps the lines are the work of a

ANONYMOUS

35 [2–3 A.D.]   FRAGMENT

Ed. pr. *Lefebvre, *Bulletin de la société royale d'archéo-
logie d'Alexandrie*, no. 14, 1912, p. 2 with Plate.   See Körte,
Archiv, vii. 1923, 141 ; Fritsch, *Neue Fragm. d. Aisch. und
Soph.*, diss. Hamburg, 1936, 14.

```
            ]ν καὶ [
    ]ν γὰρ αὐτ[ό]τευκ[τον] ἦν εν[
        ]σεν ὑψηλοῖσι θα[.  .]ούχοι[ς
. . . .]ν δὲ παῖδες οιδε[.  .]μφιμη[
        ]ν ἄρδην καυσίμοις ενδ[              5
        ]τα καὶ λοπῶντα φαρμάκου [
```

2 αὐτότευκτον Snell *ap.* Fritsch : ἀντ[ί]τευκ[τον ed. pr.
3 θα[λαμ]ούχοις ed. pr. : but unless the facsimile is misleading

ANONYMOUS

36 [4–5 A.D.]   ΓΝΩΜΗ

Ed. pr. *Vitelli, *Papiri Greci e Latini*, iv. 1917, no. 280,
p. 1.   See Körte, *Archiv*, vii. 1923, 153.

pleasure by force : and I shall try to endure my
fortune as I ought, without disgrace.

---

forger of Euripidean work, or of a slavish imitator of
Euripides, whom the youthful Apollonios thus quaintly desig-
nates Εὐριπίδης ψευδεργάτης, " a spurious Euripides."

ANONYMOUS

FRAGMENT [2–3 A.D.]

If the letters]μφιμη[*in v. 4 were supplemented to* ἀ]μφι-
μή[τορες (*see ed. pr. and Körte, loc. cit.*), *there would be some
reason to ascribe these lines to Aeschylus's* Heraclidae (*cf.
fr. 76 N.*).   *But the reading may as well have been, e.g.,* ἀμφὶ
μητέρα : *there is therefore no probability in the ascription.*

> . . .
> . . .   . . .
> . . . lofty . . .   . . .
> . . . children . . .
> . . . utterly . . . inflammable . . .
> . . . and peeling . . . of poison . . .

---

there is no room for λαμ in the gap.   4 εἰσὶ]ν δὲ παῖδες,
οἷδε[ν ed. pr. : ἀ]μφιμή[τορες Körte.

ANONYMOUS

MAXIM [4–5 A.D.]

*Vitelli debates whether these lines should be assigned to
Euripides or to Menander.   Their style and language suggest*

189

that they are Tragic, not Comic ; and Euripides is a likely author : cf. Eur. Inc. Fab. fr. 1063, 9-11 N. But it remains equally possible that the lines were part of a sen-

ὅστις νομίζει διὰ φρόνησιν εὐτυχεῖν,
μάταιός ἐστι· πάντα γὰρ τὰ τοῦ βίου
οὐ διὰ φρόνησιν, διὰ τύχην δὲ γίγνεται.

ANONYMOUS

tentious poem such as we know, e.g., Chares to have com-
posed (see Körte, Archiv, vii. p. 119 ; Powell-Barber, New
Chapters, *i. 18*).

IF a man thinks that taking thought makes him
happy, he is a fool : in life all things are brought
to pass by luck, not by taking thought.

OLD COMEDY

ΕΠΙΧΑΡΜΟΣ

37   [1 B.C.]   Probably ΟΔΥΣΣΕΥΣ ΑΥΤΟΜΟΛΟΣ

Ed. pr. Gomperz, *Mitteilungen aus der Sammlung der Papyrus Erzherzog Rainer*, v. 1889, p. 1 with Plate.   See Blass, *Fleck. Jahrb.* 1889, 257 ; *Kaibel, *Com. Graec. Fragm.* 99 ; Körte, *N. Jahrb.* 1917, 291 ; Pickard-Cambridge, *Dithyramb, Tragedy and Comedy*, 380.

[ΟΔΥΣΣΕΥΣ τῆλ’ ἀπε]νθὼν τεῖδε θωκησῶ τε καὶ
    λεξοῦ[μ’ ὅπως
  δῆλά κ’ ε]ἴμειν ταῦτα καὶ τοῖς δεξιωτέροι[ς
    δοκῆι.
  τοῖς θεοῖς] ἐμὶν δοκεῖτε πάγχυ καὶ κατὰ
    τρόπ[ον
  καὶ ἐοικό]τως ἐπεύξασθ’, αἴ τις ἐνθυμεῖν γ[α
    λῆι
  ὅσσ’ ἐγών] γ’ ὤφειλον ἐνθ[ὼ]ν ὕσπερ ἐκε-
    λή[σασθ’ ἐμὲ   5
  τῶν παρ’ ὑμέ]ων ἀγαθικῶν κακὰ προτιμάσαι
    θ’ [ἅμα
  ἅμα τε κίν]δυνον τελέσσαι καὶ κλέος θεῖον
    [λαβεῖν
  πολεμίω]ν μολὼν ἐς ἄστυ, πάντα δ’ εὖ
    σαφα[νέως
  πυθόμε]νος δίοις τ’ Ἀχαιοῖς παιδί τ’
    Ἀτρέος φί[λωι
  ἂψ ἀπαγγ]εῖλαι τὰ τηνεῖ καὐτὸς ἀσκηθὴς
    [μολεῖν.   10

EPICHARMUS

Probably ODYSSEUS THE DESERTER [1 B.C.]

The play probably told of Odysseus's entry into Troy, disguised as a beggar in order to obtain information from the enemy. This object he may have attained with the assistance of Helen (cf. Homer, Od. iv. 240-264). If our fragment is part of this play, as appears most probable, it is clear that Odysseus played a comic and by no means heroic rôle. Sent to Troy as a spy, he determined to pretend that he had fulfilled his commission, and to give a picturesque narrative of what he professed to have seen and done. In these lines he is rehearsing that narrative to himself. The sequel is altogether uncertain.

ODYSSEUS. I will retire and sit down here, and consider how my story may seem true even to the sharper wits among them.

(He rehearses his speech.) " It is, I deem, entirely right and proper that you should give thanks to Heaven, if you will only consider how—by going where you told me—I was obliged to sacrifice the comforts of your camp to misery, to fulfil a dangerous task, to win immortal glory by going to the foemen's city ; and having learnt all his secrets in full and clearly, report them home to the noble Greeks and my friend the son of Atreus, and myself return unscathed. . . ."

---

2 δῆλά D. L. P.

LITERARY PAPYRI

ΚΡΑΤΙΝΟΣ

38 [Early 2 A.D.]   ΠΛΟΥΤΟΙ

Ed. pr. (*a*) *Vitelli-Norsa, Bulletin de la société royale d'archéologie d'Alexandrie*, no. 29, 1934, p. 249 with Plate. See Goossens, *Rev. Et. Anc.* 37, 1935, 401 (revised text); Vitelli-Norsa, *Pap. Greci e Latini*, xi. 1935, no. 1212, p. 107 with Plate; Körte, *Archiv.* xi. 1935, 260. (*b*) *Mazon, *Mélanges Bidez*, ii. 1934, p. 603 with Plate. See Goossens, *loc. cit.* (revised text with Plate); Körte, *loc. cit.* 261.

From the beginning of the play. The Chorus enters and, in conversation with an interlocutor, speaks in anapaests of its anxiety about its success. The suggestion is that the judges may be too disturbed by events (doubtless of a grave political nature) to perform their duty patiently. The Chorus consists of a plurality of Plutuses : *these are the* δαίμονες πλουτοδόται *of Hesiod* (Op. *121 sqq.), once ruled on earth by Cronus, now living in the underworld but sending prosperity to men. They return in this play to Athens and judge the wealthy, whether their fortunes have been amassed unjustly. (So in fr. 208. 2 K. (the Seriphians) Cratinus turns against the* νεοπλουτοπόνηροι *at Athens.) The first case to be called is that of Hagnon, son of Nicias, from the deme Stiria. One speaker maintains that his family has long been wealthy*

(*a*)   πῶς μὲν κακό[νους εὑρήσεις;
—— ἀλλ' ἀξιόνικον [τὴν γνώμην
ἀποφαινόμεν[οι πειρώμεθ' ὅμως
τὸ τυχὸν στέργει[ν· ἀλλὰ φοβούμεθα
μὴ συντυχίαισι [βαρυνόμενοι   5
μενετοὶ κριταὶ οὐ δ[

(*Traces of two lines*)

196

CRATINUS

THE PLUTUSES [Early 2 A.D.]

another avers that Nicias was a porter in the service of
Pithias, and (presumably) left nothing to his son.

The politician Hagnon is a well-known character in
Athenian history from the Samian Revolt of 440–439 (Thuc.
i. 117) down to 413, when he became one of the Πρόβουλοι
(Lys. xii. 65). In 437–436 he was prominent in the expedi-
tion to settle Amphipolis (Thuc. iv. 102); in 430 he fell foul
of Pericles (Plut. Pericles 32). His adventures at Amphipolis
may, as Mazon suggests, have laid the foundation of his
wealth. And since his feud with Pericles, whom Cratinus
hated, would probably have earned him immunity from this
poet's attacks, the date of the play is probably to be fixed
between 437 and 430 B.C.—very likely the year was 430,
when Cratinus might well have been anxious lest the war with
Sparta should distract the mind of his judges from their
duty.

It is clear that in the Agon of this play (vv. 25 sqq.), the
Chorus was a principal actor; no parallel to this can be
found in Aristophanes.

(a) —— . . . how should you find them ill-dis-
posed ?

—— The sentiments that we declare deserve the
prize : still, let us try to be content, whatever
happens. Only we fear that our judges, oppressed
by affairs, . . . impatient . . .

(Traces of two lines)

---

5 = fr. 166 K.　　6 δικάσωσι Körte.

ὧν δ' οὕνεκ' ἐφήσαμεν [ἥκειν
πεύσεσθ' ἤδη.
Τιτᾶνες μὲν γενεάν ἐσ[μεν,
Πλοῦτοι δ' ἐκαλούμεθ' ὅτ' [ἦρχε Κρόνος·   10
τότε δ' ἦν φωνῆνθ' ὅτε π[αῖδα θεὸς
κατέπιν' ἀκόναις
κλωγμὸν πολὺν αἰνετὸς ὑ[μῖν.
—— εἶτα δὲ κλέπτεις τὸν Δία [

(*Traces of one more line, then a gap*)

(——) ἀλλὰ Ζεὺς Κ]ρόνον ἐκ βασι[λείας   15
ἐκβάλλει κ]αὶ Τιτᾶνας το[ὺς
στασιάζο]ντας δεσμ[οῖς ἀλύτοις

(*Four lines missing, and traces of one more, be-
ginning with the word* δεσμός)

ὡς δὲ τυραννίδος ἀρχῆς [στέρεται,
δῆμος δὲ κρατεῖ,
δεῦρ' ἐσύθημεν πρὸς ὅμ[αιμον τ' ὄντ'   20
αὐτοκασίγνητόν τε παλαιὸν
ζητοῦντες κεἰ σαθρὸν ἤδη.
ἀλλ' αὕτη μὲν σ]κῆψις πρώτη,
ἄλλην δέ τιν' αὖ τ]άχ' ἀκούσηι.

---

7 ἥκειν Körte.   11 φωνῆνθ Π: a doubtful form, if it
stands for φωνῆντα. παῖδα θεὸς Goossens.   16 τ[οὺς Goossens.

CRATINUS

And now you shall learn why we said that we've
come. By race we are Titans, called Riches when
Cronus was in power. It was the time when the god
devoured his son alive with a mighty gurgle, and
you cried your approval. . . .[a]
—— And then you cheat Zeus . . . ?

(Traces of one more line, then a gap)

—— But Zeus expelled Cronus from his kingdom,
and the rebellious Titans in bonds unbreakable . . .

*(Four lines missing, and traces of one more, be-
ginning with the word* band)

. . . since he is robbed of his tyrant-rule, and the
people are masters, hither we hurried to our nearest
of kin, our own brother in his old age ; decrepit now
though he may be, we search him out. This is our
first excuse ; another you shall hear anon. . . .

---

[a] So Goossens (κλωγμὸν πολύν is taken in apposition to the
action of κατέπινε παῖδα : κλωγμός = " bruit de déglutition ") :
αἰνετὸς ὑμῖν may allude to a successful scene in a recent
comedy (ἀκόναις is taken in apposition to ὑμῖν, " vous qui
êtes des pierres à aiguiser (le talent des poètes) " : this seems
to me hardly possible, and I have not translated the word) :
φωνῆντα = " vivant," cf. Hes. *Theog.* 584. This is perhaps
the best of a bad job.

---

18 στέρεται Beazley, who adds that the point of these lines is :
Zeus expelled Cronus and imprisoned the Titans ; Δῆμος,
the Populace, has now expelled Zeus, and the Titans have
been liberated ; they hasten at once to their old brother
Titan, who is *Prometheus.* Cf. Aesch. *Prom. Unbound,* fr.
190-192 N., where also a chorus of Titans has come to address
Prometheus in an anapaestic parodus.

(*b*) (*Fragments of five lines*)

ἔγειρε, θυμέ, γλῶ[τταν εὐ- 25
κέραστον ὀρθουμένην
εἰς ὑπόκρισιν λόγων.
—— μάρτυρας τοὺς προσκεκλημένο[υς παρεῖναι
βήματι
τῶιδε χρή· τοῦ Στειριῶς γὰρ εὐκτὰ τ[ὸν βίον
σκοπεῖν
ὃν καλοῦσ' Ἅγνωνα νῦν καὶ δῆμον η[30
—— οὗτος οὐ πλουτεῖ δικαίως ἐνθάδ' ὥστ[
—— ἀλλὰ μὴν ἀρχαιόπλουτός γ' ἐστὶ[ν] ἐ[ξ
ἀ]ρχ[ῆς ἔχων
πάνθ' ὅσ' ἔστ' αὐτῶι, τὰ μέν [γ'] ἐξ [οἰκι]ῶν,
τὰ δ' [ἐξ ἀγρῶν.
—— ἐξαμεινώσω φράσας [ὧδ', ὡς σα]φέστερον
μάθηις.
Νικίας φορτηγὸς ἦν κά[μν]ων πονῶν [τ' ἐν
Πειραεῖ, 35
Πειθίου μισθωτὸς [
οὗ κατέψευσται τά[δ'
—— ἀλλ' ἐγώ τοι μὰ Δία [

25 εὐ]κέραστον Goossens. 28 Goossens. 29
Goossens. 30 ἠ[γνόει πρὸ τοῦ Grégoire (pun Ἅγνων—
ἀγνοῶν: the point being that H. is a foreigner who has only
just got his name and deme. See Goossens, *loc. cit.*)

CRATINUS

(b)   *(Fragments of five lines)* [a]

—— My spirit, bestir your tongue judicial, roused
to action [b] for debate.

—— Here, on the platform, all witnesses who
have received a summons! It is most desirable to
examine the life of the man from Stiria (his name is
Hagnon now) . . . the people . . .

—— Ill-gotten are his gains at Athens, there-
fore . . .

—— Oh no! He comes of wealthy ancestors, and
had from the start [c] all that is his to-day—part from
houses, part from land.

—— Let me say so much to correct you, and
make you better informed :—Nicias was a porter,
sweating and slaving at Piraeus, in the pay of Pithias
. . . these things are falsely said of him . . .

—— But I, good heavens, . . . !

[a] Fr. 1. vv. 7-8 of ed. pr. (too fragmentary for reproduction
here) contain the ends of the lines of fr. 161 K. of this play.
[b] εὐκέραστον: well-mixed, well-balanced, impartial, "judi-
cial." ὀρθουμένην lit. "erect," as opposed to κειμένην, the
position of the tongue before speech begins.   [c] Perhaps
there is play with the meaning of ἀρχαιο-, ἐξ ἀρχῆς—he
derived his wealth *from office*! (Goossens.)

---

31 ὥστ[ε κλαύσεται Grégoire.   33 Goossens, also 34.
35 Mazon.

LITERARY PAPYRI

ΦΕΡΕΚΡΑΤΗΣ

39 [2 B.C.] FRAGMENT

Ed. pr. *Schubart-Wilamowitz, *Berliner Klassikertexte*, **v. 2**, 1907, p. 123. See Demiańczuk, *Suppl. Com.* p. 71.

ἀνὴρ γὰρ ὅστις ἀπ]οθανούσης δυσφορ[εῖ
γυναικός, οὗτος οὐκ] ἐπίστατ' εὐτυχεῖν.

ΕΥΠΟΛΙΣ

40 [(a) 4–5 A.D.]
    [(b) 3 A.D.]   ΔΗΜΟΙ

Ed. pr. (a) Lefebvre, *Catalogue générale des antiquités égyptiennes du musée du Caire*, 1911, p. 21, Plates XLIX-LIII. See *Jensen, *Hermes*, 51, 1916, 321 and literature quoted there, esp. Keil, *N.G.G.* 1912, 237 ; Körte, *Archiv*, vii. 1923, 142, *Hermes*, 47, 1912, 276 and *Ber. Sächs. Akad.* 1919, 1 ; Robert, *G.G.A.* 1918, 168 ; Platnauer, *New Chapters*, iii. 161 ; Demiańczuk, *Suppl. Com.* p. 43 ; Thieme, *Quaest. com. ad Periclem pertinentia capita tria*, diss. Leips. 1908 ; Wilamowitz, *Hermes*, 54, 1919, 69 ; Wüst, *Phil. Woch.* 1920, 385. (b) Grenfell-Hunt, *P. Oxy.* vi. 1908, no. 862, p. 172. Assigned to this play by *Schroeder, *Nov. Com. Fragm.* p. 65. See Körte, *Archiv*, vi. 232 ; Platnauer, *loc. cit.* ; Demiańczuk, p. 117. *P. Oxy.* no. 1240—fragments of 15 lines, with Πυρωνιδ[ης in v. 1—is plausibly assigned to this play.

Vv. 62-100 of my text (=fr. iii. recto and verso, ed. pr.) may possibly belong to some other play : see Jensen and esp. Robert, loc. cit. But I follow Körte in keeping it here. His

202

PHERECRATES

FRAGMENT [2 B.C.]

THE man who bears it hard because his wife has died, has no notion how to be happy.

EUPOLIS

THE DEMES [(a) 4–5 A.D.]
[(b) 3 A.D.]

argument, that this fragment is written in the same hand-writing as the rest, carries little or no weight; but it must be conceded that the references to the profanation of the Mysteries are out of place in any but an Old Comedy. Further, the address to the spectators in v. 99 strongly supports the ascription to an Old Comedy. That this Old Comedy was Eupolis's Demoi can then hardly be doubted: its content is entirely suitable, as Körte first demonstrated.

This famous play was divided (by the Parabasis) into two different but essentially connected halves. (1) In all that part which preceded the Parabasis, the scene was set in the underworld. The Chorus consisted of the old Demes, the principal actors were the great old heroes of Athens—Solon, Pisistratus, Miltiades, Aristides, Pericles and others. The plot was the δοκιμασία, or examination, of these heroes: the present state of Athens—her distress in the dark days which followed the end of the Sicilian expedition—has been reported by the last of the great generals, Myronides, who has recently died: it is determined that an embassy shall be sent from

203

LITERARY PAPYRI

*the underworld to Athens, and the action concerns the choice
of the ambassadors. Arguments were brought forward for
and against many of the great men of old. Aristides gave
evidence against Themistocles, Miltiades spoke in favour of
Pericles. In the end, five—the normal number of an Athenian
embassy—were chosen : Solon, Miltiades, Aristides, Pericles
and Myronides. [Aristides ii. 300. 11, iii. 672 Schol.,
says that Eupolis resurrected only four προστάται. The
exclusion of Myronides is natural ; he was not technically a
προστάτης at Athens, and he acts less as an ambassador than
as a ψυχαγωγός, conductor of the others, being the only one
who is but recently dead ; see Keil, pp. 241-242.] (2) In all
that part which followed the Parabasis, the scene was set in
the Ἀγορά at Athens. The Chorus consisted of the present-
day Demes,[a] the principal actors were the five ambassadors
who have now risen from Hades. The plot was probably
unfolded in a succession of scenes such as we read in vv.
62-100. The famous old heroes of Athens deal after their
own manner with living offenders, their degenerate counter-
parts in the city to-day. Aristides makes short work of
a sycophant ; no doubt Solon dealt with a moral offender,
Miltiades with an inefficient general, Pericles with a corrupt
politician.*

*In our fragments : Vv. 1-32 are from the Parabasis of the
play. The Chorus gives " a little list | of persons in society
who never would be missed." The general ground for inflict-
ing on them whatever form of maltreatment is denoted by
διαστρέφειν,[b] is apparently the fact that they have plenty to
eat, while the Chorus is starving. The dwellers in the city*

---

[a] A striking change of dress probably accompanied this
change of identity, see Keil, 248 *sqq.*

[b] On the meaning of this word, very obscure in this place,
see esp. Körte, *Ber. Sächs. Akad.* pp. 25-28 and literature
quoted, p. 26.

EUPOLIS

and the Long Walls have apparently the first pick at such supplies as come in, and the countryfolk receive only what they can glean, ὀλίγον τε φίλον τε. *Special animosity is shewn towards the Long Wall residents, who are ex-country-folk.*

Vv. 21-35. In the Epirrhema, some politician is attacked. His identity is beyond conjecture. He appears to be some sort of alien (22) ; the Attic dialect does not come naturally to him (23) ; he keeps low company ; he is a critic of the High Command, and seems to have been in some measure responsible for the expedition against Mantinea, persuading the city to take part in that enterprise although the omens were bad and the High Command adverse. (But the passage is obscure ; see notes ad loc.)

Vv. 33-60. After the Parabasis, Athenian statesmen of former days emerge from the Underworld. They are met by a Proboulos, one of the Ten Supreme Commissioners of Athens. Aristides' first request is for a meal : the Proboulos is obliging, but warns the Old Statesmen that things are not what they were, and they must not expect much to eat (again this central theme—the starvation of Athens). The Statesmen sit down, all but Myronides, whom the Proboulos and Chorus address in terms of warm friendliness and respect.

Vv. 61-100. A Sycophant comes to Aristides for justice. His story is : He saw an Epidaurian in the street with barley-crumbs sticking to his beard. That suggested that he had been sacrilegiously drinking the Sacred Soup of the Eleusinian Mysteries. The Sycophant blackmailed him for a large sum. What happened next is obscure. But it seems clear enough that the Sycophant subsequently suffered some ill treatment at the hands of the Epidaurian, and appealed to Aristides for justice. But Aristides declined to take his part. Indeed he dealt with him severely ; and warned the city that Justice was their most important virtue.

Fr. I (recto)

(*a*) [ΧΟΡΟΣ ΔΗΜΩΝ] καὶ δὴ δὲ Πείσανδ[ρον] διε-
στράφθαι χθὲς ἀριστῶντά φασ᾽,
ἐπ(ε)ὶ ξένον τιν᾽ ὄντ᾽ ἄ[σι-
τον οὐκ ἔφασκε θρέψειν.

Παύσων δὲ προσ(σ)τὰς Θεογένει   5
δειπνοῦντι πρὸς τὴν καρδίαν
τῶν ὁλκάδων τιν᾽ αὐτοῦ
κλ]έψας ἅπαξ διέστρεφεν.

α]ὐτὸς δ᾽ ἔκειθ᾽ ὁ Θεογένης
τὴν νύχθ᾽ ὅλην πεπορδώς.   10

(δια)στρέφειν οὖν πρῶτα μὲν
χρὴ Καλλίαν τοὺς ἐν μακροῖν
τειχοῖν θ᾽ ἅμ᾽, ἀ[ρ]ιστ(ητ)ικώ-
τεροι γάρ εἰσιν ἡμῶν·

Ν]ικήρατόν τ᾽ Ἀχαρνέα   15
τρώγ]ειν διδόντα χοίνικας
δύ᾽ ἤ τι πλέ]ον ἑκάστωι
                    ]ιη
τῶν χρημάτων [δὲ τἀπίλοιπ᾽
οὐδ᾽ ἂν] τριχὸς πριαίμην.   20

(*Traces of two more lines*)

Fr. I (verso)

                    ] κἀξιοῖ δημηγορεῖν.

6 πρὸς τὴν κ. is a doubtful phrase.   16-17 Körte.
19 Immisch.

---

[a] The statesman who was prominent in the following year
(411 : *Demoi* produced in 412 B.C.) in the change of constitu-
tion at Athens : Thuc. viii. 49, 68 ; Aristotle, *Ath. Pol.* 32.
Often attacked by comedians for his cowardice, venality
and appetite, Ar. *Babylonians* fr. 81 K., Athen. x. 415 d.
[b] The beggar of Ar. *Ach.* 854, *Thesm.* 949, *Plut.* 602.

EUPOLIS

Fr. I (recto)

(*a*) CHORUS. Yes, and Peisander,[a] the rumour goes,
went through the mill at breakfast yesterday ; some
poor foreigner was there half-starved, but he refused
to give him a crumb.

And Pauson [b] put Theogenes [c] through the mill,
once for all.   He was dining to his heart's content (?)
when Pauson came up to him and stole one of his
traders.[d]   As for Theogenes, he lay there all night
and broke his wind.

They all ought to go through it,—first Callias,[e]
together with the Long Wall residents,[f] for having
more to eat for breakfast than we have ; then
Niceratus [g] of Acharnae, who gives each man two or
more bushels to eat. . . . For the rest of his goods
and chattels, I wouldn't give a hair for them.

(Traces of two more lines)

Fr. I (verso)

. . . thinks himself fit to speak in public.   A day

[e] Played a rôle in the Peace of Nicias, 421 B.C. ; the butt
of Aristophanes in *Vesp.* 1183, *Pax* 928, etc.   T. was a
poor man who pretended to be wealthy.   The scholiast says
that he was called "Smoke" because he boasted much and
performed nothing.   [d] ὁλκάς may be deliberately am-
biguous here (=(1) merchant-ship, (2) prostitute) ; but prob-
ably not (Körte, *Ber. sächs. Akad.* p. 26).   [e] The
wealthy son of Hipponicus.   [f] The Long Walls were
inhabited by immigrants from rural Attica (*a*) after the
first Spartan invasions at the beginning of the Archidamian
War (Thuc. ii. 17. 3).   These returned to the land after the
Spartan disaster at Pylus, or at the latest after the Peace of
Nicias.   (*b*) After the Spartan occupation of Deceleia,
which began in the spring of 413 B.C. (Thuc. vii. 19).
Eupolis is referring to this second occasion.   [g] Not
known from other sources.

χθὲς δὲ καὶ πρώιην παρ᾽ ἡμῖν φρατέρων
  ἔρη[μος ἦν,
κοὐδ᾽ ἂν ἠττίκιζεν, εἰ μὴ τοὺς φίλους ἠισχύ-
  ν[ετο,
τῶν ἀπραγμόνων γε πόρνων κοὐχὶ τῶν
  σεμνῶν [τινας,
ἀλλ᾽ ἔδει νεύσαντα χωρεῖν εἰς τὸ κινητήρ[ιον. 25
τῆς ἑταιρίας δὲ τούτων τοὺς φίλους ἐσκ[
ταῖς στρατηγίαις δ᾽ ὑφέρπει καὶ τρυγωιδ[
εἰς δὲ Μαντίνε(ι)αν ὑμᾶς οὗτος οὐ μέμ[νησθ᾽
  ὅτι
τοῦ θεοῦ βροντῶντος ὑμῖν οὐδ᾽ ἐῶν[τος
  ἐμβαλεῖν
εἶπε δήσει(ν) τοὺς στρατηγοὺς πρὸς βίαν [ἐν
  τῶι ξύλωι;   30
ὅστις οὖν ἄρχειν τοιούτους ἄνδρας [αἱρεῖταί
  ποτε,
μήτε πρόβατ᾽ αὐτῶι τεκνοῖτο μήτε γῆ
  κ[αρπὸν φέροι.
ΑΡ[ΙΣΤΕΙΔΗΣ] ὦ γῆ πατρώια, χαῖρε· σὲ γὰρ δί[κηι
  λέγω
πασῶν πόλεων ἐκπαγλ[οτάτην καὶ φιλτάτην.
ΠΡ[ΟΒΟΥΛΟΣ] τὸ δὲ πρᾶγμα τί ἐστι; [35

---

25 The change to βινητήριον is unnecessary, cf. Eupolis fr.
233 K., Ar. Nub. 1371.   26 Leeuwen.   27 τρυγωι-
δ[ίαν δάκνει Körte, referring to Syracosius, who infringed
the liberty of comedy by a law μὴ κωμωιδεῖσθαι ὀνομαστί τινα,
Ar. Av. 1297 Schol. Schol. Raven. ibid. says that Eupolis
attacked Syracosius as a foreigner: cf. 22 above. But this,
like τρυγωιδ[εῖ τὴν πόλιν and other suggestions, seems to inter-
rupt the train of thought.   33-34 after Körte, Robert.

or two ago he couldn't find a clan[a] among us. He
wouldn't even have copied our accent, only he
was ashamed before his friends—certain non-political
pansies,—not the superior kind : why, you only had
to nod your head, and away you must go to the
knocking-shop. . . .[b] Sly attacks on the High
Command. . . . Don't you remember how, when
Heaven thundered and forbade you to assail Man-
tinea,[c] he said he would take the generals perforce
and tie them in the stocks ? Whosoever chooses
men like that to govern him, may earth never breed
him cattle nor bear him harvest.

(*Aristides, appearing from the underworld in the com-
pany of other famous Athenian statesmen, greets
his city.*)

ARISTIDES. Greetings to my native land! Of all
cities the most dreadful yet most dear, that is your
proper name.

PROBOULOS.[d] What's happening here ? . . .

---

[a] *Cf.* Ar. *Ran.* 418. The phratries were no longer of
much importance in politics : but it was still hardly respect-
able to belong to none at all.   [b] This is the best sense
that, with Beazley's assistance, I have been able to
attribute to these difficult lines (24-25) : it is less open to
objections than certain other obvious possibilities. Verse 26
may have meant : "From the company of such people he
picks himself his friends " (? ἐκκ[ρίνεται). [c] This is our
first information about bad omens before the famous battle,
and about the deference of the generals to demagogic poli-
ticians. *N.B.* in 418-417, three members of the Peace
party were made *strategoi*—Nicias (who would be distressed
by adverse portents), Nicostratus and Laches. [d] One
of the ten Commissioners who directed Athenian politics
after the disaster in Sicily, Thuc. viii. 1. 3, Aristotle, *Ath.
Pol.* 29 : *cf.* the part played by the πρόβουλος in Ar. *Lys.*

[AP.] χαίρειν δέ φη[μι

(*Traces of two more lines*)

Fr. II (recto)

[AP.   [τὸ χαλκίον
θέρμαινέ θ' ἡμῖν καὶ θύη π]έττειν τι[νὰ
κέλευ', ἵνα σπλάγχνοισι] συγγενώμεθα.

[ΠΡ. ἐμοὶ μελήσει] ταῦτα καὶ πεπράξεται.   40
ἀλλ' εὐθέως γν]ώσεσθε τοὺς δήμους ὅσωι
πάντη κάκιόν εἰ]σι νῦν διακείμενοι
ἢ πρόσθεν, ἡνί]κ' ἤρχετον σὺ καὶ Σόλων
ἥβης τ' ἐκείνης ν]οῦ τ' ἐκείνου καὶ φρενῶν.

(*The ends of eleven more lines are preserved ; in
v. 15 occurs the name* Π]υρωνίδην)

Fr. II (verso)

[XO.   ]τος γὰρ ὥσ[περ] ἄνδρες   45
ὦν κ[ιχόν]τες ἐν τοίαισιν
ἡδοναῖσι κείμεθα.

[ΠΡ. ἐπεὶ] δο[κ]ῶ τοὺς ἄνδρας ἤδη τού[σδ'] ἰ[δεῖν
καθ]ημένους, οὓς φασιν ἤκειν [π]α[ρὰ νεκρῶν,
ἐνταῦθα μὲν δὴ τῶν φίλων προστ[ήσομαι·   50
ὡ]ς ὀρθὸς ἑστηκὼ[ς] π[ά]ρ[ε]στ' αὐτῶν
[μόνος
Πυρωνίδης, ἐρώμεθ' [αὐ]τὸ[ν ὅτι θέλει.

[XO.]   εἰπέ μοι, ὦ [μάκαρ, ἔ-
μολες ἐτ[εὸν ἐκ νεκρῶν
πρὸς πολιτῶ[ν ποθητός;   55
φρά[σ]ον, τί κ[

37-39 = Eupolis fr. 108 K.   40 Schöne.   48 ἰ[δεῖν
D. L. P. : τού[σδ' ὁρᾶν Jensen ; but Π, according to him, has
ΤΟΥ . . Ι̣ . . . . at the end of this line.   52 Μυρωνίδης
Jensen.   ὅ τι θέλει Körte.   53-55 Körte.

EUPOLIS

Ar. And greetings too . . .

(Traces of two more lines)

Fr. II (recto)

Ar. Boil the kettle, tell someone to bake the cakes,
we want to come to grips with the lungs and liver.

Pr. I will look to it : it shall be done. But you
will see at once how much worse off in every way the
Demes are now, than in the good old days when you
and Solon ruled that spirit of youth, that noble mind
and heart.

*(The ends of eleven more lines are preserved ; in
v. 15 occurs the name* Π]υρωνίδην)

Fr. II (verso)

Cho. . . . like the men, whom finding we bask in
such felicity.[a]

Pr. Now since I see them sitting here, if I can
trust my eyes, these gentlemen whom rumour avers
to be come from the dead, here and now will I repre-
sent my friends. Since Pyronides [b] alone is standing
up, let us ask him what he wants.

Cho. Tell me, happy friend, are you really come
from the dead, in answer to your city's prayer ?
Speak, what . . .

[a] The word κιχόντες (*s.v.l.*: Π has κ[. . . .]τες) and the
form τοία (not elsewhere in Comedy except Ar. *Ran.* 470,
after Eur. *Theseus* fr. 383 N.) shew that this part was a
parody of the Tragic style.   [b] *i.e.* Myronides (Πυρωνί-
δης seems to be certainly the reading of Π) led the Athenian
old men and boys to victory over the Corinthians in 458 B.C.;
commanded the Athenians in victory over the Boeotians at
Oenophyta in 457 ; led an expedition to Thessaly in 454.
Thuc. i. 105, Ar. *Eccl.* 303, Diod. xi. 79.

211

[ΠΥΡΩΝΙΔΗΣ ὅ]δ' αὐτός εἰμ' ἐκεῖνος ὃν σ[ὺ παρα-
   καλεῖς,
  ὅ]ς τὰς 'Αθήνας πόλλ' ἔτη [
   ]ας τ' [ἀνά]νδρους ἄνδρ[ας
[ΧΟ.] ἦ καὶ σαφῶς οἶ[δ' ὅτι παρ' ἡμῖν ἐξ [ἔ]τη 60

Fr. III (recto)

[ΣΥΚΟΦΑΝΤΗΣ   ]τε προσμ[ένω
   ]νῦν αὐτί[χ']· ἁγνός εἰμ' ἐγώ,
  καὶ γὰρ δί]καιός εἰμ' ἀνήρ.
[ΑΡ.]   λέγ' ὅ τι λέγεις.
[ΣΥ. . . . .]ός ποτ' εἰς ἀγο[ρὰ]ν κυκεῶ
   πιὼν   65
ἐξῆλθε κρ]ίμνων τὴ[ν] ὑπήνην ἀνάπλεως
μυστηρικ]ῶν· τοῦτ' ἐννοοῦμαί πως ἐγώ·
ἐλ]θὼν δὲ ταχέως οἴκαδ' εὐθὺς τοῦ ξένου,
τί] ἔδρασας, ὦ πανοῦργε καὶ κυβευτὰ σύ;
ἔφ]ην, κελεύων τὸν ξένον μοι χρυσίου 70
δοῦν]αι στατ[ῆ]ρας ἑκατόν· ἦν γὰρ πλούσιος.
χόνδ]ρον (τότ' οὖν) ἐκ[έ]λευσέ μ' εἰπεῖν ὅτι
   πιὼν
ἐξῆλθεν· εἶπα,] κᾆτ' ἔλαβον τὸ χρυσίον.
διδοὺς δὲ ποι]είτω τίς γ' ὅ τι ποτε βούλεται.
[ΑΡ.] νὴ Δί' ἄγαμαί σε] τῆς δικαιοσύνης ὅση 75
[ΣΥ.   ]εἶπεν οὔτε πω διαστολὰ(ς)
   ]ων (ἔ)πραξεν οὑπιδαύριος
ἀλλ' ὡς ὑπε]ρφρονῶν ἀπέκλεισ(έ μ') ἐκποδών.
[ΑΡ.] ἆρ' εἰς ἀγο]ρὰν κατέλυσας ἡττηθεὶς πολύ;

57 παρακαλεῖς D. L. P.   63-75 as given by Körte.
65 'Επιδαύρι]ος Jensen (but τις indispensable), ἦλθε ξέν]ος
Körte. The omission of τις with 'Επιδαύριος is perhaps in-

EUPOLIS

Pyr. It is I indeed, the very man you summoned : who (governed) Athens many years . . . and men that are not men . . .

Cho. I know it well : six years among us . . .

Fr. III (recto)

Sycophant . . . I wait . . . now at once : my heart is pure : I am a righteous man.

Ar. Say what you have to say.

Syc. . . . came into the square. He had been drinking the Sacred Soup.[a] His beard was full of ritual barley-crumbs. I happened to notice it, and hurried to his home, and went straight up to the stranger, and asked what he had been up to, the dirty cheat. I told him to hand over £100. (He had plenty of money.) So then he urged me to say that it was ordinary gruel that he had been drinking when he came out. So I said it, and got the cash. I don't care what a man does when he pays up.

Ar. Your standards of justice are very high.

Syc. . . . . . . the Epidaurian thought it beneath his attention, and shewed me the door.

Ar. So you lodged in the agora, after your crushing defeat ?

---

[a] Barleycorn was among the ingredients of this dish, a thick soup consumed at the Eleusinian Mysteries. Clearly an echo of the recent excitement concerning the profanation of the Mysteries : barleycorns on the beard was an obvious trace of complicity ; hence the opportunity for blackmail. A remarkable passage, for Old Comedy carefully avoids this theme as a rule.

---

tolerable. Perhaps read τις for ποτ' (ΤΙΣ omitted before ΕΙΣ, ΠΟΤ inserted to fill the gap). 78 Jensen (suggested, but not adopted in his text), 79 Beazley.

[ΣΤ. ὡς οὐκ ἐπρ]αξάμην δὲ χρήματ' οὐ λέγω.   80
[ΑΡ. παρὰ τῶν]θανόντων ταῦτα χάριτος ἄξια
        ]ον εἰ σαφῶς τις ἀποθάνοι

(Traces of one more line)

Fr. III (verso)

(Traces of one line)

[ΑΡ. τί τ]οὺς θανόντας ο[ὐ]κ ἐᾶις τεθνηκέναι;
[ΣΤ. μ]αρτύρομαι· τί δ' ο[ὐκ] ἀγωνι[ο]ύμ[εθα;
    κα]λέσας με συνδεῖς κἀδι[κεῖς.]
[ΑΡ.]   ἀλλ' οὐ[κ ἐγὼ 85
    ξυνέδησά σ', ἀλλ' ὁ ξένος ὁ τὸν κυκεῶ πιώ[ν.
[ΣΤ.] δίκα[ια] δῆτα ταῦτα πάσχειν ἦν ἐμέ;
[ΑΡ.] ἐροῦ βαδίζων ἱερέα (τὸν) τοῦ Διός.
[ΣΤ.] ὕβριζε· ταῦτα δ' ο(ὐ)ν ἔτ' ὀφλήσεις ἐμοί.
[ΑΡ.] ἔτ[ι] γὰρ σὺ τοὐφείλειν λέγεις οὕτως ἔ[χ]ων; 90
[ΣΤ.] καὶ ναὶ μὰ Δία κλάοντα καθέσω σ' [ἐ]ν
    νε[κροῖς.
[ΑΡ.] καὶ τοῦτό μου τὸ χρέος καταψεύδ[ει κακῶς.
    (ἀλλ') ἀπά]γετ' αὐτὸν καὶ παράδοτ' Οἰ[νεῖ
        ταχύ,
    οὗτος γ]άρ ἐστι τῶν τοιούτων δ[εσπότης.
    ἐ[βουλ]όμην δ' ἂν καὶ Διόγνητον λ[αβεῖν 95
    τὸν ἱερόσυλον, ὅς ποτ' ἦν τῶν ἔνδε[κα,
    ὃς τῶν πανούργων ἐ[σ]τὶ τῶν νεωτ[έρων
    πολλῶι κράτιστος, ὁπόταν εὖ τὸ σῶμ'
        ἔχ[ηι.

93-94 Körte.

214

Syc. I don't say I didn't get money.

Ar. That is something for the dead to be grateful for. . . . if one should truly die . . .

(*Traces of one more line*)

Fr. III (verso)

(*Traces of one line*)

Ar. Grudge not the dead their death [a]—

Syc. Give me witnesses! A trial! First you ask me to come, then you tie me up : there's no justice!

Ar. It wasn't I who tied you up ; it was the foreigner, the man who drank the Sacred Soup.

Syc. Is it then right that I should suffer thus ?

Ar. Go and ask the priest of Zeus.

Syc. That's right, insult me! I'll pay you out one day!

Ar. You're not in a very strong position to talk of paying out.

Syc. I'll make a corpse of you, and then you'll be sorry!

Ar. A feeble falsehood : you'll never pay that debt either. Take him away, and hand him over to Oeneus [b] at once : he is the proper master for such slaves as this. I would have liked to catch Diognetus [c] too, the policeman turned temple-robber, much the toughest of the new generation of gangsters,

---

[a] Eur. *Melanippe* fr. 507 N.   [b] *i.e.* to the eponymous hero of the phyle *Oineis*, in which district was the *barathron* or execution-pit.   [c] Diognetus may be the ζητητής in the inquiry into the profanation of the Mysteries (Andoc. i. 15): identified by Blass with the brother of Nicias (*Att. Bereds.* i.² 524 A. 4). But there are other candidates.

ἐγὼ δὲ πάσηι προσαγορεύω τῆι πόλ[ει
εἶναι δικαίους, ὡς ὃς ἂν δίκαιος ἦι . . .   100

(*Traces of one more line*)

(*b*)   ]δήμου[ς . . . . .] ἠλύσ[ιον
ἑκὼν ἄν, εἰ μὴ] τοῖς ἐνερ[τέ]ροις θεοῖς
ἤρεσε, τεθνη]κὼς οὐκ ἀνεβίων οὐδ' ἅπαξ
              ]η μοι τῆς πόλεως πλεῖστον πολὺ   105
              ]αμοι διαφθείρουσι νῦν
Πείσαν]δροί τε καὶ Παρίδες ὁμοῦ
οἱ νῦν κρατοῦντες πραγμάτων] τῶν ἐνθάδε

(*Fragments of three more lines*)

107 Sudhaus *ap.* Schroeder.

ANONYMOUS

41   [1 A.D.]   ? ΕΥΠΟΛΙΣ, ΠΡΟΣΠΑΛΤΙΟΙ

Ed. pr. Vitelli-Norsa, *Bulletin de la société royale d'archéo-
logie d'Alexandrie*, no. 28, 1933, p. 137 with Plate.   Re-
published by ed. pr. in *Pap. Greci e Latini*, xi. 1935, no.
1213, p. 111.   See Goossens, *Rev. de Phil.* 61, 1935, 333
and *Chron. d'Egypte*, xi. 1936, 516 ;   Körte, *Archiv*, xi.
1935, 263.

*I follow Goossens in distinguishing three speakers in this
fragment.   The speaker of 19-20 is clearly the obstinate
αὐτός of v. 9, τοῦτον v. 12.   The speakers of v. 10 (N.B.
plurals, vv. 4, 10) are clearly to be distinguished both from
the obstinate person and from the speaker of vv. 4-9, 11-17.
The fragment now yields the following information :—B*

216

when his health permits. Now I advise the whole
city to practise justice. The just man . . .

(*Traces of one more line*)

(*b*) The demes . . . elysian . . . had it not pleased
the gods below, once dead I would never of my own
will have come to life again . . . of this city by far
the most . . .

. . . Peisanders and Parises*ᵃ* together, your
present government . . . are now corrupting you . . .

(*Fragments of three more lines*)

ᵃ *i.e.* μοιχοί, *Anth. Pal.* xi. 278, Chariton v. 2. 8.

ANONYMOUS

? EUPOLIS, *PROSPALTIANS*   [1 A.D.]

*fails to persuade A, and therefore turns to C and urges him
(or rather them) to do some task. The nature of the task is
concealed in vv. 5-7, which can be understood in more than
one way : C is either to tell someone how things are here
with the Prospaltians, or to tell the Prospaltians how things
are here. Even this does not exhaust the possibilities.
(Πρόσπαλτα was the name of a deme in the Φυλὴ ʼΑκαμαντίς, in
the south of Athens, near the city walls.) The purport of the
message, whether it be to the Prospaltians or to others on
behalf of the Prospaltians, is put in the form of an alterna-
tive :—either an army is to be sent, or some persons are to
be removed somewhither. Thus they (probably the Pros-*

217

paltians) *would be unable to complain of inaction and
wasteful expense or loss.*

Since A is obdurate in his refusal, C is requested to
undertake the mission. C accedes, and avers that they must
first consider how much (money ?) is to be sent to B. B
attempts once more to persuade A, adding force to his argu-
ment with a parody of Sophocles' Antigone 712-714. But
A persists in his refusal.

This is an obscure enough action : and many will think
that our fragment permits no conjecture at once safe and
illuminating about the matter of its context. The most that
can be said is that this was a political comedy, its subject
taken from contemporary events. With this view I agree :
but am bound to mention the brilliant—and extremely
daring—hypothesis which Goossens put forward in Rev.
de Phil. loc. cit. In brief (and space forbids me to do
him justice) :—the allusion in v. 7 is to the withdrawal of
Attic villagers and countryfolk to Athens at the start of the
Archidamian War, 431 B.C. The Prospaltians must either
send an army ᵃ or evacuate their dwellings and retire within
the walls. The obstinate man, who will not act in this matter
of army or evacuation, is none other than Pericles. B is the
spokesman of the opposition to Pericles' war-policy ; repre-
sentative of the view that the Athenians should go forth and
meet the Spartans in open battle, instead of watching them
destroy Attic farms and villages unopposed. This theory is
illustrated and supported by a number of minute and in-
genious arguments which shew that the theory is possible,
though they do not shew that it is true. Goossens further

[Α ἐ]γὼ δ' ἵν' εἰσὶν οἱ κακο[ί
.] . . . . ς δὲ χρηστῶν μ . [
ἐ]ὶ μὴ ποοίην ω . . . . [

ᵃ Why should they, or how could they, send an army ? I
suppose the demand is ironic : " either send us (to Athens)

*accepts the suggestion (of ed. pr.) that this is a fragment of
Eupolis's Prospaltians. He assigns the play to the year
429 B.C. [Normally dated much later, about 420 B.C. : but
there is nothing that proves it, v. Goossens, pp. 343-344.] It
will then be the first or second of the plays produced by
Eupolis ; and its purpose will be to attack Pericles on the
ground of his policy at the beginning of the war. For full
details I must refer to Rev. de Phil. loc. cit.*

*I have not reconstructed text and translation on this basis,
for there is no certainty in either of the two questions which
arise.—(1) What is the evidence that the action of our frag-
ment is concerned with these events ? It is simply this, that
it is possible to make the inference from v. 7, and not very
difficult to interpret the rest of the lines in the same light.
But it is absolutely clear that the inference is not necessary,
or indeed even cogent : it is easy enough to take the line in an
entirely different way. (2) What is the evidence that this
fragment comes from Eupolis's Prospaltians, however we
interpret its action ? It is simply the appearance of the
word Προσπαλτίοισι in v. 6 : this seems to me to be insufficient
evidence. As for the action according to Goossens : we learn
from Etym. Magn. 288. 19 that ἐκωμωιδοῦντο . . . Προσ-
πάλτιοι ὡς δικαστικοί (cf. ὅταν ᾖ[ι που] δ[ικῶν s.v.l., v. 14).
If the reference is to the Prospaltians of Eupolis, the state-
ment is not very easy to reconcile with Goossens' theory of the
action of the play : he is conscious of the difficulty, and
discovers a solution (pp. 344, 347) ; but I find this the least
ingenious part of his argument.*

(A) Now I . . . where the villains are . . . of good
. . . if I were not to do . . .

---

an army capable of defeating the Spartans, or leave your
territory " : since the first alternative is obviously unpracti-
cable for the Prospaltians, the command is virtually " leave
your territory."

[B] βαδίζεθ' ὑμεῖς ὡς τά[χι]στ' ἐ[ς
καὶ φράζεθ' οἷα τἀνθάδ' ἐστ[ὶ πράγματα   5
Προσπαλτίοισιν· ἢ στρατιὰν [
πέμπειν κελεύετ' ἢ κομίζεσθ[
ἵνα μὴ καθῆσθαι φῶσ' ἀναλίσκ[ειν τε πᾶν,
ὡς αὐτὸς οὐδέν, ὡς ἔοικε, πείσετ[αι.

[Γ] ἀλλ' ἐρχόμεσθ'· ἀτάρ, τὸ δεῖνα, χρὴ [σκοπεῖν 10
πόσ' ἄττα σοι πέμπωσιν. [B] εξεστι[
εἰ δεῖ γε τοῦτον ἐν κύκλωι πε[ριστρέφειν.
ἀλλ', ὠγάθ', ἔτι καὶ νῦν πιθοῦ πά[σηι
τέχνηι.
ὁρᾶις παρὰ ῥείθροισιν ὅταν ἦ[ι που] δ[ικῶν,
ἢν μέν τις εἴκηι τοῖς λόγοις, ἐκσώ(ι)ζε[ται, 15
ὁ δ' ἀντιτείνων αὐτόπρεμνος οἴχε[ται.
αὕτως δὲ ναός—[Α] ἀπό μ' ὀλεῖς, ἄνθρωπ[ε,
σύ.

[Γ] ἄνθρωπος οὗτος νοῦν ἔχοντα σ[
[Α] ἀλλ' οὐχὶ δύνατ'· εἰ γὰρ πιθοίμ[ην σοι τάδε,
τίν' ἂν τ[.]χ[.]ν ἐξ[20

[B] μέγα στένοι μεντἂν ἀκ[
ἡμεῖς δὲ ναῶν ναυτίλο[ισι προσφερεῖς

4 Goossens.   5 Körte (ἐστὶ τὰ πρ. ed. pr.).   11
perhaps ἔξ ἐστι[?ἄξια.   13 Goossens, cl. Ar. Ran. 1235.

ΑΡΙΣΤΟΦΑΝΗΣ

42   [2 A.D.]   FRAGMENTS

Ed. pr. (a) *Grenfell-Hunt, P. Oxy. ix. 1912, no. 1176,
fr. 8, col. ii. 17-19, p. 131. (b) *Ibid. fr. 39, col. ix. 25-28,
220

(B) (*To* C) Go at once to . . . and tell the Prospaltians how things are here (?). Either bid them send an army . . . or remove . . . Otherwise they will say that we are just sitting here and wasting all their . . .

He is not likely to obey a word we say.

(C) We're off,—but, by the way, you must consider how much they are to send you.

(B) . . . if I have to twist *him* round my little finger. (*To* A) Come, friend,—it is not too late—by all means do what I say ! See, when one stands before the torrent of the courts, he who yields to the argument is saved ; resist, and you perish root and branch. So with a ship,—

(A) Fellow, you'll be the death of me !

(C) This fellow . . . a man of sense.

(A) Impossible ! If I obeyed you there, what . . . ?

(B) . . . would be very sorry . . . Like sailors in a ship, we . . .

---

14 Parody of Sophocles, *Ant.* 712-714, *cf.* Antiphanes fr. 231 K.   17 αὐτομολεῖς ed. pr. : corr. Maas.   21 μεντᾶν Maas (στένοιμεν ἂν ed. pr.).

ARISTOPHANES

FRAGMENTS   [2 A.D.]

p. 152. From Satyrus's *Life of Euripides.* See Demiańczuk, *Suppl. Com.* pp. 20-21 ; Platnauer, *New Chapters*, iii. 158.

LITERARY PAPYRI

(a) δι᾽ ἧς τὰ λ[επ]τὰ ῥήματ᾽ [ἐξεσ]μήχετο.

(b)   ο[ἷ]α μὲν π[οι]εῖ λέγε[ι]ν,
τοῖός ἐστιν.

---

* The context is " Aristophanes wished to measure Euripides' tongue, by which," etc. (in a passage which praises Euripides heartily :—" he was almost as great in his soul as in his poetry," ἔτι δὲ καὶ τὴν ψυχὴν μέγας ἦν σχεδὸν ὡς ἐν τοῖς ποιήμασιν). The sense of ἐξεσμήχετο is uncertain: it seems

ΠΛΑΤΩΝ

43 [2 B.C.] FRAGMENT

Ed. pr. *Schubart-Wilamowitz, *Berliner Klassikertexte*, v. 2, 1907, p. 123. See Körte, *Archiv*, vi. 1920, 233; Demiańczuk, p. 82.

For Eudemus, v. Ar. Plut. 884 and Schol. : Eudemus was

. . . γυναῖκα κρ]εῖσσόν ἐστ᾽ ἐν οἰκίαι
ἢ φαρμακίτα]ς τῶν παρ᾽ Εὐδήμου τρέφειν.

ANONYMOUS

14 [1-2 A.D.] WOMEN CONVERSING

Ed. pr. Grenfell-Hunt, *P. Oxy.* ii. 1899, no. 212, p. 20. See *Demiańczuk, *Suppl. Com.* p. 91 ; Herwerden, *Mnemosyne*, 1900, 123 ; Weil, *Journ. des Savants*, 1900, 95 ; Wilamowitz,

. . . ὑβριζόμεναι. —— μὰ Δί᾽, ἀλλ᾽ ἐγώ [τί σοι
φράσω;

222

(*a*) " . . . by which such fine expressions were polished up." [a]

(*b*) " . . . the man is like the sentiments of his characters." [b]

to mean "scrubbed out" in the sense of "thoroughly cleansed," *cf.* Hdt. iii. 148; so here metaphorically "highly polished."　　[b] Metre apparently trochaic.　Wilamowitz compared Ar. *Thesm.* 149-150 χρὴ γὰρ ποιητὴν ἄνδρα πρὸς τὰ δράματα, ἃ δεῖ ποιεῖν, πρὸς ταῦτα τοὺς τρόπους ἔχειν.

PLATO

FRAGMENT　　　　　　　　　　[2 B.C.]

a φαρμακοπώλης, *who specialized in magic antidotes* (φαρ-μακῖται) *against snake-bites, etc.　The Scholiast quotes Eupolis,* Baptae (*415 B.C.*) *and Ameipsias ; cf. further Theophrastus,* Hist. Plant. *ix. 17.*

IT is better to keep a wife at home, than antidotes bought from Eudemus.

ANONYMOUS

WOMEN CONVERSING　　[1-2 A.D.]

G.G.A. 1900, 34 ; Fraccaroli, *Riv. di Fil.* 1900, 87 ; Platt, *Class. Rev.* 13, 440 ; Postgate, *ibid.* 441 ; Hall and Geldart, Aristoph. fr. 969.　For the argument, see Demiańczuk, p. 92.

—— . . . insulted !
—— But good gracious, what am I to tell you ?

ἢν νοῦν ἔχωμεν, σκεψ[όμεθα νῦν τοῦθ᾿, ὅπως
μηδὲν πλέον τούτου σθ[ένωσιν
—— τί οὖν γένοιτ᾿ ἄν; —— ἔχ᾿, ἀπόκριναί μοι
τόδε·
τί ἔστι τοῦθ᾿ ὃ λέγουσι τ[ὰς Μιλησίας   5
παίζειν ἐχούσας, ἀντιβολῶ, [τὸ σκύτινον;
—— φλυαρία καὶ λῆρος ὕβρε[ως ἀνάπλεως,
κἄλλως ὄνειδος καὶ κατ[αγέλως δὴ πολύς.
το[ύτ]ωι γὰρ ὥσπερ τοῖσι[ν ὠιοῖς χρώμεθα
τ[οῖς] ἀνεμιαίοις, ὅτι νεοτ[τί᾿ οὐκ ἔνι.   10
ευ[. .] δὲ καὶ τοῦτ᾿ ἐστίν· ευ[
ἐς [. . .]το χρήσει καὶ πονο[
—— κα[ὶ μ]ὴν λέγεταί γ᾿ ὡς ἐσθ᾿ [ὅμοιον ποσθίωι
ἀλη[θ]ινῶι κ[αὶ τ]οῦτο. —— νὴ Δ[ί᾿, ὦγαθή,
ὥσπερ [σ]ελήνη γ᾿ ἡλίωι· τὴν μ[ὲν χρόαν   15
ἰδεῖν ὅμοιόν ἐστι, θάλπει δ᾿ οὐ[δαμῶς.
—— οὐκ ἄξιον γάρ ἐστι. διὰ τουτον[
—— φέρ᾿, εἰ [δ]ὲ τοῖς θεράπουσι κοινωσ[αίμεθα
τὸ πρ[ᾶ]γμα, τί ἂν εἴη; λάθραι τεπια[
—— ἐγὼ μ[ὲ]ν οὔτε πιότερον [20

ANONYMOUS

45   [2 A.D.]   FRAGMENTS

Ed. pr. (a) *Grenfell-Hunt, P. Oxy. ix. 1912, no. 1176,
fr. 39, col. iv. 1-15, p. 146. (b) *Ibid. fr. 39, col. xvi. 6-17,
p. 160. See Demiańczuk, Suppl. Com. p. 95.

In (a), *Demus seems to be apologizing for being deceived by*

(a)   ο]ὐχὶ τ[ο]ῦτον τ[ὸν τ]ρόπον,

ANONYMOUS

Let's be sensible, and consider how to make . . . no
stronger than this.
—— What's to be done ?
—— Come, answer me this : quid est illud, precor,
quod Milesias dicunt feminas ludere tenentes—rem
scilicet lorinam ?
—— Rubbish and nonsense, an insult, nothing
else. A shame, too, I call it, and idiotic. Isto enim
ut ventosis quae vocant ovis utimur, quia pulli non
insunt. . . .
—— Enimvero dicitur et hoc ipsi simile esse
mentulae.
—— Ita est : ut luna soli similis—colorem aspectui
eundem, calorem minime praebet.
—— Indignum enim. . . .
—— Age, quid si rem cum servis communicemus ?
Clam . . .
—— Equidem nec pingue magis . . .

---

9 χρώμεθα Beazley.   11 εὐ[χή] δὲ . . . εὐ[θ' ἀνὴρ ἀπῆι
edd.   12 ἐς [τοῦ]το χρήσει edd.; but the original sense
of this and of v. 11 is wholly uncertain.

ANONYMOUS

FRAGMENTS   [2 A.D.]

demagogues. In (b), *the point is not clear in detail, but
the context makes it certain that the reference to Eur. is
uncomplimentary.*

(a) . . . not in that way ; nor do we make use of

LITERARY PAPYRI

ἀλλ' ο[ὐδὲ τ]ῆι πονηρ[ίαι] π[ρ]οσχρώμεθα,
ὅτ]ε τωι μάλισ[θ' ὅσ'] ἂν λέγηι πισ[τεύ]ομεν,
λέγ[οντ]ες οὐ πονή[ρ', ἀπ]αλο[ῖς] δὲ χρώ-
        [μενοι·
κἄπειτ[α τῆς] ἐκκλησία[ς κα]τηγορεῖ   5
ἕκασ[τος] ἡμῶν, ἧς ἕκασ[τος] αὐτὸς ἦν.

(b)   ] δὲ Σοφοκλ[έα] λαβών,
πα[ρ' Αἰ]σχύλου ν[. . .]ρ ὅσον [. . . . .]
        ἔσθ', ὅλον
Εὐριπίδην, πρὸς τοισίδ' ἐμβαλεῖν ἅλας,
μ[εμ]νημένος δ' ὅπως ἅλας καὶ μὴ λάλας.   10

ANONYMOUS

46   [2 A.D.]   FRAGMENT

Ed. pr. *Grenfell-Hunt, P. Oxy. ix. 1912, no. 1176, fr. 39,
col. xvii. 10-13, p. 161, Plate V. See Maas, Phil. Woch.
1912, 1077 ; Demiańczuk, Suppl. Com. p. 126.

ὅππαι καθεύδουσ' ἁ κύων τὰν ῥῖν' ἔχει.

1 ἢ ὅππαι Maas. For the synizesis, see Kühner-Blass, i.
pp. 228-229. But Beazley points out that this line may be a
comic *answer* to the question put by Euripides, *loc. cit.*, not

our knavery when someone speaks and we believe
every word he says.—We don't abuse him, we have
none but gentle phrases. And then hear one of
us accuses the assembly to which each one of us
belonged !

(b) . . . take Sophocles . . . ; from Aeschylus as
much as . . . ; the whole of Euripides, and add a
pinch of salt ; only remember, add a pinch—don't
pad an inch.

---

4 λέγ[οντ]ος οὐ πονή[ρ', ἀπ]άτ[ηι] δὲ χρω[μένου Wilam.

ANONYMOUS

FRAGMENT [2 A.D.]

From Satyrus's Life of Euripides *: the line is attached
(evidently by an humorous writer, perhaps quoting from a
Doric comedy) to Euripides'* Ino *fr. 403, 3-4 N.*

Where the bitch keeps her nose when she's asleep.

---

a continuation of the alternatives there propounded. In this
case the line—perhaps spoken by a Megarian—doubtless
comes from an Attic Old Comedy.

MIDDLE COMEDY
AND
NEW COMEDY

ANONYMOUS

47 [1 A.D.] ?ΦΙΛΙΣΚΟΣ: ΔΙΟΣ ΓΟΝΑΙ

Ed. pr. Vitelli-Norsa, *Bulletin de la société royale d'archéo-
logie d'Alexandrie*, no. 25, 1930, suppl. Republished by
ed. pr. *Pap. Greci e Latini*, no. 1175. Assigned to Middle
Comedy by Körte, *Hermes*, 65, 472, *P.-W.-K. s.v. Philiskos*,
no. 5 and *Archiv*, x. 1931, 55; Gallavotti, *Riv. di Fil.* vii.
1930, 209; Platnauer, *New Chapters*, iii. 165.

*From a prologue spoken by Rhea. She complains that her
husband Cronus is making away with all her children. He
sells them in Megara, and consumes all the money. He does
this through fear of an oracle spoken by Apollo, that he will
lose his kingdom to one of his children.*

*The date and authorship of the piece are uncertain. The
quotation from Sophocles, vv. 2-3, is known to us from O.C.*

[ΡΕΑ] τί οὖν ἐμοὶ τῶν [σῶν μέ]λει; φαίη τις ἂν
　　　ὑμῶν. ἐγὼ δ' ἐρῶ [τ]ὸ Σοφοκλέους ἔπος·
　　　πέπονθα δεινά. πάντα τοι γέρων Κρ[όνος
　　　τὰ παιδί' ἐκπίνει τε καὶ κατεσθίει,
　　　ἐμοὶ δὲ τούτων προσδίδωσιν οὐδὲ ἕν,　　　5
　　　ἀλλ' αὐτὸς ἔρδει χειρὶ καὶ Μεγαράδ' ἄγων
　　　ὅ τι ἂν τέκω 'γὼ τοῦτο πωλῶν ἐσθίει.
　　　δέδοικε γὰρ τὸν χρησμὸν ὥσπερ κύν[α λαγώς·

8 Immisch.

---

^a Possibly " gives me not a farthing's compensation for

230

ANONYMOUS

? PHILISCUS, *BIRTH OF ZEUS* [1 A.D.]

*892 : but it is a commonplace phrase which may well have
occurred in a much earlier play too : cf. Eur. Or. 1616.   In
favour of the ascription to Middle Comedy are the facts :
(1) that the subject-matter of our fragment coincides with
the plot which we assume to have deserved the title Διὸς γοναί
in a play by Philiscus ; (2) that such parody of myths about
the gods (especially about such myths as were well-known
from Tragedies) was a common feature of the Μέση.   That
the Middle Comedy was read in Egypt is proved by P. Oxy.
no. 427 (end and title of Antiphanes' Ἀνθρω]πογονία) : but
the case in favour of ascribing our fragment to Middle
Comedy in general, or to Philiscus's play in particular, must
be admitted to be singularly wanting in evidence.*

RHEA. One of you may retort " What have your
troubles to do with me ? "   I reply in the words of
Sophocles, " Dreadful my sufferings "—old Cronus is
drinking and eating all his children up.   He doesn't
give me any share in them.[a]   With his own hands he
does it [b]—takes all my babies to Megara,[c] sells them,
and swallows the money.   He is running from that

them " or " gives me no share in these (foods and drinks)."
But it probably means " gives me no share whatever
in these (children)."   [b] Possibly " does them in " : but
he seems to sell them alive.   [c] Cf. Ar. Ach. 729, a
Megarian sells his children.

231

ἔχρησε γὰρ Κρόνωι ποθ' Ἀπόλλων δραχ[μήν,
κᾆτ' οὐκ ἀπέλαβε. ταῦτα δὴ θυμὸν πνέ[ων 10
ἑτέραν ἔχρησε[ν οὐκέτι] δρα[χ]μῶ[ν ἀ]ξ[ίαν,
οὐ σκευάρια, μὰ τὸν Δί', οὐδὲ χρήματα,
ἐκ τῆς βασιλείας δ' ἐκπεσεῖν ὑπὸ π[αιδίου.
τοῦ]τ' οὖν δεδοικὼς πάντα καταπί[νει τέκνα.

11 Pfeiffer.

ANONYMOUS (? ΑΛΕΞΙΣ)

48   [3 b.c.]

Ed. pr. Wilamowitz, *Sitzungsberichte der königlich preussischen Akademie der Wissenschaften*, Berlin, 1918, p. 743. See *Zuntz, *Mnemos.* Ser. iii. 5, 1937, p. 53 (revised text) ; Körte, *Archiv*, vii. 144 and *Ber. über d. Verh. d. sächs. Akad. d. Wiss.* 71, 1919, 36 ; Platnauer, *New Chapters*, iii. 166 ; Fraenkel, *Socrates*, vi. 366.

From a scene before a temple of Demeter. Before the beginning, someone's death has lately been announced. Thereupon a speaker (A) philosophizes ; and then expresses his desire to enter the temple. It is not clear whether he does so, or is prevented by the sudden entrance of another person (B), who seeks protection from the assault of a third person (C), who is called a " guardian " (κληρονόμος). C, who is accompanied by a slave Sosias, calls B a " slaver " ; and B threatens C with physical violence : calling upon a group of men (D) to witness the fact that he is on holy ground. These men (D) express disapproval of the conduct of either B or C (probably of the former).

Zuntz suggests the following action :—B is a leno (not a slave : see vv. 19-23—in New Comedy, a slave could not so

232

ANONYMOUS

oracle, like a hare from hounds. You see, Apollo lent *a* Cronus a drachma once, and never got it back. That enraged him, so his oracle decreed a different price—no longer drachmas, nor pots and pans, dear me no, and not property either, but expulsion from his kingdom by his own child. So in a panic he's swallowing all his children.

a This word and my " decreed " below are the same word in Greek ; a pun which I cannot reproduce.

ANONYMOUS (? ALEXIS)

[3 B.C.]

threaten a freeborn gentleman) who stole a girl from her father long ago. This father, having no son, adopted C, and made C guardian of the girl when he died. Now C loved the girl, not knowing that she was his own ward : but now he has discovered her identity, and is determined to set her free from the leno's *control. In the end he will rescue and marry her.*

It has been alleged that this fragment must be part of a pre-Menandrean comedy ; for the Chorus here takes an active part in the play, outside its ordinary function in interludes (χορ[οῦ μέλος fr. 2, ed. pr.). [It is not certain that the ἄνδρες of v. 18 are really a Chorus : Zuntz compares the crowd of fishermen in Plautus's Rudens, *of advocates in his* Poenulus : *but it must be confessed that it is much more probable that a Chorus is intended.] Alexis is proposed as the author, on the ground that he is known to have used the form παλαιστρικῶς (v. 23 : Attic was παλαιστικῶς) : but unless we suppose that he alone used the form (and there is no reason for the supposition) it is impossible to attribute*

233

*importance to that evidence. The oath in v. 22 is found in
Alexis's* Τοκιστής *also : but since it occurs in Menander too,*

[Α τὸ δ]αιμόνιον τὰ τοιαῦτα τ[οῖς] φ[ρονοῦσιν εὖ
    παραδ]είγματ᾽ ἐκτίθησιν, ἀλλοτρίαν ὅτι
    ζωὴ]ν ἔχομεν ἅπαντες, ἥν, ὅταν δοκῆι,
    . . . .] παρ᾽ ἑκάστου ῥαιδίως ἀφείλετο.
    ἀλλ᾽] εἰσιὼν μετὰ τῆς ἱερείας βούλομαι   5
    τὴν] ἐπιμέλειαν τῶν προσηκόντων λαβεῖν.
[Β . . . .]γ᾽ εὐλάβει, βέλτιστε· πρὸς θεῶν, πάρες.
    διώκ]ομαι γάρ, κατὰ κράτος διώκομαι
    ὑπὸ] τοῦ καταράτου κληρονόμου, ληφθήσομαι.
[Γ . . . .] δίωκε, Σωσία, συνάρπασον   10
    τὸν ἀνδραποδιστήν, λαβὲ λάβ᾽ αὐτόν. οὐ
        μενεῖς;
[Β ὦ] φιλτάτη Δήμητερ, ἀνατίθημί σοι
    ἐμαυτόν, ἀξιῶ τε σώιζειν.
[Γ]   ποῖ σύ, ποῖ;
[Β] ἤρου ᾽με; πρὸς τὴν ἀσφάλειαν· ἐνθαδὶ
    εἵστηκ᾽ ἐμαυτὸν ἀντεταξάμην τέ σοι.   15
[Γ οὐκ] ἔστιν ἀσ[φ]άλειά που πεποιηκότι
    τοιαῦτ᾽·] ἀκολούθει θᾶττον.
[Β]   ἃ μαρτύρομαι,
    μαρ]τύρομ᾽ ὑμᾶς, ἄνδρες· ἂν τὴν χεῖρά μοι
    πα]ρ[ὰ] τῆι θε[ῶ]ι τις προσφέρηι, πεπλήξεται
    πα]ράχ[ρ]η[μά] τ᾽ εὐθὺς τἀπίχειρα λήψεται.   20
[Γ τί] φής; ὑπὸ σοῦ, μαστιγία;
[Β]   νὴ τὸν Δία
    τὸν Ὀ]λύμπιον καὶ τὴν Ἀθήναν, εὖ γε καὶ
    παλ]αιστρικῶς· πεῖραν δ᾽ ἐὰν βούληι λαβέ.

1 Suppl. Eduard Fraenkel.   4 πάλιν] too long for
space.   7 τί πο]τ᾽ Wilamowitz: but the γ is certain (Zuntz).
10 ἰού] Wilamowitz : too short for the space.   14 Punc-

234

*it gives little or no support to the ascription of our fragment
to Alexis.*

(A) Why do the powers above place these
examples before the man of sense ? To prove that
each man's life is but a loan, which they take away
with ease whenever they like. And now I want to
go indoors and, with the priestess to help me, take
charge of my duties here.

(Enter a slave furtively)

(B) . . . cautious, friend ! For God's sake, let
me pass . . . her guardian, curse him, is after me
for all he's worth—he'll get me !

(C) *(entering)*. After him, Sosias ! Grab him, catch
him, I say, catch him ! Stop thief !

(B) Demeter, dear goddess ! I dedicate myself to
you ! I beg you, save my life !

(C) *(who has not yet observed* B). Where the devil
are you going ?

(B) You ask me ? To safety, is the answer ! I
have taken my stand here, and set myself to meet
you face to face.

(C) There's no such thing as safety after what you
have done. Come with me, immediately.

(B) I appeal—gentlemen, I appeal to you ! The
man who lifts his hand against me at the goddess's
altar, shall be struck down and get his wages on
the spot !

(C) And who will strike him, scoundrel,—you ?

(B) Yes, I swear by Zeus of Olympia and Athene,
well and truly as ever wrestler threw his man. Come
and try it, if you like !

---

tuation after ἀσφάλειαν Beazley.   15 εἱστήκ' Roberts.
εἰσῆκ' Zuntz : ἔ[δω]κ' Wilamowitz, Körte.   ᾱ ᾱ Π and edd.

LITERARY PAPYRI

[Δ . . . . . .]ντες ἡμεῖς γ᾽ οἱ παρόντες ἐνθάδε

    . . . . .]ομέν σε παρανομεῖν εἰς τὴν θεόν   25

[Γ . . . . .]ο γ᾽, ἄνδρες· εὖ γε προσπαίζειν δοκεῖ

24 *e.g.* βλέπο]ντες (ὁρῶντες, ἅπαντες too short).   25
ἐάσ]ομέν Wilamowitz, too short for space. νομίζ]ομέν Zuntz,
ἀφήσομεν Warmington, κωλύσομεν D. L. P.   26 " Et
μὴ τοῦτ]ό γ᾽ et οὐκ εὔλ]ογ᾽ excedunt lacunam " Zuntz. In

ANONYMOUS

49   [Late 3 b.c.]   A FEAST

Ed. pr. *Hunt-Smyly, *Tebtunis Papyri*, iii. 1. 1933, p. 13,
no. 693. See Körte, *Archiv*, x. 265.

*This may be part of a Middle or a New Comedy, or neither :
Körte thinks an Alexandrian comedian likelier than Attic,
partly because of the non-Attic form* σευτλίον, *and the*

ἀ]λλ᾽ ἐπεὶ δοκεῖ περαίνειν τοὺς γάμου[ς ὅσον τάχος,

ἐ]π᾽ ἀγαθαῖς ἤδη τύχαισιν πρός σε [συνθήκας ποῶ.

(Here follow traces of seventeen lines : in the fourth
ἐπιδίδωμι τὸν ἀγρόν, *in the fifth* πρὸς σὲ κ[α]ὶ
πρὸς τὸν Βίων[α, *in the ninth* σ[ώφροσ]ιν¹
τρόποις ἔχαιρον; *the fifteenth line is bracketed,
perhaps for cancellation)*

π[ι]κρίδιον κ[ο]χλίον ἔπνιξεν, βολβὸς ἐπιχορεύ[εται,

φα . . σίου μικροῦ γενομένου σκόλυμος εἰσε[λήλυθε,

σευτλίον ῥυθμόν τιν᾽ (ε)ἶχεν, σιτίνης α . . ος παρ[ῆν. 5

236

ANONYMOUS

CHORUS. Are we who stand here to look on and let you offend against our goddess ?

(C) . . ., gentlemen. He thinks he's very funny. . . .

---

this line, and in v. 7 above (after βέλτιστε), ed. pr. marks a change of speaker (here after ἄνδρες). But in neither case with the support of Π, which denotes change of speaker (by leaving slight gaps between words) in vv. 13, 17, 21.

ANONYMOUS

A FEAST [Late 3 B.C.]

possibility that σιτίνης (ἄρτος) was intended for a nominative case. Perhaps from the conclusion of a Comedy. A marriage is about to take place. The speaker, who may be father of the bride, mentions certain gifts, among them a piece of land, which may have been part of the dowry. The foods mentioned later would most naturally refer to the wedding festivities.

SINCE you wish to have this marriage done without delay, here and now I make a pact with you for your good fortune : . . .

(*Here follow traces of seventeen lines including the phrases* I give you the land too . . . towards you and Bion . . . rejoiced in modest manners)

. . . stewed a bitter little shell-fish, purse-tassels came dancing to the table, . . . chopped small, golden-thistle made an entrance, beet kept a certain

---

¹ Suppl. Körte.   1-6 Suppl. Körte.   5 ἄ[ρτ]ος Körte.

237

ταῦτα καὶ τοσαῦτ' ἐπειδὴ παρεφάνη κάλ' ὀ[ψία,

(*Unintelligible remains of five more lines ; in the fourth,
οἰκίαν should perhaps be read for the unmetrical
σκιαν : the fifth is spoken by a second person,
including the phrase* χαῖρε πολλά)

ΦΙΛΗΜΩΝ

50 [2 A.D.] ΛΙΘΟΓΛΥΦΟΣ : ΑΠΟΣΠΑΣΜΑ

Ed. pr. (*a*) *Diels-Schubart, Berliner Klassikertexte*, i.
1904, p. 45. The fragment is entitled Λιθ[ο]γλύφος, an
otherwise unknown play. See *Schroeder, Nov. Com.
Fragm.* p. 60 ; Körte, *Rh. Mus.* 60, 1905, 411 ; Blass, *Archiv*,
iii. 291 ; Wendland, *G.G.A.* 1906, 366 ; Demiańczuk,
Suppl. Com. p. 71. ; Wagner, *Symbolarum ad comicorum*

(*a*) πρὸς τῶι μυροπωλίωι γὰρ ἀνθρώπων τινῶν
ἤκουσα χαλκοῦν περιπατεῖν κλέπτην τινά·
ἄπειρος ὢν δὲ τοῦ λεγομένου πράγματο[ς
'Αριστομίδην ἠρόμην παριόνθ' ὁρῶν.
ὁ δ' ἐνήλατ' εὐθύς μοι παραστὰς [τ]ῶι σκ[έ]λει 5
παίει τε λὰξ πύξ, ὥστε μ' ἐκθανεῖν· ἐπεὶ
μόλις γε φεύγων ἐξέπεσον ἄλληι λ[άθρ]α

(*b*) Εὐρι[πί]δης πού [φη]σιν οὕτως, [ὃς] μόνος
δύ[να]ται λ[έ]γε[ιν

7 λάθρα ed. pr.

* Allusion uncertain : *v.* Didymus in the sentence which
introduces this quotation, δύο 'Αριστομήδ[ει]ς εἰσίν, . . .
ἕτερος . . . 'Αθηναῖος ὁ Χαλκοῦς λεγόμενος. Perhaps Arist.

rhythm, and there was bread (?) of flour. Since all these lovely viands made their appearance . . .

(Unintelligible remains of five more lines)

PHILEMON

SCULPTOR, and a FRAGMENT [2 A.D.]

graec. historiam criticam capita IV, diss. Leips. 1905, esp. pp. 25-27 ; Platnauer, *New Chapters*, iii. 175, 177. (From the commentary of Didymus on Demosthenes.) (*b*) Grenfell-Hunt, *P. Oxy.* ix. 1912, no. 1176, fr. 39, col. vii. 32-36, p. 150. See *Schroeder, *op. cit.* p. 61 ; von Arnim, *Suppl. Eur.* p. 5 ; Demiańczuk, *op. cit.* p. 72 ; Körte, *Archiv*, vi. 249 ; Leo, *G.G.A.* 1912, 281.

(*a*) I heard some fellows near the scent-shop saying that a thief called Farthing (?) [a] was wandering about. As I didn't know what they were talking about, I asked Aristomedes,[b] whom I saw passing by. And he came straight up to me and jumped at me, on my leg, and smote me with foot and fist—I nearly fainted to death ; I ran away, and barely escaped elsewhere in hiding. . . .

(*b*) So says Euripides, who alone can speak.[c] . . .

was nicknamed " the Farthing " because he was very poor ; or because he was a miser ; or because of his kleptomania (*v.* the two pieces from Timocles below)—no sum of money was small enough to be safe from him.   [b] See below, p. 241 n. *d.*   [c] The Greek probably means " the only good *writer.*"

ΤΙΜΟΚΛΗΣ

51   [2 A.D.]   ΗΡΩΕΣ, ΙΚΑΡΙΟΙ

Ed. pr. Diels-Schubart, *Berliner Klassikertexte*, i. 1904,
p. 45. See *Schroeder, *Nov. Com. Fragm.* p. 61 ; literature
cited for Philemon above.

*The Icarians of Timocles has been inferred to be a satyric
play, since Athenaeus ix. 407 f entitles it Ἰκάριοι Σάτυροι :
but it is highly probable that this was merely the full title of
a comedy (Wagner, op. cit.) : personal allusions and attacks
have no place in a satyric drama.*

ΗΡΩΕΣ

(a) —— Ἑρμῆς δ' ὁ Μαίας ταῦτα συνδιακτορεῖ
    ἀντιπ[ρ]οθύμως· καταβέβηκεν ἄσμενος,
    χαριζόμενός γ' Ἀριστομήδηι τῶι καλῶι,
    ἵνα μηκέτ' αὐτὸν ὁ Σάτυρος κλέπτην λέγηι.

ΙΚΑΡΙΟΙ

(b) —— Μ[α]ρσύαν δὲ τὸν φ[ί]λαυλον Αὐτοκλέα
    δεδαρμέν[ο]ν   5
    γυμνὸν ἑστάναι καμίνωι προσπεπατταλευ-
       μένον
    Τηρέα τ' Ἀριστομήδην.

1 συνδιακονεῖ Körte.   2 ἀντιπρ. " zu Gegendiensten be-
reit " Körte : for the scansion in comedy, ἀντῑπρ., *cf.* Körte,
loc. cit. pp. 411-412.

ᵃ Allusion not understood.   ᵇ Marsyas, because *flayed*
(*i.e.* thrashed : the word may also suggest that he was ψωλός)
and because φίλαυλος, a lover of the flute (*i.e.* perhaps a lover
240

TIMOCLES

HEROES, and ICARIANS [2 A.D.]

[*In fr.* (b) *vv. 11-12 there is a direct address to the audience:
it is not certain that this could not occur in a satyric drama,
cf. Soph.* Ichneutae, *col. iv. 5, ed. pr.*]

About the Heroes *nothing is known. It has been con-
jectured (on very doubtful evidence, v. Wagner and Schroeder,
loc. cit.) that it was produced in or about the year 342 B.C.*

Evidently these two plays, like the Sculptor *of Philemon
(above), belong rather to Middle than to New Comedy.*

HEROES

(*a*) Hermes the son of Maea helps him conduct
his campaign, an eager enemy. He was delighted
to come down, as a favour to our pretty Aristomedes,
to stop Satyrus calling him a thief.[a]

ICARIANS

(*b*) —— . . . and Marsyas [b] the fluter—Autocles [c]
—to be flayed and stand naked and nailed to a
furnace ; also Tereus—Aristomedes.[d]

of flute-girls). Beazley has solved the mystery of the inner
meaning by a reference to Pollux vii. 108 (Ar. fr. 592 Hall):
πρὸ δὲ τῶν καμίνων τοῖς χαλκεῦσιν ἔθος ἦν γελοῖά τινα καταρτᾶν
ἢ ἐπιπλάττειν ἐπὶ φθόνου ἀποτροπῇ· ἐκαλεῖτο δὲ βασκάνια, ὡς
καὶ Ἀριστοφάνης λέγει· πλὴν εἴ τις πρίαιτο, δεόμενος | βασκάνιον
ἐπὶ κάμινον ἀνδρὸς χαλκέως. *Cf.* further Pernice, *Festschrift
für Benndorf*, p. 75. The point then is that Autocles is good
for nothing but to be a dummy or mascot, such as you
commonly saw erected on the furnace in a foundry.
[c] A fashionable ne'er-do-well, *cf.* Theophilus, *Boeot.* ii. 474
Kock, Athen. xii. 537 c.   [d] Trierarch 356-355 B.C.

241

————— διὰ τί Τηρέα καλεῖς;
————— διότι τηρ[ε]ῖν δεῖ παρόντος τοῦδε τὰ σκεύη
σφόδρα.
εἰ δὲ μή, Πρόκνη γενήσηι, κνώμενος τὸ
κρανίον,   10
ἂν ἀπολέσηις.
—————   ψυχρόν.
             ἀλλὰ πρὸς θεῶν ἐπί[σ]χετε
μηδὲ συρίξητε.

ΜΕΝΑΝΔΡΟΣ

52   [3 A.D.]   ΜΙΣΟΥΜΕΝΟΣ

Ed. pr. Wilamowitz, *Sitzungsberichte der königlich preussischen Akademie der Wissenschaften*, Berlin, 1918, p. 747. See *Körte, *Menander, reliquiae*, 3rd ed. 1938, praef. li, text p. 122 and *Ber. sächs. Akad.* 71, 1919, 28 ; Platnauer, *New Chapters*, iii. 169. Further fragments of this play :— *P. Oxy.* nos. 1013, 1605, perhaps 1238.

The attribution of this fragment to Menander's Μισούμενος *is practically certain (see Körte, loc. cit.).*

A soldier Thrasonides is in love with Crateia, his captive. Though his passion is extreme, his conduct towards her is irreproachable : yet she will have none of him.   Her father Demeas arrives, eager to purchase his daughter's freedom :

[ΓΕΤΑΣ   ]αμ' ἥκεις πρὸς ἡμᾶς. ἀλλὰ τί
παθὼν ἀνα]κάμπτεις καὶ πάλιν στέλλει διδοὺς
. . . .]ολάς; εἰ μή τι κακὸν ἡμᾶς
ποεῖς,

3 φέρειν στ]ολάς Körte : τὰς συμβ]ολάς Wilamowitz.

MENANDER

—— Why do you call him Tereus ?
—— Because, when he is about, you have to keep a sharp eye [a] on your belongings. Otherwise you'll soon be a Procne, scratching your skull,[b] if you lose them.
—— A frigid pun !
—— (*To the audience*) For God's sake, stop ! N whistling ! . . .

[a] Pun on Τηρεύς, τηρεῖν.   [b] Pun on πρό-κνη, πρό and κνῆν (scratch your head). Procne parallel because she *lost* her child.

MENANDER

UNPOPULAR   [3 A.D.]

he lodges next door to Thrasonides. In the first part of our fragment, Getas (servant to Thrasonides) is probably soliloquizing. He and his master suspect Demeas of designs upon Crateia, little knowing that he is her father. Crateia's nurse enters, and recognizes Demeas. Father and daughter now recognize each other ; but their happiness is rudely disturbed by the entry of jealous Thrasonides. The conclusion is not known but can easily be inferred : Thrasonides released Crateia, who rewarded his persevering and unselfish devotion with her consent to marriage. The play was very similar in plot and in characters to the same author's Perikeiromene.

GETAS. . . . you come to us. But what's the matter with you ?—giving me . . . and dodging and doubling back ? If you are not doing us down, why

243

τί παρεκε]λεύσω τοῦτό μ' ἐπὶ δεῖπνον πάλιν
τὸν δεσπ]ότην καλέσαντα; φανερός ἐστι γὰρ 5
. . . . . . β]αδιοῦμ' εἴσω δὲ καὶ πειράσομαι
κρύπτω]ν ἐμαυτὸν ἐπιθεωρῆσαί τι τῶν
ποιουμέ]νων ἔνδον λαλουμένων θ' ἅμα.
[ΤΡΟΦΟΣ   σοβαρώ]τερον τούτου μὰ τὼ θεὼ ξένον
οὐπώπο]τ' εἶδον. αἲ τάλας· τί βούλεται   10
ἔχειν πα]ρ' οἴκωι τὰς σπάθας τῶν γειτόνων;

(About twenty lines missing)

ἆ[ρ' ο]ὔ τιν' ὄψιν οὐδὲ προσδ[οκωμένην
ὅ[ρ]ῶ;
[ΚΡΑΤΕΙΑ]   τί βούληι, τηθία, τί μοι λαλεῖς;
πατὴρ ἐμὸς ποῦ;
[ΔΗΜΕΑΣ]   παιδίον Κράτεια.
[ΚΡΑΤΕΙΑ]   [τίς
καλεῖ με; πάππα χαῖρε πολλὰ φίλτατ[ε.   15
[ΔΗ.] ἔχω σε, τέκνον.
                [ΚΡ.] ὦ ποθούμενος φαν[είς.
ὁρῶ σ' ὃν οὐκ ἂν ὠιόμην ἰδεῖν ἔτι.
[ΓΕ.] ἐξῆλθεν ἔξω.
[ΘΡΑΣΩΝΙΔΗΣ]   παῖ, τί τοῦθ'; αὕτη τίς [εἶ;
ἄνθρωπε, τί ποεῖς οὗτος; οὐκ ἐγὼ 'λεγον;
ἐπ' αὐτοφώρωι τό[ν]δε τὸν ζητούμε[νον   20
ἔχω· γέρων οὗτός γε πολιὸς φαίνε[ται
ἐτῶν τις ἑξήκοντα· ὅμως δὲ κλαύ[σεται.
τίνα περιβάλλειν καὶ φιλεῖν οὗτος [δοκεῖς;

6 ἀδικῶν. β]αδ. Körte.   11 ἔχειν πα]ρ' Körte.   16
τέκνον: the scansion, and the absence of resolved feet in this
passage, and the style of the lines altogether, are deliberately
reminiscent of tragedy. Cf. Perikeiromene 338 sqq. Körte.
23 οὕτως Roberts, perhaps rightly.

___

[a] General sense and translation uncertain.   [b] Thraso-

did you tell me to do this after calling my master back to dinner ?[a] It's quite clear that he is . . . I will go indoors and hide myself and try to overhear what they are doing inside—as well as what they're saying.

NURSE (*entering*). Upon my word, never in my life have I seen such an impudent stranger ! Confound him, why should he want (to keep) his neighbours' swords at home ?[b] . . .

(*About twenty lines missing*)

Surely I see an unexpected vision !

CRATEIA. What do you want, Nurse ? What are you talking about ? Where's Father ?

DEMEAS. Crateia ! My little daughter !

CRATEIA. Who is calling me ? Oh Daddy, how nice to see you !

DEMEAS. My baby, in my arms !

CRATEIA. (*Tragically*) Thou art come, my heart's desire : I behold thee, whom I never thought to see again !

GETAS (*re-entering with Thrasonides*). He's[c] come out of doors !

THRASONIDES. Slave, what's all this? Who are you, woman ? You, fellow, what are you doing here ? Just what I said ! The very man I was looking for, caught in the act ! A graybeard of sixty, by the look of him, but he shall suffer for it. Here, who do you think you're cuddling and kissing ? . . .

nides, fearing a forcible attempt to kidnap Crateia, has summoned armed neighbours to his house. [c] *Sc.* Demeas : Getas is faithful to Thrasonides, and gives him immediate notice of Demeas's appearance in Crateia's company (so van Leeuwen, Körte : but the attribution of these words to Getas is by no means certain).

245

ΜΕΝΑΝΔΡΟΣ

53 [160 B.C.]   ? ΥΠΟΒΟΛΙΜΑΙΟΣ

Ed. pr. Weil, *Un papyrus inédit : nouveaux fragments d'Euripide et d'autres poètes grecs : Monuments Grecs publiés par l'association pour l'encouragement des études grecques en France*, no. 8, 1879, p. 25 with Plate. See Kock, *C.A.F.* iii. p. 420 ; Körte, *Menander, reliquiae*, 3rd ed. 1938, praef. lxiii, text p. 145 ; and esp. Herzog, *Philol.* 89, 1934, 185, *qu. v.* for further literature.

The ascription to Menander is very probable (evidence in

ἐρημία μέν ἐστι, κοὐκ ἀκούσεται
οὐδεὶς παρών μου τῶν λόγων ὧν ἂν λέγω.
ἐγὼ τὸν ἄλλον, ἄνδρες, ἐτεθνήκειν βίον
ἅπανθ᾽ ὃν ἔζην, τοῦτό μοι πιστεύετε.
πάνυ ταὐτὸ τὸ καλόν, τἀγαθόν, τὸ σεμνὸν (ἦν,) **5**
τὸ κακόν· τοιοῦτον ἦν τί μου πάλαι σκότος
περὶ τὴν διάνοιαν, ὡς ἔοικε, κείμενον,
ὃ πάντ᾽ ἔκρυπτε ταῦτα κἠφάνιζέ μοι.
νῦν δ᾽ ἐνθάδ᾽ ἐλθών, ὥσπερ εἰς Ἀσκληπιοῦ
ἐγκατακλιθεὶς σωθείς τε, τὸν λοιπὸν χρόνον 10
ἀναβεβίωκα· περιπατῶ, λαλῶ, φρονῶ.
τὸν τηλικοῦτον καὶ τοιοῦτον ἥλιον
νῦν πρῶτον εὗρον, ἄνδρες· ἐν τῆι σήμερον
ὑμᾶς ὁρῶ νῦν αἰθρίαι, τὸν ἀέρα,
τὴν ἀκρόπολιν, τὸ θέατρον, . . . 15

3 βίον Herzog, πάλαι Π: perhaps ἐγὼ τὸν ἄλλον βίον ἐτεθνή-
κειν πάλαι, or ἐγὼ τὸν αἰῶν᾽, ἄνδρες, ἐτεθνήκειν πάλαι. 15

MENANDER

Possibly THE CHANGELING [160 B.C.]

Herzog's commentary, loc. cit.) : the attribution to his Hypobolimaeus *(tentatively proposed ibid.) is a mere guess.*

The lines are evidently from the beginning of a play : a young man has come to town from the country ; studies in philosophy have opened his eyes and stimulated his imagination. He will probably find in the course of the action that his philosophy will not help him in intrigue, or protect him from distress.

WELL, here is solitude ; whatever I say, there's nobody here to listen. Gentlemen,[a] believe me : I have been dead the whole of my life so far. There seemed no difference between the beautiful, the good, the holy, and the evil,—such was the cloud of darkness that used to hang about my wits, I fancy. It hid all this from me, made it invisible.

Now that I have come here, I have come to life again for the future, like a man who lies down in Asclepius's temple and is saved ; I walk and talk and think. I never discovered the sun before—so big, so fine ! On this bright morning for the first time I see yourselves, the daylight, the acropolis, the theatre . . .

[a] Evidently he is rehearsing a speech for some occasion : otherwise this address to the "Gentlemen" would appear inconsistent with the "solitude" to which the previous lines refer.

At the foot of the piece is written αριστων φιλοσοφος μαθηματα : for which see Herzog, *loc. cit.*, Körte, praef. lxiii.

ΜΕΝΑΝΔΡΟΣ

54 [Parchment 5 A.D.] SMICRINES, CHAEREAS[a]

Ed. pr. Vitelli, *Papiri Greci e Latini*. ii. 1913, no. 126, p. 27. See Coppola, *Riv. Indo-Greco-Ital.* vi. 1922, 35 (revised text); Körte, *Archiv*, vii. 146 and **Menander, reliquiae*, 3rd ed. praef. lvi, text p. 138; Ulbricht, *Krit. und Exeg. Stud. zu Menander*, 1 (qu. v. for the case in favour of ascription to Menander); Herzog. *Hermes*, 51, 1916, 315; Wilamowitz, *Gnomon*, 5, 1929, 466; Körte, *P.-W.-K.* xv. 785; Jensen, *Menandr. reliqu.* p. 128; van Leeuwen, *Men. fab. reliqu.* p. 178.

The Prologue (doubtless preceded by an earlier scene, see Vitelli, p. 29, Körte, Archiv, 148, Menander lvii.) is spoken by Fortune. Her story is this :—An old miser Smicrines lives alone with one old woman-servant. His younger brother Chaereas lives next door (the houses of the brothers form the background of the scene). Chaereas is wealthy and popular, and has a wife and daughter. Now a certain young man (hereinafter A) went abroad and left his sister in the

(From the Prologue)

[ΤΥΧΗ] ἔχειν ἄπαντα, τοῦτο γινώσκε[ι
    καὶ ζῆι μονότροπος γραῦν ἔχων [δούλην
    μίαν.
    οὗ δ' εἰσελήλυθ' ὁ θεράπων ἐν γειτόνω[ν
    ἀδελφὸς οἰκεῖ τοῦδε τοῦ φιλαργύρου
    νεώτερός τ[ις] ὤν, προσήκων κατὰ γένος   5
    τῶι μειρακίωι, χρηστός τε τῶι τρόπωι πάνυ

---

[a] Ulbricht, p. 20, n. 37, thinks ("satis audacter," as Körte says) that the marriage to which Sm. objects is one between A and the daughter of Chaereas. See next note.
[b] Herzog thinks that A is the son of Smicrines: that he has returned from his journey, and wishes—against his

248

MENANDER

SMICRINES, CHAEREAS [Parchment 5 A.D.]

*care of Chaereas, his relative. Chaereas, observing that
A's property has greatly deteriorated in his absence, deter-
mines to repair A's fortunes by giving the sister in marriage
to his own stepson. When this prologue is done, Smicrines
appears and defends himself against the charge of avarice :
he refers to gold and silver possessions, but it is wholly un-
certain what part these played in the sequel : he announces
his intention to prevent the impending marriage.[a] The rest
of the first act and the greatest part of the second are lost in
the following lacuna of about 220 lines : in the next frag-
ment, Daos (a slave) conspires with one or two persons (one
of them surely Chaereas) to deceive and outwit Smicrines.
The essence of the stratagem is to be the fictitious death of
Chaereas. The purpose of this stratagem is a matter for (or
rather beyond) conjecture.[b] In the third act, Daos gradually
reveals to Smicrines the supposed death of his brother
Chaereas : he quotes Aeschylus and Carcinus to prepare him
for the heavy blow, Euripides to soothe him afterwards.*

(From the Prologue)

FORTUNE. . . . to have everything, as he knows. . . .
He lives all alone with one old maid-servant. Now,
in the neighbour's house, where that attendant went
in just now, lives this miser's younger brother. He
is related to our young friend, a thoroughly decent

father's will—to marry the daughter of Chaereas. The
fictitious death of Ch. is designed so that his daughter
may pass into the power of his nearest kinsman, viz.
Smicrines: this will perhaps assist A in his intention to
marry her. This view seems to me completely refuted by
Wilamowitz, *loc. cit.*, Körte, *Menander*, praef. lix.

καὶ πλούσιος, γυναῖκ' ἔχων καὶ παρθένου
μιᾶς πατήρ· [παρ'] ὧι κατέλιπεν ἔτι νέαν
ὁ μειρακίσκος τὴν ἀδελφήν· [αἱ κόραι
αὗται π[αρ' αὑ]τοῖς εἰσὶν ἐκτεθραμμ[έναι.   10
ὧν δ', [ὡς] προεῖπα, χρηστὸς οὗτο[ς τῶι
    τρόπωι,
ὁρῶ[ν κατ]ὰ τὴν ἀποδημίαν [τὰ τοῦ νέου
οἰκεῖα μ[έ]τρ[ι]α παντελῶς, τὴν παρθένον
οὗτος συνοικίζειν νεαν[ίαι τινὶ
ἔμελλεν υἱῶι τῆς γυναικός, [ὃν ἔτεκεν   15
ἐξ ἀνδρὸς ἑτέρου [

              (Twelve lines missing)

                    ] αὐτὸν οἷός ἐστ' ἀνὴρ
        ]ν ἐπὶ τἀρχαῖα. λοιπὸν τοὔνομα
το]ὑμὸν φράσαι, τίς εἰμί· πάντων κυρία
τούτων βραβεῦσαι καὶ διοικῆσαι, Τύχη.   20
ΣΜΙΚΡ[ΙΝΗΣ] ἵνα μή τις εἴπηι μ' ὅτι φιλάργυρος
    σφόδρα,
οὐκ ἐξετάσας πόσον ἐστὶν ὃ φέρει χρυσίον
οὐδ' ὁπόσα τἀργυρώματ' οὐδ' ἀριθμὸν
    λαβὼν
οὐδενός, ἑτοίμως εἰσενεγκεῖν ἐνθάδε
εἴασα· βασκαίνειν γὰρ εἰώθασί με   25
ἐπὶ παντί. τὸ γὰρ ἀκριβὲς εὑρεθή[σετ]αι,
ἕως ἂν οἱ φέροντες ὦσιν οἰκέτ[αι.
οἶμαι μὲν οὖν αὐτοὺς ἑκόντας τοῖς νόμοις
καὶ τοῖς δικαίοις ἐμμενεῖν· ἐὰν δὲ μή,
οὐδεὶς ἐπιτρέψει. τοὺς δὲ γινομένους γάμους   30
τούτους προειπεῖν βούλομ' αὐτοῖς μὴ ποεῖν.
ἴσως μὲν ἄτοπον καὶ λέγειν· οὐκ ἐν γάμοις

(About two hundred and twenty lines missing)

fellow, and well-off. He has a wife and one daughter.
In this house our friend left his sister, still a young
girl ; and in this family the two lasses have been
brought up.

Now this brother, being, I repeat, a decent char-
acter, and observing that our young friend's property
had become very modest in his absence, was about
to marry the sister to a son of his wife by her first
husband. . . .

(Twelve lines missing)

. . . him, what sort of man he is . . . to the
principal. It only remains for me to reveal my name
and identity : I am the mistress, arbiter and disposer
of all these events—FORTUNE ! *(Exit.)*

SMICRINES *(entering)*. No man shall call me
"nothing but a miser" : that is why I readily
allowed him to fetch it in here, without examining
the amount of money he brings, nor the amount of
plate, nor the quantity of anything. Everything I
do, they malign me. The exact sum will be dis-
covered anyway, so long as the carriers are my own
slaves. Well, it's my opinion that they will con-
sent to abide by law and justice. If they don't,
nobody is going to indulge them. I want to warn
them not to perform this marriage that is going on.
It may seem silly to say so, but in marriage . . .
not . . .

(About two hundred and twenty lines missing)

---

10 αὐ]ταῖς Jensen, Körte ; αὐτοῖς Vitelli.   18 νένευκε]ν
Wilamowitz, Körte.   22 ὁπόσον ἐσθ' ὃ φέρει Π, corr.
Wilamowitz, Körte.

(Beginnings of two lines)

—— ἐγὼ δὲ τοῦ[τ]ον τάδε βεβούλευμαι [παθεῖν.
—— ἀπόθνηισκ᾿ [ἀγαθῆι] τύχηι. —— ποήσω, μηδο[
ἔγωγ᾿ ἀφίεμ᾿· ἀλλὰ τηρεῖτ᾿ ἀνδρικῶς   35
τὸ πρᾶγμα. —— τίς δ᾿ ἡμῖν συ[ν]ε[ίσε]ται;
—— μόνηι
δεῖ τῆι γυναικὶ ταῖς τε παιδίσκαις φράσαι
αὐταῖς, ἵνα μὴ κλάωσι, τοὺς δ᾿ ἄλλους ἐᾶ[ν
ἔνδον παροινεῖν εἴς με, νομίσαντας . . κ . [. .
—— ὀρθῶς λέγεις. εἴσω τις ἀγέτω τουτονί·   40
ἔξει τιν᾿ ἀμέλει διατριβὴν ου[
ἀγωνίαν τε, τὸ πάθος ἂν ἐνστῆι [μ]όνον
ὅ τ᾿ ἰατρὸς ἡμῖν πιθανό[τητ]α σχῆι τινά.

χ[ο]ροϒ

[ΣΜΙΚΡΙΝΗΣ] ταχύ γ᾿ ἦλθ᾿ ὁ Δᾶος πρός με τὴν τῶν
χρη[μά]των
φέρων ἀπογραφήν, πολύ τ᾿ [ἐμοῦ] πεφρόντικε.   45
Δᾶος μετὰ τούτων ἐστί[ν. ἀλλὰ νὴ Δία,
καλῶς ἐπόησεν· πρόφασιν εἴληφ᾿ ἀσμένως
πρὸς αὐτόν, ὥστε μὴ φιλανθρώπως ἔτι
ταῦτ᾿ ἐξετάζειν, ἀλλ᾿ ἐμαυτῶι συμφόρως.
τὰ γὰρ οὐ φανερὰ δήπουθέν ἐστι διπλάσια.   50
ἐγῶιδα τούτου τὰς τ[έ]χνας τοῦ δραπέτου.
[ΔΑΟΣ] ὦ δαίμονες, φοβ[ερ]όν γε, νὴ τὸν Ἥλιον,
τὸ συμβεβ[ηκός· ο]ὐκ ἂν ὠιήθην ποτὲ
ἄνθρωπο[ν εἰς] τοσοῦτον οὑτωσὶ ταχὺ
πάθος ἐμ[π]εσεῖν. σκηπτός τις εἰς τὴν
οἰκίαν   55
ῥαγδαῖος ἐμπέπτωκε. [ΣΜ.] τί ποτε βού-
λεται;

MENANDER

(Beginnings of two lines)

—— I have made up my mind—this is what happens to him ! . . .

—— Die now, and good luck attend you !

—— I will do it ; I will not let go (?). Attend now to the business like brave men.

—— Who will be privy to our plot ?

—— Only the wife and the girls ; they must be told, to prevent their crying. The others can handle me indoors like drunkards, thinking . . .

—— Quite right. Take him indoors, somebody ! Certainly, he shall pass the time in . . . and anguish, if only the trouble will begin, and the doctor lends us some degree of plausibility . . .

(Choral Song)

SMICRINES (*entering*). Daos is soon back with the accounts for me.—His consideration for me is most touching. He is on their side ; bless my soul, I'm much obliged to him ! I am glad to get the excuse to attack him,—to examine his papers from the standpoint of self-interest, no longer like a public benefactor. If a figure's missing, multiply by two ! —I know the scoundrel's little games.

DAOS (*entering*). Ye Gods, how terrible—by the sun I do protest !—how terrible are these events ! Never would I have thought that man so suddenly could fall so deep into disaster ! How violent a thunderbolt has fallen upon the house !

SMICRINES. What on earth does he mean ? . . .

---

33 Identity of speakers here (*to v.* 43) is most uncertain : see Körte for one of several possibilities. ποήσω v. 34 is doubtless spoken by Chaereas, so probably is v. 36 μόνηι, **etc.** 39 [νε]κ[ρόν Körte. 41 οὐ[κ εὔκολον Körte.

(*Traces of ten lines*)

[ΔΑΟΣ] καὶ δ[ὴ θε]ὸς μὲν αἰτίαν φύει βροτοῖς
ὅταν κακῶσαι δῶμα παμπήδην θέληι.

[ΣΜΙΚΡΙΝΗΣ] . . . . οσα γνωμολογεῖς, τρισ-
άθλιε;

[ΔΑ.] οὐδὲν παρὰ λόγον δεινόν [ΣΜ.] οὐδὲ παύ-
σεται; 60

[ΔΑ. οὐ]δ᾽ ἔστ᾽ ἄπιστον τῶν ἐν ἀνθρώποις κακῶν,
ὡς] Καρκίν[ο]ς φησ᾽· ἐν μιᾶι γὰρ ἡμέραι
τὸν εὐτυχ[ῆ τίθη]σι δυστυχῆ θεός.
σὺ πάντα δ᾽ [εἴσηι, Σ]μικρίνη. [ΣΜ.] λέγεις
δὲ τί;

[ΔΑ.] ἀδελφός, ὦ Ζεῦ, πῶς φράσω; σχεδόν τι
σοῦ 65
τέθνηκεν. [ΣΜ. ὁ λα]λῶν ἀρτίως ἐνταῦθ᾽
ἐμοί;
τί παθών; [ΔΑ.] χολή, λύπη τις, ἔκστασις
φρενῶν,
πνιγμός. [ΣΜ.] Πόσειδον καὶ θεοί, δεινοῦ
πάθους.

[ΔΑ.] οὐκ ἔστιν οὐδὲν δειν[ὸν] ὧδ᾽ εἰπεῖν ἔπος
οὐδὲ πάθος—[ΣΜ.] ἀποκναίει[ς σ]ύ. [ΔΑ.] τὰς
γὰρ συμφορὰς 70
ἀπροσδοκήτους δαίμον[ες δι]ώρισαν.
Εὐριπίδου τοῦτ᾽ ἐστὶ το[ὐξε]υρημένον,
οὐ τῶν τυχόντων. [ΣΜ.] εἰσελήλυθ[εν] δὲ τίς
ἰατρός; [ΔΑ.] †οὐδείς· οἴχεται μὲν οὖν ὁ
Χαιρέας†

57–58 = Aesch. *Niobe* fr. 156 N.   59 τί ταῦτα πάντ]α
Jensen, Körte : text ed. pr.   61–63 quotation from
Carcinus, not otherwise known.   62 που φησ εν μιαι

MENANDER

(Traces of ten lines)

Daos. Truly " God doth create a fault in man,"
  " When he will utterly destroy his house ! "
Smicrines. . . . your strings of proverbs, confound you ?
Daos. " No terror is past reason——"
Smicrines.   Won't he stop ?
Daos. " None of man's miseries is past belief——"
  (I quote from Carcinus)—" for in one day
  God brings the happy to unhappiness."
Smicrines, you shall know all !
Smicrines. What do you mean ?
Daos. Your brother (God, how shall I tell him ?)—
your brother is at death's door.
Smicrines. What ! And only a moment ago he
was here, talking to me ! What is the matter with
him ?
Daos. Distemper, a kind of melancholy, disturb-
ance of the mind, suffocation——
Smicrines. Heaven help us, what an illness !
Daos. " There is no horror, almost, in the world,
  " Nor suffering——"
Smicrines.   You'll wear me out !
Daos.   " —For Heaven
  " Decreed man's sorrow to be unexpected."
Euripides is the inventor of these lines—none of
your second raters !
Smicrines. What doctor is attending him ?
Daos. None whatever. So Chaereas is done for. . . .

γαρ ημεραι Π, corr. Vitelli.   69-70 =Eur. *Orestes* 1-2.
70-71 quotation from Eur., otherwise unknown.   74
Corrupt.   οὐδείς· οἴχετ' οὖν ὁ Χαιρέας Körte.

? ΜΕΝΑΝΔΡΟΣ

55   [2 A.D.]   ? ΘΕΟΦΟΡΟΥΜΕΝΗ

Ed. pr. *Vitelli-Norsa, *Annali della reale Scuola normale
superiore di Pisa*, Serie ii. 4, 1935, p. 1. See Körte, *Hermes*,
70, 1935, 431, *Archiv*, xiii. 1938, 102 and *Menander, reli-
quiae*, 3rd ed. 1938, praef. xlv, text 101 ; Lesky, *Hermes*, 72,
1937, 123.

Menander's Θεοφορουμένη *has been suggested as the source
of the fragment : though the word* ἱππόπορνε *v. 4 is an
obstacle to the attribution. Such words were studiously
avoided by Menander (and indeed by New Comedy in general :
cf. however* ἐβίνησα, *p. 282, below ;* σκατοφάγος *Men.* Perik.
204, Sa. 205, *is a different type of word). Vitelli observes
that the word* ἱππόπορνος *is found thrice in Alciphron,
whose frequent dependence upon Menander is undoubted :
but this affords no legitimate inference here. The case in
favour of the ascription is this :—(1) The form* παράστα *v. 13,
attested for Menander (see Körte,* Hermes, *p. 432) and for
him alone. (2) The rare word* θεοφορεῖται *v. 10, and the
apparent presence of a divinely-possessed girl on the stage.
On this evidence we must concede that there is some, perhaps
a strong, probability that our fragment is part of Menander's
Theophoroumene : we shall not use such phrases as " end-
gültig gesichert " (Lesky, p. 124).*

*The content of the opening lines is impossible to elucidate
with certainty. Körte thinks that the first line and half the
second are spoken by the divinely-possessed girl (Theo-
phoroumene) : the next four and a half lines by Craton,
alleged to be a father who disapproves of his son's intrigue
with the girl. Craton and his friend Lysias are present
unseen by the girl, whose speech they overhear and mis-
interpret. E.g. the girl says* ἔπ[ται]σα τἀμὰ δῶρα *meaning
" I have stumbled because of my gifts," i.e. her gift of divine*

256

? MENANDER

Possibly THEOPHOROUMENE   [2 A.D.]

*inspiration : Craton thinks she means concrete literal gifts,
mistakenly. Then* τίς ἔλαβέ σε *is misunderstood—she had
used the word* ἐλήφθην *in some different sense above. I
hope that my profound disagreement with this interpretation
will not be thought inconsistent with my respect for the
interpreter : but* (1) *there is no indication in* Π *of a change
of speaker after* δῶρα *in v. 2 ; yet such a change is essential
to K.'s theory :* (2) ἔλαβε(ς) *is not a misunderstanding of
anything : coming between the words* δῶρα *and* δόντα, *it is
part of their context and means simply " received " (the
gifts) :* (3) *in K.'s view,* μαίνει *vv.* 7 *and* 8 *must be said by
Lysias to* Craton ; *yet in fact, since there is an apparently
demented woman on the scene, the words should obviously be
addressed to* her, *not to the irate father by his companion :*
(4) ἔπταισα τἀμὰ δῶρα *could not bear the meaning which
K. gives it : the plain accusative is unparalleled (*ἐὰν πταίωσί
τι *and similar phrases are of course not relevant parallels) :*
(5) *there are sundry difficulties of detail.—*τὸ δέ *v.* 3 *is un-
translatable in K.'s text : the sense given by K. to* ἔλαβε *is
only dubiously possible :* τοῦτό γ' αὐτό *v.* 8 *should =*τὸ μαίνε-
σθαι, *referring directly to the charge* μαίνει *vv.* 7, 8 ; *it
cannot do so in K.'s view : the connexion of v.* 7 τί οὖν οὐκ
κτλ. *is a little obscure (given to Craton in K.'s text).   At
least it will be admitted that Körte's view presents serious
difficulties ; that in several places (esp. in the case of the
words* ἔλαβε(ς) *and* μαίνει) *it ignores the most obvious
interpretation of the lines ; and that it is, at best, only one
among other possibilities.*

   *My own reconstruction is by no means free from diffi-
culties.   We must, I think, suppose that the Theophoroumene*

*does not overhear the proposal of a test (vv. 9-10) : perhaps,
if she is apparently mad and tearing in confusion to and fro
across the scene, this difficulty is not very great. Further,
I need hardly say that I am dissatisfied with the sense which
I give to v. 7* τί οὖν οὐκ ἔνδον ἐγκεκλειμένη [a] ; *and with the
change—slight as it is—from* τι[ς] *to* π[ως] *in v. 4 : but I do
not understand either Vitelli's* τὸ δὲ | τίς ἔλαβες *or Körte's*
τὸ δὲ | τίς ἔλαβέ σ'.—*in both, the sense of* τὸ δὲ (*and of* ἔλαβες,
ἔλαβε) *is immensely obscure. I print my own text in the
faint hope that it will prompt the reader to something better.*

[ΚΟΡΗ . .   ] κατατάξαντες οἶδ' ἀπ' ὀμ-
    [μάτων
    επ[. . .]σα· τἀμὰ δῶρα—ἀκούεις, ἡ κόρη;—
    τὰ δῶρα, φησί, τἀμά μ' ἐξεῖλον. τόδε
    π[ῶς] ἔλαβες, ἱππόπο[ρ]νε; τὸν δὲ δόν[τα
    σοι
    πόθεν οἶσθα τοῦτον; τί δὲ νεανίσκο[5
    ἢ σὺ τί λαβοῦσα στέφανον ἔξω περιπατ[εῖς;
[ΛΥΣΙΑΣ] μαίνει. [ΚΟΡΗ] τί οὖν οὐκ ἔνδον ἐγκε-
    κλειμ[ένη
[ΛΥ.] μαίνει. [Α] φλυαρεῖς· [τ]οῦτό γ' αὐτό,
    Λυσία,
    οὐ προσποεῖται; [ΛΥ.] πεῖραν ἔξεστιν
    λα[βεῖν
    εἰ θεοφορεῖται· ταῖς ἀληθείαισι γὰρ   10
    νῦν εἰς τὸ πρόσθεν ἐνθάδ' ἐκπηδᾶι [χορὸς

1 οἶδ' or οἶδ'.   2 ἐπ[ται]σα Körte.   2-3 Punctua-
tion by Beazley.   4 π[ῶς] D. L. P.: τί[ς] ed. pr.   5 τί
δὲ; νεανίσκο[ν λέγεις; ed. pr.: τί δὲ νεανίσκο[ν καλεῖς; Körte:

MENANDER

I suppose that the divinely-possessed maiden is reporting—
in wildest excitement and distress—an accusation of theft
brought against her : a young man is alleged to have been her
accomplice. Lysias (whose name has no precedent in Comedy)
proposes to his companion a test to determine whether the girl
is feigning madness or not. It is clear that without further
evidence the antecedents and sequel of these lines cannot fairly
be conjectured. (It is possible that the girl is addressing
her report to Lysias, and that A is the robbed man who
has brought the accusation against her.)

GIRL. . . . shedding (tears) from their eyes, . . .
" My presents !—do you hear, young woman ? "—he
says, " they took my presents away from me ! How
did you get *this*,[b] strumpet ? How did you come to
know this fellow who gave them to you ? What is
the lad . . ., and why are you strolling the streets
with a wreath ? "

LYSIAS. You're mad !

GIRL. Then why am I not shut up ?

LYSIAS. You're mad !

(A) Nonsense !—Surely it's just this madness that
she is assuming, Lysias ?

LYSIAS. We can take a test, to see if she has demons
in her. For here and now in very truth a choir of
the Mother of the Gods comes bounding forward, or

---

[a] Perhaps this sentence is part of the girl's reported speech,
recapitulating τί . . . ἔξω περιπατεῖς after the interruption
μαίνει. If so, there is no reason to suppose that she is address-
ing Lysias and his companion, or even aware of their presence.
This may be the simpler and preferable view.   [b] One
of the stolen gifts.

---

possibly τί δὲ (or δ' ὁ) νεανίσκο[ς ποεῖ, κτλ. D. L. P.
10 Stop after γάρ, not before ταῖς, Maas.   11-12 Suppl.
Roberts.

μητρὸς θεῶν, μᾶλλον δὲ κορυβάν[των τινῶν.
αὐλεῖ. παράστα δ' ἐνθαδὶ πρὸς τὰς θύρ[ας
τοῦ πανδοκείου. [Α] νὴ Δί', εὖ γε, Λυσία,
ὑπέρευ (γε)· τοῦτο βούλομαι· καλὴ θέα   15

13 παράστα Π, defended by Eduard Fraenkel, Maas,
Körte: παραστὰ(s) ed. pr.

ΜΕΝΑΝΔΡΟΣ

56   [2–3 A.D.]   ΓΝΩΜΑΙ

Ed. pr. *Kalbfleisch, *Papyri Iandanae*, v., *Literarische
Stücke und Verwandtes, bearbeitet von Joseph Sprey*, 1931,
no. 77, p. 180, Plate XVI. See Körte, *Archiv*, x. 1932, 56 ;
Platnauer, *New Chapters*, iii. 172.

(1) ὡς ἡδὺ φιλ[ία] μὴ λόγ[οι]s ε[
(2) ὡς χαλεπόν ἐστιν οἶ[νος, ἂν τἀνδρὸς κρατῆι.
(3) ὡς εὐάλωτος πρὸς τὸ κέρδο[s ἡ φύσις.
(4) ὡς ἡδὺ γ[ον]έων καὶ τέκνων σ[υμφωνία.
(5) ὦ παῖ, Διόνυ[σο]ν φεῦγε [κἂν] ἀλ[γῆις σφόδρα.

2, 3 Suppl. Crönert.   4 Herzog.   5 Kalbfleisch.

ΣΤΡΑΤΩΝ

57   [Late 3 B.C.]   ΦΟΙΝΙΚΙΔΕΣ

Ed. pr. Guérard-Jouguet, *Un Livre d'Ecolier : publications
de la société royale égyptienne de papyrologie, Textes et
Documents*, ii., le Caire, p. 34, Plates VIII, IX. See Körte,
Archiv, xiii. 1938, 108. and *P.-W.-K. s.v. Strato*, no. 11.

rather a crowd of Corybants.   They are playing the
flute.   Stand by the door of the inn here.

(A) Well done, by Jove, well done indeed, Lysias !
That's what I want !   A fine sight (?). . . .

MENANDER

MAXIMS   [2–3 A.D.]

*Five of ten gnomes (γνῶμαι Μενάνδρου is written at the
foot), of which the other five were already known and ascribed
to Menander.*

(1) How sweet is friendship, if not . . . by words.
(2) How hard a master is wine, if man becomes its
slave !
(3) How easily human nature yields to profit !
(4) How sweet is harmony of child and parent !
(5) Son, fly from Dionysus, though it hurt you
sorely !

STRATON

PHOENICIDES   [Late 3 B.C.]

*The first 47 lines of this fragment were already known
from Athenaeus ix. 382 c, where they are assigned to the
Φοινικίδες of Straton (=Com. Att. Fragm. iii. p. 361 Kock).
Little more is known of this poet.   Athenaeus xiv. 659 b*

LITERARY PAPYRI

*attributes the first four lines of the same piece to Philemon :
Eustathius quotes v. 34 as the work of τῶν τις παλαιῶν :
Suidas ascribes to Straton a Φοῖνιξ (doubtless the same play
as Athenaeus's Φοινικίδες) and assigns him to the Middle
Comedy, erroneously.*

*Of the 47 verses quoted by Athenaeus, our papyrus con-
tains (in whole or in part) only 28, adding at the end three
lines hitherto unknown to us. Of the missing lines, three (the
first three of the piece) were certainly written in the papyrus,
now lost in the mutilation of its beginning. Vv. 9-10, 12,
16 and 22 of Athenaeus's text were definitely unknown to, or
for some reason omitted by, the writer of the papyrus. Vv.
26-37 of Athenaeus's text are missing from the papyrus in a
lacuna which, it appears, is not large enough to have included
more than four or five of those twelve lines.*

*Further : in the lines which both texts have in common,
there are many wide divergencies in reading.*

*The first editors are clearly correct in their view that the
additional lines in Athenaeus are all, or nearly all, interpola-
tions deliberately inserted to " improve " the piece. That
the omissions in Π are not accidental, is proved by the fact
that they nowhere spoil, much less destroy, the sense of their
contexts. There seems to be no reason why the copyist of Π
should have omitted the lines voluntarily ; and the remaining
view, that the lines are not omissions from Π but additions
made later to Π's original, is supported by the fact that in
each case a clear motive for interpolation is visible. In
general their motive is, as the first editors observed, to stress
and emphasize a point or joke, so as to make it clearer to the
spectator (or reader). Thus v. 16 is virtually nothing more
than a repetition of v. 11 ; v. 12 a repetition of v. 15 ; v. 22
was evidently added to make a clearer connexion ; vv. 9-10 to
expand the joke about μέροπες (v. 10 is intelligible only in
light of the double meaning of μέροπες = (a) " mortals,"
(b) a sort of bird : here such an ambiguity goes clearly beyond*

STRATON

*the original purpose of the passage—the use of obscure
Homeric words in place of their colloquial equivalents).*

It is important to observe further that the inserting of
an interpolation leads to changes in the reading of the
context. Such changes may be either accidental, as in v. 14,
where the false reading ἀνελογιζόμην was caused simply by
a lapse in memory or attention under the influence of the
preceding ἐλογιζόμην in the interpolated v. 12 ; or deliberate,
as in v. 17 where the interpolation of v. 16 makes the reading
ὁ δ᾽ impossible—it is therefore changed to σφόδρ᾽, and this in
turn necessitates the substitution of πάνυ for σφόδρα in v. 18.
Just so the interpolation of οὐκοῦν ἔφη in v. 22 led to the
deliberate change of οὐκ οἶδ᾽ ἔφην at the end of the next line to
οὐ μανθάνω.

These characteristics of interpolation were already obvious
to us in our Greek Tragedies. The motive is especially
common—the desire to emphasize, or to explain, a point in
the original which, in a later age, might not be sufficiently, or
indeed at all, appreciated. (Cf. Schol. Soph. Ai. 839–842 τὼς
αὐτοσφαγεῖς· ταῦτα νοθεύεσθαί φασιν ὑποβληθέντα πρὸς σαφήνειαν
τῶν λεγομένων : my Actors' Interpolations, pp. 76, 117,
etc.) And the fact that interpolation might lead to con-
sequent changes in the surrounding context was already
observed in a number of tragic passages.

It cannot of course be proved that the interpolations in
Straton were made by actors : but the analogy of Tragedy
makes it probable.

As for the variations in those lines which both texts present
to us : most of them are examples of that substitution of
more or less synonymous or similar words and phrases which
is so peculiarly common in Tragedy and indeed generally in
dramatic texts, and which is most easily explained by refer-
ence to a fault of the actor's memory : no two actors reciting
500 lines of Euripides or Shakespeare will use exactly the
same words throughout : in Eur. Hec. 44 one would say

τῶιδ' ἐμὴν ἐν ἤματι, another τὴν ἐμὴν τῆιδ' ἡμέραι (see
further Actors' Interpolations, p. 100). Thus here we

Σφίγγ' ἄρρεν', οὐ μάγειρον, εἰς τὴν οἰκίαν
εἴληφ'. ἁπλῶς γὰρ οὐδὲ ἓν μὰ τοὺς θεοὺς
ὧν ἂν λέγηι συνίημι. καινὰ ῥήματα
πεπορισμένος πάρεστιν· ὡς εἰσῆλθε γάρ,
εὐθύς μ' ἐπηρώτησε προσβλέψας μέγα,   5
πόσους κέκληκας μέροπας ἐπὶ δεῖπνον; λέγε.
ἐγὼ κέκληκα μέροπας ἐπὶ δεῖπνον; χολᾶις.
τοὺς δὲ μέροπας τούτους με γινώσκειν δοκεῖς;
[οὐδεὶς παρέσται· τοῦτο γὰρ νὴ τὸν Δία]
[ἐστὶ κατάλοιπον, μέροπας ἐπὶ δεῖπνον καλεῖν]. 10
οὐδ' ἄρα παρέσται δαιτυμὼν οὐθεὶς ὅλως;
[οὐκ, οἶμαί γε, Δαιτυμών· ἐλογιζόμην·]
ἥξει Φιλῖνος, Μοσχίων, Νικήρατος,
ὁ δεῖν', ὁ δεῖνα· κατ' ὄνομ' ἐπεπορευόμην·
οὐκ ἦν ἐν αὐτοῖς οὐδὲ εἷς μοι Δαιτυμών.   15
[οὐδεὶς παρέσται, φημί. τί λέγεις; οὐδὲ εἷς;]
ὁ δ' ἠγανάκτησ' ὥσπερ ἠδικημένος
ὅτι οὐ κέκληκα Δαιτυμόνα· καινὸν σφόδρα.
οὐδ' ἄρα θύεις ῥηξίχθον'; οὐκ, ἔφην, ἐγώ.
βοῦν εὐρυμέτωπον; οὐ θύω βοῦν, ἄθλιε.   20
μῆλα θυσιάζεις ἄρα; μὰ Δι' ἐγὼ μὲν οὔ·
[οὐδέτερον αὐτῶν, προβάτιον δ'. οὐκοῦν, ἔφη,]

1-3 absent in lacuna in Π.   9-10 om. Π.   10
ἐστὶ Athen., ἔτι Dobree, Kock.   11 οὐδεὶς Athen.
12 om. Π.   14 ἀνελογιζόμην Athen.   16 om. Π.
17 σφόδρ' ἠγαν. Athen.   18 εἰ μὴ κέκλ. Athen., καινὸν πάνυ
Athen.   19 ἐρυσίχθον' Athen.   20 βοῦν δ' Athen.
22 om. Π.

---

[a] He meant, " how many *people* ": he uses the Homeric

STRATON

have the "synonymous" variants εἰ μὴ—ὅτι οὐ *v. 18,* ἄλλα ῥήματα—ἕτερα μυρία *v. 40,* ἤκουσεν—συνῆκεν *v. 41;* ταχὺ—ποτε *v. 46,* μὰ τὴν γῆν οἶδ' ὅτι—παραστᾶσ' αὐτόθι *v. 47.*

Iᴛ's the Sphinx's husband, not a cook, that I've taken into my house : bless my soul, I simply do not understand a thing he says. He's come with a stock of brand-new words. When he came in, he looked at me importantly and inquired : " Tell me, how many Articulates [a] have you invited to dinner ? "

" Articulates ? [b] Invited to dinner ? You're crazy ! Do you suppose they are acquaintances of mine, these Articulates ? [None of them will be here. Heaven above, that's the last straw, that I should invite Articulates [c] to dinner ! "]

" Then will there be no trencherman at all ? " [" Trencherman [d]? No, I think not." I thought them over :] " Philinus is coming, and Moschion, and Niceratus, and so-and-so, and what's-his-name " (I went through them by name, and I found no Trencherman among them). [" No such person will be here," I said. " What ! None at all ? "] He was annoyed, as if someone had done him an injury, just because I hadn't invited Trencherman ! Strange goings-on, to be sure ! " Then you are sacrificing no Earthbreaker ? " [e]—" Not I ! " I replied.—" No broadbrowed ox ? " " I'm sacrificing no oxen, idiot ! " " Then you are immolating wethers ? " " Good lord, no, not I ! [Neither of them ! Only a little

word μέροψ = articulate person = human being. [b] The speaker takes " Articulate " to be the proper name of an individual. [c] Play with the other meaning of μέροψ = a sort of bird. [d] He takes Trencherman to be a proper name. [e] *i.e.* ox, which helps to break, or plough, the soil.

τὰ μῆλα πρόβατα· μῆλα πρόβατ'; οὐκ οἶδ',
   ἔφην,
μάγειρε, τούτων οὐθέν, οὐδὲ βούλομαι·
ἀγροικότερός γ' εἴμ', ὥσθ' ἁπλῶς μοι διαλέγου. 25
Ὅμηρον οὐκ οἶδας λέγοντα; καὶ μάλα·
ἐξῆν ὃ βούλοιτ', ὦ μάγειρ', αὐτῶι λέγειν.
ἀλλὰ τί πρὸς ἡμᾶς τοῦτο, πρὸς τῆς ἑστίας;
κατ' ἐκεῖνον ἤδη πρόσεχε καὶ τὰ λοιπά μοι.
Ὁμηρικῶς γὰρ διανοεῖ μ' ἀπολλύναι; 30
οὕτω λαλεῖν εἴωθα. μὴ τοίνυν λάλει
οὕτω παρ' ἐμοί γ' ὤν. ἀλλὰ διὰ τὰς τέτταρας
δραχμὰς ἀποβάλω, φησί, τὴν προαίρεσιν;
τὰς οὐλοχύτας φέρε δεῦρο. τοῦτο δ' ἐστὶ τί;
κριθαί. τί οὖν, ἀπόπληκτε, περιπλοκὰς λέγεις; 35
πηγὸς πάρεστι; πηγός; οὐχὶ λαικάσει,
ἐρεῖς σαφέστερόν θ' ὃ βούλει μοι λέγειν;
ἀτάσθαλός γ' εἶ, πρέσβυ, φησίν. ἄλα φέρε·
τοῦτ' ἔσθ' ὁ πηγός, τοῦτο δεῖξον. χέρνιβον
παρῆν· ἔθυεν, ἔλεγεν ἕτερα μυρία 40
τοιαῦθ' ἃ μὰ τὴν γῆν οὐδὲ εἷς συνῆκεν ἄν,
μίστυλλα, μοίρας, δίπτυχ', ὀβελούς· ὥστ' ἔδει
τὰ τοῦ Φιλιτᾶ λαμβάνοντα βυβλία
σκοπεῖν ἕκαστον τί δύναται τῶν ῥημάτων.
ἀλλ' ἱκέτευον αὐτὸν ἤδη μεταβαλών 45

23-24 τὰ μῆλα πρόβατα. οὐ μανθάνω | τούτων οὐδέν, οὐδὲ
βούλομαι Athen.   26-37 absent in lacuna in Π.   38
φήσ', ἄλας φέρε Athen.   39 τοῦτ' ἔστι πηγός. ἀλλὰ δεῖξον
χέρνιβα Athen.   40 ἔλεγεν ἄλλα ῥήματα Athen.   41
ἤκουσεν ἄν Athen.   42 ὥστε με Athen.   43 τα του
Φιλιτα . . . βυβλία Π, τῶν τοῦ Φιλητα (Φιλιτα Α) . . . βυβλίων
Athen.   44 ἕκαστα Athen.: τῶμ βυβλίων Π.   45 πλὴν
ἱκέτ. Athen.: μεταβαλεῖν Athen.

sheep." "Well," he said,] " Aren't wethers sheep ? "
"Wethers sheep? I know nothing about it, my
dear cook, and I don't want to know anything.
I'm just a simple fellow; talk to me in plain
language." "Don't you know that Homer says
——? " "Of course; Homer, my good cook, was at
liberty to say what he liked : but what in the name
of goodness has that to do with us ? " "Attend to
the rest, now, in the style of Homer." "You want
to murder me with Homer's style ? " "I'm used to
talking like this." "Well, please don't do so in my
house !" "Am I to abandon my principles for my
four drachmas a day? "he asked.—"Bring hither the
groats !" *a* "What may they be ? " "The barley ! "
"Then why talk in circles, madman ? " "Is there
any brine ? " *a* "Brine ? Go to the devil ! Tell me
what you mean in plain language !" "Thou art a
wicked wight, old father," he replied, "bring me the
salt—*that* is what brine is, shew me where that is ! "

The holy water was ready; he did sacrifice, spoke
a myriad more words such as I swear no man on
earth could have understood—slashes, lots, doubles,
piercers *b*—till you would have had to take the works
of Philitas *c* and look each word up to find its mean-
ing. I changed my tone at once and begged him to

---

a Again the cook uses archaic Homeric words for common-
place things. The words ῥηξίχθων and (in this sense) πηγός
do not occur in our text of Homer. See ed. pr. pp. 42-43.
b *i.e.* Homeric words for slices, portions, folds (of fat or
meat), spits. μίστυλλα is meant to be plural of μίστυλλον,
as if that were a neuter noun : in fact the cook had used
μίστυλλον as 1st pers. sing. imperf. of the verb μιστύλλω.
c The celebrated Alexandrian, tutor of Ptolemy Philadelphus,
Zenodotus and others ; he is known to have composed a
glossary of obscure archaic words.

ἀνθρωπίνως λαλεῖν τι. τὸν δ’ οὐκ ἄν ποτε
ἔπεισεν ἡ Πειθὼ παραστᾶσ’ αὐτόθι.
καί μοι δοκεῖ ῥαψωιδοτοιούτου τινὸς
δοῦλος γεγονὼς ἐκ παιδὸς ἀλειτήριος
ἔπειτα πεπλῆσθαι τῶν Ὁμήρου ῥημάτων.   50

46 λαλεῖν τε. τὸν δ’ οὐκ ἄν ταχὺ Athen.   47 Πειθὼ μὰ
τὴν γῆν οἶδ’ ὅτι Athen.   48-50 om. Athen.

ΑΠΟΛΛΟΔΩΡΟΣ

58   [2 B.C.]   FRAGMENT

Ed. pr. *Schubart-Wilamowitz, *Berliner Klassikertexte*,
v. 2, 1907, p. 128.

From an Anthology. For the obscure author—probably a

οὐκ εὖ λογίζ[η]ι πλοῦτ[ο]ν, ὦ Κλ[
ἀνδρὸς [ὁ]μόνοι[α]ν κ[αὶ] γυν[α]ικὸς [οὐ κρατεῖ
            (*Fragment of one line*)
ἐπὰν ὁ μὲν θ[λιβό]μενος οἴκαδ’ [εἰσφέρηι
πάνθ’, ἡ [γ]υ[νὴ δὲ] μηθαμοῦ τἄ[ξω πονῆ]ι,
            (*Fragment of one line*)
κατά[μα]θε τ[ὴ]ν μέλιτταν, ὡ[ς οὐδὲν πον]εῖ   5
ἔξωθεν, ἀλλ’ [ἐς] ταὐτὸ ταχὺ δ[ὴ] συμφέρει
πολύ· [τ]ὸ γὰρ ε[ἰσ]ενεχθὲν ἀθ[ροί]ζ[ει δόμοις.
ἐπὰν δ’ ἀναγκασθέντες ἀν[θρ]ώπω [δύο
συνζῶ[σιν α]ὑτοῖς, ἑκάτερος [φρονῶν δίχα,

4 πονῆι Beazley.   6 End D. L. P.   7 ἀθροίζει
δόμοις D. L. P.   8 ἀνθρώπω δύο Beazley.

say something like an ordinary human being : but Persuasion herself, though she stood on the spot, could never have persuaded *him*. If you ask me, the scoundrel had been the slave of one of those rhapsode-fellows from childhood, and so got stuffed with Homeric words.

APOLLODORUS

FRAGMENT [2 B.C.]

younger contemporary of Menander—see Kaibel in P.-W.-K. *ii. 2825, s.v.* ’Απολλόδωρος, *no. 57.*

Your judgement of wealth, ..., is mistaken ; it is inferior to the harmony of man and wife. . . .

(Fragment of one line)

when the man, overworked, brings home all he earns, while the woman never works beyond her doors. . . .

(Fragment of one line)

Observe the lady-bee.[a] She does none of the out-door work, and yet her contribution to the common end is great at once, because she stores at home what the others bring in. But when two humans are forced to live together, their spirits are yet divided,

---

[a] The simile comes from Xen. *Oec.* vii. 17 (ed. pr.).

ποία[ν] κ[α]τ[ὰ λό]γον οὐσίαν σώσειαν ἄν;   10

(*Traces of one more line*)

---

^a Or "can they reasonably be expected to save?" So
Beazley, to whom the interpretation of the lines is due.
Vv. 3-4 were an illustration of the harmony of man and wife,

ANONYMOUS

59   [Late 3 b.c.]   COOKS

Ed. pr. Guérard-Jouguet, *Un Livre d'Ecolier : publica-
tions de la société royale égyptienne de papyrologie, Textes
et Documents*, ii., le Caire, 1938. (*a*) p. 27, Plate VI ;
(*b*) p. 31, Plate VII. See Körte, *Archiv*, xiii. 1938, 107-108.

(*a*) *Apparently from a monologue by a cook. He com-
plains that someone has not yet entered Simon's house, but
wastes time talking on the doorstep : Simon himself has not
even got as far as the doorstep. Then the cook narrates the
preparations which he has made. Evidently Simon and
another (ἄνθρωπος v. 1) have ordered the cook to prepare for*

(*a*)   ἄνθρωπος οὐκ εἰσέρχετ᾽ εἰς τὴν οἰκίαν,
    ἐπὶ ταῖς θύραις ἔξω δὲ διατρίβει λαλῶν
    Σίμωνος· ὁ Σίμων δ᾽ ἐστὶν οὐδ᾽ ἐπὶ ταῖς
    θύραις.
    τ . υμβουν ἔλυσα καθάπερ ἄρτι εἶπέ μοι,
    τ[. .] . ἔλ[ο]υσα, πῦρ ἐπόησα, χέρνιβον   5
    ἵμ[ησα, τ]ὸ κανοῦν ὡς προσῆκεν ἀρτίως

3 Σίμωνος ὁ Σίμων δ᾽ corrected from Σίμων ὁ Σίμωνος Π.
4 Probably τ[ρ]ύμβουν: but no such word is known. It may
have meant some sort of jar (ἔλυσα then = " I undid," *i.e.*

—and then what sort of substance are they going to save in proportion ? [a]

(Traces of one more line)

and the fragmentary line after v. 4 expressed the idea that the woman worked indoors while the man worked outside.

ANONYMOUS

COOKS [Late 3 B.C.]

some ceremony in Simon's house. The cook has prepared everything : but Simon and the other person are unreasonably slow in returning to his (Simon's) house ; the other person has got as far as the door, where he stops and passes the time of day ; Simon himself has not even come so far as that.

(b) *Also from a monologue by a cook, but almost certainly not a continuation of* (a). *The speaker narrates how he filched and pilfered morsels from the dishes which he had prepared for his master's table. Cf. Euphron fr. 1 Kock, Dionysius fr. 3 (ed. pr.).*

(a) . . . the fellow stays out of the house, spending his time chattering outside on Simon's doorstep ; as for Simon, he isn't even at the doorstep. I have undone the . . . as he told me to just now, washed the . . . made the fire, drawn the holy water, . . . the basket a moment ago, just as it ought to be, knife in

---

" removed the lid or stopper ").   5 τ[ὴν ὗν] Körte : but " after the initial τ, one can hardly supply more than two letters, three narrow letters at the most. . . . Perhaps the papyrus was corrupt," ed. pr.

LITERARY PAPYRI

ἔ[στησ'] ἔχων μάχαιραν· οὐθείς μοι λαλεῖ.
ὅσο[ν] διάφορον ἡμέρα τῆς ἡμέρας.

(*Fragments of three lines*)

(b) η.[.].τις· ἐποίησ' ἀφαν[ές]· ἐ[γ]κ[έ]φαλόν τινα
ἐνοσφισάμην· ἀπηρίθμησάν μοι κρέα·   10
ἐπόησ' ἐλάττω ταῦτα, τὸν ἀριθμὸν δ' ἴσα.
χορδῆς τις ἦν ὀβελίσκος· ἐξελὼν τόμους
ἐκ τοῦ μέσου τρεῖς, τἀπ' ἄκρωι συνήγαγον.
ἐγένεθ' ὅλη, καὶ τὸ μέσον ὠφέλησέ με.
ἰχθὺν ἀπέδωκ' αὐτοῖσι, τὴν δὲ κοιλίαν   15
ἐμέρισ' ἐμαυτῶι. τυρὸς ἦν τις· ἔσπασα.
στέαρ ἔμαρψ', ἔλαιον ἐξηρασάμην,
μέλι συμπαρέλαβον. σίλφιόν τι λοιπὸν ἦν,
ὀπός, κύμινον, νᾶπυ· τούτων σπογγιὰν
λαβὼν ἐμονθύλευσα κἀπηνεγκάμην.   20

7 ἔστησ' Beazley : or perhaps ἔθηκα D. L. P.

ANONYMOUS

60 [End of 1 A.D.]   PROLOGUE

Ed. pr. Kaibel, *Nachrichten der Gesellschaft der Wissenschaften zu Göttingen*, 1899, p. 549. Revised text in *Schroeder, Nov. Com. Fragm. 45. See Reitzenstein, *Hermes*, xxxv, 1900, 622 ; Weil, *Rev. Et. Grec.* xiii, 1900, 427 ; Olivieri, *Riv. di Fil.* xxx. 1902, 435 ; Crönert, *Archiv*, i. 515 ; Demiańczuk, p. 96 ; Legrand, *Daos*, p. 506 ; Platnauer, *New Chapters*, iii. 178.

Prologue of a New Comedy, almost complete. The playwright announces that his prologue is an innovation : it will

272

hand : nobody says a word to me. What a differ-
ence, between day and day !

(Fragments of three lines)

(*b*) . . . I made it vanish. I purloined a morsel of
brains. They numbered off the slices of meat for
me : I made them smaller, but the same in number.
There was some tripe on a spit : I took three cuts
out of the middle, and then brought the ends to-
gether ; thus it became complete again, while the
centre did me a good turn. I gave them their fish
back, but I apportioned the insides to myself. There
was some cheese : I grabbed it. I seized the suet,
I poured myself [a] oil, I took honey along with me.
There was some silphium left over, juice, cummin,
mustard : I took a sponge, stuffed [b] it full of them,
and carried it away.

[a] From ἐξεράω (Körte), not from ἐξαράομαι (ed. pr.).
[b] μονθυλεύω = ὀνθυλεύω, *cf.* Alexis fr. 273 Kock, ed. pr. p. 32.

ANONYMOUS

PROLOGUE [End of 1 A.D.]

*be very brief and strictly relevant, unlike the prevailing
fashion. The question in the last line was probably answered
briefly, as Kaibel suggests, with such a phrase as " you will
soon find out " or " because the author wished it so." The
subject of the play was probably an affair of love between the
cousins mentioned in v. 19.*

The identity of the speaker is uncertain ; it depends

273

*partly on the supplement of v. 15.   I have little doubt that he
is Dionysus (so Kaibel).*
   The fragment proves (a) that lengthy prologues were the

μηδ]ὲ μακρολόγος θε[ός,
ἕως ἂν ὕπνος τοὺς ἀ]κούοντας λάβηι.
πολλοὺς γὰρ οἶδα λιπ]αρῶς πειρωμένους
τῶν πραγμάτων λέγειν τ]ὸ πρῶτον, ὃν τρόπον
ἀρχὴν κατέστη,] καὶ τὸ δεύτερον πά[λι]ν,   5
καὶ προστιθέν]τα(ς τ)οῦδε καὶ τὰς αἰτίας
καὶ τὰς ἀπ]οδείξεις· ἐξ ἀνάγκης γίνεται
τούτων γ' ἕνε]κ' ἀγκωνισαμένοις ῥῆσιν λέγειν
μακράν, ὀ]χληράν, ἐκδιδάσκοντας σαφῶς
κἀκτιθεμ]ένους καθ' ἕκαστον ὧν εὖ οἶδ' ὅτι   10
οὐδεὶς με]μάθηκεν οὐθέν, ἀλλὰ τοῦθ' ὁρᾶι,
πότ' ἄπει]σιν. ὑμᾶς δ' ἐξ ἀνάγκης βούλομαι
πᾶν καταν]οῆσαι, καὶ θεοῦ τι, νὴ Δία,
ἄξιον ἐνε]γκεῖν αὐτός, ἀλλ' ὄντως θεοῦ
λέγω· Διον]ύσωι γάρ τι πιστεύειν ἐμοὶ   15
πρέπει τοιοῦ]το. Σωσθένης καὶ Δημέας
ἐγένοντ' ἀδ]ελφοὶ δύο ποτ'· εἰς τὰς ἐχομένας
οὗτοι δ' ἔγ]ημαν οἰκίας, καὶ γίνεται
παῖς τῶι μὲν α]ὐτῶν, θυγάτριον δὲ θατέρωι.
ἔπειτ' ἀ]ποδημία τις ἀμφοτέροις ἅμα   20
ἦν εἰς 'Α]σίαν, ἐκεῖ τε περὶ τῶν σωμάτων
κίνδυνο]ς· εἰρχθέντος γὰρ αὐτῶν θατέρου,
ἐκεῖ δίκ]ην σχόντος τιν' ἄδικον, ἅτερος
ἔπραττε] τὴν σωτηρίαν. ἔπειθ' ὁ μὲν
φεύγει λ]αθών, ὁ δ' αὐτὸν ἐκκλέψαι δοκῶν   25
δεῖται δ]ιὰ τοῦτο, καὶ γέγονεν ἑκκαίδεκα

---

1 μή πως πλανῶμαι μηδ]ὲ Schroeder.   2 Weil.   8
γ' D. L. P. (δ' Schroeder).   12 Weil.

ANONYMOUS

*early fashion of New Comedy (on the model of Euripides);
(b) that the New Comedians, like the Roman dramatists, used
the prologue as a medium for expressing their opinions
about their art.*

. . . nor god verbose, till slumber falls upon his
listeners. Many there are, I know, who diligently
try to tell their story's beginning—how it came into
being at the start [a]—then the second stage; who add
both the causes and the proofs of this: for the sake of
which they are bound to make a lengthy, tiresome,
speech, to an audience half-asleep,[b] giving the clearest
information and setting every detail forth: although
not one spectator, I am positive, has learnt anything
at all in the end; they are simply waiting for the
speaker to leave the stage. Now I want you to be
compelled to understand everything: and I, for my
part, want to produce a play that does honour to your
god—I really mean it, your *god*. For I am Dionysus;
the story which you must believe is something of
this sort:—

Once upon a time there were two brothers, Sos-
thenes and Demeas. They married into neigh-
bouring families. One of them had a son, the other
a daughter. Then they both went abroad at the
same time to Asia, where they were in danger of
losing their lives—one of them was put in prison,
suffering an unjust punishment, and the other brought
about his rescue. Thereupon the former escaped
unobserved, and the latter was put in chains on the
charge of smuggling him out. Thus their absence

[a] Or " what was the situation at the start."   [b] For
this meaning of ἀγκωνισαμένοις, see Demiańczuk, p. 10
(literally " leaning on their elbows ").

275

οὕτως] τὸ μῆκος τῆς ἀποδημίας ἔτη.
τί ἐτῶν,] τὶς ἂν φήσ(ε)ιεν, ἀμφοτέροις ἅμα
ἐχρῆν] τοσούτων; καὶ τί τἀναγκαῖον ἦν . . .;

ANONYMOUS

61   [1 A.D.]   MOSCHION, LACHES

Ed. pr. Vitelli, *Studi Italiani di Filologia Classica*, vii.
1929, p. 235. Republished with revised text by the same
editor in *Pap. Greci e Latini*, x. 1932, no. 1176 with Plate.
See Körte, *Archiv*, x. 56, *Hermes*, 72, 1937, 50 ; Vogliano,
Gnomon, vi. 1930, 113 ; Platnauer, *New Chapters*, iii. 174.

*It appears probable that these events should be interpreted
as follows :—Laches has a son Moschion and a daughter,
children of different mothers. He has arranged a marriage
between them, and himself has gone abroad for a time. He
hears during his absence that Moschion, who loves another
girl, refuses to marry the daughter : and he therefore sends
an acquaintance (C) to deal with his obstinate son. Laches
himself follows hard upon the heels of his messenger ; who
upbraids him for delegating so unpleasant and difficult a
mission. (It is possible that the daughter is the child of C,
the messenger, not of Laches.) Vv. 1-20 it appears that
Moschion has accomplices, one of whom (a slave of Laches,*

———   ] βάδιζε μὴ δεδοικὼς μηδὲ ἕν.

. . . . . .]ει μέν', ἔνδον ἐστίν, ὥστ' ἔγειρ',
ἔγειρε δὴ

2 Perhaps μῶν ἄπ]ει;

276

from home extended over sixteen years.   Why, you may ask, should both alike need so many years, and what was the necessity . . . ?

ANONYMOUS

MOSCHION, LACHES   [1 A.D.]

v. 18 δεσπότην) is warm in his support, the other intimidated by the father's imminent approach.

The authorship is (as usual) unknown.   Menander is not a specially probable candidate : certain phrases, e.g. καιρὸν εὐφυῆ λαβών v. 20, υἱῶι φέροντα περὶ γάμου v. 26, are not in the style of Menander; nor is the lengthy and circumstantial description of a storm at sea.[a]

Körte (Hermes, loc. cit.) expounds and rejects the grounds in favour of assigning this fragment to the play known as Menander's Fabula Incerta (editions of Jensen, Sudhaus, etc.).   In that play, characters named Moschion and Laches are prominent, and the action, so far as it can be discerned, is not irreconcilable with the action of our fragment, so far as it can be discerned.   But similarity of names and action in Menander do not prove identity of play : and though the actions of the two pieces are similar, there are sundry discrepancies which are not easy to explain.   See Körte, pp. 76-77 : the case, as at present expounded, is not strong enough to be worth repeating in detail here.

(A) Go ahead and never fear ! . . . Stay here—
he is indoors—so wake up, wake up,—no taking it

---

[a] Körte's observations on ὕβρισμαι ὕβρικας (*loc. cit.*) were corrected by himself in *Archiv*, x. 1932, p. 217, n. 1.

. . . σε]αυτὸν μὴ παρέργως. νῦν ἀνὴρ γενοῦ
    μέγας.
μὴ ἐγκ]αταλίπηις Μοσχίων(α). —— βού-
    λομαι, νὴ τοὺς θεούς,
καὐτός,] ἀλλ' ἀπροσδοκήτως εἰς κλύδωνα   5
    πραγμάτων
ἐμπεσ]ὼν ἠγωνίακα, καὶ πάλαι ταράττομαι,
μή πο]θ' ἡ τύχη λάβηι μου τὴν ἐναντίαν
    κρίσιν.
—— δειλὸ]ς εἶ, νὴ τὴν Ἀθηνᾶν, δειλὸς εἶ· βλέπω·
    σύ γε
τὸν π]όνον φεύγων προσάπτεις τῆι τύχηι τὴν
    αἰτίαν.
τοῖς π]λέουσιν, οὐ θεωρεῖς, πολλάκις τὰ   10
    δυσχερῆ
ἀντικεῖ]ται πάντα· χειμών, πνεῦμ', ὕδωρ,
    τρικυμία,
ἀστραπα]ί, χάλαζα, βρονταί, ναυτίαι, συν-
    α[. . .], νύξ·
ἀλλ' ὅμω]ς ἕκαστος αὐτῶν προσμένει τὴν
    ἐλπίδα
καὶ τὸ μέ]λλον οὐκ ἀπέγνω· τῶν κάλων τις
    ἥψατο
θοἰστίον] τ' ἐσκέψαθ', ἕτερος τοῖς Σαμό-   15
    θραιξιν εὔχεται
τῶι κυβερνή]τηι βοη[θεῖν], τοὺς πόδας προσ-
    έλκεται

(Traces of two lines)

ἐν κακοῖς ἥμ]εῖς ἅπασιν, εὐγενῶς προθυμ[ία]ν
αὐτὸς ἡμῖν —— ἀλλ'] ὁρῶ γὰρ τουτονὶ τὸν
    δεσπότη[ν.

easy ! Be a hero, now ! Don't leave Moschion in the lurch !

(B) Heaven knows, I should like to do as you say. But here have I suddenly tumbled into a sea of troubles, and I'm anxious : I've been worried for ages that Fortune may decide against me.[a]

(A) You're a coward, bless my soul, a coward ! I see ! You run away from trouble, and fix the blame on Fortune ! Look at sailors—constantly up against every difficulty ! Storm, gale, rain, mountainous seas, lightning, hail, thunder, seasickness, . . . darkness ! And yet every one of them awaits the gleam of Hope and despairs not of the future. One takes hold of the ropes and watches the sail, another prays the Samothracian gods [b] to assist the pilot, hauls the sheets in . . .

(Traces of two lines)

nothing but trouble all round us, support us like a gentleman—

(B) Stop ! I see the master here. So wait, wait

---

[a] So ed. pr. renders this ambiguous phrase.   [b] Cf. Diod. iv. 43. 1, *P.-W.-K.* x. 1430.

---

3 Μέγα Körte and others, but the name is unknown in Gk. Comedy, and very rare elsewhere.   9 Men. fr. 1083, 1084 εὐθὺς προσάπτει τῆι τύχηι τὴν αἰτίαν.   12 σύνα[γμα] Morel.   13 Theogn. 1144 ἐλπίδα προσμενέτω.   15 τοισαμωθραξιν Π, corr. Edwards, Wilamowitz.

μεῖνο]ν [οὖν, μεῖ]νον μετ' αὐτοῦ.   θᾶττον
εἴσ(ε)ιμ' ἐνθάδε,
κατα]φ[ανήσο]μαί τε τούτοις καιρὸν εὐφυῆ
λαβών.   20
—— ἐγὼ μὲν ὕβρισμαι, Λάχης, ὡς οὐδὲ εἷς
ἄνθρωπος ἕτερος πώποθ'· ὕβρικας δέ με
σὺ δεῦρο πέμψας.   —— μὴ λέγ' οὕτως.
                        —— Ἡρά[κ]λεις,
ἐγὼ δὲ πῶς σχοίην ἂν ἑτέρως; πολλάκις
ἔλεγον ἐκεῖ σοι· ποῖ με πέμπεις;   —— καὶ
μάλα.   25
—— υἱῶι φέροντα περὶ γάμου καὶ θυγάτερα
δώσοντ'; ἐὰν δὲ μὴ προσέχηι μοι, πῶς ἐγὼ
ἀναγκάσω σου μὴ παρόντος λαμβάνειν;

26 " Perhaps φράσοντα " (ed. pr.).

ANONYMOUS

62   [2 B.C.]   YOUTH, DAOS, SIMON

Ed. pr. Grenfell-Hunt, *P. Oxy.* i. 1898, no. 10, p. 21.
Revised text in *Schroeder, *Nov. Com. Fragm.* p. 38; see
Wilamowitz, *Gött. Gel. Anz.* 1898, 695; Blass, *Archiv*, i.
113; Demiańczuk, p. 111; Platnauer, *New Chapters*, iii.
174; Milne, *Cat. Lit. Pap. B.M.* no. 94.

*The authorship of the play is uncertain. Schroeder, loc.
cit., argues that it is the work of a later poet imitating
Menander (especially his* Andria *and* Perinthia*). But the
evidence does not permit a definite conclusion. It is perhaps*
280

with him. I'll go in here at once and take a suitable occasion to make my appearance among them. (*Departs*.)

(C) (*entering with Laches*). Laches, there was never a man alive so ill-used as I am. And it's you who have ill-used me, by sending me here.

LACHES. Don't say that!

(C) Good lord, what else can I do? Time after time I said to you there, " Where are you sending me——"

LACHES. Quite so.

(C) " ——taking a message to your son about his wedding, and giving your daughter away? Suppose he won't listen to me, how am I going to force him to take her, if you aren't here? "

ANONYMOUS

YOUTH, DAOS, SIMON   [2 B.C.]

—as Wilamowitz observed—unlikely that Menander would have used the word ἐβίνησα (v. 1, see p. 256).

A young man is about to break off his engagement to the daughter of a notable citizen, being in love with a foreign woman. He is conversing with his slave, who urges him to change his mind. When his master, still obdurate, leaves the scene, the slave determines not to abandon hope but to invent a plot to save his master—and himself—from ruin.

Simon, father of the affianced daughter, enters and prepares the wedding ceremony, which he seems to fear may be interrupted.

[ΤΡΟΦΙΜΟΣ]   οὐ γάρ, ὡς ἐγὼ]
    τὴν παρθένον] ἐβίνησ', ἐρεῖς.

[ΔΑΟΣ]   ὦ Ἡράκλεις·
    φέρ' εἰπέ μοι π]ῶς αὐτὸν οἴσειν προσδοκᾷς
    τὰ πεπραγμέν',] ἢ τίνας λόγους μετὰ ταῦτ'
    ἐρεῖν;

[ΤΡ. τί δέ;
[ΔΑ.   εἰκὸς αὐτ]ὸν ταῦτα καὶ φυλαρχίας 5
    πάλαι στερῆσ]αι νῦν τ'· ἀδόξωι [γ]ὰρ ἐφάνη
    κακῶς θυγατ]έρα σοι συνοικίζων τότε.
    τύχοι δ' ἂν] εἰπὼν ὅτι καλῶς μὲν εἴχ' ἴσως
    φιλίας χάριν] τῆς ἐκ παλαιοῦ γενομένης
    τὴν παῖδα δοῦναι] τῶν τε δοξάντων τότε, 10
    αὐτὸς δὲ νῦν οὕ]τως ἐβουλεύσω· καλῶς.
    ἴσως μὲν οὖν φ]ανήσεθ' ἕτερο[ς] ἄξιος
    τῆς παρθένου· προ]ικὸς δὲ προὔλαβες μέρος.
    ἀλλ' ἐντρέπει τιν'] ἴσως;

[ΤΡ.]   ἐμαυτόν.
[ΔΑ.]   ἴσθ' ὅτι
    φήσει τάχ'] οὗτος· ποσάκις ἐπὶ τὴν οἰκίαν 15
    παρεγίνεθ' ἡμῶ]ν. οἵ τε τούτου γνώριμοι
    φήσουσιν· οὐκ] ἔδει συνελθεῖν, οὐκ ἔδει
    ποεῖν λαθραί]ως ταῦτα. καὶ παραπείσεται
    οὕτω δικαστάς,] οὐδὲν αἰσχύνει, λέγων,
    φίλους, τίν' αἰσ]χύνει γάρ; ἔσται τ' οὐ
    φ[υγεῖ]ν   20
    δίκην σ', ἀπάν]των ἐγκαλούντων. οὐ το-
    [ρῶ]ς
    οὗτοί σε διελέγξο]υσι προσκαθημένοι
                        ]ες κύκλωι;

ANONYMOUS

YOUNG MAN. Surely you won't say that I seduced the girl!

DAOS. God bless my soul! Tell me, how do you think he's going to bear the facts, and what do you suppose he's going to say afterwards?

YOUNG MAN. Well, what?

DAOS. It's highly probable—to-day, as for some time past—that this will cost him his governorship. Marrying his daughter to a man beneath her class (you, that is!), a bad job—that's what it looked like at the time. Now he may very possibly reply that he was justified in giving his daughter for the sake of old acquaintance, and the agreement at the time; but you have now made other plans. Well and good. And now perhaps some other suitable husband for the girl will come along. Meantime you have received part of the dowry in advance.—Tell me, is there *anyone* whom you respect?

YOUNG MAN. Only myself.

DAOS. You can be sure that he will mention how often you visited his house. His acquaintances will add that you ought never to have enjoyed his company, and then to have behaved in this underhand manner. He will win the jury over: "You have no respect for your friends!" he will cry, "for tell me, whom *do* you respect?" And you won't be able to escape the penalty: all the world will be your prosecutor. They will convict you clearly, besieging you . . . in a circle. . . .

1-2 Wilam.   3 D. L. P.   5, 6 D. L. P.   9-10 D. L. P. (after Schroeder and Blass).   14 Blass. 18 λαθραίως Blass.   21 Beginning D. L. P.: το[ρῶ]s Roberts.   22 οὗτοί σε D. L. P.

[ΤΡ.] ἀλλ' οὖν ἔγωγ' ἁμόθεν γε θράσος] ἐναύσομαι.
[ΔΑ.] πάντως δὲ τοῦτ' ἀδύνατόν ἐσ]τιν.
[ΤΡ.]   ἀλλ' ὅμως   25
        δεῖ καρτερεῖν με.
[ΔΑ.]   ἆρ' οὐχ ὁρᾶι]ς τὰ τῆς ξένης;
        ἔ]στιν τι παιδισκάριον ἀ[στεῖον πάνυ·
        ὅ] δ' ἑταῖρος οἷος. ἀνατέτρα[πται πάντα
            σοι,
        ο]ὐδ' ἂν θεῶν σώσειεν ὑ[μᾶς οὐδ' ἂν εἷς.
[ΤΡ.] σώσουσιν.
[ΔΑ.]   εἰέν· καταλ[ιπών μ' ἀπέρχεται.   30
        ν]ῦν οὐ πεσόντα, Δᾶε, χρ[ή σ' ἀμηχανεῖν,
        ἀ]νανδρία γὰρ τοῦτό γ'· ἀ[λλὰ πάντα δὴ
        δε]ῖ πρότερον ἐγχε[ι]ρε[ῖν, ὅπως σε γνωρίσηι
        μ]ὴ τὸν τυχόντ' εἶναι· τ[ὸ δὲ πρᾶγμ' ἱκανὸν
            πάνυ·
        αὐλ]ητριδίου γὰρ συμπο[τικοῦ τε κατα-
            κρατεῖν   35
        κ]αὶ βουκολῆσαι δεσπό[την ἀπράγμονα
        ἔστιν νεωνήτου· μεμ[άθηκα τοῦτό που
        ἅπαξ ποτ' ἢ δίς· ταῦτα δ' [οὐ σμικρᾶς ὁρῶ
        δεόμενα φροντίδος· [μεγάλην τιμὴν πάνυ
        ἁλ]ούς τις ἂν τίσ[αι· τ]ε[λῶ δ' ἐγὼ τάδε   40
        ἔπ]αινον εὑρὼν ἢ πλ[ύνος πεποιημένος.
        διασωστέον τὸν τρόφ[ιμον. ἀδεῶς οὖν ἐγὼ
        συ]ντάξομαι, ταῦθ' ὅν[τιν' ἂν πράττηι τρόπον.
[ΣΙΜΩΝ] στεφανοῦσθ'· ἕτοιμα [πάντα· δεινὸν τῆς
            ὁδοῦ
        τὸ μῆκος· ἐξ ἀγροῦ με[τήγαγον τράγον   45
        ὑμῖν· πέραινέ μο[ι σὺ τἆλλα, Παρμένων,
        καὶ θυμία· καὶ δεῦρο π[ῦρ φερέτω ταχὺ

ANONYMOUS

Young Man. Well, I'll find encouragement some-where.

Daos. That's absolutely impossible.

Young Man. Still I must see it through.

Daos. Don't you see the situation of your little stranger girl ? " There's a very charming little lady —but oh, her sweetheart ! " You're completely ruined ; not even the gods could save you both now —not one of them !

Young Man. Oh yes, they will. (*Departs.*)

Daos. Well: he's gone off and left me. Now Daos, it's no time to lie down and wonder what to do. Cowardice, I call that. First you must try every-thing you can; he shall learn that you are no ordinary fellow. This business gives ample opportunity. To get the better of a jolly chorus-girl and cheat an easy-going master—that is a task for a slave bought only yesterday, as I have discovered once or twice before now. But *this*, I see, requires a great deal of thought. If you're caught, you may have a heavy price to pay. When I've come to the end of this road, I shall have found either compliments or a dressing-down. I have to rescue my master : I will stand fearlessly beside him, however he may act in the matter.

Simon (*entering*). Put on your wreaths ! All is prepared. — What an awful long journey ! — I've brought you a goat from the farm. Finish me the rest, Parmenon, and burn the incense. Tell a slave

---

24 D. L. P. (*cf.* Plato, *Ax.* 371 E). 29 οὐδ' ἂν εἶς C. H. Roberts after Sudhaus. 31 ἀμηχανεῖν D. L. P. 35 κατακρατεῖν D. L. P. 37-43 D. L. P. (for 41, *v.* Ar. *Plut.* 1061). 46, 48 End Beazley.

π]α[ι]δάριον ἐπὶ τὸν [βωμόν· οὐ μελλητέον.
ἀγωνιῶν γὰρ καὶ δεδ[ιὼς ἐλήλυθα

(*Fragments of two more lines*)

ANONYMOUS

63 [Early 3 b.c.] YOUTH, DEMEAS, SLAVE

Ed. pr. Grenfell-Hunt, *Hibeh Papyri*, i. 1906, no. 6, p. 29, Plate IV. See *Schroeder, *Nov. Com. Fragm.* p. 3 (revised text) ; Körte, *Archiv*, vi. 228 ; Blass, *Lit. Centralbl.* 1906, 1079 ; Fuhr, *Phil. Woch.* 1906, 1411 ; Wilamowitz, *N. Jahrb.* 1908, 34 ; Robert, *G.G.A.* 1918, 181 ; Demiańczuk, *Suppl. Com.* p. 102.

From a scene before the houses of two men, Demeas and another (A). Demeas, conversing with his servant, enters, and meets a young man and his servant. Demeas urges the young man to run away, and offers him money and provisions for the journey (this suggests that the young man is not a

[ΝΕΑΝΙΑΣ] τί γὰρ πλέον τό[δ'; ἐ]ψόφηκεν ἡ θύρα,
ἐξέρχεταί τις.
[ΔΗΜΕΑΣ] τὴν σπυρίδα ταύτην ἐν [ἧι
ἐνταῦθα τοὺς ἄρτους ἐκόμισας ἀπόφερε
ἀποδ]ός τε τῶι χρήσαντι, τῶι Νουμηνίω[ι.
. . . .]δετα . . ωι δεῦρ' ἀναστρέψας πάλ[ι]ν. 5
οὗτοι] τί λέγετε;
[ΝΕ.] τί δ' ἂν ἔχοιμεν ἄλλο πλὴν
. . . . . . π . . μεν ἀποτρέχειν ταύτας με δεῖ
. . . . αταπ . . . . . . μων μὲν οὐθὲν κωλύει.

6 D. L. P.

ANONYMOUS

to bring fire to the altar here at once.   No delay!
I've come in anxiety and alarm . . .

(*Fragments of two more lines*)

ANONYMOUS

YOUTH, DEMEAS, SLAVE   [Early 3 B.C.]

*native of the town in which Demeas lives).   The young man
is reluctant to accept this offer, and is therefore reproached
by his slave.   The young man praises Demeas warmly.   At
vv. 23-24 Demeas enters his house ; and while the young
man is waiting for his return, there emerges from the other
house its owner (A), evidently enraged because his wife has
taken a baby in.   He commands her to send it away, and
inquires whither his own daughter has disappeared.*

*The interpretation of these events is obscure and un-
certain.   It seems probable that the young man is enamoured
of A's daughter, and that the child whom A has discovered in
his house and wishes to expel, was borne by his daughter to
the young man : who now first learns of the baby's existence.
Beyond this all is mere guesswork.*

YOUNG MAN. For what's the good of it?—The
door creaked—someone is coming out!

DEMEAS (*entering*). Take away the basket in which
you brought the bread here, and give it back to
Numenius, who lent it. . . . after you come back.
(*Observing the Young Man and Slave*) Hullo, and what
are you talking about?

YOUNG MAN. What should we have to talk about,
except . . . I must run away (with?) those women
. . . there's no reason why not.

287

[ΔΗ.] οὕτω[s] δέ γ᾽ ο[ὐ]δαμῶ[s] δυνήσετ᾽ ἀπιέναι.
[ΝΕ.] πῶς; [οὐκ] ἀπῆλθεν;
[ΔΗ.]   ἡ[σύχω]s ἐπίσχετε.   10
[ΝΕ.] ὦ τᾶν, [ἔτ᾽ ἀναμε]νῶ λα[β]εῖν [τα]ύτην ἐγώ;
[ΔΗ.] πρῶτ[ον μὲν . . . . .] ἐκ πολεμίων φεύγετε.
[ΝΕ.] τὸ δὴ [μετὰ ταῦτ]α;
[ΔΗ.]   ταῦτα πράτθ᾽ ἁγὼ λέ[γ]ω.
οὐκ ἔ[στιν ἄλ]λως.
[ΝΕ.]   εἶτα πῶς δυ[ν]ή[σ]ομαι

(Fragments of five lines)

[ΔΗ.] ἐμοὶ γάρ ἐστιν πρός σε φιλό]της τήμερον,   15
εἰς αὔριον δ᾽ ἤδη πολέμιος γίνομαι.
γ]ένοιτο δ᾽ εἰρήνη ποτ᾽, ὦ Ζεῦ δέσποτα,
δι]άλυσις [ἀλγ]ε[ινῶν κακῶν τ]ε πραγμάτων.

(Fragments of three lines)

[ΔΗ.] τὸ χρυσίον δὲ [λ]άμβανε.
[ΝΕ.]   οὐ τᾶ[ν τάδε πρέποι
ἔμοιγε.
[ΔΗ.]   ἀρίθ(μ)ησον· ἐν τοσούτ[ωι δ᾽ εἰσι]ὼν 20
πρὸς τὴν γυναῖκα βούλομ᾽ εἰπεῖν [τ]ὴν ἐμήν,
εἰς τὴν ὁδόν γ᾽ ἔτ᾽ αὐτὰ τἀναγκαῖ᾽ ὅπως
ὑμῖν παρ᾽ [ἡμ]ῶν ἔνδοθεν συνσκευάσηι.
[ΝΕ.] ἔχομεν ἅπαντα.
[ΔΟΥΛΟΣ]   Ἄπολλον, ὡς ἀγροικὸς εἶ·
συσκευα[σ]άτω.
[ΝΕ.]   πέραινε.
[ΔΟ.]   παύομαι λέγων. 25

10 οὐκ Schroeder.   12 πρῶτ[ον μὲν ὥσπερ] Schr.: but
the " enemies " may be literal, not metaphorical, cf. 16-17
(Robert); cf. also fr. b ii. 92 Schr. ἐπὶ στρατόπε[δον, fr. f 119

DEMEAS. She can't possibly go away like that.

YOUNG MAN. What ? Hasn't she gone ?

DEMEAS. Gently now, contain yourselves.

YOUNG MAN. My good friend, must I still wait to get her ?

DEMEAS. First you must fly . . . from the enemy's camp.

YOUNG MAN. And then ?

DEMEAS. Then do what I tell you. There is no other way.

YOUNG MAN. And then how shall I be able . . .?

(Fragments of five lines)

DEMEAS. . . . to-day, I am your friend ; to-morrow already I shall be your foe. Grant us peace, Almighty God, at last, an end to suffering and misfortune !

(Fragments of three lines)

DEMEAS. Take the money.

YOUNG MAN. Oh, I couldn't possibly do that !

DEMEAS. Count it. Meantime I'll go indoors ; I will tell my wife to pack the bare necessities for your journey too, from the household stores.

YOUNG MAN. But we have everything !

(Demeas leaves the stage)

SLAVE. Really, your manners ! Why not let her pack ?

YOUNG MAN. That's enough !

SLAVE. I say no more.

Schr.]ω στρατῶ[ι.   13 μετὰ ταῦτα Schroeder.   14
ἔστιν Hunt, ἄλλως Schroeder.   15 D. L. P.   18
ἀλγεινῶν D. L. P., κακῶν Schroeder.   19 τὰν τάδε πρέποι
D. L. P.

LITERARY PAPYRI

[ΝΕ.] νὴ τὴν Ἀθην[ᾶ]ν καὶ θεούς, ἀγωνιῶ,
οὐκ οἶ[δ' ὅ]πως, [νῦ]ν αὐτὸς ἐπὶ τῶι πράγ-
 ματι.
Ἕλλη[ν βε]βαί[ως] φαίνεταί τις τοὺς τρόπους
ὁ Δημέα[ς ἄ]ν[θρω]πος· ἀλλὰ τῆι τύχηι
οὐθὲν δια[φέρειν] φαίνε[θ'], ὃν π[ο]εῖ κακῶς. 30
[ΓΕΡΩΝ] γύναι, τί βούλ[ει; νὴ Δί',] ἐμβ[ρόντ]ητ',
 ἄγε
νῦν πρῶτο[ν ἐκ τῆς] οἰκ[ίας τὸ π]αιδίον.
κλάεις περ[ιβα]λ[ο]ῦσ' [αὐτὸ κοὐχὶ π]ροΐεσαι;
ἔξω φέρετ' αὐτὸ δεῦ[ρό μοι 'πὶ] τὰς θύρας.
τὴν ἡμετέ[ραν] μὲν πα[ῖδα, λέγε, π]οῦ γραῦς
 ἔχει 35

(*There follow traces of numerous lines, too*
fragmentary for inclusion)

28 *Cf. P. Oxy.* 211. 33, Menander, *Perikeir.* τεκμήριον

ANONYMOUS

64 [Early 3 B.C.] STROBILUS

 Ed. pr. (1) and (4) Grenfell-Hunt, *New Classical Texts
and other Greek and Roman Papyri* (*Greek Papyri*, Series ii.),
1897, p. 18. [It is perhaps not certain whether (1) and (4)
belong to the same papyrus, see Gerhard, *op. cit.* below,
p. 41.]
 (2) Hunt, *Catalogue of the Greek Papyri in the John
Rylands Library, Manchester*, i. 1911, no. 16, p. 25, Plate V.
 (3) Grenfell-Hunt, *Hibeh Papyri*, i. 1906, no. 5, p. 24,
Plate III.
 (5) *Gerhard, *Griechische Papyri*, Heidelberg, 1938, no.

ANONYMOUS

YOUNG MAN. Heaven above, I can't tell you how nervous I am, now I am actually on the job! This Demeas really does shew himself a white man —whereas it doesn't seem to matter to Fortune, whom *she* injures!

(Enter a man, who stands at the door and speaks to his wife, off-stage)

OLD MAN. Good heavens, what is your game, woman? Bring the child out of the house, idiot, that's the first thing! What! Crying, and embracing it? You won't let it go? (*To his slaves within*) Bring it out here to the door! Now tell me, where has the old woman (hidden) our daughter? . . .

(There follow traces of numerous lines, too fragmentary for inclusion)

τοῦτ' ἐστὶν Ἑλληνος τρόπου.   31 [Δημέας] Schroeder, corr.
Robert.   35 λέγε ποῦ D. L. P.

ANONYMOUS

STROBILUS   [Early 3 B.C.]

180, p. 40. *P. Petrie*, 4 (early 3 B.C.) contains fragments of the same play (see Schroeder, p. 12): but these are not intelligible or consequent enough to be included here; the same is true of Gerhard's new fragments, except the one which I reproduce as (5).

See *Schroeder, *Nov. Com. Fragm.* p. 11; Demiańczuk, *Suppl. Com.* p. 98, 113; Fuhr, *Phil. Woch.* 1906, 1411; Leo, *Hermes*, 41, 1906, 629; Blass, *Rh. Mus.* 62, 1907, 102; Weil, *Journ. des Sav.* 1906, 514; Wilamowitz, *N. Jahrb.* 1908, 34; Körte, *Archiv*, vi. 227, 228; Milne, *Class. Rev.*

LITERARY PAPYRI

1922, 166, and *Cat. Lit. Pap. B.M.* no. 91; Kock, *Rh. Mus.* 48, 1893, 221; and esp. Robert, *G.G.A.* 1918, p. 185; Platnauer, *New Chapters*, iii. 176.

The argument appears to be :—

(1) A slave Strobilus has been commanded by his young master to make a great effort to obtain for him the company of a young woman. The slave has fulfilled his mission to the best of his ability : he has found her lodging, but not yet conversed with her.

(2) Strobilus reproaches his master for estranging himself from his father through his passion for the young woman.

(3), (4) Strobilus has discovered great abundance of treasure. His master enters, and hears what the slave has found.

(5) Strobilus converses with another slave, Daos, who offers to assist him in some enterprise or difficulty.

(1) [ΣΤΡΟΒΙΛΟΣ] . . . . σκοπεῖν, προσιέναι πᾶσι,
 πεῖρα[ν λαμβάν]ε[ι]ν
 εἰ δυνατόν ἐστι τῆς κόρης αὐτῶι τυχεῖν,
 ὅτι τῆς ἀνοίας μεστὸς ἦν τὴ[ν παῖ]δ᾽ ἰ[δών.
 ἐποίησ᾽ ἅ μοι προσέταττεν, εὗρον οἰκίαν.
 ἀδύνατον ἦν [5
 αὐτὴν νόμαρχ[

(2)   ]ας, ὦ τρόφιμε, τοιούτο[υ πατρὸς
 ἀποστερή]σας σαυτὸν ἕνεκ᾽ ἐρωμένης.
 προσέτι δοκ]εῖς ἱλαρός γε, νὴ τὸν Ἥλι[ον.

(3)   ] τρέχειν Ὀλύμπια.   10
 ἐὰν δ[ι]αφύγ[ηι]ς, εὐτυχὴς ἄνθρωπος εἶ.
 [ΝΕΑΝΙΑΣ] ὦ Ἡράκλεις, τί ποτ᾽ ἐστὶ τὸ γεγενημένον;

10 νό[μι]ζε Λά[μπ]ιδος τρέχειν κτλ. (preceded by *e.g.* θᾶττόν

ANONYMOUS

*Beyond this, nothing can be clearly discerned. Blass
maintained that these fragments are the work of Philemon,
identifying v. 21 Κροισ[with Philemon fr. 189 K. Κροίσωι
λαλῶ σοι καὶ Μίδαι καὶ Ταντάλωι. This hazardous specula-
tion, though approved by Hunt (P. Hibeh, p. 25), has natur-
ally found little support. Nor is there any likelihood in the
theory that this play was the model of Plautus's Aulularia ;
so slight is the resemblance between the two.*

*The word νόμαρχος in v. 7, being the name of an Egyptian
magistrate, has led to the plausible inference that this play
was written for performance in Egypt. But Schroeder
properly criticizes the view that it is the humble work of an
obscure poet : were this so, " mirum esset si talis comoediae
inter papyros non ita multas duo iam codices innotuissent."
See further Gerhard, op. cit. p. 48.*

(1) STROBILUS. . . . to look, to approach everyone,
to make experiments to see if he can possibly obtain
the girl ; because he went completely insane when
he set eyes on her.

I've done what he told me : I have found where
she lives. It was impossible . . . the Governor. . . .

(2) . . .(You're a fool), master, to estrange your-
self from such a father because of a mistress. And
what's more, you seem so cheerful about it !

(3) . . . to run the Olympic race. If you escape,
you're a lucky man !

YOUNG MAN. Good heavens, what has happened
here ?

σε δεῖν] at end of preceding line) Schroeder ; but in Paus.
v. 8. 7 Lampis is a victor in the pentathlon. There is no
evidence for his special fame as a runner (Robert). Schroeder
gives vv. 10-11 to Strobilus : but *v.* Robert, *loc. cit.*

[ΣΤ.] νῦν οἶδ' ἀκριβῶς, διότι τῆς οἰκουμένης
ἱερὰ σαφῶς αὕτη 'στιν ἡ χώρα μόνη
κἀνθάδε κατ[ω]ικήκασι πάντες οἱ θεοὶ   15
καὶ νῦν ἔτ' εἰσὶ καὶ γεγόνασιν ἐνθάδε.
[ΝΕ.] Στρόβιλε.
[ΣΤ.]   "Απολλον καὶ θεοί, τοῦ πνεύματος.
[ΝΕ.] παῖ δυστυχές, Στ(ρ)όβιλε.
[ΣΤ.]   τίς κέκ[λη]κέ μ[ε;
[ΝΕ.] ἐγώ.
[ΣΤ.]   σὺ δ' εἶ τίς; ὦ κράτιστε τῶν θ[εῶ]ν,
ὡς εἰς καλ[όν] σ' ἑορά[κ]α.
[ΝΕ.]   τί σ[ὺ βοᾷις ἔχων; 20

     (Fragments of four lines)

[ΣΤ.] Κροίσ[ου σε γὰρ πεπόηκα πλουσιώτερον.
[ΝΕ.] ὁ Ζε[ύς

(4) ——   ἀκηκοὼς]
γνώσει τόδ' ε]ὐθὺς συλλαβῆς μιᾶς. —— τί;
—— πῦρ.
—— τί δ' ἔστ';] ὄνομα τί τοῦτο; —— πῦρ.   25
—— ἀκήκοα.

(5) —— ἄρτοι παρὰ τούτοις οὐ [
μά]λ' ἔδεισα μή ποτ'[
π]τωχοῦ βίον ζῆις αὐτ[ὸς
     (Fragments of two lines)

21 πεπόηκε Schroeder, who ignores the *paragraphus* before
22 in Π.   πεπόηκα D. L. P.   27 μάλ' Skeat.

---

^a Strobilus thinks a divinity is calling him, and imagines
that he perceives the fragrant odour which accompanies
the advent of the gods (Eur. *Hipp.* 1391, Aesch. *P. V.* 115).

ANONYMOUS

STROBILUS. At last I know definitely that this place alone of all on earth is holy ground for certain, and all the gods reside here—born here, and still live here !

YOUNG MAN (*entering*). Strobilus !

STROBILUS. Heavens, what fragrance ! [a]

YOUNG MAN. My miserable slave ! Strobilus !

STROBILUS. Who called me ?

YOUNG MAN. I did.

STROBILUS. And who are you ? O mightiest of the gods, just when I wanted to see you !

YOUNG MAN. Why do you keep shouting ? . . .

(*Fragments of four lines*)

STROBILUS. I have made you richer than Croesus.

YOUNG MAN. Zeus . . .

(4) ? STROBILUS. Listen to one syllable, and you will know at once.

(? YOUNG MAN). What syllable ?

—— PYR.[b]

—— What word is this ?

—— PYR.

—— I heard you . . .

(5) —— (No ?) loaves in their house . . . I'm very much afraid that . . . you may live the life of a beggar . . .

(*Fragments of two lines*)

[b] Πῦρ, fire, the first syllable of πυραμίs, pyramid : Strobilus has found hidden treasure in a pyramid. Perhaps a pun on the word ἀμίs followed (for the word ἀμίs in New Comedy, see *Berliner Klassikertexte*, v. 2, no. xix, 32, p. 114).

295

LITERARY PAPYRI

[ΣΤ.] εἶέν· τί οὖν δή, Δᾶε, πρὸς τά[δ'] ἔστι μοι;
[ΔΑΟΣ] δύναμαι γενέσθαι χρήσι[μ]ος κἀγώ τί σοι
εἰς ταῦτα.   30

[ΣΤ.]   λέγε μοι, μὴ σιώπα, πρὸς θεῶν.
[ΔΑ.] τοῦτ' αὐτὸ τῶν λοιπ[ῶ]ν μὲν ἀνθρώπων
ἁπλῶς
μηθενὶ λαλήσῃς [
κάδον ἄλλον ὁ νέος δεσ[
καὶ τοῖς μεθ' αὑτοῦ συμπ[όταις   35
ἀκήκοας, Στρόβιλε, παν[
κέλε]υσον ἐλθεῖν ἐπιλ[

. . . .

ANONYMOUS

65   [About 200 B.C.]   PHAEDIMUS, NICERATUS

Ed. pr. Jouguet, *Bulletin de correspondance hellénique*,
xxx. 1906, p. 123. See *Schroeder, *Nov. Com. Fragm.* p. 29
(revised text) ; Körte, *Hermes*, 43, 1908, 37, and *Archiv*, vi.
230 ; Wilamowitz, *N. Jahrb.* 1908, 38 ; Demiańczuk, p. 104 ;
Robert, *G.G.A.* 1918, p. 180 ; Capovilla, *Bull. Soc. Arch.
d'Alex.* iv. 193 ; Platnauer, *New Chapters*, iii. 172.

*The fragment begins with a soliloquy by a slave, who
appears to have been reproached by his mistress. He says
that he fears her less than her husband, the master of the
house, who has just returned from a journey and knows
nothing of recent developments. He will soon find that his
daughter is missing from her home.*

*Phaedimus, a young man in love with the daughter, appears
and upbraids the slave as the cause of his misfortunes.*

In the brief gap which follows, the master of the house

ANONYMOUS

Strobilus. Well now, what is my part, Daos. in view of this ?

Daos. I myself can be of some use to you in the matter.

Strobilus. Tell me—for God's sake don't keep it from me !

Daos. You mustn't tell my secret to anybody else —not to anyone at all ! The young master . . . another wine-jar . . . and to his fellow-revellers . . . you have heard the whole plan, Strobilus : tell . . . to come to . . .

---

34 δεσ[πότου] Gerhard.   35 συμπόταις Kalbfleisch.
37 κέλευσον Skeat.

ANONYMOUS

PHAEDIMUS, NICERATUS   [About 200 b.c.]

enters the scene ; Phaedimus withdraws to a place of concealment to escape his notice. The master of the house laments the disappearance of his daughter, and enters his home together with the slave. Phaedimus emerges from his retreat, and is greeted by Niceratus ; with whom he quarrels vigorously, alleging that Niceratus had taken from him the girl he wished to marry. Niceratus denies the charge ; and has just persuaded Phaedimus to hear him out, when Chaerestratus (whom Phaedimus had sent on an errand) enters and informs Phaedimus that his charge against Niceratus is unjust. He promises to explain everything, if Niceratus will leave him alone with Phaedimus. Niceratus departs.

297

LITERARY PAPYRI

*It is fairly clear that what really happened was this.—
The daughter (who loved and was loved by Phaedimus),
fearing for some reason the return of her father,—perhaps
he would detect in her appearance the evidence of misconduct
--fled from her home. Niceratus thought to render his
friend Phaedimus a signal service by harbouring her in his
house which was next door, her nearest refuge. But Phaedi-
mus not unnaturally misunderstood his comrade's motives.*

[ΔΟΥΛΟΣ   ] ἧττον, ὦ δέσποινα, σὲ
  δέδοικ᾿ ἔγωγ]ε, τὸν πατέρα δὲ τουτονὶ
  τὸν ἀρτίως ἐλθ]όντα, τὸν τῶν γεγονότων
  οὐθὲν πυθόμενο]ν, ὡς ἔοικε, πραγμάτων.
  ἢ γὰρ μέγας παράλο]γός ἐστιν ἢ μάτην 5
  τὸ πᾶν πέπρακται.] τουτονὶ μὲν οὖν ὁρῶ
  προσιόντα θᾶττο]ν. χαῖρε πολλά, Φαίδιμε.
  ἥσθην μάλιστ᾿ ἔγω]γ᾿ ἀκούσας ὅτι πάρει·
  εὖ δ᾿ ἐνθάδ᾿ ἦλθες εὐ]θύς.
[ΦΑΙΔΙΜΟΣ]   οὐ μή μοι πρόσει
  ἐγγύς, πονηρέ.]
 [ΔΟ.]   διὰ τί;
 [ΦΑ.]   τοῦτ᾿ ἤρου με καὶ 10
  τολμᾶις ἀπολωλε]κώς με προσβλέπειν;
 [ΔΟ.]   ἐγώ;
 [ΦΑ.   ]ς αὐτὸν εἶδες;
 [ΔΟ.]   ο[. . . .]η Τύχη
 . . . . τ]οῖς θεοῖς δέ.
 [ΦΑ.]   μανθάνων

    (Fourteen lines missing)

[ΓΕΡΩΝ] τίνος κελεύσαντ[ος;
 [ΔΟ.   τίνος; ἆρ᾿ οὐκ] αὐτὸς ἂν
  ἠνάγκασας τοιαῦτα ποιῶν;

298

ANONYMOUS

There is no evidence to determine the further course of the action.

Language, style and metre oppose the ascription of these lively but inartistic fragments to Menander : especially disturbing are the form αὐτοῖσι in v. 41 ; the rhythm μεῖζον ἀγαθόν at the end of the line 44 ; the peculiar use of σαυτόν v. 53. The play was probably the work of a poet who lived some time after Menander ; perhaps a native of Alexandria. V. 15 of our fragments was the 100th line of the play.

SLAVE. I am less afraid of you, mistress, than of her father here. He has just arrived, completely unaware of what has happened, I imagine. Unless something very unexpected occurs, all our plans have come to nothing. Hullo, here's someone coming : I see, he is hurrying toward me. Good day to you, Phaedimus, I was delighted to learn that you're here, and I'm glad you came to me at once.

PHAEDIMUS. Don't come near me, confound you !

SLAVE. Why ever not ?

PHAEDIMUS. You ask me that, and have the nerve to look me in the eyes,—you who have ruined me !

SLAVE. I ruined you ?

PHAED. . . . you saw . . .

SLAVE. Fortune . . . but to the gods.

PHAED. I learnt . . .

(Fourteen lines missing)

FATHER. Who told you to ?

SLAVE. Who, indeed ! Your conduct would have forced me to.

---

5 D. L. P. (after Schroeder): μέγας παράλογος Thuc. iii. 16, vii. 55.   6 Schroeder.   8 μάλιστ' D. L. P. (μὲν οὖν Schroeder).   12 Ο[Υ]Ι[Μ]Η vel -[Δ]Η Schroeder.

[ΓΕ.] Ἡράκλεις, 15
τί με πεποίηκας, θύγατερ; ἄρτι μανθάνω
τὸ πρᾶγμα· ἐκεῖ νῦν ἐστιν, ὡς ἔοικε;

[ΔΟ.] ἐκεῖ.

[ΓΕ.] οἷον πεποίηκας, θύγατερ. οὐκ ἂν ᾠόμην,
θύγατερ· τί ταῦτα, θύγατερ;

[ΦΑ.] ἆρ᾽ ἀφί[στα]τ[α]ι;

[ΝΙΚΗΡΑΤΟΣ] ὡς οὐκ ἀπήντων οὐδαμοῦ τῶι Φαιδίμωι, 20
αὐτὸς μεμένηκα δεῦρ᾽ ἀναστρέψας πάλιν.

[ΦΑ.] μὴ πολὺ διημάρτηκα τὸν Χαιρέστρατον
εἰς λιμένα πέμψας.

[ΝΙ.] ἡμέτερος οὗτος φίλος
διάδ[ηλός ἐσ]τ[ι.]

[ΦΑ.] μετὰ τὸν οἰκεῖον πάλιν
ὅ γ᾽ ἐχθρός· ἀπορῶ πῶς] τε καὶ τίνα δεῖ
τρόπον 25
αὐτῶι προσελθεῖν.

[ΝΙ. χ]αῖρ᾽, [ἑ]ταῖρε φίλτατε,
περίβαλέ (μ᾽) ἱκετεύω.

[ΦΑ.] τί χρὴ νυνὶ ποεῖν;
ἡ μὲν συνήθει᾽, ἡ φιλία, [τὸ] διὰ χρόνου,
καὶ διότι μ᾽] ἠγάπηκε καὶ [πρίν] γ᾽ ἦν [ἐμοὶ
πιστός] 30

(Eight lines missing)

[ΦΑ.] ὑπερηκόντικας
ἅπαντας ὦ πιστότατε] τοῖς πεπραγμένοις.
ὑπερεπιτηδείως διάκεισαι.

[ΝΙ.] τί σὺ λέγεις;

[ΦΑ.] ἐμοῦ πρόνοιαν εἶχες;

24 Schroeder.   25 D. L. P.   32 Schroeder.

ᵃ Robert thinks *Nic.* sent Chaer. to the harbour, and

ANONYMOUS

FATHER. Heavens, my daughter, what have you done to me? At last I understand! She is there now, I suppose?

SLAVE. She is.

FATHER. My daughter, what a thing to do! I should never have thought it of you, daughter! What made you do it, my daughter? (*Departs.*)

PHAED. (*emerging from his retreat*). Is he going?

NICERATUS (*entering, aside*). Not meeting Phaedimus anywhere, I came back, and here I am, waiting.

PHAED. (*aside*). I do hope it wasn't a great mistake to send Chaerestratus to the harbour.[a]

NIC. Our old friend, large as life!

PHAED. (*aside*). First the friend, and then the enemy again! I wonder what is the best way to approach him.

NIC. Good day to you, my dear fellow, shake hands, do!

PHAED. (*aside*). What must I do now? Old acquaintance, friendship, all these years, the fact that he was fond of me, and I could trust him once. . . .

(*Eight lines missing*)

Your behaviour, loyal comrade, quite overshoots all precedent. Quite a wonderful friend, you are!

NIC. What do you mean?

PHAED. You exercised forethought on my behalf?

Phaed. is the man whom he sent Chaer. to fetch thence. This involves ignoring the *paragraphus* at v. 22 (Robert's expedient is impossible). And *v.* Introductory Note: it is most probable that Phaed. sent Chaer. to the harbour to meet and delay *the father*. It remains obscure, why no reference is made to this mission, whatever it was, at v. 70; and why Phaed. should think that he may have made a mistake in sending Chaer. there. See note on v. 69.

[ΝΙ.]   οἴομαί γε δή.

[ΦΑ.] ἀνδρειοτέρους νὴ τὴν Ἀθηνᾶν νενόμικα   35
ὅσοι δύνανται τοῖς φίλοις ἀντιβλέπειν
ἀδικοῦντες ἢ τοὺς τοῖς πολεμίοις μαχομένους.
τοῖς μέν γε κοινὸς ὁ φόβος ἐστί, καὶ καλὸν
ὑπολαμβάνουσι πρᾶγμα ποιεῖν ἑκάτεροι.
τούτοις δ' ὅπως ποτ' ἐπιτρέπει (τὸ) συνει-
      δέναι   40
αὑτοῖσι θαρρεῖν πολλάκις τεθαύμακα.

[ΝΙ.] πρὸς δὴ τί τοῦτ' εἴρηκας;

[ΦΑ.]   ὦ τάλας ἐγώ·
ὅσον διημάρτηκα τοῦ ζῆν· τοῦ βίου
τί γάρ ἐστιν ἡμῖν τῶν φίλων μεῖζον ἀγαθόν;
εἰ τοῦτο μήτ' ἔγνωκα μ[ήτ' ἐπίστ]αμαι   45
ὡς δεῖ θεωρεῖν, ἀλλὰ λα[νθάνουσί] με
οἱ μὲν ἐπιβουλεύοντ[ες οἱ δ' ἄλλ]ως φίλοι
ὄντες, τί τὸ ζῆν ὄφελός [ἐστι;

[ΝΙ.   πῶς λέγε]ις;
τί δ' ἐστὶν ὃ λελύπηκέ σε;

[ΦΑ.]   [ἤρου τοῦ]τό με;

[ΝΙ.] ἔγωγε, καὶ τεθαύμακ' οὐ μετ[ρίως σ' ὁρ]ῶν 50
συντεινόμενον πρὸς ἐμαυτόν.

[ΦΑ.]   [οἶδας, εἰ]πέ μοι,
ἐρῶντα τῆς γυναικὸς ἀνακο[ινοῦν με πᾶ]ν
πρὸς σαυτόν, οὐθὲν τῶν ἐμα[υτοῦ πρα]γ-
      μάτων
κρύπτοντα;

[ΝΙ.]   πάντ', οὐκ [ἀντιλέγω σοι.] περίμενε.

[ΦΑ.] περίμενε; ταύτην τοῦ πατρός μ' ἀ[πο]-
      στερεῖν   55
μέλλοντος ἠξίω[κας], οἶδ', [αὐ]τὴν [γ]αμεῖν.

[ΝΙ.] διαμαρτάνεις.

Nic. I should say so.

Phaed. I always did think it took more courage to face your friends after you have injured them, than to be a soldier at the front. In the latter case, each side is equally frightened, and each alike presumes that he is doing something noble. But with the former, I have often wondered how on earth their consciences give them a chance to keep their nerve.

Nic. Now what is the point of that?

Phaed. What a poor fool I am! I have completely missed the road in life. Friends are the greatest blessings of our existence; if I don't know— have never understood—that this fact must be observed,—if some of my friends are scheming against me, and others useless, and I am unaware of it—what is the good of living?

Nic. What do you mean? What has upset you?

Phaed. You ask me that?

Nic. I do. And it astounds me beyond measure to see you exasperated with me.

Phaed. Tell me, do you remember that I told you the whole story, loving the woman as I did, and concealed nothing about my own affairs from you?

Nic. You told me everything, I don't contradict you. Only have patience!

Phaed. Patience! Her father was going to take her away from me, and you have the impudence to think you would marry her! I know!

Nic. You're quite mistaken.

[ΦΑ.]   πῶς; οὐκ ἔμελλ[ε]s λαμβάνειν
αὐτήν;

[ΝΙ.]   ἄκουσον, ὦ [μ]ακάριε.
[ΦΑ.]   ἀκήκοα.
[ΝΙ.] οὐκ οἶσθας
[ΦΑ.]   οἶδα πάντα.
[ΝΙ.]   πρὶν [μ]αθεῖν; τίνα
τρόπον;

[ΦΑ.]   κατηγόρηκέ μοι τὰ πράγματα   60
ἀλλότριον ἡμῖν ὄντα σε.
[ΝΙ.]   ὦ τᾶν, Φαίδιμε,
ἐπ᾽ ἀρίστερ᾽ εἴληφας τὸ πρᾶγμα· μανθάνω
σχεδὸν γὰρ ἐξ ὧν πρός με τὴν ὑποψίαν
ἔχεις· διὰ τὸ δ᾽ ἐρᾶν σε συγγνώμην τινὰ
ὅμως δίδωμι καίπερ ἀγνοούμενος.   65
[ΦΑ.] πείθεις μ᾽ ἀκοῦσαι τὸ παράδοξον τί ποτ᾽
ἐρεῖ[s.
[ΧΑΙΡΕΣΤΡΑΤΟΣ] οὐκ ᾠχόμην εἰς λιμένα· ἀπαντήσας
με γὰρ
σύμπλους ἀνέστρεψέν τις εἰπὼν ὅτι πάλ[αι
ἀπελήλυθεν δεῦρ᾽ ἀπὸ σαω[
τίς οὗτος; ὦ, Νική[ρ]ατ[ος] καὶ [Φαίδιμος 70
αὐτός γ᾽, ἔοικε. χαῖρε πολλά, Φαίδιμε.
[ΦΑ.] νὴ καὶ σύ γ᾽, ὦ Χαιρέστρατ᾽, [εἰ σώ]σεις
φίλ[ο]ν.
χειμάζομαι γὰρ οὐ μετρίως ὑπὸ τοῦδ᾽ ἐγώ.
[ΧΑ.] τί δ᾽ ἐστίν; οὐ δήπουθεν ἠγνόηχ᾽ ὅτι
[ΦΑ.] οὐκ ἠξίουν, Χαιρέστρατ᾽, ὄντα μοι φίλον,   75
ὡς φησι

---

69 ἀπὸ Σαῶ[νο]s, ὥστε μὴ — Blass: Π has a colon (:)
before απο, hence Schroeder thinks ἀπὸ, etc., should be given

PHAED. What ! You were not going to take her ?

NIC. My dear fellow, listen to me.——

PHAED. I have listened.

NIC. You don't know——

PHAED. There is nothing I don't know.

NIC. Before you hear it ? How on earth can you ?

PHAED. The facts have exposed you in my sight as a personal enemy.

NIC. But my good Phaedimus, you have put the wrong construction on the facts. I know pretty well what makes you so suspicious of me. Misunderstood as I am, I can shew some forbearance towards you, just because you're in love.

PHAED. You win.—I will listen to the miracle—what on earth you can have to say !

CHAERESTRATUS (*entering*). I didn't go to the harbour. You see, I met a fellow-traveller who turned me back with the news that . . .*a* had come back here long ago from . . . Who is this ? Hullo, it's Niceratus, and Phaedimus himself, by the look of it. Good day to you, Phaedimus.

PHAED. And to you, Chaerestratus, if you will come to the rescue of a friend. This fellow here has upset me beyond measure.

CHAER. What's the matter ? (*To Nic.*) Surely he isn't unaware that——

PHAED. I never expected, Chaerestratus, that a man who calls himself a friend of mine——

---

a This may explain why Phaed. thought he had made a mistake in sending Chaer. to the harbour (see above, p. 301 n.) —he guessed that it might be too late.

---

to Niceratus. Change of speaker is denoted by a *paragraphus* elsewhere. 72 D. L. P. after Körte.

[ΧΑ.]   παῦσαι, μηθὲν εἴπῃς, πρὸς θεῶν,
Φαίδιμε.
[ΦΑ.]   τί δ᾽ ἐστίν;
[ΧΑ.]   μεταμ[ελήσει σοι τάχα.
[ΦΑ.] εὖ ἴσθι, βουλοίμην ἄν. ἐμὲ μὲν ῥᾴδιον
ἔσται μεταθέσθαι γὰρ μαθόντ᾽, ἀ(λλ᾽) οὑτοσὶ
[ΧΑ.] οὐκ ἂν ἐπιτρέψαιμ᾽ οὐθὲν εἰπεῖν σοι παρὼν 80
ἄτοπον, συνειδὼς τὰ περὶ τοῦτον πράγματα.
εἰ γὰρ τοιοῦτοι τρεῖς γένοιντό σοι φίλοι,
οὐκ ἔσθ᾽ ὅ τι οὐ πράξαις ἂν ἕνεκα πίστεως.
ἀλλ᾽ ἐκποδὼν ἡμῖν γενοῦ, Νικήρατε,
ἵνα μὴ παρόντος σοῦ ποιῶμαι τοὺς λόγ[ους. 85
[ΝΙ.] εἰσέρχομαι.

*(Fragments of three more lines; then end of scene
denoted by χορο]ῦ; then fragments of fourteen
lines of dialogue)*

ANONYMOUS

66   [End of 3 B.C.] FATHER, MOTHER, DAUGHTER

Ed. pr. Jouguet, *Bulletin de correspondance hellénique*,
xxx. 1906, p. 103 with Plate. See *Schroeder, *Nov. Com.
Fragm.* p. 20 (revised text); Robert, *G.G.A.* 1918, 190;
Körte, *Archiv*, vi. 229 ; Demiańczuk, p. 99.

*The story of this play does not emerge clearly from the
copious but obscure fragments.*

*(a) Reference to a plot, perhaps to secure the freedom of a
girl from her master by producing false witness that she was
freeborn.*

306

ANONYMOUS

Chaer. Stop, Phaedimus, for God's sake, not a word !

Phaed. What's the matter ?

Chaer. You'll regret it in a minute.

Phaed. Believe me, I wish I might. It will be easy enough for me to change my mind when I know better, but this fellow——

Chaer. I am not going to stand here and let you say anything silly : I know all about Niceratus. If you had three friends like him, there's nothing you could not do for want of loyalty. Now, Niceratus, out of our way, please : I don't want to tell my story in your presence.

Nic. I am going indoors. . . .

(*Fragments of three more lines; then end of scene denoted by* Choral Song; *then fragments of fourteen lines of dialogue*)

ANONYMOUS

FATHER, MOTHER, DAUGHTER [End of 3 b.c.]

(b) *A man complains that nobody except his servant Dromon has proved a trustworthy assistant.*

(c) *The speaker (perhaps Moschion) describes a conversation in which he exhorted someone to assist him in the effort to secure the freedom of the girl abovementioned.*

(d) *The recognition of the girl by her parents ; effected by means of tokens—especially the dress which she was wearing when in early childhood she was sent away to live with a childless woman abroad.*

307

LITERARY PAPYRI

(e) *The girl and her parents prepare to enter the house of a neighbour who has promised his daughter to Moschion, the girl's brother ; and has undertaken to provide the wedding feast and ceremonies. This scene may afford an important clue for the reconstruction of the plot as a whole. Schroeder observes that " in the New Comedy, nuptials prepared by parents are hardly ever fulfilled." So perhaps Moschion now refused to attend and to wed the neighbour's daughter. His motive would be that he and the girl, apparently his sister, are in love. Hence her terrified exclamation after the recognition, v. 39, " Is Moschion my brother ? " In the end it will appear that Moschion is only an adopted son, and he and the girl will marry.*

(a) . . . . γονέ]ων ἀπολεσάντων παιδίον,
  ἢ κηδεμόνι] δόντων τρέφειν, ἢ τὸν τόπον
  ὅθεν εἰσίν, ἐγ]γεγραμμένων ἄλλως ἐκεῖ.
  . . . .]όν ποτ' ἐστὶν οὕτω μαρτυρεῖν·
  μάρτυρα] τοιοῦτον ἄν τις εὕροι πολλαχοῦ 5
  . . . . . . .ἐ]ν ἄστει τοῦδ'. Ἐλευσίς ἐστι, καὶ
  τίς ὁμήγ]υρίς που, τίς νοήσει, πρὸς θεῶν,
  εἰ . . . . .]πεῖται δῆμος εἷς τις; οὐ ταχὺ
  . . . . . .] ἀφελκύσαις ἄν. εἰ δὲ περιμένω,
  . . . . . γένοιτ' ἄν] ἔτι λέγοντος ἑσπέρα 10

(b) ——   ἐξ ὅτου]περ ἐγενόμην
        οἰ]κότριψ Δρόμων·
  ἀεὶ δ' ἐτίμων αὐτὸν ὡ]ς εὐεργέτην.
  πάντας δὲ τοὺς λοιποὺς] Διόνυσος ἀπολέσαι,
  οὐδεὶς γάρ ἐστιν ὑγι]ὲς οὐδ' ἁπλοῦν φρονῶν. 15

1-10 Schroeder prints as dialogue (changes of speaker after ἐκεῖ v. 3, μαρτυρεῖν v. 4, ἄστει v. 6, που v. 7, τις v. 8, ἄν v. 9). I follow Robert in reprinting the lines as a consecutive whole ; but think it probable that there is some

ANONYMOUS

(f) *The subject-matter is altogether uncertain. It might possibly be a fragment of a scene in which somebody wished to reveal to the girl's owner (doubtless she was in the power of a leno) that she had been restored to her family.*

(g) *A son or daughter explains to his or her mother the unseemly conduct of a man (perhaps the leno) in the presence of the girl and others.*

In v. 6, Eleusis may be the Egyptian Eleusis, suburb of Alexandria, a low quarter. Hence it has been plausibly conjectured that this play was performed in Egypt, perhaps written in Egypt. (Cf. however Robert, loc. cit.: he infers from the word λαμπαδηφόρος *v. 31, that the scene is Athenian, and Eleusis therefore the Attic town.)*

(a) . . . the parents lost their baby, or gave it to a relative to bring up, or wrote their address falsely in the registers. . . . to give such evidence; you could find people to give it, almost anywhere in the city. This is Eleusis, and what assembly—goodness gracious, what assembly is going to notice if a single district . . . ? You will not easily shift me from my ground. If I wait about here, it will be nightfall before (you?) stop talking.

(b) . . . since I was born. . . . Dromon, born and bred in my house. I always respected him as my benefactor. As for all the others, may Dionyse destroy them! There's not one of them with a decent or honest thought in his head.

---

change of speaker in the last two or three lines. 1
γονέων Schroeder. 4 οὔκουν χαλεπ]όν Schroeder: καὶ τίνα
τρόπ]ον, with question-mark after μαρτυρεῖν, Roberts. 6
(A) ἐνταῦθ' ἐν ἄστει. (B) τοῦ δ' κτλ. Schroeder. 8 Perhaps εἰ μεταποεῖται. 9 μ'] ἀφελκ. Schroeder. 10
γένοιτ' ἂν Blass, perhaps preceded by οὐ σοῦ (Schroeder) or τούτου (Beazley).

(c) ——— λέγοντα τούτους τοὺς λόγους ἐπε[
ἐμοὶ δὲ καὶ τούτωι τί πρᾶγμ᾽ ἐστ[ίν; λέγων,
μὴ τοῦτον ἡμῖν τὸν τρόπον λάλε[ι σύ γε·
τολμητέον γάρ ἐστιν. ἀλλ᾽ εἴ[πε]ρ [μόνον
τούτων ἀληθὲς ὁ θεράπων τι [νῦν λέγει,   20
ἅπασιν η[. . . . .] τοῖς πολίταις ἡ κ[όρη
οὐκ ἀλλοτρία [

(d) [ΠΑΤΗΡ π]τέρυξ χιτωνίσκου γυναικείου διπλῆι·
ἔ]κρυπ[τε γὰ]ρ σῶμ᾽, ἡνίκ᾽ ἐξεπέμπομεν
πρὸς τὴν] ξένην σε, τὴν τότ᾽ αἰτοῦσαν τέκνα. 25
. . . .]όν ἐστιν ἀλλὰ τῶι βεβαμμένωι
πέπλωι, μίτρα] τ᾽ ἔχουσα χρώματος φύσιν
πέριξ ἰώ]δους, τοὐν μέσωι δὲ πορφυρᾶς,
δηλοῖ τάδ᾽· ἤ]δη καὐτὸς ἐμβλέπω σε, παῖ.
. . . .]ηται καιρὸς ὡς παρ᾽ ἐλπίδας 30
. . . .]ημι λαμπαδηφόρου
. . . .]ντος ὑπεραγωνιῶν.
[ΘΥΓΑΤΗΡ. . . . . ἐσ]τί, μῆτερ, ἀλλὰ τί
. . . . ὀνόμα]τος, ὃ νομίζω καλεῖν

(e) [ΜΗΤΗΡ] (ἴ)ωμεν εἴσω δεῦρ[ο· καὶ γὰρ Μοσχίων, 35
ἄνερ, ἐνθάδ᾽ ἐστί[ν.
[ΠΑ.   ] τὴν κόρην δώσειν (⌣)
ἡμῖν τε ποιήσειν ἕτοιμο[υς τοὺς γάμους
ἔφη προελθὼν ἐχθὲς εἰς ὁμ[ιλίαν.
[ΘΥ.] ὁ Μοσχίων ἀδελφὸς ἐμός ἐ[στιν, πάτερ;

16 ἐπε[ιθόμην Schroeder.   21 ἥ[μιν, ἥ[μειν too short:
310

(c) . . . that is what he said. . . . " What have he and I to do with each other ? " I asked. " Don't you talk to me like that ! We must be bold. If only there is a word of truth in what this servant is saying, . . . the whole city (will agree that) the girl is no foreigner."

(d) FATHER. A length of a woman's shift, in two-fold. . . .

(*Tragically*) It veiled thee, when abroad we sent thee to
That lady strange, who sought a child to love.
('Tis manifest).—Thy garment steeped in dye,
Shews it ; thy bonnet, with a violet band
About it, in the centre coloured red,
Is proof enough. Thy father looks upon thee,
His daughter ! . . .

. . . occasion, how beyond my hope
. . . of the bearing of the torch
. . . extreme anxiety.

DAUGHTER. . . . mother, but why (? may I not call you by) the name, by which I am used to call (? my foster mother). . . .

(e) MOTHER. Let's go in here. (*To Father*) Moschion's here, my love.

FATHER. When our old friend came to keep us company yesterday, he said he would give his daughter, and prepare the ceremony for us.

DAUGHTER. Moschion ! Is he my brother, daddy ?

" ἦν τάχα conatus sum " Schroeder. 23 *sqq.* Parody of Tragic Iambic style. 27 (πέπλωι), 29 D. L. P. 30 ἐπεὶ γεγένηται καιρὸς Schroeder, unlikely metre in this parody of Tragic style. 36 " In fine versus nomen aliquod fuisse puto " (*e.g.* ' Λάχης ') " Schroeder.

[ΠΑ.] ἀδελφός· ἀλλὰ δεῦρο πρὸς [τὸν γείτονα, 40
ἡμᾶς γὰρ ἔνδ[ον] προσ[δοκῶσ' οὗτοι πάλαι.
ΧΟΡ[ΟΥ]·

(f) —— ἐμοὶ τί σὺ σπουδαῖο[ν ἀγγέλλειν ἔχεις·
ὥστ' ἄξιον ταύτης [γενέσθαι τῆς ὁδοῦ,
ἣν κεκόμικάς με δεό[μενός μου τοῦ δρόμου
ἀεί τι μικρὸν ἔτι προε[λθεῖν; ἀλλ' ἐμὲ 45
ἄξιον, ἀκριβῶς ἴσθι, γιν[ώσκειν τίς εἶ.
—— τίς εἰμί; μὰ τὸν Ἥφαιστ[ον

(g) [ΠΑΙΣ ὦ μ]ῆτερ, [οὔ]τ[ω] καὶ τὰ πόλλ' ἀκήκοα
τού]του λέγοντος ἄρτι πρὸς τὸν δεσπότην.
ὁ δὲ] κόκκινος γενόμενος ὑπανεδύετο 50
καὶ π]αντελῶς ἦν βδελυρός· οὐ σφόδρ'
ἤρεσεν
. .]ειν δέ, μοιχώδης δὲ μᾶλλον κατεφάνη
.   .   .   .

42 ἀγγέλλειν D. L. P.   43 γενέσθαι Blass.   45 προ-

ANONYMOUS

67   [1 B.C.]   SLAVE, MASTER

Ed. pr. Schubart-Wilamowitz, *Berliner Klassikertexte*, v.
2, 1907, p. 113.   See *Schroeder, *Nov. Com. Fragm.* p. 43
(revised text); Demiańczuk, *Suppl. Com.* p. 97; Körte,
Archiv, vi. 231; Schmidt, *Phil. Woch.* 1908, 457; Crusius,
Lit. Centralbl. 1907, 1310.

*A slave complains that his master keeps him perpetually
occupied; and that he has no time for rest, especially when*

312

ANONYMOUS

FATHER. Indeed he is. Come on now; let's go next door. They have been waiting for us inside for hours.

(Choral Song)

(*f*) —— What important news have you to tell me, to justify this journey you have brought me?—always begging me go just a little farther up the road! Let me tell you this: I think I may properly inquire your name.

—— My name? Good heavens! . . .

(*g*) SON (or DAUGHTER). Yes, mother, it was the same with everything I heard him saying to his master just now. He turned scarlet and tried to sneak out of it. He behaved like a perfect black-guard. It disgusted . . ., he seemed still more like an adulterer . . .

.   .   .   .   .   .

ἐλθεῖν Blass, ἀλλ' ἐμὲ D. L. P.   46 τίς εἰ D. L. P. (Schroeder in 45).

ANONYMOUS

SLAVE, MASTER   [1 B.C.]

there is company to be entertained. His master loses patience and threatens him with a worse fate.

The joke about the donkey (vv. 7-14) is obscure. It is evidently an illustration of the repeated demands made upon the slave by his master. "Here comes the donkey!" was the cry raised by a patron of the baths when his place was vacated (vv. 11-12). It is most natural to suppose that the " Donkey " is a public servant at the baths, laden like a beast of burden with equipment—chiefly, no doubt, the clothes of numerous patrons (πάνθ᾽ ἑαυτῶι περιάγει v. 9). Whenever a bather leaves his place (v. 11 ἀπολειφθέντος τόπου) the Donkey brings him his clothes, and performs whatever is his duty. The departing bather shouted (ὄνος προσέρχεται has hitherto been taken as the content of the bather's shout, as

[ΔΟΥΛΟΣ   ]η, μὰ τὸν Δ[ία
                       ]αν τάχιστα φεύ[ξομαι
                    ] σχολὴν μὲν ἔχ[ειν οὐκ ἔστι μοι

            (*Traces of one line*)

     ζῆν μοι δοκῶν ἐ]ν χάρακι κοὐχὶ κ[ατὰ
     πόλ[ι]ν·
ὅτι τοῖς θεράπο]υσιν, ἡνίκ᾽ ἂν συμβῆι πότος, 5
συνεχῶς βοᾶτ᾽, α]ὐλητρίδ᾽ ἡμῖν ἀγάγετε.
          ]η βαλανεῖόν ἐστί που
         ἔγ]νωκας εἶναι παντα[χοῦ
      οὗ]τος πάνθ᾽ ἑαυτῶι περιάγ[ει·
ὅποι καλ]εῖται πρῶτον, εὐθὺς εἶσ᾽ ὄνος. 10
χὤταν] τις ἀπολειφθέντος ἀνακράγηι τόπου,
ὄνος π]ροσέρχετ᾽, εὐθὺς ἄλλος ἀνέκραγεν,
ἔπειτα δ᾽] ἕτερος πάλιν, ὄνος προσέρχεται,
μετὰ τοῦτο]ν ἄλλος. τὸ βαλανεῖόν ἐστ᾽ ὄνος.
σὲ δ᾽ εἰ] πότος τις ἢ θυσία τις γίνεται 15
ἐγὼ]ιδ᾽ ἐρεῖν, μουσουργὸν ἡμῖν ἀγάγετε·
τίς εὐτρ]επίζει; δεῖ δ᾽ ὑπάρχειν εὐτρεπῆ
. . . . . . καὶ κλί]νας.

[ΔΕΣΠΟΤΗΣ]   ἀηδίας λέγει[ς.

*it were in inverted commas : this, I think, is as awkward
as it is unnecessary*), and the poor Donkey rushed from
one place to another and one duty to another : therein re-
sembling our slave. τὸ βαλανεῖόν ἐστ' ὄνος *may, as Crusius
suggests, signify "the whole bathing-place is nothing but cries
of "Donkey." Crusius's interpretation of the joke is less
satisfactory,—bathers, laden like donkeys with bathing-gear,
waited impatiently for the vacation of "places," and joyfully
greeted the departure of the present occupants, who would
themselves be laden with gear. Thus* ὄνος προσέρχεται
*means, "Here comes a departing bather." But the bathers
themselves would not be heavily laden ; and the situation
would hardly illustrate the discomforts of our slave.*

SLAVE. . . . upon my word ! . . . I shall run away
as fast as I can . . . I cannot have leisure. . . .

(*Traces of one line*)

It seems to me I'm living in the trenches, not in the
city.   Whenever there's a party, you keep shouting
to the servants : "bring us a chorus-girl ! " . . . there
is a bath, . . . you know (the bathman ?) is every-
where . . . he carries everything round on him.
The Donkey will go straight to the first caller : when
a place is quitted, and the guest shouts—up comes the
Donkey ; another shouts at once, and then another
—up comes the Donkey ; yet another shouts—the
whole establishment is nothing but the Donkey.   So,
if there is a drinking-party or a sacrifice, I know
you'll be crying "bring us a musician.   Who is get-
ting things ready ?   The . . . and couches must be
ready there ! "

MASTER. I dislike your conversation.

---

6 Schroeder.   8 ὅ τι ἔγν. Schroeder.   10 Begin-
ning and punctuation D. L. P.: εἰσ' Beazley (εἰς ed. pr.).

[ΔΟ. οὐ κερμάτι]ον δ' ἔχοντες ἀξιοῦτ' ἐρᾶν

(Traces of one line)

] ἀλλ' οὐθέν.

[ΔΕ.]   ὦ μαστιγία,   20
τίς ὁ λῆρ]ος; ὑπομένω σε δήπουθεν πάλαι,
σὺ δ' ἀλαζονε]ύῃ πρός με καὶ σπαθᾷς ἔχων·
μή, σχέτλι', ἐπαι]ν[έ]σῃς σὺ πρώτιστος βίον
τὸν Ταν]τάλου.

[ΔΟ.]   μὰ τὸν Δί', οὐκ ὄνους ἄγων

(Traces of five more lines. The phrase δυστυχὲς
θωράκιον in the second of them may imply that the
master strikes the slave)

ANONYMOUS

68   [2–3 A.D.]   YOUTH, SLAVE

Ed. pr. Grenfell-Hunt, P. Oxy. i. 1898, no. 10, p. 21.   See
*Schroeder, Nov. Com. Fragm. p. 48 (revised text) ; Crönert,
Archiv, i. 113 ; Wilamowitz, G.G.A. 1898, p. 694 ; Demiań-
czuk, Suppl. Com. p. 110.

[A] μὴ καὶ [βλέπῃ μ' ἐντ]αῦθα.
[ΔΟΥΛΟΣ]   ὅμως δ' ἀ[μελητέον.
τῶν π[λημμελου]μένων γὰρ ἡμε[ῖς τὴν δίκην
ὑποτ[ρέομεν κο]ὺ μειράκιον ἔνθε[ρμον ὄν,
ἐρῶν· [ἐκεῖνός] μ' εἰς τὸ βάραθρον ἐμβ[αλεῖ
πρόφασ[ιν λαβὼν] μικράν· τὸ μὲν τού[τωι τὸ
πᾶν   5

2, 3 Blass.

ANONYMOUS

SLAVE. You haven't a farthing, and yet you think yourselves fit to be lovers . . .

(*Traces of one line*)

nothing else.

MASTER. What nonsense is this, you rogue? I have suffered you a long time—bragging and boasting continually to me! Be careful, you rascal, that you don't become the first man who ever thought highly of Tantalus's way of life!

SLAVE. Upon my word, not bringing donkeys . . .

(*Traces of five more lines*)

---

22 σπαθᾶις: v. Photius, s.v. σπαθᾶν· Μένανδρος Μισουμένωι· τὸ ἀλαζονεύεσθαι.   23]ΧΙ (vel ΟΝ)ΘΟΝ . ΣΗΙΣΣΥ Schroeder: either misread or corrupt.

ANONYMOUS

YOUTH, SLAVE   [2–3 A.D.]

A slave fears that the follies of his young master will bring punishment upon himself : he therefore resolves to dissociate himself from an intrigue and to secure his own immunity.

(A) . . . to prevent him seeing me there. (*Departs.*)

SLAVE. Still, inaction is my policy. It is we—not the hot-headed youth in love—who tremble at the penalty for mistakes. Our friend [a] will throw me into the Pit on the smallest pretext. Tell him [b] the

[a] The man against whom the slave and his master have been plotting.   [b] His master.

φράσαι γάρ, ἄπαγε, κρον[ι]κόν, ἀρχαίου
  τρ[όπου·
ἵνα χρηστὸν εἴπηι τις; χολὴ φιλοδεσπ[ότων,
ἔμετο[ς. τ]ὸ πλουτεῖν ἡδύ· τἄλλα δ’ ἐστὶ
  [—πάξ.
ἐκ μὲν ταπεινῶν καὶ παραδόξων ἡ[δονῆς
ὑπ]ερβολή τις. ἀλλ’ ἐλεύθερόν με δεῖ   10
πρ]ῶτον γενέσθαι, καὶ τυχόν, νὴ τ[ὸν Δία,
τὸ] νῦν με τῶν ἐνταῦθ’ ἀμελῆσαι πρα[γ-
  μάτων
ἀρχὴ γένοιτ’ ἄν· πεύσεται γὰρ αὐτίκα
ἐλθὼν ὁ τρόφιμος πρῶτον, ἡ παῖς π[οῦστί
  μοι;

ANONYMOUS

69   [2–1 B.C.]   SYMPATHETIC SLAVE

Ed. pr. Aly, *Sitzungsberichte der Heidelberger Akademie
der Wissenschaften*, v. 1914, Abh. 2, p. 1. See Körte,

[ΔΟΥΛΟΣ] (τρόφιμε, τί σύννους κατὰ μ)ονὰς σαυτῶι
  λαλεῖς;
  δοκεῖς τι παρέχειν ἔμφασιν λυπουμένου.
  ἐμοὶ προσανάθου· λαβέ με σύμβουλον
    (πόνων)·
  μὴ καταφρονήσηις οἰκέτου συμβουλίαν·
  πολλάκις ὁ δοῦλος τοὺς τρόπους χρη-
    στοὺς ἔχων   5
  τῶν δεσποτῶν ἐγένετο σωφρονέστερος·

ANONYMOUS

whole story—not I ! Too old-fashioned,[a] out of date.
Do it, to get a pat on the back ?—Lunacy of the Old
Retainer (?),—it makes me vomit ! It's nice to be
rich : the rest is—but enough ! Pleasure is doubled
when it proceeds from a humble and unexpected
source. But first I must get my freedom. And
upon my word, who knows ?—inaction in the present
crisis may be a good beginning. The first thing the
young master will ask when he arrives is, Where is
my girl ? . . .

[a] Plato, *Euthyd.* 287 β εἶτ', ὦ Σώκρατες, οὕτως εἰ Κρόνος,
ὥστε κτλ.

---

7 φιλοδεσπ[ότων D. L. P.   8 πάξ Beazley.   9 †ἐγ
μὲν† Schroeder : ἡδονῆς Blass.   14 Blass.

ANONYMOUS

SYMPATHETIC SLAVE   [2–1 b.c.]

Gnomon, i. 23, and *Archiv,* vii. 152; Wilamowitz, *Menander :
das Schiedsgericht,* p. 107; Wüst, *Burs. Jahresb.* 1926, 124.

SLAVE. Master, why so deep in thought, all alone,
talking to yourself? One might think, you present
the picture of a man in sorrow.[a] Refer it to me, take
me for fellow-counsellor in your trouble. Don't
despise the counsel of a servant—slaves of good char-
acter have often proved wiser than their masters.

[a] For this translation, see ed. pr.

---

1 Suppl. Wilamowitz, from Lucian, Ζεὺς Τραγωιδός 1.
3 πόνων add. Wilamowitz from Lucian, *ibid.* 3.

εἰ δ' ἡ τύχη τὸ σῶμα κατεδουλώσατο,
ὅ γε νοῦς ὑπάρχει τοῖς τρόποις ἐλεύθερος.

ANONYMOUS

70 [2 A.D.] NUMENIUS, SLAVE

Ed. pr. *Grenfell-Hunt, *P. Oxy.* iv. 1904, no. 667, p. 127.
See *Schroeder, *Nov. Com. Fragm.* p. 54 ; Wilamowitz,
G.G.A. 1904, 669 ; Demiańczuk, *Suppl. Com.* p. 116.

From a dialogue between Numenius and his slave, who

                              ]τρέχειν ἐκ γειτ[όνων.
[ΔΟΥΛΟΣ   δεῖ σ' ἐπιλαθέσθ', ἐάν] τι λυπήσας τύχω
    πρὸ τοῦ· τὸ γὰρ νῦν πάν]τα πειθαρχοῦντά [σοι
    ὁρᾷς με. τοῦτον τὸν] τρόπον προσιό[ντα σοι
    οὐ δῆτ' ἀπώσεις.]
[ΝΟΥΜΗΝΙΟΣ]   τίνι λαλεῖς;
[ΔΟΥ]   δίδου δ' ἐμοὶ 5
    διὰ ταῦτα τὴν ἐλευθε]ρίαν, Νουμήνιε.
[ΝΟΥ   οὐ παραφρονῶν εἶ φαν]ερός, εἰ νεῖμαί μ[ε
    δεῖ
    ἐλευθερίαν σοι, νὴ μὰ] τοὺς δώδεκα θε[ούς,

ANONYMOUS

71 [2 A.D.] FRAGMENTS

Ed. pr. *Grenfell-Hunt, *P. Oxy.* ix. 1912, no. 1176, fr. 39,
col. v. 12-15, p. 147 (=(1)) ; 16-22, p. 147 (=(2)) ; 22-27,

320

ANONYMOUS

Though fortune may have made the body a slave,
the mind still has a free man's character. . . .

ANONYMOUS

NUMENIUS, SLAVE [2 A.D.]

*asks his master to forget former delinquencies, and,
remembering his present obedience, to grant him freedom.
Numenius emphatically rejects this petition.*

NUMENIUS. . . . run out of the neighbour's house.

SLAVE. If I have annoyed you in the past, forget it.
To-day you see me wholly at your service.   You
surely won't reject such advances as these——?

NUMENIUS. Who are you talking to ?

SLAVE. ——So give me my liberty, Numenius !

NUMENIUS. You must be mad—a clear case !—if
you think that I must give your liberty, by all the
gods in heaven ! . . .

---

1 προστρέχειν edd.   2 Schroeder.   8 ἐλευθερίαν
σοι D. L. P.

ANONYMOUS

FRAGMENTS [2 A.D.]

p. 148 (=(3)).   See Schroeder, *Nov. Com. Fragm.* p. 61 ;
von Arnim, *Suppl. Eur.* p. 5 ; Leo, *G.G.A.* 1912, 281 ;
Körte, *Archiv*, vi. 249.

LITERARY PAPYRI

From Satyrus's Life of Euripides. *It is likelier that these are separate and unconnected fragments, than a continuous*

(1) ἐν ταῖς [τριό]δοις σοι [προ]σγελῶ[σ'] αὐλητρίδες.

(2) τοὺς ἀστυνόμους τίνες εἰ[σ]ὶ πυνθάνηι, [Φι]λοῖ;
    τοὺς π[τερο]κοποῦν[τ]ας [τὴν] ἐλευθερί[α]ν [λέ-
    γ]εις.

(3) οὐκ ο[ὐ]σί[αν] νενόμικας [εἶν]αι, Πά[μ]φ[ι]λε,
    [ἣν] τῶι [γ]ένηται [χρ]ήματ', ἀλλ' ἐξ[ο]υσίαν. 5

ANONYMOUS

72   [End 3 B.C.]   TWO PROLOGUES

Ed. pr. Jouguet, *Bulletin de correspondance hellénique*, xxx. 1906 : (1) p. 131; (2) p. 132. *Cf.* p. 141. See *Schroeder, *Nov. Com. Fragm.* p. 63 (revised text) ; Wilamowitz, *N. Jahrb.* 1908, 34 ; Körte, *Hermes*, 43, 1908, 40 ; Michel, *de fab. graec. argumentis metricis*, diss. Giss. 1908, 36 ; Körte, *Archiv*, vi. 1920, 230.

These two pieces are written on the verso of the papyrus whose recto contains the comic fragments nos. 65, 66 above.

(1) Ἔρως, Ἀφ[ρο]δίτης υἱὸς ἐπιεικής, [ν]έος,
    νέος ἐπιεικὴς υἱὸς Ἀφροδίτης Ἔρω[ς,
    ἐλήλυθ' [ἀ]γγελῶν τοιοῦτο πρᾶγμά τι,
    πρᾶγμ[ά] τι τοιοῦτον ἀ[γ]γελῶν ἐλήλυθα,
    κατὰ τ[ὴ]ν Ἰωνίαν πάλαι γεγενημέν[ο]ν,   5
    γεγ]ενημένον πάλαι κατὰ τὴν ['Ι]ωνίαν.

322

*and unbroken passage (e.g. a dialogue between Pamphilus
and another).*

(1) Chorus girls smile at you at the crossroads.

(2) You ask, Philo, who the policemen are ? The
men who featherclip our freedom !

(3) When a man makes money, Pamphilus, you've
always called it not property but impropriety ![a]

[a] So I render the pun. The Greek really means rather
licence, freedom in general denied to the poor man.

ANONYMOUS
TWO PROLOGUES   [End 3 B.C.]

*Each is written in a different hand, neither in the hand which
wrote the recto. In the first piece, the words of each line are
repeated in the same metre but in a different order in a
companion line. In the second, after an introductory
passage, the plot was unfolded in lines which began in order
with letters* A, B, Γ, Δ, E *and so on to the end of the alphabet.
It seems clear that neither prologue has any necessary con-
nexion with the comedy written on the recto.*

(1) LOVE, son of Aphrodite, gentle youth
   (Youth gentle, son of Aphrodite, Love)
   Is come, to tell the following romance ;
   (The following romance to tell, is come) ;
   It happened in Ionia long since ;
   (Long since it happened in Ionia);

κό]ρην νεανίσκος [ν]έαν Τροιζ[ηνία]ν,
Τροιζηνίαν [νέαν ν]εανίσκ[ος κόρην
ἐπρίατ’ [ἐρασθ]εὶς [ϵ]ὔ[πορος πωλουμένην,
πωλουμένην εὔπορος ἐ[ρασθε]ὶς [ἐπρίατο.   10
Τροιζήνιος γεγενημ[ένος κατὰ τοὺς νόμους,
κατὰ τοὺς [ν]όμους γεγε[νη]μ[ένος Τροιζήνιος,
ἔ]χων γυναῖ[κα] κατε[βίω· τὸ τέρμ’ ἔχεις.
ἔχεις τὸ τέρμα· κατ[ϵ]β[ίω γυναῖκ’ ἔχων.

(2) ἱερὸς ὁ δῆμος· ἡ λέγουσ’ ἐγὼ Κύπ[ρ]ις
ἐν τῶι τόπωι δὴ τῶιδε δι’ ἐμοῦ π[ρ]ᾶγμά τι
γεγονός, δι’ ἧς ἅπαντα γίνεται κα[λ]ά,
ἥκω φράσουσα δεῦρο· τοῦ δὲ μὴ δοκ[ϵ]ῖν
ἡμᾶς ἀγυμνάστως ἔχειν ποιητ[ικ]ῆ[ς,   5
ἅμα μὲν τὸ πρᾶγμ’ [ἐ]ροῦμεν, ἅμα δ[ὲ] π[αιγνίωι
χρησόμεθα. τῶν ἐπῶν γὰρ ὧν μέλλ[ο]μ[ϵ]ν
    [ἐρεῖν
ἕκαστον ἀπὸ τῶν γραμμάτων ῥ[ηθήσεται,
ἃ δὴ νόμωι στοιχεῖα προσαγορεύομ[ϵ]ν,
ἓν ἀφ’ ἑνὸ[ς ἑ]ξῆς κατὰ φύσ[ι]ν γεγρα[μ]μ[ένα   10
ἀκόλουθα καὶ σύμφωνα· [δι]ατρ[ι]βὴ[ν] δ[ὲ μὴ
ἔχωμεν, ἀπὸ τοῦ δ’ ἄλφα [πρ]ῶ[το]ν ἄ[ρ]ξο[μαι.
Αὐτῶν ἑταῖροι [
Β . . . την . [μ]ισθωσάμεν[ο]ι [
Γ[15
Δ[
Ε[κτλ.

ANONYMOUS

A rich young man, seeing a maid at **Trozen,**
(At Trozen, seeing a maid, a rich young man,)
A prey to love, purchased her at a sale ;
(Purchased her at a sale, a prey to love) ;
He changed his nationality by law ;
(By law his nationality he changed) ;
He lived a married man.   That is the end.
(That is the end.   He lived a married man.)

(2) Blest is this people !   I Aphrodite, who address you, am come hither to expound a matter which on this very spot I brought to pass,—as I bring all fair things to pass.   To shew you that I am not inexpert in the poet's art, we will play a little game while we tell the story.   Each line we shall utter will begin with the written characters which we are accustomed to call letters, set down one after another in their natural order, consecutive and without discord.   Let us have no delay : I will start with the letter Alpha.—

(The plot is now unfolded in such a way that the lines begin with the letters of the alphabet in order—the first line with A, the second with B, and so forth till the end of the alphabet.)

MIME

ΣΩΦΡΩΝ

73 [1 A.D.]   FRAGMENT OF A MIME

Ed. pr. Vitelli-Norsa, *Studi Italiani di Filologia Classica*, x. 1932, pp. 119 and 249.   Republished by ed. pr. in *Papiri Greci e Latini*, xi. 1935, no. 1214 with Plate.   See Körte, *Archiv*, xi. 266 ; Eitrem, *Symb. Oslo.* xii. 10 ; Latte, *Philol.* 88, 259 and 467 ; Festa, *Mondo Class.* iii. 6 ; Gow, *C.R.* 47, 113 and 168 ; Gallavotti, *Riv. di Fil.* xi. 459 ; Legrand, *Rev. Et. Anc.* 1934, 24 ; Chantraine, *Rev. Phil.* 1935, 22 ; Kerényi, *Riv. di Fil.* xiii. 1935, 1 ; Lavagnini, *L'Ant. Class.* 4, 1935, 153.

A magic ceremony taken from contemporary life.   Comparatively straightforward and unadorned : yet the omission of certain essential parts of the ritual (Eitrem, p. 28) *shews that the poet's art is studied and selective.   A female magician and her assistant are performing an occult ceremony designed to liberate a group of persons (probably women) from illness or distress inflicted by Hecate.   The scene is an inner room, of which the doors are closed, to be opened only when all is ready for the climax of the ceremony (v. 11).   The sorceress commands her patients to set down a table " just as it is," i.e. immediately.   Then they must take salt in their hands (a measure of protection against malevolent spirits) and laurel about their ears (another protective or apotropaic measure ; their ears, because just such openings to the body might give access to the demon).   Thus equipped they are to sit beside the hearth ; which here, as often, serves for an altar.   There follow preparations for the sacrifice of a dog.   The magician*

328

SOPHRON

FRAGMENT OF A MIME [1 A.D.]

*bids her assistant give her a sword—two-edged, as usual in
these ceremonies. A dog (commonly the sacrifice in a rite
concerning Hecate) is brought to her. Asphalt, a torch and
incense are held ready for the act of lustration or purification
which must accompany the sacrifice. The climax is now at
hand. The doors are opened wide, letting the moonlight in.
The patients are exhorted to keep their eyes fixed on the door.
The torch is extinguished. Auspicious silence is demanded,
and the invocation of—or imprecation against— Hecate
begins.*

Theocritus, according to the Scholiast on Idyll ii. 69,
borrowed from Sophron τὴν τῶν πραγμάτων ὑπόθεσιν : *in the
preface to the same poem, Theocritus is censured for his*
ἀπειροκαλία *in borrowing the character Thestylis from
Sophron—not necessarily from the same mime, of course.
Theocritus's model was taken to be that mime of Sophron's
which was entitled* ταὶ γυναῖκες αἵ φαντι τὰν θεὰν ἐξελᾶν :
*of which one fragment, relating to magic, survives already
(*Athen. xi. 480 b*). To this mime Kaibel assigned six other
fragments which are or may be concerned with magic. There
was however still no evidence for a fair conclusion about the
subject of the mime, or even about the meaning of its title.*

*That our fragment belongs to Sophron is made highly
probable, if not certain, by the occurrence in it of the phrase*
πεῖ γὰρ ἄσφαλτος ; *attributed to Sophron by Ammonius, de*

329

diff. 122. *That it is part of the mime entitled* ταὶ γυναῖκες *κτλ., and that it is thus the model of Theocritus's second Idyll, is proved by nothing, and suggested by nothing but the subject and the atmosphere of magic. In general, about the relation of our fragment to Theocritus's poem, I agree with Legrand (p. 28) :—the two poems differ in characters and in scene of action ; in nature and purpose of ceremony ; in details of magic accessories and utensils ; in artistic treatment of their separate themes. They have almost nothing in common except a general background of magic. It follows therefore either that Theocritus borrowed nothing but this general background, or that this is not the mime of Sophron*

τὰν τράπεζαν κάτθετε
ὥσπερ ἔχει· λάζεσθε δὲ
ἁλὸς χονδρὸν ἐς τὰν χῆρα
καὶ δάφναν πὰρ τὸ ὦας.
ποτιβάντες νυν ποτ τὰν   5
ἱστίαν θωκεῖτε. δός μοι τὺ
τὤμφακες. φέρ' ὦ τὰν σκύλακα.
πεῖ γὰρ ἁ ἄσφαλτος; —— οὖτα. ——
ἔχε καὶ τὸ δάιδιον καὶ τὸν
λιβανωτόν. ἄγετε δὴ   10
πεπτάσθων μοι ταὶ θύραι
πᾶσαι. ὑμὲς δὲ ἐνταῦθα
ὁρῆτε, καὶ τὸν δαελὸν
σβῆτε ὥσπερ ἔχει. εὐκαμίαν
νυν παρέχεσθε, ᾶς κ' ἐγὼν   15
ποτ τᾶνδε π[υ]κταλεύσω.
πότνια, δεί[πν]ου μέν τυ καὶ
[ξ]ενίων ἀμεμφέων ἀντα[

16 τᾶνδε Π, defended by Chantraine, p. 25.

*from which he was borrowing : there is of course no reason
to suppose that this was the only mime which Sophron wrote
about a magic ceremony.   N.B. further that it is not certain
that this mime portrays an exorcism of Hecate : a θεοξενία
seems equally possible, cf. vv. 17-18 (Chantraine).*

*In Ammonius loc. cit. the words πεῖ γὰρ ἀσφαλτος are
followed by ποῖος εἰλισκοπεῖται.   Kaibel, wishing to intro-
duce Thestylis from the preface to Theocr. ii., changed this to
ποῖ (or πῦς), Θεστυλί, σκοπῆι τύ ; and added it to the frag-
ment πεῖ γὰρ ἀσφαλτος.   If Ammonius's quotation from
Sophron was taken from our mime (which is not absolutely
certain : the phrase πεῖ, κτλ. may well have occurred more than
once in Sophron), Kaibel's connexion of the two clauses is now
seen to be false.*

SORCERESS. Put the table down just as it is.   Take
a lump of salt in your hands and laurel beside your
ears.   Now go [a] to the hearth and sit down.   Give
me the sword, you : bring the dog here.   Why, where
is the pitch ?

ASSISTANT. Here it is.

SORCERESS. Take the taper and the incense. Come,
let me have all the doors open ! You watch over
there.   Put the torch out, just as it is.   Let me have
silence, now, while in these ladies' name I do my
fighting.—Lady Goddess, (you have found) your
feast and faultless offerings . . .

---

[a] ποτιβάντες :   the masc. particip. here must probably
denote (or include) *men* ; instances quoted of the masc.
particip. used of *women*, cf. Kühner-Gerth, i. 82, are not
parallel to our passage : as Chantraine observes, the alleged
parallels all have a character of *generality* which is not
present here.   It is not at all unlikely that some of the
participants in Sophron's μῖμοι γυναικεῖοι, esp. mute persons,
were male : see Kerényi, p. 4.

LITERARY PAPYRI

ANONYMOUS

74 [Ostrakon 2–1 B.C.] " DRUNKARD "

Ed. pr. Reinach, *Mélanges Perrot*, 1903, p. 291; revised text in *Papyrus grecs et démotiques*, 1905, A with Plate. See Crusius, *Herodae Mimiambi*, 1914, p. 137; *Powell, *Collectanea Alexandrina*, 181; Manteuffel, *de opusculis*

[A Ὁ τλήμων γ]έγονεν μεθύων κατὰ τρό-
      πον [εὐθ]υμῶν· πρόσεχε πρόσεχε.
[B] . . . . ν, Ναῖδες ἁβρόσφυροι,
    . . . . ὑπὸ γὰρ τῶν πολλῶν προ-
          πόσεων
      βακχεύων ἅ]λλομαι.   5
[A φεῦ, τλήμω]ν.
[B] ἐπὶ δέ τινα κῶμον ὁπλίζομαι·
      τραῦμα φ]ιλίης ἔχω τι παρὰ Κύπριδος
          ἄδηλον·
      Ἔρως μ᾽ ἔλα]β᾽ ὁ γόης· εἰς τὴν ψυχήν μου
          εἰσπε-
      σὼν [ποιεῖ μ]ε παραφρονεῖν.   10
[A παροινεῖς] ἄρα· σαυτοῦ κράτει, μή τι πάθῃς.
[B ἔα μ᾽ ὁρμᾶν κ]αὶ μή με περίσπα· ὁμολογῶ
          φιλεῖν, ἐρᾶν·
      καὶ οὐκ ἀντι]δικῶ· οὐ πάντες ἁπλῶς τὸ
          (τῆς) Παφίης
      φιλοῦμεν καὶ] ἐν ἀκρήτῳ μᾶλλον; ἀνα-
          κέκαυκέ με
      ὁ θεὸς ὁ Βρόμ]ιος ὁμοῦ καὶ Ἔρως, οἷς οὐκ
          ἀντι-   15
      σχεῖν [ἔξεστι.

ANONYMOUS

ANONYMOUS

" DRUNKARD " [Ostrakon 2–1 B.C.]

graecis, p. 164; Wilamowitz, *G.G.A.* 1905, 715; Blass, *Archiv*, iii. 280.

Fragment of a mime representing a conversation between two persons, one of whom (A) is sober, the other (B) drunk. B expresses himself in vivid and semi-poetical language.

(A) . . . the poor fellow is . . . he's drunk, and cheerful as usual.[a] Hark, hark !

(B) . . . nymphs of slender ankle, . . . drinking all those healths inspires me—up and down I leap !

(A) It is a sad case.

(B) I am ready for a revel ! I have a secret wound of love from Aphrodite.—Love, the wizard, has caught me. He has sunk deep into my soul—he drives me out of my wits !

(A) Drunk, are you ? Control yourself, or you may come to harm.

(B) Let me go my way, don't distract me, I confess my love, my longing,[b]—and I don't complain about it. Don't we every one of us adore the Paphian goddess's gifts, especially in our cups ? The gods of Wine and Love together have set my heart aflame : man cannot resist them. . . .

---

[a] " κατὰ τρόπον interpretor 'ut solet'" Crusius. Perhaps " suitably." Or κατὰ τρόπον εὐθύμων, " after the manner of merry men."   [b] Or " I confess I like to be in love."

---

13 (τῆς) D. L. P.   16 ἔξεστι Beazley.

ANONYMOUS

75 [1 A.D.]   LAMENT FOR A COCK

Ed. pr. Grenfell-Hunt, *P. Oxy.* ii. 1899, no. 219, p. 39.
See Crusius, *Herodae Mimiambi*, p. 131 ; Manteuffel, *de
opusculis graecis*, p. 166 (*qu. v.*, further bibliography) ;
*Powell, *Collectanea Alexandrina*, 182 ; Crönert, *Philol.* 84,
1928, 160. On the alleged metre : Wilamowitz, *G.G.A.*
1900, 50 (denies its existence) ; Crönert, *loc. cit.* and *Rh.
Mus.* 44, 1909, 444 ; Crusius, *op. cit.* p. 132 ; Prescott, *Class.*

```
          ] ἀλέκτορά μου [δ]υνάμεθα
. . . . τη . . σασω . . ασω ἐκ περιπάτου
. . . . . . . . ιθο . . . . σαι παρ᾽ ἀλιδρόσοις
. . . . . . . κουσ . . . . νησα . τα τὸν βαρ . . . . χηι
. . . . ἐκ π]αιδὸς ἐ[φ]ύλασσεν ὁ φίλος μου Τρύφων  5
οἷά περ τέ]κνον τη[ρ]ῶν ἐν ταῖς ἀγκάλαις.
ἀπορο]ῦμαι ποῦ βαδίσω· ἡ ναῦς μου ἐ(ρ)ράγη·
τὸν κ]α[τ]α[θ]ύμιον ἀπολέσας ὄρνιθά μου κλαίω
. . . φ]έρε τὸ ἐρνίο[ν] τροφὴν αὐτοῦ περιλάβω,
τοῦ μ[αχ]ίμου τοῦ ἐπεραστοῦ τοῦ Ἑλληνικοῦ.  10
χάρ[ιν τ]ούτου ἐκαλούμην μέγας ἐν τῶι βίωι
καὶ [ἐλ]εγόμην μακάρι[ο]ς, ἄνδρες, ἐν τοῖς φιλο-
      τρόφ[οις.
ψυχομαχῶ· ὁ γὰρ ἀ[λ]έκτωρ ἠστόχηκέ μου
καὶ θακοθάλπαδος ἐρασθεὶς ἐμὲ ἐγκατέλιπε.
ἀλλ᾽ ἐπιθεὶς λίθον ἐμαυτοῦ ἐπὶ τὴν καρδίαν  15
καθ[η]συχάσομαι. ὑμε[ῖ]ς δ᾽ ὑγιαίνετε φίλοι.
```

ANONYMOUS

LAMENT FOR A COCK [1 A.D.]

Phil. **v.** 1909, 158; Platt, *Class. Rev.* 13, 440; Postgate, *ibid.* 441.

Fragment from the end of a lament for the loss of a fighting-cock. The speaker is a man, or youth. Traces of an earlier column in the left-hand margin prove that this was a fairly long piece.

. . . we can . . . my cock . . . after (?) a walk . . . beside the sea-bedewed . . . from its childhood my friend Tryphon guarded it, watching over it like a baby in his arms. I know not whither I may go : my ship is wrecked. I weep for the darling bird that I have lost ! Come, let me embrace its chick, this child of the fighter, the beloved, the gallant Greek ! For his sake I was accounted a success in life, I was called a happy man, gentleman, among those who love their pets. I fight for life—my cock has gone astray : he has fallen in love with a sitting hen, and left me in the lurch. I will set a tombstone above my heart, and be at rest. And you, my friends—goodbye to you !

---

6 Crusius.　　9 ἑρκίο[ν Crusius, Crönert.　　12 φιλο-τροφι Π, corr. Crusius.　　13 ψυχομαχωι Π, corr. edd. 14 θακαθάλπαδος Π, corr. Bechtel, *cl.* Herodes vii. 48 ὅπως νεοσσοῖ τὰς κόχωνας θάλποντες : τάχα Θάλπιδος Blass; ἐμὲν Π (*v.* Dieterich, *Unters. zur Gesch. d. gr. Sprache,* 190) 15 εματου Π, later form of ἐμαυτοῦ frequent in papyri.

ANONYMOUS

76 [2 A.D.]   CHARITION

Ed. pr. Grenfell-Hunt, *P. Oxy.* iii. 1903, no. 413, p. 41.
See Crusius, *Herodae Mimiambi*, p. 101, *N. Jahrb.* 25,
1910, 98 and *Sitzb. Bayer. Akad.* 1904, 357 ; Winter, *de
mimis Oxy.*, diss. Leips. 1906 ; Manteuffel, *de opusculis
graecis*, p. 127 ; Blass, *Archiv*, iii. 279, *Lit. Centralbl.* 1903,
1478 ; Sudhaus, *Hermes*, 41, 1906, 247 ; Knoke, *de Charitio
mimo*, diss. Kiel, 1908 ; Rostrup, *Acad. roy. sci. et lettres de
Danemark*, Bull. 1915, no. 2 ; Reich, *der Mimus*, 1903, i. and
Deut. Lit.-Zeit. 1933, 44 ; Zielinski, *Phil. Woch.* 1907, 865 ;
Wilamowitz, *Kultur der Gegenwart*, 1905, i. 8, p. 125 ;
Romagnoli, *Riv. d' Italia*, 1904, 500 ; Powell-Barber, *New
Chapters*, i. 121 ; on the musical symbols esp. Winter, *op.
cit.* 40 ; Manteuffel, *Eos*, 32, 1929, 40 ; Knoke, *op. cit.* 22 ;
on the barbarian language esp. Hultzsch, *Hermes*, 39, 1904,
37 ; Winter, *op. cit.* 23 ; Rice *ap.* Powell-Barber, *New
Chapters*, ii. 215 ; Barnett, *J. Eg. Arch.* 12, 1926, 13.
Preisendanz, *Phil. Woch.* 36, 1916, 651.   Vv. 95-98, 103-end,
Powell, *Collect. Alexandr.* p. 181.

*The scene is the coast of a barbarian country bordering on
the Indian Ocean.   The subject is the adventures of Charition,
a young Hellene woman, and a party of other Hellenes.
Charition is in the power of barbarians.   Their king (who
can speak some Greek) intends to sacrifice her to Selene, in
whose temple she has taken refuge.   Her brother has arrived
with a party of Hellenes : and they effect her rescue by
making her captors drunk.*

*This is a low sort of music-hall performance.   Such are
the lack of invention in the story, and of inspiration in the
style, that the chief sources of amusement are the dirty
humour of the Clown and the gibberish of the savages.   It is
indeed a far cry from Attic Tragedy : yet thereto it owes,
however remotely, its plot.   Euripides'* Iphigenia **in**

336

ANONYMOUS

CHARITION [2 A.D.]

Tauris *was evidently the model for the story (see Winter, p. 26 : Charition = Iphigenia ; the barbarian king = Thoas ; the foolish friend (B) = Pylades ; in both works the sister, priestess of a goddess in a barbaric country, is rescued by her brother who outwits the local king. Most striking, too, is the parallel between the theft of the sacred image in I.T. and the proposed theft of the goddess's property in our mime). Euripides' Cyclops probably suggested the detail of the heroine's escape.*

The date of the composition is uncertain : probably not much earlier than the age of the Papyrus itself ; late 1st or early 2nd century A.D. would be a likely date.

The barbarian " language " : Hultzsch (loc. cit. : cf. Sama Sastri, ap. Rice, loc. cit.) suggested that it may wholly or partly represent an ancient Indian dialect. There are, it seems, a few more or less striking coincidences, e.g. κονζει = konĉa (Dravidian, " a little ") ; πετρεκιω = pātrakke (Kanarese, " to a cup ") ; πανουμβρητικα = pānam amṛita (Sanskrit, " a drink, nectar "). But it is doubtful whether these coincidences are more significant than e.g. the equation ουενι = veni (Latin, " come "). Rice (loc. cit., cf. Knoke, p. 22) was sceptical about the theory of Hultzsch : to which Barnett, loc. cit., dealt what to the layman seems a death-blow. In any case, the ancient audiences, of course, would not have understood a syllable of the jargon ; they merely rejoiced in the exquisite humour of polysyllabic nonsense.

The characters : A is Charition, the heroine ; B is a buffoon ; Γ is Charition's brother, who rescues her ; Δ is captain of the rescue-ship ; ϛ is one of the Greek party (Winter, pp. 34-35, thinks him identical with ♀ : unlikely

and unnecessary); ♀ (ϛ *in the Papyrus*) *and* Z *are barbarians*;
whose king is designated ΒΑΣ(ΙΛΕΥΣ); *the sign* Κοι(νῇ),
"*all together,*" *denotes the unanimous voice of a group,*
whether of Greeks or of barbarians; *at v. 9 enters a group*
of barbarian women, returned from hunting.

Stage-directions: T (⊤ *in the Papyrus*) *probably refers*
to the music, and may stand for T(υμπανισμός): cf. τ(υμ-
πανισμὸς) πολ(ύς), τ(υμπανισμὸς) έ (=πεντάκις?). Κρουσ(ις)=
"*a striking*" (*of musical instruments*). *The two strokes,*
= (*curved*, ⤨, *in the Papyrus*), *which sometimes stand*
before or after T *but more often by themselves, may also*

⟦   ϛ κυρία Χαρίτιον, σύγχαιρε τούτ[ων μοι
       λελυμένωι.

   Α μεγάλοι οἱ θεοί.

   Β ποῖοι θεοί, μωρέ; Πορδή.

   Α παῦσαι, ἄνθρωπε.   5

   ϛ αὐτοῦ με ἐκδέχεσθε, ἐγὼ δὲ πορ[ευ-
       θεὶς τὸ πλοῖον ἔφορμον [
       ποιήσω.

   Α πορεύου· ἰδοὺ καὶ αἱ γυναῖκες [
       αὐτῶν ἀπὸ κυνηγίου παραγίγνοντ[αι.   10

   Β οὔ, πηλίκα τοξικὰ ἔχουσι.

ΓΥΝ[Η] κραυνου.   ΑΛ[ΛΗ] λαλλε.

ΑΛ[ΛΗ] λαιταλιαντα λαλλε αβ . . αιγμ[

ΑΛ[ΛΗ] κοτακως αναβ . ιωσαρα.

   Β χαίρετε =   15

ΚΟΙ[ΝΗΙ] λασπαθια =

   Β αἳ κυρία, βοήθει.

1-43, written on the verso of Π, are almost certainly an
actor-interpolator's rewriting of a portion of the mime on the
recto, marked there (in part) for deletion, viz. col. i. 30-36

*have some musical significance (Winter, pp. 40-42 suggests
that they are a conventional drawing of castanets ; the
straight horizontal dash — may similarly depict some sort
of flute or pipe). The word πορδ(ή), once associated with
the remarks of the Clown, is surely a stage-direction : it
may have played an integral part in the action of the farce
(Winter, p. 45 : artillery to repel the approach of the bar-
barians, cf. vv. 45-46). V. 101 καταστολή probably means
" Finale " or " Dénouement," cf. καταστροφή, p. 364 below.*

*The piece is written in vaguely rhythmical prose, with one
short metrical interval (95-98 Sotad. ; 103 iamb. ; 105-110
and 112 troch. tetr. ; 111 iamb.).*

(F) Lady Charition, rejoice with me at my escape !

Charit. Great are the gods !

Clown. The gods indeed ! Idiot ! (*Makes a vul-
gar noise.*)

Char. Fellow, less noise !

(F) Wait for me here. I'll go and bring the ship
to anchor.

Char. Go along, then. Look, here are their
women, back from hunting !

Clown. Ooh ! What huge bows they have !

A Woman. *Kraunou.*

Another Woman. *Lalle.*

Another Woman. *Laitalianta lalle . . .*

Another Woman. *Kotakos anab . iosara.*

Clown. Good day to you !

Chorus. *Laspathia.*

Clown. Lady, help me !

Hunt (too fragmentary for inclusion here), and 46-63 of
my text. I print the whole of the interpolation together at
the head of the piece, vv. 1-43.   1-25 rewrites col. i.
30-36 Hunt, 26-43 rewrites 46-63.   6-8 πορευθεὶς ποιήσω
Π, ποιήσω secl. Hunt.

A ἀλεμακα = ΚΟΙ[ΝΗΙ] ἀλεμακα. [

B παρ' ἡμῶν ἐστὶ †οὐκ ηλεω† μὰ τὴν 'Α[θήνην.

A ταλαίπωρε, δόξασαί σε πολέμι[ο]ν   20
   εἶναι παρ' ὀλίγον ἐτόξευσαν. [

B πάντα μοι κακά· θέλεις οὖν κα[ὶ ταύ]τ[ας
   εἰς τὸν Ψώλιχον ποταμὸν [ἀπελάσω;

A ὡς θέλεις. Τ. Β πορδή. [

ΚΟΙ[ΝΗΙ] μινει.   25

5 κυρία Χαρίτιον, καταρχὴν [βλέπω τοῦ
   ἀνέμου ὥστε ἡμᾶς πε[ράσαντας
   τὸ Ἰνδικὸν πέλαγος ὑπ[οφυγεῖν·
   ὥστε εἰσελθοῦσα τὰ σε[αυτῆς ἆρον,
   καὶ ἐάν τι δύνῃ τῶν ἀν[αθημάτων   30
   τῆς θεοῦ βάστασον.

A σ[ω]φ[ρό]νησον, ἄνθρωπε· ο[ὐ δεῖ τοὺς σω-
   τηρία[ς] δεομένους μετ[ὰ ἱεροσυλίας
   ταύτην ἀπὸ θεῶν αἰτε[ῖσθαι.
   πῶς γὰρ ὑπακούσουσιν αὐ[τῶν πονη-   35
   ρίαι τὸν ἔλεον ἐπισπωμ[ένων;

B σὺ μὴ ἅπτου, ἐγὼ ἀρῶ.

5 σὺ τοίνυν τὰ σεαυτῆς ἆρον.

A οὐδ' ἐκείνων χρείαν ἔχω, μόν[ον δὲ τὸ πρόσω-
   πον τοῦ πατρὸς θεάσασθ[αι.   40

5 εἴσελθε τοίνυν· σὺ δὲ ὄψον [
   διακονήσῃς ἀκρατέστερ[ον τὸν οἶνον

   διδούς, αὐτοὶ γὰρ οὗτοι πρ[οσέρχονται.]]]

.   .   .   .

19 οὐκ ηλεω unintelligible and probably corrupt : οὐ κηλεῖν

ANONYMOUS

CHAR. *Alemaka.*

CHORUS. *Alemaka.*

CLOWN. By Athene, there is no . . . from us !

CHAR. You poor fool, they took you for an enemy and nearly shot you !

CLOWN. Nothing but trouble for me ! Would you like me to drive them too away to the river Psolichus ?

CHAR. Just as you please.

(Drums. Clown imitates them)

CHORUS. *Minei.*

(F) Lady Charition, I see the wind is getting up, so we may escape across the Indian Ocean ! Go in and take up your belongings. And pick up any of the goddess's offerings you can.

(A) My good fellow, be sensible ! Those in need of salvation must not commit sacrilege in the moment of asking the gods for it. How are they going to listen to men who try to win mercy with wrong-doing ?

CLOWN. Don't you touch it—I will take it up !

(F) Well, take up your own things then.

CHAR. I don't need them either : all I want is to see my father's face.

(F) Go in, then. As for you (*to the Clown*), serve their food, give them their wine rather strong. Here they come in person ! ⎤⎤

.   .   .   .   .   .

---

is possible, but hardly makes sense (Hunt, who suggests that there may have been some play on αλεμακα v. 18). οὐκ ᾔδειν Crusius.   22-23 Crusius.   26 Π has αγων[in left-hand margin. A stage-direction ἀγωνία, ἀγώνισμα seems hardly appropriate at this point. Perhaps misplaced, see Manteuffel *ad loc.*

B δοκῶ χοιριδίων θυγατέρες εἰσί· ἐγὼ καὶ
    ταύτας

    ἀπολύσω. Τ. πορδ(ή). κοι[νηι] αι αρ-
    μινθι = — Τ.   45

B καὶ αὗται εἰς τὸν Ψώλιχον πεφεύγασι.

Γ καὶ μάλα, ἀλλὰ ἑτοιμαζώμεθα [ἐ]ὰν σωθῶμεν.

B κυρία Χαρίτιον, ἑτοιμάζου ἐὰν δυνηθῆις τι
    τῶν ἀναθημάτων τῆς θεοῦ μαλῶσαι.

A εὐφήμει· οὐ δεῖ τοὺς σωτηρίας δεομένους με- 50
    θ' ἱεροσυλίας ταύτην παρὰ θεῶν αἰτεῖσθαι.
    πῶς γὰρ ὑπακού(σ)ουσι ταῖς εὐχαῖς πονηρίαι
    τὸν ἔλεον μελλόντων παρ[ασπᾶ]σθαι; τὰ τῆς
    θεοῦ δεῖ μένειν ὁσίως.

B σὺ μὴ ἅπτου, ἐγὼ ἀρῶ. A μὴ παῖζε, ἀλλ'
    ἐὰν παρα-   55
    γένωνται διακόνει αὐτοῖς τὸν οἶνον ἄ[κ]ρατον.

B ἐὰν δὲ μὴ θέλουσιν οὕτως πίνειν;

Γ μωρέ, ἐν [τ]ούτοις τοῖς τόποις οἶνος [οὐ]κ
    ὤνι[ος,
    λοιπὸν [δὲ] ἐὰν τοῦ γένους δράξω[ν]τα[ι]
    ἀπειρ[ί]αι πο-
    θοῦντ[ες] ἄκρατον πίνουσιν.   60

B ἐγὼ αὐτοῖς καὶ τὴν τρυγίαν διακο[ν]ῶ.

45 ? ἀπελάσω.   47 Sudhaus.   50 Cf. Alciphron

CLOWN. Daughters of little swine, I call them. I will get rid of them too.

(*Drums. Clown imitates them*)

CHORUS. *Ai arminthi.*

(*Drums*)

CLOWN. So they too have run away to the Psolichus!

(C) They have indeed. But let's get ready, if we are to escape.

CLOWN. Lady Charition, get ready, see if you can tuck under your arm one of the offerings to the goddess.

CHAR. Hush! Those in need of salvation must not commit sacrilege in the moment of asking the gods for it. How are they going to listen to the prayers of those who mean to snatch mercy through wrongdoing? The goddess's property must remain in sanctity.

CLOWN. Don't you touch it—I will take it up.

CHAR. Don't be silly. Serve them their wine neat, if they come here.

CLOWN. Suppose they refuse to drink it so?

(C) Idiot, wine is not for sale in this country [a]: it follows that if they get their hands on this kind of thing, inexperience whets their appetite,—they drink it neat.

CLOWN. I'll serve them, dregs and all!

---

[a] Wine has never been produced in India (see Winter, *op. cit.* p. 25) except sparsely in a very few districts (Strabo, p. 694).

---

3. 46. 3 τὸ χειρόμακτρον ὑπὸ μάλης λαβὼν ἐξηλλόμην (Winter). 52 ὑπακουουσι Π, corr. D. L. P.; *cf.* v. 35. 53 παρασπᾶσθαι Sudhaus. 59 End Manteuffel.

Γ αὐτοὶ δὲ οὗτοι λελουμένοι μετὰ **τῶν**
 [. . . . . . .]
 παραγίγνονται. Τ ἀναπεσ( ). Τ δίς
 μέσος. Ϋ. . . . . οσαλλ[

ΒΑϹ[ΙΛΕΥϹ] βραθις. ΚΟΙ[ΝΗΙ] βραθεις. Β τί
 λέγου[σι;

 Γ εἰς τὰ μερίδια, φησί, λάχωμεν. Β λάχω-
 [μ]εν. Τ.   65

ΒΑϹ[ΙΛΕΥϹ] στουκεπαιρομελλοκοροκη. Β βάσκ᾽,
 ἄλαστε.

ΒΑϹ[ΙΛΕΥϹ β]ραθιε = Τ. βερη· κονζει· δαμυν· πε-
 τρεκιω
 πακτει· κορταμες· βερη· ιαλερω· δεπωμενζι
 πετρεκιω· δαμυτ· κινζη· παξει· ζεβης· λολω
 βια· βραδις· κοττως. ΚΟΙ[ΝΗΙ] κοττως.   70

 Β κοττως ὑμᾶς λακτίσαιτο. ΒΑϹ[ΙΛΕΥϹ] ζοπιτ.
 Τ.

 Β τί λέγουσι; Γ πεῖν δὸς ταχέως.

 Β ὀκνεῖς οὖν λαλεῖν; καλήμερε, χαῖρε. = Τ.

ΒΑϹ[ΙΛΕΥϹ] ζεισουκορμοσηδε. Τ. Β ἆ, μὴ ὑγι-
 αίνων.

 Γ ὑδαρές ἐστι, βάλε οἶνον. Τ πολ(ύς).   75

 Ϙ σκαλμακαταβαπτειραγουμι.

---

63 Perhaps for ἀναπαισ[τικός] Hunt : ἀναπλασ(σόμενος)
Manteuffel. Τ δισ(σὸς) μέσο(ς) Manteuffel, who writes also
ὁ[τόπ]ος ἀλλ[άσσεται.   76 γουμμι ed. pr., -γουμ Knoke.

 ª So ed. pr.: perhaps "Don't, if you are in your senses!"

(C) Here they come, bathed, with . . .

(Drums, twice, mouerate)

KING. *Brathis.*
CHORUS. *Bratheis.*
CLOWN. What do they say ?
(C) " Let us draw lots for portions," he says.
CLOWN. Yes, let us !

(Drums)

KING. *Stoukepairomellokoroke.*
CLOWN. Get away, confound you !
KING. *Brathie.*

(Drums)

*Bere konzei damun petrekio paktei kortames bere ialero
depomenzi petrekio damut kinze paxei zebes lolo bia
bradis kottos.*
CHORUS. *Kottos.*
CLOWN. May *Kottos* kick you hard !
KING. *Zopit.*

(Drums)

CLOWN. What do they mean ?
(C) Give them a drink, hurry up.
CLOWN. So you won't talk ? Good day to you,
hullo there !

(Drums)

KING. *Zeisoukormosede.*

(Drums)

CLOWN. Not if I know it ! [a]
(C) It's watery : put some wine in.

(Drums, loud)

♀ *Skalmakatabapteiragoumi.*

345

z τουγουμμι = νεκελεκεθρω.   ϙ ειτουβελ-
    λετρα

    χουπτεραγουμι.   Β αἴ = μὴ ἀηδίαν· παύ-
        σασθε.   Τ. =

    αἴ = τί ποιεῖτε; z τραχουντερμανα.

ϙ βουλλιτικαλουμβαι πλαταγουλδα = βι[80
    απυλευκασαρ.   Τ. Β[ΑΣ(ΙΛΕΤΣ)] χορβονορ-
        βοθορβα[

    τουμιωναξιζδεσπιτ πλαταγουλδα = βι[
    σεοσαραχις.   Τ. ΒΑΣ[ΙΛΕΤΣ] . . . οραδω =
        σατυρ[Τ.

ΒΑΣ[ΙΛΕΤΣ] ουαμεσαρεσυμψαραδαρα = ηι = ια = δα[
    Β   μαρθα = μαριθουμα εδμαιμαι = μαιθο[85
        θαμουνα μαρθα = μαριθουμα. Τ. . . . . τυν[
ΒΑΣ[ΙΛΕΤΣ] μαλπινιακουρουκουκουβι = — καρακο
        . . . ρα
ΚΟΙ[ΝΗΙ] αβα. ΒΑΣ[ΙΛΕΤΣ] ζαβεδε = — ζαβιλιγι-
        δουμβα. ΚΟ[Ι(ΝΗΙ)].

    αβα ουν[
ΒΑΣ[ΙΛΕΤΣ] πανουμβρητικατεμανουαμβρητουουενι.   90
ΚΟΙ[ΝΗΙ] πανουμβρητικατεμανουαμβρητουουενι.

    παρακουμβρητικατε[μ]ανουαμβρητουουενι
    ολυσαδιζαπαρδαπισκουπισκατεμαν = αρει-
        μαν[

    ριδαου = — ουπατει[ ]α = — Τ έ.

ΒΑΣ[ΙΛΕΤΣ βά]ρβαρον ἀνάγω χορὸν ἄπλετον, θεὰ 95
        Σελή[νη,

    πρὸς ῥυθμὸν ἀνέτωι ῥήματι βαρβάρωι [προ-
        βαίνων.

ANONYMOUS

Z *Tougoummi nekelekethro.*
♀ *Eitoubelletra choupteragoumi.*
CLOWN. Oh ! Stop your dirty tricks !

(Drums)

What are you doing ?
Z *Trachountermana.*
♀ *Boullitikaloumbai platagoulda bi . . . apuleukasar.*

(Drums)

KING. *Chorbonorbothorba toumionaxizdespit plata-goulda bi . . . seosarachis.*

(Drums)

KING. . . . *Orado satur . . .*

(Drums)

KING. *Ouamesaresumpsaradara.*
        Ei   ia   da
CLOWN. *Martha marithouma edmaimai maitho . . . thamouna martha marithouma.*

(Drums)

. . . *tun* . . .
KING. *Malpiniakouroukoukoubi karako . . . ra.*
CHORUS. *Aba.*
KING. *Zabede zabiligidoumba.*
CHORUS. *Aba oun . . .*
KING. *Panoumbretikatemanouambretououeni.*
CHORUS. *Panoumbretikatemanouambretououeni para-koumbretikatemanouambretououeni olusadizapardapiskou-piskateman areiman . . . ridaou oupatei . a.*

(Drums, five times)

KING. Barbaric, unconfined the dance I lead, O goddess Moon !—advancing with barbaric step, in-

347

Ἰνδῶν δὲ πρόμοι πρὸς ἱ[ε]ρόθρουν = δότε [
[Σ]ηρικὸν ἰδίως θεαστικὸν βῆμα παρα-
λ[.] . . Τ πολ(ύς), κροῦσ(ις). ΚΟΙ[ΝΗΙ]
ορκισ[.] Β τί πάλι
λέγουσι;   100

Γ ὄρχησαί φησι. Β πάντα τὰ τῶν ζώντων.
Τ. Πορδ(ή).

Γ ἀναβαλόντες αὐτὸν ταῖς ἱεραῖς ζώναις κατα-
[δήσα]τε. Τ πολύς. Καταστολή.

Β οὗτοι μὲν ἤδη τῆι μέθηι βαροῦνται.

Γ ἐπαινῶ. σὺ δέ, Χαρίτιον, δεῦρο ἔξω.

Α δεῦ[ρ', ἀδ]ελφέ, θᾶσσον· (ἆρ') ἄπανθ' ἕτοιμα
τυγχάν[ει;   105

Γ πάντα γ[ά]ρ· τὸ πλοῖον ὁρμεῖ πλησίον· τί
μέλλετε;
σοὶ [λέ]γω, πρωρεῦ, παράβαλε δεῦρ' ἄγων
τὴ[ν ναῦν ταχύ.

Δ ἐὰν ἐγὼ π[ρ]ώτως κελεύσω

Β   πάλι λαλεῖς, καταστροφεῦ;
ἀπο[λ]ίπωμεν αὐτὸν ἔξω καταφιλεῖν (τὸν)
πύνδ[ακα.

Γ ἔνδον ἐστὲ πάντες; ΚΟΙ[ΝΗΙ] ἔνδον. Α
ὦ τάλαιν[α συμφορᾶς,   110
τρόμος πολύς με τὴν παναθλίαν κρατεῖ.
εὐμενής, δέσποινα, γίγνου· σῶ(ι)ζε τὴν σὴν
πρό[σπολον.

97 [κροταλισμόν Winter.   108 εαν π[ρ]ωτος εγω ὁ κυ-
βερνήτης κελεύσω Π; corr. Hunt, Crusius (ὁ κυβερνήτης is
probably a gloss on ἐγώ).   110 Sudhaus.

temperate in rhythm! Chieftains of India, bring
the drum of mystic sound! The frenzied Seric step
. . . severally . . .

(Drums, loud : clapping)

CHORUS. *Orkis* . . .
CLOWN. What are they saying again?
(C) He says, dance.
CLOWN. Just like real men!

(Drums. Clown imitates them)

(C) Hoist him up and bind him with the sacred
girdles!

(Drums, loud : Dénouement)

CLOWN. Well, they're heavy now with the drink——
(C) Good! Charition, come out here!
CHAR. Come, brother, quickly! Is everything
ready?
(C) Yes, everything. The boat is at anchor not
far away. What are you waiting for? Helmsman!
I tell you to bring the ship alongside here at once!
SHIP'S CAPTAIN. If I give the order first——
CLOWN. What, talking again, you bungler? Let's
leave him outside to kiss the ship's behind!
(C) Are you all aboard?
CHORUS. All aboard.
CHAR. Woe is me! A mighty trembling masters
me, unhappy! Grant us your favour, Lady goddess!
Save your handmaiden!

ANONYMOUS

77 [2 A.D.] ADULTERESS

Ed. pr. *Grenfell-Hunt, *P. Oxy.* iii. 1903, no. 413, p. 41.
See Crusius, *Herodae Mimiambi*, p. 110 ; Sudhaus, *Hermes*,
41, 1906, 247 ; Knox, *Philol.* 81, 243 : Manteuffel, *de opus-
culis graecis*, pp. 46 and 138, *qu. v.* for further bibliography ;
Powell-Barber, *New Chapters*, i. 122 ; Reich, *der Mimus*, i. ;
Lynghy, *Eranos*, 26, 52 ; Winter, *op. cit.* p. 49 ; Knoke, *op.
cit.* (revised text), p. 35.

*I follow Crusius's text in the distribution of parts from
vv. 60-end (except in v. 61, where he makes no change of
speaker after γελάσω). This distribution, however incorrect
it may be in detail, is certainly correct in principle. The
division of the piece into separate scenes is based upon no
explicit indication in Π, but appears to be a necessary ex-
pedient. I suppose a pause of only a few seconds at the end
of each scene : longer intervals are unlikely. The Archi-
mima leaves the stage at v. 10 εἰσελεύσομαι ; there is an
interval after εἰσελθόντες v. 19 ; again after ἔλθετε v. 26
the Adulteress departs, and returns almost immediately,
ἐξιοῦσα v. 26 ; she leaves again at εἰσελθέ v. 35, at ἀπελ-
θόντες καὶ ἡμεῖς v. 44, at εἰσελθοῦσα v. 51, and at εἰσελθόντες
v. 56. A break in the performance is most clearly indicated
by v. 10 ; the slaves remove their victims, and the Adulteress
says that she will go indoors ; but in the same line the slaves
have evidently returned, their mission accomplished (or
rather frustrated) ; clearly there was a pause in the action
after εἰσελεύσομαι v. 10, during which the Adulteress left the
scene for a moment. Cf. vv. 25-26 : the Adulteress orders
the execution of Aesopus,—and at once inspects his corpse ;
again, there was a brief interval for the fulfilment of her
commands.*

It is probable that all the rôles were enacted by one Archi-

350

ANONYMOUS

ADULTERESS [2 A.D.]

mima (*Winter, p. 54*) : *for the sake of clearness, I write as though the separate characters were portrayed by separate actors. The plot appears to be* :—

Scene I—The Adulteress (hereinafter A) has made advances to a slave Aesopus, who refuses her. She condemns him to death, together with his mistress Apollonia. Slaves remove the convicts : A goes indoors to await their report.

Scene II—The slaves, who have probably released their fellows through compassion, report that Aesopus and Apollonia have escaped, apparently through divine intervention. A demands that they be caught and brutally executed. She withdraws again.

Scene III—Apollonia returns and is arrested ; her execution and the arrest of Aesopus are commanded.

Scene IV—Aesopus is brought, apparently dead, to the door. A mourns him.

Scene V—A plots with Malacus (a slave who is eager to enjoy the favour of his mistress) to poison her husband. They withdraw together.

Scene VI—A inspects the body of Apollonia, who has been brought in—apparently dead—and laid beside Aesopus. A sends a parasite to summon her doomed husband, and departs to prepare the fatal table.

Scene VII—A announces that all is ready, and goes indoors to accomplish her murderous designs.

Scene VIII—The husband is carried on to the scene, apparently dead. The Archimima has now finished the rôle of the Adulteress, and begins to enact a dialogue between the minor characters. The parasite laments the passing of his master ; Malacus interrupts and begins a dirge ; but

351

LITERARY PAPYRI

*suddenly the husband, who was only feigning death, leaps up
and orders Spinther to belabour Malacus. The husband now
perceives the figure of Aesopus, and inquires who he is : from
the reply it appears that Aesopus and Apollonia are both
alive and well.*

This is a fine piece of writing in its class. The construc-

I

ὥστε, παῖδ(ες), συνλαβόντ(ες) τοῦτον
ἕλκετε ἐπὶ τὴν
πεπρωμένην. προάγετε νῦν κἀκείνην ὡς
ἔστιν
πεφιμωμένη. ὑμῖν λέγω, ἀπαγαγόντες αὐ-
τούς
κατὰ ἀμφότερα τὰ ἀκρωτήρι[α κ]αὶ τὰ
παρακείμενα
δένδρα προσδήσατε, μακρὰν διασπ[ά]σαντες 5
ἄλλον ἀπ᾽ [ἄ]λλου καὶ βλέπετε μή πο(τε) τῶι
ἑτέρωι
δείξητε, μὴ τῆς ἀλλήλων ὄψεως [πλ]ησθέντες
μεθ᾽ ἡδον[ῆ]ς ἀποθάνωσι. σφαγιάσαντες δὲ
αὐτοὺς
πρός με ἔσω ἀντᾶτε. εἴρηκα· ἐγὼ δ᾽ ἔνδον
εἰσ-
ελεύσομα[ι].

II

τί λέγετε ὑμ(εῖς); ὄντ(ως)
ο[ἱ] θεοὶ ὑμῖν   10
ἐφαντάσθ(ησαν), [κ]αὶ ὑμεῖς ἐφοβήθ[ητ]ε,
κα[ὶ . . . . .
γεγόνασι; [ἐ]γὼ [ὑ]μῖν καταγγ[έλλω], ἐκεῖ-
νοι

ANONYMOUS

*tion is elaborate and dramatically good ; the language is
powerful, picturesque, sometimes even poetical. This author,
who probably lived near the end of the 1st century A.D.,
controls the Greek language easily, and affects a pleasing
directness and economy of style. This Archimima has
indeed an excellent part to play, varied and vivid,—first
furious and vindictive, then repentant and sentimental ;
first exultant, then subtly cunning and sinister.*

*The writer's model was clearly the fifth Mime of Herodes:
and it may not be fanciful to detect the influence of Euripides'
Medea upon the character of the Archimima.*

Scene I

(A) So seize him, slaves, and drag him to his doom.
Now bring out the woman too, gagged, just as she is.
I order you to take them away to the two promon-
tories and bind them down to the trees there ; drag
them far apart from each other, and see that you
don't shew one to the other, lest they die rejoicing,
feasting their eyes upon each other ! When you
have cut their throats, come and meet me inside.
That is all. I'm going indoors.

Scene II

(A) What are you saying ? Oh really, the gods
appeared to you, and you were frightened, and they
(escaped) ? . . . I can tell you this, that even if they

---

11 κα[ὶ ἐκεῖν](οι) ἀόρατ(οι) Knoke, Crusius.   12 κατ-
αγγέλλω Crusius.

εἰ καὶ ὑμᾶ[ς] δ[ιέ]φυγον τοὺς ὀρε[ο]φ[ύλ]ακας
    οὐ μὴ λάθωσι.
νυνὶ δὲ τοῖς θεοῖς ἀπαρᾶσ(θ)αι βούλομαι,
    Σπινθήρ·
ὄμοσον· ἔπιπ . . . σ . . . . ινόμενα.
λ[έγ]ετε   15
τὰ πρὸς τὰ[ς] θυσίας. ἐπειδὰν οἱ θεοὶ καὶ
    ἐπ᾽ ἀγαθῶι
ἡμῖν φα[ί]νεσθαι μέλλω(σιν) ὡς προσέχ(οντες)
    ὑμνήσ(ατε)
τοὺς θεού[ς]. μαστιγία, οὐ θέλ(εις) ποιεῖν
    τὰ ἐπιτασσόμε(να);
τί γέγονε[ν; ἦ] μαίνη(ι); εἰσελθόντ(ες) ἴδετε
    τίς ἐστιν.

III

τί φησιν; (ἦδ᾽) ἦν ἄρα; ἴδετε μὴ [κ]αὶ ὁ
    ὑπερήφανος   20
ἔσω ἐστί. ὑμῖν λέγω, ἀπαλλά[ξα]ντες ταύ-
    την πα-
ράδοτε τ[οῖς] ὀρεοφύλαξι καὶ εἴπατε ἐν
    πολλῶι σιδήρωι
τηρεῖν ἐ[π]ιμελῶς. ἕλκετε, σύρετε, ἀπάγετε.
καὶ ὑ[μ]εῖ[ς δ]ὲ ἐκεῖνον ἀναζητήσαντες
    ἀποσφα-
γιάσαντές τ]ε προβάλετε ἵνα [ἐγ]ὼ αὐτὸν
    νεκρὸν ἴδω.   25
ἔλθετε Σπι]νθήρ, Μάλακε, μετ᾽ ἐμοῦ·

IV

                    ἐξιοῦσα
. . . . . . ἀκρ]ιβῶς νῦν ἰδεῖν πειράσομαι εἰ
    τέθνηκε

escaped you, they certainly will not evade the
mountain-police. Now I want to ask the gods their
mercy, Spinther. Swear . . . say the sacrificial
prayers. When the gods are about to appear to us
with good omen, sing their praises as if you meant
it.[a] Villain, won't you do as you're told? What's
happened to you? Are you mad? (*A noise, off-
stage.*) Go indoors and see who it is.

Scene III

(A) What does he say? Oh, it's she,[b] is it? See
if our high and mighty friend[c] isn't indoors too.
I tell you, take this woman away, hand her over to
the mountain-police, tell them to load her with chains
and watch her carefully. Pull her—drag her—away
with her! As for you, go and look for the man;
kill him, and throw the corpse down before me, so
that I may see him dead. Spinther and Malacus,
come with me.

Scene IV

(A) Out I come . . . I will try to see for certain if

---

[a] Lit. " like people paying attention." [b] Apollonia.
[c] Aesopus.

---

13 δ[ιε]φυγεν G.-H., corr. Crusius.   19 Suppl. Sud-
haus.   20 (ἤδ') ἦν ἄρα Crusius.

ἐκεῖνος, ὅ]πως μὴ πάλιν πλανῆι μ' ἔρις. ὧδε
   μὲν
. . . .]καμαι τὰ ὧδε. ἐέ, ἰδ[ο]ῦ οὗτος·
   αῖ ταλαί-
πωρε, σὺ γὰρ] ἤθελες οὕτω ῥιφῆναι μᾶλλον ἢ
   ἐμὲ   30
φιλεῖν; κε]ίμενον δὲ κωφὸν πῶς ἀποδύρομαι;
   νεκρῶι
εἴ τίς ποτ]ε γέγονεν, ἦρται πᾶσα ἔρις. ἀνά-
   παυσον
. . . . κ]εκ[α]ρμένας φρένας ἀρῶ.
Σπινθήρ, πόθεν σου ὁ ὀφθαλμὸς ἡμέρωται;
   ὧδε ἄνω
συνείσελθέ μοι, μαστιγία, ὅπως οἶνον διυ-
   λίσω. εἴσελθε,   35
εἴσελθε, μαστιγία· ὧδε πάρελθε. ποταπὰ
   περιπατεῖς;
ὧδε στρέφου.

V

                ποῦ σου τὸ ἥμισυ τοῦ
   χιτωνί(ου), τὸ ἥμισυ;
ἐγώ σοι πάντα περὶ πάντων ἀποδώσω. οὕτω
   μοι
δέδοκται, Μάλακε· πάντας ἀνελοῦσα καὶ
   πωλήσασα
τὰ ὑπάρχοντά πού ποτε χωρίσεσθαι. νῦν
   τοῦ γέροντ(ος)   40
ἐγκρατὴς θέλω γενέσ(θαι) πρίν τι τούτ(ων)
   ἐπιγνοῖ· καὶ γὰρ εὐκαίρως
ἔχω φάρμακον θανάσιμον ὃ μετ' οἰνομέλιτος
   διηθήσασα

he is dead, so that I mayn't be bothered with jealousy
again. . . . Oh, look! here he is! Poor fool, so you
preferred to be cast out like this, rather than be my
lover? Deaf he lies—how shall I mourn him?
Whatever quarrel I may have had with this dead
man, now it is all over! Stop! . . . I will ease
my ravished heart! Spinther! Why looking so
subdued? Come up here to me, confound you! I
want to strain some wine. Come in, come in, con-
found you, come in here! Where (?) are you walk-
ing? This way!

Scene V

(A) Where's the half of your tunic—the half of it,
I say? I will pay in full for everything. My mind
is made up, Malacus.—I will kill them all and sell
the property and retire somewhere. What I want
now is to get the old man into my power, before he
has any notion of the plot. I have a fatal drug—it
comes in most conveniently!—which I will strain

---

28 πλανῆι μέ τις Sudhaus, and Π acc. to Knoke.　　29
οὐ γὰρ ἐπίσ]ταμαι Crusius.　　30 σὺ γὰρ Manteuffel.
32 Sudhaus.

δώσω αὐτῶι πεῖν. ὥστε πορευθεὶς τῆι
   πλατ(ε)ίαι θύραι κά-
λεσον αὐτὸν ὡς ἐπὶ διαλλαγάς. ἀπελθόντες
   καὶ ἡμεῖς
τῶι παρασίτωι τὰ περὶ τοῦ γέροντος προσ-
   αναθώμεθα.   45

VI

παιδίον, παῖ· τὸ τοιοῦτόν ἐστιν, παράσιτε·
   οὗτος τίς ἐστι;
αὕτη δέ; τί οὖν αὐτῆι ἐγένετο; ἀ[ποκ]ά-
   λυψον ἵνα ἴδω
αὐτήν. χρείαν σου ἔχω. τὸ τοιοῦτόν ἐστιν,
   παράσιτε.
μετανοήσασ(α) θέλ(ω) τῶι γέροντ(ι) διαλ-
   λαγ(ῆναι). πορευθεὶς οὖν
ἴδε αὐτὸν καὶ ἄγε πρὸς ἐμέ, ἐγὼ δὲ εἰσελ-
   θοῦσα τὰ πρὸς τὸ   50
ἄριστον ὑμῖν ἑτοιμάσ[ω].

VII

                     ἐπαινῶ, Μάλακε,
   τὸ τάχος.
τ[ὸ] φάρμακον ἔχεις συγκεκραμένον καὶ τὸ
   ἄριστον
ἕ[τοι]μόν ἐστι; τὸ ποῖον; Μάλακε, λαβὲ
   ἰδοὺ οἰνόμελι.
τάλας, δοκῶ πανόλημπτος γέγονεν ὁ παρά-
   σιτος· τάλας, γελᾷ.
σ[υν]ακολουθήσ[α]τε αὐτῶι μὴ καί τι πάθηι.
   τοῦτο μὲν ὡς   55

together with mead and give him to drink. So go and stand at the broad gate and call him—say, for a reconciliation. Let us too withdraw, and take the Parasite into our confidence about the old man.

Scene VI

(A) Slave ! Slave, I say ! The case is like this, my dear toady.—Who is this ? And who is she ? What's the matter with her, then ? Uncover her so that I can see her.—I want your help ; the case is like this, my good toady :—I have repented, and want a reconciliation with the old man. So go and see him, and bring him to me, and I will go in and prepare your lunch.

Scene VII

(A) Thank you, Malacus, for being so quick. You have got the drug mixed, and the lunch is ready ? I beg your pardon ? Here Malacus, take the mead. Poor fellow, I think the devil has got into our toady ! —He's laughing, poor fool. Follow him, and see that nothing happens to him. So that is settled as I

ἐβ[ο]υλόμην τετ[έ]λεσται· εἰσελθ[όν]τες περὶ
    τῶν λοιπῶν
ἀσφαλέστερον βουλευσώμεθα. Μάλακε,
    πάντα ἡμῖν κατὰ
γνώμην προκεχώρηκε, ἐὰν ἔτι τὸν γέροντα
    ἀνέλωμεν.

VIII

παράσιτε, τί γέγονεν; αἴ πῶς; μάλιστα,
    πάντων γὰρ
ν[ῦ]ν ἐγκρατὴς γέγονα. [ΣΠΙ.] ἄγωμεν,
    παράσιτε. τί οὖν θέλεις;   60
[ΠΑΡ.] Σπινθήρ, ἐπίδος μοι φόνον ἱκανόν. [ΣΠΙ.]
    παράσιτε, φοβο[ῦ]μαι
μὴ γελάσω. [ΜΑΛ.] καὶ καλῶς λέγεις.
    [ΠΑΡ.] λέγω· τί με δεῖ λέγειν;
πά[τ]ερ κύριε, τίνι με καταλείπεις; ἀπολώ-
    λεκά μου τὴν
παρρησ(ίαν,) τὴν δόξ(αν), τὸ ἐλευθέριον φῶς.
    σύ μου ἦς ὁ κύριος. τούτωι——
[ΜΑΛ.] ἄφες, ἐγὼ αὐτὸν θρηνήσω. οὐαί σοι,
    ταλαίπωρε, ἄκληρε,   65
ἀ[λγ]εινέ, ἀναφρόδιτε· οὐαί σοι· [ΔΕΣΠ.] οὐαί
    μοι· οἶδα γάρ σε ὅστις
π[οτ]ὲ εἶ. Σπινθήρ, ξύλα ἐπὶ τοῦτον. οὗτος
    πάλιν τίς ἐστιν;
[ΣΠΙ.] μένουσι σῷοι, δέσποτα.

•   •   •   •   •   •   •

61 φαιὸν ἱμάτιον Knox.   64 ἦς = ἦσθα, as usual in com-
mon speech at this time.   65 Above ἄφες κτλ. Π has

wanted it. We shall plan the rest more securely if
we go indoors. Everything has gone as I intended,
Malacus, if we also make away with the old man.

Scene VIII

(A) My dear toady, what has happened ?—Oh !
How ?—Certainly, for I now have all I want. (*The
body of the Old Man is introduced on a bier.*)

Spinther. Come along, toady ! What is it you
want ?

Toady. Spinther, give me sufficient means of
death !

Spinther. Toady, I'm afraid I shall laugh !

Malacus. Quite right too !

Toady. I say—well, what should I say ? (*Tragic-
ally*) Father and master, to whom are you leaving
me ? I have lost my freedom of speech, my reputa-
tion, my light of liberty. You were my master.
To him——

Malacus. (*Ironically*) Let me sing him his dirge.
Woe to you, miserable, hapless, troublesome, un-
lovable man ! Woe to you !

Old Man. (*Leaping from his bier : he had only been
pretending to be dead*)—Woe to me !—I know who you
are ! Spinther, bring the stocks for him. (*Catching
sight of Aesopus.*) Who is this again ?

Spinther. Master, they are still safe !

. . . . . .

μόνον ἀληθῶς οὐ λέγω. Perhaps σοι· οἶδα.   67 Above
Σπινθήρ Π has μεισό(υ)μενε.   π[οτ]ε Sudhaus.

LITERARY PAPYRI

ANONYMOUS

78 [2 A.D.] A QUARREL

Ed. pr. Körte, *Archiv für Papyrusforschung*, vi. 1913,
p. 1 with Plate. See Milne, *Cat. Lit. Pap. B.M.* no. 97, p.
67; Crusius, *Herodae Mimiambi*, p. 117; Manteuffel, *de
opusculis graecis*, p. 146 and *Hermes*, 65, 126; de Stephani,
Phil. Woch. 1914, 253; Knox, *Philol.* 81, 243; Körte,
Archiv, vii. 153; Srebrny, *Journ. Minist. Nar. Prosw.*,
Petrograd, 1917 and *Eos*, 30, 1927, p. 401; Powell-Barber,
New Chapters, i. 123.

*About this fragment speculation has exceeded all reason-
able bounds. Readers may peruse the piece and decide
whether there is the least evidence for the greater part of*
e.g. *Crusius's interpretation :—" muliercula iuvenem amans
atque divitiis sibi devinciens ; iuvenis mollis et asotos, ei
non tribuens quod postulat sed* πυγίζων [*this word depends
on an unnecessary correction*]. *Vir senescens* Ἴων *πατήρ
cinaedologus cum iuvene Veneris masculae vinculo con-
iunctus, mulierculae infestus. Iuvenis frater, homo frugi sed
qui mulierem divitem a patre commendatam a fratre spretam
domo recipere non dedignetur "—more follows, even more
widely separated from the evidence. Manteuffel does not
recede so far from the facts until the end, when he bases
inferences upon the most questionable supplements of* vv. 19,
21, 24.

*If we return to the fragment itself, we shall not diverge
very much from the sober conclusions of the first editor.
This much is certain :—*

(a) *At least five characters are designated in* Π : A, B,
Γ, Δ *and some sort of group or " chorus " denoted by the*

A ποῦ τὸ δίκαιον;
B παρὰ τοῖς ἀλλήλους [π]υτίζουσι.

362

ANONYMOUS

ANONYMOUS

A QUARREL [2 A.D.]

marginal direction Κοι(νῆι). *Γ is evidently named " Father
Ion " (v. 7) ; A is probably a woman (ταύτης v. 3) ; Δ is a
man (v. 25), probably a young man (v. 17, he refers to his
father) ; another man is referred to several times (v. 13
αὐτοῦ, v. 15 τούτωι, v. 18 τούτου) ; this could be, but is not
necessarily, B (I refer to him hereafter as X). B may
possibly be a buffoon, like the clown in P. Oxy. 413. The
identity of the " chorus " is quite uncertain.*

*(b) There is a dispute between Δ and X : possibly con-
cerned with A, who complains of unjust treatment. Γ acts
as arbiter in the quarrel ; he is a friend of the father of X,
and seems likely to give his verdict in favour of X. X has
recently suffered a misfortune (possibly the death of his
father, vv. 15, 18), and Γ has come to sympathize with him.*

*Beyond this point I perceive no reference which is both
legitimate and important. Two young men are quarrelling,
probably about a woman ; an older man is arbitrating
between them : he is predisposed in favour of one of the two
disputants. The cause of the quarrel probably lay in the
question of the possession of the woman : the result of it is
altogether beyond conjecture.*

*[This fragment is inscribed ἐκ βιβλιοθήκης Πρασίου
Ἡρακλείδης : evidently the texts of these wretched and
ephemeral pieces were circulated for the delectation of the
reading public.]*

(A) Where is justice to be found ?
(B) Among people who spit at each other.

---

2 [κο]πίζουσι (=ψευδομένοις) Manteuffel: π]υγίζουσι Crusius.

LITERARY PAPYRI

Δ ἄγε, περὶ ταύτης σ[υνῆ]κα τὴν γνώμ[ην,
   . . . . . .
   τῶν κοσμίων [. . . . . .] τί βουλεύεσθ[ε;
Γ .]ταιτ . [. . . . .]να.   5
ΚΟΙ[ΝΗΙ] δικαί[ως.
Δ πάτερ Ἴων, οὐ χρῶμαί σοι οὔτε κριτῆι [οὔτε
   παρακρήτωι. [Α] παρακλήτωι.
Γ διὰ τί;
Δ ὅτι ὅλος ἐξ ἐκ[εί]νο[υ το]ῦ μέρους εἶ. ο[ὐ . . . 10
   οὐδ’ εἰς β[ιασμὸ]ν ἁρπάζομαι.
Γ συγγνώμην μ[οι ἔχε, ἄ]κομψος σ[ύ· τοῦ
   πατρὸς
   αὐτοῦ γέγονα φ[ίλ]ος ἀναγκαῖος, [καὶ νῦν
   ὡς ἀκούσας τὴ[ν] μεταλλαγὴ[ν ἥκω
   τούτωι συλλυπηθησόμενος.   15

ΚΑΤΑΣΤΡΟΦΗ

Δ λέγ[ε] μοι, πάτερ Ἴων, [τὸν . . .
   πατέρα ἡμῶν ἤιδεις;
Γ τὸν τούτου ἤιδειν.
Δ ἄγ’, ε[ἰ] σῶιος (ὁ) πατὴρ ἦν, [οὐ . . .;
Γ οὐ μὰ τὴν ἐμὴν σω[τ]ηρίαν.   20
Δ π[ῶ]ς . . .
Γ π[ό]θεν; ἐκείνη (ἡ) γυνὴ ἀξιω[. . . . . . .
   προσφι-
   λεστάτη.

3-4 περὶ δὲ] τῶν κοσμίων [τούτων] Körte: τὴν] τῶν κοσμίων
[ἀλλὰ] Crusius.   5 ἑταῖρα[ί εἰσ]ν Körte: εταιτα[. . . .]ινα
Bell: ἑταίρας, [πα]ιδία Manteuffel.   The fifth letter is certainly
not a P, almost certainly a T.—ἑταίρα[ν παρε]ῖνα[ι Crusius,
ἔ(σ)ται ταῦτα δεινά Knox.   6 Bell: δίκαι[ον Körte.   11
364

ANONYMOUS

(D) Come now, I understand your view about her ; what are you deciding . . . these gentlewomen ?

(C) . . . .

CHORUS. Quite right, too !

(D) Father Ion : I am not using you as judge or banister.

(A) Barrister, you mean.

(C) Why not ?

(D) Because you're wholly on the other side. I am not . . ., or dragging her off to violate her.

(C) Pardon me, my vulgar friend : I am a comrade and kinsman of his father. So now, hearing of his reverse, I have come to sympathize with him.

DÉNOUEMENT

(D) Tell me, Father Ion, you knew our father ?

(C) I knew *his* father.

(D) Come now, if my father were alive, would you not . . .

(C) Damn me if I would.

(D) How . . .

(C) Why on earth ? That lady will naturally (claim your) affection.

Perhaps β[άσανο]ν.　　15-16 καταστροφή: *cf.* καταστολή, p. 348.　　19 οὐκ [ἐδίδου ἄν; Körte: οὐκ [ἐδέξατ' ἄν; Crusius: ἄγ', ε[ἰ] ἐμὸς πατὴρ ἦν οὐκ ὁ[τεθνηκὼς ἤδη; Manteuffel; but ἐμὸς is wrong and οὐκ very doubtful: the ὁ after it is not in Π.　　21 π[ῶ]ς; ἆρ' ἐμὲ ἔλεγ' ἂν ὁ σαίν[ων αὐτήν; Manteuffel, but the end of this cannot be reconciled with the evidence of Π. πῶς ἐμὲ ἐδενο . . ν . . . . . Körte; πῶ[ς ἄρ]α ἐμὲ ἔλεγ' ἂν ὁ[πυ]ί[ειν αὐτήν; Crusius, after Bell ; the letters are not legible, and can be forced into various combinations.　　22 ἀξίω[ς ἔσται σοι Manteuffel, ἀξιώ[σει ἡ τούτωι Crusius.

Δ   .] μοιχ[.]υτ[. . .] . . . [
     ὅμοιός εἰμι;   25
Γ   τυχόν.
Δ   οὐκ ἀρέσκει μοι οὔτ[ε
     †σαπραλμεια†

     .   .   .   .   .   .

     24 οὐ] μοίχ[ο]υ τ[ιν᾽ ε]ὐνὴ[ν ζητῶ· οὐ γὰρ τοῦ ἀδελφοῦ Crusius:

ANONYMOUS

79   [3 A.D.]   DAMSEL IN DISTRESS

Ed. pr. *Milne, *Catalogue of the Literary Papyri in the British Museum*, 1927, no. 52, p. 39, and Addenda, p. xv. See Schubart, *Gnomon*, iv. 1928, 398 ; Wüst and Crönert, *Philol.* 84, 1928, 153 ; Körte, *Archiv*, x. 62 ; Manteuffel, *Eos*, 32, 1929, 34 and *de opusculis graecis*, p. 56 and p. 161 ; Knox, *J.E.A.* 15, 140.

Interpretation of this fragment has gone beyond the bounds of legitimate inference. In the following account I include only so much as I judge to be certain or highly probable.

(1) *The Characters.* (a) *A young girl (παρθένος v. 17, κόρη v. 18) ; (b) a brother, or sister, or both (σύγγονε v. 4, φιλάδελφε v. 6). φιλάδελφε is so sharply contrasted with σύγγονε βάρβαρε that two persons are probably intended. These may be a brother and a sister, or two brothers (less probably two sisters, for vv. 8-16 (especially 12-16) are much more suitable to a brother). (c) A nurse (τροφέ v. 5), who is probably included in the μαινόμεναι v. 1 : that plural proves the presence of more than one woman beside the maiden ; for their identity, there is no need to look beyond the nurse and the sister whose presence we have doubtfully*

ANONYMOUS

(D) Do I look like (a man who is going to marry)
an adulteress ?

(C) Perhaps you do.

(D) It is not my idea of fun . . . stale fish *a* . . .

. . . .

a Cf. Athen. iii. 119 e, 132 e (Crusius).

ἢ μοιχ[ε]υτ[ρία]ν λη[ψομέναι Srebrny, Manteuffel.   28
σαπρὰ (ἅ)λμια (or σαπράλμια) Körte, proverbial, like " faule
Fische " in German.

ANONYMOUS

DAMSEL IN DISTRESS   [3 A.D.]

inferred under (b) *above.* (d) *The young woman's father
(πάτερ v. 27 : Wüst reads μᾶτερ, but πάτερ seems to be fairly
certain in* II).

(2) *The distribution of the lines among the characters.
The Papyrus gives no indication of change of speaker. It is
certain that the maiden speaks vv. 1-7, probable that her
brother speaks vv. 9-16.*

*It is natural to suppose that the speaker changes where the
metre changes ; the whole being performed by one Archimima,
and the transition from one character to another being made
clearer to the audience by a simultaneous change of metre. I
have followed precedent in distributing the parts on this
assumption : though neither this nor any other distribution
is free from objections. In a good author, v. 17 and v. 18
would naturally be spoken by different characters (λέγε
παρθένε 17, εἰπὲ κόρη 18). Yet if change of metre is to
accompany change of speaker, and vice versa, these lines
must be said by the Nurse. For on this theory, the brother*

367

LITERARY PAPYRI

*must speak vv. 9-16, and therefore cannot speak vv. 17-21;
the sister would not address her own sister as παρθένε, κόρη;
the father could not speak v. 20.*

*The plain fact is that the evidence is not sufficient to allow
a certain, or even a highly probable, distribution of the lines.
The original assumption, that change of metre denotes change
of speaker, may be wholly false. All we can say is, that any
other distribution (e.g. that of Wüst) departs still farther
from the available evidence and produces no better a result.*

(3) *The nature of the plot. The maiden is being ques-
tioned against her will by distracted womenfolk. Someone
—probably her brother—reproaches her for want of con-
fidence in him. Others coax her to reveal her secret, which is
suspected to conceal a love-affair. The end is uncertain.
There is a reference to a carousing reveller, who is a light o'
love; and to a festival by night. All that we may fairly
conclude from this is:—the maiden has been violated at a
midnight festival; she is deeply distressed, but ashamed to
confess to her womenfolk, who sorrow and sympathize with*

[ΠΑΡΘΕΝΟΣ μὴ δε]ίρατε σώματα, μαινόμεναι,
  καὶ μὴ καθυβρίζετε τρόπον ἐμόν.
  τί περὶ σφυρά μου δέμας ἐβάλετε;
  ἐμέ, σύγγονε βάρβαρε, παρακαλεῖς;
  ἱκέτις, τροφέ, ναί, πέπτωκας ἐμοῦ;   5
  φιλάδελφε, πρόνοια· λόγων ἀνέχῃι.
  πειραζομένη βασανίζομαι.
[ΑΔΕΛΦΟΣ] οὕτω τι . [. . . . .]ω . ν . . το . . . . μενη
  ναι.
  καὶ πρόσωπα τύπτει
  κ[αὶ] πλοκαμοὺς σπαράσ(σ)ει.   10
  νῦν ἔμαθον ἀληθῶς
  ὅτ[ι πλ]εῖον οὐ ποθεῖς
  μετελθοῦσά τι λέξαι.

her ; or to her brother, *who is annoyed that she has not had
confidence in him.* It is probable that she will discover that
her unknown violator is none other than the youth whom she
anyway desires to marry. (*The resemblance to the plot of
Menander's* Epitrepontes *is obvious.*)

*Beyond this all is uncertain. Nothing is gained by intro-
ducing Mothers and Friends into a fragment which itself
affords no evidence of their participation ; nothing is gained
by elaborating the plot beyond this point. Above all, infer-
ences based upon vv. 25-27 are worthless ; so doubtful is the
reading of the text there.*

(4) *The Metres.* 1-7 anap. dim., partly full, partly with
(resolved) iambic end = ἀπόκροτα, Wilam. Gr. Versk. 374.
9-16 ithyph.: aristoph.: ithyph.: iamb.: 2 pherecr.:
iamb. dim.: adonius. 17-21 " mouse-tailed " hexameters,
see Crönert, loc. cit., Higham, Greek Poetry and Life,
p. 299. N.B. these lines avoid paroxytone endings. 22-end,
reading is so uncertain that nothing is worth saying about
the metre (cf. however Crönert, loc. cit.).

GIRL. Stop flaying yourselves,[a] you crazy creatures,
and stop insulting my character !—Why have you
thrown yourselves about my ankles ? Cruel brother,
do you call to me ? Is it to entreat me, nurse—
yes ?—that you have fallen here ? Loving sister,
have a care ! [b]—refrain from speech ! [c] I am put to
trial and torture !

BROTHER. . . . and beats her brow, and tears her
hair ! Now I know for certain that you don't want
to come to me or tell me anything more. You should

---

[a] The women (sister, nurse) are beating their breasts and
tearing their hair for sorrow. *Cf.* v. 9.   [b] πρόνοια, *sc.*
ἔστω ; *cf.* εὐφημία ἔστω, etc.   [c] ἀνέχηι I take (with
Crönert) to be a subjunctive equivalent to an imperative.

---

1 μὴ δε]ίρατε Manteuffel.   6 Punctuation D. L. P.

ἔδει σ᾽ ἐμὲ λι[τα]νεῦσαι,
καὶ οὗ παρῆν ἐμοὶ ποιεῖν   15
πάντα κελεῦσαι.
[ΤΡΟΦΟΣ] θρῆνον ὑπερθεμένη λέγε, παρθένε, μή τινα
      ποθεῖς;
   εἰπέ, κόρη, φανερῶς ἀλγηδόνα, μηδ᾽ ἔ[μὲ]
      φοβοῦ.
   εἰ θεός ἐστιν ὁ σὰς κατέχων φρένας, [οὐ]δὲν
      ἀδικεῖς.
   κοὐκ ἔχομεν γενέτην ἀγριώτατον· ἥμερα
      φρονεῖ·   20
   καὶ καλός ἐστιν ἔφηβος ὁ σὸς τάχα, καὶ σὺ
      δὲ καλή.
[ΠΑΡΘΕΝΟΣ] ἐπικωμάζει καὶ μεθύει,
   κοινῆς δὲ φέρων πόθον ᾿Αφροδίτης
   αὐτός τ᾽ ἐφηβῶν ἄγρυπνον
   ὑπὸ κάλαμον †ανομαλοντε.†   25
   καὶ τοῦτον ἐῶ· βραχύτατον ἦν
   ζ[ήλω]μα, πάτερ, γινώσκω.
   ἕτερον . . . . ἕτερον
   παρὰ παννυχίσιν [
      .   .   .   .   .

have entreated me, and commanded me wherever I had power to act.

Nurse. Put off lament and tell me, maid, you're not in love ? Tell me, daughter, the secret of your pain, and have no fear of me. If it's a god that possesses your heart, you do no wrong. We have no ferocious father : he is a gentle soul. And your young man is handsome, it may be ; you're pretty, too !

Girl. He revels and carouses : his desire is for loves that are given to all. He, in the bloom of youth, to the wakeful flute . . . Him too I dismiss : that was but the briefest craze, father, I recognize. One . . . another . . . at the festival by night . . .

. . . . . .

17 μοι Milne (for μή). 25-end: the readings of Π are extremely difficult and doubtful; contrast Milne, Manteuffel, Crönert. 25 ἄνομα λέγει coni. Milne. 26 καὶ τοῦτο νέωι Milne, later.

LYRIC POEMS

ANONYMOUS, probably ARCHILOCHUS

80 [3 B.C.]

Ed. pr. *Milne, *Catalogue of the Literary Papyri in the British Museum*, 1927, no. 54, p. 42, Plate IVa. See Körte, *Archiv*, x. 43; Manteuffel, *de opusculis graecis*, p. 60; Maas, *Zeitschr. f. vergleich. Sprachforschung*, 60, 1932, 286.

]νται νῆες (ἐ)ν πόντωι θοαὶ
π]ολλὸν δ᾽ ἱστίων ὑφώμεθα
]ντες ὅπλα νηὸς οὐρίην δ᾽ ἔχε
]ρους ὄφρα σέο μεμνεώμεθα
] ἄπισχε μηδὲ τοῦτον ἐμβάληις   5
]ν ἵσταται κυκώμενον
]μης ἀλλὰ σὺ προμήθεσαι
]υμος . . .

. . . .

ΣΑΠΦΩ

81 [Ostrakon ? 3 B.C.]   BOOK I

Ed. pr. Norsa, *Annali della reale Scuola normale superiore di Pisa, Lettere, Storia e Filosofia*, Serie ii. vol. vi. 1937, fasc. i-ii, pp. 8-15 with Plate. See Pfeiffer, *Philol.* 92, 1937, 117 with Plate; Theander, *ibid.* 465; Schubart, *Hermes*, 73, 1938, 297; Vogliano, *Pap. d. r. Univ. di Milano*, 1937, 374

ANONYMOUS, probably ARCHILOCHUS [3 b.c.]

Dialect, style, spirit, metre and subject-matter (cf. fr. 56 Diehl) are consistent with the attribution to Archilochus.

. . . swift ships in the sea . . .
. . . take in the sail . . .
. . . ship's harness, and keep the fair wind . . .
. . . that we may remember you . . .
. . . keep it away, cast it not in (?)
. . . rises in turmoil . . .
. . . but do you take heed . . .

. . . .

7 προμήθεσαι: 2nd pers. sing. med. imper., Maas and L. & S.

SAPPHO

BOOK I [Ostrakon ? 3 b.c.]

1, p. 271; Schadewaldt, *Antike*, 14, 1938, 77; Körte, *Archiv*, xiii. 1938, 90.

The reading of the first line is too uncertain to permit a probable inference about its subject-matter. In the rest, there follows a reference to a temple in a grove, and altars fragrant with incense. "*Cold water sounds through the apple-branches*"—*perhaps from a stream or waterfall behind them ; roses bloom, and the leaves rustle. There is also a meadow, and flowers therein. Aphrodite, wreath in hand, pours nectar into golden cups.*

This clearly enough includes a description of a shrine of Aphrodite in the country. Theander reminds us of Ἀφροδίτη Ἄνθεια, who (according to Hesychius) was worshipped at Cnossus in Crete. If Κρῆτες or ἐκ Κρήτας were read in v. 1, the poem might be a description of a shrine of this divinity ; and Sappho's poem might (but not necessarily) have been written in Crete on her way either to or from exile in Sicily. There is no other reference to Cretans in Sappho, unless fr. 12

> †δευρυμμεκρη† . . . πρ[   ] νάον
> ἄγνον, ὄππ[αι τοι] χάριεν μὲν ἄλσος
> μαλί[αν], βῶμοι δὲ τεθυμιαμέν-
> οι λιβανώτω,
> ἐν δ' ὕδωρ ψῦχρον κελάδει δι' ὕσδων   5
> μαλίνων, βρόδοισι δὲ παῖς ὁ χῶρος
> ἐσκίαστ', αἰθυσσομένων δὲ φύλλων
> κῶμα κατέρρει,
> ἐν δὲ λείμων καλ(λ)ίβοτος τέθαλεν
> ἠρίνοισιν ἄνθεσιν, †αιανητοι†   10
> μέλλιχα πνέοισιν . . .
>
> . . . . . .
>
> ἔνθα δὴ σὺ στέμ[ματ'] ἔλοισα, Κύπρι,
> χρυσίαισιν ἐν κυλίκεσσιν ἄβρως

1 δευρ' υμως (?) †κρητες† Pfeiffer: δευρυμμεισρητας Schubart: πυρυμμεκρητες ed. pr. Hence δεῦρύ μ' ἐκ Κρήτας Theander, δεῦρ' ὔμ' ἐς ῥήτας Schubart. πρ[ολίποισα] Theander. νάον Lobel.   2 ὄππαι Lobel, τοι D. L. P.   3 μαλίαν
376

incerti auctoris (*Lobel, p. 73*) *is ascribed to her. In that fragment, Cretan women dance around an altar in a meadow of flowers* (v. 2 ἀμφ' ἐρόεντα βῶμον, v. 3 πόας τέρεν ἄνθος μάλακον ματείσαι). *It is easy to infer that both fragments describe the worship of the same goddess—Aphrodite of the Flowers, at Cnossus, whose altar stands in a grove with a meadow beside it* (cf. *no. 88* (a) *below*). *But decisive evidence is wanting, since it is not certain either that v. 1 of our fragment has any reference to Cretans (though it is probable), or that Sappho is the author of the other fragment.* Vv. 5, 7-8 = *Diehl*, Anth. Lyr. (1935), *Sappho no. 5*; vv. 13-16 = *no. 6.*

HITHER, . . . the holy temple, where is a pleasant grove of apple trees, and altars fragrant with frankincense.

And there cold water sounds through the apple-branches, and all the place is shadowy with roses, and from the whispering leaves comes slumber down.

And there a lovely meadow blooms with flowers of springtime, and the . . . breathe the sweet scent . . .

There, Aphrodite takes up wreaths and pours nectar

Lobel. βῶμοι ΔΕΜΙ : corr. ed. pr.: δ' ἔνι θ. Pfeiffer. **4** διανωτω Π, corr. Pfeiffer. 6 μαλιαν Π, corr. Pfeiffer. 7 ἐσκίασται, θυσσ. ed. pr., corr. Schubart. 8 κῶμα κὰτ ἴρρον ed. pr.: κατέρρον Pfeiffer: καταιριον Schubart, *i.e.* καταιρι + ON from following EN (καταιρι = κατέρ(ρ)ει). 9 ΙΔΔ . ΑΟΤΟΣ ed. pr.: † ι . . ιδοτος Pfeiffer: ἱππόβοτος Schubart, Lobel. But Π does not resemble Λ elsewhere in this text, and it is questionable if horses should have any place in the sacred meadow, *cf.* Eur. *Hipp.* 73-77. ΚΑΛΙ-ΒΟΤΟΣ D. L. P. 9-10 τεθαλε τ . τινφριν | νοις ανθεσιν ed. pr.: τεθαλε τωτηριριν|νοις Schubart, *i.e.* perhaps a combination of two readings, λωτίνοισιν and ἠρίνοισιν, into λωτηρι(ρι)νοις. αἱ δ' ἄνητοι edd. : but ἄνητος (for ἄνητον) is found nowhere else. 13 δὸς μεδέοισα Κύπρι Schubart. 14 Π has ἀκρως (Lobel).

ἐμ(με)μειχμένον θαλίαισι νέκταρ   **15**
οἰνοχόεισα

.   .   .   .   .   .

ΚΟΡΙΝΝΑ

82   [1 A.D.]   ΟΡΕΣΤΑΣ

Ed. pr. Coppola, *Introduzione a Pindaro*, p. 231. Revised
text in *Vitelli-Norsa, *Papiri Greci e Latini*, x. 1932, no.
1174, p. 140 with Plate. See Diehl, *Anthol. Lyr.*[2] i. fasc. iv.
p. 201 ; Bowra, *Class. Qu.* 1936, 130 ; Körte, *Archiv*, xiii.
1938, 95.

(Small fragments of seven lines)

ΟΡΕΣΤΑΣ

ῥο]ὰς μὲν Ὠκιανῶ λιπῶσα τ[
   ] ἱαρὸν φάος σελάνας πασα[
   ]ω· Ὥρη δ' ἐς Διὸς ἄμβροτυ [
   ] Γέαρος ἐν ἄνθεσι γεγα[
   ]συν χορὸς ἀν' ἑπτάπουλον [**5**

.   .   .   .   .   .

ΠΙΝΔΑΡΟΣ

83   [(a) 2 A.D.]   **FRAGMENTS OF TWO POEMS**
     [(b) 1 A.D.]

Ed. pr. Grenfell-Hunt, *P. Oxy.* xv. 1922, (a) no. 1791,
p. 84, Plate III ; (b) no. 1792, p. 86. See *Bowra, *Pindari*

378

gracefully in golden cups, mingled with the festive
joy . . .

. . . . . .

CORINNA

ORESTES [1 A.D.]

*This fragment suggests that Orestes had a place among the
native heroes of old Boeotian tradition : cf. Pindar, P. ix.,
and full discussion in Bowra, loc. cit., Coppola, loc. cit.*

(Small fragments of seven lines)

ORESTES

. . . Leaving the streams of Ocean . . .
. . . the holy light of the moon . . .
. . . the immortal Hours . . . from Zeus . . .
. . . rejoice in the flowers of spring . . .
. . . choir through the city of seven gates . . .

. . . . .

PINDAR

FRAGMENTS OF TWO POEMS [(a) 2 A.D.] [(b) 1 A.D.]

Carmina, Paeanes, xi., xii.; Körte, *Archiv,* vii. 137 ; Schroeder,
Pindarus, Carmina, pp. 345-346 ; Schmidt, *G.G.A.* 1924, 2.

(a) *The reference is to the second and third temples at*

LITERARY PAPYRI

Delphi, and to the story (Paus. x. 5. 9) that the former of these was sent to the Hyperboreans : the latter is described

(a)   ναὸν τὸν μὲν Ὑπερβορ[έαις
    αὔραις ζαμενὴς ἔμειξ[εν,
    ὦ Μοῖσαι, τοῦ δὲ παντέχ[νοισιν
    Ἀφαίστου παλάμαις καὶ Ἀθ[ά-
    νας] τίς ὁ ῥυθμὸς ἐφαίνετο;   5
    χάλκεοι μὲν τοῖχοι, χάλκεαί θ'
    ὕπο κίονες ἔστασ[αν·
    χρύσεαι δ' ἐξ ὑπὲρ αἰετοῦ
    ἄειδον κηληδόνες.
    ἀλλά νιν ηρονετη. [10
    κεραυνῶι χθόν' ἀνο[ίξαις
    Ζεὺς ἔκρ[υ]ψεν [ἀπ]άντως

        (Fragments of eight more lines)

(b)   ]με[
        ]οισιν εννε[
     ]αλα δ' Ἀρτέμιδ[. . . . . .]ονας [
    λέχος ἀμφεπό[λει . .]α τοιαῦτ[
    .]υμνήσιος δρέπ[. .] ἅμα δὲ φ[5
    Ναξόθεν λιπαροτρόφων θυσί[ας
    μή]λων Χαρίτεσσι μίγδαν
    Κύ]νθιον παρὰ κρημνόν, ἔνθα
    κελαινεφέ' ἀργιβρένταν λέγο[ντι
    Ζῆνα καθεζόμενον κορυφαῖ-   10
    -σιν ὕπερθε φυλάξ[αι χρ]όνον,
    ἁνίκ' ἀγανόφρων
    Κοίου θυγάτηρ λύετο τερπνᾶς
    ὠδῖνος. ἔλαμψαν
    δ' ἀελίου δέμας ὅπω[ς   15
    ἀγλαὸν ἐς φάος ἰόντες δίδυμοι

in detail (vv. 3-9) ; its destruction by a thunderbolt was the subject of vv. 10-12.

(b) *Ascribed to Pindar on grounds of style and vocabulary (see ed. pr. p. 87). The subject is the birth of the twin children of Zeus and Leto.*

(a) One temple in his violence he [a] brought near to the Northern Winds. But for the other,—tell, Muses, what grace was this, fashioned by the handicraft of Hephaestus and Athene ? Walls of bronze, bronze pillars supported it ; in gold above the gable sang six enchantresses. But . . . Zeus rent the earth asunder with a thunderbolt, and hid it utterly from sight. . . .

(Fragments of eight more lines)

(b) (Vv. 5 sqq.) . . . and also from Naxos (brought) sacrifices of fat sheep for all the Graces on the crags of Cynthus, where they say the dark-clouded wielder of the bright thunderbolt, Zeus, sitting on the peaks above, watched the time when Coeus's gentle daughter [b] was released from the travail that was her joy. Bright they shone as the sun, when to the glorious daylight they came, twin children : and

---

[a] Apollo.   [b] Leto.

(a) 10 νιν [β]ρον[ταῖ τε καὶ Körte.

LITERARY PAPYRI

παῖδες· πολὺν ῥόθ[ο]ν ἴεσαν ἀπὸ στομ[άτων
'Ε]λείθυιά τε καὶ Λά[χ]εσις·

(Fragments of eight more lines)

.   .   .   .   .   .

ANONYMOUS, perhaps BACCHYLIDES
(or possibly SIMONIDES)

84   [2–3 A.D.]

*Ed. pr. Vogliano, *Papiri Greci e Latini*, x. 1932, no. 1181,
p. 169. See Milne, *Class. Rev.* 47, 1933, 62 ; Snell, *Bacchy-
lides* fr. dub. 60, 61 ; Severyns, *Bacchylide*, 1933, p. 142 ;
Davison, *Class. Rev.* 1934, 205 and literature quoted there
and by Snell, *loc. cit.* ; Bowra, *Class. Rev.* 1933, 440 ; Körte,
Archiv, xiii. 1938, 92 ; Snell, *Hermes, Einzelschr.* 5, 1937, 98.

*Ascribed to Bacchylides on grounds of style : especially
because of the abundance of compound adjectives, and the
preference for new formations (cf. in the first three lines
of the second piece ἰοδερκής, νεοκέλαδος). Further : the
fragments seem to be a continuation of the alphabetically
arranged Dithyrambs of Bacchylides in the B.M. papyrus.
The latter run in order down to the letter Ι : the second of
our pieces begins with the letter Λ ; and it is not unlikely
that the first begins with the letter Κ (Κάβειροι, or Κάστωρ
καὶ Πολυδεύκης). But it must be confessed that the subject-
matter of the first piece is uncertain (Milne may be right in
detecting a reference (vv. 12-15) to the story of divine twins,
one of whom was to dwell in Hades, the other on earth. Castor
and Polydeuces would then be the most natural subject :
though others—e.g. the Cabiroi—cannot be excluded from
consideration). Further, Davison is justly sceptical about*

ANONYMOUS

Lachesis [a] and Ilithyia sent forth a great clamour
from their lips. . . .

(Fragments of eight more lines)

. . . . . .

[a] Lachesis as goddess of childbirth elsewhere only Isyll.
Paean 18.

ANONYMOUS, perhaps BACCHYLIDES
(or possibly SIMONIDES)

[2–3 A.D.]

*the coincidence that " a papyrus discovered at Oxyrhynchus in
1928 should fit so closely on to the end of a papyrus discovered
in a tomb at Meir in 1896."*

*Davison argues for the ascription to Simonides. But the
evidence is not much, if at all, stronger. Simonides wrote a
poem about women in exile (Plutarch, On Exile 8, 602 C–D);
" that poem included at least one lament in direct speech."
Now the first of our pieces also may be interpreted to be a
poem about women in exile (from Troy); and their lamenta-
tions are in direct speech (1–5). So far the ascription to
Simonides rests on the supposition that his treatment of this
subject in this manner must have been unique. But Davison
observes further that the metre of our fragment corresponds
in part with that of Plutarch's quotation (fr. 28 Diehl):—*

$$\left. \begin{array}{l} \breve{\upsilon}\pi o \ \pi\epsilon\nu\theta\epsilon o\varsigma \ \eta\mu\epsilon\nu\alpha\iota \\ \iota\sigma\chi\epsilon\iota \ \delta\epsilon \ \mu\epsilon \ \pi o\rho\phi\upsilon\rho\epsilon\alpha\varsigma \end{array} \right\} \textit{Telesill.}$$

$$\left. \begin{array}{l} \kappa\rho\upsilon o\epsilon\nu\tau\iota \ \gamma\alpha\rho \ \epsilon\nu \ \pi o\lambda\epsilon\mu\omega\iota \\ \alpha\lambda o\varsigma \ \alpha\mu\phi\iota \ \tau\alpha\rho\alpha\sigma\sigma o\mu\epsilon\nu\alpha\varsigma \end{array} \right\} \textit{? Anap.}$$

LITERARY PAPYRI

Plutarch's next word, ὀρυμαγδός, *can hardly be made to correspond to* Π's διμενακα[, *whatever that may stand for* (Δὶ μὲν ἄκαι[ρον *Milne). Davison suggests that it may be a case of a choriamb corresponding to an ionic a minore: but there is no parallel (Simon. fr. 13, v. 7 = v. 21 is far too hypothetical to be used as evidence here). We must then*

ὑ]πὲρ ἀμετέρ[ας νεό-
τατος ἐρατυ[. . ὄμ]ματα
δ]υσμενέω[ν, ἀνε]χοίμεθα
ἀκρίτοις αν[
ὑπὸ πένθε[σιν ἤ]μεναι·   5
κρυόεντι γὰρ [ἐν π]ολέμωι

(Fragments of eight lines)

μάλ' ἔγε[ιρε] τοι[α]ῦτα φάτις
ἐπεὶ δοκ[. . .]κια[. .]ν
ἐπεὶ πολυ[δεν]δρέ[ω]ν αι[.]ων
κῦμα πό[ρευσ’] ἀπ’ Ἰλίου   10
θεῶν τι[ς ἀ]μ-
φανδὸ[ν εἶπε τὸν μὲν
αὖθι μένε[ιν . . . . .]ερ[.]μιδι
τὸν δ’ οὐλόμε[νον . .]ειμεν
προφυγεῖν θά[νατ]ον.   15
ἐ]πασσύτεραι δ’ ἰα[χαὶ
οὐρανὸν ἷξον [
ἀέλπτωι περὶ χάρ[μα]τι [
οὐδ’ ἀνδρῶν
θώκοισι μετε[. . . .]τω[ν μέλος   20
ἄναυδον ἦν,
νέαι δ’ ἐπεύχο[ν]τ[ο . . .]λλαι
ἰὴ ἰή.

ANONYMOUS

suppose that Plutarch has " omitted either a word equivalent to one long syllable, . . . or a whole line, before ὀρυμαγδός."

The coincidences of subject-matter, treatment, and metre[a] are admittedly curious: but in my opinion they fall far short of proof of Simonidean authorship. It is tenable, too, that the style of the fragments as a whole is by no means reminiscent of Simonides.

" . . . in defence of our youth, checks the glance of foemen upon us, we should endure to sit beneath an infinite load of sorrow.   For in bitter war . . .

(*Fragments of eight lines*)

Such the utterance that aroused . . .

For . . . of many trees, the wave carried . . . from Ilium, a god declared openly that one should abide there . . . but the other should escape accursed death.   And multitudinous cries . . . went up to Heaven for unexpected joy, and the song of men . . . on seats . . . was not silent; and young women prayed . . . Iê, Iê.

---

[a] The coincidence of metre depends, of course, on the scansion of πορφυρέας: it may seem more natural to scan

ἰσχει δε με πορφυρεας αλος αμφιταρασσομενας ορυμαγδος, a sequence of lyric dactyls : if so, there is no metrical coincidence at all, and the case for Simonides becomes very weak indeed.

---

4 ἀν[εχοίμεθα repeated, Beazley.   9 Maas.   ακ[τ]ων Milne, but " αἰγῶν e ἀκτῶν vanno esclusi " ed. pr.   ἀιόνων Beazley.   12 D. L. P. (after Milne).   13 π]αρ' ῎Αιδι Milne, impossible acc. to text of ed. pr.

ΛΕΤΚΙΠΠ[ι]ΔΕΣ

ἰοδερκεῖ τελλόμεναι
Κύπριδι νεοκέ[λ]αδον   25
ε]ὐειδέα χορόν
.   .   .   .

ANONYMOUS

85   DIVERS FRAGMENTS OF EARLY LYRIC
[1–2 A.D.]   POETRY

Ed. pr. Grenfell-Hunt, *P. Oxy.* ii. 1899, no. 220, p. 41,
Plate VI. See *Powell, *Collectanea Alexandrina*, p. 194 ;

(a) ἡ Λῆμνος τὸ παλαιὸν εἴ τις ἄλλη

(b) εὐξά]μην τάδε τοῖς θεοῖσ' ἅπασι

(c) πτέρα δ' ἄγνα παρ' Ἔρωτος 'Αφρόδιτα

(d) παρθένον κόρην
.   .   .   .

ANONYMOUS

86   [Early 3 B.C.] SCOLIA, perhaps ATTIC

Ed. pr. *Schubart-Wilamowitz, *Berliner Klassikertexte*,
v. 2, 1907, p. 56, Plate VIII. See Diehl, *Anth. Lyr. Graec.*
ii. p. 189 ; Powell, *Collect. Alexandr.* p. 190 ; Körte, *Archiv*,
1913, 552 ; Schroeder, *Phil. Woch.* 1907, 1446 ; Schmidt,
Phil. Woch. 1908, 430 ; Maas, Crusius, *Lit. Centralbl.* 1907,
1319 ; Powell-Barber, *New Chapters*, i. 58.

Two scolia, *or drinking-songs, destined for recitation at*
386

ANONYMOUS

Leucippides

We arise and (begin) a fair dance of new song for
the Cyprian violet-eyed. . . .

. . . . . .

ANONYMOUS

DIVERS FRAGMENTS OF EARLY LYRIC
POETRY   [1–2 A.D.]

Leo, *N.G.G.* 1899, 499 ; Diehl, *Anth. Lyr. Gr.*² I. iv. 215,
219 ; Lobel, Σαπφοῦς Μέλη *Inc. Auct.* 19.

(*a*) Lemnos, of old, of all cities . . .

(*b*) Thus I entreated all the gods . . .

(*c*) Aphrodite . . . holy wings from Eros . . .ᵃ

(*d*) A virgin girl . . .

. . . . . .

ᵃ Perhaps a line of Sappho.

ANONYMOUS

SCOLIA, perhaps ATTIC   [Early 3 B.C.]

*symposia or banquets. Cf. the collection of Attic scolia in
Athenaeus xv. 694 c (Diehl, Anth. Lyr. Gr. ii. p. 181;
Bowra, Greek Lyric Poetry, ch. ix.).*

In (*a*) *the interpretation of the title* Εὐφωρατ[. .], *and
identity of the* παρθένος *of vv. 3 sqq. are uncertain. Ed. pr.
supplements* Εὐφωρατ[ίς] (*or* Εὐφωρατ[ώ]) *and appears to under-*

387

*stand by this title " the Scout's Goddess " ; she is then to be
identified with the* παρθένος *of vv. 3 sqq. It is however
perhaps more probable that the supplement should be* Εὐφώ-
ρατ[ος] *" The Easy Prey," a synonym for Homer's Dolon,
who is in fact the subject of the song. The identity of the*
παρθένος *will then remain uncertain ; though Athene is the
most natural candidate, since she is especially the goddess
who protects and prospers Odysseus, the captor of Dolon ; cf.
Homer, Il. x. 245, 277, 284, 295, where Athene's influence in
this episode is particularly stressed ; cf. further, Il. x. 507,*

Εὐφώρατ[ος][1]

(a)   ἐ]γκέρασον Χαρίτων κρατῆ[ρ'] ἐπιστ[ε-
φέα κρ[ύφιόν τε π]ρόπι[ν]ε [λό]γον.
σήμαιν', ὅτι παρθένων
ἀπείροσι πλέξομεν ὕμνοις
τὰν δορὶ σώματι κειραμέναν   5
Τρ[οί]αν κάτα [τ]ὸν παρὰ ναυσὶν ἀειμνά-
σ]τοις ἁλόντα
νυκτιβάταν σκοπόν.

(b)   Μνημοσύνη

Μουσᾶν ἀγανόμματε μᾶτερ
συνεπίσπεο σῶν τέκνων [. . .]ωι [. . .]ωι·
ἄρτι βρύουσαν ἀοιδὰν
πρωτοπαγεῖ σοφίαι διαποίκιλον
ἐκφέρομεν.   5

[1] Εὐφώρα[τος] D. L. P. : -τίς or -τώ ed. pr.   (b) 1 ὦ
Μοῦσ' ἀγανόμματε, corr. ed. pr.   2 [ἀγν]ῶι [γόν]ωι ed. pr.

[a] *i.e. of poetic beauty.*   [b] *i.e. the " toast " (the poem*

ANONYMOUS

578.   *Whether the praise of Athene should then lead to
the inference that these* scolia *are, like those of Athenaeus,
Attic songs, remains uncertain* (N.B. *the dialect of the elegy
which follows these songs in* Π, *no. 103 below, is "so gut
wie ganz attisch," ed. pr.*).

(b) *A song entitled "Μνημοσύνη." The virtues of the
composition are pompously advertised in the 3rd-5th lines:
then the proper theme begins—the sailor is advised to hug
the shore and make for safety when the south-wind blows
a gale.*

THE EASY CAPTURE

(a) Pour a bowl brimful of Graces,[a] drink a riddle [b]
for a toast.   Give notice, that we are going to weave
in boundless [c] chants that Maiden [d] who in presence [e]
with her spear at Troy destroyed the spy [f] caught
by night beside those vessels unforgettable.

MEMORY

(b) O mother of the Muses, with gentle eyes,
follow the . . . of your children: we bring out a
song but lately flowering forth, bedight with new-
fashioned art.

which follows) is to be obscurely phrased, to take the form of
a γρῖφος or riddle: hence the obscurity of the phrases which
follow.   [c] Perhaps "boundless *in their praise of
Athene*" (after ed. pr.): or "songs that shall have no
limit or end," *i.e.* shall be sung everywhere for ever:
or "rings (wreaths) of song," *cf.* Pindar, *Nem.* viii. 15
(Beazley).   [d] Probably Athene.   [e] An "improve-
ment" on Homer: who however strongly implies a more or
less direct intervention of Athene in this episode.   The poet
only suggests that Athene was invisibly present, guiding the
spear of Odysseus (and Diomedes).   Possibly δορὸς οἴματι,
"with the dart of a spear."   [f] Dolon, the Trojan spy in
Homer, *Il.* x.

389

νῆά τ]οι τέγξαν Ἀχελώιου δρόσ[οι.
παῦε] παραπροιών, ὑφίει πόδα,
λῦ' ἑανοῦ πτέρυγας, τάχος ἵεσο
λεπτολίθων [ἐπ' ἀγῶ]ν·
εὖ· καθόρα πέλαγος,   10
παρὰ γᾶν ἔκφευγε νότου χαλεπὰν
φοβερὰν [διαπο]ντοπλανῆ μανίαν.

· · · · · ·

(b) 7 πέρα προιών coni. ed. pr.

―――――――――――――――――――――

ᵃ The dew of Achelous : rain, acc. to ed. pr. ; but see
Callim. *Hymn. Dem.* 13, Schol. T on Hom. *Il.* xxi. 195, Dion.

ANONYMOUS

FRAGMENTS OF DITHYRAMBIC
87 [c. 1 B.C.]   POETRY

Ed. pr. Oellacher, *Mitteilungen aus der Papyrussamm-
lung der Nationalbibliothek in Wien : Papyrus Erzherzog
Rainer, Neue Serie, Erste Folge*, Wien, 1932, no. xxii. p. 136.
See Körte, *Archiv*, xi. 1935, 246 ; Crönert, *Symb. Oslo*. 14,
1935, 126 ; Powell, *Class. Rev.* 46, 1932, 263, and *New
Chapters*, iii. 210.

Fragments of Dithyrambic poetry embedded in a prose

(a)   ἀναβόασον αὐτῶι.

Διόνυσον ἀ[ύ]σομεν

390

ANONYMOUS

The dews of Achelous *a* have bathed our ship:
cease faring further, relax the sheet, release the
wings of linen,*b* swiftly speed to the light shingle of
the shore! Hurrah! *c* Keep a watch on the ocean,
hug the shore and avoid the harsh dreadful sea-
roving frenzy of the south-wind!

.   .   .   .   .   .

Perieg. 433, *Epic. Adesp.* 5. 2 (Powell) and Panyasis fr. 1 in
Powell, *Collect. Alex.* p. 248: in all these places Ἀχελῶιος =
ὠκεανός.   *b* The sails.   *c* εὖ is divided in Π from
the preceding and following words by English colons (:), the
significance of which is here uncommonly obscure. (Often
used to denote change of speaker; this is improbable here,
as ed. pr. observe.)

ANONYMOUS

FRAGMENTS OF DITHYRAMBIC
POETRY   [*c.* 1 B.C.]

*text, which may have been a treatise on the great Dithy-
rambic poets of the turn of the 5th and 4th centuries B.C., or
a commentary on one such poet; written about the end of the
3rd century B.C.   Philoxenus and Melanippides are men-
tioned by name.*

(Crönert, loc. cit., appears to attribute (f) *to Timotheus: I
do not know why).*

(*a*) . . . lift up your voice to him! We will sing

(*a*) 2 possibly ᾀ[εί]σομεν: but it is better to avoid the
strange form.

ἱεραῖς ἐν ἀμέραις
δώδεκα μῆνας ἀπόντα.
πάρα δ' ὥρα, πάντα δ' ἄνθη   5

(b)   Ζ[ε]ὺς μὲν ἐπέβρεμε βάρβαρα βροντᾶι
γᾶν δ' ἐτίναξε Ποσειδὰν
χρυσεόδοντι τριαίναι [

(c)   ] καρπῶι
ἀγ[ν]ὰ δρῦς·
φύετο στάχυς ἄμμιγα κριθαῖς
πασπερμεί,
ἀνθεῖ καὶ λευκοχίτων   5
ἅμα ζειὰ κυανότρι[χι

(d)   Ἄ]μμωνος ἀ[.]εθλ[. .
ἐπ]έβα τηλωπὸν ἱδρυθεὶς
ἀ[νύ]δρου Λιβύας
ἀσπάσιος ποσὶ λειμώ-
νων τέρεν' ἄνθεα τείρας   5
σῶμ' ἀκαμάτου

(e)   νύμφαν φοινικοπ[τέρ]υγα·
†κράτει† δ' ὑπὸ γᾶς θέτο
βριαρὸν τέκνον μαστοῖς
Ἄρεως πεφρικὸς
πα[ί]δευμ' ἀτυχίας   5

(f)   ]ε μαλακόμματος ὕπ-
νος [γ]υῖα περὶ πάντα βαλὼν

(a) 5 πάρα δῶρα ed. pr., πάρα δ' ὥρα ibid. in note.   (b) 1

ANONYMOUS

of Dionysus on holy days. Twelve months he was away: now the season is here, and all the flowers[a] . . .

(b) Zeus roared with a savage thunderclap: Poseidon shook earth with his golden-fanged trident.[b]

(c) . . . fruit . . . sacred oak; there grew a corn-ear mixed with barley, all seeds together; there flowers the white-coated[c] wheat together with the dark-haired (barley) . . .

(d) . . . of Ammon . . . made his home far away and set foot on desert Libya; rejoicing, crushed underfoot the slender flowers of the meadows, even he, unwearied[d] . . .

(e) . . . nymph purple-winged.[e] Beneath the earth (?) she set upon her breast the strong child of Ares trembling,[f] the nursling of Misfortune . . .

(f) Sleep soft-eyed, encompassing all his limbs; as

---

[a] Evidently from an annual cult-song for Dionysus, performed on certain holy days, hinting at an Epiphany of the god, who has been absent since last year's festival. [b] Cf. Homer, Il. xx. 57. [c] The coat is the husk surrounding the fruit on the ear. [d] Subject possibly Heracles, or epiphany of local divinity; but the evidence seems insufficient for conjecture. [e] A new, and here unintelligible, compound. Possibly a Siren, Harpy or other winged female is the subject (ed. pr.). [f] Perhaps Penthesilea: ἀτυχίας will then refer to her name, compound partly of πένθος, "mourning." (Beazley). I suspect that the ridiculous ΚΡΑΤΕΙ in v. 2 may be a corruption or misreading of ΚΛΕΙΘ, the name of Penthesilea's nurse. But the general sense is extremely doubtful.

βαρβαραβροντᾶι ed. pr.: but see Körte, *loc. cit.*   (e) 3
Perhaps βριαροῦ.   (f) 1 ἦλθεν δ]ὲ Crönert.

ὡσεὶ μάτηρ παῖδ' ἀγαπα-
τ]ὸν χρόνιον ἰδοῦσα φίλωι
κ]όλπωι πτέρυγας ἀμφέβαλεν   **5**

· · · · · · ·

ANONYMOUS

FRAGMENTS OF DITHYRAMBIC POETRY

88   [3 A.D.]

Ed. pr. Grenfell-Hunt, *P. Oxy.* i. 1898, no. 9, p. 14, Plate III. See *Powell, *Collectanea Alexandrina*, pp. 192-193; Diehl, *Anth. Lyr. Gr.* ii. pp. 166-167; Wilamowitz, *G.G.A.* 1898, 698 and *Gr. Versk.* 67, 294; Jan, *Phil. Woch.* 1899, 478 and *P.-W.-K.* ii. 1063; Muenscher, *Hermes*, 54, 1919, 42; Reinach, *Rev. Et. Gr.* xi. 399; Powell-Barber, *New Chapters*, i. 54.

(*a*)   ἔνθα δὴ ποικίλων ἀνθέων ἄμβροτοι λείμακες
βαθύσκιον παρ' ἄλσος ἀβροπαρθένους
εὐιώτας χοροὺς ἀγκάλαις δέχονται.

(*b*)   ὅστις εὐθυμίηι καὶ χοροῖς ἥδεται.

(*c*)   φίλον ὥραισιν ἀγάπημα, θνα-
τοῖσιν ἀνάπαυμα μόχθων.

(*d*)   φέρτατον δαίμον' ἀγνᾶς τέκος
ματέρος ἂν Κάδμος ἐγέννασέ ποτ' ἐν
ταῖς πολυόλβοισι Θήβαις.

(*c*) 1 (ὦ) φίλον Powell.

a mother, seeing her darling son after many days,
casts her wings about him on her loving breast . . .

.　　　.　　　.　　　.　　　.　　　.

ANONYMOUS

FRAGMENTS OF DITHYRAMBIC
POETRY　　　[3 A.D.]

*Fragments quoted in a treatise on metre identified by
ed. pr. with the Ῥυθμικὰ Στοιχεῖα of Aristoxenus of Tarentum.
Quotations probably from 4th-century Dithyrambs ((e) per-
haps from a Partheneion ; in (b), the Ionic εὐθυμίηι renders
doubtful the ascription to a Dithyramb). With the grove
and meadows of (a), compare the fragment of Sappho above.*

(a)　Where the fields　Which decay　Not, nor fade
　　　Receive in their embrace by shady woodland
　　　　deeps
　　　Delicate　　Maiden-throngs　　Celebrating Bac-
　　　　chus.[a]

(b)　Who soe'er　Pleasure takes　In good cheer
　　　And the dance.

(c)　To the Hours　Cherishèd delight, to men
　　　Respite for a space from labour.

(d)　All-revered　God, a chaste　Mother's child,
　　　Hers, who of old　Was in the wealth-　Teem-
　　　　ing renowned
　　　City of Thebes　Born to Cadmus.

　[a] The translations, intended to reproduce the original
metres, are taken from ed. pr.

LITERARY PAPYRI

(e)   βᾶτε βᾶτε κεῖθεν αἰδ᾽
         ἐς τὸ πρόσθεν ὀρόμεναι·
         τίς ποθ᾽ ἀ νεᾶνις; ὡς
         εὐπρέπης νιν ἀμφέπει

.   .   .   .   .   .

ANONYMOUS

89   [3 B.C.]   ? DITHYRAMBIC POEM

Ed. pr. *Gerhard, *Griechische Papyri; Urkunden und Literarische Texte aus der Papyrus-Sammlung der Universitätsbibliothek Heidelberg*, 1938, no. 178, p. 26. See Roberts, *Class. Rev.* liii. 1939, 89.

The evidence for the connexion of these fragments with some parts of the story of Odysseus is as follows :—

(1) *V. 48* πολυαινο[. . .]σεν. πολυαιν᾽ Ο[δυσ]σεν *is a possible supplement ;* πολύαινος *is used by Homer of Odysseus only.*

(2) *V. 20* Κίρκας, *the only other proper name in the piece, is clearly consistent with the above connexion.*

(3) *There is some evidence that vv. 47* sqq. *are concerned with the underworld, cf.* Εὐμενιδᾶν, ὑπὸ ζόφου δ᾽ ἀερό[εντος, φθιμένων βασιλῆα πανδ[οκέα. *Now in v. 43 the speaker addresses his mother,* μᾶτερ ἐμά: *these words, and also the words in the next line* ἀλλ᾽ ἄγε μοι τόδε, *occur also in the scene in Homer where Odysseus addresses his mother* (Od. *xi. 164, 170). The coincidence in phraseology is not very surprising ; but in a scene relating to the underworld, and one already conjectured on other grounds to deal with Odysseus, the coincidence becomes not altogether negligible.*

(4) *The adjectives* πολυπλανής *v. 32,* δολομήτας *v. 33*

396

ANONYMOUS

(e)   Onward, onward now ye maids,
       Come ye speeding on to the front.
       Who then can that maiden be ?
       With what grace about her flows . . .

.   .   .   .   .   .

ANONYMOUS

? DITHYRAMBIC POEM   [3 B.C.]

*describe Odysseus aptly. And the references to wanderings
over the sea, v. 36 ἀνὰ κύματα πόντια . . . ἀλαλημένος,
after v. 46 σὺν ναὶ μελαίναι πλαγχθείς suit his story well.*

*The evidence for the connexion of vv. 1-31 with the story
of Elpenor is (1) the reference to Circe v. 20, from whose roof
he fell to his death, (2) references to death and a burial in the
fragments. This is therefore a possible, though hazardous,
speculation.*

*Ed. pr. assigned these fragments to Timotheus : who
(according to some MSS. of Etym. Magn.) wrote an Odyssey
in four books. We know that he wrote four dithyrambs on
the story of Odysseus—Elpenor fr. 4 Wilam., Cyclops
fr. 5-8 Wilam., Scylla fr. 17-19 Wilam., Laertes fr. 9
Wilam. It is natural to suppose (with ed. pr.) that these
four dithyrambs constituted the four books of the Odyssey.
But if this is so, it is unlikely that our fragments are part of
that poem ; for though the reference to Elpenor (if there is
one) would suit this theory well, there is no room in the above
scheme of Timotheus's Odyssey for the Νέκυια, or scene in
the underworld ; which is the only scene which can be inferred
with probability from our fragments.*

Further, the style of these fragments does not recall

*Timotheus. We miss the bold—indeed the ludicrous—
metaphors and paraphrases of the poet of* The Persians ; *we
miss the extravagant compound adjectives (κρατεραυγής is
bold ; βαθύπορος, βαθύπολος, θρασύαιγις, εὐερίστης are com-
paratively tame). And we can hardly believe that Timotheus
wrote so simply and clearly, or that he copied Homeric
epithets and turns of phrase so submissively. This is the*

```
        ]μ μέλεος δ[ . ]ο . . [
        ἔ]κφυγον ἀλκα[
        ]ατα μὲν σκοτεα[
        ]αις δὲ πότμο[
        ]αρμενος ὤλε[                          5
    κα]ταστορέσας β[
        κ]εδρινὸν π . [
        ] ἀποσφαλτ[
        ] . σιυπεν[

            ]ειδμ[                            10
    φ]αεσφόρ[ο]ν ἀελ[ιόυ] δρόμον ἐν[
    ἐ]πὶ νέρτερον αὐγὴν νυκτ[
    ]ερισμ' ἀντεφαε . . ννεκ[
    ] τέκνον ὦ τέκνον ε[.] . . [
    ]αλλα τας Δαρδανι[                        15
        ]υγοτα τε δεα[
```

(Traces of two lines, including] . ορα—'Ελπήν]ορα
ed. pr.)

```
    ]μπροχέω λόγοις ἐμῶν
    ] . αμοις οἶδα γὰρ ὡς πα[
    ]υ κυαναυγέος εὖ ἄγε[ι]ν
    ] Κίρκας εν . [.]μεε . [. . .] . .         20
    ]σεη δὲ τάφου στηρίγματι
    ] τέκνων ἱκέτας προχέων
```

ANONYMOUS

*lucid writing of a straightforward and comparatively un-
ambitious poet, who calls a wave κῦμα, the sun ἀέλιος, a
tomb τάφος, deception ἀπάτα, etc. Metre, where discernible,
proves nothing decisive. There is in fact no strong evidence
in favour of the ascription to Timotheus, some evidence
against it.*

. . . unhappy . . .
. . . escaped . . . strength . . .
. . . dark . . .
. . . doom . . .
. . . perished . . .
. . . strewed . . .
. . . of cedar . . .
. . . tripped (?) . . .

.   .   .   .   .   .

.   .   .   .   .   .

. . . the course of the sun that brings light . . .
. . . to the nether rays of night . . .
. . . shone against . . .
. . . child, my child . . .
. . . but . . . Dardanian . . .

.   .   .   .   .   .

(Traces of two lines)

. . . pour forth . . . with words . . . of my . . .
. . . for I know how . . .
. . . of the dark-shining . . . to bring safely . . .
. . . of Circe . . .
. . . to the foundation of a tomb . . .
. . . of children . . . suppliant pouring forth . . .

---

12 ἐπὶ D. L. P.   13 Fort. ἐν νέκυσιν or ἐν νεκροῖς.
16 Fort. πεφε]υγότα.   17 συμπροχέω, vel fort. στοναχω]μ
προχέω.

οἳ μὲν βαθύπορον α[
πολ]υδέγμονα παι[. .]ν
] . α στε[να]χὰς παθέων [25
] . ρας δ . . ιαι δ' ἤγειρον [
]γη μυχὸν αιλο[
]ηρ' αἰαῖ ἡ δὲ νέα
] θεοὶ
]μένα ψυχὰ   30
] . . ιδα.

πολυπλανῆτα δ[
ἀπάται δολομήτας δ[
κτόνα πήματα δ[
ὅδ' ἐμὲ λυγρὰ κώλυσεν αλ[35
ὡς ἀνὰ κύματα πόντια [
ροις ἀλαλημένος ἤλυ[θ
οσ . . . νας ὑψιτύπου π[
β[. . . .]ε κρατεραυγέσι γορ[γ
[. . . .]ατόπνευστος αὔρα [40
[. . .]η δ' ὑποερείφθη γ . [
[. .] . ἔπνευσε νεκυοπο . .[
[μ]ᾶτερ ἐμά, θάμα το[
[ἀ]λλ' ἄγε μοι τόδε τ[
[. .]νομοι ἔννεπεν δα[45
[. . .]εασυστα θανατ[

(Fragments of nine lines, including σ]ὺν ναὶ μελαίναι
πλαγχθείς . . . ἀνέμοις, λίφ' ἑκὼν . . . .
ἔλιπον . ματερ . . .)

]νας καὶ Εὐμενιδᾶν ε . . ω . . . ὑπὸ ζόφου
δ' ἀερό-
[εντος   ]σμον μύθων ὅρμαν . . . ε τάδε δὴ
πολύαιν' Ὀ[δυσ]σεῦ

ANONYMOUS

. . . some . . . the deep crossing . . .
. . . Receiver of the Multitudes . . .
. . . groans . . . of sorrows . . .
. . . collected . . .
. . . recess . . .
. . . alas ! and the young . . .
. . . gods . . .
. . . soul . . .

.   .   .   .   .   .

The Wanderer . . .
by deceit the crafty schemer . . .
sorrows . . .
he stopped me . . . grievous . . .
as in the waves of the sea . . .
wandering came . . .
. . . lofty . . .
. . . bright strong . . .
. . . -blown breeze . . .
. . . was dashed down . . .
. . . breathed . . . corpse- . . .
My mother, often . . .
But come., . . . me this . . .
. . . spoke . . .
. . . death . . .

(Fragments of nine lines)

. . . and of the kindly Goddesses . . . beneath the
misty darkness . . . of speech . . . impulse . . . this,

---

23 οἱ D. L. P.   25 στεναχὰς D. L. P.   27 Fort.
κυαναυ]γῆ μυχὸν ῎Αιδο[ς.   35 ὅδ᾽ ἐμὲ D. L. P.   37
ἤλυθον, -ε.   40 ? κυματόπνευστος D. L. P.   42
νεκυοπόμπ- ?   48 ᾽Οδυσσεῦ not at all certain.

LITERARY PAPYRI

] . δώματα καὶ φθιμένων βασιλῆα πανδ[οκέα]
]μεν προφυγὼν θάνατον θρασυαίγιδα τ[. . . .]αν 50
] δι' ἀπείρονα κύ[μα]τα

(*Fragments of eight-and-a-half lines, including* μυχὸν
. . . ἄντρου, λώβαν . . . οὐκ εἶδον οὐδ' ἐδό-
κευσα νόωι (*cf. Od. xii. 258-259*), εὐεριστα[. . .
θαλερὰν φρένα ἐδρέψατο, βαθυπόλων, συνθεὶς
κλίμακα)

.   .   .   .   .   .

ΦΙΛΙΚΟΣ

90   [End 3 b.c.]   HYMN TO DEMETER

Ed. pr. Norsa, *Studi Italiani di Filologia Classica*, N.S. v.
1927, p. 87+Gallavotti, *ibid.* ix. 1931, p. 37. See Powell-
Barber, *New Chapters*, ii. 61 and iii. 195 ; Maas, *Gnomon*,
1927, 439 ; Körte, *Archiv*, viii. 1927, 255 and **Hermes*, 66,
1931, 442 ; Stoessl, *P.-W.-K. s.v. Philiskos*, no. 4.

*The ascription to Philicus is based on Hephaestion, Ench.
p. 30, 21 :* Φίλικος δὲ ὁ Κερκυραῖος, εἷς ὢν τῆς Πλειάδος,
ἑξαμέτρωι (sc. χοριαμβικῶι) συνέθηκεν ὅλον ποίημα· τῆι χθονίηι
μυστικὰ Δήμητρί τε καὶ Φερσεφόνηι καὶ Κλυμένωι τὰ δῶρα :
*i.e. Philicus wrote a Hymn to Demeter in choriambic
hexameters ; our fragment, on the same subject and in the
same peculiar metre, is almost certainly a portion of that
Hymn. The cult of Demeter was at this time very popular
in Alexandria : new details of ritual had been instituted by
royal command* κατὰ μίμησιν τῶν Ἀθηνῶν (*Schol. Callim.
Hymn vi. 1*). *But it is clear that our poem was not a cult-
song. It was an exercise in poetry—especially in metre—
intended for a learned audience* (*Gallavotti, p. 56, Körte,*

402

PHILICUS

illustrious Odysseus . . . houses and king of the dead,
their host, . . . escaping death . . . of the bold
aegis, . . . through the boundless waves . . .

(Fragments of eight-and-a-half lines)

•   •   •   •   •   •

PHILICUS

HYMN TO DEMETER [End 3 B.C.]

*p. 443 : evidence of the line quoted by Hephaestion, almost
certainly from the beginning of our poem, καινογράφου
συνθέσεως τῆς Φιλίκου, γραμματικοί, δῶρα φέρω πρὸς ὑμᾶς).
So far as we can see, the poem was obscurely learned, varied
in incident, original in metre.[a]*

*The action from vv. 4-15 is fairly clear. A woman (or
goddess) has just finished speaking. The Nymphs and Graces
and a crowd of mortal women do homage to Demeter, in the
manner of subjects doing obeisance to an Eastern potentate.
They honour her, as mortal victors at pan-Hellenic contests
were honoured, by showering leaves over her—only they must
throw whatever plants or grasses they can find : there are no
leaves, for Demeter has made the earth unfruitful. Then
from Halimous—here apparently located among the hills of
Attica—comes Iambe (there was a shrine of Demeter and
Persephone at Halimous, Paus. i. 31. 1). The poet, inspired*

---

[a] The metre had been used before (by Simias) ; but so far
as we know, no poem had even been—or ever was again—
composed *solely* in lines of this metre.

*by the Homeric Hymn to Demeter, 202 sqq., now warns us
that what follows is comic : Iambe addresses the women and
Demeter with rough and ready familiarity, apologizes for her
uncouth manners, admits that she has no gifts such as the
goddesses and women offer, but promises to find a remedy for
Demeter's sorrow.*

*The action of the 50 fragmentary verses which precede
v. 4 in the papyrus is excessively obscure. It is probable
enough that the first 21 lines narrated some part of Demeter's
search for Persephone, and told how the earth was rendered
unfruitful. Vv. 22-50 have been, and can be, variously
interpreted.*

*Körte argues, with habitual skill, that they are a speech
by Peitho (Persuasion), who consoles Demeter, forecasts the
institution of the Eleusinian mysteries, and offers her
assistance in recovering Persephone from the underworld.
But great difficulty is caused by the fragments of lines 24-27*

. . . . κλῦ]θι λιτὰς μητρόθεν αὐταδέλφους
. . . . ἥτ]ις ὁμόσπλαγχνον ἔθρεψα Κύπριν
. . . . Ὠκεαν]ίνη γάλα σοι, μητρὶ δ' ἐγὼ σύναιμος
. . . . μ]εγάλας κοινοπάτωρ λοχεύει.

*If the supplement in the third line is correct, the line is
most naturally taken as an address to Zeus, reminding him
that Amalthea, daughter of Oceanus, was his nurse. But
who is then the speaker ? Neither Demeter nor Peitho can*

] ἄγου Φερσεφόνην ὑπ' ἄστρα
]ασιν ἡγησαμένης οὐθὲν ἐμοῦ σφαλήσει.
ἀλλὰ σ]ὺ πεύκας ἀνελοῦ, λῦε βαρεῖαν ὀφρύν.
ἦ μὲν [ἔ]ληγεν [κατακούουσι δ]ὲ Νύμφαι τε δικαίας
    Χάρ[ι]τές τε Πειθοῦς,
π]ᾶς δὲ γυναικῶν ἅ[μα κύκλωι τε π]έριξ θ' ἐσμὸς
    ἐθώπευσε πέδον μετώποις.

PHILICUS

say μητρὶ δ' ἐγὼ σύναιμος : *Peitho, because it would not be true ; Demeter, because she had the same father (Cronus), as well as the same mother, as Zeus ; possibly the next line continued* πατρί τε, *or* καὶ πατρί ; *but the phrase* μητρόθεν αὐταδέλφους *suggests that the speaker is sister of the listener on the mother's, not on the father's, side ; it may also be said that* μητρὶ δ' ἐγὼ σύναιμος *is a most unnatural phrase for a sister to use to a brother—it should mean " I am of the same kin as your mother." Further, neither Peitho nor Demeter can—so far as we know—say* ὁμόσπλαγχνον ἔθρεψα Κύπριν. *Körte admits these objections, but can do nothing to remove them.*

*So far as I can discover, the only figure in mythology who suits the four fragmentary lines quoted above is Dione. She is sister of Rhea, Zeus's mother (*μητρὶ δ' ἐγὼ σύναιμος : μητρόθεν αὐταδ. *will then =of your mother's sister) : she brought up Aphrodite (*ἔθρεψα Κύπριν : ὁμόσπλαγχνον *obscurely referring to the fact that she is daughter in common to Zeus and Dione) : further, Dione is anciently a daughter of Oceanus and Tethys (Hes. Theogon. 353 : a Nereid, Apollod. i. 12), therefore a sister of Amalthea (*'Ωκεαν]ίνη γάλα σοι) ; *so, although she is here regarded as daughter of Uranus, her connexion with the Oceanids may have remained close. But I have no evidence for a close connexion of Dione with Demeter, and therefore no reason why she should intercede in this poem on Demeter's behalf.*

" . . . bring Persephone to the starlight . . . you shall never stumble, where I lead. . . . Take up the torches, unknit your heavy brow."

She ceased : . . . the Nymphs and Graces hearkened to righteous Persuasion, and together in a ring around her all the swarm of women did

---

2 ἄμβ]ασιν Beazley. 4 κατακούουσι Beazley.

405

φυλλοβολῆσαι δὲ θεὰν [. . . . .]ν ἔσχον τὰ μόνα
　　ζώφυτα γῆς ἀκάρπου.
τὴν δὲ γεραιὰν παν[άπυ]στον μὲν ὀρείοις ʼΑ[λ]ιμοῦς
　　ἤθεσι, καιρίαν δέ,
ἔκ τινος ἔστειλε τύχ[ης· τοῖσι δὲ] σεμνοῖς ὁ γελοῖος
　　λόγος ἆρ' ἀκερδῆ[ς;
στᾶσα γὰρ ἐφθέγξατ' [ἄφαρ θα]ρ[σ]αλέον καὶ μέγα·
　　μὴ βάλλετ(ε) χόρτον αἰγῶν·
οὐ τόδε πεινῶντι θεῶι [φάρμα]κον, ἀλλ' ἀμβροσία
　　γαστρὸς ἔρεισμα λεπτῆς.　　　　　　　　　　　　10
καὶ σὺ δὲ τῆς ʼΑτθίδος, ὦ δ[αῖμ]ο[ν], ʼΙάμβης
　　ἐπάκουσον βραχύ μού τι κέρδος.
εἰμὶ δ' ἀπαίδευτα χέα[σ' ὡς ἂ]ν ἀποικοῦσα λάλος
　　δημότις· αἱ θεαὶ μὲν
αἵδε, θεά, σοι κύλικας [. . . . .]ε καὶ στέμματα
　　καὶ [β]απτὸν ὕδωρ ἐν ὑγρῶι,
ἐκ δὲ γυναικῶν π[έλεται νῦ]ν βοτάνη δῶρον ὀκνηρᾶς
　　ἐλάφου δίαιτα.
οὐθὲν ἐμοὶ τῶνδε [πάρεστιν γ]έρας· ἀλλ' εἰ χαλά-
　　[σ]ε[ις] π[έ]νθος, ἐγὼ δὲ λύσω. . . .　　　　　　　15
　　　　　　　　．　　　　　　．

6 [ἄθλιο]ν Gallavotti, [πότνια]ν Powell.　　7 πανάπυστον
Gallavotti.　　8 τοῖσι δὲ Lobel.　ἆρ' ἀκερδῆ[ς; Norsa.
11 ὦ δαῖμον Schmid, Pohlenz.　Various punctuations of the
end of the line.　　12 End αιδεαιμεν Π, corr. Lobel.
13 αιδεθεαι Π : θεά, Powell.　χα[λά τ]ε Gallavotti.　　14
πέλεται νῦν Vogliano.

obeisance with their foreheads to the ground. For
leaves to throw upon the goddess, plants from the
barren earth—all that was left—they had.

Now by some chance Halimous sent forth that old
woman, all unknown among her mountain-haunts,
yet timely come. The tale of humour is good for the
solemn spirit.—She stood there and cried at once
aloud and boldly " Don't throw her the fodder of
goats ! That is no remedy for a starving god ; it is
ambrosia that supports her delicate belly ! Now do
you, great Spirit, give ear to Iambe from Attica.
I have some benefit to offer. I have given [a] tongue
to foolish chatter like a country-cousin gossip. These
goddesses have given you, Goddess, chalices and . . .
wreaths and water drawn in the stream [b] : and now
from these women your gift is the grass, the diet of
the timorous deer. Not one of such boons is mine
to give : yet, if you will relax your sorrow, I will set
free. . . ."

.   .   .   .   .   .

[a] For the constr. εἰμὶ χέασα cf. S. O.T. 90, Kühner-Gerth, i.
38 A. 3.   [b] Cf. Eur. Hipp. 123 βαπτὰν κάλπισι ῥυτὰν
παγὰν προιεῖσα (sc. πέτρα) : " a flowing stream, dipped into
with pitchers." So here " water dipped-into (with—or by
—pitchers) in the flood." But I have no great confidence
in my rendering here and elsewhere in this piece. For
another view see Powell, loc. cit. p. 199.

ANONYMOUS

91 [3 B.C.]   HYMN TO DEMETER

Ed. pr. *Roberts, *Aegyptus*, xiv. 1934, p. 447. See Körte, *Archiv*, xiii. 1938, 89.

The chief interest of this poor composition lies in its metre: the regular combination of dactylic hexameter and tetrameter is familiar to us from Horace, Carm. i. 7. 28, but unique in Greek literature. Ed. pr. observes that the writer seems in vv. 3-10 to be contradicting Callimachus, who (Hymn to Zeus 57-66) had denied that the three gods cast lots for their empires, maintaining that Zeus won his place of honour by his own prowess. The poem may have gone on

ὕ]μνον Δήμη[τρ]ος πολυωνύμου ἄρχομαι ἱστ[ᾶν
   δί]πλακ᾽, ἀκούσατε, δεῦτε, μέλισσαι.
καὶ τὸν ἐν ἀθανάτοισι θεοῖς μέσατόν ποτ᾽ ἔθεντο
   κλῆρον, τίς τίνα χῶρον ἀνάξει.
πρώτωι δ᾽ ἦλθε λαχεῖν πόντον βαθὺν ἁλμυροδίνη   5
   χερσὶ τρίαιναν ἔχοντα Ποσειδᾶν·
Ζεὺς δ᾽ ἔλαχεν Κρονίδης μέγαν οὐρανὸν ἀστερόεντα
   ἀενίαν ἵν᾽ ἔχηι βασιλείαν·
Ἀγεσίλας δ᾽ ἔλαχεν τὸν Τά[ρταρον οὖ]ρον ἔπεσθαι.
   καὶ πᾶσιν μακάρεσσι τά[δ᾽ ἧρκει.   10
καὶ τότ᾽ ἀπὸ κλήρων μὲν ἀφίκετο δ[

   (*Traces of one more line*)

·   ·   ·   ·   ·   ·

9 εὐ]ρὺν Körte.

ᵃ Lit. " bees ": *cf.* Pindar, *P.* iv. 60 and Schol.   ᵇ *Sc.* the gods. An ungainly sentence, *cf.* next note.   ᶜ κλῆρος

ANONYMOUS

ANONYMOUS

HYMN TO DEMETER [3 B.C.]

to tell how Pluto stole Persephone, and how Demeter sought her.

This piece is not "literature" in the narrower Alexandrian sense : it is the work of an amateur, e.g. a schoolmaster or public servant : it is interesting to observe how quickly and how far the work of Callimachus (and others) penetrated and provoked imitation. Here the influence of learned Alexandrian poetry is clear from both metre and style (e.g. Ἀγεσίλας for the king of Hades ; μέλισσαι for the priestesses of Demeter ; the form Ποσειδᾶν accus. and the compound (new) ἁλμυροδίνης).

To raise a twofold hymn to Demeter of many names I start—hither and hear it, priestesses ! [a] Once on a time they [b] cast the lot amidst the immortal gods, which one should rule which district. To him first came the lot,[c] that he—Poseidon,[d] who holds the trident—should receive the salt eddies of the deep sea. Zeus, the son of Cronus, won the wide starry heaven to hold forever as his kingdom. And Agesilas [e] won Tartarus to be the district of his tendance. And all the gods were satisfied therewith. And then from the lots arrived . . .

(*Traces of one more line*)

.   .   .   .   .   .

is the subject of ἦλθε, λαχεῖν epexeg. infin.   [d] Ποσειδᾶν accus., Ar. *Ach.* 798.   [e] Form of name known only from Kaibel, *Epigr. Gr.* 195 ; Callim. *Hymn* v. 130 ; *cf.* Lactantius, *de fals. relig.* i. 11 Plutoni, cui nomen Agesilao, pars occidentis obtingeret (ed. pr.).

LITERARY PAPYRI

ANONYMOUS

FOUR HELLENISTIC FRAGMENTS

92 [About 100 B.C.]

Ed. pr. Grenfell-Hunt-Smyly, *The Tebtunis Papyri*, i. 1902, no. 1, p. 1, Plate I. See *Powell, *Collectanea Alexandrina*, p. 185 ; Diehl, *Anth. Lyr. Gr.* ii. p. 296 ; Wilamowitz, *Timotheos : die Perser*, p. 82, n. 3 ; *Gr. Versk.* p. 343 ; Powell-Barber, *New Chapters*, i. 56, ii. 62.

(a) *Brief lyric poem, presumably incomplete, in which Helen complains that Menelaus is deserting her after their return from Troy.*

(a) ὦ φανεὶς χάρμα μοι   (στρ.)
    φίλιον, ὅτ᾽ ἔμ᾽ ἠγάπας,
    ὅτε δόρατι πολεμίωι
    τὰν Φρυγῶν
    πόλιν ἐπόρθεις, μόνον   5
    τἀμὰ κομίσαι θέλων
    λέχεα πάλιν εἰς πάτραν.
    νῦν δὲ μούναν μ᾽ ἀφεὶς   (ἀντιστρ.)
    ἄλοχον, ἄστοργ᾽, ἄπεις,
    ἣν Δαναιδᾶν λόχος   10
    (μετ)έμολεν,
    ἧς ἕνεκα παῖδα τὰν
    ἄγαμον εἷλ᾽ Ἄρτεμις
    σφάγιον Ἀγαμέμνονι.

(b) ξουθὰ δὲ λιγύφωνα
    ὄρνεα διεφοίτα (τ᾽)
    (ἀ)ν᾽ ἐρῆμον δρίος, ἄκροις (τ᾽)
    ἐπὶ κλωσὶ πίτνος ἦμεν᾽

ANONYMOUS

ANONYMOUS

FOUR HELLENISTIC FRAGMENTS
[About 100 B.C.]

(b) *An elaborate and " dithyrambic " description of dawn in the country : the writer displays his considerable knowledge of bees.*

(c) *and* (d) *Couplets of an epigrammatic sort, in a combination of lyrical metres, concerned with sundry aspects of the passion of love.*

Extracts from an anthology, according to ed. pr. : but, if so, it was a curiously heterogeneous collection. Wilamowitz thinks that the papyrus may be the result of a writing-lesson (pieces dictated by a master to a pupil learning orthography). Our four extracts are followed in Π by fragments of two more—one poetical, of the same sort as (c) *and* (d), *the second (obscene) in prose.*

(a) You were a vision of love and joy to me, when you cared for me, when with foeman's spear you sacked the Phrygian city, eager only to bring me back, your wife, to my native land. But now, heartless, will you begone, leaving your wife lonely,[a] whom the band of Danaids pursued, for whose sake Artemis took that unwedded maid [b] her victim from Agamemnon ?

(b) Birds nimble and musical were flitting through the lonely woodland ; perched on the topmost pine-

---

[a] This poem is our only evidence for the desertion of Helen by Menelaus after their return to Sparta.   [b] Iphigenia.

(a) 5 μονα Π : possibly μόνας (gen. sing. fem.).

ἐμινύριζ' ἐτιττύβιζεν   5
κέλαδον παντομιγῆ, καὶ
τὰ μὲν ἄρχετο, τὰ [δ' ἔμ]ελλεν,
τὰ δ' ἐσίγα, τὰ δὲ βωστρεῦντ'
ἀν' ὄρη λαλεῦσι φωναῖς,
φιλέρημος δὲ νάπαις(ιν)   10
λάλος ἀνταμείβετ' ἀχώ.
πιθαναὶ δ' ἐργατίδες σιμοπρόσωποι
ξουθόπτεροι μέλισσαι
θαμιναὶ θέρεος ἔριθοι
λιπόκεντροι βαρυαχεῖς   15
πηλουργοὶ δυσέρωτες
ἀσκεπεῖς τὸ γλυκὺ νέκταρ
μελιτόρρυτον ἀρύουσιν.

(c)   ἐρῶντα νουθετοῦντες ἀγνοεῖθ' ὅτι
       πῦρ ἀνακαιόμενον ἐλαίωι θέλετε κ[οι]μίσαι.

(d)   ἐρῶντος ψυχὴ καὶ λαμπάδιον ὑπ' ἀνέμου
       ποτὲ μὲν ἀνήφθη, ποτὲ δὲ πάλι κοιμίζεται.

(b) 8-9 τὰ δ' ἐβώστρει· τότ' ὄρη Powell, after ed. pr. : ταδε-
βωστευοντοτορη Π¹, ταδεβωστρευοντανορη Π² : corr. Wilamo-
witz.   10 Or νάπαις (ά).

ANONYMOUS

93   [1 A.D.] LATE HELLENISTIC ANAPAESTS

Ed. pr. *Schubart-Wilamowitz, *Berliner Klassikertexte*,
v. 2, 1907, p. 131. See Powell, *Collectanea Alexandrina*,
p. 187 ; Schmidt, *Phil. Woch.* 1908, 465 ; Powell, *New*

ANONYMOUS

branches they chirped and twittered in loud sweet
jargoning, some beginning, some pausing, some silent,
others sang aloud and spoke with voices on the hill-
sides ; and Echo talkative, that loves lonely places,
made answer in the glades. The willing *a* busy bees,
snub-nosed, nimble-winged, summer's toilers in a
swarm, stingless,*b* deep-toned, clay-workers,*c* unhappy
in love,*d* unsheltered, draw up the sweet nectar
honey-laden.

(c) When you rebuke a lover, you know not that
you seek to quench with oil a blazing fire.*e*

(d) A lover's spirit, and a torch in the wind, are
now kindled, and now die down again.

a Vergil, *G.* iv. 154 certis sub legibus (Powell).   *b* See
Powell.   *c* References to a variety of bees (found in
Egypt) " which build cells of mud against stones in sheltered
situations," ed. pr.   But see Powell, *New Chapters*, ii. 63
" the epithet πηλουργός is particularly appropriate to the
species Chalicodoma, which visibly collect, prepare, trans-
port and mould into shape their building materials. ἀσκε-
πεῖς are wild bees which have no hive."   *d* " Averse
from love," as being " non-mating and so producing no
offspring," *cf.* Vergil, *G.* iv. 198-199 (Powell).   *e* I
agree with ed. pr. that the second line of this and the first
of the next fragment should not be converted into iambic
trimeters.

ANONYMOUS

LATE HELLENISTIC ANAPAESTS [1 A.D.]

Chapters, i. 57 ; Körte, *Archiv*, v. 557 ; Diehl. *Anth. Lyr.
Gr.* ii. p. 310 ; Schubart, *Pap. Graec. Berol.* Plate XIb,
preface xii.

LITERARY PAPYRI

(a) *A catalogue of districts in Hellas : all of them praise Homer, who is then extolled as the creator of all poetry. The description of the places is indifferent work : Aetolia is Elean because its hero was Elean Endymion ; the Locrian coast is " near the sea," a quality which it shares with other coasts ; Achaea is " the wave" of Dyme because it borders the sea ; Boeotia is represented by the obscure Teumessus (this trait borrowed from Antimachus, cf. Strabo ix. 409, Wilam.) ; Athenians are "children of Erichthonius," a commonplace description.*

(b) *May be part of the same poem as (a), with an easy transition from Homer to Cassandra. We know nothing of*

.   .   .   .   .   .

(a)   Αἰτωλῶν τ' Ἠλ[εῖον] ἔθνος
        Δύμης τε κλυδών, γλαύκης τε πέλ[ας]
        Λοκρίδες ἀκταί, τό τε Κρισαίων
        ζάθεον τριπόδων ὑ[μ]νωιδὸν ὄρος,
        Τευμησιάδ[ες] τ' ἄνετοι σκοπιαί,   5
        τό τ' Ἐριχθονίου βλάστ[ημ'] ἀρότων,
        οὓς Παλλὰς ἄνασσ' ἔξοχα θνητῶ[ν
        δορὶ κἂν σοφίαις ἀνέγραψεν,
        σῶ]ν πάντες, Ὅμηρ', αἰνετὸν ὕμνων
        φύσιν [ἡρ]ώιων λογάσιν μερόπων   10
        παραδεξάμενοι μεγαλύνουσιν
        τήν τ' ἀπὸ Μουσῶν ἄφθιτον αὐδὴν
        ἣν σὺ μερίμναις ταῖσιν ἀτρύτοις
        καθυφηνάμενος πόντος τις ὅπως
        ἔπτυσας ἄλ[λο]ις [ο]ὐ [μυθητοῦ]ς   15
        φωσὶν ἐπ' ἀκτάς

(b)   . . . ἦλθ[ε]ν ὑπ' αὐτὴν ζεῦγλαν ἀνά[γκης·
        πρ]όσπολον οἰκτρᾶς μετὰ παρθενικ[ῶν
        παίδων ἰαχῆς μέλος οἰμώξασ',

414

ANONYMOUS

this kind of composition. We observe in it monotony of metre ; lack of taste in phraseology, and of imagination in sentiment and description. The time and place of such work is unknown, but doubtless vaguely Hellenistic.

The influence of Timotheus is obvious in the phraseology (cf. τόσον ὠδίνων σχῆμα λοχευθέν = σχῆμα τοσούτων τέκνων : vv. 25 sqq. are a periphrasis for τίς ἔτικτέ με ;). The writing of anapaestic lyrics survived in Tragedy after other lyrical forms became obsolete (see no. 30 above) ; and the metre was popular for many different kinds of composition in the 1st century A.D. This specimen is remarkably similar in form and subject-matter to no. 30 above, and to Eur. Tro. 767, etc., which must still have been its acknowledged model. It is curious that this part of ancient drama still inspired imitation so long after every other part of it had ceased to do so.

(a) . . . and Elean race of Aetolians, the wave of Dyme, the Locrian shores near the grey sea, and the sacred hill of song at Crisa's tripods, and the desert peaks of Teumessus, and the men that grow in the fields of Erichthonius, whom above other mortals Queen Pallas has recorded among men valiant and wise : all these, Homer, inherit and exalt the nature of your heroic song, praised by the chosen among men ; and praise too your deathless voice, gift of the Muses, which with such unwearying labour you wove to a pattern : then like the sea you spewed it forth upon the shore [a] for men that have no poetry. . . .

(b) She came beneath the very yoke of Necessity, together with her maiden daughters wailing a song that went in hand with cries of woe : she sped to

---

[a] *Cf.* Aelian, *V.H.* xiii. 22, a painter ὃς ἔγραψε τὸν μὲν Ὅμηρον αὐτὸν ἐμοῦντα, τοὺς δὲ ἄλλους ποιητὰς τὰ ἐμημεσμένα ἀρυτομένους (ed. pr.): ἐμοῦντα is coarse, ἔπτυσας is not (*cf.* *Iliad* iv. 426).

ἵετ' ἐ[π'] ἀκτὰς [συνμι]υρομένας   20
δεσπότις ἡ πρ[ὶ]ν σκήπ[τρων ἀρχ]ός,
δούλη Δαναῶν ἐπίσημ[ο]ς.
σ[ῆς] γὰ[ρ γεν]εᾶς ὁ πα[λ]αιὸς ἰὼν
θεσμὸς ἐ[λέ]γχει τό[σον ὠ]δίνων
σχῆμα λοχευθέν. τίς δ' ἤροσ' [ἐμὴν   25
φύσ]ιν, ἢ τίν[ι δὴ] τὸν [ὑ]πὸ ζώνης
δεσμ[ὸν] ἔλυσεν πότ[νι' Εἰλ]ήθυι',
Ἄτροπ[ο]ς νεα[ρά; και]ρὸς ἀνοίγειν
τὸν ὑ]πὸ σκοτίαις β[ύ]βλοισι λόγον
κρυπ[τόν], ἀνάγκη πρὸς [φ]ῶς μ' ἀ[σαι·   30
παρ' ἔμοιγε, [πάτ]ερ, πίστιν θνητοῖς
πᾶσι βε]βαίαν ῥίζ[ωσ]εν ἄναξ
σῆς ἀπ[ὸ φύτλης εὐώ]δινος
μούνηι. λυγρὰν εὗρεν ἀοιδ[ὴν
πρὸ πυ]λῶν [ἱερῶν κτ]ύπον ἀλγούσηι   35
χαλ[κῆς] κανα[χῆς, στυγνὸν ἀ]χόρδου
μέλος ἁ[ρμονίας,] μυστί[δα δ' ὀμφὴν
ὁ] λύραι συνετὴν [Μοῦσαν] ἀείσας
θεσμ[

(Obscure fragments of six more lines)

.   .   .   .   .   .

ANONYMOUS

94   [End 2 A.D.] A VISIT TO THE UNDERWORLD

Ed. pr. Grenfell-Hunt-Hogarth, *Fayum Towns and their Papyri*, 1900, no. 2, p. 82. See Crönert, *Archiv*, ii. 358; *Weil, *Journal des Savants*, 1901, p. 25.

the shores that moaned in unison with her, once a sceptred Queen and ruler, now illustrious slave of Danaans. For the ancient Doom of your house has found out in its course all the fair children of your travail-pangs.

Who was ploughman of the fields that grew me? For whom did gracious Ilithyia loose the bond beneath the girdle, Doom in another guise? The time has come to reveal the word that lies hidden in the darkness of the Book, now must I sing it to the sunlight. In me alone of your noble race, my father, the Master planted knowledge that all men should trust. A dismal incantation he found for me, when I shuddered before the holy gate at the clash of the din of bronze,[a] the hateful song of stringless symphony: he who sang upon the lyre a hymn of wisdom . . . a mystic oracle. . . .

(Obscure fragments of six more lines)

.   .   .   .   .   .

[a] She refers to the beginning of the Trojan War. In vv. 25 *sqq.* above, I do not know why she should be in doubt about the identity of her parents.

22-23 ἐπὶ σημ[αί]ας . [δὴ] γὰ[ρ ed. pr.: text Schubart. 31-32 Schubart.

ANONYMOUS

A VISIT TO THE UNDERWORLD [End 2 a.d.]

Adventures of a man who descended to the underworld in order to converse with a woman, now dead, formerly no doubt

417

LITERARY PAPYRI

his wife or mistress. His life has evidently been brought to ruin. He blames the woman, and seeks her out among the dead to upbraid her : he accuses her of deceit (τί δέ μ' ἐξαπατῶσα ; in the scraps of 17 lines which follow our fragment— itself preceded by scanty remains of 2 columns) and complains of her luxurious living (σπαταλῶσα, ibid.).

There are other descriptions of a voyage to the underworld in Greek and Latin literature, and other stories of men who descended alive to Hades in pursuit of a woman : but this fragment's description of the journey is gruesome and horrible beyond any other, and the motive for the pursuit is (so far as I know) unique. The details of the journey also diverge considerably from traditional lines. Traditionally (e.g. in Vergil, Aen. vi. ; Lucian, Menippus ; cf. Homer, Νέκυια ; Ar. Frogs ; and other sources : Helm, Lucian und Menipp, 1906, Kap. 1, and authorities quoted there), the living visitor to the underworld must first undergo a certain preparation and ritual. When all is ready for the adventure, he crosses the Acherusian lake, sacrifices, and invokes the gods. There follows an earthquake ; the visitor enters the underworld through a chasm. He must now soothe Cerberus, and per- suade Charon to ferry him across the Styx. He then arrives at (1) the Plains of Sorrow, lugentes campi, where the ghosts await their turn for trial by Minos, (2) the place where guilty ghosts are punished, (3) the place where the pure, or adequately punished, souls have their abode. So much for the traditional outline, apart from details.

In our poem, several stages of the visitor's journey can be

λοξὴν δ' ἀτράπου τρίβο[ν ἑρπύσας
τόπον ἦλθε τὸν οὔ[τ]ι[ς ἐπῆλθ' ἑκών.

ᵃ Col. ii. 6 ἔμ]ολεν πύλην, no doubt the entrance to Hades. Here he meets a divinity whom he addresses, col. ii. 9 προ- [σελ]ήλυθά σοι, μάκαρ. The divinity should traditionally be

*discerned. First, an oblique road—perhaps the steep entrance
to Hades* [a] *—leads to a place where dogs are devouring bodies.
The position and description of this place do not suit the
Acherusian lake ; it is then probably the nearer side of a
river encircling Hades ; the bodies may be those of the un-
buried dead, who cannot be conveyed across the river. The
visitor continues his journey across this river. Having
passed through a " toilsome land " (which may be the region
just described, or a further stage of the journey) the visitor
arrives at the Shores of Ugliness. Here he sits on a rock and
tries to catch a fish.—Why ? Because some part of it is to
be an accessory in his evocation of the dead woman with
whom he wishes to converse ? I know no evidence for it, and
think it an improbable act at this stage of the journey. This
grisly fishing remains a dark mystery. The visitor is now
on the verge of a field, wherein he observes a multitude of
corpses violently dead and cruelly punished.*

*It is clear that the poet has departed far from the firm
tradition about visits to the underworld. He ignores
Cerberus, dispenses with the aid of Charon, sees nothing of
the Seat of Judgement.*

*The language and style of the poem preclude a date of
composition much earlier than the date of the papyrus itself.
N.B. especially τραχηλοκοπῶ (Plutarch, Arrian, Epictetus),
τάδην (new in literature), σκολοπίζω " impale." Rare uses
are ἄνετον " consecrated," ἀχανής " vast," ἔμφοβος " fright-
ened." The author was using highly poetical language,
borrowed from classical and post-classical literature of
different kinds.*

. . . Along the oblique pathway he crept, and
came to a place whither no man ever came of his

Hecate, *cf.* Lucian, *Menippus* ; Verg. *Aen.* vi. 258 ; Helm,
Lucian und Menipp, p. 29. For μάκαρ vocat. femin. *cf.*
Eur. *Hel.* 375, *Ba.* 565, etc.

ἐφοβεῖτο· φόβος γόνυ δεῖ ['μ]φοβο[ν·
κατὰ πᾶσαν ἐτύγχανε σώματ[α·
πολλοὶ δὲ κύνες περὶ τοὺς νεκροὺς   5
θοίνης χάριν ἦσαν ἀφιγμένοι.
ἄνετον (δ)ὲ πόνοις κραδίαν φέρων
ἐπλόιζε πρόπαντα δέος μεθείς·
†ὡς αὐτὸν ἔχων ερρωδι πόρον.†
κ[α]ὶ δὴ χθόνα δυστράπ[ελ]ον φθάσας   10
ἀ[σ]χήμονας ἦλθε παρ' ἠιόνας.
ἐνθένδε πέτρα[ν] καθίσας, ὅτε
κάλαμον μὲν ἔδησε νεκρᾶι τριχί,
δέλεαρ δὲ λαβών, καὶ ψωμίσ[α]ς
ἄγκιστρον, ἀνῆκε βαθεῖ βυθῶι,   15
τὴν νηχομένην δ' ἔ[λκ]ων [τρίχ]α,
ὡς οὐδὲν ὅλως τότ' ἐλάμβανεν,
[[κατὰ τὸν βυθὸν]]
κατὰ θυμὸν ανεσ . ο . [. . . .]ένως.
ἀχανὲς γὰρ ἔκειτ[ο τάδ]ην πέριξ   20
δάπεδον γέμον αἰνομόρων νεκρῶν
πελεκιζομένων, σταυρουμένων·
λυγρὰ σώματα δ' [ἵστ]αθ' ὑπ[ε]ρθε γῆς
τετραχηλακοπημ[έ]να προσφάτως·
ἕτεροι πάλιν ἐσκολοπισμένο[ι   25
ἐκρέμαντο τροπαῖα πικρᾶς τύχης.
Ποιναὶ δ' ἐγέλων μέλ[ε]ον νεκρῶν
θανάτου τρόπον ἐστεφανω[μέναι.
μιαρὰ δὲ λύθρου τις ἐκεῖ πνοή.
ὁ δὲ φρικαλέον δέμας ἑλκύ[σας   30

.   .   .   .   .

own will. Afraid was he—fear bound his affrighted
knees. Bodies there were all over the path: and
many dogs had come around the corpses to feast
upon them. Yet—for his heart was dedicated to
labours—he put terror aside, and floated through all
the region, . . . So swiftly he came to that toilsome
land, the Shores of Ugliness. There, sitting on a
rock, when he had bound a reed with corpse's hair,
he took bait and feeding the hook sent it down
to the deepest depths. Yet when he drew forth
the swimming hair, since he could then catch
nothing at all, . . . For stretched around there
lay a vast plain, full of corpses of dreadful doom,
beheaded or crucified. Above the ground stood
pitiable bodies, their throats but lately cut. Others,
again, impaled, hung like the trophies of a cruel
destiny. The Furies, crowned with wreaths, were
laughing at the miserable manner of the corpses'
death. There was an abominable stench of gore.
He, dragging his shuddering frame along, . . .

.   .   .   .   .   .

---

3 'μφοβον Beazley.   8 επλοεριζε Π: ἐπόδιζε Weil.
9 Possibly a conflation of two lines, one beginning ὡς αὐτὸν
ἔχων . . ., the other ending . . . ὀρρωδεῖ πόρον.   17 ὡς
(δ') Weil.   18 Cancelled in Π.

ANONYMOUS

95 [11–111 A.D.] METAMORPHOSES

Ed. pr. Bilabel, *Philologus*, lxxx. 1925, p. 331. See
Körte, *Archiv*, viii. 256 ; Powell, *New Chapters*, iii. 201.

A description of trees and plants with references to the
legends—evidently for the most part stories of metamorphosis
—with which they were associated. Thus (a) 1-3 the πίτυς
introduced an allusion to Attis (for his connexion with the
tree, see ed. pr. 335-336) ; and v. 4 another tree brings in
the story of Tereus ; μ]ετὰ Τηρέω[ς *appears in a small*
fragment of a line below) ; and in a fragment too slight

διὰ τοῦτο πίτυς καὶ ἀ[ρεστὸς ἦν
φιλογαλ[λ]οβραχειονοτυμπ[άνωι
Κορύβαντι κολυθροφιλάρπαγ[ι.
αἴγειρος ἔπειτά τις ἦν ἐκεῖ,
δισσοῖ[σι] κλάδοις δεδιχασμέν[η·   5
ἑνὸς ἐκ στελέχους δύο δ᾽ ἦν φυ[τά.
ἐπὶ τ[ήν]δε βλέπουσ᾽ ἀπεθαύμ[ασεν,
ἐπὶ δ[εξι]ὰ πλευρὰ χελιδόνα
μελ[ανο]πτεροφαιολοσώματ[ον

.   .   .   .

ἐπ᾽ ἀρισ[τερὰ δ᾽ ἔβ]λεπ᾽ ἀηδόνα   10
γοεροστ[ονοθρ]ηνολαλήμονα.
ἰκτὶν δὲ νεοσσίον ἁρπάσας
γαμψωνυχοπαντοφιλάρπαγος
διφυοῦ[ς στ]ελέχους μέσος ἵσταται·
στόμασιν δὲ κατήσθιε κα[ὶ γνάθοι]ς.   15
ἐσιδοῦσα δ᾽ ἔκραξεν ἀηδο[νίς·
τὸν Ἴτύν, τὸν Ἴτὺν κατακλ[

.   .   .   .   .   .

ANONYMOUS

ANONYMOUS

METAMORPHOSES [11–111 A.D.]

for inclusion here the story of Myrrha's passion for her father was told in connexion with the tree which was named after her (στε)λέχους μύρρης πικρᾶς precedes το]ὺς ἀσεβεῖς γάμους). The trees are introduced one after another with a more or less fixed formula, cf. ed. pr. frag. B. 3]ειτα πίτυν βλέπω, ibid. C. 2] ἄλλο φυτὸν βλέπω, ibid. C. 11]τε βλέπω τι φυτὸν καλόν, v. 4 αἴγειρος ἔπειτά τις ἦν ἐκεῖ. The metre consists of anapaestic dimeters, of which the second closes in an iambic. Remarkable are the long compound adjectives: other fragments too small for inclusion here present the surprising words—σηματοποίκιλος, τρυγοσώματος, φιλομυρτο-φαγήκομος.

. . . And therefore the pine found favour with the Corybant, the lover of the tympanum that clashes on the arm of Cybele's priest, the lover of theft of figs. Next, there was a poplar, split into twofold branches; from one stem there came two shoots. She looked at it, and was amazed, on the right side by a swallow, black feathers on all its body of dark hue . . .

. . . on the left she saw a nightingale, the moaner and mourner; a kite had snatched its young —kite of hooked talons, lover of all thieving—and stood in the middle of the twofold stem; its beak and jaws devoured the brood; and the nightingale saw it, and shrieked with a cry for her Itys, her Itys.

. . . .

---

10 Beazley.   11 Beazley: γοεροστ[εναχ]ηνολαλ. ed. pr.: but -ηνο is then unintelligible.   12 νεοσσίον Powell for (τὸ) νοσσίον (ed. pr.).   17 Prob. κατακλ[άεται.

LITERARY PAPYRI

ANONYMOUS

96   [3 A.D.]   RECORD OF A CURE BY SARAPIS

Ed. pr. Abt, *Archiv für Religionswissenschaft*, xviii. 1915,
p. 257 with Plate. See Körte, *Archiv*, vii. 140; *Wilamo-
witz, *Gr. Versk.* p. 150 (revised text).[a]

(1) *There is no doubt that our fragment is incomplete at
both ends. Abt thought that v. 1 was the first line of the
poem: but* τῶι Λιβυκῶι φράσας *v. 2,* τοῦ πένητος *v. 5, the
obscure line v. 4, and vv. 8-9 all presuppose information
which must have been given in lines preceding v. 1. (Nor is
there any reason to suppose that our fragment was the first
column of the roll, see Wilam. p. 150 in reply to Abt, p. 257.)*
(2) *There is no doubt that the poem is not to be dated much,
if at all, earlier than the papyrus itself. Ed. pr. thought it
might still be a late Hellenistic piece: but it is certain (apart
from linguistic evidence[b]) that this poem did not survive in
circulation for several centuries. For the metre (iamb. trim.
catal. and phalaec.), see Wilam. ibid. pp. 137 sqq.*
(3) *The action (according to Wilamowitz):—Sarapis
gives two oracles, one to a Libyan (v. 2), one to a pauper (v. 5).
The god undertakes to transfer to the pauper the destiny
which Fate had intended for the Libyan, and vice versa: the
Libyan has been given a deceptive oracle, and the pauper's
malady will be transferred to him. Perhaps the transfer will
be facilitated by the fact that both patients were born under
the same constellation (v. 9). Thrason (the pauper: Abt
thinks he is the Libyan) is now commanded to fast, and in the
morning to intoxicate himself with wine, then go to sleep:*

[a] One word about the text: ed. pr. is not completely
accurate in the details of transcription, as may be seen from
the facsimile and by comparison of Wilam.'s text. Neither,
unhappily, is the latter completely accurate. I have ven-

424

ANONYMOUS

RECORD OF A CURE BY SARAPIS [3 A.D.]

*when he wakes up he will be cured (v. 19). Perhaps similar
advice had been given to the Libyan—only he, when he wakes
up, will find that the pauper's malady has been transferred to
him. Wilamowitz takes οὗτος in vv. 24, 25, 27 to refer to
Thrason, νῆστις v. 22 to the Libyan.*

*With this view I agree, except in the assignment of parts.
It seems (as Abt thought) more probable that vv. 10 sqq. are
a report of the deceptive instructions which Sarapis gave to
the Libyan. If this is so, the supreme difficulty in Wilam.'s
view—the necessity of making οὗτος in vv. 24, 25, 27 all
refer to the same person—can be avoided.[c] The pauper has
been told to fast and abstain, the Libyan to indulge himself.
Their separate acts of conduct are then described in alternate
lines. The abstinence of the pauper is to coincide in time
exactly with the indulgence of the Libyan (v. 23). ὁ μὲν 21,
ἐκεῖνος 23, οὗτος 25 and 27 are the Libyan (Thrason) ; ὁ δὲ
22, οὗτος 24, and the subject of 26, are the pauper. Vv. 6-7
I take to be the conclusion (τέρμα) of an oracle previously*

tured to make the very few trivial corrections which appeared
necessary. στραφεὶς for τραφεὶς in v. 24 is not so trivial. I
have had nothing but the facsimile to guide me, and shall
therefore be the object of universal objurgation. But Wilam.
says nothing about addition of new fragments to the text :
and if he had none, his transcription of vv. 4, 18, 25 is
undeniably in need of minute correction.

[b] The language aims at poetical style, which it maintains
in a simple way with a few lapses. The poet soared aloft to
the invention of ἐξαδόχος v. 17 (here only, *s.v.l.* : Abt read
ἐξ ἀδόλου, but the facsimile supports Wilam.).

[c] The contrast is clear not only from the use of οὗτος, but
also from the obvious opposition μένει κραταίως—μεθύει, ὑπο-
μένει—πίπτει.

425

(i.e. *before our fragment begins*) *given to the pauper.* In *that oracle, the pauper had been advised to fast and abstain:* *vv. 6-7 give the end of it, and the ground* (*hence* γάρ, *v. 6*) *for* *it* (*because the pauper will thus be cured by transference of his malady to the Libyan*).

I *think we must suppose that the Libyan has somehow offended Sarapis;* cf. *the records of cases at Epidaurus, esp.* A *III, IV,* B *XXXVI* (*Herzog, "Wunderheil. von Epidauros,"* Philol. Suppl. 22, 3). *Although there is no instance*

. . . .]των ὁ Σάραπίς ἐστι σωτὴρ
]ι τῶι Λιβυκῶι φράσας ἀπέστ[η
] . . . δεχομεν . . προρε . [
καὶ τοῦ τ[ὸ] δακτυλείδιον κρατοῦν[τος.
τοῦ χρησμοῦ δὲ τὸ τέρμα τοῦ πένητ[ος·   5
ἀπὸ τῆς γὰρ αὔριον Λίβυς τις ἀνὴρ
πάσχει νόσον ξένην, δι' ἧς σε σώζω.
οὗτος δ' ἦν ὁ Λίβυς ὃν ὁ θεὸς εἶπεν,
κοινὴν συναστρίαν ἔχων ἐκείνω(ι).
τῆι νυκτὶ παραφανεὶς ὁ θεὸς ἔλεξε·   10
τῆς μοίρης ἀπέχεις, Θράσων, τὸ τέρμ[α,
οὐ]χ ὡς ἤθελε μοῖρα, παρὰ δὲ μοῖρα[ν,
τὰς] μοίρας γὰρ ἐγὼ μεταμφιάζω.
. . . . .] . . ρε δ' αὔριον, μετὰ δὲ τετάρτην
μέθυε] καὶ πρόπειε, πολὺ παραμείν[ας   15
μηδὲν] γευσάμενος, μόνον δ' ἄκρατο[ν
χύτρ]ας ἐξαδόχου, μετὰ δὲ τὸ πείνε[ιν
. . . . συ]ντυχίας βαλὼν κάθευ(δ)ε.
κοιμώ]μενον δ' ἐγώ σ' ἀποθεραπεύσω.

3 δεχομεν . . . . προρε . [Abt: δεχομενπ . προσε . [Wilam.:
εχο very doubtful.   4 κρατοῦντος Wilam. : κρατοῦν[τος
426

ANONYMOUS

*of transference of a disease from one man to another, there
are records of cases in which the god visits a healthy offender
with sickness (Herzog, p. 124 : the god usually cured the
offender in the end : so here, the Libyan may have been
healed in the end : the miracle-cures of Sarapis were founded
on those of Asclepius, Herzog, p. 47. Beazley refers me
to an interesting and apposite passage in Artemidorus,*
Oneirocriticon v. 94).

. . . Sarapis is the saviour. . . . told the Libyan
and departed. . . . and of him who possessed the
ring.

The conclusion of the pauper's oracle was this :
" —since, from to-morrow, a certain Libyan shall
suffer a strange malady, through which I shall save
you." Now this was the Libyan of whom the god had
spoken, who had the same constellation as the pauper.
The god appeared in the night beside him, and
spoke : " Thrason, you have in full the upshot of
your Fate ; not as Fate desired, but against the
will of Fate : for I change the Fates about.[a] . . . to-
morrow, and after the fourth hour [b] souse and drink
deep—having waited long without a taste of any-
thing—nothing but unmixed wine from a full-sized [c]
pitcher ; and after drinking . . . lie down and sleep.
While you lie at rest, I will cure you." . . .

---

[a] Lit. " I change the clothes of Destiny."   [b] Quite
early in the morning.   [c] Lit. " of six measures," a
new word.

Abt and II.   9 εκειν[ω Abt, Wilam.: half the ω is
clearly visible.   12 μοῖραν Wilam.: μοῖρα[ν Abt and II.
14 ανεγ]ειρε Fahz, Abt: imposs. acc. to Wilam.   18 ἐκ
τῆ]ς συντυχ. Wilam.: . . . . συ]ντυχ. Abt and II.   κάθευδε
Wilam., καθευε II.

. . . . . .] δὲ τοῦτον †ου πειραν . λως σχη[† 20
ὁ μὲν οὗ]ν ἀνίσταται λαβὼν τὸ πεί'ειν,
ὁ δὲ νῆστις ἀν[α]μένει θεῶ(ι) κελευσθείς,
ὥραν λαβ[ώ]ν, ἐκεῖνος ἦν ἐτάχθη·
οὗτος δὲ μὴ στραφεὶς μένει κραταίως,
πεί]νει δ' οὗτος ἄκρατα καὶ μεθύει   25
. . . . .]ουσαν δ' ὑπομένει . . . [
πίπ]τει δ' οὗτος ἐκεῖ καρηβ[αρήσας

.   .   .   .   .   .

20 ουπειρεν . λωσσεχη[Wilam.: οὖ πεῖραν [ὅ]λως σχ[ῇις
Abt.   Perhaps *e.g.* δρᾶσον] δὲ τοῦτ', ἐμοῦ πεῖραν [ὅ]πως σχῇ[ις.

ANONYMOUS

97   [2–3 A.D.]   SAILOR'S SONG

Ed. pr. *Grenfell-Hunt, *P. Oxy.* iii. 1903, no. 425, p. 72.
See Crusius, *Herodae Mimiambi*, p. 134; Powell, *Col-
lectanea Alexandrina*, p. 195; Wilamowitz, *G.G.A.* 1904,
670; Crusius, *Philol.* 66, 1907, 315; Maas, *Philol.* 68,
1909, 445; Crönert, *Rh. Mus.* 64, 1909, 445; Powell, *C. Qu.*
v. 177; Grenfell-Hunt, *P. Oxy.* xi. p. 236; Manteuffel, *de
opusculis graecis*, p. 180; Blass, *Archiv*, iii. 276; Powell-
Barber, *New Chapters*, i. 58; Eitrem, *Symb. Oslo.* 17, 1937,
105.

There is a clear contrast between (a) ocean-going sailors,

Ναῦται βαθυκυμα[τ]οδρόμοι
ἁλίων Τρίτωνες ὑδάτων
καὶ Νειλῶται γλυκυδρόμοι
τὰ γελῶντα πλέοντες ὑδάτη,

428

ANONYMOUS

So then the one took the drink and arose : the other waited fasting, as the god commanded, at the hour to which the Libyan had been appointed. The pauper stood his ground firmly without turning : the other drank neat wine and got drunk. . . . the one stood firm . . . the other collapsed on the spot with a headache . . .

．　　　．　　　．　　　．　　　．　　　．

21 ὁ Θράσω]ν Wilam.: text D. L. P.　　　24 μὴ τραφεὶς Wilam.: the facsimile shews μὴ στραφείς: μή for οὐ common at this era.　　　25 πεινει] Wilam.: πείν]ει Abt: πει]νει Π. 27 πίπ]τει Wilam.: Π must then have had πειπ]τει.

ANONYMOUS

SAILOR'S SONG　　　　　　[2–3 A.D.]

and (b) *Nile-sailors.　The poem is an invitation to these two groups of men to compete with each other in song or play, the subject of the competition being " the comparison (or rather contrast)" of ocean and Nile.　Crusius* (Her. Mimi. p. 134) *recalls the* κωμασταὶ Νείλου *of* P. Oxy. iii. 1903, no. 519 (b) 10, p. 255.

Metrically the lines are μύουροι (μείουροι), *here enoplia with iambus instead of spondee or trochee at the end : all the lines close with paroxytone words.*

SAILORS who skim deep waters, Tritons of the briny waves, and Nilots who sail in happy course upon

4 ὑδάτῃ: v. Maas, loc. cit.

LITERARY PAPYRI

$$\tau \dot{\eta} \nu \ \sigma \acute{\upsilon} \gamma \kappa \rho \iota \sigma \iota \nu \ \epsilon \breve{\iota} \pi \alpha \tau \epsilon, \ \phi \acute{\iota} \lambda o\iota,$$ 5
$$\pi \epsilon \lambda \acute{\alpha} \gamma o\upsilon\varsigma \ N \epsilon \acute{\iota} \lambda o\upsilon \ \tau \epsilon \ \gamma o\nu \acute{\iota} \mu o\upsilon.$$

6 καὶ νείλου γονίμου Π: corr. Powell (and Eitrem).

ANONYMOUS

98   [3 A.D.]   SAILOR'S SONG

Ed. pr. *Grenfell-Hunt, *P. Oxy.* xi. 1915, no. 1383, p. 236.
See Powell, *Collectanea Alexandrina*, p. 195 ; Schmidt,
G.G.A. 1918, 123 ; Draheim, *Phil. Woch.* 1918, 310 ;
Deubner, *Sitzb. Heidelb. Akad.* 1919, Abh. 17, p. 11 ;
Preisendanz, *Phil. Woch.* 1920, 1130 ; Crönert, *Philol.* 84,
159 ; Manteuffel, *de opusculis graecis*, p. 181 ; Powell-
Barber, *New Chapters*, i. 59 ; Körte, *Archiv*, vii. 141 ;
Eitrem, *Symb. Oslo.* 17, 1937, 104; Wilamowitz, *Hermes*,
60, 1925, 314 and *Gr. Versk.* p. 374.

'Ροδίοις ἐκέλευον ἀνέμοις
καὶ μέρεσι τοῖς πελαγίοις
ὅτε πλέειν ἤθελον ἐγώ,
ὅτε μένειν ἤθελον ἐκεῖ,
ἔλεγον μέρε(σιν) πελαγίο(ις)·   5
μὴ τύπηι τὰ πελάγη·
ἀλ' ὑποτάξατε ναυσιβά[τ]αις.
ὅλος ἄρ' ἄνεμος ἐπείγεται.
ἀπόκλειε τὰ πνεύματα καί, Ν[ύ]ξ,
δὸς τὰ [. .]ατ' εὔβατα.   10

2 σοῖς Π.   **6** τύπη(τε), πελάγη· Preisendanz.   **8**
γὰρ (for ἄρ') Deubner.   επιγεται Π: ἐπιγελᾶι Schmidt.

430

the smiling waters, tell us, friends, the comparison
of the ocean with the fruitful Nile.

Crönert defends II, scanning a choriamb at the end
(-$\bar{\upsilon}\upsilon$ $\gamma ον\acute{\iota}μου$); Maas defends the scansion $N ε\acute{\iota}λου$ $\gamma ον\acute{\iota}μου$.

ANONYMOUS

SAILOR'S SONG [3 A.D.]

*This is not (as it has sometimes been alleged) a magic
incantation : it is (as the imperfect tenses suggest) the song
of a Rhodian sailor, sung by him when returned to Rhodes.
" When I wanted to sail (to Rhodes), and to stay there (in
Rhodes), I used to ask the winds to control the seas (so that I
might enjoy fair weather to Rhodes)."*
'Ρο$δ\acute{\iota}οις$ $\mathring{α}ν\acute{ε}$[$μοις$ *is written in the right-hand margin.*

I USED to command the Rhodian winds and the
quarters of Ocean, when I wanted to sail, when I
wanted to stay there, I used to say to the quarters of
Ocean, " Let not the seas be smitten ! Subdue the
Ocean to the seafarers ! Lo, in full strength the wind
is rising ! Shut up your storm-winds, Night, and
make the waters smooth to cross ! "

---

9 $ν\acute{υ}ξ$, $κα\grave{\iota}$ Wilamowitz.   10 [$\ddot{υ}δ$]$ατ$' ed. pr. : [$\acute{α}β$]$ατ$' Prei-
sendanz.   [$κ\acute{υ}μ$]$ατ$' is too long for the space. $δ\acute{ο}ς$ prob. = $θ\grave{ε}ς$
(*cf.* Pseudo-Euripides, *I.A.* 629, Herodas vi. 1).

ANONYMOUS

99 [3 A.D.] HYMN TO FORTUNE

Ed. pr. *Schubart-Wilamowitz, *Berliner Klassikertexte*,
v. 2, 1907, p. 142. See Schmidt, *Phil. Woch.* 1908, 457 ;
Körte, *Archiv*, v. 557 ; Powell, *Collectanea Alexandrina*,
196 ; Diehl, *Anth. Lyr. Gr.* ii. p. 313.

πολύχροε ποικιλόμορφε πτανό[πους
θνατοῖς συνομέστιε παγκρατὲς Τύχα·
πῶς χρὴ τεὰν ἰσχύν τε δεῖξαι καὶ τ[
τὰ μὲν ὑψιφαῆ καὶ σεμνὰ εἰς τεὸν ὄμ[μα
ὑπήρικας ποτὶ γᾶν, νέφος ἀμφιθηκαμέν[α σκότιον, 5
τὰ δὲ φαῦλα καὶ ταπεινὰ πολλάκις πτερο[ῖ]σ[ι
εἰς ὕψος ἐξάειρας, ὦ δαῖμον μεγάλα.
πότερόν σε κλήζωμεν Κλωθὼ κελαιν[άν,
ἢ τὰν ταχύποτμον Ἀνάγκαν,
ἢ τὰν ταχὺν ἄγγελον Ἶριν ἀθανάτων;   10
πάντων γὰρ ἀρχὰν καὶ τέλος †ἄγιον† ἔχεις.

1 πολυχιροε Π, corr. Schmidt (πολύχειρε ed. pr.) : πτανόπους
D. L. P. : the reference is to the swiftness of Fortune's muta-
tions. 3 τεαν τ[Π : I omit τεάν, following Wilam. τ[
may be read as π[: the reading then was probably π[ύσιν,
i.e. φύσιν. 10 ταχνάγγελον Schmidt. 11 ἄγιον

ANONYMOUS

100 [4 A.D.] A SCHOOLBOY'S RECITATION

Ed. pr. Vitelli, *Studi Italiani di Filologia Classica*, xii.
1912, p. 320 ; and xiv. 1914, p. 126. See Wilamowitz,
Griech. Versk. 611 ; Crönert, *Gnomon*, 1926, 663 ; *Powell,
New Chapters, iii. 208 ; Blass, *Archiv*, iii. 487.

ANONYMOUS

HYMN TO FORTUNE [3 A.D.]

Hymn to Fortune, of uncertain but late era. Ed. pr. aptly compares Diehl, Anth. Lyr. Gr. ii. p. 158, fr. mel. chor. adesp. 4 (τύχα, μερόπων ἀρχὰ καὶ τέρμα resembles v. 11 : σὰν πτέρυγα χρυσέαν may have suggested πτανο[v. 1).

GODDESS of many hues and many guises and wingèd feet, partner of man's hearth and home, almighty Fortune ! How may one demonstrate your power and . . . ? That which is high and mighty against your countenance you dash *a* to the ground with a cloud of darkness set around it ; the mean and lowly you often exalt on your wings aloft, O mighty spirit. Shall we call you gloomy Clotho, or Necessity of sudden doom, or Iris, swift messenger of the immortal gods ? Of all things the beginning and the end are yours.

a ὑπήρικας is intended to be active transitive aorist of ὑπερείκω (ed. pr.).

---

almost certainly the reading of Π : ed. pr. suggests emendation to ἄκρον : πάντων Maas, Crusius.

ANONYMOUS

A SCHOOLBOY'S RECITATION [4 A.D.]

" Something of the nature of an occasional or prize-poem by a schoolboy, perhaps to be recited on a ' Speech Day ' " (Powell).

ἑ[ται]ρικῆς [θ᾽ ἑορ]τῆς
θαλύσιον κομίζω.
ἐρῶ μὲν οὖν ἐς ἥβης
τάχιστα μέτρον ἐλθεῖν,
διδασκάλου τ᾽ ἀκούων   5
πολὺν χρόνον βιῶναι.
φυὴ δὲ κ[οσμί]α τις
σοφό[ν τε νοῦ φρόνημα
γένοιτό μοι, [μάθησιν
κ]υ(κ)λουμένη[ν περῶντι·   10
μετάρσι[ος θέλοιμ᾽ ἂν
Διὸς δόμο[ις πελάσσαι

.   .   .   .   .   .

ANONYMOUS

. . . and I bring the harvest-offerings of our common festival. I long to come with all good speed to the fullness of young manhood, and to live many years the pupil of my teacher. A nature well-behaved and wise imaginings be mine, as I pass through the circle of my studies ! I yearn to rise aloft and knock upon the gates of Heaven ! . . .[a]

.   .   .   .   .   .

[a] *Cf.* Eur. fr. 911 (Wilam.).   He means " I hope to go to the University later on."   V. 10 refers to the ἐγκύκλιος παιδεία, the routine of education.

---

10 περῶντι D. L. P. : περῆσαι Crönert, with heavy punctuation after φρόνημα v. 8.

ELEGIAC AND IAMBIC POEMS

ΜΙΜΝΕΡΜΟΣ

101   [1 A.D.]   ΣΜΥΡΝΗΙΣ

Ed. pr. Vogliano, *Papiri della reale Università di Milano*,
vol. 1°, 1935, p. 13.   See *Wyss, *Antimachi Colophonii
Reliquiae*, p. 83 ; Bowra, *Early Greek Elegists*, 1938, p. 29 ;
Körte, *Archiv*, xiii. 1938, 81.

This fragment comes from a commentary on Antimachus,

ὡς οἱ παρ᾽ βασιλῆος, ἐπε[ί ῥ᾽] ἐ[ν]εδέξατο μῦθο[ν,
ἤ[ιξα]ν, κοίληι[σ᾽ ἀ]σπίσι φραξάμενοι.

•   •   •   •   •   •

EPICHARMEA

      [(*a*) 2 B.C.]
102   [(*b*) 3 A.D.]   Probably by AXIOPISTUS
      [(*c*) 3 B.C.]

Ed. pr. (*a*) *Schubart-Wilamowitz, *Berliner Klassikertexte*,
v. 2, 1907, p. 124.   (*b*) *Wilamowitz, *Sitzungsberichte der
königlich preussischen Akademie der Wissenschaften*, 1918,
p. 742 (ostrakon).   (*c*) *Grenfell-Hunt, *Hibeh Papyri*, i.
1906, no. 1, p. 13, Plate I.   See Crönert, *Hermes*, 47, 1912,
408 ; Powell, *Collectanea Alexandrina*, p. 219 and *New
Chapters*, i. 18 ; Pickard-Cambridge, *Dithyramb, Tragedy
and Comedy*, p. 369 ; Milne, *Cat. Lit. Pap. B.M.* no. 56.

MIMNERMUS

SMYRNEIS

in which we are told that Mimnermus wrote a Smyrneis *; cf.*
Paus. ix. 29. 4.   Mimnermus wrote elegiacs about the war
between Smyrna and the Lydians under Gyges.   This war
occurred a generation before the time of Mimnermus ; who is
therefore the first Greek known to have written an historical
poem about events in the recent past.

So from the king, when he made known his order,
they darted, fenced in their hollow shields.

· · · · · ·

EPICHARMEA

Probably by AXIOPISTUS

[*Hibeh Papyri*, i. no. 2 omitted, as too fragmentary for
inclusion : *cf.* however Crönert, *loc. cit.*]

(c) *Preface to a book of* Sententiae, *perhaps the work of*
one Axiopistus (Athen. xiv. 648 d Φιλόχορος . . . 'Αξιόπιστον
. . . τὰς γνώμας πεποιηκέναι φησίν), *who flourished about*
300 B.C.: this papyrus is dated between 280 and 240 B.C.

*Crönert shews that the extant Γνῶμαι ascribed to Epicharmus
can easily be distributed under the headings of the opening*

(a)   τοὺς τρόπους χείρω γυναῖ]κά φαμ' ἐγὼ τῶν
        θηρ[ίων
    εἶμεν· ὅστις γ]ὰρ λέοντι σῖτον ἢ ποτὸν [φέρει
    ἢ κυσὶν Μολοσσικοῖσ[ιν ἢ
    θῆρε]ς αἰκάλλοντι το[ῖ]σι[ν εὖ ποεῦσιν εὐ-
        μενεῖς.
    ἁ [γ]υνὰ δὲ τὸν τρέφοντα [πρῶτον εἴθισται
        δακεῖν.   5

(b)   †ταλεας† γάρ ἐσθ' ὁ φρόνιμος. ὡς δὲ τοῦθ'
        οὕτως ἔχει,
    χῶρος οἰκία τυραννὶς πλοῦτος ἰσχὺς καλλονὰ
    ἄφρονος ἀνθρώπου τυχόντα καταγέλαστα
        γίνεται.
    ἀδοναὶ δ' εἰσὶν βροτοῖσιν ἀνόσιοι λαιστήριοι·
    καταπεπόντισται γὰρ εὐθὺς ἀδοναῖς ἀνὴρ
        ἁλούς.   5

(c)   τεῖδ' ἔνεστι πολλὰ καὶ παν[τ]οῖα, τοῖς
        χρήσαιό κα
    ποτὶ φίλον, ποτ' ἐχθρόν, ἐν δίκαι λέγων, ἐν
        ἁλίαι,
    ποτὶ πονηρόν, ποτὶ καλόν τε κἀγαθόν, ποτὶ
        ξένον,
    ποτὶ δύσηριν, ποτὶ πάροινον, ποτὶ βάναυσον,
        αἴτε τις
    ἀλλ' ἔχει κακόν τι, καὶ τούτοισι κέντρα
        τεῖδ' ἔνο.   5
    ἐν δὲ καὶ γνῶμαι σοφαὶ τεῖδ', αἷσιν αἰ
        πίθοιτό τις,

lines of this fragment (ποτὶ φίλον, ποτ᾽ ἐχθρόν, κτλ.), *and maintains that they are parts of the book to which our fragment is the preface. Fr. 254 (Kaibel) may belong to the end of this preface.*

(*a*) In character, I tell you, women are worse than animals. Give food or water to a lion, or Molossian dog, or . . ., and the beasts wag their tails and make friends with their benefactors. But the first hand the woman bites is the one that feeds her.

(*b*) The wise man is . . . Here is a proof : lands and houses and kingdoms and wealth and strength and beauty, if they fall to a fool, become absurd. Pleasures are the godless pirates of mankind : let pleasure catch you, and you sink at once.

(*c*) Within this book are many and manifold advices for you to use towards a friend or foe, while speaking in the courts, or the assembly, towards the rogue or the gentleman, towards the stranger, towards the quarrelsome, the drunkard, and the vulgar, or any other plagues that you may find—for them too there's a sting within my book.

Within it too are maxims wise ; obey them, and

(*b*) 1 ταλεας hopelessly corrupt. (*c*) 5 ἔνο: *cf. Anecd. Oxon.* i. 160. 126 ἐξὸ ῥῆμα παρὰ Δωριεῦσιν ἀντὶ τοῦ ἔξεστιν ; 176. 12 (ἐν) παρὰ τὴν Αἰολίδα καὶ Δωρίδα διάλεκτον ἐνὸ γίγνεται (ἔνο Thumb), ὁπόταν καὶ ἀντὶ ῥήματος.

LITERARY PAPYRI

δεξιώτερός τέ κ' εἴη βελτίων τ' ἐς πά[ν]τ'
ἀνήρ.
κο]ὔτι πολλὰ δεῖ λέγειν, ἀλλ' ἓν μόνον
[τ]ούτων ἔπος,
ποττὸ πρᾶγμα περιφέροντα τῶνδ' ἀεὶ τὸ
συμφέρον.
αἰτίαν γὰρ ἦχον ὡς ἄλλως μὲν εἴην δε-
ξιός,   10
μακρολόγος δ' οὔ κα δυναίμαν ἐν β[ρ]αχεῖ
γνώμα[ς λέγ]ειν.
ταῦτα δὴ 'γὼν εἰσακούσας συντίθημι τὰν
τέχναν
τάνδ', ὅπως εἴπηι τις, 'Επίχαρμος σοφός τις
ἐγένετο,
πόλλ' ὃς εἶ]π' ἀστεῖα καὶ παντοῖα καθ' ἓν
ἔπος [λέγων,
πεῖραν] αὐταυτοῦ διδοὺς ὡς καὶ β[ραχέα
καλῶς λέγοι.   15
εὖ δὲ τάδ]ε μαθὼν ἅπας ἀνὴρ φαν[ήσεται
σοφός,
οὐδὲ ληρ]ήσει ποτ' οὐδέν, ἔπος ἄπ[αν μεμνα-
μένος.
εἰ δὲ τὸν λαβ]όντα λυπήσει τι τῶνδ[ε τῶν
λόγων,
οὔτι μὰν ἄσκεπτ]α δρῶντα τοῖσδ[έ θ' ἧσσον
ὁμότροπα,
ἀγαθὸν ἴστω σύμφ]ορόν τε πολυμαθῆ [νόον
τρέφειν   20

(Traces of two lines)

ἄλλος ἄ]λλωι γὰρ γέγαθε, κοὔτι ταὐ[τὰ
κρίνομες.

442

you will be a cleverer and a better man for all events.
You need no lengthy speech, only a single one of
these proverbs ; bring round to your subject which-
ever of them is apt.   Men used to censure me because,
though shrewd enough in other ways, I was a lengthy
speaker—could not express my thoughts with brevity.
To this charge I lent an ear, and I composed this book
of rules,[a] to make the world exclaim " Epicharmus
was a philosopher, who uttered many witty sayings of
many kinds in single verses : himself he lets us test
his skill in brevity of speech as well ! "

He who learns these maxims well shall appear a
wise man to the world, and never talk but good sense,
if he remembers every word.   If one who takes this
book shall be offended by some word within it—not,
of course, because his own conduct is ill-considered
and in conflict with my counsel—let me tell him, a
broader mind is a blessing and a boon. . . .

(*Traces of two lines*)

Different people, different pleasures : we do not all

[a] " Work of art " (ed. pr.).

(*c*) 15-23 Crönert (16 εὖ δὲ τάδε, 17 οὐδὲ, 19 θ´, 22 ἑκάστωι
φαίνεται, 23 συμφέρειν and ἐλευθέρως D. L. P.).

. . . . δ]ὲ πάντα δεῖ τάδ' ὡς ἑ[κάστωι
  φαίνεται
συμφέρειν, ἔ]πειτα δ' ἐν καιρῶι λέ[γειν
  ἐλευθέρως.

. . . .

ANONYMOUS

103   [3 B.C.] EPIGRAM FOR A MERRY COMPANY

Ed. pr. *Schubart-Wilamowitz, *Berliner Klassikertexte*,
v. 2, 1907, p. 62, Plate VIII. See Powell, *Collect. Alex.*
p. 192 ; Diehl, *Anth. Lyr. Gr.* ii. 237 ; Powell-Barber, *New*

χαίρετε συμπόται ἄνδρες ὁμ[ήλικες, ἐ]ξ ἀγαθοῦ γὰρ
  ἀρξάμενος τελέω τὸν λόγον [ε]ἰς ἀγ[αθό]ν.
χρὴ δ' ὅταν εἰς τοιοῦτο συνέλθωμεν φίλοι ἄνδρες
  πρᾶγμα, γελᾶν παίζειν χρησαμένους ἀρετῆι
ἥδεσθαί τε συνόντας ἐς ἀλλήλους τε φ[λ]υαρεῖν   5
  καὶ σκώπτειν τοιαῦθ' οἷα γέλωτα φέρει.
ἡ δὲ σπουδὴ ἐπέσθω ἀκούωμέν [τε λ]εγόντων
  ἐν μέρει· ἥδ' ἀρετὴ συμποσίου πέλεται.
τοῦ δὲ ποταρχοῦντος πειθώμεθα· ταῦτα γάρ ἐστιν
  ἔργ' ἀνδρῶν ἀγαθῶν εὐλογίαν τε φέρει.   10

ΠΟΣΕΙΔΙΠΠΟΣ

104   [160 B.C.]   TWO EPIGRAMS

Ed. pr. Weil, *Un papyrus inédit : nouveaux fragments
d'Euripide et d'autres poètes grecs : Monuments Grecs publiés*
444

judge alike. Each man should . . . these advices, as he deems expedient; then speak them freely as the time requires.

. . . . . .

ANONYMOUS

EPIGRAM FOR A MERRY COMPANY [3 B.C.]

Chapters, i. 58; Jurenka, *Wien. Stud.* 29, 1908, 326; Taccone, *Riv. di Fil.* 38, 1910, 18.

An early Hellenistic epigram, preface to the opening of a sympotic gathering, and to the recitation of further pieces suitable to the occasion. Cf. Xenophanes fr. 1, Theognis 467.

HAIL to you, companion revellers! With good omen I begin, and with good omen I will end my speech. When friends are come together for such purpose, they must laugh and play, behaving bravely, and rejoice in their company, and make sport of each other and utter such jests as bring laughter with them. Earnest converse must follow, and we must listen to each speaker in his turn : therein is the virtue of a merry company. And let us give ear to the leader of our revels : such is the conduct of good men, and the source of honest reputation.

POSEIDIPPUS

TWO EPIGRAMS [160 B.C.]

par l'association pour l'encouragement des études grecques en France, no. 8, 1879, p. 28 with Plate. See *Hiller von

LITERARY PAPYRI

Gaertringen, *Histor. Griech. Epigr.* no. 92, p. 38, no. 95, p. 40 and literature quoted there; Schott, *Poseidippi Epigrammata*, no. 1, 2; Powell-Barber, *New Chapters*, i. 107; Reitzenstein, *Epigramm und Skolion*, pp. 163-164; Blass, *Rh. Mus.* 35, 1880, 90.

(a) *Epigram composed to celebrate the erection (282-281 b.c.) of the lighthouse on the island Pharos (which was said to have been dedicated to Proteus, cf. v. 1), in the reign of Ptolemy I Soter. (See Suidas, s.v. Φάρος, Strabo xvii. 791,*

(a)   Ἑλλήνων σωτῆρα, Φάρου σκοπόν, ὦ ἄνα
       Πρωτεῦ,
          Σώστρατος ἔστησεν Δεξιφάνου[ς] Κνί-
          διος.
       οὐ γὰρ ἐν Αἰγύπτωι σκοπαὶ οὔρεά θ' οἷ' ἐπὶ
       νήσων,
       ἀλλὰ χαμαὶ χηλὴ ναύλοχος ἐκτέταται.
       τοῦ χάριν εὐθεῖάν τε καὶ ὄρθιον αἰθέρα
       τέμνων   5
          πύργος ὅ[δ'] ἀπλάτων φαίνετ' ἀπὸ στα-
          δίων
       ἤματι· παννύχιος δὲ θ[έ]ω[ν] σ[ὺ]ν κύματι
       ναύτης
       ὄψεται ἐκ κορυφῆς πῦρ μέγα καιόμενον,
       καί κεν ἐπ' αὐτὸ δράμοι Ταύρου κέρας, οὐδ'
          ἂν ἁμάρτοι
       σωτῆρος, Πρωτεῦ, Ζην[ὸ]ς [ὁ] τῆιδε
       πλέων.   10

(b)   μέσσον ἐγὼ Φαρίης ἀκτῆς στόματός τε
       Κανώπου
          ἐν περιφαινομένωι κύματι χῶρον ἔχω

*ed. pr. p. 28 for details.) This famous building stood on the
eastern extremity of the island, in front of the port of
Alexandria. The architect was Sostratus of Cnidus. See
esp. Thiersch, Pharos, pp. 82-83.*

(b) *Epigram composed to celebrate the foundation of a
shrine to his wife Arsinoe by Ptolemy II Philadelphus. The
building was a chapel (ναίσκος) containing an image of
Arsinoe, who was worshipped there as Arsinoe-Aphrodite: it
stood on Cape Zephyrium, between Alexandria and Canopus.
(See Strabo xvii. 800, Athen. vii. 318, ed. pr. p. 29.) For
Callicrates v. Hiller von Gaertringen, p. 40.*

(a) Lord Proteus : the saviour of Hellenes, this
watchman of Pharos, was built by Sostratus, son of
Dexiphanes, a Cnidian. In Egypt there are no
mountain-peaks, as in the islands : but low lies the
breakwater where ships may harbour. Therefore
this tower, cleaving the sky straight and upright,
shines in the daytime countless leagues [a] away : and
all night long the sailor who runs with the waves shall
see a great light blazing from its summit. And he
may run even to the Bull's Horn,[b] and yet not miss
the God of Safety,[c] O Proteus, whosoever sails this
way.

(b) Midway between the beach of Pharos and the
mouth of Canopus I have my place amid surrounding

─────

[a] Lit. "from boundless furlongs": ἀπλάτων here=ἀπλέ-
των, see L. & S. s.v.   [b] One of the narrow and danger-
ous channels leading to the port of Alexandria; Pliny, N.H.
v. 31 (128) Alexandria tribus omnino aditur alveis mari,
Stegano, Poseideo, Tauro.   [c] The lighthouse was in-
scribed θεοῖς σωτῆρσιν.

(a) 3 σκοπαὶ οὔρεά θ' οἳ' ἐπὶ Blass ap. ed. pr. p. 59. ΣΚΟ-
ΠΑΙΟΥΡΗΣΟΙΕΠΕΙ Π.   (b) 2 κύματι Π: κ[λί]ματι H.-G.

τήνδε πολυρρήνου Λιβύης ἀνεμώδεα χηλὴν
τὴν ἀνατεινομένην εἰς ἰταλὸν ζέφυρον.
ἔνθα με Καλλικράτης ἱδρύσατο καὶ βασι-
λίσσης   5
ἱερὸν ᾿Αρσινόης Κύπριδος ὠνόμασεν.
ἀλλ’ ἐπὶ τὴν Ζεφυρῖτιν ἀκουσομένην ᾿Αφρο-
δίτην
῾Ελλήνων ἀγναὶ βαίνετε θυγατέρες,
οἵ θ’ ἁλὸς ἐργάται ἄνδρες· ὁ γὰρ ναύαρχος
ἔτευξεν
τοῦθ’ ἱερὸν παντὸς κύματος εὐλίμενον.   1ο

ANONYMOUS

105 [Late 3 b.c.]   TWO EPIGRAMS

Ed. pr. Guérard-Jouguet, *Un Livre d'Ecolier : publications
de la société royale égyptienne de papyrologie, Textes et
Documents*, ii., le Caire, 1938, (a) p. 20, Plate V, (b) p. 25,
Plate VI. See Körte, *Archiv*, xiii. 1938, 106-107; Schweitzer,
*Festgabe zur Winckelmannsfeier des arch. Sem. der Univ.
Leipz. am 10. Dezember 1938*.

(a) *Description of a fountain, written by an Alexandrian
epigrammatist in the 3rd century b.c. Among the sculptures
there were images of the king (v. 12 :* cf. Πτολεμ[αι- *v.* 2) *and
of the queen* (᾿Αρσινόην *v.* 13 : *Arsinoe Philadelphus or
Philopator*).

The details of the description are **very** *obscure. I append
a few notes to justify my renderings :—*

V. 5. " *Having set free* (ἐκποδίζω, *here only, presumably
the antithesis of* ἐμποδίζω) *the bright water-drop* " : *see ed.
pr. p.* 22 *for reference to epigrams which were written in
celebration of the revival of obsolete fountains. See further
my note, ad loc., below.*

448

waters, this windy breakwater of pastoral Libya, facing the western wind from Italy. Here Callicrates established me and called me the Temple of Queen Arsinoe-Aphrodite. Chaste daughters of Hellenes, hither come to her that shall be named Zephyritis-Aphrodite [a] : come, men that labour on the seas. Our Captain [b] has made this temple a safe harbour from all the waters.

[a] From Zephyrion, name of the promontory on which the temple stands. [b] Callicrates ; *cf.* Callim. *ap.* Athen. vii. 318.

(b) 3 τηοδε Π : corr. Reitzenstein.

ANONYMOUS

TWO EPIGRAMS   [Late 3 b.c.]

Vv. 6-9. The following is a brief and inadequate summary of the views of Professor D. S. Robertson. I am most grateful for his assistance, and fortunate to be able to publish so important a contribution to the understanding of this obscure passage.

(1) ζωνή is the low semicircular bounding-wall of the basin ; this wall carried one or more columns (it is possible, perhaps likely, that one of a set of identical columns is being described as a typical example). The semicircle may be conceived as projecting in front of a straight rear wall.

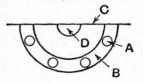

A = column
B = semicircular bounding-wall
C = rear wall
D = mouth through which water flows

LITERARY PAPYRI

(2) πέζαν ἰωνι τύπωι means "column-base in the Ionic style."

(3) Punctuate after τύπωι, and abolish ed. pr.'s comma after ἔντος. For the consequent postponement of δέ, see Denniston, Greek Particles, pp. 185 sq.

(4) ῥάβδος κοίλη is the characteristic cavetto moulding of the typical Attic-Ionic base.

(5) πτερναί are also parts of this base—presumably the two convex mouldings which frame the cavetto moulding.

(a) θοινα[   ]τε φλεγετ[

σιγηλου[   ]ηρια καὶ Πτολεμ[αι

ἀσπάσιοι βα[   ] δέχοισθε γέρας

ὃς καὶ λάινον [ἔργον ἐθ]ήκατο δαψιλὲς οἴκωι

κτίσμα, πά[ρος λ]ευκὴν ἐκποδίσας στα-

γόνα,   5

εἰς ἡμίσφαιρο[ν τ]εύξας θέσιν· ἡ δὲ λυχνῖτις

ζωνὴ στυλοῦται πέζαν ἰωνι τύπωι·

ῥάβδου κοίλης ἔντος ἀποστίλβει δὲ συνηνὶς

στικτὴ πρὸς πτερναῖς· κιόνος ἥδε θέσις.

(a) 3 βα[σιλεῖς τοῦτο], or Βα[λάκρου (proper name required as antecedent to ὃς v. 4) ed. pr.   4 ἔργον D. L. P.   5

ANONYMOUS

(6) θέσις v. 9 means "foundation" or "base" in a non-technical sense, i.e. all that has hitherto been described as the support for the column-shaft.

(b) *An epigram, composed in the same era as the preceding one, celebrating a person distinguished in poetry and warfare. This person is undoubtedly Ptolemy IV Philopator, who won a great victory over Antiochus III at Raphia in 217 B.C., and was at the same time ambitious in the world of letters, writing a tragedy* Adonis (*Schol. Ar.* Thesm. *1059*) *and setting up a temple to Homer* (Aelian, V.H. *13. 22*). *This poem refers to a dedication to Homer* (vv. 2-5) : *we can hardly suppose it to be other than the dedication of that temple to Homer. The parents of* vv. *6-7 are then Ptolemy III Euergetes* (*hence* εὐεργέται v. 6) *and his wife Berenice.*

(a) (Vv. 3 *sqq.*) Gladly ... accept the gift ... who also set up a work in stone, an ample building for your house, having first set the bright water free. He made it into the form of a semicircle ; the Parian [a] boundary-wall supports the column-base in Ionian style, and within the hollow moulding speckled Syenite [b] glistens near the heels [c]; such is the foundation of the column.

[a] Lit. " the lamp-stone," because Parian marble was quarried underground by lamplight.　　[b] The dappled granite of Syene.　　[c] For the sense of ῥάβδος and of πτερναί, see Introd. Note.

Πά[ρου ed. pr.: "having set free the white water-drop of Paros" must mean "having quarried Parian marble." But σταγών is a most unnatural word to use here with reference to marble (despite the stalactites in the underground galleries of the Parian quarries); the sense of ἐκποδίσας is very strained ; and in this description of a fountain, σταγών must surely refer to the water of the spring. πά[ρος D. L. P. 6 Ed. pr. thinks ἡμισφαίρο[υ] a more probable reading. 7 στυλουσαι Π, corr. ed. pr.

ἡ δ' ἀφ' Ὑμηττοῦ πέτρος ἐρευγομένη πόμα
κρήνης   10
ἐκδέχεται σπιλάδων ὑγρὰ διαινομένη.
εἰκόνα δ' ὑμετέρην ἐτυπώσατο πίονι λύγδωι
πρηύνας, μέσσην δ' ἥρμοσ[ε]ν Ἀρσινόην
σύγκληρον νύμφαις κατὰ πᾶν ἔτος. ἀλλ'
ἐπὶ πηγὴν
τήνδε μετ' εὐνομίης βαίνετε Κρηνιάδες.   15

(b)   ]των ουρ[   ]ιναν α[
εὐαίων Πτολεμ[αῖος   τοῦ]το δ' Ὁμήρωι
εἴσαθ' ὑπὲρ διδ[   ]ατοναρτεμενος
τῶι πρὶν Ὀδυσσείας τε [καὶ Ἰλι]άδος τὸν
ἀγήρω
ὕμνον ἀπ' ἀθανάτων γραψ[α]μένωι πρα-
πίδων.   5
ὄλβιοι ὦ θνατῶν εὐεργέται, [οἳ] τὸν ἄριστον
ἐν δορὶ καὶ Μούσαις κοίρανον ἠρόσατε.

11 Perhaps διαινομένων: but the last two words are still a
feeble addition. ἐρευγομένης Schadewaldt (ὑγρὰ being then
the object of ἐκδέχεται).   (b) 2 τοῦ]το D. L. P.   3
]α τὸν Ἀρτέμονος ed. pr.: ὑπὲρ διδ[αχῆς, γνοὺς (?) κ]ατ' ὄναρ,
τέμενος Körte.   Körte is clearly right in his view that the

ANONYMOUS

EPIGRAM ON THE DEATH OF PHILICUS

106   [3 B.C.]

Ed. pr. Wilamowitz, *Sitzungsberichte der königlich
preussischen Akademie der Wissenschaften*, Berlin, xxix.
452

ANONYMOUS

Through stone[a] from Hymettus gushes forth the draught of springwater, taking up the flood from caves, itself drenched therewith. Your[b] image he modelled from rich white marble, smooth-wrought, and in the midst he set Arsinoe, who shares the Nymphs's fortune every year.[c] Come with good order to the fountain, Nymphs of spring-waters!

(b) Blessed Ptolemy . . . set this up to Homer . . . who wrote of old the ageless song of *Iliad* and *Odyssey* from his immortal mind. O happy benefactors of mankind! You sowed the seed of a king who excels with spear and among the Muses!

---

[a] Fashioned, evidently, into the shape of a lion's head, through which the water poured.   [b] The king's and queen's.   [c] Possibly a reference to an annual ceremony in which Arsinoe was associated with the Nymphs of the spring. But we know nothing of such an association; and κατὰ πᾶν ἔτος might mean (as ed. pr. understand it) " all the year round."

---

traces suit ενος better than ονος at end of line: but his διδαχῆς introduces an unpoetical word, and he himself is dissatisfied with γνούς. κ]ατ' ὄναρ τέμενος is very probably the correct reading of the end, but the preceding lacuna is hard to fill.

ANONYMOUS

EPIGRAM ON THE DEATH OF PHILICUS

[3 B.C.]

1912, p. 547. See Körte, *Archiv*, v. 1913, 547; *Powell, *New Chapters*, iii. 200.

*An epigram on the death of Philicus(for whom see no. 90),
written by a rather tedious and affected contemporary. N.B.
the form of the name Φίλικος (not Φιλίσκος). Interesting for*

ἔρχεο δὴ μακάριστος ὁδοιπόρος ἔρχεο καλοὺς
   χώρους εὐσεβέων ὀψόμενος, Φίλικε,
ἐκ κισσηρεφέος κεφαλῆς εὔυμνα κυλίων
   ῥήματα, καὶ νήσους κώμασον εἰς μακάρων,
εὖ μὲν γῆρας ἰδὼν εὐέστιον Ἀλκινόοιο   5
   Φαίηκος, ζώειν ἀνδρὸς ἐπισταμένου·
Ἀλκινόου τις ἐὼν ἐξ αἵματος [
     ἀπ]ὸ [Δη]μοδόκου

   .   .   .   .   .

ᵃ εὐέστιον from ἑστία (not εὐεστώ), cf. Callim. Del. 325.

AMYNTAS, LEONIDAS, ANTIPATER
107 [1 A.D.]   OF SIDON

Ed. pr. *Grenfell-Hunt, *P. Oxy.* iv. 1904, no. 662, p. 64.
See Wilamowitz, *G.G.A.* 1904, 669 ; Powell, *Aegyptus*, xiv.
1934, p. 468 and *New Chapters*, iii. 188 ; Milne, *Cat. Lit.
Pap. B.M.* no. 61.
[I omit the two fragmentary and obscure lines of Amyntas
which head col. ii. (vv. 21-22) in ed. pr. : *cf.* however Powell,
Aegyptus, loc. cit.]

*The first column of this Π contains ends of lines of epi-
grams by Leonidas (= Anth. Pal. vii. 163) and Antipater
(= Anth. Pal. vii. 164). The second column contains two
poems by Amyntas (a poet hitherto unknown : evidently an
Alexandrian epigrammatist of the 2nd century B.C.) ; one
concerned with a Samian woman named Prexo, who is the
subject of the two epigrams in col. i. (and also of Anth. Pal.*

454

the reference to the poet's convivial habits and cheerful tem-
perament in old age (Philicus was a " Phaeacian " as well in
character as by birth). See further ed. pr. pp. 548-549.

Go your path, blest wayfarer, go your path,
Philicus, to see the fair land of the god-fearing dead.
Your head crowned with ivy, rolling forth your lines
of lovely song, begone with revel to the Islands of
the Blest. Happy, that you saw the festive [a] old-
age of an Alcinous, the Phaeacian, a man who
knew how to live. Born of Alcinous's line . . . from
Demodocus . . . [b]

. . . . . .

[b] It was evidently suggested that descent from Homer's
Demodocus explained the poetic genius of Philicus.

AMYNTAS, LEONIDAS, ANTIPATER
OF SIDON   [1 A.D.]

vii. 165, ascribed to Antipater or Archias) ; the other con-
cerned with the capture of Sparta by Philopoemen in 188 B.C.
(a variant of Anth. Pal. vii. 723). The third column con-
tains two new dedicatory epigrams by Leonidas and Antipater,
composed for one Glenis ; and the first word (or two words) of
another epigram, apparently also by Leonidas ; at this point
the scribe stopped abruptly, and wrote no more in this column.
    Thus it is clear that this anthology was arranged by sub-
ject-variation (i.e. poems which were variations on the same
theme were put together). And it is also clear (from the
evidence of the first column) that this anthology was an
ancestor, however partial and remote, of the Palatine Antho-
logy. Now it is commonly believed that the celebrated

LITERARY PAPYRI

Anthology of Meleager *was arranged* κατὰ στίχον, i.e.
alphabetically, according to the first letter of the poem
(*Schol.* on Anth. Pal., *ms.* P, *p. 81,* συνέταξεν δὲ αὐτὰ κατὰ
στοιχεῖον). *We must therefore either revise our views about*

ΑΜΥΝΤΑΣ

(1)   φράζε, γύναι, τίς ἐοῦσα καὶ ἐκ τίνος, εἰπέ
            τε πάτρην,
        καὶ ποίας ἔθανες νούσου ὑπ' ἀργαλέης.
    οὔνομα μὲν Πραξὼ Σαμίη, ξένε, ἐκ δὲ γονῆος
        Καλλιτέλευς γενόμαν, ἀλλ' ἔθανον τοκε-
            τῶι.
    τίς δὲ τάφον στάλωσε; Θεόκριτος, ὧι με
            σύνευνον   5
        ἀνδρὶ δόσαν. ποίην δ' ἦλθες ἐς ἡλικίην;
    ἑπταέτις τρὶς ἑνὸς γενόμαν ἔτι. ἦ ῥά γ'
            ἄτεκνος;
        οὔκ, ἀλλὰ τριετῆ παῖδα δόμωι λιπόμαν.

(2)   τὰν πάρος ἄτρεστον Λακεδαίμονα, τᾶς χέρα
            μούνας
        πολλάκι τ' ἐν πολέσιν δῆριν ἔφριξεν
            Ἄρης,
        . . . .
    νῦν ὑπ' ἀνικάτωι Φιλοποίμενι δουρί τ'
            Ἀχαιῶν
        πρήνης ἐκ τρισσᾶν ἤριπε μυριάδων
    ἄσκεπος. οἰωνοὶ δὲ περισμυχηρὸν ἰδόντες   5
        μύρονται, πεδίον δ' οὐκ ἐπίασι βόες.
    καπνὸν δ' ἐκθρώισκοντα παρ' Εὐρώταο
            λοετροῖς
        Ἑλλὰς δερκομένα μύρεται ἀκρόπολιν.

456

*the nature of the arrangement of poems in Meleager's antho-
logy, or admit that there existed early in the 1st century A.D.
a different collection of Alexandrian epigrams, which (like
Meleager's) was taken up into the corpus which ultimately
developed into our* Palatine Anthology.

AMYNTAS

(1) Say, lady, who you are, and who your father,
and tell your country, and of what grievous sickness
you died.
" Stranger, my name is Praxo, of Samos ; I was
the daughter of Calliteles ; but I died in childbirth."
Who set up the tomb ? " Theocritus, to whom
they gave me as wife." To what age did you come ?
" Thrice seven and one years old was I." Child-
less ? " No ; I left at home a child three years
of age."

(2) Lacedaemon, of old the dauntless, at whose
single-handed might and warfare many a time and
oft the War-God shuddered . . . now is cast head-
long and defenceless by thrice ten thousand foes,
beneath unconquered Philopoemen and the Achaean
spears. The birds look on the smoking ruins and
mourn, and the oxen go not upon her plain. And
seeing the smoke leap up beside Eurotas where men
bathe, Hellas mourns her citadel.

---

(1) 8 ουκαλλιτεληστριετη Π, corr. Ed. Fraenkel.   (2) 2
πολλακις Π, corr. D. L. P.   πολλάκις ἄμ πολέμου Powell, πολ-
λάκις ἐν πολέμωι θοῦριν Milne.   After this line, syntax
demands a lacuna (of at least two lines): unless we read ἃ
or αἱ πάρος ἄτρεστον v. 1 (Powell).   6 Read by Milne.
7 Read by Wilam.   8 Read by Milne.   The last two
couplets seem to be *alternatives, cf.* the repetition ἰδόντες
μύρονται, δερκομένα μύρεται.

ΛΕΩΝΙΔΑΣ

(3) Ἀκρωρίται Πανὶ καὶ ενπα[. . . . .] νύμφαις
Γ]λῆνις ὁ συγγείτων δῶρα κ[υνηγεσί]ης,
ταύταν τε προτόμαν καὶ δ[. . . . . . .]ησ[. .]ι
βύρσαν καὶ ῥοθίους τούσ[δ᾽ ἀνέθηκε]
πόδας.
Πὰν ὦ καὶ νύμφαι, τὸν δ[εξιὸν ἀγ]ρευτῆρα 5
Γλῆνιν ἀεξήσαιθ᾽ αιεδ[. . . . . . .]ς.

ΑΝΤΙΠΑΤΡΟΣ

(4) Σιληνῶν ἀλόχοις ἀντρήισιν ἠδὲ κερασταῖ
ταῦτ᾽ Ἀκρωρίται Πανὶ καθηγεμόνι,
καὶ προτόμαν ἀκμῆτα καὶ αὐτὸ νέον τόδε
κάπρου
δέρμα, τὸ μηδ᾽ αὐτῶι ῥηγνύμενον
χάλυβι,
Γλῆνις ἀνηέρτησε καλᾶς χαριτήσ[ιο]ν ἄγρας 5
δεικνὺς ἰφθίμου κοῦρος Ὀνα(σι)φάνε[υ]ς.

(3) 1 Prob. [ἀντρήισι] νύμφαις : but ενπ[remains unintelligible.   5 ὦ Πᾶν Powell. δεξιὸν Beazley.   6 End

ANONYMOUS

108   [3 B.C.]   EPIGRAM

Ed. pr. *Schubart-Wilamowitz, *Berliner Klassikertexte*,
v. 1, 1907, p. 77.   See Körte, *Archiv*, v. 547.

ἀκμῆι] δρεπάνου θῆκε τεμὼν ῥόπαλον
]τεχνᾶτο γὰρ εὖ μέγα· τοὶ δ᾽ ἀνα-
θέντ[ες,
σηκὸν ὅπου λαὸς τ]εὐχ[ε] παληοσέβης,

ANONYMOUS

LEONIDAS

(3) To Pan of Acroria *a* and the . . . nymphs, neighbour Glenis dedicated gifts from the chase :— this head and . . . hide and these swift feet. O Pan, O nymphs, prosper the clever hunter Glenis . . . !

ANTIPATER OF SIDON

(4) To the Silens' mates *b* that dwell in caves, and to their chieftain, horned Pan of Acroria, a scatheless *c* head and this new boarskin, that not even steel has rent, were hung up by Glenis, son of mighty Onasiphanes, who shewed these thank-offerings for a fine quarry.

a Acroria : name of a mountain in Sicyon ; Acroreites was local epithet of Dionysus (Steph. Byz.).　　*b* The nymphs.　　*c* ἀκμῆτα "uninjured" as in *Anth. Pal.* ix. 526 πύλαι ἀκμῆτες (" permanent ").

prob. ['Ονασιφάνεν]ς, but αἰεδ[remains unintelligible: may have been an error for υἱόν.　　(4) 2 καθηγεμόνι Wilam. 3 αὐαλέον or αὐσταλέον Wilam.: αὐτὸ is meaningless and probably corrupt.

ANONYMOUS

EPIGRAM　　　　　　　　　　　[3 B.C.]

Fragment of a long epigram, of Hellenistic date, composed in praise of a dedicated statue.

. . . cut with a sickle's edge, and made it a club (?) . . . wrought it to a fine size. You dedicators in the shrine fashioned by a folk god-fearing of

νικᾶτ᾽ ἀν]τιπάλους ἀπτῶσί τ᾽ ἐλέγχετε π[αντᾶι
εὐτεχνίαις] πλάσταν καὶ τὸν ἀριστοπάλαν·   5
. . . .] χρυ[σ]ῆν θηήσατο Κ[ύπ]ριν ᾽Απελλῆς
γυμνὴν ἐκ μέλανος πό]ντου ἀνερχ[ομ]ένην

(*Fragments of two more lines*)

. . . .

5-6 ἀριστοπάλαν, [ὅς ποτε καὶ] ed. pr.: but Apelles was not
a πλάστης. ἀριστοπάλαν . [οὐδ᾽ ὅς τὴν] or [εἰ δ᾽ ἄρα τὴν] Beazley.

ANONYMOUS

109 [3 B.C.]   TWO EPIGRAMS

Ed. pr. *Edgar, Catalogue général des antiquités
égyptiennes du musée du Caire*, iv. p. 1.   See Wilcken,
Archiv, vi. 453 ; Powell, *New Chapters*, i. 107.

*Two epitaphs for a dog named Tauron, who died from his
wounds after killing a wild boar which attacked his master
Zenon.   Zenon was the agent of Apollonius, who was
financial minister to Ptolemy Philadelphus and Ptolemy*

(1) ᾽Ινδὸν ὅδ᾽ ἀπύει τύμβος Ταύρωνα θανόντα
         κεῖσθαι, ὁ δὲ κτείνας πρόσθεν ἐπεῖδ᾽
            ᾽Αΐδαν·
       θὴρ ἅπερ ἄντα δρακεῖν, συὸς ἥ ῥ᾽ ἀπὸ τᾶς
            Καλυδῶνος
       λείψανον εὐκάρποις ἐν πεδίοις τρέφετο
       ᾽Αρσινόας ἀτίνακτον, ἀπ᾽ αὐχένος ἀθρόα
            φρίσσων,
          λ]όχμαις, καὶ γε[ν]ύων ἀφρὸν ἀμεργό-
            μενος·   5

460

old, you conquer your antagonists, and, with skill
that never lets you down, in every point you
vanquish even the champion sculptor in the ring.—
Apelles, who once beheld the golden Cyprian rising
naked from the dark sea . . . . [a]

(Fragments of two more lines)

.   .   .   .   .   .

[a] The Anadyomene of Apelles.

ANONYMOUS

TWO EPIGRAMS [3 b.c.]

*Euergetes : he had been sent to Fayum (the nome of Arsinoe,
cf. v. 5) to superintend the work on a great estate given to
Apollonius by the king.*

*These are good compositions ; probably the work of a pro-
fessional Alexandrian poet. It is likely that both pieces were
inscribed on the dog's tombstone. The composition of two
epitaphs, one elegiac and the other iambic, was a common
practice at this time (Wilamowitz ap. Wilcken, loc. cit.
quotes Kaibel, Epigr. Gr. 325, 462, 502, 546, 550).*

(1) This tomb proclaims that Indian Tauron lies
dead. But his slayer saw Hades first.—Like a wild
beast to behold,[a] like a relic of the Calydonian boar,
it grew in the fertile plains of Arsinoe immovable,
shaking from its neck the mane in masses in its lair,
and dashing the froth from its jaws. Engaging the

[a] Since the boar *was* a θήρ, I do not know what is meant
by saying that it was *like* one.

461

σὺν δὲ πεσὼν σκύλακος τόλμαι στήθη μὲν
    ἑτοίμως
ἠλόκισ’, οὐ μέλλων δ’ αὐχέν’ ἔθηκ’· ἐπὶ
    γᾶν,
δρα]ξάμενος γὰρ ὁμοῦ λοφιᾶι μεγάλοιο
    τένοντος
ο]ὐ πρ[ὶ]ν ἔλυσεν ὀδόντ’ ἔσθ’ ὑπέθηκ’
    Ἀίδαι.   10
σώιζει δὲ] Ζ[ήνω]να πόν[ων] ἀδίδακτα
    κυναγόν,
καὶ κατὰ γᾶς τύμβωι τὰν χάριν ἠργά-
    σατο.

(2)   σκύλαξ ὁ τύμβωι τῶιδ’ ὕπ’ ἐκτερισμένος
Ταύρων, ἐπ’ αὐθένταισιν οὐκ ἀμήχανος·
κάπρωι γὰρ ὡς συνῆλθεν ἀντίαν ἔριν,
ὁ μέν τις ὡς ἄπλατος οἰδήσας γένυν
στῆθος κατηλόκιζε λευκαίνων ἀφρῶι,   5
ὁ δ’ ἀμφὶ νώτωι δισσὸν ἐμβαλὼν ἴχνος
ἐδράξατο φρίσσοντος ἐκ στέρνων μέσων
καὶ γᾶι συνεσπείρασεν· Ἀίδαι δὲ δοὺς
τὸν αὐτόχειρ’ ἔθναισκεν, Ἰνδὸν ὡς νόμος.
σώιζων δὲ τὸν κυναγὸν ὧι παρείπετο   10
Ζήνων’ ἐλαφρᾶι τᾶιδ’ ὑπεστάλη κόνει.

ANONYMOUS

110   [3 B.C.]   ELEGY ABOUT A WAR

Ed. pr. Wilamowitz, *Sitzungsberichte der königlich preussischen Akademie der Wissenschaften*, 1918, p. 736. See *Powell, *Collectanea Alexandrina*, p. 131, *Class. Rev.* 1919, 462

fearless dog, readily it ploughed a furrow in its breast: then immediately laid its own neck upon the ground. For Tauron, fastening upon the massive nape, with mane and all, loosed not his teeth again until he sent it down to Hades. So he saved hunter Zenon from distress, unschooled [a]; and earned his gratitude in his tomb below the earth.

(2) A dog is buried beneath this tomb, Tauron, who did not despair in conflict with a killer. When he met a boar in battle face to face, the latter, unapproachable, puffed out its jaws and, white with froth, ploughed a furrow in his breast. The other planted two feet about its back, and fastened upon the bristling monster from the middle of its breast, and wrapped him in the earth. He gave the murderer to Hades and died, as a good Indian should. He rescued Zenon, the hunter whom he followed; and here in this light dust he is laid to rest.

[a] It was a very young dog, cf. σκύλαξ v. 7, (2) v. 1.

---

(1) 10 ἔλυσεν D. L. P.: ἔμυσεν ed. pr. 11 σώιζει D. L. P. (σώσας and πονῶν ed. pr.).

ANONYMOUS

ELEGY ABOUT A WAR [3 B.C.]

90 and *New Chapters*, i. 106 ; Momigliano, *Boll. Fil. Class.* 1929, 151 ; Körte, *Archiv*, vii. 122 ; Diehl, *Anth. Lyr. Gr.* ii. p. 236.

LITERARY PAPYRI

This much is certain : (a) *part at least of the poem was
addressed to a returned ambassador, v. 2,* (b) *whose report is
made to a king, v. 6.* (c) *The news exasperates the king,
who utters threats against the persons about whom the ambas-
sador reported, vv. 7-10.* (d) *There is a reference to Medes
and to a Gaul, vv. 13-14. To the further question, can we
identify the king and the occasion, we must return an emphatic
negative. It is possible that the Gaul is the object of the
king's anger (Wilam., Momigliano, Powell, Körte) ; and that
the king threatens him with the fate which had previously
befallen the Medes. If so, the king cannot be Attalus,[a] but
may still be a Macedonian, a Seleucid, or even a Ptolemy
in Egypt (reference to Gallic mercenaries of Ptolemy Phila-
delphus, Paus. i. 7. 2, Powell). But it is only one possibility :
it is not a necessary inference from the text. As the lines
stand, it is more probable that the king is saying that he, who
defeated the valiant Gauls before, will now easily overcome
the effeminate Medes. In that case the king would probably*

. . . . πρ]όσθε πύλης καὶ τείχεος α[
. . . . . .]ην ταύτην ἤνυες ἀγγελίην.
. . . .]νης, ὦ[ν]α, διὰ στόματος λόγου [ἀρχή,
        ἱ]ερῆς ἔρνεα φυταλίης
. . . . ὀ]πίσω ῥυπαρῆς στάχυες τρι[βόλοιο. 5
εἶπας ἀ]παγγέλλων εἰς βασιλῆα λόγο[ν.
χὼ μὲν] ἐπεὶ μάλα πάντα δι' οὔατος ἔκλ[υε μῦθον,
  ὠργίσθη, βρι]αρὸν δ' αὐτίκ' ἀνέσχε λόγο[ν·
ἀνέρε]ς ὑβρισταί τε καὶ ἄφρονες, ἀλλὰ μ[άλ' ὦκα
  οἴσουσι]ν ταύτης μισθὸν ἀτασθαλίης· 10
γνώσον]ται δὲ μαθόντες, ἐπεὶ καὶ ἀρεί[ονας ἄλλους
  ἡμεῖς εἰς κρατερὴν δουλοσύνην ἔθεμ[εν
. . . . .]ης Μήδοισι βαθυκτεάνοισιν ὁμ[οίως
. . . .]σασθαι θοῦρος ἀνὴρ Γαλάτης.

  8 ἄνεχε λόγον Eur. *El.* 592.   11 παθόντες Beazley.

464

ANONYMOUS

be a Seleucid ; but might still be Ptolemy Philadelphus, e.g.
on the occasion of his irruption into the Seleucid empire.

*If the Gauls are here the objects of the king's anger, the
identity of the king and the date of the occasion are still
impossible to determine. The poem might refer to the war of
Antiochus I against the Gauls in 277–276, again in 275 ;
or to the revolt of Ptolemy II's Gallic mercenaries in 274 ;
or to any one of numerous conflicts between the Seleucid
empire and those Gauls who, since 275, had been settled in
northern Asia Minor ; or to the war of Attalus against the
Gauls in 230 ; or possibly even to a war of Antiochus III
against the Gauls (Momigliano, quoting Suidas*, s.v. Σιμωνίδης
Μάγνης). *There are other interesting possibilities ; but
enough has been said to shew that without further evidence
a precise identification of the king and of the occasion is
absolutely impracticable.*

. . . in front of the gate and wall . . . you fulfilled this
embassage . . . " . . . my king, the beginning of speech
upon my lips . . . shoots of an holy plant . . . crops
of dirty (weed ? [b]) . . ." . . . you brought back the
message to your king, and thus you spoke. But he,
when he heard all, was angry, and lifted up his voice
in strong utterance :—" The men are insolent and
fools, but they shall quickly win the wages of their
presumption. They shall learn and understand,
since we have set others better than them to harshest
slavery. . . . Alike to the wealthy Medes . . . the
valiant Gaul. . . . in purple raiment, nor amid per-

---

[a] Successors of Attalus are excluded by the age of the
papyrus. [b] τρίβολον: described by Dioscorides iv. 15,
Pliny xxi. 98. The point of this obscure couplet may have
been, " the beginning of my report is pleasant, but there is
bad news at the end (ὀπίσω)," or " the king's message was
noble, the answer to it is mean and base."

LITERARY PAPYRI

. . . . πο]ρφυρέοισιν ἐν εἴμασιν οὐδὲ μύροισ[ιν   15
  ] μαλακὸν χρῶτα λιπαινόμενο[ς,
. . . . χά]μευνα Διός τε καὶ αἰθριάα[ι] ἐνι[αυτόν
      .   .   .   .   .   .

ANONYMOUS

POEM IN PRAISE OF AN OFFICER

111 [End 3 B.C.]

Ed. pr. *Crönert, *Nachrichten der Gesellschaft der Wissenschaften zu Göttingen*, 1922, p. 31.   See Körte, *Archiv*, vii. 257 ; Wüst, *Burs. Jahrsb.* 1926, 124 ; Platnauer, *New Chapters*, iii. 178; Knox, *Herodes* (Loeb Classical Library), p. 254.

      ἀγαπᾶτε ταῦτα πάντες ὅσ’ ἔχει· τἀγαθὰ
      ἅπαντ’ ἐν αὐτῶι· χρηστός, εὐγενής, ἁπλοῦς,
      φιλοβασιλεύς, ἀνδρεῖος, ἐν πίστει μέγας,
      σώφρων, φιλέλλην, πραύς, εὐπροσήγορος,
      τὰ πανοῦργα μισῶν, τὴν [δ’ ἀ]λήθειαν σέβων. 5
      .   .   .   .   .   .

1 τοῦτον πάντες ὃς ἔχει τἀγαθὰ . . . αὐτῶι Knox.

ANONYMOUS

PREFACE TO AN ASTRONOMICAL
112 [2 B.C.]   TREATISE

Ed. pr. Letronne, *Papyrus grecs du Louvre : Notices et extraits des manuscrits de la bibliothèque imperiale et autres bibliothèques*, i. 1850, p. 46.

466

fumes . . . letting his soft skin grow sleek, . . . his
bed (*fragments of a line*) . . .

. . . . . .

---

15 οὐ γὰρ πορφ. ed. pr.   16 κοιμᾶται ed. pr.   **17**
ἀλλὰ χάμ. ed. pr.

ANONYMOUS

POEM IN PRAISE OF AN OFFICER
[End 3 B.C.]

*Fragment of an Hellenistic poem, praising an officer of the
royal court at Alexandria.   Probably not part of a drama :
but Tragic models in Eur. Hic. 860-908, esp. 867-871 ; Or.
918-922.*

EACH man admire his many virtues !   All goodness
lives in him : good, noble, and honest, loyal to his
king, courageous, great in trust, modest, a patriot,
gentle, affable, hater of wickedness, worshipper
of truth.

. . . . . .

ANONYMOUS

PREFACE TO AN ASTRONOMICAL
TREATISE   [2 B.C.]

*An acrostic preface, in correct " tragic " iambics, to a treat-
ise on astronomy by Eudoxus.   Vv. 6-8 mean : " There is one
line for each month of the year [there are in fact 12 lines]*

and each letter counts one day " [*in fact each line contains 30 letters ; except the last, which consists of 35. Total, 365 = a Great Year* (μέγας χρόνος *v. 8, here simply a year of 365 days, as opposed to the lunar year of 364). Thus ed. pr.*].

Ἐν τῶιδε δείξω πᾶσιν ἐκμαθεῖν σοφὴν
Ὑμῖν πόλου σύνταξιν, ἐν βραχεῖ λόγωι
Δοὺς τῆσδε τέχνης εἰδέναι σαφῆ πέρι.
Οὐδεὶς γάρ ἐστιν ἐνδεὴς γνώμης ὅτωι
Ξένον φανεῖται, ταῦτ᾽ ἐὰν ξυνῆι καλῶς.   5
Ὁ μὲν στίχος μείς ἐστι, γράμμα δ᾽ ἡμέρα.
Ὑμῖν ἀριθμὸν δ᾽ ἴσον ἔχει τὰ γράμματα
Ταῖς ἡμέραισιν ἃς ἄγει μέγας χρόνος·
Ἐνιαύσιον βροτοῖσι περίοδόν τ᾽ ἔχει
Χρόνος διοικῶν ἀστέρων γνωρίσματα.   10
Νικᾶι δὲ τούτων οὐθὲν ἕτερον, ἀλλ᾽ ἀεὶ
Ἥκει τὰ πάντα ἐς ταὐτὸν ὅτε ἀνέλθηι χρόνος.

4 οὕτως (Beazley) is perhaps necessary instead of ἐστίν.

ANONYMOUS

113   [1 A.D.]   EPIGRAM

Ed. pr. Kenyon, *Revue de Philologie*, N.S. 19, 1895, p. 177. See Weil, *ibid.* p. 180 ; Milne, *Cat. Lit. Pap. B.M.* no. 62 ; *Keydell, *Hermes*, 69, 1934, 420 ; Powell, *New Chapters*, iii. 189.

An epigram to a statue of Actian Apollo erected at

468

ANONYMOUS

The first letters of the lines spell perpendicularly ΕΥΔΟΞΟΥ
ΤΕΧΝΗ *("Eudoxus' Book of Rules") : for parallels to this
"acrostic" cf. Nicander (Lobel, C. Qu. 22, 114), Dionysius
Periegeta (Leue, Philol. 42, 175), P. Oxy. 1795 ; P. Amh. 23.*

HEREWITH I will reveal to you all the subtle com-
position of the heavens, and give you certain know-
ledge of our science in a few words.   There is nobody
so wanting in intelligence that it will seem strange to
him, if he understands these verses well.   The line
stands for a month, the letter for a day ; the letters
provide you with a number equal to the days which
a Great Year brings.   Time brings to men a yearly
circle, as it governs the starry signs : of which none
outrivals another, but always all come to the same [a]
point, when the time comes round.

   [a] *i.e.* the same as on the same day of the year before.

---

5 τῶιδε ἀν ed. pr. : corr. D. L. P.   7 ἴσον ed. pr. :
corr. D. L. P.   11 οὐθεὶς ἔτερον ed. pr. : corr. D. L. P.
(to restore metre and 30 letters).   12 αὐτὸ ὅτ᾽ ἀνέλθηι ὁ
χρόνος ed. pr. : corr. D. L. P.

ANONYMOUS

EPIGRAM   [1 A.D.]

*Alexandria in commemoration of the victory of Octavian
(= Caesar, v. 1) at the battle of Actium : which battle was
fought in sight of a temple of Apollo, cf. " Apollo Actius "
on Greek coins of Nero's era.*

469

Ἄκτιον ἀμ[φιέπων, ἄνα ν]αύμαχε, Κ(αί)σαρος
  ἔργων
μνῆμα κ(αὶ) ε[ὑτυ]χέων μαρτυρίη καμάτων,
Αἰῶνος σ[τό]μασιν βεβοημένε· σοὶ γὰρ Ἄρηος
π[νεῦμα]τα καὶ σακέων ἐστόρεσεν πάταγον,
Εἰρήνης μόχθους εὐώπιδος ἔνθα κλαδεύσας   5
  γῆν ἐπὶ Νειλῶτιν νίσε(τ)ο γηθαλέος,
εὐνο[μίης] φόρτοισι καὶ εὐθενίης βαθυπλούτου
  βρι[θό]μενος βύζην Ζεὺς ἅτ' ἐλευθέριος,
δωροφόροις δὲ χέρεσσιν ἐδέξατο Νεῖλος ἄνακτα
  κ(αὶ) δάμαρ ἡ χρυσέοις πήχεσι λουομένη   10
ἀπτόλεμον καὶ ἄδηριν ἐλευθερίου Διὸς ὄμβρον,
  ἀτρεκὲς ἐσβέσθη δ' οὔνομα κ(αὶ) πολέμου·
χαῖρε, μάκαρ Λεύκᾱτα, Διὸς [Κρον]ίδαο Σεβαστοῦ
  νικ(αί)ων ἔργων ἓν πρυτάνευμα καλόν.

6 νίσε(τ)ο Weil, Keydell.

ᵃ Egypt.   ᵇ The " arms " are the floods which the
Nile puts forth to embrace the land ; " golden," because of

ΠΟΣΕΙΔΙΠΠΟΣ

114 [1 A.D.]   ELEGY ON OLD AGE

Ed. pr. Diels, *Sitzungsberichte der königlich preussischen Akademie der Wissenschaften*, Berlin, 1898, p. 845 with Plate. See Crönert, *Archiv*, ii. 517 ; Schubart, *Pap. Graec. Berol.* 1911, Plate XVII and Text, and *Symbolae philologicae O. A. Danielsson octogenario dicatae*, Upsala, 1932, p. 290.   Text on wooden tablets.

From a poem about the misfortune of old age.   The writer asks the Muses to come to Thebes : therefore he is writing the

470

POSEIDIPPUS

MASTER of Actium, sea-fighting lord, memorial of
Caesar's deeds and witness of his prosperous labours;
whose name is on the lips of Time, for in your honour
Caesar calmed the storm of war and the clash of
shields, and there he cut short the sufferings of
fair Peace, and came rejoicing to the land of Nile,
heavy-laden with the cargo of Law and Order, and
Prosperity's abundant riches, like Zeus the god of
Freedom; and Nile welcomed his lord with arms of
bounty, and his wife,[a] whom with golden arms [b] the
river laves, received the shower, apart from stress or
strife, that came from her Zeus of Freedom,[c] and
truly the very name of war was extinguished.—
Hail, Lord of Leucas, one and only noble president at
the victorious deeds wrought by Augustus, our Zeus
the son of Cronus!

the cornfields and other bright harvests which arise: the
χρυσ. πήχ. are the same as the δωρ. χέρ. of the previous line.
[c] The blessing of the flooding of the Nile was commonly
ascribed to the king: Kaibel, *Ep. Gr.* 981, Keydell, *loc. cit.*

POSEIDIPPUS

ELEGY ON OLD AGE [1 A.D.]

*poem in Thebes.   The tablets were found in Egypt : therefore
Thebes is Egyptian Thebes, unless we suppose that the author,
a Macedonian (vv. 14, 16), is writing his poem during a tem-
porary residence in Boeotian Thebes, and later travels to
Egypt, taking his poem with him.   Schubart's supposition,
that " Pimplean Thebes " may stand here for some Mace-
donian town, is altogether unconvincing.   He objects to the
reference to Egyptian Thebes on the grounds (1) that that city*

LITERARY PAPYRI

*was a place of small importance in the 1st century A.D. ;
(2) that its market-place was so insignificant that statues of
poets were not likely to be set up in it ; (3) that the outlook
of vv. 14-15 is that of a man living in Hellas, or in
Macedon, not in Luxor or Karnak. These are surely in-
sufficient grounds : the city was small enough, but still people
lived there ; the market-place to which the poet refers may
well be that of his native town in Macedon ; the outlook of the
Macedonian does not change because he happens to be staying
for a time in Egypt.*

εἴ τι καλόν, Μοῦσαι πολιητίδες, ἢ π[α]ρὰ Φοίβου
   χρυσολύρεω καθαροῖς οὔασιν ἐκλ[ύε]τε
Παρνησοῦ νιφόεντος ἀ[ν]ὰ πτύχ[α]ς ἢ παρ' Ὀλύμ-
   πωι,
   Βάκχωι τὰς τριετεῖς ἀρχόμεναι θυμέλας·
νῦν δὲ Ποσειδίππωι στυγερὸν συναείσατε γῆρας   5
   γραψάμεναι δέλτων ἐν χρυσέαις σελίσιν.
λιμπάνετε σκοπιὰς Ἑλικωνίδες, εἰς δὲ τὰ Θήβης
   τείχεα Πι(μ)π[λ]είης βαίνετε (Κα)σταλίδες.
καὶ σὺ Ποσείδιππόν ποτ' ἐφίλα(ο), Κύνθιε, Λητοῦς
   υἱὲ . . .   10

  •   •   •   •   •   •   •

(φήμη, τῆι νιφόεντ' οἰκία τοῦ Παρίου·
τοίην ἐκχρήσαις τε καὶ ἐξ ἀδύτων καναχήσα[ις
   φωνὴν ἀθα(νά)την ὦ ἄνα καὶ [κα]τ' ἐμοῦ,)
ὄφρα με τιμήσωσι Μακεδόνες οἵ τ' ἐπὶ νήσ[ων
   οἵ τ' Ἀσίης πάσης γείτονες ἠιόνος.   15

8 ΠΙΠ[.]ΗΚΙΣ, Πι(μ)π[λ]είης Schubart, cf. Hesych. *s.v.*
472

POSEIDIPPUS

*The composition is seen, since Schubart's drastic revision of
the text (in which e.g. v. 16 ποιήμασιν ἦγον Ὀλύμπωι Diels
becomes ἕοιμι δὲ βίβλον ἑλίσσων Schubart !), to be conven-
tional enough in metre and diction, though παρηιδος is
eccentric, and there are some faults which Beazley thinks
(and I am loath to disagree) could never have been part of
the original text, esp. 11 (τοῦ Παρίου), 13, 16-17. Vv.
11-14 were savagely crossed out in a moment of grace—not
necessarily by the author himself.*

MUSES[a] of our city, if you have heard a song of
beauty from Phoebus, god of the golden lyre, listeners
undefiled, in the ravines of snowy Parnassus or at
Olympus, starting for Bacchus his triennial cere-
monies,[b]—now join Poseidippus in his song of hateful
Age, inscribing the golden leaves of your tablets.
Leave your peaks, Muses of Helicon, and come,
Castalian maids, to the walls of Pimplean[c] Thebes.
You also, god of Cynthus, loved Poseidippus once,
son of Leto . . . an utterance, where the snow-white
house of the Parian[d] stands. With such immortal
speech make answer, and let your voice, O lord, ring
loud from the sanctuary, even in my ears : that the
Macedonians and the peoples of the islands and the
neighbours of all the Asiatic shore, may honour me.

[a] These, the local Muses of the town in v. 1, return to
Parnassus—or Olympus—in v. 3, shift to Helicon in v. 7,
and to Delphi in v. 8.   [b] For the sense of θύμελαι see
L. & S.⁹, *s.v.*   [c] If the text is sound, ="city of the
Muses."   [d] Apollo, god of the Delphic temple, so called
because his statue there was made of Parian marble? Apollo
is to declare from his shrine that Poseidippus is a great poet.

Πίπλιαι.   13 ὦ ἄνα Beazley (ὠτία Schub., ὦνα καὶ ἵετ'
ἐμοί Diels).

Πελλαῖον γένος ἀμόν· ἔοιμι δὲ βίβλον ἑλίσσων
 ἄμφω λαοφόρωι κείμενος εἰν ἀγορ[ῆι.
ἀλλ' ἐπὶ μὲν παρηῖδος ἀηδόνι λυγρὸν ἐφ[
 νᾶμα· κατ' ἀχλὺν ἐὼν δάκρυα θε[ρ]μὰ χέω,
καὶ στενάχω, ναί, ἐμὸν δὲ φίλον στόμα [20

 μηδέ τις οὖν χεύαι δάκρυον· αὐτὰρ ἐγὼ
γήραι μυστικὸν οἶμον ἐπὶ 'Ραδάμανθυν ἱκοίμην
 δήμωι καὶ λαῶι παντὶ ποθεινὸς ἐών,
ἀσκίπων ἐν ποσσὶ καὶ ὀρθοεπὴς ἀν' ὅμιλον,
 καὶ λείπων τέκνοις δῶμα καὶ ὅλβον ἐ[μ]όν.   25

16-17 It is hard to believe that the text is sound here : ἄμφω has to mean " with both hands." 19 νᾶμα Diels: λῆμα Schubart, =λήμη (" rheum "). ΚΑΤΑΚΛΥΝΕΩΝ corr. Diels (κατὰ γληνέων coni. Schubart).

ANONYMOUS

115   [140–141 A.D.]   MORAL FABLE

Ed. pr. *Jouguet-Lefebvre, Bulletin de correspondance hellénique, xxviii. 1904, p. 201, Plate X. See Blass, Archiv, iii. 487.

Fragment of a moral fable. A school text of a type very

π]ατήρ ποθ' υἱὸν εὐποροῦντα τῶι βίωι
καὶ μηδὲν αὐτῶι τὸ σύνολον δωρούμενον
ἐπὶ τὸν Σκύθην 'Ανάχαρσιν ἦγεν εἰς κρίσιν.
ἐβόα δ' ὅ γ' υἱὸς μὴ θέλων τοῦτον τρέφειν·
οὐκ οἰκίαν οὐ κτήματ' οὐ πλούτου βάρος;   5
ποῖός τις οὖν τύραννος ἢ ποῖος κριτὴς
ἢ νομοθέτης ἀρχαῖος ἐνδίκως ἐρεῖ

ANONYMOUS

Pellaean [a] is my family : may I be set in the crowded
market-place, unwinding in both hands a book.[b] Yet
on the nightingale's [c] cheek there are the floods of
mourning ; I sit in darkness, and warm tears I shed,
and I make moan, yes, my own lips . . . So none
must shed a tear ; no, I am fain in old age to go the
mystic path to Rhadamanthys, missed by my people
and all the community, on my feet without a stick to
support me, sure of speech, among the throng, leav-
ing to my children my house and my happiness.

[a] Macedonian, from Pella, the royal seat.   [b] The poet
desires that his statue, as a poet, book in hand, may be
erected.   [c] *i.e.* the songster (himself).

ANONYMOUS

MORAL FABLE   [140–141 A.D.]

*popular at this era, represented by the fables of Babrius,
maxims of Menander, extracts from Hesiod, sayings of wise
men, etc. After the end of our fragment there doubtless
followed the reply of Anacharsis—a philosophic maxim pre-
ferring the simple life to luxury, piety to pride.*

A FATHER once took his son, who was wealthy but
refused him any gift at all, to Scythian Anacharsis
for judgement. The son, unwilling to keep his father,
cried : " Has he not a house and properties and loads
of gold ?   What tyrant, then, what judge or ancient
lawgiver will justly say . . . ?

* * * * *

4 ὁ υἱὸς τοῦτον μὴ θέλων τρέφειν Π, corr. D. L. P. (or perhaps
simply οὐ for μή).

LITERARY PAPYRI

ANONYMOUS

116   [4 A.D.]   MORAL MAXIMS

Ed. pr. *Jouguet-Perdrizet, *Studien zur Palaeografie und Papyruskunde, herausgegeben von C. Wessely*, vi., Leipzig, 1906, p. 158. Republished by Collart, *Les Papyrus Bouriant*, Paris, 1926, no. 1, p. 17, literature quoted p. 18.

(1)   ἀρχὴ μεγίστη τοῦ φρονεῖν τὰ γράμματα.
(2)   γέροντα τίμα τοῦ θεοῦ τὴν εἰκόνα.
(3)   ἔρως ἁπάντων τῶν θεῶν παλαίτατος.
(4)   κάλλιστά φημι χρημάτων τὰ κτήματα.
(5)   λαβὼν πάλιν δός, ἵνα λάβῃς ὅταν θέλῃς.
(6)   ὁ νοῦς ἐν ἡμῖν μαντικώτατος θεός.
(7)   πατὴρ ὁ θρέψας κοὐχ ὁ γεννήσας πατήρ.
(8)   σῶσον σεαυτὸν ἐκ πονηρῶν πραγμάτω(ν).
(9)   χάριν φίλοις εὔκαιρον ἀπόδος ἐν μέρει.
(10)   ὦ τῶν ἁπάντων χρημάτων πλείστη χάρις.

---

[a] *Cf. γνώμ. μονόστ.* 317.   [b] *Cf. γνώμ. μονόστ.* 452, and Wilhelm Busch's " Vater werden ist nicht schwer; Vater sein dagegen sehr."

ANONYMOUS

EPITAPHS FOR EUPREPIUS, BY
117   [3 A.D.]   HIS DAUGHTER

Ed. pr. *T. L. *Papiri Greci e Latini*, i. 1912, no. 17, p. 35. See Körte, *Archiv*, vii. 124.

A series of epitaphs written for one Euprepius, apparently by his daughter. Euprepius is described as a tall man, distinguished in service of state and court. He was wealthy,

476

ANONYMOUS

MORAL MAXIMS [4 A.D.]

Ten of 24 monostich sententiae (the other fourteen were already known to us) : from a schoolboy's copybook.

(1) Letters are the first and foremost guide to understanding.

(2) Honour the agèd man : he is the image of your god.

(3) Love is the oldest of all the gods.

(4) Possessions, I say, are the fairest things of all.

(5) Receiving, give again : that you may receive whenever you will.[a]

(6) Our mind is our greatest god of divination.

(7) Father is he who rears, not he who begets.[b]

(8) Your own hand must rescue you from evil estate.

(9) Render a timely service back to your friends in turn.

(10) O gratitude, most abundant of all riches !

ANONYMOUS

EPITAPHS FOR EUPREPIUS, BY HIS DAUGHTER [3 A.D.]

and is alleged to have been wise. His daughter may have had these pieces composed by a professional poet : however that may be, the epitaphs, though uninspired, are tolerably free from technical flaws. They imitate the style of the " Ionic " epigram at Alexandria :—direct, simple phrases, pointed conclusion. Here and there emerges something original and

477

powerful, e.g. *the phrase* ἐν μακάρων ἀγοραῖς (*here only*), **cf.** *the adaptation of Callimachus's* θνήισκειν μὴ λέγε τοὺς ἀγαθούς

(1)   ἀγ]γέλλει τὸ σχῆμα κ(αὶ) ἴ[νδαλμ'] οὐ
      βραχὺν ἄνδρα·
      τοῦτο γ[. . .]ου[. . . . .]δρυ[. . . .]η
      θυγά[τηρ·
      ἀλλὰ διαρρήδην ἐπισημ[ότατον] καὶ ἄριστον
      ὄλβωι καὶ πλού[τωι], τοὔνομα δ' Εὐ-
      πρέπιον.

(2)   ἐνθάδε μὲν κεῖται τῆς εἰκ[όνος] ἡ γραφὴ
      αὕτη
      Εὐπρεπίου· ψυχὴ δ' ἐν μακάρων ἀγο-
      ραῖς.
      οὐ γάρ πω τοιοῦτος ἀνήλυθεν εἰς Ἀχέροντα·
      τῶν ὁσίων ἀνδρῶν Ἠλύσιον τὸ τέλος·
      ἔνθα διατρίβειν ἔλαχεν πάλαι ἔκ τινος
      ἐσθλῆς   5
      μοίρης· οὐδὲ θανεῖν τοὺς ἀγαθοὺς λέ-
      γεται.

(3)   τόνδ' ἐσορᾶις, ὦ ξεῖνε, τὸν ὄλβιον ἀνέρα
      κεῖνον,
      τ(ὸν) σοφὸν Εὐπρέ[π]ιον καὶ βασιλεῦσι
      φίλον.
      ἡ θυγάτηρ δ' ἀνέθηκε τάδε θρεπτήρια δοῦσα
      καὶ φθιμένωι· χάριτος δ' οὐδὲν ἔλειψεν
      ἐμοί.

(4)   εἰ καὶ μὴ φωνὴν ὁ ζωιγράφος ὧδ' ἐνέθηκεν,
      εἶπες ἂν ὡς ἤδη φθέγγεται Εὐπρέπιος·
      εἰ γάρ τις παριὼν τῆς εἰκόνος ἐγγύθεν ἔλθοι,
      οὔατα παρθήσει ὥσπερ ἀκουσόμενος.

*in 2, 6 ; cf. too the attempt—not altogether unsuccessful—
at an immortal verse in* τῶν ὁσίων ἀνδρῶν Ἠλύσιον τὸ τέλος : *
an essay in Ionic wit in* οὐ βραχὺν ἄνδρα (which has a
double meaning).*

(1) The form and figure proclaim him no small
man, . . . daughter . . . but the very best and
brightest in prosperity and wealth ; and his name,
Euprepius.

(2) Here is set up the painting of the likeness of
Euprepius ; but his soul is in the gatherings of the
Blessed. Never yet went such a man to Acheron :
for holy men, Elysium is the end. To live there was
the lot he won of old from some blessed Destiny.
And it is said that good men do not die.

(3) Here, stranger, you behold that happy man,
Euprepius the wise, the friend even of kings. His
daughter made this dedication, even to the dead
repaying her debt of nurture : I was not found
wanting in gratitude.

(4) Even though the painter has not placed in him
a voice, still you would have said that Euprepius is
speaking now. For if a passer-by should come near
the portrait, he will give ear as though about to
hear.

---

(2) 2 Punctuation after Εὐπρεπίου and δ' after ψυχὴ from
the interlinear alternative mentioned below. (4) 1 μὴ
D. L. P. : τὴν Π (which is nonsense). Possibly οὐκ (or οὐδ')
for ὧδ', retaining τὴν (Roberts).
Interlinear *variae lectiones* occur in Π in the following
places :—(2) 2 Εὐπρεπίωι· ψυχὴ δ'. (3) 2 . . . πάντων
ἁψάμενον γεράων is the text : here, following ed. pr., I have
printed the *v.l.* (3) 4 πᾶσαν τὴν χάριν ὧδ' ἀπέχω.

(5) Εὐ]πρέπιος μὲν ἐγών, ὁ δὲ νήπιός ἐστι
     [θυγα]τρὸς

(6) ο]ὐ γὰρ ἐν ἀνθρώποισιν ἐὼν ἐβάδιζεν ἐκείνην
     τὴν ὁδὸν ἣν ἀρετῆς οὐκ ἐκάθηρε θέμις·
     ἔνθεν ἐς ἀθανάτους καὶ ἀείζωο[ν] βίον ἦλθεν,
     τοῦτο τὸ μοχθηρὸν σῶμ' ἀποδυσάμενος.

(5) 1 ὅδε δ' ἔκγονός ἐστι.   (6) 3 τοὔνεκα ῥηιδίως.

ANONYMOUS

(5) Euprepius am I; the little one is my daughter's . . .

(6) When he was among men, he trod not that path which the law of Virtue has not purified. Wherefore he departed to heaven and immortality, putting off this offending flesh.

---

(6) 4 ἄσμενος οὐλομένην ὠσάμενος γενεήν and (alternative to σῶμ' ἀποδυσάμενος only) φῦλον ἀπευξάμενος.

HEXAMETER POEMS

ΠΑΝΥΑΣΙΣ

118   [2 A.D.]   ΗΡΑΚΛΗΙΣ

Ed. pr. *Grenfell-Hunt, *P. Oxy.* ii. 1899, no. 221, col. ix.

πῶς δ' ἐπορεύθης ῥεῦμ' Ἀχελωίου ἀργυροδίνα,
Ὠκεανοῦ ποταμοῖο δι' εὐρέος ὑγρὰ κέλευθα;

.   .   .   .   .   .

ANONYMOUS

119   [2–1 B.C.]   FRAGMENT

Ed. pr. Aly, *Sitzungsberichte der Heidelberger Akademie der Wissenschaften,* v. 1914, Abh. 2, p. 1.   See *Powell, *Collectanea Alexandrina,* 251 ; Maas, *Gnomon,* 1927, 692.

Fragment of an hexameter poem of uncertain date and subject.   The Epic Cycle is probably excluded by reason of

ὡς δ' ἁλιεὺς ἀκτῆι ἐν ἁλιρράντωι ἐπὶ πέτρηι
ἀγ(κ)ίστρου ἕλικος δελεουχίδα μάστακ' ἀείρας

.   .   .   .   .

(Fragments of two more lines)

2 δ' ἕλικος Π.   τελιουχίδα Π, corr. Powell.

PANYASIS

HERACLES [2 A.D.]

8-11, p. 64. See Wilamowitz, *G.G.A.* 1900, 42 ; *Powell, *Collect. Alexandr.* p. 248.

How did you come to the stream of Achelous's silver eddies, through the watery ways of the broad river Ocean ?

.　　.　　.　　.　　.　　.

ANONYMOUS

FRAGMENT [2–1 B.C.]

such a word as δελεουχίδα (*or* τελιουχίδα) : *the relation to Homer is closer than would be expected in an Hellenistic poem. Antimachus and his 4th-century posterity are possible authors : but the evidence is too meagre to permit a definite conclusion.*

LIKE a fisherman on a rock on the sea-washed shore, lifting the enticing bait of his curved hook . . .

.　　.　　.　　.　　.

(Fragments of two more lines)

ΗΡΙΝΝΑ

120   [1 B.C.]   ΑΛΑΚΑΤΑ

Ed. pr. Vitelli-Norsa, *Papiri Greci e Latini*, ix. 1929, no. 1090, p. 137, Plate IV. See Maas, *Hermes*, 69, 1934, 206 ; Vitelli, *Gnomon*, 1928, 455 and 1929, 172 and 288 ; Körte, *Archiv*, x. 21 ; Bowra, *New Chapters*, iii. 180 and **Greek Poetry and Life*, p. 325 (*qu. v.* for full discussion).

This beautiful fragment is part of Erinna's Distaff, ᵃ

                         ἐς βαθ]ὺ κῦμα
λε]υκᾶν μαινομέν[οισιν ἐσάλαο π]οσσὶν ἀφ' ἵ[π]πω[ν·
ἀλ]λ', ἴσ[χ]ω, μέγ' ἄυσα, φ[ίλα. τὺ δ' ἔοισα]
    χελύννα
ἀλ]λομένα μεγάλας [ἔδραμες κατὰ] χορτίον αὐλᾶς.
τα]ῦτα τύ, Βαῦκι τάλαι[να, βαρὺ στονα]χεῖσα γόημ[ι· 5
τα]ῦτά μοι ἐν κρα[δίαι τεῦς, ὦ κό]ρα, ἴχνια κεῖται
θέρμ' ἔτι· τὴν[α δ' ἃ πρὶν ποκ' ἐπα]ύρομες ἄν-
    θρακες ἤδη.
δαγύ[δ]ων τ' ἐχ[όμεσθα νεαν]ίδες ἐν θαλάμοισι
νύμ[φαι]σιν [προσόμοιοι ἀκηδ]έες· ἅ τε πὸτ ὄρθρον
μάτηρ, ἃ ἔ[ριον νέμεν ἀμφιπόλ]οισιν ἐρίθοις,   10
τήνα σ' ἦλθ[ε κρέας προκαλευμέ]να ἀμφ' ἁλίπαστον.
αἳ μικραῖς τ[όκα νῶιν ὅσον] φόβον ἄγαγε Μο[ρμ]ώ,
τᾶ]ς ἐν μὲν κο[ρυφᾶι μεγάλ' ὤ]ατα, ποσσὶ δ' ἐφοίτη
τέ]τρασιν, ἐκ δ' [ἑτέρας ἑτέραν] μετεβάλλετ'
    ὀπωπάν.

6 τεῦς, ὦ κόρα D. L. P., *cf.* Theocr. xi. 25.

ᵃ The paragraph refers to the game described by Pollux ix. 125 : one girl (called the Tortoise) sat among others and spoke with them in alternate lines. At the end of the last line the Tortoise leapt up and tried to catch, or touch, one

ERINNA

THE DISTAFF   [1 B.C.]

poem written in sorrow for the death of Baucis, a friend of her girlhood. Erinna herself is said to have died at the age of nineteen : and this poem, which (according to Suidas) consisted of 300 hexameters, was perhaps her only published work.

. . . From white horses with madcap bound into the deep wave you leapt : " I catch you," I shouted, " my friend ! " And you, when you were Tortoise, ran leaping through the yard of the great court.[a]

Thus I lament, unhappy Baucis, and make deep moan for you. These traces of you, dear maid, lie still glowing in my heart : all that we once enjoyed, is embers now.

We clung to our dolls in our chambers when we were girls, playing Young Wives, without a care. And towards dawn your Mother,[b] who allotted wool to her attendant workwomen, came and called you to help with the salted meat. Oh, what a trembling the Bogy brought us then, when we were little ones ! —On its head were huge ears, and it walked on all fours, and changed from one face to another !

of the others—who would then take her turn as Tortoise. The last two lines are given by Pollux as : (Girls) ὁ δ' ἔκγονός σου τί ποῖων ἀπώλετο ; (Tortoise) λευκᾶν ἀφ' ἵππων εἰς θάλασσαν ἅλατο " from white horses into the sea he *leapt* " (on the last word the Tortoise leaps up) : hence the first line here.
[b] I suspect that the " Mother " here and below (v. 16) is Erinna herself, playing " Mothers and Children " with Baucis : the " attendant toilers " would be a row of dolls, or imaginary. Both references to " Mother " seem thus more charming and apter to their contexts.

487

LITERARY PAPYRI

ἀνίκα δ' ἐς [λ]έχος [ἀνδρὸς ἔβας, τ]όκα πάντ'
    ἐλέλασο   15
ἄσσ' ἔτι νηπιάσα[σα] τ[εᾶς παρὰ] ματρὸς ἄκουσας,
Β]αῦκι φίλα· λάθα[ν ἄρ'] ἔ[νὶ φρεσὶ θῆκ'] Ἀφροδίτα.
τῶ τυ κατακλαίοισα τὰ [κάδεα νῦν] παραλείπω·
οὐ [γ]άρ μοι πόδες [ἐντὶ λιπῆν] ἄπο δῶμα βέβαλοι,
οὐδ' ἐσιδῆν φάε[σσι πρέπει νε]κυν οὐδὲ γοᾶσαι 20
γυμναῖσιν χαίταισιν, [ἀτὰρ φο]ινίκεος αἰδὼς
δρύπτει μ' ἀμφι . . [

. . . .

ΕΥΦΟΡΙΩΝ

121 [(a) Parchment 5 A.D.]   **THREE FRAGMENTS**
     [(b) Papyrus 1–2 A.D.]

Ed. pr. (a) *Schubart-Wilamowitz, *Berliner Klassikertexte*,
v. 1. 1907, p. 57. See Schubart, *Pap. Graec. Berol.*, Plate
43 b, Text xxx.; Wilamowitz, *Hermes*, 63, 1928, 376; Scheid-
weiler, *Euphorionis Fragmenta*, diss. Bonn, 1908, frr. 62,
95; Körte, *Archiv*, v. 536; Powell, *Collect. Alex.* pp. 31, 40
and *New Chapters*, i. 110; Ludwich, *Phil. Woch.* 1907, 490;
Morel, *Phil. Woch.* 1927; Robert, *Hermes*, 42, 508. (b)
Vitelli-Norsa, *Annali della reale Scuola normale superiore di
Pisa*, II. iv. 1935, p. 3. See Maas, *Gnomon*, xi. 1935, 102;
Lobel, *Riv. di Fil.* xiii. 1935, 67; Latte, *Philol.* 90, 1935,
129; Cazzaniga, *Rend. Ist. Lomb.* 68, 1935, fasc. xi-xv;
Körte, *Archiv*, xiii. 1938, 84; Pfister, *Phil. Woch.* 55, 1935,
1357.

A further fragment of Euphorion (one line) was recovered
from Didymus's commentary on Demosthenes by Wilamo-
witz, *Hermes*, *61*, *p. 289.*

    (a) *1. The conclusion of a passage concerned with the*

But when you went to a man's bed, you forgot all
that you heard from your Mother, dear Baucis, in
babyhood: Aphrodite set oblivion in your heart.
So I lament you, yet neglect your obsequies *a*—my
feet are not so profane as to leave the house, my eyes
may not behold a body dead, nor may I moan with
hair unbound, yet a blush of shame distracts me . . .

. . . .

a Probably, as Bowra suggests, Erinna was " a priestess
or a devotee of some cult which forbade her to look on dead
bodies." ἀτὰρ v. 21 proposed by Beazley.

EUPHORION

THREE FRAGMENTS $\quad\begin{bmatrix}(a)\text{ Parchment 5 A.D.}\\(b)\text{ Papyrus 1-2 A.D.}\end{bmatrix}$

*labours of Heracles, especially the bringing of Cerberus
from Hades.*

2. Perhaps from the Ἀραὶ ἢ Ποτηριοκλέπτης; *in which,
as in our fragment, the robbed complainant himself appeared
and cursed the thief (i.e. using the first person), as we learn
from the only hitherto surviving fragment*

ὅστις μευ κελέβην Ἀλυβηΐδα μοῦνος ἀπηύρα (*ed. pr. p. 63*).

(b) *From a roll which contained several poems of Euphorion
arranged in alphabetical order. In fr. i. col. ii. of ed. pr.
is a fragment of a poem entitled* Ἱππ]ομέδων με(ί)ζων (*cf.
frr. 30-31 Powell*): *this perhaps dealt with the adventures of
Odysseus and the Thracian King Poltys (Latte, p. 132;
Serv. Aen. ii. 81, iii. 16). It is preceded in* Π *by fragments
of the* Thrax, *which included the stories of Clymenus and*

*Harpalyce (Parthenius xiii.) and of Apriate and Trambelus
(Parthenius xxvi.).   The extant portions of the former story
refer to the metamorphosis of Harpalyce into a bird (the*
χαλκίς) ἑτέροισιν ἀπεχθομένην ὄρνισι, *and the suicide of
Clymenus, who, because of the terrible banquet* (ἀεικέος
αἴκλου), *died on his own sword* (ἑῶι θάνεν ἀμφὶ σιδήρωι).
*The scene of the second story is Lesbos.   Where our frag-
ment begins, Apriate is scornfully rejecting the advances of
enamoured Trambelus.   Then she leaps into the sea : it is
uncertain whether she is rescued by dolphins or not.   There-
after begins the story of Trambelus's death at the hands of
Achilles.   Finally the moral is pointed at some length :—
that Justice always pays in the end ; this conclusion is
supported briefly by two more instances from mythology.*

*Since my text contains some new readings, derived from a
study of a photograph, I prefix the following notes.   My debt
to Mr. Lobel is very great.*

V. 4. ακτωρ (*the reading is certain*) *has so far defied inter-
pretation.   There is no evidence that the word can mean
" suitor," and its usual sense seems irrelevant here.   I have
written the word as a proper name, but it remains as obscure
as before.   Leipephile, who was the daughter of Iolaus and
wife of Phylas (Hesiod fr. 142), has no connexion in our
tradition with anyone named Actor.*

*Apart from this difficulty, the sense of the passage as a
whole is not very clear.   It looks as though Apriate is taunt-
ing Trambelus while refusing to yield to his passion : " Go
and court a Leipephile, or marry a Semiramis—you will
never marry me ! "—Why should she advise him thus ?   The
sense may be " I hope that you may make a disastrous
marriage " : for Semiramis notoriously slew her lovers the
next morning* (Diodorus ii. 13. 4 πάντων τῶν εἰς τρυφὴν
ἀνηκόντων ἀπολαύσασα, γῆμαι μὲν νομίμως οὐκ ἠθέλησεν, εὐλα-
βουμένη μή ποτε στερηθῆι τῆς ἀρχῆς, ἐπιλεγομένη δὲ τῶν
στρατιωτῶν τοὺς εὐπρεπείαι διαφέροντας, τούτοις ἐμίσγετο, καὶ

πάντας τοὺς αὐτῆι πλησιάσαντας ἠφάνιζε).   *How Leipephile*
fits into such a context we cannot tell, though it is easy
enough to guess.   Her name is known to Hesiod : it was
therefore not originally a nomen ex facto, *a nickname*
given because she " left her lovers " ; but an Euphorion
may, for his own purpose, have chosen so to interpret her
name—though no such interpretation is necessary, if the
story of Actor's courting of Leipephile was in itself a record
of a disastrous suit.

But I admit that I leave this part almost, if not quite, as
obscure as I found it.

V. 5.   At the end of the line, ἀγκάσσαιτο (*suggested to me*
by Mr. Lobel) is almost entirely legible in the photograph.
αὐτὴ ἕλοιτο *ed. pr.,* ἀγκὰς ἕλοιτο *Latte : in both,* ἕλοιτο
should be ἕλοι.

V. 7. ΠΟΔΙΚΡΑΤΕΟΙΤΕ . . Ε . . . *is the reading of the*
text. (ἀ)πο δικρατεί τάμοι ἔγχει *Latte : but* ἀποτέμνειν τινά
is not a convincing phrase here, and the a *and* o *of* τάμοι *are*
hardly to be reconciled with the traces in the text.   Read
ποδὶ κροτέοι τε[θν]ε[ῶτα (κροτέοι *Lobel) " stamp your corpse*
with her foot."   For the sense and construction of κροτέω
cf. Eur. Ba. *188* γῆν θύρσωι κροτεῖν.

V. 8. ἢ ν[ύ το]ι (*Latte) is definitely too long for the space.*
ν[έον] (*Lobel) is clearly best.   At the end of the line, Lobel's*
ὧ κ[υνάπαι]δες *fits the traces very well, and is indeed mostly*
legible (the π *in the middle is far more probable than* ν,
otherwise κυνάναιδες *might seem the preferable reading.*
For κυνάπαιδες, *see Norsa-Vitelli in* Stud. It. Fil. *x. 121,*
249.)

V. 9. ἢ δ' [ὅτε] *ed. pr. and Latte.   But the* δ *is almost*
certainly κ, *and* οτε *is too long for the gap.   Read* ἦ, κ[αὶ]
" she spoke, and . . ."

V. 13. α[.]ορδ[.]ν *seems certain.   Unless* ἀφόρδιον *is*
relevant, no known word seems to fit.   I can only suggest
ἀ[μ]ορδ[ή]ν. ἀμορδή, *" deprivation," related to* ἀμέρδομαι *as*

πορδή to πέρδομαι. *For the rhythm* cf. (a) 2, 11 above, γυναικῶν ἐμπελάτειρα.

Latte's view, that the poet is saying " the dolphins did not rescue her," seems to me improbable. The connexion of vv. 13-14 is very obscure. It is likely enough that αὖθις . . . αὖθι δὲ . . . are co-ordinated : but the evidence fails us here altogether. (Perhaps the sense was : " dolphins rescued her, so we may sing again (or hereafter) the escape of Apriate from the sea, and sing again (or hereafter) the fate of Trambelus, etc.")

V. 21. τὸ γρήιον, τι γρήιον, τε γρήιον edd. *The first iota is certain. The word is, as Lobel first printed it,* τιγρήιον :

(a) (1)

(*Fragments of four lines*)

οἱ δ᾽ ὄπιθεν λασίῃ ὑπὸ γαστέρι πεπ[τηῶτες
οὐραῖοι λιχμῶντο περὶ πλευρῇσι δρά[κοντες.
ἐν καί οἱ βλεφάροις κυάνωι ἠστράπτετο
    [πέμφιξ·
ἤ που Θερμάστραις ἤ που Μελιγουνίδι τοῖαι
μαρμαρυγαί, αἴρησιν ὅτε ῥήσσοιτο σίδηρος, 5
ἠέρ᾽ ἀναθρώσκουσι, βοᾷ δ᾽ εὐήλατος ἄκμων,
ἤ Αἴτνην ψολόεσσαν, ἐναύλιον Ἀστερόποιο.
ἵκετο μὴν Τίρυνθα παλιγκότωι Εὐρυσθῆι
ζωὸς ὑπὲξ Ἀίδαο δυώδεκα λοῖσθος ἀέθλων,
καί μιν ἐνὶ τριόδοισι πολυκρίθοιο Μιδείης 10
ταρβαλέαι σὺν παισὶν ἐθηήσαντο γυναῖκες.

(2)
                                   ] ὄπισθε
                              ]α φέροιτο
                    αὐτό]θι κάππεσε λύχνου
                    ]α κατὰ Γλαυκώπιον Ἔρσηι

(a) (1) 3 Suppl. Wilam. *Hermes, l.c.*: ἠστράπτετο[ν ὄσσε Schubart.   (2) 3 αὐτόθι Roberts.

this piece was written soon after the first tiger was brought to Alexandria.

Vv. 24-25. The transitive use of ἀγηνορέω occurs nowhere else, but is unavoidable here. The sense is " who treat with arrogance their feeble parents, having dismissed with scorn (στύξαντες : edd. ignore the tense) the advice of the living and the dead."—The advice of the living and the dead is the wise counsel of present and past poets and moralizers, who exhort men to love and respect their parents. [There can be no truth in a view which equates the " living and dead " with the parents of v. 24 : for (1) it cannot be done grammatically, (2) the parents are not dead (v. 24, they are feeble, but still alive), (3) what advice do dead parents give ?]

V. 32. [θ]ῆρ Lobel. The corpse of Comaetho was doubtless thrown to the dogs and vultures.

(a) (1)

(Fragments of four lines)

Behind, under his shaggy belly cowering, the serpents that were his tail darted their tongues about his ribs. Within his eyes, a beam flashed darkly. Truly in the Forges or in Meligunis[a] leap such sparks into the air, when iron is beaten with hammers, and the anvil roars beneath mighty blows,—or up inside smoky Etna, lair of Asteropus. Still, he[b] came alive to Tiryns out of Hades, the last of twelve labours, for the pleasure of malignant Eurystheus ; and at the crossways of Mideia, rich in barley, trembling women with their children looked upon him . . .

(2) (Vv. 4 sqq.) . . . to Hersa[c] at the Glaucopium,

[a] Lipara. [b] Cerberus. [c] Hersa and Aglauros threw themselves to death from the Athenian acropolis, being maddened after opening the basket in which lay Erichthonius, the nursling of Athena.

493

οὕνεκ' 'Αθ]ηναίης ἱερὴν ἀνελύσατο κίστην 5
. . . . .]ης. ἢ ὅσσον ὁδοιπόροι ἐρρήσσοντο
Σκε]ίρων ἔνθα πόδεσσιν ἀεικέα μήδετο
χύτλα
ο]ὐκ ἐπὶ δήν· Αἴθρης γὰρ ἀλοιηθεὶς ὑπὸ παιδὶ
νωιτέρης χέλυος πύματος (ἐ)λιπήνατο λαιμόν.
ἢ καί νιν σφεδανοῖο τανυσσαμένη ἀπὸ τόξου 10
Ταιναρίη λοχίῃσι γυναικῶν ἐμπελάτειρα
Ἄρτεμις ὠδίνεσσιν ἑῶι ταλάωρι μετάσποι.
ὀκχοίη δ' 'Αχέροντι βαρὺν λίθον 'Ασκα-
λάφοιο,
τόν οἱ χωσαμένη γυίοις ἐπιήραρε Δηώ,
μαρτυρίην ὅτι μοῦνος ἐθήκατο Φερσεφο-
νείηι. 15

(b)   ] κενεον μετὰ λέκτρον ἵκοιο.
ἀ]λλὰ σύ γ' 'Ακ . . δ . . ν δαίσα[ις] γάμο-
[ν . .]εφ . [. .]ρος
ἢ Ἰφικλείδαο δαιθρασέος 'Ιολάου
Ἄκτωρ Λειπεφίλην θ[α]λ[ε]ρὴν μνήσαιο
θύγατρα,
καὶ δέ σ' ἐράσμιο[ν ἄ]νδρα Σεμείραμις
ἀ[γκ]άσσαιτο, 5
ὄφρα [τ]οι εὐ[ό]δμοιο [π]αρὰ πρόδομον
[θ]α[λάμοιο
πα[ρ]θέν[ιον χ]αρίεντα ποδὶ κροτέοι τε-
[θν]ε[ῶτα.
ἢ ν[έον] 'Απριάτη(ι) [τ]εύξω γάμον, ὦ
κ[υνάπαι]δες.
ἢ, κ[αὶ] Τραμβήλοιο λέχος Τελαμωνιάδαο
εἰς ἅλα δειμήνασα κα[τ' αἰ]γίλιπος θόρε
πέτρ[ης. 10

EUPHORION

because she opened the sacred coffer of Athene: or as
wanderers were dashed to pieces, where Sciron in-
vented an unnatural washing for his feet,—but not for
long: crushed by the son of Aethra,[a] he was himself
the last to fatten the gullet of our [b] tortoise: or may
Taenarian [c] Artemis, who comes to women in their
pangs of travail, stretch her violent bow and reach
him [d] with her shaft therefrom: and on the Acheron
may he bear the heavy boulder of Ascalaphus,[e] which
Demeter in her anger fastened upon his limbs, be-
cause he alone bore witness against Persephone. . . .

(b) " . . . may you come to a . . . bed. Go, cele-
brate a wedding with . . . or like Actor woo some
fair Leipephile, daughter of Iolaus the warrior son
of Iphicles. Or may a Semiramis embrace you, her
pretty husband, that on the threshold of her fragrant
boudoir she may trample the corpse of her charming
bridegroom. Now, shameless wretch, a new sort of
wedding [f] will I make for Apriate!"

She spoke; and for terror of the bed of Trambelus,
son of Telamon, leapt from a steep rock into the sea.

---

[a] Theseus.   [b] Euphorion *may* be speaking: for
Megaris τῆς Ἀθηναίων ἦν τὸ ἀρχαῖον (Paus. i. 39. 4), *cf.* Hellad.
ap. Phot. *bibl.* 532, 18 (Körte).   [c] Perhaps simply
"Lacedaemonian" (Artemis Orthia).   [d] Or *her.*
[e] See Apollod. i. 5. 3.   [f] *i.e.* "I will marry *Death*"
(or "*the Sea*").

(a) (2) ὁ δεσποίν]ης K. F. W. Schmidt, too long for space
(five letters), acc. to Wilam. and Schubart.   (b) 1 κε νέον
or κενεόν.   2 Ακ . . δ . ων ed. pr.: but δ . ον seems just
as likely.   5 ἁ[γκ]άσσαιτο Lobel.   7 κρατεοι Π,
corr. Lobel: τε[θν]ε[ῶτα D. L. P.   8 νέον, τεύξω,
κυνάπαιδες Lobel.   9 ἤ, κ[αὶ] D. L. P.

495

. . .] μ[ιν ἔ]τι πνείο[υσαν
δελφῖνες [π]ηγοῖο δ[ι' ὕδ]ατος ἐγκονέεσκον
αὖθις ἵν' ἀεί[δ]ωμεν α[.]ορδ[.]ν ἰχθύσι [
αὖθι δὲ Τραμβήλοι[ο μ]όρον Ἀχιλῆι δ[α-
μέντος
ξεινοφόν[15

*(Fragments of sixteen lines, followed by a gap of
about eight lines)*

Πα[νδ]ώρη κακόδ[ωρ]ος ἑκούσι[ον] ἀνδράσιν
ἄλγ[ος.
Ἄ]ρ[ης] νωμήσειεν ἑῶι ἐπίχειρα ταλάντωι,
αὖτις δὲ κρυόεντος ἐρωήσας πολέμοιο
Εἰρήνην πολύβοιαν ἐπ' ἀνέρας ἰθύσειεν,
ἐν δ' ἀγορῆι στή[σ]αιτο Θέμιν, τιμωρὸν ἑάων, 20
σὺν δὲ Δίκην ἥ τ' ὦκα τιγρήιον ἴχνος
ἀεί[ρ]ει,
σκυζομένη μετὰ ἔργα τέων τ' ἐπιδέρ(κ)εται
ἀ]νδρῶ[ν,
οἵ ῥα θεοὺς ἐρέθωσι, παρὰ ῥήτρας δ' ἀγά-
γωντ[αι
ἠ]πεδανοὺς ἢ ο[ἵ] κεν ἀγη[ν]ορέωσι τοκῆας,
[σ]τύξαντες ζώων τε παραιφάσιάς τε καμόν-
[των,   25
ἤ]τοι ξείνια δόρπα Διός τ' ἀλίτωσι τράπεζαν.
οὔ κεν ὁ κουφότατος ἀνέμων ἄλληκτον
ἀέ[ντων
ῥε[ῖα φύ]γοι λαιψηρὰ Δίκης ὅτε γούνατ'
ὅρηται.
οὐ γάρ κ' ἔ[ν] νήσοισιν Ἐχινάσιν ἐσκίμψαντο

(b) 11 οὔ] μ[ιν Latte: but it is not improbable that they *did*
rescue her. *Cf.* Propertius ii. 26. 17 delphinum currere vidi.

EUPHORION

And . . . dolphins hastened through the dark waters
(to rescue) her still alive ; that we might sing here-
after [a] . . . and hereafter [a] the fate of Trambelus,
vanquished by Achilles . . .

*(Fragments of sixteen lines, followed by a gap of
about eight lines)*

. . . Pandora, donor of evil, man's sorrow self-
imposed. Ares allot them their wages in his scales,
and rest again from chilling warfare, and send
Peace with her Prosperity to men ! And in the
market let him set Themis up, requiter of good deeds :
and, beside her, Justice, who leaps up like a tiger at
once in anger at the deeds of men upon whom she
looks—even them who provoke the gods and turn
their commandments aside, and such as treat their
feeble parents with arrogance, scorning the counsel
of the living and the dead ; or sin against the hospit-
able feast and the table of Zeus. The lightest of
winds that blow unceasing could not easily escape the
swift knees of Justice when up she leaps. Never in
the island Echinades had the companions of Cephalus [b]

[a] Or, " again."   [b] Amphitryon, accompanied by the
Athenian Cephalus, led an expedition against the Taphians
and Teleboans. Alcmena (later, wife of Amph.) would
marry nobody but the avenger of her brothers, who were
killed in conflict with the Teleboans while these were driving
the cattle of Electryon (father of Alcmena) out of the Argolis.
The name *Teleboans* suggests that they got " cattle from afar."

13 ? ἀμορδήν.   14 Τραμβήλο[υ πρόμ]ορον Latte, too long.
22 ΤΕΩΝΤΕΠΙΕ̂ΣΤΑ[Π. ἐπιδέρκεται (Lobel, Latte) is the
only plausible restoration so far suggested. τέων = ὦν Callim.
fr. 9, 60 Pf.   25 πτύξαντες looks impossible, στύξαντες is
probable : τεύξαντες was not in Π, but τ(ε)ύξαντες is just
possible. παραφφασίας Π. θανόν[των Π, with καμ written
above θαν.   27 οὔ, 28 ῥεῖα φύγοι Lobel.

LITERARY PAPYRI

οι . [. .] νε[ῶ]ν Κεφάλοιο καὶ 'Αμφιτρύωνος
  ἀμο[ρβοί,   30
ἔκ [τε] τρίχα χρυσέην κόρσης ὤλοιψε Κο-
  μ[αιθὼ
πα[τρ]ὸς ἑοῦ, ὡς [θ]ῆρ ἄταφος τάφος εἷο
  πέλοιτο,
εἰ μὴ [λ]ῃιδίῃσι γύας ἐτάμοντο βόεσσι
Τηλεβόαι, διὰ πόντον ἀπ' 'Αρσίνοιο μο-
  [λόντες·
οὐδ[. . . . . .]μα . . . ες ἐπεφράσσαντο νέ[εσθαι 35
τέτ[μον τ'] ἐν βοτάνῃσιν 'Αχαιΐδος ἴχ[νια
  μόσχου,
εἰ μὴ . . [.] . ια . ρ . . θεν ἐκείρατο δούρα[τ
οὕνεκ[α] τὸν μὲν ἔολπα κακώτερα γῆ[ς ὕπο
  πράσσειν,
ὃς σέο λ[αυ]κανίην ἡμάξατο, κάμμορ[
σοὶ δ' [ὀλίγ]ὴ μὲν γαῖα, πολὺς δ' ἐπικείσε[ται
  αἶνος.   40
χ[αίροις, εἰ] ἐτεόν τι πέλει καὶ ἐν "Αιδι
  χ[άρμα.

. . . . . .

(b) 30 ὅι Π.   32 θῆρ Lobel.   *Cf.* Catullus 64. 83 funera

ANONYMOUS

122   [2 A.D.]   OLD WOMAN'S LAMENT

Ed. pr. *Grenfell-Hunt, *P. Oxy.* xv. 1921, no. 1794, p. 110.
See Powell, *Collectanea Alexandrina*, p. 78 and *New Chapters*,
ii. 45 ; Körte, *Archiv*, vii. 117 ; Schmidt, *G.G.A.* 1924, 9 ;
498

ANONYMOUS

and Amphitryon pressed on their vessel's . . ., nor
had Comaetho [a] cut the golden hair from her father's
temple, that a wild beast might be her monstrous tomb
—had not the Teleboans cleft the field with stolen oxen,
coming over the sea from Arsinus [b] ; nor would . . .
have thought to go . . . nor found among the pastures
the tracks of that Achaean cow, had not the spear-
point cut [c] . . . Therefore I expect he suffers still
worse below the earth,—he who steeped your throat
in blood, ill-starred. . . .

For you, light shall be the earth and weighty the
praise that will be upon you.   Farewell—if truly in
Hades there is any faring well.

.   .   .   .   .   .

[a] Comaetho, daughter of the Teleboan king Pterelaus,
fell in love with Amphitryon and betrayed her country to
him.   She cut off that lock of her father's hair which rendered
him immortal and his kingdom secure.   Amphitryon
executed Comaetho, instead of rewarding her ; and pre-
sumably threw her body to the dogs and vultures.   [b] A
form of Erasinus, the river near Argos.   [c] Obscure
allusion to some murderer and his companions, who were
driven from their native land, and led by a cow to the place
where they must found a city.

. . . nec funera.   33 ληιδίηισι Maas.   38 πράσσειν
D. L. P.   40-41 Latte.

ANONYMOUS

OLD WOMAN'S LAMENT   [2 A.D.]

Crönert, *Lit. Centralbl.* 73, 1922, 400 ; Morel, *Phil. Woch.*
46, 351.

From a speech by an elderly woman to a youth. She observes the mutability of fortune, and says that she was

φῆ δέ οἱ ἆσσον [ἰοῦσα, τέ]κος τέκο[ς, ο]ὔ σε ἔοικε
δευόμενον τ . . . . . . τόσον παρ[ὰ π]αῖδα νέεσθαι,
τῶι οὐ χεὶρ ὀ[ρ]έ[γ]ειν σῖτ'] ἀρκέε[ι], οὐ[δ]ὲ μὲν αὐδὴ

(Fragments of three lines)

            ] ἐλπωραὶ δ' ἐάγησαν
ἡμετέρης βιοτῆ[ς, αὖ]ον δέ μοι οἶκος ἀυτεῖ.   5
ἄλλοτε γὰρ ἄλλο[ι]ς ὄλβ[ο]υ λάχος ἀνθρώποισιν·
οἵη τοι πεσσοῖο δίκη, το[ὶ]ήδε καὶ ὄλβου·
πεσσ[ὸ]ς ἀμειβόμενος [π]οτὲ μὲν το[ῖς], ἄ]λλοτε τοῖσι[ν
εἰς ἀγαθὸν πίπ[τει] καὶ ἀφνεὸν αἶψα τίθησι
πρόσθεν ἀνολβείοντ', εὐηφενεόντ[α] δ' ἄνολβον·   10
τοῖος διν(η)τῆσι περ[ιστ]ρέφεται πτερύγεσσιν
ὄ]λβος ἐπ' ἀνθρώπους [ἄλ]λον δ' ἐξ ἄλ[λο]υ ὀφέλλει.
ἡ δ' αὐ[τ]ὴ πολέεσσι π[οτὸ]ν καὶ σῖτον ὄρεξα
τὴν ὁράᾳς, ἐπεὶ οὔτι λιπ[ερ]νῆτις πάρος ἦα,
ἔσκε δέ μοι νειὸς βαθυλ[ή]ιος, ἔσκεν ἀ[λ]ωή,   15
πολλὰ δέ μοι μῆλ' ἔσκε, [τ]ὰ μὲν διὰ πάντα κέδασσεν
ἠδ' ὀλοὴ βούβρωστις, ἐγὼ δ' ἀκόμιστο[ς ἀ]λῆτις
ὧ]δέ ποθι πλήθουσαν ἀνὰ πτόλιν ε[. . . ἕ]ρπω

     •   •   •   •   •   •   •

rich once but now is poor. A good composition, by an Alexandrian poet indebted to Callimachus's Hecale *and* Hymn to Demeter *(see ed. pr.).*

SHE went near to him and said : " Son, my son, not to a child should you go . . . in the hour of need ; his hand cannot proffer you food, nor his voice. . . .

(Fragments of three lines)

the hopes of my life are broken, my house rings hollow. The lot of prosperity falls now to one man, now to another ; the way of wealth is as the way of dice—dice bring in turn a lucky throw to-day to one, to-morrow to another, and swiftly make the poor man rich, and the rich man poor. Even thus on wheeling wings prosperity goes up and down among men, and makes first one thrive and then another. I myself, whom you behold, have proffered drink and food to many, for of old I was no outcast : fields of deep corn were mine, and a threshing floor, and many sheep : this fatal famine has made havoc of them all, and I—uncared for, vagabond—creep thus about the crowded city . . .

.   .   .   .   .   .

18 ἐ[ξ ἕω ἕ]ρπω Morel.

LITERARY PAPYRI

ANONYMOUS

123 [3–4 A.D.]   BUCOLIC

Ed. pr. *Oellacher, *Griechische Literarische Papyri*, i. p. 77, 1932 (*Mitteilungen aus der Papyrussammlung der Nationalbibliothek in Wien: Papyrus Erzherzog Rainer, Neue Serie, erste Folge*). See Körte, *Archiv*, xi. 222; Collart, *Rev. Et. Grec.* 46, 1933, 168 (whom I follow in reversing ed. pr.'s order of the two fragments); Powell, *Class. Rev.* 46, 1932, 263 and *New Chapters*, iii. 208.

From a bucolic poem, probably of the Alexandrian era (see Collart, loc. cit.). Vv. 1-23, Pan has lost his pipe: wherefore Silenus approaches and taunts him : in his catalogue of ironic possibilities, the last one is true—Pan hid his pipe from the Satyrs, but they stole it nevertheless. Vv. 24-

τὸν] δὲ ἰδών, γ[α]λερὸν προσέφη Σιληνὸς [ἀναιδής·
εἰπ]έ μοι, ὦ νομέων μέγα κοίρανε, πῶς ἀ[ν ἔποιτο
αἰχ]μητὴς μενέχαρμος ἄτερ σακέων πόλ[εμόνδε;
πῶς δὲ χ]ορῶν ἐπ' ἀγῶνας ἄνευ σύριγγ(ο)ς ἱκά[νεις;
πῆι σ]οι πηκτὶς ἔβη, μηλοσκόπε, πῆι σέο φ[όρμιγξ; 5
π[ῆι] μελέων κλέος εὐρύ, τὸ καὶ Διὸς οὔατ' ἰα[ίνει;
ἦ ῥα σεῦ ὑπν(ώο)ντος ἀπειρεσίη[ν] μετὰ θ[οίνην
κλέψε τεὴν σύριγγα κατ' οὔρεα Δάφνις ὁ βού[της,
ἢ Λυκίδας ἢ Θύρσις, 'Αμύντιχος ἠὲ Μεν[άλκας;
κεῖνο(ι)ς γὰρ κραδίην ἐπικαίεαι ἠιθέοισ[ιν· 10
ἦ[έ] μιν ἔ(δ)νον ἔδωκας ὀρεσσιπόλωι τινι ν[ύμφηι;
σὸν γὰρ ὑπὸ πτερύγεσσιν ἀεὶ φέρετ' ἦτορ ["Ερωτος·
πάντηι γὰρ γαμέεις, πάντηι δέ σε θ[. . .]ρι[

1 ἀναιδής D. L. P.   2 ἔποιτο D. L. P.: ἴοι τις ed. pr. in note.   6 ἰαίνει Powell.   9 ηλυδοσητοι Π, corr. Maas.

ANONYMOUS

ANONYMOUS
BUCOLIC   [3–4 A.D.]

*end, Pan makes himself a new flute with wax from an oak-
tree. Dionysus and perhaps Bacchanals are present. One
of the latter tries the pipe in vain ; she throws it aside,
but Pan picks it up and plays on it.*

*Evidently Dionysus has engaged Pan to play at a contest
(v. 4 χορῶν ἐπ' ἀγῶνας refers to a definite competition). The
Satyrs, led by Silenus, have stolen Pan's pipe ; Dionysus will
therefore be enraged against Pan (vv. 20 sqq.). Pan makes
himself a new one, but has difficulty in commanding it to
any utterance of harmony. Doubtless Pan triumphed over
the Satyrs in the end.*

*It is probable that Vergil's Sixth Eclogue (vv. 13 sqq.) is
based upon this poem, or upon a common ancestor.*

Now seeing him, thus cheerfully spoke Silenus [a] un-
abashed.—" Tell me, great lord of shepherds, how
could a warrior steadfast follow into battle without
a shield ? How then come you to the dancing-match
without your pipe ? Where is your lute gone, shep-
herd, where your lyre ? Where the wide fame of your
songs, that delight even the ear of Zeus ? Did they
steal your pipe upon the hills while you slept after
feasting without limit, Daphnis the cowherd or
Lycidas or Thyrsis ? Amyntichus or Menalcas ?—
For those young men your heart is set afire. Or have
you given it for a wedding gift to a nymph upon the
mountains ?—your heart flies ever beneath the wings
of Love ; and everywhere it is your wedding-day,

[a] A character not found in the poems of Theocritus, Bion,
Moschus.

ἢ σὺ λαβὼν σύριγγα τε[ὴν κ]νέφα[ς ἀμφὶ καλύψας
δειμαίνων σατύρο(υ)ς [15
μή τί σε κερτομέωσιν ἐπὴν [
εὐύμνων προχέοις κεχρημέ[νος
μούνους δ' ἀμφὶ νομῆας ἀϊδρι[ά]ς ἐσσ[ι
οἳ σέ(ο) θάμβος ἔχουσι καὶ οὔν[ομ]α [. . .]σι[
πῶς οὔ τοι φόβος ἐστὶ μέγα[ς, μ]ὴ Β[άκχος ἐπελθὼν 20
οἷον ἄναυδον ἴδοιτο καὶ οὐκ ἀλέγ[οντα χορείης,
καὶ λασίας σέο χεῖρας ἀ[ν]ώγει[
δήσ(ε)ι' οἰοπόλοισιν ἐν οὔρεσιν [
          .   .   .   .   .
κοίλης δ'] ἐκ φη[γ]οῖο λαβὼν εὐαν[θέα κηρὸν
τὸν μὲν πρώτο]ν ἔθαλψεν ὑπ' ἠελίοιο [βολαῖσιν   25
          ] πωτᾶτο φιλόδροσος . . . . μέλισ(σ)α
          ]όμευσα τὸ κηρίον ὠδίνουσα
ἀμφὶ Διω]νύσοιο καρήατι, πίμπλατο δὲ δρῦς
ἔργου τεχνήεντος· ἐν ἀνθεμόεντι δὲ κηρῶι
. . . . . . ἐ]υτρήτοις μέλι λείβετο (. . . . . . .)   30
αὐγαῖς δ' ἠελίοιο τακεὶς ὑπελύ(ύ)ετο κηρὸς
          ]δε ῥέειν ἀτάλαντος ἐλαίωι
π]ηκτίδα πῆξε (. . . .) χρίσας λάσιος Πὰν
          ]κοιησιν, ὅπως μένοι ἔμπεδα κηρός.
          ]πρόσθεν ἀπ' αἰθέρος ἵπτατο Περσεὺς   35
          ἵκ]ανε καὶ ἔκτισεν ἀγλαὸν ἄστυ
          ]ιδ[. . .]ορωεν† κεκμηῶτες
          ]φιλω[. . . . .]μοιατα Βάκχαις
          π]ερὶ Πανὸς ἐπήδα
          ὁρμω]μένη ἐς χορὸν ἐλθεῖν   40
χείλεσσι]ν ἐφήρμοσεν ἀκροτάτοισι
ἀ]φέηκε, θεοῦ δ' ἐνιφυσιόωντος
ἰσ]χυρὸν ὑπ' ἄσθματος αὐχένος ἶνες
          ]εσνεχροις† ἐντέτατο χρώς·

504

ANONYMOUS

and everywhere . . . Or did you take your pipe and hide it about with darkness, fearing the Satyrs . . ., lest they taunt you, when . . . you should pour forth . . . of noble songs, wanting . . .? Only about the ignorant shepherds you are . . ., who hold you in wonder, and . . . name. Why are you not alarmed, lest Bacchus may approach and see that you only are voiceless and heedless of the dancing, and . . . fetter your hairy arms on the lonely hills ? . . . "

.   .   .   .

. . . took the bright wax from a hollow oak. First he warmed it in the rays of the sun . . . flew a bee that loves the dew . . . the honeycomb, in travail . . . about the head of Dionysus, and the oak was filled with its cunning work. In the flowery wax . . . honey was distilled in porous cells. Melted by the rays of the sun, the wax dissolved . . . to flow like olive-oil . . . Shaggy Pan, anointing . . ., fashioned a pipe . . . so that the wax should stand fast. . . . Perseus flew from the sky of old . . . came, and founded a glorious city . . . wearied . . . to Bacchanals . . . was leaping around Pan . . . starting to go to the dance . . . fitted it to the edge of her lips . . . let go, and while the god blew therein . . . strongly the sinews of his neck (swelled up) as he

---

30 Incomplete in Π : ⟨κυτταρίοισιν⟩ ed. pr.   36 Ἄργος ἱκ]ανε ed. pr.   43 *e.g.* οἰδαίνουσ᾽ or ὠιδηνάν τ᾽ ἰσχυρὸν Beazley, *cf.* Theocr. i. 43 ὧδέ οἱ ὠιδήκαντι κατ᾽ αὐχένα πάντοθεν ἶνες.

LITERARY PAPYRI

πλατ]άνοιο μελίζεμεν ἀρχόμενος Πὰν   45
]βαιον ἐπήιε χεῖλος ἀμείβων
π]άλιν ἔπνεεν εὐρυτέροισι

.   .   .   .   .   .

ANONYMOUS

124   [2 A.D.]   GEORGIC

Ed. pr. *Grenfell-Hunt, *P. Oxy.* xv. 1921, no. 1796, p. 116.
See Körte, *Archiv,* vii. 118 ; Schmidt, *G.G.A.* 1924, 10.

*From a poem about Egyptian botany.   First the cyclamen,
then the persea, described.   A good enough piece of writing,*

αἰσθάνετα[ι] ποταμοῦ γὰρ ἐπήλυσιν· ἢν δ' ἀπολείπηι,
ῥίζηισιν μεγάληισιν ἅτε φρονέοντι λογισμῶι
πλεῖον ὕδωρ ἕλκουσα πολυπληθεῖ τότε καρπῶι.
ἀλλ' οὐκ ἔσθ' ὅτε καρπὸν ἐφεδρεύσουσι λαβέσθαι
ἄνθρωποι χα(τέ)οντες ἐ[υ]τραφέων κυκλαμίνων·   5
πολλὴ γὰρ Νείλοιο χύσις πολλὴ δ' ἐπὶ σίτωι
ἀφθονίη τετάνυσται, ἐποίησεν δὲ γελῶσα
εὐθενίην, οὗ καρπὸς ἐπὶ χθόνα πᾶσαν ὁδεύει.
ὠγύγιος νόμος οὗτος ἀπ' ἀρχαίων ἔτ' ἀνάκτων,
θέσθαι δένδρεα κεῖνα παρ' ἀλλήλοισι κολώναις,   10
χώματος εὐύδροιο πέδην ἀλκτῆρά τε λιμοῦ.

3 πολυπλήθει ed. pr., corr. Beazley.   5 χάοντες Π,
defended by Schmidt.   7 γελῶσα(ν) Schmidt.

ᵃ The reference to *trees* seems awkward, interrupting as it
506

blew . . . flesh stretched . . . of the plane-tree, **Pan**
starting to play . . . ranged over, shifting his lips
. . . breathed again with broader . . .

. . . . . .

ANONYMOUS

GEORGIC [2 A.D.]

*concise and forceful, with some imaginative touches and
obvious avoidance of the monotony to which the theme natur-
ally lends itself : the style and technique are not dissimilar
to Vergil's in the* Georgics. *There seems to be no reason to
deny to this fragment an Hellenistic date : but it is possible
that is much later.*

. . . for she feels the advance of the River : if it
should fail, through her long roots she draws—as if
by conscious reasoning—more water, and thereafter
produces abundant fruits. But never will men be
watching and waiting in need to seize the fruit of the
full-grown cyclamen; for great is the flood of Nile,
and great the Abundance that is spread over the
corn, and smiles, and brings fertility ; the fruits
thereof go forth to every land. This is an im-
memorial law, surviving still from our lords of old :
—to set those trees *a* side by side upon hills, to bind
the watery mound and ward famine off.

does the discussion of cyclamen and persea. Perhaps these
trees (perhaps the ἄκανθα, Housman *ap.* Hunt) had been
mentioned already in connexion with the cyclamen, one kind
of which grew especially ὑπὸ τὰ δένδρα, Dioscor. ii. 193-194.
More probably the lines are simply misplaced (Beazley).

507

περσ(ε)ίη δ' ἄκμητος ὑπὸ χλοεροῖσι πετήλοις
εὐφορέοι καρπῶι περικαλλέι μηδὲ πεπαίνοι
μεχρὶς ἐπανθήσουσι κλάδοι πρότερον περὶ καρπόν·
πίπτοι μηδ' ἄρα νυκτὸς ὅτ' ἐγγύθεν ὄρνυται ὕδωρ   15
περσ[ε]ίης ἄπο καρπὸς ἀτὲρ βαρυηχέος αὔρης.
συμφέρεται μούνη γὰρ ἀθωπεύτωι δὲ γέγηθεν
ἀδροσίηι· καρπὸν γὰρ ὑπ' ἀδροσίηισι πεπαίνει.
σῆμα καὶ ἡμερίης εὐειδέος ἐγγὺς ἰδέσθαι·
Νείλου πλημύροντος ὕδωρ νέον εὖτε πιοῦσα   20
καρπὸν ἀπ' ὀφθαλμοῖο ν[έ]ωι συνανήκατο βλαστῶι
ἠέρος ἀκρισίηισι [

· · · · · ·

14 πρότεροι Π, corr. Hunt.

ᵃ Because evergreen, Theophr. *H.P.* iv. 2-5 ; for the
persea see further Nicander, *Al.* 99 ; Strabo xvii. 823 ;

ANONYMOUS

125 [1 A.D.] DRINKING-SONG

Ed. pr. Grenfell-Hunt, *P. Oxy.* xv. 1921, no. 1795, p. 113.
See *Powell, *Collect. Alex.* p. 199 ; Higham, *Greek Poetry
and Life*, 299 ; Körte, *Archiv*, vii. 140 ; Maas, *Phil. Woch.*
1922, 581 ; Manteuffel, *de opusculis graecis*, 177 ; Wilamo-
witz, *Gr. Versk.* 364 ; Crönert, *Philol.* 84, 1928, 162 ;
Schmidt, *G.G.A.* 1924, 10.

*Fragment of a series of stanzas written for a merry com-
pany, a sort of* scolion *or drinking-song : so arranged that
the first stanza began with the letter* A, *the second with the
letter* B, *and so forth to the end of the alphabet ; our frag-
ment preserves the series from* I *to* Ξ. *Cf. P. Oxy. i. no. 15,
a similar " acrostic " scolion, composed some two centuries
later. The metre is " tapering " hexameter, whether* μύουροι
or μείουροι *(probably the former is correct, Higham, p. 305 ;*

ANONYMOUS

The unwearying [a] persea should be fertile with
lovely fruits under leaves in the green : it should not
ripen till the twigs bear foliage about the former [b]
fruit. Nor should fruit fall from the persea in the
night when rain rushes near, without a violent wind.
For it alone agrees therewith, and rejoices in harsh
want of dew : when no dew is there, the fruit is
ripened.[c] A proof of its fair culture [d] is near to see :
when Nile is in its first flood, drinking the water
and sending forth from the bud new fruit and shoot
together, in the changes of the climate . . .

. . . .

Pliny, *N.H.* xiii. 9, 15. It is *Mimusops Schimperi.* [b] *i.e.*
do not pick the first crop until the flowers of the second crop
appear. [c] Deriving enough moisture from the rains, it
is prepared for the dry season. [d] σῆμα ἡμερίης = σῆμα,
ὡς ἡμέρα (worth cultivating) ἐστί.

ANONYMOUS

DRINKING-SONG [1 A.D.]

qu. v. *also p. 315 for explanations of the curious refrain*
αὔλει μοι, *and p. 323 for a beautiful translation into English*).

*It is not, I think, to be supposed that these stanzas compose
together a single complete poem, nor yet that each stanza was
intended to be an entirely separate song. Though each
stanza, sung in its turn, is in fact more or less self-contained
and independent, yet all are connected and bound together by
the occasion on which they are recited and by a common
subject-matter—the philosophic toper's Design for Living.
The work is thus something less than a single complete poem,
and something more than a series of independent songs. Cf.
the Harmodius and Aristogiton songs in Athenaeus's collec-
tion of Attic scolia.*

[Θ] . . . . . .
μηδ' ἀδικεῖν ζήτει, μηδ' ἂν ἀδι[κῆι πρ]οσερίσηις·
φεῦγε φόνους καὶ φεῦγε μάχας, φ[εῖ]σαι διαφρονε[ῖ]ν,
εἰς δ' ὀλίγον πονέσεις, καὶ δεύτερον οὐ μεταμέλῃ.
                              αὔ[λει μοι.   5

Ἴδες ἔαρ, χειμῶνα, θέρος· ταῦτ' ἐστι διόλου·
ἥλιος αὐτὸς [ἔδυ], καὶ νὺξ τὰ τεταγμέν' ἀπέχει·
μὴ κοπία ζητεῖν πόθεν ἥλιος ἢ πόθε[ν] ὕδωρ,
ἀλλὰ π[ό]θεν τ[ὸ] μύρον καὶ τοὺς στεφάνου[ς]
     ἀγοράσηις.
                              αὔλει μο[ι.   10

Κρήνας αὐτορύ[το]υς μέλ[ιτ]ος τρεῖς ἤθελον ἔχειν,
πέντε γαλακτορύτους, οἴνου δέκα, δ[ώδε]κα μύρου,
καὶ δύο πηγαίων ὑδάτων, καὶ τρεῖς χιονέων·
παῖδα κατὰ κρήνην καὶ παρθένον ἤθελον ἔχειν.
                              αὔλει μο[ι.   15

Λύδιος αὐλὸς ἐμοὶ τὰ δὲ Λύδια παίγματα λύρας
κα[ὶ] Φρύγ[ιο]ς κάλαμος τὰ δὲ ταύρεα τύμπανα
     πονεῖ·
ταῦτα ζῶν ᾆσαί τ' ἔραμαι καὶ ὅταν ἀποθάνω
αὐλὸν ὑπὲρ κεφαλῆς θέτε μοι παρὰ ποσ(σ)ὶ δὲ
     λύρη[ν.
                              αὔλει μοι.   20

Μέτρα τί[ς] ἂν πλούτου, τίς ἀνεύρατο μέτρα πενίας
ἢ τίς ἐν ἀνθρώποις χρυσοῦ πάλιν εὕρατο μέτρον;
νῦν γὰρ ὁ χρήματ' ἔχων ἔτι πλε[ί]ονα χρήματα
     θέλει,
πλούσιος ὢν δ' ὁ τάλας βασανίζεται ὥσπερ ὁ πένης.
                              αὔλ[ει μοι.   25

ANONYMOUS

Nor seek to do a wrong, nor strive in answer if a wrong be done to you. Stay far from slaughter, far from strife, forbear to quarrel. So shall your pains be brief, with no after-care. Play me a song. . . .

You saw the spring, the winter and the summer: these are for ever. The sun himself is gone to rest, night has her portion due. Labour not to seek whence comes the sunshine, whence the rain—but whence you may buy the scent and wreaths of flowers. Play me a song. . . .

I wish I had three natural springs of honey, five of milk, ten of wine, of scent a dozen, two of fountain-water, and three from snow. I wish I had a lass and lad beside the fountain. Play me a song. . . .

For me, the Lydian pipe and play of the Lydian lyre, the Phrygian reed and oxhide timbrel toil for me. In life these songs I love to sing: and when I die, set a flute above my head, beside my feet a lyre. Play me a song. . . .

Who ever found the measure of wealth or poverty? Who, I repeat, found out the measure of gold among mankind? For now, he that possesses money desires more money still: and rich though he is, poor wretch he is tormented like the poor. Play me a song. . . .

---

3 The δε before διαφρονεῖν in Powell is merely an oversight (repeated by Manteuffel).   6 *i.e.* (ε)ἶδες.   11 ἤθελον: tense as in ὤφελον (Higham): *cf.* Goodwin, pp. 157-158.

511

Νεκρὸν ἐάν ποτ' ἴδηις καὶ μνήματα κωφὰ παράγηις
κοινὸν ἔσοπτρον ὁρᾶι(ς)· ὁ θανὼν οὕτως προσεδόκα.
ὁ χρό[ν]ος ἐστὶ δάνος, τὸ ζῆν πικρός ἐσθ' ὁ δανίσας,
κἂν τότ' ἀπαιτῆσαί σε θέληι, κλαίων [ἀ]ποδιδοῖς.
                                        αὔλει μοι.   30

Ξέρξης ἦν βασιλε[ὺ]ς ὁ λέγων Διὶ πάντα μερίσαι,
ὃς δυσ(ὶ) πηδαλ[ί]ο[ι]ς μόνος ἔσχισε Λήμνιον ὕδωρ.
ὄλβι(ο)ς ἦν ὁ Μίδας, τρὶς δ' ὄλβιος ἦν ὁ [Κ]ινύρ[α]ς,
ἀλλὰ τίς εἰς Ἀίδα ὀβολοῦ πλέον ἤλυθεν ἔχων;
                                        αὔλει μοι.   35

. . . .

29 ποτ' Hunt.

---

[*] *i.e.* with a single ship: the rudder consisted of two large

ANONYMOUS

126 [1 A.D.]   HERO AND LEANDER

Ed. pr. *Roberts, *Catalogue of the Greek Papyri in the
John Rylands Library, Manchester*, iii. 1938, no. 486, p. 98,
Plate VI : the earliest extant text in Greek literary papyri
which divides words one from another : the division doubt-
less made by a young pupil in a school.

*Fragment of a poem about Hero and Leander, the earliest
appearance of that story in Greek literature (where it was
hitherto known first from Musaeus in the 5th century A.D.).
Is this the Hellenistic poem which scholars postulate as the
common source of Ovid,* Heroides *17, 18 and Musaeus ? The
fragment is too meagre to permit a certain conclusion.
Hardly more than two dozen words are more or less com-*

ANONYMOUS

Whenever you see a body dead, or pass by silent tombs, you look into the mirror of all men's destiny: the dead man expected nothing else. Time is a loan, and he who lent you life is a hard creditor: if he wants to ask you for his money back, you repay him to your sorrow. Play me a song. . . .

Xerxes the king it was, who said he shared the universe with God—yet he cleft the Lemnian waves, deserted, with a single rudder.[a] Blessed was Midas, thrice-blessed was Cinyras : but what man went to Hades with more than one penny piece ? Play me a song. . . .

. . . . . .

oars fastened aft. Xerxes entered Europe with a vast army across a bridge of boats: he returned, defeated and deserted, in a single vessel.

ANONYMOUS
HERO AND LEANDER [1 A.D.]

pletely preserved : so far as they go, there is perhaps nothing inconsistent with Hellenistic style and technique, except the break after the first short syllable of the fourth foot in v. 9. (The Plate makes it clear, I think, that γένοισθε v. 2, καὶ ἀστ[v. 6 come after the feminine caesura in the third foot of their lines ; not, as seemed likely at first, after the similar caesura in the fourth foot.) The two vocatives Ἕσπερε v. 5 and Λάα]νδρε v. 6 are not easy to combine, but may of course have been wholly free from objection in the original text.

Our poet has in common with Musaeus (1) the word τηλε- σκόπος v. 10, Mus. 237, (2) the address to Leander in the

513

second person, vv. 6, 9, Mus. 86, (3) *the appeal to the Evening Star to assist Leander*, v. 5, Mus. 111.

The form of Leander's name Λάανδρος " which appears in this text and is nowhere else used of the hero of this story, may be explained either as a pseudo-archaism or as a scribal error " (ed. pr.). The lines appear to describe Leander's

[ἀστέρες . . .
ἀντομένηι ν]εύσαιτε, γένοισθε δὲ τυφ[λο
μήνη, σὸν τ]αχινῶς καταδυνόμενον [φάος ἔρροι.
ὡς φάτ', ἐπεὶ] Λάανδρον ἰδεῖν μόνον ἦνδα[νε θυμῶι.
καὶ σὺ τότ' ἀ]ντιάαις· πάλιν, Ἔσπερε, λάθρ[ιος
    ἔρποις,   5
ὧδ' εὔχηι Λάα]νδρε, καὶ ἀστ[έρες] ἱππευ[όντων
πάντες, ὅπως σκοτάσ]ει νὺξ οὐρανὸς ἠέλιο[ς γῆ.
δαίμονι πάντα δι]δοὺς ὁπλίζεαι ἔν περ [ὀλέθρου
οὐδῶι, καρτερόθυμ]ε Λάανδρε· [τ]έτηκε γὰρ α[ἰνῶς
λύχνος ὁ πρὶν φα]έθων τηλέσκοπος· ειπε[10

   ·   ·   ·   ·   ·

2 ν]ευσητε Π. τυφλοι ⌣⌣‒×, or a compound of τυφλο-. 3 τ]αχινως possible in Π; -ος perhaps likelier. καταδυνεομενον Π.   5 Or *e.g.* λάθρ[α σύ τ' αὐτός (λάθρᾶ *h. Cer.* 240, Eur. fr. 1132. 28).   7 May the reader find a better word here

ANONYMOUS

127   [2 A.D.] SAYINGS OF THE SEVEN WISE MEN

Ed. pr. Vitelli-Norsa, *Bulletin de la société royale d'archéologie d'Alexandrie*, 24, 1929, p. 4: republished *Papiri Greci e Latini*, ix. 1929, no. 1093, col. i. 1-6, p. 154. See Körte, *Archiv*, x. 224.

*final journey and death. " The first two lines are probably
spoken by Hero, an appeal to the elements to favour her
lover, in particular to the stars not to shine and vie with the
light of the lamp. . . . The rest would then be a description
. . . in which the Evening Star is invoked as Leander's
helper " (ed. pr.). My hazardous supplements endeavour to
restore this sense to the text.*

" STARS, bow to my prayer, and become sightless ;
Moon, suffer your light to sink swiftly and depart ! "
So she [a] spoke, for to see Leander was all her
heart's desire. Then did he too make supplication :
" Back, Hesperus, to hiding ! " (thus prayed Leander).
" Ride [b] backward, all the stars, that night and heaven
and sun and earth may grow dark ! "
Entrusting all to Heaven, you gird yourself even
on the threshold of death, Leander lion-hearted ;
for sorely dwindles the lamp that was bright before
and looked afar. . . .

. . . . .

[a] Hero.   [b] For Hesperus and other stars as youths
on horseback, ed. pr. refers to *P.-W.-K.* viii. 1. 1253 : *cf.*
Eur. *Hic.* 990-994.

---

than σκοτάζω.   8]λους or]δους Π : οπλισ[σ]εαι Π. Or
πάντα θεοῖσι δι]δούς.

ANONYMOUS

SAYINGS OF THE SEVEN WISE MEN [2 A.D.]

*Fragment, quoted in a monograph on maxims, from a
poem in which perhaps the Seven Wise Men met at a sym-
posium and each in turn expressed a profound sententia.*

Cf. *Plato,* Protagoras *343 .t, the earliest passage in which the Seven Wise Men are mentioned together—Thales, Pittacus, Bias, Solon, Cleobulus, Myson and Chilon* (ἕβδομος ἐν αὐτοῖς ἐλέγετο Λακεδαιμόνιος Χίλων : *the phraseology suggests that he was decidedly less illustrious than the others ; no doubt it was just this passage of Plato which " canonized " him*). *Plato refers to the* ῥήματα βραχέα ἀξιομνημόνευτα

$$] \ \dot{a}\gamma o\rho\epsilon\acute{v}\epsilon\iota\nu.$$

Χί]λων [δ᾿ ἦ]ρχε λόγου Λ[α]κεδαίμονα πατρίδα
    ναίων,
ὅς ποτε καὶ Πυ[θ]οῖ τὸ σοφὸν ποτὶ [νη]ὸν ἔγραψεν,
του . . .

· · · · · · ·

ΠΑΓΚΡΑΤΗΣ

128   [2 A.D.]   ANTINOUS

Ed. pr. *Grenfell-Hunt, *P. Oxy.* viii. 1911, no. 1085, p. 73. See Milne, *Cat. Lit. Pap. B.M.* no. 36, p. 30 ; Körte, *Archiv,* v. 539 ; Schmidt, *G.G.A.* 1912, 643 ; Müller, *Phil. Woch.* 1916, 672 ; Schmid-Stählin, *Gr. Lit.* ii. 2, 673.

Pancrates of Alexandria, an acquaintance of Athenaeus, suggested to the emperor Hadrian that a certain lotus should be named after his favourite Antinous ; averring that it had sprung from the blood of a lion which the emperor had killed near Alexandria. Hadrian approved the conceit, and rewarded Pancrates. Athenaeus (xv. 677 d-f) quotes four lines from the poem which Pancrates wrote :—

οὔλην ἔρπυλλον λευκὸν κρίνον ἠδ᾿ ὑάκινθον
πορφυρέην γλαύκου τε χελιδονίοιο πέτηλα
καὶ ῥόδον εἰαρινοῖσιν ἀνοιγόμενον ζεφύροισι·
οὔπω γὰρ φύεν ἄνθος ἐπώνυμον ᾿Αντινόοιο.

PANCRATES

ἑκάστωι εἰρημένα, which probably formed the basis of our
poem. If indeed the poem did describe a meeting of the
Seven Wise Men, this passage of Plato was probably the
ultimate source of the plot, cf. 343 A–B κοινῆι συνελθόντες
ἀπαρχὴν τῆς σοφίας ἀνέθεσαν τῶι Ἀπόλλωνι εἰς τὸν νεὼν τὸν
ἐν Δελφοῖς, γράψαντες ταῦτα ἃ δὴ πάντες ὑμνοῦσιν, γνῶθι
σεαυτὸν καὶ μηδὲν ἄγαν.

. . . to hold forth. Now Chilon, whose fatherland
was Lacedaemon, began to speak : he it was who
once at Delphi wrote the wise saying [a] on the
temple . . .

.   .   .   .   .   .

[a] γνῶθι σεαυτόν (know yourself).

PANCRATES

ANTINOUS   [2 A.D.]

*Our fragment, in which the slaying of a lion by Hadrian and
Antinous is described, presumably comes from the same poem.
It is a poor enough composition ; exaggeration ruins the
realism at which it aims.   A stale and conventional lion does
everything at once—except move : we cry to him " Fellow,
leave thy damnable mouthings, and begin ! "*

*That Hadrian was an experienced hunter of lions, we
knew already.   The commonest method was to drive the
beast into a net ; pits and poisons were probably only em-
ployed by those whose purpose was to take the lion alive (for the
amphitheatre) or merely to destroy it as a danger to life and
property.   Frontal attack, whether on horseback as here or
on foot as in Oppian, Cyn. ii. 474-478, was too dangerous a
method to be employed by any but the boldest or those who
had no alternative in a chance encounter.   See further Butler,
Sport in Classic Times (1930), 88-97.*

517

ἵππου] δ' Ἀδρ[ή]στοιο θοώτερον, ὅς ποτ' ἄνακτα
ῥηιδί]ως φεύγοντα κατὰ κλόνον ἐξεσάωσε.
τοῖ]ον ἐφεζόμενος δαμασήν[ο]ρα μίμνε λέοντα
Ἀ]ντίνοος λαιῆι μὲν ἔχων ῥυτῆρα χαλινόν,
δεξιτερῆι δ' ἔγχος κεκορυθμένο[ν] ἐξ ἀδάμαντος.   5
πρῶτος δ' Ἀδριανὸς προιεὶς χαλκήρεον ἔγχος
οὔτασεν, οὐδὲ δάμασσεν· ἑκὼν γὰρ ἀπήμβροτε
      θ[ηρός·
ε]ὐστοχίης γὰρ πάμπαν ἐβούλετο πειρηθῆναι
Ἀ]ργειφοντιάδαο μεγηράτ[ου Ἀντι]νόοιο.
θ]ὴρ δὲ τυπεὶς ἔτι μᾶλλον [ὀ]ρίνετο, ποσσὶ δ'
      ἄμυσσ[ε   10
γαῖαν τρηχαλ[έ]η[ν] θυμούμ[ε]νος· ἐκ δὲ κονίη
ὧ[ς ν]έφ[ος] ἱσταμένη φ[άος ἤ]χλυεν ἠελίοιο.
μαίνετο δ' ὡς ὅτε κῦμ[α] πολυκλύστο[ι]ο θαλάσσης
Στρυ[μ]ονίου κ[α]τόπισθεν ἐγειρομένου Ζεφύρ[οιο.
ῥί]μ[φα δ' ἐ]π' ἀμφοτέροισιν ἐπώρορε, μάστιε δ'
      οὐρ[ῆι   15
ἰσχία κ]αὶ πλευρὰς σφετερῆι μάστιγι κε[λαινῆι
. . . . .]ος· ὄσσε δὲ δεινὸν ὑπ' ὀφρύσι πῦρ φ[λε-
      γέθεσκον,
ἐκ δ' αὖ λ]αβροβόρ[ω]ν στομάτων πο[λὺν ἀφρὸν
      ὀδόντων
ἐξανίει] συναρασσομένων ἔντοσθεν ἐς [αἶαν,
κρατὸς δ'] ἐκ μεγάλοιο καὶ αὐχένος ἐκ λασιο[ῖο   20
χαίτη] ἀειρομένη κατεσείετο· ἡ μὲν ἀπ' ἄ[λλων
δάσκιος] ἦν μελέων ἅτε δένδρεα, ἡ δ' ἀπὸ ν[ώτου
. . . .]μένη θηκτοῖσιν ὁμοίιος ἦεν ἀκω[καῖς.
ὣς ὅ γ' ἔβη] κατέναντα θ[εοῦ] κλυτοῦ Ἀντι[νόου τε,
οἷα γιγαντ[ο]λ[έταο] Διὸς πά[ρο]ς ἄντα Τυφωεύ[ς   25

(*Fragments of fifteen more lines*)

PANCRATES

. . . swifter than the steed of Adrastus,[a] that once
saved its master easily, when he was fleeing through
the press of battle. On such a horse Antinous
awaited the manslaying lion ; in his left hand he held
the bridle-rein, in his right a spear tipped with
adamant. Hadrian was first to shoot forth his bronze
spear ; he wounded, but slew it not, for it was his
intent to miss the animal, wishing to test to the full
how straight the other aimed—he, lovely Antinous,
son of the slayer of Argus.[b] Stricken, the beast was
yet more aroused ; with his paws he tore the rough
ground in anger ; forth rose a cloud of dust, and
dimmed the sunlight. He raged like a wave of the
surging sea, when the West wind is awakened after
the wind from Strymon.[c] Lightly upon both he leapt,
and scourged his haunches and sides with his tail,
with his own dark whip. . . . His eyes flashed dread-
ful fire beneath the brows ; he sent forth a shower
of foam from his ravening jaws to the ground, while
his fangs gnashed within. From his massive head
and shaggy neck the mane rose and quivered ; from
his other limbs it fell bushy as trees ; on his back it
was . . . like whetted spear points. In such guise
he went against the glorious God and Antinous, like
Typhoeus of old against Zeus the Giant-Killer. . . .

.   .   .   .   .   .

(Fragments of fifteen more lines)

[a] Adrastus was saved by his horse Arion in the battle of
the Seven against Thebes : Homer *Il.* xxiii. 346-347, Apollod.
iii. 6. 7.   [b] *i.e.* son of Hermes. *Inscr. Gr. Ital.* 978 (a)
Kaibel, Antinous is called νέος θεὸς Ἑρμάων : Hermes appears
on the reverse of a coin struck in honour of Antinous in
Bithynia (Eckhel vi. p. 532).   [c] The North Wind, Boreas.

2 ῥηιδίως Schmidt.   15 ῥίμφα δ' Schmidt.   23
φρισσομένη Schmidt : ῥωσαμένη Müller.

LITERARY PAPYRI

ANONYMOUS

129 [3 A.D.] DIONYSUS AND LYCURGUS

Ed. pr. Zereteli, *Nachrichten der Russischen Akademie der Wissenschaften*, Petrograd, 1918, 873-880 ; 971-1002 ; 1153-1180 (in Russian) : republished *Papyri Russischer und Georgischer Sammlungen* [*P. Ross.-Georg.*], ed. Zereteli-Krueger, i. (Literarische Texte), Tiflis, i. 1925, no. 11, p. 69. See Körte, *Archiv*, viii. 254.

Fragment of a hymn to Dionysus, composed in the 3rd century A.D. Our papyrus is the author's own copy, left incomplete.

Where our fragment begins, the countryside is by a sudden miracle rendered waste and desert. Lycurgus is terrified. Dionysus appears and assails him with thunder and lightning. Maenads and Satyrs assault his person, and Dionysus distracts his soul with madness. Lycurgus fights against imaginary serpents : believes that his sons, Astacius and Ardys, are serpents, and so destroys them. His wife Cytis is

. . . . σάτυ]ροι φιλοπαί[γμονε]ς ἐξεγένοντο.
οὐδὲ παρὰ πτελέ]ην κρήνη νάεν οὐδ' ἔσαν ἀρδμοί,
οὐ πάτοι, οὐ θρι]γκοί, οὐ δένδρεα, πάντα δ' [ἄ]ισ[τα·
μοῦνος δὲ πλα]ταμὼν λ[εῖ]ος πάλιν ἐξεφαάν[θη.
λειμὼν δ' ἧι πάρος] ἔσκε, παρῆν ἆσσον Λυκόοργος 5
κῆρ μεγάλωι τάρβ]ει βεβολημένος ἀμφασίηι τε·
καὶ γὰρ ἀάσχετ]α πάντα καὶ ἀνδράσιν οὐκ ἐπιει[κ]τὰ
θνητοῖσιν παλίνορσα μ]ετατράπετ' ἀμφα[δὸν] ἔργα.
ἀλλ' ὅτε δὴ γίγνωσκε] Διὸς [γό]νον ἀγλ[αὸν] ὄντα,
ἔμπεσεν ὧι θυμ]ῶι χλω[ρ]ὸν δέος, [ὧι δὲ] πονεῖτο 10
θείνων, ἔκπεσέν οἱ] βουπλῆ[ξ] χερὸς ἄντα ποδοῖιν,

ANONYMOUS

ANONYMOUS

DIONYSUS AND LYCURGUS [3 A.D.]

*rescued by Dionysus, on the ground that she had always
attempted to check her husband in his career of wickedness.
Lycurgus regains his senses : but his punishment has yet
hardly begun. He is bound with vines and conveyed to the
underworld, where he must perpetually attempt to fill with
water a leaking vessel. The last few lines, which were left
unfinished, were meant to be an epilogue. They seem to
contain a reference to a Dionysiac ceremony : so that our
poem may be a cult-hymn intended for recitation at a par-
ticular festival.*

*The treatment of the story is to a great extent dependent
upon older epic and tragic poetry : new to us are the punish-
ment of Lycurgus in the underworld, and a few details such
as the names of his wife and children. Language and metre
(e.g. τῖσις twice) forbid us to consider the attribution of the
piece to an era earlier than the 3rd century A.D.*

. . . (whence) the playful Satyrs were born. Neither
flowed the spring beside the elm, nor were there ways
of watering, nor paths nor fences nor trees, but all had
vanished. Only the smooth plain appeared again.

Where a meadow was before, close came Lycurgus,
heart-stricken with mighty fear and speechlessness.
For irresistibly, beyond mortal defence, all their
works were upset and turned about before their
eyes. But when Lycurgus knew him for the glorious
son of Zeus, pale terror fell upon his spirit ; the ox-
goad, wherewith he had been at labour smiting, fell

7-8 ἦν γὰρ ἀάσχετα and θνητοῖς, οἷα τότ' αἶψα ed. pr. : text
D. L. P.

521

οὐδέ τι ἐκφάσθ]αι ἔπος [ἤθ]ελεν οὐδ' ἐρέεσθ[αι.
καί νύ κε δὴ τά]χα δειλὸς ὑπέκφυγε κῆρα κελαιν[ήν,
ἀλλὰ τότ' οὐκ ἐ]δέησε θεὸν μήνιμα μεθεῖναι.
ἄτην δ' οἱ παρ]εοῦσαν ἑῶι [π]ρο[νοή]σατο θυμῶι, 15
ὡς εἶδ' οἱ ἐλ]θόντα μετ' ἀ[στε]ροπ[αῖ]s Διόνυσον,
αἱ πυκναὶ σ]ελάγιζον ὑ[π]ὸ β[ρον]τῆισι θαμείαις
οὐ γόνου ἔργ' ἀί]δηλα Δι[ὸ]ς μέγα κυδαίνοντος.
ὤτρυν' οὖν Διόν]υσος ὀπάονας, οἱ δ' ἄρ' ὁμαρτῆι
θ]ύσθλοισιν χλοεροῖσιν ἐπαίσσοντες [ἔ]θε[ι]νον. 20
ἔ]στη δ' ἀστεμφὴς πέτρηι ἶσος, ἥ ῥά τε προ[βλὴ]ς
εἰ]ς ἅλα μαρμαρέην στεναχίζεται, ἥν τις ἀη[τ]ῶν
ὀρ]νύμενος πνεύσηι, θείνοντά (τε) κύματα μίμ[νει.
ὣ]ς ὅ γε θεινόμενος μέ[νεν] ἔμπεδον οὐ[κ ἀ]λεγίσ-
        [σας.
μ]ᾶλλον δ' ἀ[ζηχὴ]ς ἐνεδ[ύ]ετο παῖδα Θυ[ώνη]ς 25
μ]ηνιθμὸς κραδί[η]ν, κραιπνῶι δέ μιν οὔτι μενοίνα
αἱρήσειν θανάτωι, δο[λιχ]α[ῖ]ς δ' ἄταισιν ἐρ[είκ]ει[ν,
ἀργαλέην ἵνα τῖσιν ἔτι ζώων ἀποτίσηι.
ὦ]ρ[σ]ε δέ οἱ [μα]νίην, ὀφίων δ' ἰνδαλμὸν [ἔ]χευ[ε]ν,
ὄφρ' ἀπαλεξή[σ]ων τρίβηι χρόνον, ἄχρις [ὀλοι]ὴ 30
φήμη τ[ῆ]ς μα[νί]ης πτηνὴ Θήβην ἀφίκ[η]ται
Ἄρδυν τ' Ἀσ[τ]άκιόν τε δύω π[αῖ]δα[ς] καλέουσα
καὶ Κύτιν ἥ οἱ γή(μ)ατ' ἐν ἀγκοίνηισι δαμεῖσα.
οἱ δ' ἐπεὶ οὖν ἀφίκοντο πολυγλώσσο[υ] δ[ιὰ] φήμης
ἄρτι νέον λήγοντα πόνου κιχέτην [Λυκό]οργον 35
τρυόμενον μα[νίηι], περὶ δ' αὐτῶι χεῖρ' ἐβ[άλ]οντο
κείμενο[ν] ἐν κ[ο]νίηι, μέγα νήπ[ιοι]· ἦ γὰρ ἔμελλον
φθίσεσθ[αι] ὑπὸ πατρὸς ἐναντίον ὄμμασι μητρός.
οὐ γὰρ δὴν πάλι Λύσσα κελεύοντος Διονύσου
ὀρθῆισ[ιν μ]αν[ίη]ισιν ἀνήγειρεν Λυκόοργον. 40

from his hand before his feet.   He had no will to utter
or to ask a word.   Now might that poor wretch have
escaped his gloomy fate : but he besought not then the
divinity to abate his wrath.   In his heart he foresaw
that doom was nigh to him, when he saw Dionysus
come to assail him amid lightings that flashed mani-
fold with repeated thunderclaps, while Zeus did great
honour to his son's destructive deeds.

So Dionysus urged his ministers, and they together
sped against Lycurgus and scourged him with rods
of foliage.   Unflinching he stood, like a rock that
juts into the marble sea and groans when a wind
arises and blows, and abides the smiting of the seas :
even so abode Lycurgus steadfast, and recked not of
their smiting.   But ever more unceasing wrath went
deep into the heart of Thyone's son : he was minded
not at all to take his victim with a sudden death, but
rather to break him under a lengthy doom, that still
alive he might repay a grievous penalty.   He sent
madness upon him, and spread about the phantom
shapes of serpents, that he might spend the time fend-
ing them away, till baneful Rumour of his madness
should arrive at Thebes on wings and summon Ardys
and Astacius, his two sons, and Cytis who married
him and was subdued to his embrace.

They, when led by Rumour's many tongues they
came, found Lycurgus just now released from suffer-
ing, worn out by madness.   They cast their arms
around him as he lay in the dust—fools ! they
were destined to perish at their father's hand before
their mother's eyes !   For not long after, madness,
at the command of Dionysus, aroused Lycurgus yet

---

37 Perhaps κειμένω[ι] should be read : but Π has κείμενο[ν].

φῆ δ' ὄ[φια]ς θείν[ε]ιν, τεκέων δ' ἐξείλατο θυμόν.
κ]αί νύ κ[εν] ἀμφ' αὐτοῖσι Κύτις πέσεν, ἀλλ' ἐλε-
      [αί]ρων
ἤ]ρπαξε[ν] Διόνυσος, ἔθηκε δὲ νόσφιν ὀλέθρ[ο]υ,
οὕνεκα [μ]αργαίνοντι παραίφασις ἐμμενὲς ἦ[εν.
ἀλλ' οὐ π[εῖσ]εν ἄθελκτο[ν] ἑὸν πόσιν· ὅς [ῥα λυ-
      θ]εί[σης   45
λα]ιψ[ηρῆς] μανίης πείρηι παθέων θεὸν [ἔγν]ω.
ἀλλ' [ο]ὔ θ[ην] Διόνυσος ἐ[παύε]το μηνιθμ[οῖο,
ἀ]τ[ρέ]μα [δ' ἐ]στειῶτι δυη[πα]θίηι τ' ἀλύοντι
ἄ]μπ[ελον] ἀμφὶς ἔ[χευ]ε καὶ ἄψεα πάντ' ἐπ[έδη]σε.
σ]τεινό[με]νος δὲ δέρην [δο]ιο[ύς] θ' ἑκάτερθε
      τ[ένοντας   50
οἴκτι[στ]ον κάμεν οἶτον ἐπιχθονίων ἀνθ[ρ]ώπ[ων.
καὶ νῦν ἐς χῶρον τὸν δυσσεβέων εἴδωλον
ὀ]τλε[ύει κά]ματον τὸν ἀνήνυτον ἐς πίθον ἀν[τλ]ῶν
ῥω]γαλέο[ν], τὸ δὲ πολλὸν ἐς Ἅιδος †ἔκχυται†
      ὕδωρ.
τοίην [οὖν] ἐρίδ[ου]πος ἐπεκραίαινε Κρονίων   55
ἀνδρ[άσι] θ[ε]ιομάχοι[σ]ι δ[ί]κηην, ἵνα τίσις [ἔπ]ητ[αι
ἀ[μ]φότερον ζωοῖ[σ]ιν ἀτὰρ πάλι τεθνηῶσιν.

(*Traces of four obscure lines, evidently referring to a
    present festival of Dionysus. Then three lines of
    prose—perhaps a sketch for future verses*)

. . . .

45 πεῖσεν ἄθελκτον Beazley.   48 This line is omitted

again with real frenzy. He thought that he was
smiting serpents ; but they were his children from
whom he stole the spirit forth. And now would Cytis
have fallen about them : but in compassion Dionysus
snatched her forth and set her beyond the reach of
doom, because she had warned her lord constantly in
his storms of evil passion. Yet she could not per-
suade her master, too stubborn ; he, when his sudden
madness was undone, recognized the god through
experience of suffering. Still Dionysus abated not
his wrath : as Lycurgus stood unflinching, yet frenzied
by distress, the god spread vines about him and
fettered all his limbs. His neck and both ankles
imprisoned, he suffered the most pitiable doom of
all men on earth : and now in *a* the land of Sinners
his phantom endures that endless labour—drawing
water into a broken pitcher : the stream is poured
forth into Hades.

Such is the penalty which the loud-thundering son
of Cronus ordained for men that fight against the
gods ; that retribution may pursue them both living
and again in death. . . .

*(Traces of four obscure lines, evidently referring to a
present festival of Dionysus. Then three lines of
prose—perhaps a sketch for future verses)*

.   .   .   .

a ἐς χῶρον=ἐν χώρωι: characteristic of the date of com-
position.

---

from ed. pr.'s supplemented version of the poem, but dis-
cussed (and restored) in note.   54 ἐκχέεθ' ed. pr. (doubt-
ful metre).

ANONYMOUS

130   [3 A.D.]   PRAISE OF THEON

Ed. pr. *Grenfell-Hunt, *P. Oxy.* vii. 1910, no. 1015, p. 11.
See Schmid-Stählin, *Gr. Lit.* ii. 2, 675 ; Wagner, *Philol.* 77,
1921, 256 ; Abert, *Archiv f. Musikwiss.* i. 1919, 313 ; Körte,
Archiv, v. 540.

*These conventional and uninspired verses are described at
the foot and in the left-hand margin (opposite vv. 8-9) as
Ἑρμοῦ Ἐγκώμιον: but in both places the name Ἑρμοῦ has been
obliterated, and higher up in the left-hand margin (opposite
vv. 4-5) the same hand has written εἰς τὸν ἄρχοντα. It is
clear that the poem, though it devotes its first nine lines to
Hermes, is essentially a panegyric of one Theon, who appears
to have made a benefaction to his community. Evidently*

αὐτός μοι τεὸν ἀεῖσαι ὑποφήτορα παῖδα,
Ἑρμεία, σπεύσειας, ἀοιδοπόλωι δ᾽ ἐπαρήγοις
ἑπτάτονον χείρεσσι λύρην πολυηχέα κρούων,
τὴν αὐτὸς τὰ πρῶτα κάμες παρὰ ποσσὶ τεκούσης
ἄρτι πεσών, λύτρον δὲ βοῶν πόρες Ἀπόλλωνι·   5
τοὔνεκα μουσοπόλόν σε νέοι κλείουσιν ἀοιδοί,
ἀγρονόμοι δὲ θεὸν νόμιον κληίζουσι βοτῆρες,
Ἑρμῆν δ᾽ ἐν σταδίοις ἐναγώνιον ἀθλητῆρες,
γυμνασίων δὲ πολῆες ἐπίσκοπον ἀείδουσιν.
ἔνθα σε καὶ πάις οὗτος, ἄναξ, ἱερῶι ἐνὶ δήμωι   10
πίδακ᾽ ἐ[λ]αιόρυτον προχέων ἀστοῖσι γεραίρει.
οὐ γάρ σε πρώτιστα, Θέων, μετὰ παισὶν ἑταίροις
ἀρχεύοντα νέον γινώσκομεν, ἀλλ᾽ ἔτι τηλοῦ,

6 Corrected from μὲν ἀνυμνείουσιν ἀοιδοί in Π.   7
κλήιζουσι is a substitute for κλείουσι in Π.   10 Corrected
from τίων ἐνὶ δήμωι in Π.

ANONYMOUS

PRAISE OF THEON [3 A.D.]

Theon, who had previously supplied oil for the men's gymnasium, has now supplied it for the boys' also. " Probably . . . Theon was a young man whose wealth had led to his early appointment to the office of gymnasiarch " (ed. pr., after Wilamowitz).

In vv. 6-7, 10, 19 there are interlinear improvements on the text. These are not corrections of misprints, but deliberate alterations made, probably, by the author himself. It is not likely that such a poem was often republished : probably our text is the author's copy, incorporating his own δεύτεραι φροντίδες.

WITH your own lips, Hermes, hasten to sing to me about your young interpreter [a] : assist the minstrel, let your fingers strike the seven strings of the tuneful lyre, which your own hands first fashioned, when you were new-dropped at your mother's feet ; and you gave it to Apollo in ransom for his oxen. Therefore do latter-day minstrels celebrate your service of the Muse, and herdsmen in the fields proclaim you Pastoral God, and athletes in the Stadium call you Hermes, Governor of the Games,[b] and cities hymn you as Guardian of their Gymnasiums. Here this youth also, great master, honours you among your hallowed people in pouring forth a fountain of oil for our townsfolk. It is not lately that we knew you first, Theon, holding high office among your youth-

---

[a] Theon was evidently a man of literary tastes (*cf.* the end of the poem): hence " interpreter of H." (who invented the lyre). [b] ἐναγώνιος Ἑρμᾶς Pind. *P.* ii. 10, *N.* x. 52-53.

ἠμὲν ἐλαιοχύτοισιν ἀλειφόμενοι κοτύλῃσιν,
ἠδὲ καὶ αἰνύμενοι δώρων Δημήτερος ἁγνῆς.   15
κεῖνα μὲν ἐσθλὰ φίλος δήμωι πόρες, ἐσθλὰ δ' ἐπ'
     ἐσθλοῖς
ἐνθάδε νῦν παίδεσσι διδοῖς καὶ ἀμείνονα ταῦτα.
ἤτοι μὲν γὰρ κεῖνα καὶ ἀφνειὸς πόροι ἀνήρ,
πλούτου γὰρ κενεοῖο πέλει κενεαυχέα δῶρα·
ταῦτα δὲ Μουσάων σοφίης δεδαημένος ἀνήρ.   20
τῶι σ' ἐπὶ τοῖσι μάλιστα γεραίρομεν ἤ περ ἐκείνοις,
οὕνεκα κεῖνα πατήρ σε διδάξατο, ταῦτα δὲ Μοῦσαι.

19 κεν. δῶρα written above μειλίγματα κεῖνα in Π.

ANONYMOUS

131 [3 A.D.]   TREATISE ON METRES

Ed. pr. *Schubart-Wilamowitz, *Berliner Klassikertexte*,
v. 2. 1907, p. 140.   See Wilamowitz, *Gr. Versk.* p. 69, n. 1;
Körte, *Archiv*, v. 540.

τ]ῶν αὖ Πρωτεσίλαος ἀρήιος ἡγεμόνευε,
τ]ῶι δ' ἅμα τεσσαράκοντα μέλαιναι νῆες ἕποντο.

ἡ]νίκ' ἂν ἦ(ι) σπονδεῖο[ς] ὁ δεξιὸς ἂν [τε τ]ροχαῖος
σὺν τούτωι κατ' ἴαμβον, ἐνόπλιος ὣ[ς] διάκειται.

1 Quoted under the lemma [ἄ]λλος in Π, so v. 3 under the
unintelligible ἄλλον.

──────────────

ᵃ =Homer, *Il.* ii. 698 and 710.   ᵇ The first foot
of the line, see ed. pr.   ᶜ See ed. pr.: the writer
is explaining that the first six syllables of the first of

528

ANONYMOUS

ful comrades ; but from long ago,[a] anointing our-
selves from oil-vessels, or sharing the gifts of chaste
Demeter. Those blessings of your favour you be-
stowed upon your people ; and here to-day you give
blessings upon blessings, more precious yet, to our
young men. The others a rich man might provide,
since vainglorious are the gifts of vain riches ; but
these come only from a man learned in the Muses'
arts.[b] So we honour you more highly for these than[c]
for the others, for those were taught you by your
father, these by the Muses.

[a] τηλοῦ temporal Oppian, *Hal.* ii. 495. [b] δεδ. with
genitive Homer, *Il.* xxi. 487. [c] μάλιστα . . . ἤ . . . Ap.
Rhod. iii. 97.

ANONYMOUS

TREATISE ON METRES [3 A.D.]

*From a treatise, itself metrical, on Greek metres : parallel
to the work of Terentianus Maurus in Latin.*

" Of them, warlike Protesilaus was commander ;
forty dark ships followed in his company." [a]
When the right foot [b] is a spondee, if there is a
trochee with it beside an iambus, it is like an
enoplion.[c]

the two Homeric lines are " like an enoplion ": *i.e.* a
" spondee " followed by a " trochee " followed by an
" iambus," $- - | - \cup | \cup - |$: not what is usually understood
by *enoplion,* but the term was used to cover several similar
metrical units (or complexes).

529

κρητικὸν ἂν προσθῇς πόδα τῶι τρι[μ]έτρωι,
τ[ετράμετρος   5
γίνεται, ἐν ῥυθμῶι τε τροχαίωι κλί[ν]εται οὗτος.
εἶδος δ᾿ αὐτοῦ ἐγὼ δείξω, σὺ δὲ μάνθαν᾿ ἀκ[ούων·

εἶα νῦν, ἐπεὶ σχολὴ π[άρεσ]τι, πα[ῖ Μενοιτίου

. . . .

---

^a The writer is shewing that the addition of a cretic – ‿ –
transforms an iambic trimeter into a trochaic tetrameter.

ANONYMOUS

132 [4 A.D.]   PRAISE OF MAXIMUS

Ed. pr. *Gerstinger, *Griechische Literarische Papyri*, i.
p. 83, 1932 (*Mitteilungen aus der Papyrussammlung der
Nationalbibliothek in Wien : Papyrus Erzherzog Rainer,
Neue Serie, Erste Folge*). See Körte, *Archiv*, xi. 224.

*It is natural to suppose that the iambics are part of a
preface to the hexameters, cf. the Epicedeion on the Professor
at Berytus below : but this is by no means certain, v. Körte,
loc. cit. p. 225.*

*The iambics : the subject had been ordered to represent his
city at Rome (v. 14 ἐν Ἰταλοῖς, v. 17 παρ᾿ Ἰταλοῖσι). His
appointment was a compliment to his intelligence, his talent
for oratory and his perseverance. He impressed his superiors
by the celerity of his journey to Rome ; and we may safely*

(a)   ] ἦλθες· ἔστ[ε γαῖά] σε
    ἡ τῶν βασι[. . . .] εὐμενὴς ἐδέξατο·
    ἐν ἧι στρατεύων [κ]αταδεηθέντος ποτὲ
    τοῦ τότε κρατοῦντος· ἦν δὲ τοῦ νι[. .]μεν[. .

2 βασι[λέων] ed. pr.   4 νι[κω]μέν[ου] ed. pr.

530

ANONYMOUS

If you add a cretic foot to the trimeter, it becomes
a tetrameter ; and this descends in trochaic rhythm.
I will shew you its type, if you will listen and learn :—
"Come now, since we have leisure, offspring of
Menoetius." [a]

.   .   .   .   .   .

N.B. the example lacks the diaeresis normal in troch. tetram.
The iambic trimeter recurs *T.G.F.* fr. adesp. 138 Nauck[2]
(assigned to Sophocles, Wilam. *Gr. Versk.* 69 n.).

ANONYMOUS
PRAISE OF MAXIMUS   [4 A.D.]

*conjecture that he was not unsuccessful in his mission. The
first five lines remain obscure,—on his way to Rome he
arrived at some country where he was welcome, and where he
engaged in a military campaign at the request of the local
government.*

*The hexameters : Maximus is applauded because he did
not forget his city and succumb to the temptation to stay in
the capital, as many had done in the past. He is described as
" leader of the Tyrians and their neighbours," and his ser-
vices to Anatolian cities are commemorated. Probably this
poem was composed in Tyre, and Tyre is the city which
entrusted Maximus with his mission to the capital (v. 12).*

*Since (in the iambics) the central imperial court is evidently
still in Italy, the composition is to be dated before the end of
the 3rd century A.D.*

(*a*) . . . you came, until the land of . . . received
you with friendly welcome. Campaigning there,
as he who then was in command requested, . . .[a]

[a] The general sense of vv. 4-5 is at present quite uncertain.

531

ἀνδρός· παρὰ τὸν ἀδελφὸν αὐτὸν ἱε[5
οὐ παντὸς ἀνδρός, ἀλλὰ τεχνικωτάτου
καὶ νοῦν ἔχοντος, ὀξύτητι μὲν φρενῶν
δρόμωι δὲ γλώττης εὐστ[ό]χως κ[ε]χρημένου
δε[ι]νοῦ δὲ κάμνειν· ει δε . ιτι . . ηκαμεν
ρω[. . . . .]υτ[. . . .]ουτιηω[. .]ωντος σι[.]-   10
   σο[. .]ουν
μηδ' εἰς αναπα[. .]αν· πᾶσιν ἐρρῶσθα[ι φ]ρ[ά-
   σα]s
τούτωι [. . . .]ξας· τοῦ μεμαρτυρηκότος
τὴν ψ[ῆ]φον οὐκ ἔδειξας ἡμαρτημένην,
ἀλλ' ἧς ἐν Ἰταλοῖ[s] πρίν γε τὸν πεπομφότα
τουτὶ πεπεῖσθαι τοῦ χρόνου σταθμώμενον   15
ὃν [χ]ρὴ δαπανῆσαι καὶ τὸν ὀξέως πάνυ
ὁδοιπορούντ[α·] παρ' Ἰταλοῖσι δ' ἐν
   βραχεῖ . . .

(b) πατρίδος ἐξελάθοντο καὶ αὐτόθι [ναιετάεσκον,
οἱ δ' ὁπόταν θ[υ]ρέοις [. . .]των πτόλι[
ἄψορροι στ(ε)ίχουσιν [ἐὴ]ν ποτὶ πατρί[δα
   γαῖαν
μᾶλλον ἀγαυότεροι, ναέτῃσι δὲ χ[άρμα
   π]έλονται.
τοὺς αὐτὴ δέχεται πα[τρ]ὶς μέγα [κα]γχα-
   λόωσα,   5
μήτηρ οἷα Λάκαινα σὺν ἀσπίδι π[αῖδ]α
   λαβοῦσα
αὖτις ἀφ' αἱματόε[ν]τος ἀνερχόμενον πο-
   λέμοιο.
εὖ γὰρ δὴ τόδε ἴστε π[ο]λὺ [π]λέον ἤπερ
   ἔγωγε,
οἳ καὶ ἐπειρήσασθ[ε καὶ] ὄμμασι θηήσασθε,

ANONYMOUS

It was not the task of every man, but only of the skilful, the intelligent, the man of sharp wits and fluent speech that hits the mark, a man strong to endure. . . . You took your leave of all, . . . you did not prove your sponsor's vote mistaken. You were in Italy before the man who sent you could believe it, when he measured the time that even the swiftest traveller must consume. Among the Italians in a short space . . .

(*b*) . . . forgot their country and dwelt even there. The others, when . . . with shields . . ., come back to their country more glorious than ever, and to the dwellers there rejoicing comes with them. Exultant their own country gives them welcome, like a Spartan mother receiving back her son with his shield when he returns from bloody warfare. For this you know well—far better than I —you who have put it to the proof and seen it with

---

(*a*) 5 ἰϵ[το ed. pr.

πῶς ὅδ᾽ ἀν[ὴρ] ἐ[φ]έπε[σκ]ε κατ᾽ ἀντολίην
   ἐρατεινὴν   10
ἠώιαις πτολίεσσι[ν ἐυ]κτιμένηι[σιν ἀρ]ήγων,
Μάξιμος ἀντίθεος, Τυρ[ί]ων ἀγὸς ἠδὲ πα-
   [ροίκων,
φαίνων εὐνομίης ἱερὸν φάος· ἔργα δ᾽ [ὕ]φ[ην]ε
καλὰ καὶ ἀμφιβόητ[α], τὰ μὴ φθίσει ἄσπετο[ς
   αἰ]ών·
ἀλλὰ] τὰ μὲν μολπῇσιν [ἐ]ν εὐρυτέρῃσι[ν
   ἀείσω.   15

.   .   .   .   .   .

ANONYMOUS

133   [3 A.D.]   ? ASTYOCHE

Ed. pr. *Grenfell-Hunt, *P. Oxy.* ii. 1899, no. 214, p. 27.
See Powell, *Collect. Alex.* p. 76 ; Platt, *C.R.* 13, 439 ; Weil,
Journal d. Savants, 1900, 96 ; Crönert, *Archiv,* ii. 516 ;
Powell-Barber, *New Chapters,* i. 110 ; Milne, *Cat. Lit. Pap.
B.M.* no. 39 ; Bolling, *A.J. Phil.* 20, 1901, 63 ; Schmid-
Stählin, *Gr. Lit.* ii. 2, 965.

*The first five lines refer to part of Telephus's adventures,
and describe how nearly he destroyed the Achaeans when they
mistook their way to Troy and landed at Mysia. The speaker
(of v. 8 sqq., and doubtless of the preceding seven lines too)
is a Trojan (v. 9) woman (v. 14 ed. pr., αὐτή) : perhaps
Astyoche, mother of Telephus. She prays for a treaty
between Trojans and Achaeans. From this prayer (esp.
v. 11) it seems certain that the Trojan war has already
begun, and that the allusion to the adventures of Telephus is*

your eyes, how this hero dealt in the fair Orient
bringing succour to the nobly-founded cities of the
East,—he, godlike Maximus, leader of the Tyrians
and their neighbours, revealing to them the holy
light of Law and Order. Noble and renowned are
the deeds that he wrought, and countless ages shall
not destroy them.

But of this I would sing anon in ampler melo-
dies. . . .

.   .   .   .   .   .

ANONYMOUS

? ASTYOCHE [3 A.D.]

retrospective: prayer for a treaty between Trojans *and*
Achaeans *would be irrelevant in the course of the war of*
Telephus *and his Mysians against the Achaeans. An obvious
possibility is the story of Eurypylus, the son of Telephus,
defeated in single combat at Troy by Neoptolemus (see p. 17
for the story): fear for her son's fate would be sufficient
reason for the anxiety of Astyoche, and her prayer for
heaven-sent peace. But there are doubtless other possibili-
ties: and the problem is complicated by the verso of this
papyrus, which contains fragments of 22 hexameters—
probably belonging to the same speech—dealing with the
dangers of travel by sea. (See further Robert, ap. ed. pr.)*

*The date of composition is uncertain. But there is nothing
Alexandrian in the style, and the ascription to the 3rd century
A.D. is probable enough. The poem may then be the work of
a writer who represents that tradition which reached its*

535

*climax in the poetry of Quintus Smyrnaeus : simple and
direct narrative, in the Homeric style—a tradition which*

ἐ]ξαπίνης ἐπέδησεν ἀνωίστο[ισι κλάδοισι,
οὔ] κεν ἔτι ζώοντες ἐς Ἴλιον ἦλθον ['Αχαιοί·
ἔ]νθα δὲ καὶ Μενέλαος ἐκέκλιτο, ἔν[θ' 'Αγαμέμνων
ὤ]λετο, καὶ τὸν ἄριστον ἐν 'Αργείοις ['Αχιλῆα
Τήλεφος ἐξενάριξε πρὶν Ἕκτορ[ος ἀντίον ἐλθεῖν   5

(*Fragments of two more lines*)

εἰ καὶ ἀπ' 'Αργείοι(ο) λάχεν γέν[ος] Ἡρακλῆος
[[Τ]ήλεφον ἐν θαλάμοις πολέμων ἀπάνε[υθε . . . . .]]
κλ]ῦτέ μοι ἀθάνατοι [Ζ]εὺς δ[ὲ π]λέον ὃν γενετῆρα
Δαρδάνου ἡμετέροιο καὶ Ἡ[ρα]κλῆος ἀκούω·
καὶ τούτων φράσσασθε μ[αχῶ]ν λύσιν, †ἶσα δὲ
      μύθοις†   10
σ]υνθεσίη Τρώεσσι καὶ 'Α[ργ]είοισι γε[ν]έσθω

(*Fragments of eight more lines*)

6 η καὶ Π, corr. Bolling.   7 Del. Bolling.   8 The
word γενετήρ, hitherto unknown before Nonnus (but see v. 6
of no. 136 below), supports the ascription of the poem to
the 3rd century A.D. (Pratt). The plural κλῦτε in a prayer
is against the older epic convention (Bolling).   11 For
a tentative restoration of the first three of the next eight

ΔΙΟΝΥΣΙΟΣ

134   [4 A.D.]   ΒΑΣΣΑΡΙΚΑ

Ed. pr. Kenyon, *Album Gratulatorium in honorem Henrici
van Herwerden*, 1902, p. 137.   See Crönert, *Archiv*, ii. 351 ;
Ludwich, *Phil. Woch.* 23, 1903, 23 ; *Milne, *Archiv*, vii. 3
(revised text, with notes by Wilamowitz) and *Cat. Lit. Pap.*
536

soon fought a losing battle against the loud and pretentious followers of Nonnus.

. . . suddenly ensnared him in branches that he looked not for,[a] the Achaeans would not have come to Ilium still alive. There had Menelaus been laid low, there had Agamemnon perished, and Telephus had slain Achilles, noblest among the Argives, before he came face to face with Hector. . . .

(Fragments of two more lines)

. . . if truly he got his descent from Argive Heracles, . . . [Telephus, in his chambers, apart from warfare]. . . . Hear me, immortals, and especially Zeus, who is father—they tell me—of our Dardanus and Heracles : devise an end to these battles too, and let there be agreement,[b] . . . between the Trojans and the Argives. . . .

(Fragments of eight more lines)

[a] Allusion to the story that Dionysus caused Telephus to stumble over a vine in his pursuit. [b] ἶσα δὲ μύθοις is unintelligible : " chose qui ressemble à une fable," Weil. Perhaps, as Beazley suggests, a line is missing after v. 10.

lines, see Bolling : his readings are not to be reconciled with the evidence of Π.

DIONYSIUS

BASSARICA [4 A.D.]

B.M. no. 40 ; Morel, *Archiv*, ix. 222 ; Bidez, *Rev. de Phil.* 27, 1903, 82 ; Keydell, *Phil. Woch.* 1929, 1101 ; Maas, *Byz. Zeitschr.* 29, 383 ; Wifstrand, *Eranos*, 1930, 102 ; *cf.* Knaack, *P.-W.-K. s.v. Dionysius*, no. 95.

LITERARY PAPYRI

From the Bassarica *of Dionysius (first identified by* Keydell, loc. cit.). *Written long before the time of Nonnus, this poem anticipated the theme of his* Dionysiaca—*the Indian expedition of Dionysus—and even the name of his Indian king, Deriades.*

Three men (Thrasius, Prothous and Pylaon) slay a stag and skin it at the command of a fourth (Bombus). They dress the corpse of an enemy (Modaeus) in the skin. A

δὴ γάρ μιν Πρόθοός τε Πυλάων τε Θράσιό[ς τε
Βόμβου κεκλομένοιο διαθρώισκοντα κιχ[όντες
σφάξαν, ἀτὰρ δείραντε καὶ ἐκ δέρος εἰρύσ[αντε
κόσμεον ἀνέρα λυγρὸν ἀπὸ κρατός τε καὶ ὤ[μων,
ἀμφὶ δέ οἱ νεόδαρτος ἐνὶ χροῖ δύετο ῥῖνος   5
ἐντυπάς, αὐτὰρ ὕπερθε κ[έ]ρα πάμφαινεν ἰδ[έσθαι
τηλόθεν, οὐδέ τι θηρὸς ἐ[λ]είπετο δερκομέ[νοισιν.
ὣς οἱ μὲν ποιητὸν ἐπ' ἀνέρι θῆρα τίθ[ε]σκ[ον.
ἡ δὲ Μεθυμναίοιο βαθύπτε[ρ]ον οὐλοσυθ[
ἐς κλισίην ἵκετ' ἄρτι πε[ρ]ι[ζα]φελὲς βοοῶ[σα,   10
τὸν δ' εὗρ' ἐν λεχέεσσιν . . . . . θ[ρ]ωισκον[
κείμενον οὐδέ μιν ἐγ[γὺ]ς ἄναξ] ἐφρά[σσ]ατ' [ἰοῦσαν,
ἀλλά ἑ χαιτάων ὄπιθ[εν λάβεν αἰ]ξασα.
αὐτὰρ ὁ αἶψ' ἀνόρουσε [καὶ ἔκθορε]ν ἠύτε π[ῶλος
ῥοίζωι ὑπὸ σφεδαν[ῶι . . . .] προχέε[ι α[.]π[15
βουκόλωι εἰδόμεν[ος . . . .]κ νόον ἠερεθ[
αὐτίκα δ' εὐαστὴ[ρ θεὸς ἔσσυ]το, τοὺς δ' ἐνόη[σε
Βόμβον ἐὺν Πρόθοόν [τε Πυλ]άονά τε Θράσιό[ν τε
Μωδαίωι τανύοντα[ς ἔπι σκέπ]ος, αὐτὰρ [ὕπερθεν
ἱερὰ λήνεα πλεκτά, τά τ' α[. . . .] κικλή[σκουσι·   20

7 οὐδ' ἔτι Milne, with Π: οὐδέ τι ed. pr.   10 L. & S.⁹
quote as περιζαφελῶς, wrongly.   12 D. L. P.   16
παρὲ]κ Milne.   17 D. L. P.   20 Some obscure word
is wanting, *e.g.* ἀ[ργέτα] (Beazley, see L. & S. *s.v.* ἀργής).
538

woman (whose name may be concealed in the end of v. 9)
awakens Dionysus. He approaches the four men, and
decrees that the corpse shall be eaten by its compatriots. He
leaps into the midst of his enemies' army, and tells their
leader, Deriades, that they shall not escape unless they rend
an animal apart and eat its flesh raw. Therefore he offers
them the corpse dressed in a stag-skin. Deriades, whose
men fall eagerly upon it, says that he would rather eat the
flesh of Dionysus. [For the matter of numerous other small
fragments belonging to our II, see esp. Wilamowitz, l.c.]

As it [a] leapt through, Prothous and Pylaon and
Thrasius came upon it at the call of Bombus and slew
it : they flayed it, and stripping off the skin, arrayed
the wretched man from head and shoulders down.
The new-flayed hide clave to his body, moulded to
the flesh ; above, the horns gleamed to be seen afar ;
to one that beheld him, he wanted nothing of the wild
beast's form. Thus did they set a counterfeited
animal upon a man.

Now she, . . ., came with furious cries to the deep-
winged [b] tent of Methymna's god.[c] And him she
found lying in his bed . . . ; her master marked her
not as she came close ; but she rushed forward and
seized him by the hair behind. Then up he leapt,
and jumped from his bed like a colt at a violent
whistling . . . pours forth . . . in the guise of an
oxherd. . . . Straightway the Bacchanal god set
forth, and he observed them—strong Bombus and
Prothous and Pylaon and Thrasius—stretch the
covering upon Modaeus, and sacred fillets on his
head of twisted wool, which they call . . . But the

[a] A stag.   [b] *i.e.* a tent with wide " flaps " at the door.
[c] Dionysus.

ἀλλά σφεας κατέεργε καὶ [ἀσχ]αλόων φά[το μῦθον·
μηκέτι νῦν ἔργωι δηθύ[νετ]ον ἑστειῶτ[ες,
μηδὲ πέλας βωμοῖο θεῶ[ν . .]αινεμεν [
ἀλλὰ ἑ δυσμενέεσσιν ἕλωρ καὶ κύρμα [γενέσθαι
δώσομεν, ὥς κεν ἔτηισιν ὑπὸ σφετέροι[σι   25
φῆ καὶ μέσσον ὄρουσεν ἀνὰ στρατόν, ἔν[θα μάλιστα
Κηθαῖοι πυρίκαυτον ἐπὶ μόθον ἐκλο[νέοντο,
σ]τὰς [δ'] ὅ γε Δηριαδῆα καὶ ἄλ[λου]ς ἴαχ[εν αὐδῶν·
ὢ]δ' ἄρα νῦν φράζεσθε γυναικ[ῶ]ν ἀτμέ[νες Ἰνδοί,
Δ]ηριάδηι δ' ἔκπαγλον ἐ[πιστάμ]ενος τ[άδε φράζω· 30
ο[ὐ] γάρ κεν πρὶν τοῦτο κατ[ὰ στ]ένος αἴθο[πος
          ὁρμὴν
οἴνου ἐρωήσαιτε καὶ ἐκ κακότητα φύ[γοιτε,
πρίν κε θοῆι ἐνὶ νυκτὶ διάλλυδις εἰρύσ[σαντες
ὠμάδια κρέα θηρὸς ἀπὸ ζωοῖο φάγη[τε.
ἀλλ' ἄγετ' ὀρθόκερων ἔλαφον μέγαν, ὅσ[τις ἄριστος 35
Ἑλλάδος ἐξ ἱερῆς σὺν ἄμ' ἕσπετο, θαῦμ[α ἰδέσθαι,
ἑλκεμέναι κρειῶν ἀγαθὴν [ἔ]ριν ὁρμη[θῆτε.
αὐτὰρ ἐπὴν νὺξ ἥδε τέκηι φάος, αὐτίκ' [ἔπειτα
κίσταις λείψανα θηρὸς ἐν ἀργυρέηισι β[άλωμεν,
ὄφρα κε νοσφισθεῖεν ὑπ' ἠλέκτωρι [φαεινῶι.   40
φῆ ὅ γε, τοὶ δὲ καὶ αὐτοὶ ἐπὶ κρεάεσσι π[
ἀνδρομέοις λελίηντο καὶ ἵμερον ἄ[σπετον ἆσαι,
λύσσηι ὑπ' ὀξείηι βεβολημένοι. α[ὐτὰρ ἔπειτα
Δηριάδης Διὸς υἱὸν ἀμειβόμενος [προσέειπεν·
αἲ γὰρ δὴ μελειστὶ διὰ κρέα σεῖο τάμ[οιμι,   45
ὠμὰ καταβρῶξαι μὲν ὀίομαι ου[

god stayed them, and spoke in distress : " Delay
no longer at your task, idly standing, nor by the
altar of the gods . . . but we will give him up to
be the spoil and prey of our enemies, that he may
be (devoured) by his own comrades." He spoke, and
leapt into the midst of the army, where most of all
the Cethaeans were rushing to the flame of battle.
There stood he, and cried aloud to Deriades and the
rest : " Slaves of women, Indians, consider now this
way : to Deriades above all I speak this of my know-
ledge :—You shall not, in your present straits, with-
stand the onslaught of the gleaming wine[a] and escape
your evil fate, before in the swift night you tear apart
the raw flesh of a living animal and eat it. This tall
stag straight of horn, the finest that followed us from
holy Hellas, a marvel to behold,—come, hasten to
rend it in good conflict for its flesh. And when this
night gives birth to brightness, straightway let us
cast the animal's remains into silver coffers, that they
may be removed under the beaming sunshine."
He spoke ; and they of their own accord were fain
to fall upon human flesh, and to appease their bound-
less desire, smitten by eager madness. And then
Deriades answered the son of Zeus and spoke :
" Would that I might cut your body limb from limb :
to swallow it raw. . . ."

---

[a] *i.e.* the attack of Dionysus's army inflamed with wine.

---

25 δαμείη at end edd.   42 D. L. P.

ANONYMOUS

PERSIAN WAR OF DIOCLETIAN
135 [Early 4 A.D.] AND GALERIUS

Ed. pr. *Reitzenstein, *Zwei religionsgeschichtliche Fragen, nach ungedruckten griechischen Texten der Strassburger Bibliothek*, Strassburg, 1901, p. 47. See Cumont, *Rev. Et. Anc.* iv. 1902, 36 ; Bidez, *Rev. Phil.* N.S. 27, 1903, 81.

The fragment opens at the conclusion of a fiery speech. Soldiers are stirred to frenzy and fly to arms. Their infinite numbers are related. The news spreads rapidly throughout the world.

This is an era when the Roman Empire stands under four masters. Two of them, Diocletian and Galerius, are about to begin a war with Persia. The other two would have rushed to their assistance, had not one (Constantius Chlorus)

. . . β]ού[λο]μαι. [οἵ] ῥα μανέντες ὑπὸ πληγῆισιν
Ἐννο[ῦς
ἰ]οδόκου[ς] μὲν ἅπαντες ἀν[ε]ζώσαντο φα[ρ]έτ[ρ]ας
τόξα δὲ χερσὶν ἕκαστος ἐκαρτύναντο καὶ αἰχμάς,
πᾶσά τε [Ν]ησαίη πεδιημάχος ἵππος ἀγέρθη,
ἵ]ππος ὅσ[η]ς οὐδ' ἴχνος ὑπὲρ πόντοιο θεούσης   5
πρόσθεν [ἐ]πὶ πλωτῶν δρ[υ]όχων ἠνέγκατο Νηρεύς.
οὐ γὰρ ὅσος στεινωπὸν ὑπ[ὸ π]τύχα Θερμο-
πυλάων
Μῆδος Ἄρης ἤχησεν ὑπ[ὸ σ]τρατιῆισι Λακώνων,
τόσσος ἐμοῖς βασιλεῦσ[ιν ἐ]πήιεν ἀντιβολήσων,
ἀλλὰ πολὺ πλείων τε κα[ὶ ἀ]σχαλό]ων ὑπ' [ὁμ]ο-
κλῆς.   10

7 ὅσον στεινωπός Π.

542

ANONYMOUS

ANONYMOUS

PERSIAN WAR OF DIOCLETIAN
AND GALERIUS   [Early 4 A.D.]

*been busy in Britain, the other (Maximian) engaged in Spain
(of which fact this fragment is our first evidence: but we
knew that in 296 he was fighting the Germans on the Rhine,
in 297 the Moors in Africa; perhaps he went to Africa
through Spain, driving the Moors before him).*

*The correct language and metre of this competent but
unexciting piece suggest an Alexandrian model: for which
v. ed. pr. p. 51 n. 3.   The poem is representative of a common
literary genre:—the hymn in celebration of a general's
victories.   Cumont compares the poems written in honour of
the campaigns of Constantine (Julian, Or. i. p. 2 d) and of
Julian (Zosimus iii. 2. 4).*

" . . . it is my will." They, maddened by Enyo's
lash, all girded on their quivers full of arrows, each
armed his hand with bow and spear, and all the
Nesaean[a] cavalry that fights upon the plain as-
sembled,—no fraction[b] of their number speeding
across the sea did Nereus ever bring of old on
floating rafts. Not such as the Persian arms that
rang beneath the Spartan host in the narrow cleft
of Thermopylae,[c]—not such the numbers that ad-
vanced to meet my kings, but greater far, and
stung by the battle cry. . . .

---

[a] *i.e.* from Media : Oppian, *Cyn.* i. 310-311 πανυπείροχος
ἵππος Νησαῖος.   [b] οὐδ' ἴχνος, "not even a trace," I
take (with Beazley) to mean "not even a fraction."
[c] This parallel, and the next sentence, shew that it is the
Persian (not the Roman) army whose gathering is described.

543

LITERARY PAPYRI

*(Fragments of the beginnings of nine more lines, referring
to the spread of the news throughout the world. Cf.*
χῶρος ἅπας Κάσιαί τε [πύλαι, Ἀραβίης ὑπὸ
χέρσον [, οὐδὲ καὶ Ἑλλὰς ἄπυστ[ος, κτλ.

τ[η]λεθάοντα κατηιώρησε κορύμβω[ν.
τῶι δέ κ]εν Ἰταλίηθεν ἐπερρώοντο καὶ ἄλλοι
κοίρανοι, εἰ μὴ τὸν μὲν ['Ι]βηρικὸς εὔρυεν Ἄρης,
τῶι δὲ μόθος νήσοιο Β[ρ]εταννίδος ἀμφιδεδήει.
οἷα] δ' ὁ μὲν Κρήτηθεν, ὁ δ' εἰναλίης ἀπὸ Δήλου, 15
εἰσι Ζεὺς ὑπὲρ Ὄθρυν, ὁ [δ'] ἐς Πάγγαιον Ἀπόλ-
λων,
τοῖν δὲ κορυσσομένοιν ὅμαδος πέφρικε Γιγάντω[ν,
τοῖος ἄναξ πρέσβιστος [ἄ]γων στρατὸν Αὐσονιήων
ἀντολίην ἀφίκανε σὺ[ν ὁ]πλοτέρωι βασιλῆι.
καὶ γὰρ ἔσ[αν μακάρεσσιν ὁ]μοίιοι, ὃς μὲν ἐοικὼς 20
αἰθερίωι [Διὶ κάρτος, ὁ δ'] Ἀπόλλωνι κομήτηι

·   ·   ·   ·   ·   ·

ANONYMOUS

136   [Early 4 A.D.]   CREATION OF THE UNIVERSE

Ed. pr. *Reitzenstein, *Zwei religionsgeschichtliche Fragen,
nach ungedruckten griechischen Texten der Strassburger
Bibliothek*, Strassburg, 1901, p. 53 (*qu. v.* for full interpreta-
tion and discussion : the cosmogony is Grecized Egyptian).
See Bidez, *Rev. Phil.* N.S. 27, 1903, 81.

*A successful poem, grand in conception and quite forceful
in execution. Not much is missing from the head of our
fragment. There was a description of God and of the four
elements : then God determined to make a* Κόσμος *out of the*

544

ANONYMOUS

(Fragments of the beginnings of nine more lines)

. . . hung blooming (garlands) from the sterns of ships. Other kings also would have sped from Italy to help him; but one [a] was stayed by war in Spain, and round the other [b] blazed the flame of battle in the isle of Britain. Even as one divinity goes from Crete, the other from seagirt Delos—Zeus over Othrys, Apollo to Pangaeus—and as they gird their armour on, the throng of Giants trembles: in such guise came our elder [c] lord, beside the younger king,[d] to the Orient with an army of Ausonians. Like to the blessed gods they were, one in strength a match for Zeus above, the other for long-haired Apollo . . .

. . . . . .

[a] Maximian.   [b] Constantius Chlorus.   [c] Diocletian.
[d] Galerius.

ANONYMOUS

CREATION OF THE UNIVERSE [Early 4 A.D.]

elements, and (where our fragment begins) creates of himself a second god, Hermes, to perform this task.

Hermes brings to an end the conflict of the elements, and creates out of them the sky with its planets and constellations, and the earth with its rivers and seas.

The gap after v. 41 is probably quite a small one. In the interval, Hermes decided that Life must be created : and that he will then transform himself into the sun.

When the fragment begins again, Hermes is looking for a place where he may set life down when he has created it. He

*determines to build a city. In the fragments which follow,
he decides (at some length) against the extremes of north
and south.*

*In the end, of course, his choice fell upon Egypt (tradi-
tionally—even among the Greeks—the first part of the world
to be inhabited by men).*

ἐ]ξερύσας τινὰ μοῖραν ἑῆς πολυειδέος ἀλκ[ῆς.
κεῖνος δὴ νέος ἐστὶν ἐμὸς πατρώιος Ἑρμῆς·
τῶι μάλα πόλλ᾽ ἐπέτελλε καμεῖν περικαλλέα
   κ[όσμον,
δῶκε δέ οἱ ῥάβδον χρυσέην διακοσμήτειραν,
πάσης εὐέργοιο νοήμονα μητέρα τέχνης.   5
σὺν τῆι ἔβη Διὸς υἱὸς ἑ[οῦ] γενετῆρος ἐφετμὴν
πᾶσαν ἵνα κρήνειεν· ὁ δ᾽ ἥμενος ἐν περιωπῆι
τέρπετο κυδαλίμου θηεύμενος υἱέος ἔργα.
αὐτὰρ ὁ θεσπεσίην φορέων τετράζυγα μορφὴν
ὀφθαλμοὺ[ς κάμ]μυσε . . . . . . ομένης ὑπὲρ αἴγλης 10
         ]ς εἶπέ τε μῦθον·
κέκλυτε . . . . αἰ]θέρος . . . . αὐτὸς
λη]γέμεναι προτέρης ἔριδος στοιχε[ῖα κελεύει.
δαι]μονίηι πείθεσθε διακρίνεσθέ (τ᾽) [ἐφετμῆι.
λ]ωιτέρη δέ τις ὕμμι συνήλυσι[ς ἔσσετ᾽ ἔπειτα. 15
τεύξω γὰρ φιλότητα καὶ ἵμερον [ἀμφὶς ἐοῦσιν
ὕ(μμι) μετ᾽ ἀλλήλοισιν ἀρειοτέρηι ἐ[πὶ μοίρηι.
ὣς εἰπὼν χρυσέηι ῥάβδωι θίγεν [
εὐκήλωι δὲ τάχιστα κατείχε[το πάντα γαλήνηι
παυσάμενα στοιχεῖα πολυσ[20
ἔστη δ᾽ εὐθὺς ἕκαστον ὀφειλ[ομένωι ἐνὶ χώρωι,
μαρμαρυγὴν [
δηναίης [δὲ διχοστασίης λάθετ᾽ ἀρθμηθέντα.

ANONYMOUS

Bidez, loc. cit., *plausibly suggests that these fragments are from the introduction to a lengthy encyclopaedic poem, of which the ultimate purpose is the narration of the historical founding of a particular city. The attribution of the poem (and of the previous one : they probably proceed from the same hand) to Soterichus is very speculative.*

. . . having drawn forth a portion of his manifold power [a] : that is the Hermes of my fathers in his youth. To him he gave full many a command, to make an Universe of fairest Order, and gave him a golden wand, his regulator, wise parent of every serviceable art. With this the son of Zeus went forth to accomplish all his father's bidding ; Zeus sat on a place of vantage, and rejoiced as he beheld the works of his illustrious son. He, clad in wondrous fourfold shape,[b] closed his eyes [c] . . . over the brightness . . . and spoke :—" Hearken . . . of air . . . (Zeus) himself bids the elements cease their former strife. Obey the word of God, and fall apart ! Hereafter you shall come together in better sort : for I will create mutual friendship and love among you in your day of separation, towards a better destiny." So he spoke, and with his golden wand he touched . . . and quietude and peace at once prevailed over all the elements, and they ceased . . . and straightway stood each in his appointed place, the gleam . . . united, they forgot their immemorial conflict. Now

[a] *i.e.* having created Hermes from his own person.
[b] This mystical expression means that Hermes represented each of the four elements in himself.   [c] When Hermes closes his eyes, darkness falls upon the universe ; when he opens them, light (so the Egyptian Thot, with whom H. is identified here. *Cf.* Homer, *Od.* v. 47 : Hermes has a staff with which he can open or close the eyes of men).

20 πολυσ[χιδέων καταμιγμῶν ed. pr.

αὐτὰρ ὁ παγγενέτα[ο θεοῦ
πρῶτα μὲν αἰγλήεν[τα . . . . αἰθέρα 25
ἀρρήτωι στροφάλιγγ[ι] π[α]λιν[δ]ί[νητον
οὐρανὸν ἐσφαίρωσε κατεστραφ[
ἑπτὰ δέ μιν ζώναις διεκόσμ[εεν, ἑπτὰ δ᾽ ἐπῆσαν
ἄστρων ἡγεμονῆες, ἄλη ὢν [τείρεα δινεῖ·
ἄλλου νέρ[τ]ερος ἄλλος ἐπήτρ[ιμοι ἠλάσκουσι.   30
πάντοθι δ᾽ αἴθον ὁμοῦ περὶ χ[
μέσσην γαῖαν ἔπ[η]ξ[εν] ἀκι[νήτοις ἐνὶ δεσμοῖς,
ἐς δ᾽ αἴθωνα νότ[ον] κρυμώ[δεά τ᾽ ἄρκτον ἔτεινε
λοξὸν ἀκινήτοιο [κ]αὶ ἡ[σύχου ἄξονος οἶμον.
καὶ ποταμοῦ κελάδοντος [35
μαινομένην ἀχάλινον ἀν[
ἀλλὰ μέσαις ἕνα κόλπον ἀολ[λ
μακραῖς ἠιόνεσσι χάραξε δ[
ἡ δὲ πολυπλάγκτων π[
νήχεται ἠπείροιο κασιγνήτης ε[40
ἄξονα δὲ σφίγγουσι δύω πόλοι [ἀμφοτέρωθεν.

(*Traces of five more lines*)

οὔπω] κύκλος ἔην Ὑπερίονος, οὐδὲ καὶ αὐτὴ
εἰλι]π(ό)δων (ἐτίνασσε) βοῶν εὔληρα Σελήνη,
νὺ]ξ δὲ διηνεκέως ἄτερ ἤματος ἔρρεε μούνη
ἄστρων λεπταλέηισιν ὑποστίλβουσα βολῆισι.   45
τὰ φρονέων πολιοῖο δι᾽ ἠέρος ἔστιχεν Ἑρμῆς
οὐκ οἶος, σὺν τῶι (γ)ε Λόγος κίεν ἀγλαὸς υἱός
λαιψηραῖς πτερύγεσσι κεκασμένος, αἰὲν ἀληθής,
ἁγνὴν ἀτρεκέεσσιν ἔχων ἐπὶ χείλεσι πειθώ,
πατρώιου καθαροῖο νοήματος ἄγγελος ὠκύς.   50
σὺν τῶι ἔβη γαιάνδε με[τ. . . . . Ἑρμῆς
παπτ[αίνων

the son of the God who created all things . . . first . . .
the bright air . . . revolving round and round, whirl-
ing unspeakably, . . . the heavens he made a sphere,[a]
. . . and he divided it into seven zones, and to govern
each were seven leaders of the stars. Their wander-
ing revolves the constellations ; one below another
they roam in close array. And on all sides blazed at
once around. . . . He fastened earth in the centre
with unmovable bonds ; to the burning south and
the frosty north he stretched the oblique path of
the peaceful and unmoving[b] axis . . . of the re-
sounding river . . . mad, unbridled . . . but one
gulf[c] in the midst . . . dug with long coastlines
. . . of far-wandering . . . swims . . . of the sister
mainland . . . two poles bind fast the axis at each
end. . . .

(Traces of five more lines)

The circle of Hyperion was not yet, nor yet the
Moon shook the reins of her shambling oxen : but
night without day flowed on alone unbroken, faintly
gleaming under the thin rays of the stars. With this
in mind went Hermes through the grey skies—not
alone, for with him went Reason, his noble son,
adorned with swift wings, ever truthful, with holy
persuasion on lips that never lie : he is the swift
herald of his father's pure intention.

With him went Hermes to the earth, looking about

[a] By whirling the sky round and round.   [b] Earth
revolves about its axis, which itself does not revolve.
[c] Prob. the Mediterranean.

---

26 ἀνάγκην at end ed. pr.   29-30 Commas after δινεῖ
and ἄλλος, ἠλάσκοντες ed. pr. : text D. L. P.

χῶρον [εὔκρη]τον διζήμενος, ἔνθα πολίσσηι
ἄστυ [. . . . . . .]

ANONYMOUS

137   [3-4 A.D.]   ODYSSEY

Ed. pr. *Roberts, *Catalogue of the Greek Papyri in the John Rylands Library, Manchester,* iii. 1938, no. 487, p. 100.

This fragment is almost (v. P. Oxy. no. 1821) unique, inasmuch as it treats a theme taken directly from the Odyssey. Probably Odysseus is relating the adventures of himself and his friends in the first two lines : he is perhaps speaking to Laertes or to Eumaeus (cf. μάκελλαν, βώλωι at the ends of lines verso 13, 15 : so ed. pr., but from v. 6 Philoetius seems as likely a candidate). Vv. 3 sqq., Odysseus convinces somebody (perhaps Philoetius, probably not Eurycleia) of his identity by revealing the scar on his thigh. He reassures

δύσμορ[ο]ς Ἐλπήνωρ, τ[ὸ]ν ἀφήρπασε δώματα
    Κίρκης.
ἴκελ[α] Ἀν[τ]ιφάτηι καὶ ἀνδροφάγωι Πολυφήμωι
. . . .
        ἀ]θλήματα [Πη]νελοπείης.
μὴ σύ γ' ἄπιστος ἐῃις ὡς οὐ νόστησεν Ὀδυσσεύς,
οὐλὴν εἰσοράαις τὴν μηδ' ἴδε Πηνελόπεια.   5
παύεο νῦν σταθμοῖο, Φιλοίτιε, κ[α]ί σε μεθήσω
μνηστῆρας τρομέοντα τεαῖς σὺν βουσὶν ἀλᾶσθαι·

2 (τε) καὶ Beazley.

550

. . . seeking a temperate clime where he might found a city. . . .

・　　・　　・　　・　　・　　・

ANONYMOUS

ODYSSEY [3–4 A.D.]

Philoetius, and promises him freedom. Then he persuades his supporters to arm themselves against the suitors.

Like some details of the story, the words and phases are sometimes independent of their model : e.g. ἴκελα vv. 2, 11, here only adverbial ; ἀθλήματα here only in epic poetry, and with this sense ; the sense of παύεο in v. 6. Apart from these differences the style, metre and vocabulary are fairly conventional. This is the work of a competent poet, whom we may tentatively assign to the 3rd century A.D., thus placing him in the tradition of which Quintus of Smyrna is the most celebrated representative, and from which the school of Nonnus made so violent a reaction.

. . . unhappy Elpenor, whom Circe's palace stole away.[a] . . . like Antiphates and Polyphemus who devoured men.[b] . . .

・　　・　　・　　・　　・

" . . . the hardships of Penelope. That you may not be mistrustful, thinking that Odysseus has not returned, you see the scar which not even Penelope has seen. Leave now your stable, Philoetius, and I will set you free from fear of the suitors, to fare afield

[a] *Odyssey* x. 552 sqq.   [b] *Ibid.* 199–200 μνησαμένοις ἔργων Λαιστρυγόνος Ἀντιφάταο | Κύκλωπός τε βίης μεγαλήτορος ἀνδροφάγοιο.

LITERARY PAPYRI

στήσω σοι τεὸν οἶκον ἐλεύθερον. ἀλλὰ καὶ ὑμεῖς
ἀμφ' ἐμὲ θωρήσσεσθε κατ' Εὐρυμάχοιο καὶ ἄλλω(ν)
μνηστήρων· κακότητος ἐπειρήθητε καὶ ὑμεῖς,   10
ἴκελα Τηλεμάχωι καὶ [ἐχέφρονι Πηνελοπείηι.

.   .   .   .   .   .

*(Traces of two more lines, then fragments of five more
lines, probably the beginning of another extract)*

11 Or [ἀμύμονι Πηνελοπείηι, *cf. Od.* xxiv. 194.

ANONYMOUS

138   EPICEDEION FOR A PROFESSOR OF THE
[4 A.D.]   UNIVERSITY OF BERYTUS

Ed. pr. *Schubart-Wilamowitz, *Berliner Klassikertexte*,
v. 1, 1907, p. 82. See Körte, *Archiv*, v. 547 ; Schemmel,
Phil. Woch. 42, 1923, 236 ; Schubart, *Pap. Graec. Berol.*
Plate XLIIIa, Text xxix.

*Fragments of an Epicedeion spoken at Berytus about a
dead Professor* (Βη[ρυτῶι ed. pr. 1, col. 2, v. 40, Β]ερόης πέδον
II recto v. 9, *in portions too small to be included here). Vv.
1-29, in comic iambics, are a preface to an hexameter eulogy.
(Thereafter follows—too fragmentary for inclusion here—a
similar performance :—an elegiac Epicedeion to which the
same iambic introduction, slightly abbreviated at the end,
is prefixed.)*

*The iambic prologue falls into two parts. Vv. 1-12 are
more or less specially adapted to the occasion ; vv. 12-end
were a stereotyped passage frequently used for this purpose
with little or no change. Thus vv. 12-24 recur at the end
of the prooimion to the second Epicedeion (there however*

552

with your cattle.*a* I will set you up your house in
freedom. But do you also arm yourselves beside
me against Eurymachus and the other suitors. Evil
days *b* you too have known, like Telemachus and
steadfast Penelope."

.   .   .   .   .

*(Traces of two more lines, then fragments of five more
lines, probably the beginning of another extract)*

a Or (lit.), " I will release you, that now tremble at the
suitors, to fare," etc.   *b* Or, "their evil ways you too
have known," etc.

ANONYMOUS

EPICEDEION FOR A PROFESSOR OF THE
UNIVERSITY OF BERYTUS [4 A.D.]

*vv. 22-24 are abbreviated to two lines). In vv. 1-12, 10-12
are written in the margin ; not in the text, which may there-
fore also be a stereotype, to which vv. 10-12 could be added
at will if appropriate (i.e. in the case of an ex-professor).*

*The dead professor was a native of Smyrna, and held his
appointment at Berytus. He went to Constantinople on
private business, and died just when he was about to be
appointed professor there. Thus the poem affords a brief
insight into the famous School at Berytus in the middle of
the 4th century. We learn that the pupils studied (among
other subjects) Attic comedy ; Plato ; Demosthenes ; Thucy-
dides ; Homer. And at first sight we are impressed by the
affection of the class for its teacher, and its remarkable
esprit de corps. But closer scrutiny reveals the artificiality
of the piece and the formality which it implies. The class*

of students is clearly highly organized, especially for such business as this. And we may doubt whether all the virtues ascribed to the professor in his obituary were acknowledged in him in his lifetime. The sentiments of praise are indeed empty ; it is not easy to discern profound affection or even respect underlying the commonplace expressions. And the portrait which the grateful pupils had painted was not a singular token of esteem for an individual ; as much was done for the subject of the second Epicedeion, and we shall not be surprised to find it proven of yet others, if further compositions of this kind are unearthed. Only in one respect, perhaps, may we detect a difference : this prooimion is extended (in comparison with the second one) by several lines which quote Demosthenes and Thucydides in a somewhat precise and pedantic manner ; it is possible that these lines were added here in mimicry of some quaint mannerism of an individual.

. . . . . .
λυπη[σό]μεσθα μὴ βλέποντες ἐνθ[άδε
τὸν το[ῦ θε]άτρου δεσπότην, τὸν ῥήτο[ρα
οὗ χ[ωρὶς] οὐδεὶς σύλλογος ἐγεγόν[ει] ποτέ,
δι' ὅν τε δεῦρο συνελέγημεν πολλάκις.
ὑ[με]ῖς τε πάντες ὑποθέσεως ἄλλης ὅρον   5
ο]ὐκ ἂν προθύμως ἡδέως τ' ἠκ[ού]ετε,
εἰ μὴ τὸν ἄνδρα [τ]ουτονὶ τεθνηκότ[α
λόγοις [ἐτί]μων, οἷς ἐτ[ί]μα πολλάκις
ἄλλ[ο]υς [ἐκ]εῖνος· καὶ γὰρ ἦν δεινὸς λέγειν.
οὐκ ἴστε, πρώιην πῶς ἑτέραν ᾑρημένος   10
ὁ]δὸν τραπέσθαι [

.   .   .
ἐπαινετέον δὲ τῶν μαθητῶν τὸν χορὸν
εὐγνωμοσύνης τῆς ἀμφὶ τὸν διδάσκαλον.
ἄλλως γὰρ αὐτὸν οὐκ ἔχοντες εἰσορᾶν

ANONYMOUS

Schemmel's article on the School at Berytus is relevant and interesting (I paraphrase a section of his admirable work) :—

"*The life of students [in the Eastern schools] was nowhere creditable to them. But of all universities, the lowest reputation was enjoyed by Berytus. Our sources are unanimous in praise of the beauty of the city, and in admiration of its magnificent buildings and brilliant festivals, no less than of the refinement and culture of its inhabitants : but they are equally unanimous in censure of its luxury and vice. . . . The student had 1-2 hours of classes ; then came bath and breakfast, where he gambled with dice ; he was expected to visit the theatre daily to see the latest mime ; in the evening there were drinking-parties in the company of courtesans. He participated eagerly in the numerous festivals of the city, e.g. races and animal-fights. Temptation was great, and the Christian therefore took the precaution to postpone baptism until his studies were over : he considered that baptism washed away all previous sins, whereas for sins committed after baptism there could be no atonement.*"

Berytus was almost entirely destroyed by an earthquake in A.D. 554.

. . . we shall grieve, no longer seeing him here, the master of our Theatre, the Teacher without whom no meeting ever yet occurred, and for whose sake we assembled hither so many times. None of you would gladly or willingly be listening to any other programme, if I were not speaking to honour this departed soul, as he often spoke to honour others; for he was an able orator. Do you not remember how, a little while ago, chosen to turn another way . . .?

.   .   .   .   .   .

Now I must praise the circle of his pupils for courtesy toward their teacher. Unable to look upon

ἔσ]τησαν ἐν γραφαῖσιν εἰκόνων δύο,   15
ὧ]ν τ[ὴ]ν μὲν ἠργάσαντο παῖδες ζω[γ]ρά[φων,
ἡ] δ᾽ [ἦν] ἐν ἑκάστωι κατὰ φύσιν γεγραμμένη
ἔ]ν τῆι δ[ι]ανοίαι. νῦν δ᾽ ἐγὼ ταύτην τρίτην
ἔ]μπνουν ἀναθήσω καὶ λαλοῦσαν εἰκόνα,
οὗτοι διατήξας κηρὸν ἀλλ᾽ ε[ἰ]πὼν ἔπη.   20
ἐὰν δὲ δόξω τῶι πάθει νικώμενος
π]ολλαῖς ἐπαίνων ἐμπεσεῖν ὑπερβολαῖς
τι]μῶν τὸν ἄνδρα, μηδὲ εἷς βασκαινέτω.
φ]θόνος γὰρ οὐδείς, φησί που Δημοσθένης
ἐκ] τοῦ παλαιοῦ συγγραφέως ἀποσπάσας,   25
πρὸς τ]οὺς θανόντας τοῖς ἔτι ζῶσιν τέως.
καὶ νῦ]ν ἰά[μ]βων κωμικῶν πεπαυμέν[ος
ἡρῶι᾽ ἔπη τ]ὸ λοιπὸν εἰσκυκλήσομ[αι.
. . . . . .

         ] σὲ δ᾽ οὐ τόσον εἵλετο πένθος
οὐδ᾽ [ὅτε σὸν κατὰ κύκ]λον ὑπώκλασε γαῖα χα-
    νο[ῦσα   30
καὶ σέο πάντα τίναξε θεμείλια, σοῖς δ᾽ ἐπὶ λαοῖς
πολλοῖς ἔπλεο τύμβος ἐρικλαύτοισι πεσοῦσα·
ὡς ὁπότ᾽ [ἀγγ]ελίη χαλεπὴ σέο τύψεν ἀκουὰς
δῖον ἐς] Ἕρμον ἰοῦσα νεοκτιμένη[ς] ἀπὸ Ῥώμης
κλεινοτάτο]υ ναετῆρος ἀπαγγέλλουσα τελευτήν.   35
ἐκ τοῦ θε]σπέσιον κλέος ἦραο, τῶι ἐπὶ μούν[ωι
πρόσ]θε μέγα φρονέεσκες ἐν Ἀντολίηι περ ἐόντι
ἀλλοδάπην ἀνὰ γα[ῖ]αν· ἐπεὶ καὶ τοῖο ἕκητι
εἰσέτ᾽ ἀριστοτόκον σε βροτοὶ καλέεσκον ἅπαντες.
τρεῖς γὰρ σεῖο γένοντο περικλήεστατοι υἷες,   40
εἷς μὲν ἀοιδοπόλος, δύο δὲ ῥητῆρες ἀγαυοί.
ἤ τοι ὃ μὲν φίλος υἷος ἐϋρρείταο Μέλητος
κῆρ]υξ ἀθανάτων τε καὶ ἀνδρῶν θεῖος Ὅμηρος
Ἴλι]ον ὅστις ἔθηκεν ὑπ᾽ ὀφθαλμοῖσιν ἁπάν[των
556

him otherwise, they have set up his image in two por-
traits—one made by the sons of painters, the other
naturally drawn in the mind of each. And now I will
dedicate this third portrait, breathing and articulate,
not by melting wax but by speaking words. If,
conquered by our calamity, I seem to fall often into
excess of praise while honouring him, let none look
askance upon me. " No malice can be," says Demos-
thenes (taking it from the ancient chronicler), " from
the still living to the dead." And now I have made
an end of Comedy's iambics : for the rest, I shall wheel
on to the stage my Heroic verse.

. . . not such the grief that gripped you,[a] even when
earth gaped and sank about your mural round, and
shook all your foundations; down upon your own
folk you fell, and became a tomb for many, deeply
mourned,—not such, as when the grievous tidings
struck upon your hearing, coming to divine Hermus
from new-founded Rome,[b] bringing back the tidings
of the death of our illustrious inhabitant.

Through him you gained wondrous glory, for his
sake alone your pride used to be great, though he
dwelt in the Orient, on foreign soil : because of him,
all men still called you Mother of Noblest Sons.

For three most illustrious sons were born of you ;
one a singer, two glorious orators. One was the dear
son of the fair stream of Meles, the herald of immortals
and men, divine Homer, who set Ilium before the

[a] The reference is to the city of Smyrna.   [b] Con-
stantinople.

---

36 Beginning D. L. P.

πλ]αγκτοσύνην τ' Ὀδυσῆος ἰδεῖν ὑποφήτ[ορι
    Μούσηι,   45
οἳ] δὲ δύω ῥητῆρες Ἀριστείδης τε καὶ α[ὐτὸς
πάντα μάλ' ἀ]λλήλοισιν ὁμοῖοι, ἶσα δὲ [δῶρα
γλώσσης ἀμφ]οτέροισι, δι' ἧς ῥέεν ὡ[ς μέλι
    φωνή

. . . .

ἀ]λλ'] οὔ [ο]ἱ τάδε πάντα κακὴν ἀπέερ[γε τελευτήν,
ο]ὐδ' ὁ πολὺς γλώσσης ῥόος ἤρκεσεν [ὧστ' ἀπ-
    αμῦναι   50
Μοῖραν νηλεόθυμον ἀμειδέ[
ἀλλά ἑ χαλκ[εί]η θανάτ[ου] κοίμ[ησεν ἀνάγκη
Κ[ωνστ]αντινιάδος νεο[θή]λε[ο]ς [ἐν χθονὶ Ῥώμης.
το[ν] δὲ πόλις βασιλῆος ἐμύρ[α]τ[ο νεκρὸν ἰδοῦσα
ἀχνυμένη, πᾶσαι δὲ γόωι πλήμυρον ἀ[γυι]α[ί,   55
τοῖον ἐπεὶ σίγησε λιγὺ στόμα, τοῦ κλέος εὐρὺ
τηλόθεν α[ἰ]ὲν ἄκουσε, λ[ι]λαίετο δ' ἐγγ[ὺς ἀκούειν
φθεγγομένου, καὶ ἔμελλεν ἀκουέμ[εν·] ἦ[λθε γὰρ
    αὐτὸς
Θρηικίην ποτὶ γαῖα[ν] ἑὸν χρέος ὥς κε τελέσσηι·
τὸν δὲ μετὰ χρειὼ ζαθέη πόλις αὖ[θι κατασχεῖν   60
ἤθελε παρπεπιθοῦσα, νέων ἵνα πῶυ [νομεύσηι,
ἀνθρώπων εὐη[γ]ε[ν]έων ἀγανόφ[ρ]ονας υἷα[ς],
οἵ μιν ναιετάουσιν, ἀπειρεσίαις ἐνὶ τιμαῖς
πολλοὺς κυδιόωντες ἀριζήλοισι θοώκοις.
ἀλλὰ τά γ' οὐκ ἐτε[λεῖ]το· τὸ καὶ νέκυν ἀνδρὸς
    ἰδοῦσ[α   65
ἡ πάρος αἰὲν ἄδακρυς ἐδάκρυσεν τότε Ῥώμη,
Θρηικίαι δὲ γόων ἁλιμυρέες ἔκλυον ἀκταὶ
μυρία] κοπτόμεναι ῥοθίωι πλήσσοντ[ι θ]αλάσ[σης
κλυζομένης] παρὰ θῖνα ῥοώδεος Ἑλλ[ησ]πόντου.
ὣς ποτ' Ὀ]λυμπιάδες κοῦραι Διὸς ἐννέα Μοῦσα[ι   70

eyes of all mankind and the wanderings of Odysseus,
with the Muse to inspire him ; the two orators were
Aristides and he,[a] in all ways alike, and equal the gifts
of their tongues, through which there flowed a voice
like honey . . .

Yet all this kept not evil doom from him, nor
availed the broad flood of his speech to avert relent-
less unsmiling Fate ; the brazen doom of death laid
him to sleep in the land of the new-born Rome of
Constantine. The city of the king mourned in
sorrow when she saw him dead, and all the streets
were a flood of lamentation—such the clear voice
that was silenced : whose widespread glory she had
heard ever from afar, and yearned to hear it speaking
near by, and was about to hear. Himself he had
gone to Thrace to accomplish his own need ; and
after it, the holy city wished to induce him to stay
there to be shepherd of her youthful flocks, the
gentle sons of those noblemen who dwell in her and
glorify so many men with countless dignities in
Chairs of Honour. But these things came not to
pass : so, seeing his corpse, Rome, that never wept
before, wept then ; her groans were heard by the
sea-coasts of Thrace, smitten unendingly by blows of
breakers from the ocean that dashed high beside the
shore of rapid Hellespont.

As once the Muses nine, Olympian maids of

---

[a] *Sc.* the person who is subject of this *epicedeion*.

48 γλώσσης D. L. P., *cf.* 50. Ἀτθίδος ed. pr.   51
ἀμειδέ[ος Ἀιδωνῆος ed. pr.

πενθάδε]ς ἀμφὶ Θέτιν Νηρηίδα κωκύεσκον
υἱέα Μυρμ]ιδόνων ἡγήτορα δα[κρυχέουσαι

---

^a Achilles.

ANONYMOUS

139   [4 A.D.]   EPITHALAMION

Ed. pr. *Hunt, *Catalogue of the Greek Papyri in the John
Rylands Library, Manchester*, i. 1911, no. 17, p. 28. See
Schmidt, *G.G.A.* 1912, 58 ; Körte, *Archiv*, v. 541.

A wretched composition of an uncertain, but certainly late,

νυμφίε, σοὶ Χάριτες γλυκεραὶ καὶ κῦδος ὀπηδ[ε]ῖ·
Ἁρμονίη χαρίεσσα γάμοις γέρας ἐγγυάλιξε.
νύμφα φίλη, μέγα χαῖρε διαμπερές· ἄξιον εὗρες
νυμφίον, ἄξιον εὗρες, ὁμοφροσύνην δ᾽ ὀπάσε[ιε]ν
ἤδη που θεὸς ὔμμι καὶ αὐτίκα τέκνα γενέ[σ]θαι,   5
καὶ παίδων παῖδας καὶ ἐς βαθὺ γῆρας ἱκέσθ[αι.

ANONYMOUS, perhaps PAMPREPIUS OF PANOPOLIS

140   [About 500 A.D.]   TWO POEMS

Ed. pr. *Gerstinger, *Pamprepios von Panopolis ; Sitzungs-
berichte der Akademie der Wissenschaften in Wien, Phil.-
Hist. Klasse*, 1928, 208, 3, with Plate. See Maas, *Gnomon*,
1929, 250 (corrections and improvements in the text, includ-

ANONYMOUS

Zeus, wailed in mourning around Thetis, daughter
of Nereus, weeping for her son, the leader of the
Myrmidons,[a] . . .

. . . . . .

ANONYMOUS

EPITHALAMION [4 A.D.]

*era. A cento of epic words and phrases, whether suitable or
not : adequate condemnation by Schmidt, loc. cit. Cf.
Theocritus xviii. 49-53.*

BRIDEGROOM, the sweet Graces and glory attend
you ; gracious Harmonia has bestowed honour upon
your wedding. Dear bride, great and abiding joy
be yours ; worthy is the husband you have found,
yea worthy. May Heaven now give you concord, and
grant that you may presently have children, and
children's children, and reach a ripe old age.

. . . . . .

ANONYMOUS, perhaps PAMPREPIUS OF PANOPOLIS

TWO POEMS [About 500 A.D.]

ing some by Keydell) ; Horna, *Anz. d. Wien. Akad. d. Wiss.*
1929, 19, 257 (revised text) ; Schissel, *Phil. Woch.* 1929,
1073 ; Körte, *Archiv,* x. 25 ; Barber, *Class. Rev.* 43, 237 ;
Graindor, *Byzantion,* 4, 469.

LITERARY PAPYRI

(a) *The poem opens with a prologue in comic iambic tri-meters* (cf. pp. 552, 554). *The six lines of this probably repre-sent only a fragment of the original composition.* (*On the topic of these prologues see ed. pr. pp. 8-10, corrected and modified by Schissel, loc. cit.*) *The theme of the poem is announced in the fifth line of the preface. It is " to sing of the hours and tell of their actions " ; that is, to describe the successive stages of a single day and the activities of country life appro-priate to each stage. It is in general a peculiar sort of bucolic idyll :—the events of a single day described against a background of the changes of weather ; which strikes a fairly impressive undertone of the struggle between light and dark, between storm and sunshine. The season is early winter, in November (see Maas, Byz. Zeitschr. 1934, p. 76).*

An introductory passage, 9-26, blends with the beginning of the theme. Against a background of a storm the poet tells of a shepherd in the early morning driving his herds to shelter. Rain is pouring already, and he expects a hailstorm ; he takes cover beneath a cliff, and plays his pipe (27-38).

The scene then shifts when the storm breaks and attacks the Tree-Nymphs, scattering their twigs and foliage and swelling the streams around them (39-48).

Then the storm begins to clear. The sun gradually breaks through, and the world rejoices in light and warmth. The snow melts and floods the springs and streams. A Tree-Nymph addresses a Spring-Nymph with good humour :—" I am already drenched by the storm ; the work of your swollen streams is superfluous ; reserve your energies against the time of summer heat, when they will be very welcome " (49-85).

The events of the day in the sunlit afternoon are next described. The countryfolk gather to honour Demeter with song and dance and sacrifice. Then they return to their proper tasks : the ploughman and sower are working in the fields, hedges are built, and the birds are scared from the

562

seed. And a farmer sings of the coming harvest. His melody is repeated by a maid tending her flocks at eventide ; she dries her hair and clothes still drenched by the storm of the morning (86-139).

The sun goes down, and a violent thunderstorm gathers in the twilight ; here the proper theme of the poem closes (140-150).

There follow six lines of epilogue in which the poet begs the favour of his audience and announces that he has been summoned to Cyrene (151-end).

In general we may say of this poem that its theme and structure are well-planned and highly poetical ; but the composition itself is weak and vicious. The writer is of the school of Nonnus, to whom he owes his excessive ornament and fullness of description, his strained and too ingenious phraseology, erotic colouring, monotonous rhythms, and inclination to grotesque allegory. Vv. 144-148, in which the sentimental may seem to find a touch of true tenderness, are in fact a conventional copy of an outworn tradition, and a vulgar appeal to susceptible emotions. The poem is carefully, indeed laboriously, written by a person eager above all to impress an audience with his cleverness ; in that limited ambition he cannot fairly be said to have failed.

The structure of the piece, which we praised so highly, was not altogether the invention of this author. It follows the rules of a recognized literary type, the ἔκφρασις συνεζευγμένη, *defined by Aphthonius (37, 17):* συνεζευγμέναι δὲ ὡς αἱ πράγματα καὶ καιροὺς ἅμα συνάπτουσαι.

(b) *This is a fragment of a poem in honour of one Patricius Theagenes, perhaps composed by the author of the previous piece (ed. pr. supplements its title as* τοῦ αὐτο]ῦ εἰς τὸν Πατρίκ[ιον Θ]εαγενῆ Ἰχθ[υόνος). *There is no doubt that it is only a fragment of a complete poem, not a beginning left unfinished by its author ; for our papyrus is a portion of a published book, not a writer's rough and incomplete auto-*

graph. (*See Schissel*, loc. cit., *against ed. pr. p. 18.*) *We do not know, but may provisionally assume, that the poem in its fullness obeyed the strict rules which used to govern this kind of composition (for which see* Buecheler, Rh. Mus. N.F. *xxx. 1878, 57, 73 ;* Reichel, *Quaest. Progymnast. 1909, 89). It is, as it should be, a direct address to the object of its eulogy ; it begins conventionally with an account of Theagenes' immensely distinguished ancestry, and probably went on to describe next his ἀνατροφή, then his πράξεις, ending at last with a σύγκρισις.*

Theagenes is identified by the first editor with the Athenian archon of that name who, according to Suidas and Photius, was a wealthy and ambitious politician of good family and varied service to the state. He lived in the second half of the 5th century A.D.

This identification is reasonably certain ; that of the poet himself is not. He is alleged by the first editor to be one Pamprepius of Panopolis (biography by Asmus, Byz. Zeitschr. *xxii. 1913, 320), a pagan Egyptian poet born in the year A.D. 448, who came to Athens and lived there under the patronage of Theagenes. Later he quarrelled with his patron*

(a)   χ[ρὴ τοὺς] θ[εατὰς εὐνο]εῖν [μ]ελωιδίαι·

     ὅπου γὰρ [. . . .]ν συντρέχουσιν οἱ λόγο[ι,

     τὸν ποικίλον νοῦν τῶν ποιητῶν σωφρόνως

     ἕλκουσιν, ἐκφέρουσιν εἰς εὐτολμίαν

     ὥρας μελίζειν καὶ λέγειν τὰ πράγματα, 5

     ὡσὰν παρασπ[ά]σωσιν αἱ μεληδόνες.

    σήμερον ἀμφ' ἐμὲ κῶμος ἀείδεται, οὐχ ὅσον

     αὐλῶν,

    2 [εὐνῶ]ν Gerstinger : but *v.* Schissel, *loc. cit.*

and departed to Constantinople, where he became a crafty diplomat ; a favourite at the court of Zenon ; executed for treason in an Isaurian fortress, A.D. 488.

Now (assuming that both poems are the work of one author) ed. pr. legitimately infers (1) from (a) 155 sqq., that the poet had connexions with Egypt ; (2) from (a) 86-100, where Demeter's relation to Athens and Attica are broadly under-lined, that the scene of the poem's recitation is Athens ; further (b) was certainly recited at Athens ; (3) from the tone of (b) 4, that the poet was a pagan, as was also probably Theagenes ; (4) from (b) as a whole, that he stood in some close personal relation to Theagenes.

It is therefore clear that the evidence of the poems is in no way at variance with anything we know of the career of Pamprepius. But it is equally clear that Theagenes may have protected a score of other persons, whose names are lost, whom the evidence might fit just as well. Any such person would of course have recited at Athens, would have been a pagan, and might very well have been summoned to Cyrene (which is all that is proved by (a) 153).

We therefore concur with Schissel, who properly criticizes the first editor for entitling his book Pamprepios von Pano-polis, *as if there were no difference between a certainty and a possible hypothesis.*

(a) . . . The audience must be friendly to my song. When the words come together [a] . . . they draw the poet's subtle mind discreetly with them, they lead him on to have the courage to sing the hours and tell their deeds, however anxiety may distract him.

To-day a revel [b] is ringing round about me, not of

[a] " When the (applauding) words of (well-disposed) listeners accompany the recital," Gerstinger; " When the (poet's) words (and ideas) are assembled," Schissel.
[b] κῶμος here " song," ὅσον = ὅν: this poem naturally con-tains many usages of later Greek.

οὐχ [ὅσ]ον ἑπτατόνοιο λύρης ἀναβάλλεται
    ἠχὼ
ἡδὺν ἀμειβομέ[ν]η μελέων θρόον, οὔθ' ὃν
    ἀείδε[ι
οὔρεος ὀμφήεν[το]ς ὑπὸ κλίτος ἠχέτα κύ[κ]νος 10
γηραλέης σει[ρ]ῆν[ο]ς ἀκήρατον ἄχθος ἀμεί-
    βων,
ἀκροτ[άτ]οις πτερύγεσσιν ὅτε πνείουσιν
    [ἀ]ῆτα[ι·
ἀλλ' ὅσον [ἐκ] Θρήικης νιφετώδεος ἔμπνοος
    [α]ὔρη
χειμερίοις πελάγεσσιν ἐ[π]ι[σ]κα[ίρ]ουσα θα-
    λάσσης
ὄρθριον ἀείδει ῥοθ[ί]ωι μ[έλο]ς· ἡδὺ δὲ
    μέλπει   15
χιονέην Φαέθοντος ἐ[ριφλεγέος πυρὸς αἴγλην
χεύμασιν ὀμβρο[τόκων σβεῖσαν διεροῖς νεφε-
    λάων
καὶ κυνὸς ἀστραίοιο πυρ[αιθέα
ὑγροπόροις νιφάδεσσι κατασβε[σθέντα
χεύματι γὰρ χλο(ά)ουσι καὶ ἀστέρες, οὐ[κέτι
    μήνην   20
σύνδρομον ἠελίωι κυανώπιδα πό[τναν ὁρῶμεν
ψυχομένωι νεφέεσσι καλυπτομενο[
οὐκέτι νυκτὸς ἔρευθος ἴτυν περίβαλλ[εν
    ἑῶι]ον.
ἄρτι μὲν ἀντολίης χιονώδεες ἐπρ[.]σ[. .
    αὖρ]αι
αἰθερίων γονόεσσαν ἀμελγομέ[νην χύσι]ν
    ὄμβρων·   25
Π]ηιάδ[α]ς δ' ἔκρυψε παλίνσ[τροφος αἰθέρ]ος
    ἄξων

the flute, nor that which the sound of the lyre's seven strings awakens, responding in sweet utterance of song, nor that which on the slope of the prophetic mountain [a] is sung by the tuneful swan, changing to freshest youth his burden of melodious old age,[b] when the breezes blow through his feather-tips [c]; but a song which the blast of wind from snowy Thrace, dancing upon the wintry waves of the sea, sings to the surge at dawn. And sweetly it sings how the snow-white brightness of the blazing sun is quenched by the liquid streams of rainclouds, and the fiery . . . of the dog-star is extinguished by the watery snowstorms. For even the stars go pale before their streams, no longer do we see the Moon, the dark-eyed Lady that treads upon the heel of the sun, who is frozen among the clouds . . . no longer did the redness of the dawn embrace the circle of the night.

Lately the snowy winds from the East had . . . the fruitful downpour of rain from heaven as it were milk ; the revolving axis of the sky hid the Pleiads . . .

---

[a] Parnassus.   [b] Reference to a notion that the swan did not die, but was rejuvenated in extreme old age, like the Phoenix.   Here periphrased as " he changes the load of old age's song so as to be undefiled (*sc.* by age)."   [c] The song of the swan was sometimes ascribed to the sound of the wind in its feathers.   See Gerstinger.

---

9 οὐδ' Gerstinger (coni. Radermacher), but Schissel rightly retains Π's οὔθ'.   11-12 Punctuation by Maas.   ἀκρο-τάτοις D. L. P. : ἀκροκόμοις Gerstinger, admitting its weak-ness : ἀκροκέροις dubiously Horna.   13 Π acc. to Horna. 22 ψυχομένωι coni. Keydell ; Π acc. to Horna.   24 ἔ-πρ[ε]σ[α]ν ed. pr.   25 For ἀμελγ. see Gerstinger, p. 103.

*(Fragments of seven lines, then a gap of about ten
lines, then fragments of four lines)*

ἔνθα τις ὑετίων νυμφήιος ὄμβρος ἐρώτων
ἔδνα τελεσσιγόνοιο χέων ἐπὶ δέμνια γαίης
ἐλπίσιν εὐαρότοισι φερέσβιον ὄγ[μ]ον ἀφάσ-
        σει·
καί τις ὀρεσσινόμων ἀγεληκόμο[ς] ἄγχι
        βοαύλων   30
ἐκ νεφέων πρηστῆρα χαλαζήεντα [δο]κεύων,
α]ἴσιον ὀμβροτόκοιο προάγγελον Εἰλιθυείης,
π]όρτιας ἀρτιτόκοισιν ὑπ᾽ ὠδίνεσσιν ἀνείσας
ἤ]λασεν ὑψίκρημνον ἐς ἄβροχον α[ὐλι]ν
        ἐρίπνης·
κ]ύκλα δὲ (λα)χνήεντα βοοκραίροιο χ[ιτῶ]νος 35
ζ]ωσάμενος περὶ νῶτον ἐδύσατο δειράδα
        πέτρης
συρί]ζων ἀγέλῃσι· μόγις δ᾽ ἀνεβάλλετο
        [σ]ῦρι[γξ
ἄσθμ]ασι λεπταλέοισιν ὑπωροφίης μέλος
        ἠχοῦς

        (Fragments of eight lines)

ἡ μὲν ἀν[ειλίσσου]σα πολύπλοκον ὄζον
        ἐθείρης
πάντοθι π[ορφυρέ]ης ἀπεσείσατο φυλλάδα
        χαίτης,   40
ἡ δὲ νιφοβλ[ήτ]οιο παρὰ πρηῶνα κολώνης
ἀπτόρθοις παλάμῃσιν ἀρύετο παρθέν[ο]ν
        ὕδωρ.

        (Fragments of three lines)

        ] χιὼν ἐ[π]ιδέδρομε νύμ[φ]ῃ

ANONYMOUS

(Fragments of seven lines, then a gap of about ten lines, then fragments of four lines)

There a bridal shower of Love-gods in the guise of rain, pouring their wedding-gifts upon the couch of Mother Earth, embraces the fertile furrow with hope of lucky ploughing. A herdsman, near the mountain-stables, expecting a hailstorm from the clouds, propitious harbinger of a goddess that brings rain to birth, drives his heifers lately relaxed from the pangs of travail to a dry resting-place high up among the crags. The shaggy circles [a] of ox-horn [b] coat he bound about his back, and went under the cliff, piping to his herds. The pipe hardly struck up the music of its song beneath the roof, so meagre came his breath. . . .

(Fragments of eight lines)

One (nymph) unwound the twisted shoots that are her hair, and shook off the leafage of her bright tresses on every side.[c] Another on the foreland of a snowbound hill drew virgin water with arms bereft of twigs [d] . . .

(Fragments of three lines)

Snow rushed upon the nymph, mingled with

---

[a] Circles, merely because it goes *round* him.   [b] He means only "made from the hide of a horned ox."   [c] The tree, here identified with a Dryad, shook (in the wind) its twisted branches, and the leaves fell off.   [d] This monstrous phrase means that the tree (here a nymph) turned snow to water on its branches, from which the storm had broken off the twigs.

---

35 Maas.

συμμιχθεῖσα ῥόο]ισ[ι] πολυψηφῖδο[ς] ἐέρσης.
ἀλ[λ᾽ ο]ὐ φορ[μὸν ἔ]ρυ[κ]ε λιθώδεα, γηθομένη
    δὲ   45
δέξατο χιονόπεπλον ἀναγκαίην [τρ]οφὸν ὕλης.
οὐκ ἄρα δηρὸν ἔμ[ε]λλεν ἀερτάζε[ιν ῥ]όθον
    ὄμβρων,
οὐδ᾽ ἔτι χιονέης ὑδατώδεα δεσμ[ὰ] κ[α]λ[ύ]-
    πτ[ρ]ης.
ἤδη γὰρ νεφέων ἀνεφαίνετο μέσσοθι κύκ[λος
ἄκρον ἐρευ[θιόων], λεπτὴ δ᾽ ἀνεθήλεεν
    αἴ[γλη   50
βοσκομένη τινὰ χῶρον, ὅσον νέφος ἐκτὸς
    ἐρύκει,
ἠ]ερίην δ᾽ [ὤι]ξε[ν] ἀνήλυσιν· ἠελίου δὲ
αὐγὴ πρῶτο]ν ἔλ[α]μψε βοώπιδος οἷα σε-
    λήνης,
ὑψίπορος] δ᾽ ἤστραψεν οἰστεύουσα κολώνας
ἀκ[τάς τε κλον]έουσα· μόγις δ᾽ ἐκέδασσεν
    ὀμίχλην   55
ὑψόθε[ν ἀμφι]έλικτον, ἀλαμπέα μητέρα
    πάχνης.
πᾶσα [δὲ γαῖα γ]έλασσε, πάλ[ιν] μείδησε
    γαλήνη.
ἠέρ[α δ᾽ ἠέλιος πυριλαμπέ]ος ἔμπλεον αἴ-
    [γ]λης
θέρμε [τε καὶ πέλαγος· νηυ]σὶν δ᾽ ἀνεπάλ-
    λε[τ]ο δελφὶς
ἡμιφανὴς ῥο[θίοισιν ἐν] ἠέρι πόντον ἐρέσσων. 60
στέρνα δὲ ν[υ]μφάων ἐζώσατο παντρόφον
    αἴγλην
μαρναμένην χιόνεσσι, φύσις δ᾽ ἤμειπτο
    χαλάζης

streams of a rain of hailstones. Yet she beat not
away that stony cloak,[a] nay, rejoicing she welcomed
that snowclad nurse, thus forced upon her, who would
help her wood to grow. She was not destined long
to support the rainy surge, nor long the wet veil of
snow that bound her head. For already a circle ap-
peared amid the clouds, red about its rim, and a thin
gleam grew, pasturing so much of the space as the
clouds hold off,[b] and opened a path back into the
sky. The light of the sun shone first like the glow
of the ox-eyed moon, then soaring it blazed, routing
the shores and hills with arrows of light. Hard it
must fight to scatter the mist that rolled around on
high, the rayless mother of the frost. There was
laughter in all the land, and peace smiled again.
The sun filled the air and ocean with a fiery brilliance,
and made them warm. The dolphin leapt up, half-
seen by ships, with splashes in the air as it rowed
across the sea. Nymphs girt their breasts with
the brightness[c] that fought against the snow and
made the world to flourish. The nature of hail was

---

[a] The "stony cloak" is the thickly-falling hail which
covers her like a cloak. φορμός is a seaman's cloak of coarse
plaited material. [b] The gleam " grazes on " the patch
of white sky which the clouds " excluded " from their society.
[c] Exposed themselves to the sun.

---

45 Horna, except ἔρυκε (D. L. P.: ἔρεικε Horna, which I
do not understand). 48 For ὑδατώδεα see Gerstinger,
p. 103. 49 Horna's reading of Π. 52 ἠ]ερίην
Horna. 57 Maas. 61 ἐζώσατο coni. Keydell; Π
acc. to Horna.

εἰς ῥόον ὀμβρήεντα, χιὼν δ' ἐτινάσσετο
    γαίηι,
φέγγει νικ[η]θεῖσα· βιαζομένη δὲ γαλήνηι
ἔρρεε ποικιλόδ[α]κ[ρ]υς ἀνηναμένη μ[ό]θο[ν]
    αἴγλης.   65
πηγάων δὲ τένοντες ἐμυκήσαντο ῥ[εέ]θροις
στεινόμενοι νιφάδεσσι διιπετέων προχοάων,
μαζοὶ δ' ἐσφ(ρ)ιγόω[ν]το ῥοώδεες· ἐκ δὲ
    χαράδρης
ὦρτο ῥόος παλ[ίνο]ρσος, ὅπηι πιτυώ[δε]ος
    ὕλης
νειόθεν ἐρρίζωντο συνήλικες ἔρνεσι νύμφαι.   70
τοῖα δ' Ἀ[μα]δρυάδων τις ὑπερκύπτουσα
    πετήλων
ἔννεπ[ε π]ηγαίηι ῥοδοπ[ήχ]ει γείτονι νύμφηι·
χαῖρέ μοι, ἀρχεγόνοιο φίλον τέκος Ὠκεανοῖο,
φυταλιῆς βασίλεια· τί μ[οι χρέος] ἐστὶ
    ῥοάων
βριθομένηι γεράεσσι με[λανστέρνω]ν νεφε-
    λάων;   75
οὐχ ὁράαις, ὅσος ὄμβρο[ς ἐμὴν προχυθεὶς
    κατὰ] λόχμην
ἡμετέρης ἔντοσθεν ἀποστ[άζει πλο]καμῖδος;
ἔνθεν ἔχεις τόσον οἶδμα, τάλαν· τ[ί δὲ μῦθ]ον
    ἐγείρω;
θυμοδακὴς ὅτι μῦθος, ἔπειτα δὲ μῆτι[ς
    ἀμείνων.
ἐγγύθι γὰρ χρόνος οὗτος, ὅταν ποτὲ Σε[ίριος
    αἴθηι,   80
ἔνθα τεῶν γεράων τιμήορος ἔσσετ[αι ὥρη.
ναὶ τότε, πότνα, τίταινε φυτοσπόρον [ἀρδμὸν
    ἀλωαῖς

changed to a showery stream. Snow was shaken to
the ground, vanquished by the light ; forced by fair
weather it flowed away in myriad changeful tears
declining battle with the brightness. The sinews
of the springs roared loud, hard-pressed by the
snowfloods of the heavenly outpour ; their breasts
were taut with the streams. And from its bed
the stream arose and turned again, back to where the
nymphs, coeval with the trees, were rooted in the
depths of the pinewood.

There spoke an Hamadryad, peeping forth from
the foliage, to her rosy-armed neighbour, a fountain-
nymph : " Good morrow, dear daughter of father
Ocean, queen of the Plantation ! How should I
need your streams, laden as I am with the bounty
of the black-breasted clouds ? Do you not see how
great a shower, poured upon my bushes, drips down
from within my tresses ?—That is why you have so
deep a flood, my dear ! Why am I aroused to speak ?
Because speech touches to the heart, and thereafter
plans are better formed. For that time is near, when
the dog-star burns : then will be the season when
your bounties are helpful—then, lady, spread your

63 γαίηι coni. Keydell : Π acc. to Horna.   64 γαλήνη
Gerstinger.   68 Cf. Joh. of Gaza 2. 127 ῥόωι σφρι-
γόωντι.   78 τόσον Maas (τὸ σὸν G).   82 ἀρδμὸν
ἀλωαῖς Horna.

ε[ἰ]σέ[τ]ι διψαλέηισιν, ὅπως χάρις εὔχαρι[ς
εἴη.

ἡ μὲν ἔφη γελόωσα, χάρις δ᾽ ἀπελάμπετο
π[ολλὴ

εἰ]ς ἔριν ὀρν[υμέν]ηι φιλομειδέα [85

(Fragments of six lines)

ἔν]θα μετ᾽ αἰθερίων χιονώδεα κῶμο[ν ἐρ]ώ-
    των

ἴδ]ρει γειοπόνωι νυ[μ]φεύεται ὄμπνια Δηώ.

π]άντες δ᾽ εὐχε[τόω]ντο, θύος δὲ μέμηλεν
    ἑκάστωι,

β]ωμὸν ἀν[ιστάμ]ε[να]ι Δηώιον. ἐς δὲ θυηλὰς
. . . .]ς σκοπέλοισι καλαύ[ροπι . . . . .]ο
    ταῦρος.   90

αἰγι]δ[ίων] δὲ φάλαγγες ἐπερρώοντο βοτῆρι

ἀψ]αμένωι θυόεσσαν Ἐλευσινίης φλόγα
    πεύκης.

ἀγρο]νόμοι δ᾽ ἀγέροντο, περιστέψαντο δ[ὲ
    β]ωμὸι

ἀζαλ]έον τινὰ κόσμον ἀμαλλήεντα τιθέντ[ες

αἴσιον] ἐσσομένης σταχυώδ[ε]ος ἄγγελον
    ὥρη[ς.   95

μέλπεσκο]ν δὲ γέροντες, ἐπωρχήσαντο δὲ
    κοῦ[ροι

ἀ[ζόμε]νοι μεγάλοιο φιλοξενίην Κ[ε]λ[ε]οῖ[ο·

Ῥα[ριά]δος μέλποντο φιλοφροσύνην [βασι-
    λείης

(Fragments of two lines)

fertile waters over gardens ever thirsty, that your
favour may be favourable indeed ! " Smiling she
spoke, and abundant grace shone forth from her as
she sped to laughing conflict. . . .

(Fragments of six lines)

There, after the snow-dance of the Gods of love
from the sky, Deo the goddess of the corn is wedded
to the skilful tiller of the soil.   All men were praying,
and each had the sacrifice at heart, to raise up an
altar to Deo.   The bull that (rejoices) in the crags
(obeyed) the crook toward the sacrifice.   The troops
of kids pressed hard upon the herdsman who kindled
the fragrant torch of Eleusinian pine.   The country-
folk forgathered, and encircled the altar, laying upon
it a fair offering of dry sheaves, propitious omen of
the harvest-time to come.   The old men sang, the
young men danced in time, with reverence for the
generosity of great Celeus [a] : they chanted the kind-
liness of the goddess of the Rarian [b] plain . . .

(Fragments of two lines)

---

[a] See Hom. *Hymn to Demeter*.   [b] Demeter.   See
Allen and Halliday, *The Homeric Hymns*, 2nd ed., pp. 114 *sqq.*

---

83 εἴη Maas.   88 δ' ἐμέμηλεν Gerstinger, corr Horna.
89 θυηλὰς coni. Keydell ; Π acc. to Horna (θυρίδας G).
90 ἀχθόμενος . . . ἕσπετο Gerstinger : βοσκόμενος . . . κόπτετο
Horna : πλαζόμενος Keydell, βάλλετο Maas.   Possibly γηθο-
συνὸ]ς σκοπέλοισι καλαύ[ροπι πείθετ]ο.   95 αἴσιον Maas.
96 μέλπεσκον Horna.   98 βασιλείης Maas.

Τριπτολέμωι ζεύξασα δρακον[τ(ε)ίοιν ζυγ]ὰ
    δίφροιν,
θεσμοφόρον δ' ἐτέλεσσεν ἀγήνορα δῆμον
    Ἀθήνης.   100
καὶ τὰ μὲν ἐν θυέεσσι· βόες δ' ἀροτῆρι
    σιδ[ή]ρωι
νειὸν [ἐ]πισπέρχοντο μεταλλεύοντες ἀρούρης.
μαστίζων δ' ἑκάτερθε συνωρίδος ἴχνια
    ταύρων
γηπόνος ἡνιόχε[υ]εν ἐπ' ἰξύος ἡνία τείνων
ῥινὸς ἐυτρήτ[οιο] περισφίγγοντα κελεύθους.   105
οὕτω πανδαμάτειρα φύσις πειθή[μο]νι τέχνηι
ἐξ ὀρέων ἐς ἄροτρα βοῶν ἐβιήσατο [φύ]τλην
. . .]οβόρωι τίκτου[σα]ν ἐοικότα τέκνα
    [. . .]είηι.
ὀρ]θαδίην δ' ἐχάραξε τανυπλεύρου πτύχα
    γαίης
σ]τοιχάδα δινεύων ἐριβώλακα, βαιὰ δὲ
    βαίνω[ν   110
χ]ε[ι]ρῶν ἄχθος ἔρειδεν ἐς αὔλακα, μή ποτ'
    ἀρότρωι
τρα]χὺς ὑπαντιόων κρύφιος λίθος ἔργον
    ἐρύκηι.
. . . .]βωτοισιν ανα[. . . . .] ἀρδμὸν
    ὁδεύων
ἀνδρ]ομέης ἔσπειρ[ε γύην θρε]πτῆρα [γ]ε-
    νέθλης,
ῥ]αίνων ἔνθα κα[ὶ ἔνθα φυτοσπ]όρα δῶρα
    θεαίνης.   115
τέ]μνε δὲ πυρο[φόρον πέδο]ν ἔρκεσι· μίμνε
    δὲ βάκτρωι

100 θεσμ. Π acc. to Horna.   108 αἱμοβόρωι . . . τεκνία

576

ANONYMOUS

yoking for Triptolemus a dragon-chariot, and made
the proud people of Athene law-bringers (?).[a]

Thus was it with the sacrifices. The oxen went
speedily turning up the fallow-land with iron plough;
the labourer whipped them, now one of the pair, now
the other, and steered the steps of his pair of bulls;
and upon his hips he stretched the reins that bound
fast the passage of their tunnelled nostrils. Thus did
Nature omnipotent, by Art's persuasion, drive the
race of oxen from the mountains to the plough; and
they create offspring like to . . . He cut open a
straight fold in the broad earth, turning the rich soil
in rows; taking short steps he pressed his heavy hands
toward the furrow, lest a rough stone hidden should
meet the plough and stay his labour; . . . walking . . .
water . . . he sowed the field that must nourish the
race of men, sprinkling this way and that the fruitful
gifts of the goddess; he cut off the wheatland with
hedges, and stayed warding off with his staff the

---

[a] θεσμοφόρος here obscure: usually epithet of Demeter
and Persephone.

'Ρείηι Gerstinger: but Π acc. to Horna has τέκνα [. . .]είηι
at the end.   114 ἀνδρομέης Maas: γύην D. L. P. (ἀγ-
ρὸν Horna).   115 ῥ]αίνων Keydell; (.]αινων Π acc. to
Horna).

πυρ]οβόρων γ[εράνω]ν πολεμήιον ἑσμὸν ἐρύ-
    κων
        ] τόσσην δ' ἀνεβάλλετο μολπὴν
        ] θαλύσιον ὕμνον ἀείδων.

(*Fragments of nine lines, including a reference to*
ὄργια Κῶια)

τοῖα γέρων μ[έλπ]εσκε· μέλος δ' ἀπαμείβετο
    νύμφη   120
ἐγγύθι βουκολέουσα, λάθεν (δ') ἄρα θῆλυς
    ἐοῦσα
ἀνέρος εἷμα φέρουσα καὶ ἄ[ρσ]ενα δ[εσ]μὰ
    πεδίλων.
πᾶσα μὲν ἐσφήκωτο καλυψαμ[έν]η χρό[α]
    π[έπ]λοις,
ποιμενίωι ζωστῆρι περίπλοκος· ἐκ δὲ καρήνου
χαίτην ἀμφιέλισσαν ἀποθλίψασα κομάων   125
ἀ]νδρείην ἐδίηνεν ὅλην ῥάχιν, οὐδέ μιν αἴγλη
ἐσ]περίη(ν) ἴ[σχ]ναινεν ἀποστάζουσαν ἐέρσην.
ἡ δ' ἄρ' ἀλυσκ]άζουσα πάτον κρυμνώδεος
    ὕλης
γήλοφον αἰ]γλήεντα μετήλυθεν, ἠελίωι δὲ
κύ[κλα νι]φοβλήτοιο περιστείλασα χιτῶνος 130
ἄκρα [μελ]ῶν γύμνωσεν ἐς εὐφυέων πτύχα
    μη[ρῶν.
οὐδ' [ἀγέλης ἀ]μέλησεν, ἀλωομένην δὲ
    τιθήνη[ν

       (*Fragments of three lines*)

ἦκα περι[σ]φίγξασα πολύρρυτον ἄντυγα
    μαζῶν
εἷλκε ῥόον γλαγόεντα καὶ ὤπασε Πανὶ
    θυηλήν.

hostile swarm of cranes that devour the wheat.
. . . awoke so great a song . . . singing a hymn of
harvest. . . .

(Fragments of nine lines)

So the old man sang.   A maid sent back a melody
in answer, tending a herd near by, and concealing
her womanhood with a man's attire and a man's
sandals bound upon her feet.   Her body was all
hidden and tightly bound in raiment, a shepherd's
girdle twisted round her.   From her head she squeezed
the flowing tresses of her hair, and her manly back
was all a-streaming ; nor could the sunlight make
her dry, as she dripped with water in the evening.
Evading the path of the chill forest, she went to
a gleaming hill-top.   Fastening the snow-beaten
vest around her, she bared to the sun the top of
her body down to the cleft of her shapely thighs.[a]
Still she was not forgetful of her flock : the straying
mother-ewe . . .

(Fragments of three lines)

lightly gripping the roundness of its streaming udder,
drew forth a milky flood and gave it for an offering
to Pan.

[a] The poet has in mind such figures of Aphrodite as
Vatican Gabinetto delle Maschere 433 and its many replicas
and variations ; *v.* Amelung, *Vat. Kat.* ii. 696-698 ; Brendel,
die Antike 6, 41-64 (Beazley).

---

117 γεράνων Maas.   127 ἑσπερίην Maas.   132
ἀγέλης Maas.   133 περισφίγξ. coni. Maas ; Π acc. to
Horna (ἐπισφ. G).

ἤδη μὲν Φαέθοντος ἐφ᾽ ἑσπερίης πόμα
    λίμνης   13
αἰθερίην κροτέοντες ὑπ᾽ ἴχνεσιν ἀτραπὸν
    ἵπποι
ἄντυγα μυδαλέην λιποφεγγέος ἕλκον ἀπήνης.
ἠέρι δ᾽ ἠγερέθοντο πάλιν νεφελώδεες ἀτμοὶ
ἐκ χθονὸς ἀντέλλοντες, ἀποκρύπτοντο δὲ
    πάντα
τείρεα πουλυθέμεθλα καὶ οὐκέτι φαίνετο
    μήνη.   14
ὑψιπέτης δ᾽ ὄρ[μαι]νε μέ[γ]ας βρονταῖος
    ἀήτης
λάβρος ἐπαιγίζων, νεφέων δ᾽ ἐξέσσυτο δαλὸς
ῥηγν[υμ]ένων ἑκάτερθε καὶ ἀλλήλοισι χυθέν-
    των.
παῖδα δὲ νηπιάχοντα πατὴρ ἐπὶ κόλπον
    ἀείρας
οὔασι χεῖρας ἔβαλλεν, ὅπως μὴ δοῦπον
    ἀκούσηι   14
ὑψόθεν ἀλλήλησιν ἀρασσομένων νεφελάων.
αἰθὴρ δ᾽ ἐσμαράγησεν, [ὀ]ρινομένη δὲ καὶ
    αὐτ[ὴ
παρθένος ἑλκεσίπεπλος ἑὴν ἐκάλεσσε τιθή-
    ν[ην.
γαῖα δὲ καρποτόκων λαγόνων ὠδῖνας ἀνέ-
    σχ[εν
αἰθέρι καὶ νεφέεσσιν ἐπιτρέψασα γ[ενέ]θλη[ν. 15
ἀλλά μοι εὐμενέοιτε καὶ ἐξ Ἑλ[ληνος ἀρού-
    ρης
πέμπετέ με σπείσαντες ἐφισταμεν[
Κυρήνη καλέει με, βιαζόμενος [δέ με Φοῖβος
ἕλκει θηροφόνοιο φίλης ἐπὶ γούνατα [νύμ]φης.

Already the steeds of Phaethon, beating the path of heaven beneath their hooves, were drawing the dew-moist rail of their twilight chariot toward their drinking-pool in the western sea. And again the cloud-mists were gathering in the sky, rising from earth, and all the deep-rooted stars were hidden, and the moon was seen no more. A great thunderstorm was speeding on high, fiercely rushing, and a torch leapt from the clouds as they burst on either side and mingled one with another. A father lifted upon his lap his infant child, and put his hands upon its ears, that it might not hear the crash of cloud bursting on cloud above. The heavens rang loud. A little maiden too, in trailing robe, was aroused and called her nurse. Earth yielded the fruits of her teeming flanks, and committed her children to the sky and clouds.

Grant me your favour, and speed me from the soil of Hellas with libation. . . . Cyrene calls me, and Phoebus constrains me and drags me to the knees

---

146 ἀλλήλησιν Maas (-οισιν G). 152 ἐφιστάμεν[ον νέωι
ἔργωι Gerstinger. 153 Maas.

δ[εῦτε], φίλοι, πρὸς ἔδεθλον ἀρειμανέος
    Πτ[ολ]εμαίου,   155
ἔν]θα με [κικ]λή[σ]κουσι Λιβυστίδες εἰσέτι
    [Μο]ῦσαι.

(b) Ἑλλ]άδος ἁγνὸν ἄγαλμα, Θεάγενες, [ὧι ἔνι
       πάντων
  ἔ]μπεδον Ἑλλήνων   θαλέθει   πανδή[μιος
       ὄ]λβος,
  εὔ]διον ὑμνοπόλου γενεῆς σκέπας, ὧι [ἔν]ι
       πάσας
  ὕβρει γηράσκων Ἑλικὼν ἀνεθήκατο Μούσας,
  ἄλσος ἀκηράσι[ον] ξεν[ίο]υ Διός, ὧι ἔνι
       πάντων   5
  π]ᾶσα πολυπλάγκτων μερόπων ἀμπαύεται
       ὁρμή·
  αἰ]ετὸς αἰγιόχοιο [Διὸ]ς βασιλήιος ὄρνις
  αἴ]θριον ἠελίοιο βολὴν χρυσάμπυκος αἴγλης
  ἧ]ς εὐηγενίης ἐπιμάρτυρον οἶδε καλέσσαι·
  Γερ]μανοὶ δ᾽ ἐφέπουσι θεμιστοπόλου πο-
      ταμοῖο   10
  μάρ]τ[υν] ἀμωμήτοιο δικασπόλον οἶδμα γε-
      [νέθλης.
  σῆς δ᾽ εὐ]ηγενίης ἐπιμάρτυρα πᾶσι φυλάσ-
      σ[εις
  Ζῆνα γ]ιγαντοφόνοιο κυβερνητῆρα χορείη[ς·
  Ζῆν]α γὰρ αὐτὸν ἄνακτα καὶ Αἰακὸν ἀμφι-
      πολ[εύεις
  φύτλης] ὑμετέρης [γεννήτο]ρας, ἧς ἄπο πᾶσα 15
  πάσα[ις ἐν πολέεσσιν Ἀ]χαιιάς ἐστι γεν[έθλα.
  ποῖον σ[. . . . .]ος ποίην δὲ
      τ[ιταίν]ων

of that dear nymph and huntress. Up, friends, to
the seat of Ptolemy the Warrior, where the Libyan
Muses are still calling me.

(b) Pride of Hellas, revered Theagenes, in whom
all the wealth of all the Hellenes prospers abidingly,
a calm shelter for the race of poets ; in whom
Helicon, grown old with insults, has dedicated all
her Muses ; undefiled grove of Zeus the Stranger's
God, wherein every adventure of wandering mortals
comes to rest ! The eagle, royal bird of aegis-bearing
Zeus, knows how to call for witness of his noble birth
the heavenly ray of the Sun's golden gleam [a] ; the
Germans use the stream of the river, their judge
that ministers the law, as their witness of irreproach-
able descent.[b] You, as proof of noble birth, have
Zeus in safe keeping, in the sight of all ; Zeus, the
leader of the dance that slew the Giants. For you
are servant of Zeus himself, your lord, and Aeacus,
the founders of your race, from which proceeds every
Achaean breed in every city.

What . . . or what lyre of seven strings shall I

---

[a] Julian, *Ep.* xv. : the eagle takes its fledgelings forth
from the nest and displays them to the sky, as it were calling
the God to witness that his brood is legitimate.   [b] *Ibid.*
The Celts put babies into the river : bastards sink, the
legitimate float.

(b) 1 End Maas.   2 End Horna.   5 ξεν[ίο]υ Maas
(and prob. Π acc. to Horna) (ξεί[νο]υ G).   9 ῆς Horna
(and prob. Π) (σῆς G).   13 Beginning Horna (Ζῆν]α
γιγ. G).   14 End Maas.   16 πάσαις ἐν πολέεσσιν
Horna.   17 τιταίνων Maas.

ἑπτάμιτον φόρμιγγα τεὰς ἀκτῖνας [ἀ]είσω;
πατρίδα σὴν πρώτην παρελεύσομαι· εὐ[ε]πίης
    μὲν
χε[ύμ]ατα φωνήεντα τεαὶ νικῶσιν Ἀθῆναι.   20
ἔνθα γὰρ αἰγλήεις ἀνεθήκατο μάντις Ἀπόλ-
    λων
καὶ κιθάρην καὶ τόξα καὶ ἔρνεα θέσκελα
    δάφνης.
ἀλλά οἱ εὐρύτ[ε]ρόν τι μέλος μετὰ τοῦτο
    φυλάσσω
σὸν πόθον εὐκελάδοιο φέρων ἡγήτορα μολπῆς.
ἐκ δὲ τεὸν μέλπειν φέ[ρο]μαι γένος· ἀλλὰ
    λιγαίνειν   25
δειμαίνω, γενεῇ γὰρ ἐμ[ὴ]ν σειρῆν[α] καλύπ-
    τεις.
εἰ μὲν ἐυφθόγγοισιν ἀνύμνεον ἄλλον ἀοιδαῖς
ἀνέρα τιμήεντα βοώμενον, ἢ τάχα κέν μ[ι]ν
ἠ]γαθέοις ἤειδον ἀριστήεσσιν ἐίσκων
Ἑλ]λάδος εὐκαμάτοιο· σὲ δ᾿ Ἑλλάδα πᾶσαν
    ἀείδων   30
ἀγν]ώσσω τίνα τοῦτον ἐν [ἥ]ρώεσσι καλέσσω.
Αἰακὸ]ν αὐδήσω· Τελαμώ[νι]ον αἷμ[α] κομί-
    ζεις.
Κέκρο]πα κικλήσκω καὶ Ἐρεχθέα δῖον
    ἐνίψω·
νείατ]ον ἀμφοτέρων γένος ἔπλεο. Νέστορα
    λέξω·
Νέστο]ρο[ς αἷ]μα φέ[ρε]ι[ς]. Λαπίθην δέ σε   35
    Καινέα φαίην
        ]ησας· ἀπ᾿ Ἀρκαδίης σε βοήσω·
ἀρχ]εγόνοιο Λυκάονος ἐς γένος ἕρπεις.
Ἀτρέα σ᾿ ἀλκή]εντα καὶ Ἡρακλῆα καλέσσω·

ANONYMOUS

stretch to sing your radiance ?   Your fatherland first
I will pass by.   Your Athens is beyond a poet's flow
of praise ; for there bright Apollo the prophet hung
up his lyre and bow and divine shoot of laurel.   But
I keep an ampler song for Athens after this one,
since you have charged me .with your heart's desire,
that is the mover of melodious song.

Now I am inspired to sing of your descent.   But
I fear to voice it, for your nobility obscures my
song.[a]   If I were hymning in tuneful melody some
other honoured and famous man, my song would
perhaps compare him with noble heroes of Hellas
rich in famous deeds.   But singing you I sing all
Hellas, and know not whom among her heroes I may
summon to play this part.[b]   Aeacus I will call you :
you carry the blood of Telamon.   I name you Cecrops,
and speak of you as divine Erechtheus : you are the
latest descendant of both.   I will call you Nestor :
you bear the blood of Nestor.   I might call you
Lapith Caineus . . .   I will cry that you are from
Arcadia. . . . You go back to the race of Lycaon, the
founder of the line.   I will name you strong Atreus

---

[a] *i.e.* is too splendid for my song, puts my song in the
shade.   [b] τοῦτον : to be this object of comparison.

---

18 τεὰς ἀκτῖνας Π acc. to Horna (πασακτεινας† G).   29
ηειθεν Π : ἤειδον Arnim (ἤ εἶτεν G). εἴσκων Π (ἔισκον G).
32 Αἰακὸν Maas (Αἴαν G).   37 ἀρχεγόνοιο Keydell (]ε
τόκοιο G).   38 Ἀτρέα Horna, σ' D. L. P. (Θησέα G):
ἀλκήεντα Horna.

585

γνήσι[ος ἀντ]έλλεις Πελοπήιος. ἄλλον ἀείσω
Μιλτιάδ[η]ν· καὶ τόνδε φέρεις ἡγήτορα
    φύτλ[η]s.   40
αὐδήσω [σ]ε Πλάτωνα· Πλατώνιδός ἐσσι
    γενέθλ[ης.
ἐν σοὶ π[ά]ντα(ς) ἔχεις, πάντων [μέρος αὐτὸ]ς
    ἐτύχθ[ης,
σῆς ἐ]ὑηγενίης προτερηγενὲς εὖχος ἀέξων.
εἰ [δ᾽ ἐθ]έλεις, δείξοιμι τεῆς κρήδεμ[να]
    γενέθλης.
Ἀζειόν ποτε κοῦρον ἐγείνατο κυσαμένη
    Χθὼν   45
Τιτήνων μεγάλοισι συνηβήσαντα κυδοιμοῖς.
Ἀζειὸς δὲ Λύκωνα γίγας τεκνώ[σα]το
    νύμφης
ἀντήσας ἐς ἔρωτα, Λύκων δ᾽ [εὐ]ώπιδα
    κούρην
ἥρως Δηιάνειραν. ἀεξομ[ένη]ς δὲ [Πε]-
    λασγὸς
εἰς λέχος εὖ[στρωτόν ποτ᾽ ἀνῄιε Δ]ηια-
    ν[εί]ρης,   50
Ζηνὸς ἐλευ[θερίοι]ο φίλος [γό]νος, ἧς ἀπὸ
    λέκτρων
Ἀ[ρ]καδίης ἐ[φύτευσ]ε Λυκάονα ποιμένα
    γαίης.

.   .   .   .   .   .

(*Fragments of five more lines*)

ANONYMOUS

and Heracles : you rise a true born son of Pelops. I
will sing you as a second Miltiades : him also you have
for leader of your family. I will call you Plato : you
are of Plato's line. All these men you have within you,
yourself you were created a part of all, increasing
the ancient glory of your noble family. If you de-
sire, I will lift the veil from your remotest ancestry :
Earth teemed of old and bore a son Azeius, who
grew to manhood amid the mighty battles of the
Titans. Giant Azeius encountered a nymph with
lover's intent, and begot Lycon ; and hero Lycon
loved a fair maiden Deianeira. Now Pelasgus of old
went up to the fair couch of Deianeira when she was
growing to womanhood ; he was the dear son of
Zeus the god of Freedom ; and from her bed he
got Lycaon, shepherd of the land of Arcadia. . . .

. . . . . .

(Fragments of five more lines)

---

42 πάντας Maas (πάντα G). 44 δείξοιμι Maas (δέξ. G).
48 εὐώπιδα Keydell (εὐέλπιδα G). 50 D. L. P. (εὐ[ποίη-
τον ἀνήλυθε G).

LITERARY PAPYRI

ANONYMOUS

141 [5 A.D.] PRAISE OF A ROMAN GENERAL

Ed. pr. *Schubart-Wilamowitz, *Berliner Klassikertexte*,
v. 1, 1907, p. 114. See Körte, *Archiv*, v. 540 ; Schmidt,
Phil. Woch. 1908, 462.

A Roman general has been put in command of Egyptian

. . . .

Θ[ήβ]η μὴ τρομέοις, οὐκ ὄρχαμος ἄλλος ἀμ[είνων.
κ[οί]ρανος Αἰγυπτίων ἔτι φείδεται ἀχνυμε[ν
ο]ὔ[πω] γηραλέοιο λιτὰς ἠρνήσατο Νείλ[ου.
Πέρσα[ι] ἀναπνεύσωσι Θεμιστοκλῆα φυγόν[τες.
ἔμπαλιν ὀτρύνων σε νέμειν ἔτι πείσματα Θ[ήβης   5
γράμματά σο[ι] προίαλλεν ἄναξ χθονὸς ἠδὲ θ[αλάσ-
    σης.
τί πλέον αἰνήσω σε, τὸν ἤνεσε θεσπεσίη [ὄψ;
δείξας δ' ἀθανάτοιο χαράγματα παμβασι[λῆος
χάρμα πόρες ναετῆισι δι' ἄστεος ἵππον ἐλ[αύνων,
σῆς στρατ[ιῆ]ς δὲ φάλαγξ χλαινηφόρος ἤθελ[10

2 ἀχνυμέ[νων περ ed. pr. : ? better ἀχνύμε[νός περ.   5
Θηβῶν ed. pr. : Θήβης D. L. P.   7 ΗΝΗΣΩΣΕ Π, αἰνήσω
σε D. L. P. (form common in late Greek : *cf. P. Oxy.* 1793,
col. x. 5) : ἠνήσω Schmidt.

---

a Perhaps the Blemyes ; see the next piece, and the poem
in praise of Johannes in *B.K.T.* v. 1 (Dioscorus of Aphrodito).

ANONYMOUS

PRAISE OF A ROMAN GENERAL   [5 A.D.]

Thebes, which is threatened by enemies.[a] *Small fragments after v. 10 refer to the Thebans' welcome of their general; then to a battle ending in treaty between Rome and her enemy. That was the end.   Sober hexameters of the Homeric type, written probably early in the 5th century A.D.*

THEBES, be not afraid; there is no better ruler. The king spares Egypt yet . . . in grief, and has not yet gainsaid the prayers of ancient Nile. The Persians may breathe again, for they have escaped their Themistocles.[b]

The lord of land and sea sent a letter to you, bidding you again to take in hand the stern-cables of Thebes.[c]   Why should I praise you more, whom that wondrous voice has praised ?   You revealed the letter of the immortal monarch, and brought joy to our citizens, riding through the town.   And your cloaked company wished . . .

.   .   .   .   .   .

[b] The hero of the poem has perhaps just returned from a campaign in Persia.   [c] πείσματα are cables most commonly used to make a vessel fast from the stern to the shore. The meaning then may be "to hold the city secure, not to let it slip away (into the seas of trouble, or the power of the enemy)."

LITERARY PAPYRI

ANONYMOUS

142 [5 A.D.] PRAISE OF GERMANUS

Ed. pr. *Schubart-Wilamowitz, *Berliner Klassikertexte*,
v. 1, 1907, p. 108. See Schmid-Stählin, *Gr. Lit.* ii. 2, 959 ;
Dräseke, *Phil. Woch.* 33, 1915, 15.

*Description, in the style of Homer, of the conquest of the
Blemyes on the Nile by one Germanus, a Roman commander
hitherto unknown. The names of the soldiers are chosen at*

δεξιτε]ρῆι κραδάων δολιχόσ[κιον ἔγχος ἔτυψεν
γαστ[έ]ρα· τῆι δ' ἐνὶ χαλκὸς ἐλήλα[το
ἀσπίδα δαιδαλέην χαμάδις βάλ[ε, κάππεσε δ' αὐτὸς
ὕπτιος ἐν κονίηισι, κυλινδομέν[ου δ' ὑπὸ χα]λκῶι
γαστρὸς ἀποθρώσκοντα κατέρρεε[ν] ἔ[γκατ]α γαίηι. 5
Περσίνοος δ' ὄλεκεν Δολίον κρατερόν τε Πυλάρτην
Λαμπετίδην τε Φάληρον 'Αγήνορά τ' αἰολομήτην·
Αἴνιος αὖτε Μίμαντα δαήμονα θηροσυνάων
Ν]ειλώιης προβλῆτος ἰδὼν ἐπιάλμενον ὄχθης
ἀκ]ροτάτης κεφαλῆς κατὰ ἰνίον οὖτασε χαλκῶι· 10
πρηνὴς δ' ἐς ποταμὸν προκυλίνδετο, [μίσ]γετο δ'
    ὕδ[ωρ
αἵμ]ατι, τῆλε δέ οἱ προλιπὼν χρόα θ[υμὸς ἀπέπτη
ἠΰτ]ε κοῦφος ὄνειρος, ἐπερρώο[ντο δὲ νεκρῶι
ἰχθ]ύες, ἀμφὶ δ' ἄρ' αὐτὸν ἀγηγ[έρατ' ἔνθα καὶ ἔνθα,
ἔσ]θοντες σάρκας τε κ[αὶ] ἔγ[κατα πίονα φωτός. 15
Αὐτ]ομέδων δ' ὑσμῖν[
καὶ γ]ὰρ δὴ Βλεμύων πυκιναὶ κλονέ[οντο φάλαγγες·
ἔν]θ' ἔβαλ' Αἴσυμνον κατὰ γαστέρα, τ[ῆς δὲ διαπρὸ
ὠκυ]πετὲς κατέδυ δόρυ [χάλκ]εον, [αὐτὰρ ὅ γ' ἥρως

14 End D. L. P.

ANONYMOUS

PRAISE OF GERMANUS [5 A.D.]

random from Homeric catalogues : with the subtle implica-
tion that Germanus is another Achilles (cf. ῥηξήνωρ v. 48, in
Homer of Achilles only). The events however are certainly
historical. The Blemyan wars occurred at the end of the
4th century A.D., and this poem was written in the same era.
Homeric hexameters of the school of Quintus Smyrnaeus.

In his right hand brandishing his far-shadowing
spear he smote him in the belly : therein the bronze
was driven . . . his shield of curious device he cast
upon the ground, and himself dropped supine in the
dust : he reeled beneath the blow of bronze, and his
entrails leapt from his belly and flowed down upon
the earth. Persinous slew Dolius and strong Pylartes,
and Phalerus, son of Lampetus, and Agenor, shifty
schemer ; Aenius, again, seeing Mimas the skilled
huntsman leaping upon the bank of a promontory of
Nile, wounded him with bronze in the back of the
head, upon the crown ; into the river he rolled for-
ward prone, the water was mingled with blood, his
spirit left his flesh and flew far away lightly as a
dream ; fishes swarmed upon his corpse and gathered
round him on this side and that, devouring his flesh
and fat entrails.

Automedon . . . battle . . . For truly the dense
ranks of Blemyes were being routed. There smote
he Aesymnus in the belly ; the bronze spear, flying
swiftly, sank through it, and the hero stood helpless,

591

ἔστ]η ἀμηχανέων, χολ[άδες δέ οἱ αὐτίκα πᾶσαι   20
χύν]το χαμαί, [

. . . .

       ] τέταται νέφος, οὐδ' ἐσορῶ[μαι
       ]αινὴν ὁδόν, ἡ δέ μ[οι] ἔξω
στηθέων ταρβαλέη] κραδίη ἀναπάλλεται ἤδη,
πάντα δ[. . . . . .]λυται χρόα δείματι. τίς κεν
     ἀλύξαι   25
ἀνέρα τό[νδ'] οὗπέρ τε μένος καὶ χεῖρες ἄαπτοι
ἀ]τρεκέως πεφύασιν ἀπ' ἀκαμάτοιο σιδήρου;
ἦ ῥ]α καὶ ἐς φόβον ὦρτο κατὰ φρένα θυμὸν ἀλυίων,
οἱ] δ' ἄλλοι κατὰ μέσσον ἐελμένοι ἠύτε κάπροι
. .]θόμενοι κατ' ὄρεσφι λίνων ὕπο θηρητήρων   30
       ] τεκέων ὕπερ, ἔρρεε δ' ἠχὴ
τῶν μὲν ἀπολλυμένω]ν τῶν δ' αὖ φεύγοντας ὀπίσσω
θεινόντων ξίφεσίν τε] καὶ ἔγχεσιν, ἔκτυπε δ' αἰθ[ήρ

(Fragments of three lines)

καὶ τίνα δὴ πρῶτον, τί]να λοίσθιον ὤλεσεν ἥρω[ς,
ὡς Βλέμυας φεύγον]τας ἀπεσκέδασεν πολέμο[ιο;   3̣5̣

ἀλλ' οὐδ' ὣς] ἀπέληγε μάχης [
ἀλλ' ἐπιὼν Β]λεμύων κλισίας τ[ε κ]αὶ ἕ[ρκεα πυκνὰ
ῥῆξέ τε] καὶ κατέκηε καὶ οὓς κατέμαρπτε κα[τέκτα,
πρὸς δ'] ἔθεεν πέτρας τε καὶ οὔρεα καὶ μέλαν [ὕδωρ
εὐνά]ς λειπομένων διζήμενος εἴ που ἐφ[εύροι.   4̣0̣
ὡς δ]ὲ λέων νομίηι ἐπὶ φορβάδι θυμὸν ἀλυίων
αἶψα] βοῶν ἀγέλην μετανείσεται ἤματι μέ[σσωι,
οὐδέ] μιν ἰσχανόωσι κύνες δεδαημέν[οι ἄγρης
δύμε]ναι ἕρκεα πυκνά, τεθήπασιν δὲ β[οτῆρες,
αὐτὰρ ὅ] γ' αἶψα βόαυλον ἀμαιμακέτηι ὑ[πὸ λύσσηι 45

and straightway all his intestines were poured upon
the ground . . .

. . . . . .

. . . " a cloud stretches, nor do I see . . . path,
and already my fearful heart leaps forth from my
breast, and . . . all my flesh with terror. Who could
escape such a man as this, whose spirit and hands
invincible are truly created of untiring steel ? " He
spoke, and started for flight, distraught of mind.
The rest, penned in the centre like boars, . . . on the
hills by hunter's nets, . . . defending their offspring ;
far floated the clamour as these were slain, those
smote with sword and spear the fugitives ; loud rang
the skies . . .

(Fragments of three lines)

Whom first, whom latest did that hero slay, as he
routed the flying Blemyans from the battlefield ? . . .

. . . . . .

Not even so would he stay his hand from battle . . .
attacking the tents and thick fences of the Blemyans,
he broke them and burned them, and slew those
whom he overtook ; and he ran to the rocks and the
hills and the black waters, searching to find them
while they left their beds. Even as a lion, raging in
heart against a cow in the pastures, swiftly pursues a
herd of cattle at midday ; the trained hunting-dogs
cannot restrain him from entering the thick fences,
and the herdsmen are aghast ; swiftly the lion leaps
into the stalls, driven by fury irresistible, and blood

ἔσθορε, τ]αυροφόνον δὲ γένυν περιάγνυτ[αι αἷμα·
ὣς κλισίαις Γερμανὸς] ἐπέχραεν, οἱ δ' ἐπ[

. . . .

ὣς ἄρα Γ]ερμανῶι ῥηξήνορι χαλκοκορύστ[ηι
τῆι μὲν θ]ῆλυς ὅμιλος εὐπλέκτοις ἐνὶ δεσμο[ῖς
τῆι δὲ καὶ] αἰζήων στρατὸς ἕσπετο, τοὺς [κατὰ
    χώρην   50
ζώγρησ' ἐκ] πολέμοιο πεφυζότας. ἔστενε δὲ χθ[ὼν
στειβομέν]η πρυλέεσσι καὶ ἀκ[α]μάτων ποσὶν
    ἵππω[ν
στεινομένων ἅ]μυδις, λιγυρὴ δ' ἀνεβόμβεε σάλ[πιγξ
πατρίδι ση]μαίνουσα μάχης πολυγηθέα νίκ[ην·
οὐδὲ φυλα]κτῆρες πυλέων ψαῦ[ε]σκον ὀχῆε[ς   55

. . . .

ANONYMOUS

143 [5 A.D.] APPEAL TO A ROMAN GENERAL

Ed. pr. Vitelli, *Atene e Roma*, vi. 1903, p. 149. See
*Comparetti, *Papiri Fiorentini*, no. 114 (revised text),
Plates IV, V.

*This very difficult piece, obscure in phraseology and some-
times barbarous in prosody, was written in the 5th century
A.D. by an inhabitant of Egyptian Thebes. Ostensibly its
purpose is panegyric, but an ulterior motive is clearly dis-
cernible. The hero whom it praises is absent ; and the poem
is an illiterate but powerful appeal to him to return and save
his country once again. The enemy—perhaps the Blemyes
again—have taken advantage of his absence to renew their
predatory incursions. The hero, compared successively to
Perseus, Achilles and Odysseus, is exhorted to return and*

594

splashes upon its jaws that bring the oxen death.
Even so Germanus fell upon the tents, and they . . .

.   .   .   .   .   .

Thus they followed Germanus, the bronze-mailed
breaker of the ranks—on one side a throng of women
in strong-twisted bonds, on the other a host of young
warriors whom on the field he had taken alive, fugi-
tives from battle.   Earth moaned beneath the steps
of men-at-arms and hooves of tireless horses crowded
close together; shrill blared the trumpet, heralding
to the fatherland the joyous victory of battle : nor
did the bars, that guard the gates, touch . . .

.   .   .   .   .   .

53 στεινομένων D. L. P.

ANONYMOUS

APPEAL TO A ROMAN GENERAL   [5 A.D.]

*conquer ;   and to bring with him a son, like Achilles'
Neoptolemus, to succeed him in his valiant command.   The
mixture of panegyric and petition has a good parallel in the
poem addressed to Johannes, B.K.T. v. 1, p. 117 (6 A.D. :
probably Dioscorus of Aphroditopolis).*

*The detail is often obscure and sometimes unintelligible.
Vv. 1-8 : the hero and the Muses, who are to celebrate his deeds,
fight together steadfast in battle.   The hero and his brother
were both taught the arts of war from early youth.   In the
gap after v. 8, the sense may have been :—" When you went
away, you left your brother in command ; but meantime the
enemy has invaded us again, and your brother has failed us."*

595

LITERARY PAPYRI

Then vv. 9 sqq., " He is not moved by the spectacle of women violated by barbarous victors."   Fragmentary lines beginning παρθένο[ὁπλοτερ[γήραος [*suggest a detailed catalogue of injured persons :* [οὐκέτι . . .] Θήβη καγχα[λόωσα *implies a reference to a change from laughter to sorrow in Thebes. Vv. 25-35 : the hero is reminded of his former services : how he repelled the onset of the enemy, restored freedom to*

οὐκ ἄρα μοῦνον ὅδ' [ἦν μ]ενεδήιος, ἀλλὰ καὶ αὐτα[ὶ
Μοῦσαι ἀριστεύου[σαι] ἀεὶ βασίλειαν ἀοιδή[ν·
οὐ τέκε Καλλιόπην χ[αλ]κάσπιδα πότνια μήτη[ρ;
καὶ σὲ μάχην ἐδίδα[ξα] μέν, ἀμφοτέρω δ' ἐλίτ[αινον,
φῆ μὲν Πηλείδης [ἐνοπ]ῆς ἀποπειρηθέντα   5
καὶ μεγάλην αἰεὶ στ[. . . . ἀ]ερτάζοντα βοείη[ν.
εἰς ὅσον ἀργυρέην [φρουρ]εῖς Νειλωίδα δίνη[ν,
σὺν σοὶ ἀλεξίκακο[s . . . .] σοὶ καὶ ὁμόφρω[ν

  .   .   .   .   .   .

                                      ] οὐδὲ γυναικῶν
οἰ]μωγὴν ἀλέγυνεν ὀ[δυρ]ομένων θέμις εὐνῆς,   10
αἳ]σι βίηι μίσγοντο· βίη [δ' οὐ]κ ἔστιν ἐρώτων·
ἱ]μερτὸς θεός ἐστιν· [ἔρω]ς δ' οὐκ οἶδεν ἀνάγκην·
πολλά τις ἑλκομένη πε[ρ] ἑὸν βοάασκεν ἀκοίτη[ν·
ο]ὐδὲ †φόβος† χραίσμησε, φόβος δ' ἐπέδησεν
  ἀκουήν.
ἣ δὲ καὶ οὐκ ἐθέλουσ[α] τό[σ]ην ὑπέμεινεν [ἀ]νάγ-
  κην,   15
δείδιε γὰρ μὴ τοῦτο[ν . . . . . . μ]ῦθον ἀκούσηι
καὶ πόσιν αἰσχύ[νηι] τε καὶ υἱάσι μῶμον ἀνάψηι.

1 [ἐμμ]ενε δήιος edd.: text D. L. P.   4 Beazley.
5 πηι Π: corr. Beazley.   6 " ἄρρηκτον is nearer the remains ; but Αἴαντος would make better sense " (Beazley).
7 φρουρεῖς Beazley.   10 ἀλέειινεν Π, corr. Beazley (error of pronunciation).   13 πολλάκις Π, corr. D. L. P.   14

ANONYMOUS

the city. " A Heracles is nothing to the land of Egypt!"—
the only distinguished phrase in this sordid composition.
Our hero once brought back the head of the enemy's leader
on the point of his spear, and there was rejoicing throughout
Thebes. Vv. 36-end: so now he is implored to return and
save his city again. [Such metrical errors as those in vv. 4,
18, 35, 43, 46 need not be removed: nor should γὰρ δέ v. 27
be altered.]

Not only was he a steadfast fighter—so also are
the Muses, who ever excel in kingly song. Did not
her lady mother bear Calliope to carry shield of
bronze? I taught you the arts of battle, and im-
plored you both, when you ventured the battle cry
like the son of Peleus, and lifted the mighty (un-
broken) shield of oxhide. As long as you stayed
beside the silver tides of the Nile, by your side . . .
defender against evil, one with you in spirit,[a] . . .

. . . .

nor heeded the groan of women lamenting the rights
of their marriage-bed. Perforce they lay with them:
but force has no part in Love; he is a god of Desire;
Love is ignorant of compulsion. Often one cried
for her mate, in the moment of her ravishing; . . .
was of no avail—terror took his hearing captive.[b]
Another endured such constraint even against her
will,[c] for she feared lest . . . should hear the word,
and she disgrace her husband and bring reproach

[a] The reference may be to the hero's brother. [b] Ter-
ror made him (the husband) turn a deaf ear to his wife's cries.
[c] The contrast is really between the one who cries out and
the other who does not: perhaps βοᾶν should be understood
with οὐκ ἐθέλουσα.

ὑπέδησεν Π, corr. Beazley. For the first φόβος, perhaps
read βοή.

οὐ μία τις βιότοιο γὰ[ρ ἔμ]φασις, οὐ χορὸς αὐτοῖς,
οὐχ Ἑλικών, οὐ Μοῦσα· βέβηκε γὰρ ἶσα θυέλλαις.
ἥρως, οὐδέ σε τοῦτο παρήρ[α]μεν, ἀλλ' ἔτι καὶ νῦν 20
ἐνναέται Θήβης σταχυωδέο[ς] εὐ[υ]μνέουσιν
Ἄρει τειρ]ομένοισιν ἀλεξίκακόν σε φανέντα.
ἔτλη γὰρ πρηνής (σ)ε κυλινδο[μ]ένη παρὰ ποσσὶ
πολλὰ πόλις λιταν[
.   .   .   .   .

τοῦτο πάρος τολύπευσας ἐλευθερίαν ἀγα[π]άζω[ν, 25
κῦδος ἔχειν ἐθέλων καὶ κέρδεος οὐκ ἀλεγίζω[ν.
ὅσσοι γὰρ δ' ὑπὸ χεῖρα σαόπτολίν εἰσι μαχη(τ)αί,
ῥύσαο καί σφιν ἔδωκας ἀναιρέμεν [
οὐδὲν ἐς Αἰγυπτίων Ἡρακλέες· ου[
.   .   .   .   .

καὶ κεφάλη στονόεντος [30
δουρὸς ἀπ' ἀκροτάτου δ[
ὧι δαίδων ἄσβεστον ἀεὶ [σέλας, ὧι τε πανῆμαρ
τερπωλὴ κατὰ ἄστυ καὶ απ[
οὕνεκα δῖα πόλις πάλιν ὀλβ[ία . . . .]οις
μυρίοι δ' ἐστέψαντο γεγηθότε[ς, οὕνεκα δή σφιν 35
δηναίην βαρύδεσμον ἀπ' οἵ[κων τρέψας ἀνί]ην.
τοῖα μὲν ἀνθρώποις πέλε χάρμα[τα· . . . . . .] εστη
δεύετο νόσφιν ἐόντος, ἔπος τ' ἔ[φατ' αὐτίκα τ]οῖ[ο]ν·
ζ[η]λήμων, τί παθοῦσα φίλον γόνο[ν ἀμὸν ἀπ-
η]ῦρ[α]ς;
ἡ]μετέρας ὠδῖνας ἀφήρπασας· εἰ [δὲ μεγαίρ]εις, 40
οὕ]νεκα πωτήεντα πόρον ποτὲ Περσέα δ' ἄλλον

(*Lacuna of at least one line*)

20 παρήραμεν, like ἀναιρέμεν v. 28, is a solecism (intended
to be forms of παραιρέω, ἀναιρέω).   22 Beazley.   26
ἀλογίζω[ν Π: corr. D. L. P.   32 D. L. P.   35-40
(and lacuna after 41) Beazley.

upon her sons. For these men, life has no significance (?): they have no dancing, no Helicon, no Muse —she is gone swift as the storm-winds. Great hero, we have not taken this honour from you—still to-day the citizens of Thebes' cornlands sing your praises, how you appeared as their defender against evil, when they were hard-pressed in war. The city endured to fall prone and roll before your feet, with many a prayer . . .

. . . .

This you fulfilled of old, from your love of liberty, eager for glory and heedless of gain. The warriors beneath this hand that saved their city—them you rescued all, and granted them to destroy. . . . A Heracles is nothing in the land of Egypt ! [a] . . .

. . . .

And the head of the mournful . . . from the spear-tip . . . light of torches for ever unquenchable . . . and . . . because the holy city . . . happy again ; and myriads wreathed their heads, rejoicing that you had turned from their homes the long-enduring heavy chains of woe. So greatly did men rejoice : (and now again your city) was in need of you, but you were far away ; and thus at once she spoke [b] : " Jealous, what made you steal our dear son away ? You have taken from us the child of our own womb. If you begrudge us, because of old . . . winged journey, another Perseus . . . . Perseus re-

[a] *i.e.* we want no Heracles ; we have *you*. (I take Ἡράκλεες nom. plur., ἐς Αἰγ.=ἐν Αἰγ. γῆι.) [b] Thebes is speaking to the distant city in which our hero is now detained.

LITERARY PAPYRI

Περσεὺς καὶ μετὰ Νεῖλον ἐς οἰκία νόστιμος ἦλθεν.
δεῦρο, τέκνον, σπεύδοις σέο πατρίδα καὶ συνοίκ(ους).
ἐξ οὗ μητρ]ὸς ἔφυς, αἰεὶ μερόπεσσιν ἀρήγεις·
νῦν ἀπόν]οσφι μένεις, πατρὶς δ' ἔτι σεῖο χατίζει. 45
ὡς 'Αχιλεὺς] πάρος ἤιεν ἐς οἰκία Δηιδαμείης,
πατρίδι Π]ύρρον ἄγοις Πριάμου τεκέων ὀλετῆρα
] ππ[ολ]ιπόρθιος· ὡς 'Οδυσῆι

· · · · · · ·

44-45 D. L. P.

ANONYMOUS

144 [5 A.D.] VICTORY OF A ROMAN GENERAL

Ed. pr. *Vitelli, *Papiri Greci e Latini*, iii. 1914, no. 253,
p. 112.

Hexameters by a poet of the school of Nonnus. Evidently

] ἐπέ[ρ]ρεεν Αὐσονι[ή]ων
ὁρμῆι μαινομέν]ηι ποταμοῦ παρὰ γείτονας ὄχθα[ς.
καὶ πάλιν ἐφθέγξα]το δυσηχέος "Αρεος αὐλοί,
β[. . . . . το]ξοβόλο[ι] [. . . .]σα[ν ἀ]κόντων,
κ[αὶ γο]ερὸ[ν θαν]άτοιο μέλος σύρ[ιζον] ὀιστοί. 5
. . . .] δ' οκ[. . . . . . .]λακων νέφος· [αἰ]ψα δὲ πᾶσαν
ἠ[έρα] γηγε[νέος] κονίης ἐπύκαζ[ε κ]αλύπτρη,
καὶ πῶλοι χ[ρεμ]έτ[ι]ζον ἐθήμονος "Αρεος οἴστρωι,
ὑγρῆ δ' αἱ[μα]τόεντι ῥόωι φοινίσσετο γαῖα.
αὐτὰρ ὁ δυσ[μ]ενέεσσιν ἄναξ ἄτλητος †ἀρούρας† 10
ἀνδροφόνο[υ] βάκχευεν 'Εννα[λίοι]ο χορείην.
φῶτα μὲν ὠ[κή]εντος ὑπὲρ ῥάχιν ἥμενον ἵππου

10 *αρουρας* cancelled in Π.

600

turned home even after his visit to Nile. Hither, my son, hasten to your country and fellows. From the day of your birth, you are for ever helping mortal men : but now you abide afar, and your country still has need of you. As Achilles went of old to the home of Deidameia, so bring a Pyrrhus to your country, the slayer of Priam's children . . . sacker of cities . . .: as to Odysseus. . . .

. . . .

ANONYMOUS

VICTORY OF A ROMAN GENERAL [5 A.D.]

a description of a battle in which Romans (v. 1) are engaged. Probably a panegyric of the same kind as no. 143.

This text, which contains corrections made by the first hand, is perhaps the writer's own copy.

. . . flowed on . . . of the Ausonians . . . with furious onset by the neighbouring riverside. Again spoke the harsh music of martial flute, . . . archers . . . of javelins . . . the hiss of arrows was a mournful melody of death . . . a cloud . . ., and straightway a veil of earth-born dust hid all the sky from sight ; steeds neighed at the goad of the familiar God of War, and the ground was moist and purple with a stream of blood. Now the king, whom no foeman could endure, danced the fling of Enyalius the Killer of Men. One hero, seated on the back

601

LITERARY PAPYRI

τύψεν [ἀ]λοιητῆρος ὑπὸ ῥιπῇσι σιδήρου·
ἐτμήθη δὲ φά[ρ]υγξ, κεφαλὴ δ' ὑπὲρ ἔδραμεν ὤμων,
καὶ πέσεν ἀσπαί[ρο]υσα· τὸ δ' [ἄ]πνοον ὑψόθι σῶμα 15
οὐ πέσεν, [ἀλλ' ἐπέμε]ινε, καὶ οὐ μεθέ[η]κε χαλι-
    νούς.
              .   .   .   .   .
. . . . ἱππήεσσι καὶ αὐτοκέλευστος ὁδίτης,
φεύ[γων ἐγγ]ὺς ἐόντας, ἐπεσσυμένους δὲ δι[ώ]κων,
ψευδόμενος πεζοῖσι[ν ἀ]λ[ή]μοσι μέτρα πορείης.
ὃς πάσης προνένευκεν ὑπ' ἠέρα μάρτυς ἀρ[ούρ]ης, 20
πεπταμένης χθονὸς ἔργα λόφωι προβλῆτι φυλάσσων,
ἀκροτάτωι δὲ τένοντι Πύλης ἐπαφώμενος ἄστρων,
ὀμβροτόκους ὠδῖνας ἐλαφρίζειν νεφελ[ά]ων
              .   .   .   .   .

20 ἀρούρης Cammelli, ap. ed. pr.

ANONYMOUS

145 [5 A.D.]   FRAGMENT

Ed. pr. *Wilcken, *Sitzungsberichte der königlich preussischen Akademie der Wissenschaften zu Berlin,* 1887, p. 819.

The interpretation of these comical lines is difficult. Two kings, one Trojan and one Achaean, meet in the house of a third party. The Trojan is " seeking to discover the race (pedigree) of a horse " (for γενεὴ ἵππου cf. Iliad v. 265, 268), the Achaean brings a colt with him. The third person is comically surprised.

τίπτε δύω βασιλῆες ὁ μὲν Τρώων ὁ δ' Ἀχαιῶν
οἵ]κοθ' ὁμοφρονέοντες ἐμὸν δόμον εἰσανέβητε;
602

of his swift steed, he smote with the blows of threshing
steel; the throat was severed, the head ran over his
shoulders and fell quivering; the body above, bereft
of breath, fell not but stayed there, and let not loose
the reins. . . .

. . . . .

. . . foot soldier, . . . to the horsemen, and un-
welcome, flees them when they are near, pursues
them when they charge, deluding them in the
distance of the march, by the tactics of the roving
infantry. He[a] who leans forward into the sky,
surveying all the farmland, with his projecting ridge
watching the fields stretched out beneath. Pyles, with
his topmost spur touching the stars, (ready) to relieve
the clouds of their pangs that give birth to rain . . .

[a] This difficult sentence appears (as Professor Beazley first
observed) to refer to a mountain named Pyles, hitherto
unknown.

ANONYMOUS

FRAGMENT [5 A.D.]

*The date, context, and literary associations of these curious
lines are uncertain. It is unlikely that they refer to the
celebrated Wooden Horse. Beazley suggests as a possible
background the story of the mares which Zeus gave to
Laomedon in recompense for the rape of Ganymede, and
which Laomedon refused to give to Heracles in recompense
for the rescue of Hesione.*

" Why have you two monarchs—one of the Trojans,
the other of the Greeks—come up to my house,
in harmony of spirit at home ?—one seeking to dis-

ἤτοι ὁ μὲν γενεὴν ἵππου διζήμενος εὑρεῖν,
αὐτὰρ ὁ πῶλον ἄγει· τί νυ μήδεαι, ὦ μεγάλε Ζεῦ;

* * * * *

ANONYMOUS

146   [? 5 A.D.] INCANTATION TO CURE HEADACHE

Ed. pr. *Schubart-Wilamowitz, *Berliner Klassikertexte*, v. 2, 1907, p. 144.

An *incantation intended to dispel headache.* *In the first five lines an analogy is adduced* : *the house of certain Mystics was burning on a hill, but seven maidens prayed to seven*

(*Small fragments of seven lines*)

        μ]υστοδόκος κατεκα[ύθη
         ]δ' ἐν ὄρει κατεκαύθ[η
       ]ων κρήνας ἑπτὰ [   ]ντων
ἑπτὰ δὲ παρθε[νικαὶ κυα]νώπιδες ἠράσαν[το
. . . . .]σι κυανέαισ(ι) καὶ ἔσ[βεσαν ἀκάμ]ατον πῦρ. 5
καὶ κεφ]αλῆς ἐπαοιδῆισ[ιν φεύγει τ' ἀλεγει[νὸν
πῦρ ἐκ τῆς κ]εφαλῆς, φεύγει δὲ [

* * * * *

(*Obscure fragments of four more lines*)

ANONYMOUS

147   [5–6 A.D.]   ADDRESS TO THE NILE

Ed. pr. *Norsa, *Papiri Greci e Latini*, vii. 1925, no. 845, p. 149. See Keydell, *Hermes*, 69, 1934, 420.

cover the descent of a horse, while the other leads **a**
colt ! What now are you devising, mighty Zeus ?

. . . . . .

ANONYMOUS

INCANTATION TO CURE HEADACHE [? 5 A.D.]

*Spring-nymphs and extinguished the fire. In the next two
lines it is suggested that this incantation shall extinguish the
fires that burn in the sufferer from headache. Ed. pr.
compare P. Amherst, ii. 11. A crude composition, unlikely
to achieve its object.*

(Small fragments of seven lines)

(the house) of the Mystics . . . burned down, . . .
burned down on the mountain. . . . Seven foun-
tains . . ., and seven dark-eyed maidens prayed to
the dark (nymphs of the fountains), and put out the
unwearying fire. Even so the grievous head-fire flies
from the head before this incantation, flies too . . .

. . . . . .

(Obscure fragments of four more lines)

ANONYMOUS

ADDRESS TO THE NILE   [5–6 A.D.]

*Vv. 7–9 are addressed to the Nile, here as elsewhere[a] con-
ceived as the groom of his bride Egypt. Cf. Nonnus (of
whose school our poet is a member) vi, 341 ; xxvi, 229.*

[a] See the poem in praise of Johannes, *B.K.T.* **v.** 1 (Dios-
corus of Aphrodito), and Keydell, *loc. cit.*

δεῦρο λύρη μ[ὲν ἄ]ειδε παρ' ἠιόνεσσ[ι] θαλάσσης,
δεῦρο μὲν [ἠιόν]εσσιν ἀείσομεν ἄ[σθ]ματα μολπῆς·
κυδαίνειν ἐδ[άη]ν τὴν οὐ δεδάασι γυναῖκες.
θηλυτέρης δὲ νόος χαλεπώτερός ἐστ[ι θ]αλάσ[σης·
Ὀρφείηι καὶ πρόσθεν ὑπείκαθε πόντ[ος ἀοιδῆι,   5
καὶ θῆρες θέλγοντο, καὶ οὐ θέλγοντο [γυναῖκες.

. . . .

νυμφίε μὴ δήθυνε, τεὸν δ' ἐπ[
ἄνθει κυμα[τ]όεντι φερέσταχ[υν] ἄμφεπε νύμφην,
ὑμετέρων [δ' ἀ]πόναιο πολυρροθ[ίων] ὑμεναίων.

3 Keydell : εδ . . η and δεδιασι ed. pr.   5 Keydell.
9 δ' ἀπόναιν Keydell : .[. .]πονηο ed. pr.

ANONYMOUS

HITHER, my lyre, and sing by the sea-shore, hither
and let us sing the breath of melody [a] to the shore ;
I have learnt to honour one [b] whom women have not
learnt to honour.—A woman's [c] mind is harsher than
the sea. Ocean once yielded to the song of Orpheus,
and wild animals were charmed, but women were
not charmed . . .

.   .   .   .   .   .

Tarry not, bridegroom, . . . attend your bride,
that bears the corn ear, with the bloom of your waves [d];
enjoy the blessing of the wedding of your roaring
waters. . . .

[a] ἄσθματα μολπῆς Nonnus, *D.* ii. 18.   [b] The context
suggests that Μοῦσαν, the Muse, should be understood.
[c] θηλυτέρη = woman Nonnus, *D.* xlii. 147.   [d] Alcman fr.
94, 3 Diehl : κύματος ἄνθος.

607

INDEX OF PROPER NAMES

(OCCURRING IN THE GREEK TEXT)

608

INDEX OF PROPER NAMES

INDEX OF PROPER NAMES

INDEX OF PROPER NAMES

INDEX OF PROPER NAMES

INDEX OF PROPER NAMES

INDEX OF *EDITIONES PRINCIPES*

INDEX OF *EDITIONES PRINCIPES*

INDEX OF *EDITIONES PRINCIPES*

INDEX OF *EDITIONES PRINCIPES*

INDEX OF *EDITIONES PRINCIPES*